International Economics, Sixth Edition

The latest edition of **International Economics** improves and builds upon the popular features of previous editions. The graphs, tables and statistics are of course all updated, but also added are improved sections on topics including:

- new developments in international trade agreements and the latest round of international trade talks
- international financial crisis
- a new section on current controversies in the international monetary system

With impressive pedagogy, learning objectives and summaries, this impressive clearly written book will be another winner with students of international economics and international business.

Robert M. Dunn, Jr is Professor of Economics at the George Washington University, USA.

John H. Mutti is Sydney Meyer Professor of International Economics, Grinnell College, Iowa, USA.

International Economics
Sixth edition

Robert M. Dunn, Jr.
George Washington University

John H. Mutti
Grinnell College

Routledge
Taylor & Francis Group

LONDON AND NEW YORK

First published 2004
by Routledge
11 New Fetter Lane, London EC4P 4EE

Simultaneously published in the USA and Canada
by Routledge
29 West 35th Street, New York, NY 10001

Routledge is an imprint of the Taylor & Francis Group

© 2004 Robert M. Dunn & John H. Mutti

Typeset in Goudy by
Keystroke, Jacaranda Lodge, Wolverhampton
Printed and bound in Great Britain by
T.J. International Ltd, Padstow, Cornwall

British Library Cataloguing in Publication Data
A catalogue record for this book is available from the British Library

Library of Congress Cataloging in Publication Data
A catalog record for this book has been requested

ISBN 0–415–31153–5 (hbk)
ISBN 0–415–31154–3 (pbk)

Contents

Figures

Tables

Boxes

Exhibits

Preface

This book is an introduction to international economics, intended for students who are taking their first course in the subject. The level of exposition requires as a background no more than a standard introductory course in the principles of economics. Those who have had intermediate micro and macro theory will find that background useful, but where the tools of intermediate theory are necessary in this book they are taught within the text.

The primary purpose of this book is to present a clear, straightforward, and current account of the main topics in international economics. We have tried to keep the student's perspective constantly in mind and to make the explanations both intuitively appealing and rigorous.

Reactions from users of the first five editions – both students and faculty – have been encouraging. The passage of time, however, erodes the usefulness of a book in a constantly evolving area such as international economics, and we have consequently prepared a sixth edition.

The book covers the standard topics in international economics. Each of the two main parts, International Trade and Trade Policy (Part One) and International Finance and Open Economy Macroeconomics (Part Two), develops the theory first, and then applies it to recent policy issues and historical episodes. This approach reflects our belief that economic theory should be what J.R. Hicks called "a handmaiden to economic policy."

Whenever possible, we use economic theory to explain and interpret experience. That is why this book contains more discussion of historical episodes than do most other international economics textbooks. The historical experience is used as the basis for showing how the theoretical analysis works. We have found that students generally appreciate this approach.

This is the second edition of this book with John Mutti as co-author and with Routledge as the publisher. John Mutti replaced James Ingram, who is now Emeritus at the University of North Carolina, Chapel Hill, who authored the first two editions alone, and who co-authored the next two with Robert Dunn. Both authors of this edition would like to express their great appreciation for the help which Jim Ingram provided, including his permission to carry over some material which he wrote for previous editions. It would have been impossible to continue this project without Jim's help, and his spirit and many of his concepts remain central to the book.

Changes in the coverage of international trade

In the first half of the book some important changes in the presentation of conceptual material should be noted, in addition to the inclusion of several more recent developments in commercial policy and multilateral trade negotiations. Chapter 3 pays greater attention to common extensions of the Heckscher–Ohlin framework for analyzing patterns of trade. It gives a more systematic presentation of the effects on patterns of production from growth in factor endowments, and it addresses the conditions for factor price equalization more formally. Chapter 5 extends the analysis of tariffs to consider tariff escalation and tariff-rate quotas, and it assesses US safeguard protection in the steel industry and EU export subsidies for sugar.

Following the treatment of arguments for protection in Chapter 6, the order of the next three chapters changes. Chapter 7 now presents the analysis of regional trade blocs. The decision of the European Union in 2002 to offer membership to ten additional countries raises several important issues of governance and economic policy that are discussed there. With respect to the North American Free Trade Agreement, because a longer time frame is available to observe the consequences of its creation, the scope of adjustments faced by US industries is put in better perspective. Chapter 8 now reviews world commercial policy. It especially notes significant issues that arose in initiating the Doha Development Round of multilateral trade talks in 2001, and it notes others that will be addressed in the negotiations. Chapter 9 now covers issues of capital mobility, immigration, and multinational corporations.

Chapter 10 on trade and growth pays particular attention to the position of the least developed countries. Chapter 11, which discusses issues of public economics, notes the advance of the Kyoto Protocol to the Climate Change Convention, in spite of US opposition, and the success of the Irish in international tax competition.

Changes in the discussion of international finance and open economy macroeconomics

First, all graphs and tables have been updated to what was available in early 2003. Within Chapter 12, the coverage of intertemporal trade has been moved forward from an appendix into the main text. The discussion of what assets constitute foreign exchange reserves has been extended, and the discussion of the IMF format for the balance of payments accounts made more thorough. In Chapter 13 the discussion of various means of evading exchange controls has been made far more complete, and now includes a discussion of hawala banking. The fact that all of these techniques are relevant for criminal or terrorist groups which wish to move money in undetected ways, makes this topic of greater importance than it was before September 11, 2001.

In Chapter 14 the discussion of foreign exchange options, which some readers found to be confusing, has been rewritten and extended, with an emphasis on intrinsic and time values in determining premiums on foreign exchanged puts and calls. In Chapter 16, the treatment of currency boards has been extended, with an emphasis on why Argentina's institution failed. Dollarization is also covered more thoroughly. Chapter 17 now includes far more on the disastrous effects of currency mismatches when a country devalues. If banks and other firms in a country have large liabilities denominated in foreign exchange without offsetting foreign exchange assets of other forms of cover, a devaluation can produce a wave of insolvencies and create something approaching a depression, as Argentina discovered very unhappily. The diagram developed by Trevor Swann to analyze a devaluation has been added at the end of this chapter, with the accompanying discussion emphasizing how both the exchange rate and domestic macroeconomic policies must be adjusted to produce both payments equilibrium and an acceptable level of GDP. In Chapter 19, the "impossibility trinity" of "trilemma," which is associated with Robert Mundell is introduced. If a country wishes to have a stable price level through a fixed exchange rate, an independent national monetary policy, and free mobility for international capital flows, it can have any two of the three, but not the third. In theory a fixed rate and independent monetary policy are possible through rigid exchange controls, but if one believes that such controls are not likely to succeed, the options decline to two. A country can have an independent monetary policy at the cost of living with a floating exchange rate and some price instability, or it can have a fixed exchange rate and stable prices if it gives up all monetary policy independence, perhaps through a currency board.

The largest changes in the second half of the book are in what were the last two chapters. Chapter 20 in the fifth edition has been combined with Chapter 21 to produce a new Chapter 20. The discussion of the history of the international financial system before 1973 had to be considerably reduced in length to stay within the planned length for the book. The treatment of the eurodollar, or eurocurrency, market has, however, been fully retained. The section on the history of floating exchange rates has, of course, been updated to early 2003. The European Monetary Union, which is now in full operation, is covered far more thoroughly than was the case in the previous edition. The main change in this chapter, however, is in the discussion of developing country debt crises. Less emphasis is put on the Latin American crisis of the 1980s, and far more is put on the events in Asia during 1997–9. Recent research on such crises, including the issue of crisis contagion, is covered. Late in the chapter, the so-called New Financial Architecture is introduced, with the Basel I and proposed Basel II accords. Sovereign bankruptcy for heavily indebted developing countries, as proposed by Anne Krueger at the IMF, is also introduced. The chapter closes with a list of likely international policy issues during the next decade. Some of those issues are carried over from the fifth edition, but a number of them are new. Finally, the Glossary has been updated and new terms have been added.

Instructors' options for the use of this book

Those instructors using this book for a full-year course can cover the entire volume and assign a supplementary book of readings. Those who choose to use this book for a one-semester (or one-quarter) course will probably want to eliminate some chapters. The core chapters are 2 through 7, and 12 through 19. For a one-semester chapter emphasizing trade, Chapters 1 through 11 provide a compact, self-contained, unit. For a one-term course emphasizing international finance and open economy macroeconomics, Chapter 1 and Chapters 12 through 20 are the appropriate choice.

In writing this book, we have accumulated a number of obligations: to our students and colleagues, and to international economists too numerous to mention whose work is drawn upon in preparing a textbook such as this. We also gratefully acknowledge the economics editors and outside reviewers both at Wiley and at Routledge: for the second edition, Maurice B. Ballabon of Baruch College, Elias Dinopoulos of the University of California at Davis, Geoffrey Jehle of Vassar College, Marc Lieberman of Vassar College, Don Shilling of the University of Missouri, and Parth Sen of the University of Illinois at Champaign/Urbana; for the third edition, Robert Gillispie of the University of Illinois at Champaign/Urbana, Henry Goldstein of the University of Oregon, Gerald Lage of Oklahoma State University, Robert Murphy of Boston College, William Phillips of the University of South Carolina, and Henry Thompson of Auburn University; for the fourth edition, Ron Schramm of Columbia University, John Carlson of Purdue University, Wayne Grove of the College of William and Mary, Oded Galor of Brown University, Chong Kip of Georgia State University, Chi-Chur Chao of Oregon State University, Zelgian Suster of the University of New Haven, Mark Shupack of Brown University, Paolo Pesenti of Princeton University, and Francis Lees of St. John's University; for the fifth edition, Keith Bain of the University of East London, Christopher Dent of the University of Lincoln and Humberside, Miroslav Jovanovic of the Economics Commission for Europe, United Nations, Jean-Claude Léon of the Catholic University of America, Richard Schatz of the Nanjing University, China, and Houston Stokes at the University of Illinois at Chicago. We would like to thank Professor Ronald Shone of Stirling University in the United Kingdom, and Walter Vanthielen of Limburg University in Belgium for their help in reviewing drafts of this edition.

Finally, we thank users of the first five editions of the book who made useful comments and suggestions.

Robert M. Dunn, Jr.
George Washington University
Washington, DC

John H. Mutti
Grinnell College
Grinnell, Iowa

July 2003

1 Introduction

Learning objectives

By the end of this chapter you should be able to understand:

- the extent to which international trade in goods and services and international capital flows have increased more rapidly than output over the past several decades for the world as a whole;
- why barriers to the free flow of goods, labor, and capital are central to the study of international trade;
- why separate currencies and national business cycles are central to the study of international finance;
- how information about international economic events is available from a variety of sources, including the Internet.

Although world trade shrank in 2001 as a result of economic recession in the largest economies, a general characteristic of the entire post-World War II period has been a remarkable expansion of trade. In fact, global trade and investment has grown much more rapidly than output. The process of globalization has left ever fewer countries isolated or unaffected by worldwide economic conditions outside their own borders. While some protest the destruction of traditional ways of life and the challenge to national sovereignty caused by greater trade and investment, others note that trade and investment have been engines of growth that allow rising standards of living.

What explains this expansion of global commerce? **Tariffs** have fallen substantially. Latin American countries that in the past avoided multilateral trade organizations such as the **General Agreement on Tariffs and Trade (GATT)** have become members, a signal of their commitment to a different approach to trade. Former communist states and many countries in the developing world whose previous goal was to be self-sufficient have become active traders. Transportation and communication costs have continued to fall, making it less expensive to reach foreign markets. Consumer incomes have risen, and correspondingly, their demand for variety and foreign goods has risen. Rapid technical change generates new products whose innovators aggressively seek new markets. Multinational corporations, rather than produce complete products in a single plant or country, have located stages of the production process where the inputs necessary at that stage are cheaper. Many host countries now seek out rather than penalize such investment. These are just some of the reasons that the globalization process shows no sign of reaching a plateau.

Yet, this process is not proceeding at the same pace everywhere. The figures in Table 1.1 suggest why this trend has been particularly newsworthy in the United States. Trade in goods and services as a share of national output more than doubled in the past 30 years, from 11 percent in 1970 to 26 percent in 2000. Perhaps the US rate of increase appears large because the country started from a small initial base. In the case of Canada, however, in spite of the fact that the country was much more reliant on trade in 1970, the increase in its trade/output ratio from 43 percent to 86 percent represents an even bigger change in the share of the economy attributable to trade. For most European economies, a similar expansion of trade occurs. Surprisingly, the Japanese figure has changed little. Does this signify an advantage to Japan as being less subject to external shocks, or does it represent a lost opportunity to gain from the type of trade enjoyed by other advanced nations? We hope succeeding chapters provide insights into the various questions raised in this introductory chapter.

Other important trends also appear in these figures. For developing countries such as Korea and Malaysia that have relied upon **export-led growth** in recent decades, the ratio of trade to national output is higher than for other developing countries, and it has grown over the past 30 years. We might initially puzzle over the figures for Malaysia, which show a trade to output ratio that exceeds 100 percent. The explanation rests on the rapid rise of imports of intermediate goods that are assembled into products for export; while the output term in the denominator depends upon the income generated in the process of assembling goods, the trade term in the numerator includes the value of inputs produced elsewhere, and that has increased even more quickly.

Prior to 1991 India pursued a strategy of **import substitution**, based on the goal of becoming self-sufficient and avoiding dependence on a few primary exports. The larger the country, the more feasible the goal, and the figures in Table 1.1 suggest that some countries have held trade to a comparatively small share of their economies. Has this turned out to be a strategy that has effectively protected those economies from major swings in economic fortunes, and has it required any sacrifice in how rapidly their standard of living grows?

Table 1.1 Exports plus imports of goods and services as a share of GNP (percentage)

Country	1970	1975	1980	1985	1990	1995	2000
United States	10.8	15.8	20.5	17.1	20.4	23.3	26.0
Canada	42.5	46.8	54.7	54.0	50.8	71.3	85.8
United Kingdom	43.8	52.5	52.0	56.6	50.6	57.1	58.1
Japan	20.3	25.6	27.9	25.0	19.8	16.8	20.1
Germany	43.2	49.5	55.1	63.8	61.6	48.2	67.1
France	31.1	36.9	43.2	46.8	43.6	43.6	55.8
Italy	30.5	39.1	44.1	45.4	39.4	50.0	55.7
Ireland	81.9	91.5	112.6	117.6	109.3	141.6	175.6
Netherlands	91.3	96.4	99.9	112.2	99.6	95.4	129.6
Korea	37.7	62.9	152.7	65.0	59.4	61.9	86.5
Malaysia	90.5	92.6	112.6	104.6	146.9	192.1	229.6
India	8.0	13.5	16.6	14.0	15.7	23.2	—
China	—	—	—	28.8	34.5	39.7	—
Brazil	14.9	18.1	20.2	19.3	15.2	17.2	23.2
Mexico	17.4	16.5	23.7	25.9	40.7	58.1	64.0

Source: Calculated from International Monetary Fund, *International Financial Statistics*.

Countries such as Mexico have faced major financial crises over this period and have changed policies. These changes were not simply political pronouncements that were easily reversed. Rather, Mexican trade liberalization during the 1980s shows up in a rapid increase in the role of trade from 26 percent in 1985 to 64 percent in 2000. More gradual liberalization, as in the case of China, still demonstrates a pattern substantially different from that of India.

These trends are noteworthy, but we should not automatically conclude that this experience represents a major aberration compared to the past. Figure 1.1 shows UK experience over a longer period, tracing out the ratio of imports plus exports of goods to GDP from 1850 to 1990. Current figures do not represent a peak, but rather a return to a degree of openness that existed prior to the devastating effects of depression and war. The pattern for the United States is similar, but the increase in trade since 1970 has been even more marked. The expansion of the post-war period is significant, but the view that in earlier times economies were more sheltered from the outside influence of trade is simply inaccurate.

The composition of trade, however, has changed. At the start of the post-war period, agricultural trade fell and manufactures rose as a share of total trade. Those trends have continued at a slower pace over the past 25 years. A more recent phenomenon has been the expansion of trade in services, such as banking, insurance, telecommunications, transportation, tourism, education and health care; they have grown faster than trade in goods. That change has not had a uniform effect across countries, either. Even within the three largest developed economies, a different picture emerges. For example, between 1985 and 1997 the United States' net exports of services rose by $74 billion, while its net imports of goods rose by $77 billion. Conversely, over that same period, Japan's net exports of goods rose by $37 billion while its net imports of services rose by $44 billion. In the case of Germany, net exports of goods rose by $64 billion and net imports of services rose by $34 billion. While all three countries may seem similar because they are net exporters of high-technology products and their producers often compete against each other in international markets, the pattern of trade in goods versus services should serve as a warning against any presumption that industrialized countries as a bloc have identical production patterns and trading interests.

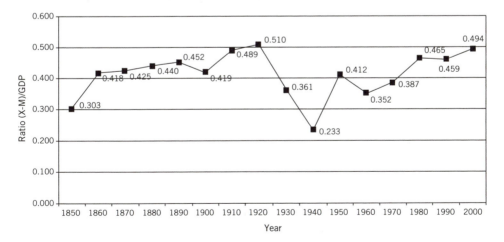

Figure 1.1 Trade in goods as a share of GDP in the United Kingdom 1850–1990.

Source: B.R. Mitchell, *International Historical Statistics, Europe 1750–1993*, 4th edn, (London, Macmillan Reference Ltd, 1998).

Another major aspect of the globalization process has been the explosion of international investment. Economists refer to one category of this investment as "foreign direct investment." This label applies when multinational corporations control how assets are used. Generally it is motivated by longer-run considerations, because such investments cannot be easily reversed in the short run. Figure 1.2 shows that a traditional image of investment by multinational corporations (MNCs) being dominated by a few developed countries is no longer very accurate. Such investments now come from companies headquartered in a variety of developed countries and even some developing countries. Also, they do not flow in one direction only, with a country being only an importer or only an exporter. The United States, for example, is not simply an important source of foreign direct investment in other countries, but also a major recipient of investment by MNCs based in other countries. Some countries appear to discourage such inflows that entail foreign control, as in the case of India, Japan, and Korea, while others, such as Malaysia, appear to encourage such inflows as a way to gain access to technology and marketing networks. Countries such as Brazil and Mexico appear to have changed both their receptiveness and their attractiveness to foreign investors over the past two decades. What explains these variations across countries?

An even larger share of international investment is accounted for by purchases and sales of stocks and bonds and by deposits and loans from financial institutions when one of the parties to the transaction is a foreigner. Often, the time horizon that motivates such investments is quite short and the volatility of such investment flows has given them the

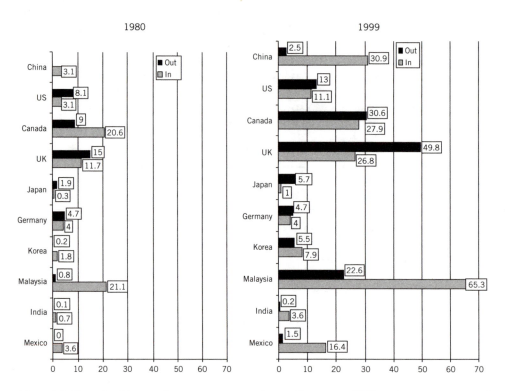

Figure 1.2 The role of foreign direct investment in the world economy (FDI stock as a percentage of GDP).

Source: United Nations, *World Investment Report 2001*, Annex Table B.6, pp. 325–55.

pejorative label "hot money." Financial liberalization has allowed the growth of such flows to accelerate, as national capital markets become integrated into a world market where savers have many more options regarding the assets they acquire. Critics of globalization fault the rapid pace at which financial markets in developing countries have been liberalized, because it has occurred without adequate supervision. Not only have banking systems been adversely affected by rapid increases and decreases in the availability of funds from abroad, but national governments face more constraints over the way they conduct macroeconomic policy.

In part, the expansion of capital flows can be attributed to changing economic circumstances and government policies. For example, the rapid rise in oil prices that the OPEC **cartel** achieved in the 1970s led to a major increase in international financial intermediation. Major petroleum exporting countries such as Saudi Arabia were able to deposit large amounts of funds in banks in industrialized countries, who in turn recycled or lent them to developing countries. In the 1980s, Japanese regulations of financial institutions were liberalized to allow them to acquire foreign assets, just at the time the United States ran large government budget deficits and attracted large capital inflows. In the 1990s, however, Japanese economic recession, bad loans and near bankruptcy of many financial institutions slowed the rapid expansion of its capital flows in the earlier decade. Many developing countries and transition economies experienced large inflows of private capital in the 1990s, which often came from countries such as Germany or the United States, even though those countries themselves were net borrowers internationally.

Table 1.2 reports balance-of-payments measures of three categories of capital flows: direct investment, already examined in Figure 1.2; portfolio investment, applicable when foreign buyers of stocks or bonds have no management control; and other investment, which includes operations of banks and other financial institutions. Consider first the total figures. Aside from Japan, they indicate that the rate of growth of international capital flows was much greater than the rate of growth of trade in goods over all of the decades shown. For example, in Germany and the United Kingdom trade flows measured in dollars increased by a factor of five over the decade, but capital flows started from a small base and rose by a much greater multiple. In the United States, the same pattern can be observed, although it is not as pronounced.

Table 1.2 also demonstrates that while portfolio investment rose in importance, the role of banks and other financial institutions remains a dominant factor. The fact that these four countries have both large capital inflows and large capital outflows likely indicates that they play a role as intermediaries of international investment flows, accepting deposits from sources that seek security and making loans to riskier borrowers. How should such risk-taking be regulated, and who should bear the consequences of failed loans?

These snapshots of aggregate inflows and outflows from major economies do not adequately reflect the rapidity with which capital flows can shift from one country to another, thereby affecting the value internationally of a country's currency (its exchange rate), standards of living, and the competitive positions of goods produced in different locations. Also, we have said nothing of the way macroeconomic policies in individual countries may affect incentives to invest in a country and influence the exchange rate, or the freedom that countries have in determining those policies.

In the 1950s and 1960s, for example, capital flows were often regulated but exchange rates were fixed; countries were not free to pursue any domestic monetary policy that they chose if they were to maintain a stated exchange rate. In the 1990s, exchange rates were no longer fixed between many countries, but capital flows internationally were much less restricted.

Table 1.2 International capital flows and trade

	Capital outflows				Capital inflows				Trade in goods	
	Direct investment	Portfolio investment	Other investment	Total	Direct investment	Portfolio investment	Other investment	Total	Exports	Imports
Germany										
1971	1.20	-0.16	0.91	1.95	1.09	0.57	2.78	4.44	38.39	33.87
1980	4.70	4.19	19.41	28.30	0.33	-3.98	33.17	29.52	191.16	183.22
1990	24.20	15.17	74.67	114.04	2.53	13.44	43.28	59.25	410.92	341.88
2000	52.05	197.52	74.83	324.40	189.18	36.46	115.49	341.13	549.17	491.87
Japan										
1980	4.90	8.77	25.53	39.20	0.19	13.22	24.23	37.64	126.74	124.61
1990	48.05	40.20	89.14	177.39	1.76	35.39	118.70	155.85	280.85	216.77
2000	31.53	83.36	4.15	119.04	8.23	47.39	10.21	65.83	459.51	342.8
US										
1970	6.53	1.08	3.27	10.88	1.26	2.25	2.73	6.24	42.45	39.86
1980	19.23	3.57	57.12	79.92	16.93	14.15	28.13	59.21	224.25	249.76
1990	29.95	28.80	13.73	72.48	47.92	22.02	52.24	122.18	388.71	498.34
2000	152.44	124.94	303.27	580.65	287.68	474.59	261.96	1024.23	774.86	1224.43
UK										
1970	1.68	0.32	1.16	3.16	1.49	0.33	-0.18	1.64	19.51	19.54
1980	11.23	7.79	81.22	100.24	10.12	2.88	79.74	92.74	109.62	106.27
1990	19.32	32.63	94.58	146.53	32.43	24.82	118.48	177.73	181.73	214.47
2000	266.25	99.89	411.54	777.68	119.93	258.34	423.31	801.58	284.38	330.27

Source: International Monetary Fund, *International Financial Statistics.*

Because of that greater capital mobility, countries still faced constraints on the type of macroeconomic policy they pursued. For example, a country may have little freedom to fight a recession by following an expansionary fiscal policy, if any tendency for interest rates to rise results in a capital inflow that causes its currency to appreciate and reduce foreign demand for its goods.

Additionally, events outside the borders of a country can have a significant impact on its economic performance and policy choices. For example, recession in Europe in 1992 slowed Japanese and US recovery at that time. Financial turmoil in Asia and in Russia in 1997–8 gave industrialized countries an incentive to pursue more expansionary macro-economic policies to spur domestic demand.

An asymmetry in the international financial system exists because the US dollar plays the role of a reserve currency. Other countries can acquire reserves by selling more goods and assets to the United States than they buy from it. When the European Union introduced the euro in January 1999, many expected it to challenge the role of the US dollar as the dominant reserve currency. Weakness of the euro after its introduction, however, meant that this challenge did not materialize during the first four years of its existence.

Why international economics is a separate field

International trade theory and domestic microeconomics both rest on the same assumption that economic agents maximize their own self-interest. Nevertheless, there are important differences between domestic and foreign transactions. Similarly, international finance is closely tied to domestic macroeconomics, but political borders do matter, and international finance is far more than a modest extension of domestic macroeconomics. The differences between international and domestic economic activities that make international economics a separate body of theory are as follows:

1 Within a national economy labor and capital generally are free to move among regions; this means that national markets for labor and for capital exist. Although wage rates may differ modestly among regions, such differences are reduced by an **arbitrage** process in which workers move from low- to high-wage locations. There are even smaller differences in the return to financial capital across regions because investors have lower costs (the price of a postage stamp) of moving funds from one location to another. As a result, domestic microeconomic analysis generally rests on the assumption that firms competing in a market pay comparable wages and borrow funds at comparable interest rates.

   International trade is quite different in this regard. Immigration laws greatly limit the arbitraging of wage rates among nations, so that wage rates differ sharply across the world. Labor in manufacturing can be hired in Sri Lanka for 40 rupees per hour. Industrial wages in the United Kingdom, including fringe benefits, are typically over £11 per hour, implying a ratio of the UK to the Sri Lankan wage rate of about 30:1. Although capital flows among nations more easily than does labor, exchange controls, additional risks, costs of information, and other factors are sufficient to maintain significant differences among interest rates in different countries. Therefore, international trade theory centers on competition in markets where firms face very different costs.

2 There are normally no government-imposed barriers to the shipment of goods within a country. Accordingly, firms in one region compete against firms in another region of the country without government protection in the form of tariffs or **quotas**. Domestic microeconomics deals with such free trade within a country. In contrast, tariffs, quotas,

and other government-imposed barriers to trade are almost universal in international trade. A large part of international trade theory deals with why such barriers are imposed, how they operate, and what effects they have on flows of trade and other aspects of economic performance.

3 Domestic macroeconomics normally deals with monetary and fiscal policy choices that address cyclical economic fluctuations that affect the country as a whole. With one currency used throughout the country, establishing a different monetary policy or interest rate for different regions is not possible. While there are differences across regions in the way central government spending is allocated and in the location of interest-sensitive industries, essentially fiscal and monetary policies that exist in one part of the country also prevail in other parts.

   International finance, or open economy macroeconomics, is about a very different situation. Different countries have different business cycles; the significance of strikes, droughts, or shifts in business confidence, for example, regularly differs across countries. Because some countries may be in a recession while others enjoy periods of economic expansion, they generally choose different monetary and fiscal policies to address these circumstances. These differences in macroeconomic conditions and policies among countries have major consequences for trade flows and other international transactions. The second half of this book, which deals with international finance, discusses these issues.

4 A country normally has a single currency, the supply of which is managed by the central bank operating through a commercial banking system. Because a New York dollar is the same as a California dollar, for example, there are no internal exchange markets or exchange rates in the United States.

   International finance involves a very different set of circumstances. There are almost as many currencies as there are countries, and the maintenance of a currency is typically viewed as a basic part of national sovereignty. The choice of eleven European nations to give up some of this sovereignty in forming the European Monetary Union and launching the euro in 1999 represents a remarkable political achievement. International finance is concerned with exchange rates and exchange markets, and the influence of government intervention in those markets.

The organization of this volume

This book is divided into two broad segments, the first of which deals with international trade, and the second with international finance. Chapters 2 to 4 examine alternative explanations of the pattern of trade among countries and the potential economic gains from trade. We pay particular attention to differences in technology, the availability of capital, labor and other factors of production, and the existence of **economies of scale**, all of which are important determinants of trade.

   Chapters 5 and 6 assess the consequences of policies to restrict international trade and consider possible motivations for protectionist policies that are chosen. Some policy decisions that affect international trade are taken unilaterally by a single country, but often these choices are made by several countries acting together. Chapter 7 treats preferential trade agreements, a form of trade liberalization that favors members of a trade bloc but discriminates against nonmembers. Chapter 8 addresses multilateral trade agreements, tracing progress since the 1930s to establish nondiscriminatory rules for international trade and to reduce trade barriers.

Chapter 9 extends the basic framework for analyzing trade in goods to treat trade in factor services, including capital flows, labor migration and the operations of multinational corporations. Chapter 10 considers the relationship between international trade and economic growth, and includes an analysis of trade and investment policies particularly relevant to developing countries. Chapter 11 recognizes that devising an efficient trade policy while ignoring the existence of other national and international distortions may leave a country worse off, and therefore it addresses areas where domestic policy choices over environmental regulation and government taxation have important implications for the design of trade policy.

The treatment of international finance begins with Chapter 12 and continues through the remainder of the book. It begins with a discussion of balance-of-payments accounting. Chapters 13 and 14 discuss foreign exchange markets. Initially we focus on the relationship between what is occurring in the balance-of-payments accounts and events in exchange markets, and then consider in more detail the financial instruments, commonly referred to as derivatives, that have resulted in greater interdependence among national financial markets.

Chapters 12 to 16 focus on the problem of balance-of-payments disequilibria, primarily under the assumption of a fixed exchange rate. This early emphasis on a regime of fixed exchange rates may seem strange because countries such as Britain, Japan, and the United States do not attempt to maintain fixed exchange rates among their currencies. This organizational approach has been adopted for two reasons. First, the vast majority of the countries of the world do not have fully flexible exchange rates, but instead maintain some form of parity or very limited flexibility. More important still, students find it much easier to understand a fixed exchange rate system than a regime of floating exchange rates. Once students understand the problems of balance-of-payments disequilibria and adjustment under fixed exchange rates, they will find it much easier to learn how a flexible exchange rate system operates.

Chapter 17 discusses changes in otherwise fixed rates, that is, devaluations and revaluations. Chapter 18 deals with open economy macroeconomics for countries with fixed exchange rates. The theory of flexible exchange rates is then covered at some length in Chapter 19, with particular emphasis on open economy macroeconomics in such a setting. Chapter 20 applies the previously developed theory to historical and current events.

A glossary follows Chapter 20. The first time a word in the glossary appears in the text it is printed in bold type. Readers encountering terms in the text that are unclear should refer to the glossary for further help. The inclusion of a glossary and a detailed index is intended to make this book useful to readers long after a course in international economics has been completed.

This book is designed for students whose previous exposure to economics has been limited to a two-semester principles course, but it also attempts to teach the theory of international economics with some rigor. Each chapter begins with a statement of learning objectives to alert you to the main ideas to be covered in it. At the end of the chapter we include a summary of key concepts, a set of questions to give you practice in explaining concepts and applying principles presented in the chapter, and suggestions for further reading. Some of the tools of intermediate microeconomics and macroeconomics are presented in the text and are used to treat international issues. Offer curves and Edgeworth boxes are introduced in the trade theory chapters, and the IS–LM model, modified to include the balance of payments, is taught in the international finance chapters. These analytical tools are treated in self-contained sections separate from the main text. Students and instructors who wish to omit these entirely self-contained sections can do so, because the main text is designed to be understood without necessary reference to this material. However, the student will gain a fuller understanding of the theory by working through these graphical explanations.

A web site that students have found useful in supplementing material presented here is maintained by Professor A.R.M. Gigengack of the University of Groningen, the Netherlands, at http://www.eco.rug.nl/medewerk/gigengack.

Information about international economics

A course in international economics will be both more enjoyable and better understood if an attempt is made to follow current events in the areas of international trade and finance. Both areas are full of controversies and are constant sources of news. We note here some useful sources of current information, some of which are available through the Internet. In many cases they provide extensive access to the most current publication without requiring a user subscription.

Publication	Web site
Financial Times (daily newspaper)	http://www.ft.com/
The Economist (a weekly magazine)	http://www.economist.com
The New York Times (financial section, daily newspaper)	http://nyt.com/
The Wall Street Journal (daily, international news in section 1, market data in section 3)	http://online.wsj.com/

Important sources of current and historical statistics in the areas of international trade and finance are given below. We first list international organizations, which compile comparable information for a broad range of countries and issue regular reports. These agencies often provide working papers on selected topics that can be downloaded; they usually charge for electronic access to their data.

Organization	Reports
Bank for International Settlements • http://www.bis.org/wnew.htm	• *Annual Report*
International Monetary Fund • http://www.imf.org/	• *Annual Report* • *Balance of Payments Statistics Yearbook* • *Direction of Trade Statistics* • *Government Finance Statistics Yearbook* • *International Financial Statistics*
Organization for Economic Cooperation and Development • http://www.oecd.org	• *Main Economic Indicators* • *Economic Country Surveys* • *Revenue Statistics of OECD Countries*
United Nations • http://www.unctad.org/	• *International Trade Statistics Yearbook* • *Monthly Bulletin of Statistics*

- http://unstats.un.org/unsd/mbs/

- *World Investment Report*
- *Trade and Development Report*

World Bank (International Bank for Reconstruction and Development)
- http://www.worldbank.org

- *Finance and Development* (quarterly, by the IMF and the World Bank)
- *World Development Report* (annual)
- *World Tables* (annual)
- *Global Development Finance* (annual)

World Trade Organization
- http://www.wto.org

- *Annual Report*
- *International Trade Statistics*
- *Country Trade Policy Reviews*
- *Dispute Resolution Activity*

In its statistics directory, the WTO site provides links to national statistical offices. We include some common ones here:

Country	Web site
Australia	http://www.abs.gov.au/
Canada	http//www.statcan.ca/start.html
European Union	http://www.europa.eu.int/comm/eurostat/
United Kingdom	http//www.ons.gov.uk/ons_f.htm

US data sources and agency reports that are particularly relevant for international economists are:

Agency	Web site
Bureau of Labor Statistics (*Export and import price indices*)	http://www.bls.gov/
US Bureau of the Census (*Trade and balance of payments data*)	http//www.census.gov/
Federal Reserve Board (*Exchange rates and financial flows*)	http://www.federalreserve.gov/releases/
US Department of Commerce, International Trade Administration (*Trade data, unfair trade cases*)	http://www.ita.doc.gov/
US Department of State, (Country Reports: Economic Policy and Trade Practices)	http://www.state.gov/www/issues/economic/ trade_reports/
US International Trade Commission (*Investigations and trade cases*)	http://www.usitc.gov/

A particularly useful compilation of international data for 1950–92 on real output and prices, created by Professors Heston and Summers of the University of Pennsylvania, is accessible in a form that allows you to download data and view it graphically:

Penn World Tables   http://datacentre.chass.utoronto.ca:5680/pwt/

Commercial investment houses often provide current financial information and analysis. For example:

Company	**Web site**
J.P. Morgan	http://www.jpmorgan.com/
Bloomberg	http://www.bloomberg.com/

Many non-profit organizations or "think tanks" publish studies on international economic issues. Groups in this category include:

Nonprofit organization	**Web site**
The Brookings Institution	http://www.brook.edu
The Cato Institute	http://www.cato.org
The Center for Economic Policy Research	http://www.cepr.org/home_ns.htm
The Institute for International Economics	http://www.iie.com

Summary of key concepts

1   Since 1970 international trade in goods and services has grown faster than national income in most industrialized countries. The pattern among developing countries is more mixed, but since 1980 trade has become more important to a larger number of developing countries.

2   Foreign direct investment has grown more rapidly than national income in most industrialized countries since 1980. Other capital flows have grown rapidly, too, due to the liberalization of government restrictions previously imposed on them.

3   In a world with complete factor mobility and free trade, there would be less reason to study international trade as a separate field. Because it is costly to move labor, capital, and technology internationally, international economists study the incentives for trade in goods that exist, as well as government intervention to influence these trade patterns.

4   In a world with a single currency and economic shocks that affected all parts of the world equally, there would be less reason to study international finance as a separate field. Because economic shocks have different impacts on individual countries, and governments often choose to maintain their own currencies to help address those shocks, international economists study the way exchange rates between currencies are determined and the effectiveness of macroeconomic policy in an open economy.

Questions for study and review

1   Table 1.1 shows that trade plays a bigger role in smaller economies such as Ireland and the Netherlands than in larger economies such as Germany, Japan, and the United States. What do you think explains such differences? Why is a small country less likely to be self-sufficient?

2   In 2000 exports as a share of gross national income were 31 percent in Israel and 88 percent in Ireland. Both countries have populations less than 7 million. What other factors might explain the different role of trade in the two countries? How is the opportunity to trade with neighboring countries relevant to your answer?

3   In Figure 1.2, for which countries do you observe a change greater than 10 percentage points between 1980 and 1999 in the value of inward foreign direct investment as a share of GDP? . . . a change greater than 20 percent? In 1980 over three-fourths of foreign direct investment occurred between industrialized countries. Explain whether you would expect that number to have fallen in 2005.

4   Of the four countries shown in Table 1.2, which one experienced a net outflow of capital in 2000? Was German and UK experience more or less the same? To evaluate the effect of capital flows on a country, in what cases might we be more interested in the flow of dollars, and when might we want to express this flow as a share of the country's income?

Suggested further reading

For a collection of accessible articles by leading economists that elaborate many of the issues addressed in this textbook, see:
- King, Philip, *International Economics and International Economic Policy, a Reader*, 3rd edn, New York: McGraw-Hill, 1999.

A concise and sharply worded critique of many popular but misleading pronouncements about international economics is:
- Krugman, Paul, *Pop Internationalism*, Cambridge, MA: MIT Press, 1996.

For debate over globalization issues as framed by economists, see:
- Bhagwati, Jagdish, *The Wind of the Hundred Days*, Cambridge, MA: MIT Press, 2000.
- Rodrik, Dani, *Has Globalization Gone Too Far?* Washington, DC: Institute for International Economics, 1997.
- Stiglitz, Joseph, *Globalization and its Discontents*, New York: Norton, 2002.

Part One

International trade and trade policy

The patterns of international trade and investment cited in Chapter 1 sometimes vary considerably from year to year, but they also demonstrate general trends over time. Factors that determine the volatility in the short run often differ from factors that determine the long-run trends. In the first half of this book, we pay primary attention to the longer-run determinants of these trends in international trade and investment. Economists often refer to these relationships as pertaining to the "real side of the economy." The goods a country trades typically are independent of whether the country fixes the value of its national currency in terms of gold, or euros, or the dollar. Likewise, a country's choice of monetary policy is not likely to have a permanent impact on whether it exports airplanes and imports shoes. Although such financial relationships are a significant part of our discussion of international finance in the second half of this book, we largely ignore them in our treatment of trade theory and trade policy.

Chapter 2 begins with the ideas classical economists Adam Smith and David Ricardo presented 200 years ago to support the claim that there were mutual gains from trade, a major contrast to the prevailing mercantilistic view that exports allowed a country gain while imports represented a loss. Chapter 2 also develops the analytical framework of production-possibility curves and community indifference curves that economists have subsequently come to use in demonstrating a country's willingness to trade and its potential gains from trade. Although the classical framework assumed differences in productivities across countries caused differences in costs internationally and created the basis for trade, two Swedish economists, Eli Heckscher and Bertil Ohlin, proposed an alternative reason for costs to differ across countries: differences in the availability of factor inputs. That theory is presented in Chapter 3. Economists have found this a useful approach, not only to predict how a country's pattern of trade may change as its factor endowments change, but also to explain how trade benefits abundant factors used intensively in export production and hurts scarce factors used intensively in import-competing production. The theoretical completeness of this model makes it attractive, but it appears to be most applicable in explaining trade between countries with dissimilar endowments, as in the case of industrialized versus developing countries. The large volume of trade among industrialized countries is not well explained by it. Therefore, Chapter 4 presents a different analytical framework where trade is based on economies of scale and imperfect competition. Although gains from trade still exist and are even likely to be magnified, there also are circumstances where trade may leave a country worse off.

Chapters 5 and 6 examine the consequences of trade barriers that reduce but do not eliminate trade. In a world with competitive markets, trade barriers reduce economic efficiency and leave a country worse off, as shown in Chapter 5. When a country is large enough to affect prices internationally or when distortions in the domestic economy exist, restrictions may make a country better off, as analyzed in Chapter 6. To successfully implement such a policy in a political setting where there are many competing claimants for protection is a tall order indeed, and this reasoning provides little support for a highly interventionist government policy.

Regional trade blocs, such as the European Union or the North American Free Trade Area, are agreements to reduce trade barriers on a preferential or discriminatory basis for members only. Chapter 7 assesses whether such blocs are likely to increase welfare, because they liberalize trade, or reduce welfare, because they divert production to less efficient producers. Advocates of multilateral trade liberalization fear the losses from such trade diversion and point to the benefit of a trade system open to all countries. Chapter 8 presents developments in commercial policy to move closer to that goal within international organizations such as the GATT and its successor, the WTO.

The principles of trade in goods are closely related to the incentives for trade in factors of production when labor and capital mobility are considered, as is done in Chapter 9. The reallocation of capital internationally, labor migration, and the operations of multinational corporations are key topics addressed there.

Chapter 10 examines the way growth affects trade and vice versa. The chapter pays particular attention to the prospects for developing countries and the potential consequences of dependence on primary product exports, on attempts to become self sufficient in industrial products, and on diversification into non-traditional exports.

Chapter 11 recognizes that much of the recent controversy in debates over international trade and investment policy arises when the standards established in those areas collide with domestic policies, such as regulatory measures to deal with a polluted environment or tax policies to finance government expenditures. These traditional issues from public finance will claim more attention of international economists in the future, and for that reason they are included in this text.

2 Patterns of trade and the gains from trade
Insights from classical theory

Learning objectives

By the end of this chapter you should be able to understand:

- how both countries gain from trade based on absolute advantage;
- how both countries gain from trade based on comparative advantage;
- why a country's willingness to trade is based on its domestic production capabilities and consumption preferences;
- how the determination of prices internationally depends upon the willingness to trade of all countries;
- how the comparative advantage model appears to predict patterns of trade successfully.

Nations (or firms in different nations) trade with each other because they benefit from it. Other motives may be involved, of course, but the basic motivation for international trade is that of the benefit, or gain, to the participants. The gain from international trade, like the gain from all trade, arises because specialization enables resources to be allocated to their most productive uses in each trading nation. Everyone recognizes that it would be foolish for a town or a province to try to be self-sufficient, but we often fail to recognize that the benefits of specialization and the division of labor also exist in international trade. The political boundaries that divide geographic areas into nations do not change the fundamental nature of trade, nor do they remove the benefits it confers on the trading partners. Our goal in this chapter is to establish and illustrate this basic truth, which was developed by the classical economists of the late eighteenth and nineteenth centuries.

Absolute advantage

Adam Smith's original statement of the case for trade, contained in his epic *The Wealth of Nations* (1776),[1] was couched in terms of absolute cost differences between countries. That is, Smith assumed that each country could produce one or more commodities at a lower real cost than its trading partners. It then follows that each country will benefit from specialization in those commodities in which it has an **absolute advantage** (i.e. can produce at lower real cost than another country), exporting them and importing other commodities that it produces at a higher real cost than does another country.

"Real cost," for Smith, meant the amount of labor time required to produce a commodity. His analysis was based on the labor theory of value, which treats labor as the only factor of production and holds that commodities exchange for one another in proportion to the number of hours required for their production. For example, if 10 hours of labor are required to produce a shirt, and 40 hours to produce a pair of shoes, then four shirts will exchange for one pair of shoes. The labor embodied in four shirts equals the labor embodied in one pair of shoes. This argument holds for a given market area within which labor can move freely from one industry to another and one place to another.

Within a single country, competition ensures that commodities exchange in the market in proportion to their labor cost. In our example of shirts and shoes, no one would give more than four shirts for one pair of shoes because that would entail a cost of more than 40 hours of labor to obtain a pair of shoes. One instead can obtain a pair of shoes directly by expending 40 hours of labor. No one would accept fewer than four shirts for one pair of shoes for the same reason. Competition in the market, and the mobility of labor between industries within a nation, thus cause goods to exchange in proportion to their labor cost.

Because of legal and cultural restrictions, however, labor does not move freely between nations. To simplify the analysis, we make the classical economists' assumption that labor is completely immobile between nations. If labor requirements differ across countries, then in the absence of trade, prices of goods will differ across countries. Adam Smith ignored the way an equilibrium price might be reached among trading nations. He instead demonstrated the proposition that a nation benefited from trade in which it exported those commodities it could produce at lower real cost than other countries, and imported those commodities it produced at a higher real cost than other countries.

An arithmetical example helps to illustrate the case of absolute cost differences. Suppose that, as shown in Table 2.1, in Scotland it takes 30 days to produce a bolt of cloth and 120 days to produce a barrel of wine, whereas in Italy it takes 100 days to produce a bolt of cloth and only 20 days to produce a barrel of wine. (Each commodity is assumed to be identical in both countries, which ignores the problem of the likely quality of Scottish wine.) Clearly, Scotland has an absolute advantage in cloth production – it can produce a bolt of cloth at a lower real cost than can Italy – whereas Italy has an absolute advantage in wine production. Consequently, each country will benefit by specializing in the commodity in which it has an absolute advantage, obtaining the other commodity through trade. The benefit derives from obtaining the imported commodity at a lower real cost through trade than through direct production at home.

In the absence of trade, in Scotland one barrel of wine will exchange for four bolts of cloth (because they require equal amounts of labor); in Italy one barrel of wine will exchange for one-fifth of a bolt of cloth. Scotland will benefit if it can trade less than four bolts of cloth for one barrel of wine, Italy if it can obtain more than one-fifth of a bolt of cloth for one barrel of wine. Clearly, both countries can gain at an intermediate ratio such as one barrel

Table 2.1 An example of absolute advantage

Days of labor required to produce	Country	
	Italy	Scotland
Wine (1 barrel)	20	120
Cloth (1 bolt)	100	30

of wine for one bolt of cloth. By shifting 120 days of labor from wine to cloth, Scotland could produce four additional bolts of cloth, worth four barrels of wine in trade with Italy. Scotland gets four barrels of wine instead of one. Italy obtains a similar gain through specialization in wine.

The nature of the possible efficiency gains for the combined economies of Scotland and Italy in this situation can be seen by noting what will happen if each country shifts 600 days of labor from the production of the commodity in which it is inefficient toward one it produces efficiently. If Scotland moves 600 labor days from wine production to cloth, while Italy shifts 600 labor days in the opposite direction, the production changes shown in Table 2.2 will occur in each country. With no increase in labor inputs, the combined economy of the two countries gains 14 bolts of cloth and 25 barrels of wine. These gains in the production of both goods resulted from merely shifting 600 labor days in each country toward more efficient uses. If 1,200 labor days were shifted by each country instead of 600, the gains would be twice as large.

Table 2.2 The gain in output from trade with an absolute advantage

	Italy	Scotland	Total
Wine (barrels)	30	−5	25
Cloth (bolts)	−6	20	14

Total output of both goods rises when Italy shifts 600 labor days from cloth to wine production and Scotland shifts 600 labor days from wine to cloth production.

This explanation based on absolute advantage certainly suffices to account for important segments of international trade. Brazil can produce coffee at a lower real cost than can Germany; Florida can produce oranges at a lower real cost than Iceland; Australia can produce wool at a lower real cost than Switzerland. But what if a nation (or an individual) does not have an absolute advantage in any line of production? Does trade then offer it no benefit?

Comparative advantage

David Ricardo clearly showed, in his *Principles of Political Economy* (1817),[2] that absolute cost advantages are not a necessary condition for two nations to gain from trade with each other. Instead, trade will benefit both nations provided only that their relative costs, that is, the ratios of their real costs in terms of labor inputs, are different for two or more commodities. In short, trade depends on differences in comparative advantage, and one nation can profitably trade with another even though its real costs are higher (or lower) in every commodity. This point can best be explained through a numerical example.

Ricardo presented the case of potential trade in wine and cloth between Portugal and England, which we have modified here by using a different set of numbers. The costs of producing a bolt of cloth or a barrel of wine in each of the two countries, measured in terms of days of labor, are given in Table 2.3. As can be seen in this table, England is more efficient at the production of both goods. Less labor is required to produce either good in England than in Portugal. That fact is irrelevant, however. What is important is that Portugal has a comparative advantage in wine, whereas England has a comparative advantage in cloth.

Table 2.3 An example of comparative advantage

Days of labor required to produce	Country	
	Portugal	England
Wine (1 barrel)	3	2
Cloth (1 bolt)	10	4

England can produce either two barrels of wine or one bolt of cloth with the same amount of labor (4 days). By shifting labor from wine to cloth production, it can transform two barrels of wine into one bolt of cloth. Portugal, however, can produce either 3.33 barrels of wine or one bolt of cloth with the same labor (10 days). Therefore by shifting labor from cloth to wine production, Portugal can transform one bolt of cloth into 3.33 barrels of wine. In comparative terms, cloth is inexpensive in England and expensive in Portugal, whereas wine is cheap in Portugal and costly in England. A bolt of cloth costs only two barrels of wine in England, but the same bolt of cloth costs 3.33 barrels of wine in Portugal. When viewed from the perspective of wine, we see that a barrel costs one-half of a bolt of cloth in England, but only one-third of a bolt of cloth in Portugal. These differences in the relative costs of one good in terms of the other create Portugal's comparative advantage in wine and England's in cloth.

The efficiency gains that this pattern of comparative advantage makes possible can be seen by imagining that Portugal shifts 60 days of labor from the production of cloth to employment in the wine industry, whereas England shifts 36 days of labor in the opposite direction, that is, from wine to cloth production. Given the labor costs presented in Table 2.3, the result of these shifts of labor use would be as shown in Table 2.4. The combined economies of Portugal and England can drink two more barrels of wine and wear clothes using three more bolts of cloth, even though there has been no increase in labor use. Note that to guarantee that total output of both goods rises, Portugal must shift more labor days than England because Portugal produces less efficiently in absolute terms. If both countries had shifted the same number of labor days, there would have been a far larger increase in cloth production and a small reduction in wine output.

Another way to understand the nature of these gains is to imagine that someone had the monopoly right to trade between London and Lisbon. If the labor costs presented in Table 2.3 prevailed and labor were the only input, the price ratios faced by the monopoly trader in the two countries would be as shown in Table 2.5.

In Portugal a bolt of cloth is 3.33 times as expensive as a barrel of wine, whereas in England cloth is only twice as costly as wine. The difference in these two barter ratios creates an enormously profitable opportunity for the monopoly trader. Starting out with 100 bolts

Table 2.4 The gain in output from trade with comparative advantage

	Portugal	England	Total
Wine (barrels)	20	–18	2
Cloth (bolts)	–6	9	3

Total output of both goods rises when Portugal shifts 60 labor days from cloth to wine production and England shifts 36 labor days from wine to cloth production.

Table 2.5 Domestic exchange ratios in Portugal and England

	Portugal	England
Wine (barrels)	3.33	2
Cloth (bolts)	1	1

of cloth in London, the trader ships that merchandise to Lisbon, where it can be exchanged for 333.3 barrels of wine. The 333.3 barrels are put on the ship back to London, where they are bartered for 166.7 bolts of cloth. The trader started out with 100 bolts of cloth and now has 166.7 bolts, thereby earning a return of 66.7 percent minus shipping costs by simply trading around in a circle between London and Lisbon.[3]

The monopoly trader merely took advantage of the differing price ratios in England and Portugal, which were based on differing relative labor costs, and made an enormous profit. Now imagine that the monopoly has been eliminated and that anyone who wishes to do so can trade between London and Lisbon. As large numbers of people purchase cloth in London, with the intention of shipping it to Lisbon, they will drive the English price of cloth up. When these same people arrive in Lisbon and sell this large amount of cloth, they will depress the price. As these same traders buy large amounts of Portuguese wine to ship to London, they will drive the Lisbon price of wine up. When they all arrive in London to sell that wine, they will push the price down.

As a result of trade, the price ratios are converging. As the price of cloth rises in London and falls in Lisbon, while the price of wine rises in Portugal and falls in England, the large profits previously earned by the traders decline. In a competitive equilibrium, the differences in the price ratios would be just sufficient to cover transport costs and provide a minimum competitive rate of return for the traders. For simplicity we will ignore transport costs and the minimum return for the traders; free trade will result in a single price ratio that prevails in both countries. That price ratio will be somewhere between the two initial price ratios in Portugal and England.

Does this mean that the gains from trade, which were previously concentrated in the profits of the monopoly trader, have disappeared? No, it merely means that these gains have been shifted away from the trader and toward the societies of Portugal and England through changes in the price ratios. When the monopolist controlled trade between the two countries, England had to export one bolt of cloth to get two barrels of wine. Now that competition prevails, the English price of cloth has risen while the price of wine has declined. Consequently, a bolt of cloth exported by England will pay for considerably more wine, or significantly less exported cloth will pay for the same amount of wine. England now has an improved standard of living because it can have more wine, or more cloth, or both. The same circumstance prevails for Portugal. In Lisbon the price of wine has risen and the price of cloth has declined; thus the same amount of wine exported will purchase more cloth, or the same amount of cloth can be purchased with less wine. Portugal also has an improved standard of living because it can consume more cloth, or more wine, or both.

This demonstration, that the gain from trade arises from differences in comparative cost, has been hailed as one of the greatest achievements of economic analysis. It may seem, on first acquaintance, to be a rather small point to warrant such extravagant praise, but it has proven to have a great many applications in economics and in other fields of study as well. Ricardo appealed to a common-sense application in another of his examples:

Two men can make both shoes and hats, and one is superior to the other in both employments, but in making hats he can only exceed his competitor by one-fifth or 20 per cent, and in making shoes he can excel him by one-third or 33 per cent; – will it not be for the interest of both that the superior man should employ himself exclusively in making shoes, and the inferior man in making hats?[4]

It is the principle of comparative advantage that underlies the advantages of the division of labor, whether between individuals, firms, regions, or nations. We specialize in those activities in which we have a relative advantage, depending on others to supply us with other goods and services. In this way real income can increase as a result of the growing economic interdependence among countries.

Additional tools of analysis

That gains from trade exist is a conclusion that holds much more generally than in the world represented by the labor theory of value. To substantiate this claim, we will consider several more formal economic models here and in the next two chapters. Rather than repeat all the qualifying assumptions each time we introduce a new model, it is useful to clarify at the outset what common set of circumstances is to apply in each trading nation. Recognizing what conditions actually are imposed should help us to appreciate how broadly our results may apply and to recognize when exceptions to our conclusions might arise. These assumptions are:

1　perfect competition in both commodity and factor markets: costs of production determine pre-trade prices, and flexibility of factor prices ensures that factors are fully employed;
2　fixed quantities of the factors of production: we do not consider capital formation or growth in the labor force;
3　factors of production are perfectly mobile between industries within each country but completely immobile between countries;
4　a given, unchanging level of technology;
5　zero transport costs and other barriers to trade: a good will have a single price internationally;
6　given tastes and preferences: the sharpest distinctions can be made when tastes are identical across countries and a rise in income increases consumption of all goods proportionally;
7　balanced trade, where the value of imports equals the value of exports.

The concept of opportunity cost

One way to avoid dependence on the labor theory of value is through the use of the now familiar concept of **opportunity cost**.[5] The opportunity cost of a unit of commodity A is the next best alternative given up in order to obtain it. In a two-good world, that is the amount of commodity B given up to obtain a unit of A. If just enough land, labor, and capital are withdrawn from B to permit the production of an extra unit of A, the opportunity cost of the additional (marginal) unit of A is the amount by which the output of B declines. A country has a comparative advantage in commodity A if it can produce an additional unit of A at a lower opportunity cost in terms of commodity B than can another country.

The production-possibility curve with constant opportunity cost

This view of cost leads directly to the concept of a production-possibility curve. Suppose that Germany can produce only two commodities: wheat and steel. If it puts all its productive resources into wheat, let us suppose that it can produce 100 million tons. Suppose further that German conditions of production are such that the opportunity cost of a ton of steel is 1 ton of wheat. Starting from an initial position in which Germany is fully specialized in wheat, as resources are shifted into steel the output of wheat will drop by 1 ton for each additional ton of steel produced. When all German resources are devoted to steel production, its total output will be 100 million tons of steel and no wheat. Table 2.6 summarizes the alternative combinations of wheat and steel that Germany can produce.

Table 2.6 German production of wheat and steel (millions of tons)

Wheat	100	90	80	70	60	50	40	30	20	10	0
Steel	0	10	20	30	40	50	60	70	80	90	100

This situation can also be shown in a diagram (Figure 2.1). The straight line AB represents the production-possibility curve for the German economy. Points along the line AB represent alternative combinations of wheat and steel that Germany can produce at full employment. At A, it produces 100 million tons of wheat and no steel; at B, 100 million tons of steel and no wheat; at P, 60 million tons of wheat and 40 million tons of steel. The constant slope of AB represents the constant opportunity cost or internal ratio of exchange (one wheat for one steel). The line AB, therefore, represents the highest attainable combinations of wheat and steel that the German economy can produce at full employment. All points above and to the right of AB, such as J, represent combinations of wheat and steel that exceed current German productive capacity. Points to the left of AB, such as K, represent the existence of unemployment or the inefficient use of resources.

More can usefully be said about the slope of the production-possibility curve. Because Germany's economy is fully employed at both points P and P', the additional cost from

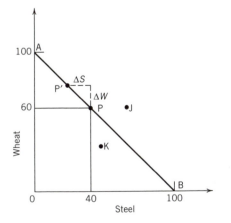

Figure 2.1 Germany's production-possibility curve. This figure illustrates the combinations of wheat and steel that can be produced with a fixed available supply of labor. The slope of that line represents the ratio at which steel can be transformed into wheat.

increasing the production of steel by ΔS (i.e. that change in quantity times the marginal cost of steel) must equal the cost saving from reducing the production of wheat by $-\Delta W$ (i.e. minus one times that change in quantity times the marginal cost of wheat), which can be expressed as $\Delta S \cdot MC_s = -\Delta W \cdot MC_w$. This formulation can also be written in terms of the absolute value of the slope of the production-possibility line, $\Delta W / \Delta S$, where we omit the minus sign in representing this slope as

$$\frac{\Delta W}{\Delta S} = \frac{MC_s}{MC_w}$$

and note that it equals the ratio of the marginal cost of steel to the marginal cost of wheat. This ratio of marginal costs, which represents the rate at which the German economy can transform steel into wheat, is called the **marginal rate of transformation** (MRT).

The fact that AB in Figure 2.1 is a straight line indicates that the relative costs of the two goods do not change as the economy shifts from all wheat to all steel, or anywhere in between. This case of constant costs, or a constant marginal rate of transformation, is most applicable when there is a single factor of production and when that factor is homogeneous within a country. Labor is the only input in Germany, for example, and all German workers have the same relative abilities to produce steel and wheat. Constant costs also may exist when more than one factor input is necessary to produce both goods, but the proportions in which the inputs are required must be identical in the two industries.

When two countries have straight-line production-possibility curves with differing slopes, their relative costs differ. This situation creates a potential for mutual gains from trade under comparative advantage. In this case, labor is the only input in each country, and labor is homogeneous within countries but not between countries. That is, all workers in Germany are alike and all workers in the other country are alike, but workers in Germany differ from the workers in the other country. For some unspecified reason, the workers in Germany are relatively more efficient at producing one good, while the workers in the other country are relatively more productive at the other good. These assumptions, though not particularly realistic, are none the less maintained for the next few pages because they make it easier to illustrate some basic concepts in international trade theory.

The production-possibility curve AB thus provides a complete account of the supply side of the picture in our hypothetical German economy. To determine which one of all these possible combinations Germany will actually choose, we will have to deal with the demand side of the picture.

Demand conditions and indifference curves

The classical economist John Stuart Mill recast the analysis of Smith and Ricardo to consider how the equilibrium international ratio of exchange is established.[6] He introduced demand considerations into the analysis by noting that at the equilibrium ratio of exchange, the amount of the export good one country offers must exactly equal the amount the other country is willing to purchase. He referred to this equilibrium as one characterized by equal reciprocal demands. If trade is to balance, as we assume here, this condition must be met for each country's export good.

Within the bounds set by the different opportunity cost ratios in each country, the equilibrium ratio of exchange will be determined by demand in each country for the other country's export. Mill discussed how this outcome is influenced by the size of each country and by the elasticity of demand. We develop those ideas here, but with the use of some additional analytical tools that help clarify why different outcomes arise.

One useful tool is an indifference curve, which economists use to represent consumer preferences. For example, the indifference curve i_1, in Figure 2.2, shows the alternative combinations of food and clothing that give an individual the same level of satisfaction, well-being, or utility. Suppose the individual initially consumes the bundle of food and clothing represented by point A.

Now suppose that one unit of food (AR in Figure 2.2) is taken away from our consumer, thus reducing their level of satisfaction or utility. How much additional clothing would it take to restore him or her to the same level of satisfaction or utility that they enjoyed at point A? If that amount is RB units of clothing in Figure 2.2, then at point B the consumer will be just as well satisfied as at A. We can say that they are indifferent between the two commodity bundles represented by points A and B, and therefore these two points lie on the same indifference curve, i_1.

Proceeding in a similar way, we can locate other points on i_1. Conceptually, we wish simply to determine the amount of one commodity that will exactly compensate the consumer for the loss of a given amount of the other commodity.

Thus far we have derived only a single indifference curve, but it is easy to generate others. Starting back at point A, suppose we give the consumer more of both commodities, moving him or her to point E. Since both commodities yield satisfaction, E represents a higher level of utility than does A – that is, it lies on a higher indifference curve, i_2. We can then proceed as before to locate other points on i_2. In this way, a whole family of indifference curves can be generated, where movement to a higher indifference curve implies a higher level of welfare, utility, or real income.

Furthermore, because E lies along i_2, we can conclude that the individual is better off than at B, which lies along i_1, even though they have less clothing at E than at B. Note also that indifference curves are convex to the origin – that is, they bend in toward the origin. This curvature simply reflects the fact that, as the consumer gives up more food, it takes more and more clothing to compensate him or her and to maintain the same level of satisfaction. In other words, the marginal rate of substitution between food and clothing, which is the ratio

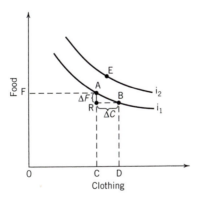

Figure 2.2 Consumer indifference curves. Consumers are at the same level of welfare with any combination of food and clothing along i_1. The curvature of that line results from the law of diminishing marginal utility: the more of a good one has, the less extra units of it are worth.

of AR to RB, is falling as the consumer moves down the indifference curve. Finally, indifference curves cannot intersect each other. If two indifference curves intersected, it would imply that people were indifferent between more of both goods and less of both goods, which is impossible if they value both goods. The reader can draw intersecting indifference curves to confirm that this situation would imply such an indifference between more and less of everything.

Returning to the slope of the indifference curve, note that since consumers have the same level of welfare at point A as at point B, they must view the smaller amount of food $-\Delta F$ as having the same value as the additional amount of clothing ΔC. This means that if they exchanged $-\Delta F$ of food for ΔC of clothing, they would have the same standard of living. Thus the slope of the indifference curve, AR over RB (or $-\Delta F$ over ΔC), represents the relative values that they place on the two goods. This can be expressed as

$$-\Delta F \cdot MU_f = \Delta C \cdot MU_c$$

where MU represents marginal utility, which is the value consumers place on an additional unit of a product. The previous statement then says that the change in the quantity of food $(-\Delta F)$ times the value of one less unit of food equals the change in the quantity of clothing (ΔC) times the value of one additional unit of clothing. We can rearrange these terms and express the absolute value of the slope of the indifference curve as

$$\frac{\Delta F}{\Delta C} = \frac{MU_c}{MU_f}$$

Thus the slope of the indifference curve equals the ratio of the marginal utilities of the two goods. That ratio is called the **marginal rate of substitution**, or MRS. The marginal rate of substitution is the rate at which consumers are willing to substitute one good for the other and become neither better nor worse off.[7]

Can this representation of an individual's preferences and well-being be applied analogously to talk of a nation's preferences and well-being? Only under very specific circumstances does that happen to be true. Several complications may arise when we try to add together or aggregate the preferences of two different individuals. Two types of issues are relevant.

First, if individuals have different preferences, then the total quantity demanded of a good will depend upon how income is distributed in the economy. If individuals with a strong preference for clothing receive a larger share of income, for example, then society will demand more clothing than when a larger share of income is received by those who prefer food. To predict society's demand for a good we need to know how income is distributed in a society and how changing circumstances, such as a change in the international ratio of exchange, may alter that income distribution.

Another way to make this point is to note that if the distribution of income within a country changes, the shape of the community's indifference curves will also change to favor the good that is preferred by those who have gained higher incomes. Indifference curves for one distribution of incomes could easily intersect indifference curves for a different distribution of incomes. Since free trade will change the distribution of income within a country, it could be expected to change the shape of the country's indifference curves. We would need to know the relevant set of indifference curves for each distribution of income to predict the combination of goods that society demands at the new price ratio.

Second, if individuals in fact had the same tastes and spent their incomes in the same proportions on the two goods, our **community indifference curves** would not cross as income was redistributed. That would mean we could predict total product demands in the economy in response to relative price changes, without having to pay attention to changes in the income distribution. If we try to judge whether the price change made society worse off, however, we confront another difficulty: the satisfaction or utility enjoyed by one individual cannot be compared with the utility enjoyed by another. Utility cannot be measured cardinally in units that are the same for all individuals.

If some individuals gain from trade while others lose, we have no way to make interpersonal comparisons of utility that would tell us how to weigh these separate effects. Therefore, economists typically talk of potential improvements in welfare, where gainers could compensate losers and still become better off as a result of trade.

One way to escape from these difficulties is to assume that every individual has exactly the same tastes and owns exactly the same amount of each factor of production. Then any price change leaves the distribution of income unchanged and everyone is harmed or benefited to the same degree. In that extreme situation, it is possible to conceive of community indifference curves just as we have described them for a single person, and the reader may find it useful to apply that simplifying assumption to our subsequent discussion of the effects of trade. Alternatively, our approach can be interpreted as assuming that any differences in tastes between individuals are so small that nonintersecting community indifference curves are appropriate and that any conclusions about improvements in welfare rest upon the convention of potential welfare improvements. We discuss these assumptions to demonstrate how restrictive they must be.[8]

International trade with constant costs

We are now ready to bring supply and demand conditions together and to demonstrate how and why trade takes place. Figure 2.3 shows the initial equilibrium in a closed economy, before trade. Community indifference curves for Germany are superimposed on its production-possibility curve from Figure 2.1. Under competitive conditions, the closed-economy or autarky equilibrium of the German economy will be at point P, where 60 million tons of wheat and 40 million tons of steel are produced. That is where Germany reaches the highest possible indifference curve (level of welfare) it can attain with its given productive resources. At the point of tangency P between the production-possibility curve WS and the community indifference curve i_2, the slopes of the two are equal, which means that the marginal rate of transformation is exactly equal to the community's marginal rate of substitution. At any other production point, it is possible to reallocate resources and move to a higher indifference curve. At N, for example, Germany is on i_1. By shifting resources from steel to wheat, it can move to P and thus reach a higher indifference curve, i_2.

Although we speak of Germany shifting resources from steel to wheat, in a competitive economy it is actually individual firms that are making these decisions and taking the necessary actions. Their motivation comes from price signals in the market. At N, the opportunity-cost ratio facing producers is not equal to the slope of the indifference curve, i_1. Consumers are willing to swap, say, two tons of steel for one of wheat, whereas the opportunity cost in production is one ton of steel for one of wheat. When prices reflect this

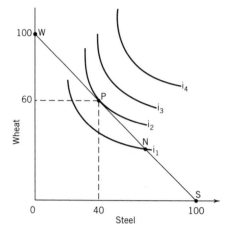

Figure 2.3 Equilibrium in a closed economy. If WS is the production-possibility frontier, producing and consuming at point P results in the highest possible level of welfare for a closed, or nontrading, economy.

difference, producers are led to expand wheat production, and a move from N toward P occurs.

Given the initial closed-economy equilibrium at P, now suppose that Germany has the opportunity to trade with the rest of the world (ROW) at an exchange ratio different from its domestic opportunity cost ratio (1S:1W). Specifically, suppose the exchange ratio in ROW is 1S:2W, and suppose that Germany is so small relative to ROW that German trade has no effect on world prices. Comparing Germany's domestic ratio to the international exchange ratio, we can see that Germany has a comparative advantage in steel. That is, its cost of steel (measured in forgone wheat) is less than the cost in ROW. Note that we do not need to know whether German labor is efficient or inefficient compared to labor in other countries. In fact, we do not need to know anything at all about the real cost in terms of labor hours, land area, or capital equipment. All that matters to Germany is that by trans-ferring resources from wheat to steel, it can obtain more wheat through trade than through direct production at home. For every ton of wheat lost through curtailed production, Germany can obtain 2 tons through trade, a smaller cost in resources than it would incur at home. An opportunity for a gain from trade will exist provided the exchange ratio in ROW differs from Germany's domestic exchange ratio. That is, with a domestic ratio of 1S:1W, Germany can benefit, provided it can get anything more than 1 ton of wheat for 1 ton of steel. If 1 ton of steel buys less than 1 ton of wheat in ROW, Germany will benefit from trading wheat for steel. Only if the international exchange ratio is exactly equal to Germany's domestic ratio will there be no opportunity for gainful trade.

This example can be given a useful geometric interpretation, as in Figure 2.4, in which we add to Figure 2.3 the "consumption-possibility line" or barter line, SB, drawn with a slope equal to the autarky price ratio in ROW (1S:2W). Once they have the opportunity to trade at the ROW ratio, German producers will shift from wheat to steel. With constant opportunity costs, they will continue to shift until they are fully specialized in steel (at S in Figure 2.4). German firms will have an incentive to trade steel for wheat, moving along the barter line to reach the highest possible level of welfare, which will be found at the point of tangency between an indifference curve and the line SB. That is point T in Figure 2.4. At

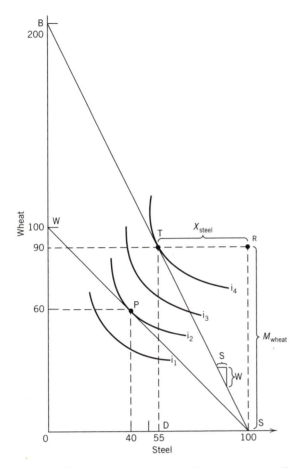

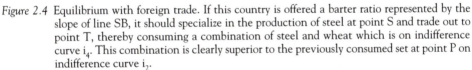

Figure 2.4 Equilibrium with foreign trade. If this country is offered a barter ratio represented by the
slope of line SB, it should specialize in the production of steel at point S and trade out to
point T, thereby consuming a combination of steel and wheat which is on indifference
curve i_4. This combination is clearly superior to the previously consumed set at point P on
indifference curve i_2.

T, the price ratio is again equal to the marginal rate of substitution in consumption as
represented by the slope of the indifference curve i_4 at that point.

In the final equilibrium position, Germany will produce at point S and consume at point
T. It will produce OS of steel (100 million tons), keeping OD (55 million tons) for its own
use and exporting SD of steel (45 million tons) in exchange for imports DT of wheat (90
million tons). Recognize what we will call the "trade triangle," TRS, where TR = steel
exports and RS = wheat imports, and the slope of the third side, TS, represents the relative
price of steel.

Germany's gain from trade can clearly be seen in the final column of Table 2.7. Compare
the amounts of wheat and steel that are available for domestic consumption before and after
trade: 30 million more tons of wheat and 15 million more tons of steel are available after
trade. Because population and resources employed remain the same, while more of both
goods are available, Germany clearly can increase economic welfare in the sense of providing
its population with more material goods than they had before trade began.

Table 2.7 German production and consumption

	Before trade		
	Production (net national product)	=	Consumption
Wheat:	60 million tons	=	60 million tons
Steel:	40 million tons	=	40 million tons

	After trade (millions of tons)						
	Production (NNP)	−	Exports	+	Imports	=	Consumption
Wheat:	0	−	0	+	90	=	90
Steel:	100	−	45	+	0	=	55

Another demonstration that Germany gains from foreign trade is the fact that it reaches a higher indifference curve: the movement from i_2 to i_4. This point is important because it may well be that a country will end up with more of one commodity and less of another as a result of trade. As we have seen, indifference curves enable us to determine whether or not welfare has increased in such cases.

Thus far we have focused on the position of one country and have assumed that it has the opportunity to trade at a fixed relative price of steel. We assumed that Germany's offer of steel on the world market did not affect the international exchange ratio. We will now consider how the international exchange ratio is determined. Our example uses two countries of approximately equal size. Again, we find that both countries can gain from international trade.

Our two countries are Germany and France. German supply and demand conditions remain the same as in Figure 2.3. We assume that France can produce 240 million tons of wheat or 80 million tons of steel if it specializes fully in one or the other. The French production-possibility curve, HG, drawn as a straight line to indicate a constant marginal rate of transformation of 1S:3W, is shown in Figure 2.5, along with community indifference curves to represent French demand. In complete isolation, the French economy is in equilibrium at point K, where 120W and 40S are produced and consumed.

Before trade, the domestic exchange ratios differ in our two countries: in Germany 1S:1W, in France 1S:3W. As noted, the fact that these ratios are different is enough to show that comparative advantage exists. Steel is cheaper (in terms of forgone wheat) in Germany than it is in France; hence Germany has a comparative advantage in steel and France in wheat. Note that we need not compare the resources used in each country in order to determine comparative advantage; we need only to compare their opportunity-cost ratios. If these are different, a basis for trade exists.

Germany will benefit if it can exchange 1S for anything more than 1W, and France will benefit if it can obtain 1S for anything less than 3W. Therefore, when trade begins between these two countries, the international exchange ratio may lie anywhere between the two domestic ratios: 1S:1W and 1S:3W. Just where the international exchange ratio will settle depends on the willingness of each country to offer its export commodity and to purchase imports at various relative prices. To explain this process, we will first show the conditions that must prevail for an equilibrium to exist in our illustrative example, and then we will present a more general approach.

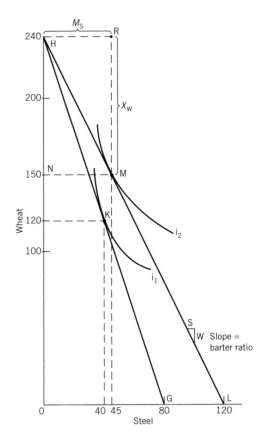

Figure 2.5 France: equilibrium before and after trade. Production is specialized in wheat at point H, and trade occurs along barter line HL to point M, producing a higher level of welfare on indifference curve i_2, than existed before trade at point K.

We have already determined Germany's demand for imports (90W) and its offer of exports (45S) at the intermediate exchange ratio 1S:2W. Those amounts are shown in Figure 2.4. How much wheat is France willing to export for how much steel at that exchange ratio? In Figure 2.5, we draw the line HL to represent France's barter line. It originates at H because France will specialize in wheat production. We see that by trading wheat for steel, France can barter along HL and attain a higher level of welfare than it can reach in isolation. At M, it reaches the highest possible indifference curve. At that point France will export 90W and import 45S, as indicated by its trade triangle, HRM.

Thus, it turns out that France is willing to export, at the exchange ratio 1S:2W, just the amount of wheat that Germany wants to import. And France wants to import just the amount of steel that Germany is willing to export. Geometrically, this equality can be seen by comparing the two trade triangles, TRS and HRM in Figures 2.4 and 2.5. They are identical, which means that we have hit upon the equilibrium terms-of-trade ratio. Note carefully the conditions that are necessary for the exchange ratio 1S:2W to be an equilibrium ratio: each country must demand exactly the amount of its imported commodity that the other country is willing to supply.

Before proceeding to a more general case in which countries do not have constant costs and therefore do not have straight-line production-possibility curves, we pause to note that

Table 2.8 The gain from trade: production and consumption before and after trade

	Wheat					Steel				
	P	− X	+ M	= C		P	− X	+ M	= C	
Situation before trade										
France	120			120		40			40	
Germany	60			60		40			40	
Total world	180			180		80			80	
Situation after trade										
France	240	− 90	+ 0	= 150		0	− 0	+ 45	= 45	
Germany	0	−	+ 90	= 90		100	− 45	+ 0	= 55	
Total world	240			240		100			100	
Gain from trade										
France			+	30				+	5	
Germany			+	30				+	15	
Total world			+	60				+	20	

Legend: P = Production, X = Exports, M = Imports, C = Consumption.

both France and Germany benefit from international trade. This is shown most directly by the fact that both countries end up on higher indifference curves in the trading equilibrium in Figures 2.4 and 2.5. The gain in this particular case can also be shown arithmetically in Table 2.8, which contains a summary of the world position before and after trade. Before trade, world outputs of wheat and steel were 180W and 80S; post-trade outputs are 240W and 100S. One may ask by what magic has world output of both commodities increased without the use of any additional resources. The answer is that specialization – the use of each nation's resources to produce the commodity in which it possesses a comparative advantage – has made possible a larger total output than can be achieved under self-sufficiency.

International trade with increasing costs

So far, we have assumed that opportunity costs in each country remain unchanged as resources shift from one industry to another. We now drop this assumption of constant costs and adopt the more realistic assumption of increasing costs. That is, we will now assume that as resources are shifted from, say, wheat production to cloth production, the opportunity cost of each additional unit of cloth increases. Such increasing costs could arise because factors of production vary in quality and in suitability for producing different commodities. Business firms, in their efforts to maximize profit, will be led through competition to use resources where they are best suited. Thus, when cloth production is increased, the resources (land, labor, and capital) drawn away from the wheat industry will be somewhat less well suited to cloth production than those already in the cloth industry. Hence, for a given increase in cloth output the cost in forgone wheat will be larger – that is, the marginal opportunity cost of cloth rises as its output increases. Also, if more than one factor of production exists, increasing opportunity costs arise when the two industries require the inputs in different proportions. That situation is examined more carefully in Chapter 3. For both reasons, it seems intuitively plausible to expect increasing costs to exist as a country moves toward greater specialization in a particular product.

Increasing costs give rise to a production-possibility curve that is bowed out (concave to the origin) as in Figure 2.6. At any point on the production-possibility curve, WC, the slope of the curve represents the opportunity-cost ratio (real exchange ratio) at that point. As the production point moves along the curve from W toward C, the slope of the curve becomes steeper, which means that cloth costs more in terms of forgone wheat. In isolation, the country will seek to reach the highest possible indifference curve, which means that it will produce at point P in Figure 2.6. At P, the line RR is tangent to both the production-possibility curve, WC, and the indifference curve u_1. The slope of the tangent RR represents the internal barter ratio, the marginal rate of transformation, and the marginal rate of substitution. At P, which is the optimum situation for this country as a closed or nontrading economy, the country produces and consumes OC_1 of cloth and OW_1 of wheat, and the following condition holds:

$$\frac{P_c}{P_w} = \frac{MC_c}{MC_w} = \frac{MU_c}{MU_w}$$

Within this country, the price ratio for the two goods equals the marginal rate of transformation, which equals the marginal rate of substitution. When this is true, the country is operating at maximum efficiency as a closed economy.

A further comment on this solution is warranted, because this is a barter economy without money prices. Therefore, rather than talk of separate prices for wheat and cloth, we are limited to the relative price ratio, or the price of cloth in terms of how many units of wheat are given up to obtain a unit of cloth. If the price line RR is steeper, the relative price of the good along the horizontal axis, cloth, is higher. Alternatively stated, we can think of P_w remaining constant at a value of one because all other prices are measured in terms of units of wheat. An increase in the ratio P_c/P_w then indicates that the price of cloth has risen. As RR becomes steeper, the point of tangency along the production-possibility curve will be further to the right, because a higher price for cloth justifies the higher cost of expanding cloth output.

As we apply this framework to a situation where trade is possible, most of the analysis developed in the case of constant costs also applies to the case of increasing costs. The major difference is that we must allow for the changing internal cost ratios in each country as trade

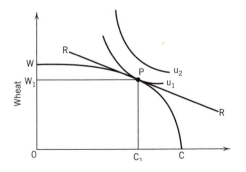

Figure 2.6 Increasing costs: equilibrium in a closed economy. With increasing costs of specialization, represented by the curvature of the production-possibility curve WC, this country maximizes welfare at point P as a closed economy.

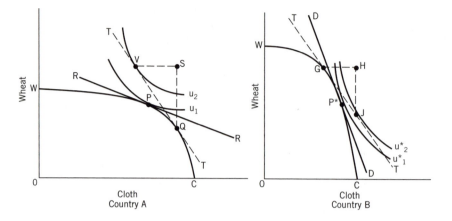

Figure 2.7 Equilibrium trade in a two-country case (increasing costs): (a) Country A, (b) Country B. With trade, each country can consume a set of goods that is superior to that which occurred without trade. Country A shifts production from point P to Q and then trades to consume at point V, which is on a higher indifference curve. Country B produces at point G and trades to reach point J, which is also on a higher indifference curve.

begins to cause resources to shift toward employment in the comparative-advantage industry. Let us consider a two-country, two-commodity example as depicted in Figure 2.7.

The pre-trade equilibrium

In Country A, the pre-trade or autarky equilibrium is at point P in Figure 2.7a with production and consumption of cloth and wheat represented by the coordinates of point P. Country A's domestic exchange ratio is represented by the slope of RR, and its level of welfare by u_1. In Country B, the pre-trade equilibrium is at point P* in Figure 2.7b, with production and consumption of cloth and wheat represented by the coordinates of that point. B's domestic exchange ratio is represented by the slope of DD, and its level of welfare by u^*_1.

Because the slopes of the autarky price lines are different in Countries A and B, it is clear that a basis for mutually beneficial trade exists. In this case, cloth is relatively cheaper in A than in B, and wheat is relatively cheaper in B than in A. Hence A has a comparative advantage in cloth, and B in wheat. The difference in the slopes of the autarky price lines creates the following condition:

$$\frac{P^B_c}{P^B_w} = \frac{MC^B_c}{MC^B_w} = \frac{MU^B_c}{MU^B_w} > \frac{P^A_c}{P^A_w} = \frac{MC^A_c}{MC^A_w} = \frac{MU^A_c}{MU^A_w}$$

The equalities within each country mean that each closed economy is operating at maximum efficiency; it is the inequality in the middle that informs us that Country B has a comparative advantage in wheat, that Country A has a comparative advantage in cloth, and that mutually beneficial trade is therefore possible. If, by some chance, the two countries started out with the same slopes for their barter price lines, and therefore with an equals sign in the middle of the above statement, there would be no comparative-advantage basis for trade.

The post-trade equilibrium

When trade is opened up, producers in A will find it profitable to shift resources from wheat to cloth, moving along the production-possibility curve in Figure 2.7a from P toward Q, and exporting cloth to B for a higher price than they were getting at home, in isolation. How far this shift will go depends on the final international exchange ratio. Similarly, producers in B find it profitable to shift resources from cloth to wheat, moving from P* toward G in Figure 2.7b, and exporting wheat to A.

Trade will be in equilibrium at an exchange ratio at which the reciprocal demands are equal – that is, where A's exports of cloth precisely equal B's imports of cloth, and conversely for wheat. In Figure 2.7, the equilibrium exchange ratio is shown as the slope of the line TT, common to both countries. At this ratio, the trade triangles SVQ and HGJ are identical. Thus A's cloth exports, SV, exactly equal B's cloth imports, GH; and A's wheat imports, SQ, exactly equal B's wheat exports, HJ. Country A produces at Q and consumes at V; Country B produces at G and consumes at J. Note that by trading both countries are able to reach higher indifference curves than in isolation.

Given the opportunity to trade, each country tends to specialize in the commodity in which it has a comparative advantage, but this tendency is checked by the presence of increasing costs. Country A does not fully specialize in cloth; instead, it continues to produce much of the wheat its population consumes. Similarly, B retains part of its cloth industry – the more efficient part, in fact.

The effect of trade

We pause to review and summarize the effects of trade. First, trade causes a reallocation of resources. Output expands in industries in which a country has a comparative advantage, pulling resources away from industries in which it has a comparative disadvantage. Graphically, we see this effect as a movement along the production-possibility curve – for example, the movement from P to Q in Country A in Figure 2.7a. Under conditions of increasing costs, as resources move into the comparative-advantage industry, marginal opportunity cost increases in that industry and falls in the industry whose output is contracting. The shift in resources will stop when the domestic cost ratio becomes equal to the international exchange ratio, as at Q in Figure 2.7a. Thus complete specialization normally will not occur. In the constant-cost case, however, where marginal costs do not change as resources move from one industry to another, complete specialization is likely.

This discussion of resource shifts throws into sharp relief the long-run nature of the theory we are discussing. Clearly, it will take much time for workers to be retrained and relocated and for capital to be converted into a form suitable for the new industry. The shift we show so easily as a movement from P to Q on a production-possibility curve may in fact involve a long and difficult transition period, with heavy human and social costs. These matters will be discussed more fully in later chapters; here we wish only to remind the reader to think about the real-world aspects of the adjustment processes we are describing.

A second effect of trade is to equalize relative prices in the trading countries. (We still ignore transport costs.) Differences in relative pre-trade prices provide a basis for trade: they give traders an incentive to export one commodity and import the other. When trade occurs, it causes relative costs and prices to converge in both countries. In each country, the commodity that was relatively cheaper before trade tends to rise in price. Trade continues until the domestic exchange ratios become equal in the two countries, as at the international exchange ratio, TT, in Figure 2.7.

A third effect of trade is to improve economic welfare in both countries. Through trade, each country is able to obtain combinations of commodities that lie beyond its capacity to produce for itself. In the present analysis, the gain from trade is shown by the movement to a higher indifference curve.

In the final equilibrium, because the slope of TT is the same in both countries, the following condition holds:

$$\frac{P^B_c}{P^B_w} = \frac{MC^B_c}{MC^B_w} = \frac{MU^B_c}{MU^B_w} = \frac{P^A_c}{P^A_w} = \frac{MC^A_c}{MC^A_w} = \frac{MU^A_c}{MU^A_w}$$

The price ratios, the marginal rates of transformation, and the marginal rates of substitution are all equal across the two countries. When this condition holds, further trade will not create additional gains.

The division of the gains from trade

The division of the gains from this exchange between Countries A and B depends on the ratio at which the two goods are exchanged, that is, on the international exchange ratio that causes the quantity that one country wants to export to just equal the quantity that the other wants to import. Of particular interest is what causes this international exchange ratio to be closer to the closed-economy exchange ratio that held in Country A or in Country B. We will analyze this question using two different diagrammatic approaches. First, we utilize supply and demand curves, because they are likely to be more familiar. In a separate boxed section we introduce **offer curves**, which can be derived explicitly from the production-possibility curves and community indifference curves we have utilized thus far.

Figure 2.8 shows the domestic demand and supply curves of cloth for each country. The price of cloth is given in terms of units of wheat per unit of cloth, which means we are still in a world of barter where we must talk of relative prices. The supply curves slope upward

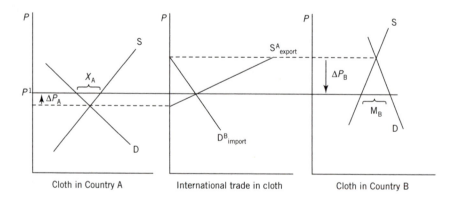

Figure 2.8 Equilibrium price determination. The equilibrium international price, P^1, is determined by the intersection of A's export supply curve with B's import demand curve where the quantity of cloth supplied by A exactly equals the quantity of cloth demanded by B. A's export supply is the residual or difference between its domestic quantity supplied and domestic quantity demanded. B's import demand is the residual or difference between its domestic quantity demanded and domestic quantity supplied.

because there are increasing opportunity costs of production in each country. Such a supply curve differs, however, from the supply curve economists use to represent a single industry that is too small to influence wages or the prices of other inputs. Here, in our two-good world, any additional inputs into cloth production must be bid away from wheat producers. The supply curve for cloth includes the adjustments that occur as inputs are reallocated and input prices change in the process. Economists refer to that outcome as a general equilibrium solution, in contrast to a partial equilibrium solution that ignores such adjustments outside the industry being considered.

On the basis of the demand and supply curves in A, we can derive a residual export supply curve, which shows the quantity of cloth A is willing to export when price exceeds the autarky value P_A. At such a price, the corresponding quantity supplied to the export market equals the difference between the quantity produced domestically and the quantity consumed domestically. That export supply curve is shown in the center panel of Figure 2.8. Similarly, we can derive B's residual import demand curve, which shows the quantity of cloth B seeks to import when price is lower than its autarky value P_B. It represents the difference between the quantity demanded domestically and the quantity produced in B at a given price.

The equilibrium price is given by the intersection of A's export supply curve and B's import demand curve. At that price (P^1), the volume of cloth that Country A wishes to export matches the volume that B wants to import. In this example, B gets most of the gains from trade, because its price of cloth falls sharply, whereas the price in A rises only slightly. B's import price falls much more than A's export price rises. Country B is able to purchase a great deal more cloth for a given amount of wheat, whereas Country A gains less because the cloth it exports does not purchase a great deal more wheat. Nevertheless, Country A's price of cloth rises slightly in terms of wheat, meaning that its price of wheat falls. Thus, Country A does consume a combination of wheat and cloth which is superior to the combination it had without trade.

These graphs also reveal that Country B's enjoyment of particularly large gains from trade result from its relatively inelastic supply and demand functions. Because both of those curves are so inelastic, B's residual import demand curve is inelastic. Country A gains less from trade because its supply and demand functions are more elastic. As a consequence, its residual export supply curve is quite elastic. The general conclusion is that in trade between two countries, most of the gains go to the country with the less elastic supply and demand functions. The common-sense intuition of this conclusion is that the existence of inelastic functions means that large price changes are needed to produce significant quantity responses. Country B would not export much more wheat or import much more cloth unless prices changed sharply, whereas Country A was willing to import a large volume of wheat (and export a large amount of cloth) in response to only modest price changes. As a result, large price changes and the larger gains from trade occur in Country B.

We seldom observe a country that shifts away from a position of no trade and we seldom have enough information about the prices of all the goods actually traded to verify how large price changes happen to be. One such study by Richard Huber for Japan suggests that they can be very large.[9] He found that the prices of goods that Japan exported after its opening to trade with the outside world in 1858 rose by 33 percent, while the prices of goods it imported fell by 61 percent. Both of these measures are based on prices in terms of gold; the price ratio that represents Japan's terms of trade (export prices divided by import prices) rose from 1.0 to 3.4, a significant gain.

If we relate this outcome to the situation shown in Figure 2.8, what is the cause of the large change in Japan's prices relative to those in the rest of the world? Exports from the rest of the world did not rise in price very much because the extra demand created by Japan was such a small share of current world supply. Think of analogous cases where this situation can be interpreted in terms of elasticities of supply and demand. A single consumer's demand for apples has little or no effect on the market price of apples, because that buyer faces a very high or perfectly elastic supply of apples. If suppliers do not receive the market price from this single buyer, they have many other customers to whom they can sell. Similarly, Japan faced a very high elasticity of supply of the goods it imported, because producers could easily divert supply from other countries to sell to Japanese buyers. We can generalize this result to say that a small country is particularly likely to benefit from abandoning an autarky position of no trade.

Box 2.1 Offer curves

Offer curves, which are also known as "reciprocal demand curves," provide a more thorough means of illustrating how the equilibrium relative price ratio and the volume of trade in both commodities for our two countries are determined. An offer curve for one country illustrates the volume of trade (exports and imports) that it will choose to undertake at various terms of trade that it could be offered. By combining the offer curves for both countries and noting where they cross, we obtain an equilibrium price ratio and the volume of both goods traded.

An offer curve can be derived in a number of ways. One of the more straightforward approaches is to begin with the earlier production-possibility curve and indifference curve set for Country A, shown in the top panel of Figure 2.9, and to note what happens to that country's trade triangles as its terms of trade improve. Starting from autarky at point 1, as the price of cloth rises relative to the price of wheat, Country A shifts it production to point 2, point 3, and finally to point 4. Consumption shifts from point 1 to 5, 6, and finally 7. The three trade triangles, drawn with dotted lines, show how much Country A will choose to export and import at each of the three exchange ratios. In the bottom panel of Figure 2.9, the horizontal axis represents cloth exported

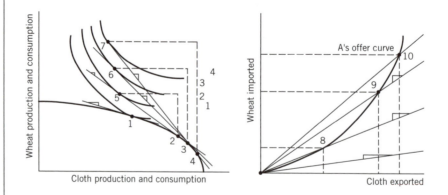

Figure 2.9 Derivation of Country A's offer curve. As Country A's terms of trade improve in the left panel, that country's willingness to trade increases, as shown by the three trade triangles. These trade triangles are then shown in the right panel as points 8, 9, and 10, which represent Country A's willingness to export cloth and import wheat at the same three barter ratios shown in the left panel.

by Country A, and the vertical axis is wheat imported. Exchange ratios are then shown as the slopes of rays from the origin; as the price of cloth increases, these rays become steeper. The flattest ray represents Country A's exchange ratio in autarky. As the price of cloth rises and the rays from the origin become steeper, Country A exports more cloth and imports more wheat.

The dimensions of the trade triangles in the upper panel are then used to derive the volume of trade undertaken by Country A at each exchange ratio. Point 8 in the bottom panel represents the volume of trade that is based on production point 2 and consumption point 5 in the upper panel; point 9 corresponds to A's offer at the improved terms of trade that results in production at point 3 and consumption at point 6. A's offer of cloth for wheat is shown for each of the three prices represented in the upper panel, and connecting those points in the lower panel traces out A's offer curve.

Country B's offer curve could be derived in the same manner. As shown in Figure 2.10 however, it curves in the opposite direction. At point 1 in Figure 2.10, where the offer curves cross, Countries A and B agree on the volumes of wheat and cloth to be exchanged, as well as on the exchange ratio for the two goods, which is shown as the slope of the ray from the origin. At any other exchange ratio, there would be no such agreement and the markets for the two goods would be out of equilibrium. If the barter line were steeper, for example, A would choose to import more wheat than B would be willing to export, while A would export more cloth than B would be willing to import. The excess demand for wheat, which is an excess supply of cloth in a world of barter transactions, indicates that the price of wheat must rise relative to the price of cloth. The barter line becomes flatter. If the countries are out of equilibrium, the automatic adjustments of prices will bring them back.

Why spend time on this complication derivation when the same basic point was made with simple supply and demand curves? Offer curves allow us to see more

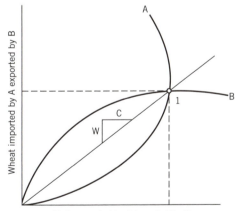

Figure 2.10   Offer curves for Countries A and B, with the equilibrium barter ratio and trade volumes. At point 1, with a barter ratio represented by the slope of the ray from the origin, the two countries agree on the quantity of the two goods to be exchanged. There is no other barter ratio at which that is true, which means there is no other barter ratio at which the market for these goods can clear.

explicitly how all the information in the production-possibility curves of the two countries and in the two sets of community indifference curves are relevant in determining the equilibrium volumes of trade and the international exchange ratio. The differing productive abilities of the two countries and the preferences of their consumers are all combined to determine the equilibrium point in Figure 2.10. Offer curves also will prove useful later to illustrate some important theoretical aspects of the impact of tariffs and the relationship between trade and economic growth.

In those later applications an important factor will be the elasticity of the offer curve. Therefore, before moving on, we consider how the offer curve is related to the more familiar import demand curve and the price elasticity of demand for imports. The left panel of Figure 2.11 shows an offer curve where the price of cloth has risen high enough that the amount of cloth A offers to trade for wheat actually declines. That is, when the price of cloth rises from 0a to 0b, A offers two more units of cloth in exchange for two more units of wheat, but when the price rises from 0b to 0c, A offers two fewer units of cloth in exchange for two more units of wheat. Is such behavior unusual or inconsistent?

The right panel of Figure 2.11, which shows A's demand for imports of wheat, is intended to remind us why a reduction in the quantity of cloth offered is not unexpected. Each point along the import demand curve has the same label as the corresponding point along the offer curve. For example, at point a the import demand curve shows that A will demand two units of wheat from B when the price is three units of cloth per unit of wheat. A's total spending on wheat imports is six units of cloth, and along the offer curve we note that A offers six units of cloth for two units of wheat. At point c, A will demand six units of wheat from B at a price of one unit of cloth per unit of wheat. A's total spending on wheat imports again is six units of cloth, but along the offer curve this corresponds to A's offer of six units of cloth for six units of wheat.

As we move downward along A's import demand curve, the price elasticity of demand (the percentage change in the quantity of wheat demanded divided by the

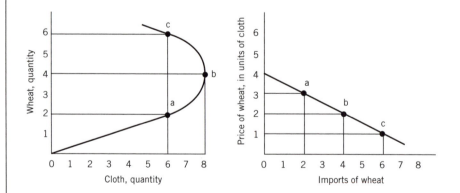

Figure 2.11 The elasticity of Country A's offer curve. A's offer curve of cloth for wheat shown in the left panel is based on the same behavior as A's demand for imported wheat shown in the right panel. The maximum offer of cloth occurs when the elasticity of demand for imported wheat is unitary.

percentage of change in price) declines in absolute value, which you can confirm as shown in the endnote.[10] You can also confirm that A's maximum offer of cloth occurs at b, where the elasticity is –1.0. At any price of wheat lower than at point b, demand is less elastic, and price will fall by a larger percentage than the quantity of wheat demanded increases. Consequently, total spending on imported wheat (A's offer of cloth) declines. At any price higher than at point b, demand is elastic. Price will rise by a smaller percentage than the quantity demanded falls, and total spending on imported wheat again declines. Therefore, as price rises or falls from point b, A offers less cloth for wheat.

Comparative advantage with many goods

In order to make the argument clear, thus far we have presented comparative advantage for only two countries and two goods, with the assumption of no transport costs. The real world, of course, includes thousands of goods, almost 200 countries, and significant transport costs. How is a country's trade pattern established in this more realistic situation?

A single country in a world with many goods can be viewed as rank-ordering those products from its greatest comparative advantage to its greatest comparative disadvantage. We want this ranking to reflect the marginal cost of production in Country A relative to the marginal cost of production in Country B (which represents the rest of the world), for each of the many goods that can be produced. Consider again the special case of the classical labor theory of value, where labor is the only input. This ranking of relative costs will depend upon the relevant labor productivities in each country, if we can assume labor earns the same wage wherever it is employed within the country. Let us demonstrate this outcome by considering how wages and labor productivity determine costs of production. We pay special attention to this case because it is one that has been used in testing the relevance of this theory to real-world trade patterns.

The marginal cost of cloth production (MC_c) equals the wage rate (w) times the amount of labor required per unit output (L/Q_c):

$$MC_c^A = w^A (L/Q)_c^A$$

As we found earlier, for a barter economy, the price of cloth is the amount of wheat given up to buy one unit of cloth. Wages also are measured by this same standard, the amount of wheat that labor receives per hour of work. With respect to the expression for marginal cost, we can see that A's marginal cost of production will be higher when its wage rate is higher and lower when its labor productivity is higher, because labor productivity (output per hour of labor input) is just the inverse of labor required per unit of output. We can write the same relationship for country B:

$$MC_c^B = w^B (L/Q)_c^B$$

and form the ratio of these two marginal cost terms:

$$\frac{MC_c^A}{MC_c^B} \quad \frac{w^A (L/Q)_c^A}{w^B (L/Q)_c^B}$$

It is the ranking of these ratios across all goods that we want to consider in predicting the pattern of trade that will emerge.

Suppose we can calculate this ratio of marginal costs for cloth, oats, and steel, and the ranking turns out to be

$$\frac{w^A \, (L \, / \, Q)^A_c}{w^B \, (L \, / \, Q)^B_c} < \frac{w^A \, (L \, / \, Q)^A_o}{w^B \, (L \, / \, Q)^B_o} < \frac{w^A \, (L \, / \, Q)^A_s}{w^B \, (L \, / \, Q)^B_s}$$

We can see that A has the greatest productivity advantage in cloth production, which gives it a relatively lower marginal cost in cloth, and the least advantage in steel. As long as there is a single wage rate in each country, the ratio (w^A/w^B) is simply a constant term that does not affect the comparative advantage ranking across industries; relative labor productivities determine the ranking.

From our discussion of reciprocal demand and the determination of equilibrium prices internationally when each country's trade must be balanced, we have the necessary framework to determine the demand for output and labor in each country and the ratio of wages in A and B. The greater the world demand for cloth, for example, where Country A has a comparative advantage, the higher the wage in Country A will be relative to Country B. Correspondingly, Country A will be more likely to import both steel and oats from Country B.[11]

From the standpoint of a single country considering what to trade with the rest of the world, we predict that it will export goods at the top of the list and import goods at the bottom of the list. Most small countries will export large amounts of a few goods and import smaller amounts of many goods. A country will tend to trade primarily with those countries that normally import its strongest comparative-advantage goods and/or export its strongest comparative-disadvantage goods. Trade volumes will be larger with countries that represent particularly large markets for exports or sources of imports, that is, countries with large populations and high levels of GNP per capita.

There will be a number of goods, most likely in the middle of a country's comparative-advantage rank-ordering, that it will neither export nor import (nontradables), because its comparative advantage or disadvantage in these products is too slight to overcome transport costs. Such products will be produced domestically in sufficient volume for local consumption. The heavier or bulkier products are, the more likely they are to be nontradables: for example, very few countries export or import gravel and sand. Transport costs will also mean that a country will tend to trade more with its neighbors and somewhat less with more distant countries.

Empirical verification in a world with many goods

Attempts to test the predictions of the models discussed in this chapter have rested on the many-good framework just discussed. The case of constant opportunity cost derived from the classical labor theory of value suggests a very direct test of the comparative-advantage model: countries will export goods in which their productivity relative to other countries is high. The prediction is clearcut in the classical case, because opportunity costs of production will be the same before and after trade occurs. The fact that economists do not observe relative costs of production before trade occurs does not matter, because the same relative cost rankings will prevail after trade occurs.

One of the earliest systematic tests was reported by G.D.A. MacDougall.[12] He based his analysis on labor productivity in 25 different US and British industries and their exports in 1937, which were largely made to third-country markets. While MacDougall only had comparable trade and labor productivity information for industries that represented a little over half of each country's total exports, he found that for 97 percent of the trade covered, the UK exported more than the United States whenever the US advantage in labor productivity was less than twice UK productivity, whereas the United States exported more than the UK whenever the US labor productivity was more than twice UK productivity. Because the US wage rate on average was twice the British rate at that time, this relationship confirmed that relative labor costs determined the pattern of trade, as suggested by the chain of comparative advantage presented above. For example, US labor productivity in cotton spinning and weaving was 1.5 times UK productivity, but with US wages 1.7 times UK wages, US producers had a price disadvantage relative to UK producers. British exports in this industry were nine times US exports.

MacDougall found that this relationship was linear when expressed in logarithms or shown on a logarithmic scale as in Figure 2.12. Note that the regression line he estimated did not show that US exports equaled UK exports exactly where US productivity was twice UK productivity. Rather, the US productivity advantage needed to be somewhat greater. MacDougall suggested that this result might be due to UK Imperial Preferences in its trade or to a smaller US productivity advantage in nontraded inputs such as public utilities and domestic transportation that were part of the cost of the traded goods considered.

The linear relationship found by MacDougall (the greater the relative US productivity advantage, the greater the US/UK export ratio) is not particularly what the pure classical model would predict. In a world with constant opportunity costs, the country with the lower relative cost of producing a good should be its only producer. MacDougall's result does make sense if we relax some of the assumptions of the classical model. For example, if we allow for transportation costs internationally or quality differences in the goods produced by different countries, we can justify the existence of more than one producer. France may choose to import from the UK while Canada may choose to import from the United States if UK and US labor costs are similar and any production cost difference is offset by a greater difference in transportation costs. Or, differences in product qualities may play a role if some French consumers prefer American cigarettes while other French consumers prefer British cigarettes. Nevertheless, we can see why a progressively larger US productivity advantage, and

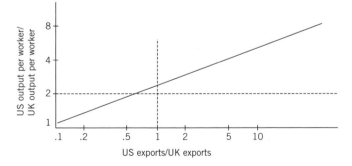

Figure 2.12 An empirical demonstration of the relationship between relative labor productivities and trade. For a greater US productivity advantage relative to the UK, US exports relative to UK exports tend to rise.

consequently more favorable price, could come to overshadow transport costs or quality differences and result in a larger US share of the export market.

A final fact to note is that even though the United States had an absolute advantage in all of the industries examined, that did not prevent the UK from having a comparative advantage in industries where the United States had a higher opportunity cost of production. The US opportunity cost was higher in British export industries such as cotton textiles because of the high demand for US labor in other industries where its relative productivity was much greater, such as automobiles. The high demand for labor in auto production bid up US wage rates and raised the cost of producing US cotton textiles.

The fact that the model of comparative advantage based on the labor theory of value predicts trade so well is rather remarkable. Some of the simplifying assumptions made, such as a nationwide wage rate or the existence of only a single factor of production, seem extreme. We must remind ourselves, however, that economists do not judge a model by the reasonableness of its assumptions, but by its ability to explain observed behavior and predict future behavior. From that standpoint, the classical model has shortcomings because it allows us to ask only a limited set of questions. For instance, it does not address why differences in productivity arise across countries or how they might change in the future. There is no basis for considering whether a government can affect the country's autarky cost conditions. While a favorable climate may provide a permanent basis for comparative advantage in some industries, a more general appeal to differences in technology, which for some reason exist but cannot be transferred from one country to another, is not likely to give us much insight into likely changes in what is traded internationally. In the next two chapters we present models that can better address these issues and also raise other issues that are overlooked in the classical approach.

Summary of key concepts

1   Adam Smith demonstrated that the potential to gain from specialization applies not only to the assignment of tasks within a firm but also to trade between countries. A country should export products in which it is more productive than other countries: that is, goods for which it can produce more output per unit of input than others can and in which it has an absolute advantage. The country should import those goods where it is less productive than other countries and has an absolute disadvantage. Trade makes it possible for world output to rise, even though individuals are working no harder than before trade.

2   Ricardo extended this insight to demonstrate that the basis for gains from trade is the existence of comparative advantage, not absolute advantage. A country that is less productive in two goods still can gain from trade by exporting the good in which its relative disadvantage is smaller, because its relative price of this good before trade will be lower than abroad. A country that has an absolute advantage in both goods gains by specializing in the production of the good in which its relative advantage is greater. It can gain from trade by importing the product in which its relative advantage is smaller, because the foreign opportunity cost of producing it is lower.

3   When there are increasing opportunity costs, gains from trade based on comparative advantage still exist. The tendency to specialize in production, however, is not as great as under constant opportunity costs.

4   Wherever pre-trade prices in two countries differ, gains from trade are possible. The

gains are greater the larger the improvement in a nation's terms of trade (the ratio of its export price to its import price) relative to its autarky position. A large improvement in a nation's terms of trade is more likely for the country that faces an elastic foreign supply curve and has a less elastic demand for imports.

5   Early tests of the classical model with constant opportunity costs suggest that trade between countries can be explained by the principle of comparative advantage. Relative labor productivities appear to be useful predictors of the pattern of trade in different goods. Classical theory, however, does not explain why labor productivities differ across countries.

Questions for study and review

1   "It is unlikely that Myanmar, a relatively closed economy, would gain from trade with Japan because Japan would have a comparative advantage in all goods." Do you agree? Explain.

2   Given two countries, A and B, and two products, cloth and wheat, state whether each of the following statements is true or false, and show why.

(a) If Country A has an absolute advantage in cloth, it must have a comparative advantage in cloth.

(b) If Country A has a comparative advantage in wheat, it must have an absolute advantage in wheat.

3   What is meant by the terms of trade? What is meant by an improvement in a country's terms of trade?

4   Assume a classical world of two goods and two countries where labor is the only input. One day of labor will produce the following amounts of output in each country:

Country	Cloth (meters)	Wheat (kilograms)
Metropolitano	20	30
Ruritania	5	15

(a) What pattern of comparative advantage exists?

(b) Ruritania has an absolute disadvantage in each good. Nevertheless, it can still gain from trade. If the equilibrium exchange ratio is two bushels of wheat per 1 yard of cloth, explain how Ruritania gains from trade.

(c) If Ruritania discovers a new way of producing cloth and its labor productivity rises to 10 yards per day, how does that affect the potential gains from trade?

5   In a two-country, two-commodity case, how do both supply and demand factors determine the exact exchange ratio that will prevail in free trade? Explain.

6   How do increasing-cost conditions affect the extent of international specialization and exchange? Explain.

7   In isolation, Country A produces 12 million tons of rice and 8 million tons of beans. One ton of rice exchanges for 2 tons of beans, and there are constant costs.

(a)   Construct Country A's production-possibility curve, and label your diagram.
(b)   Suppose Country A now has the opportunity to trade with Country C. It can trade at the exchange ratio (terms of trade) 1R: 1B, and in equilibrium Country A consumes 10 million tons of beans.

(i)   What will Country A produce after trade?
(ii) What will Country A consume after trade? Show its consumption point and its trade triangle.
(iii) What is the gain from trade (in real terms) to Country A?

8   "Trade theory assumes that resources are fully employed both before and after trade and that technology remains unchanged. But if the same amounts of resources are actually used, both before and after trade, world production must also be the same. There can be no gain to the world as a whole." Critically evaluate this statement.

9   Suppose Togo can produce 120 million bushels of wheat if it uses all of its productive resources in the wheat industry, or 80 million yards of cloth if it uses all of its resources in the cloth industry. Use a diagram to illustrate your answers to the following questions. Label the diagram and explain in words.

(a)   Assuming constant opportunity costs, draw Togo's production-possibility curve.
(b)   With no trade, suppose Togo's consumers choose to consume 70 million bushels of wheat. How much cloth will Togo then be able to produce?
(c)   What is the real exchange ratio (terms of trade) in Togo?
(d)   Now suppose that Togo has the opportunity to engage in foreign trade and that the world terms-of-trade ratio is 1W:1C. What will happen to the allocation of resources in Togo? Explain why.
(e)   If Togo consumes 75 million bushels of wheat, after trade begins, how much cloth will it consume?
(f)   What is the gain from trade to Togo?

10 (a)   Draw an offer curve for Guatemala that shows its offer of coffee for wheat. Include both an elastic and inelastic range in Guatemala's offer curve.
(b)   Draw an offer curve for the United States that shows its offer of wheat for coffee. Show this US curve intersecting the Guatemalan offer curve in the inelastic range of the Guatemalan curve. Note the equilibrium terms of trade established.
(c)   Compare the equilibrium international price you found in question (b) to the autarky prices in Guatemala and in the United States. (You can find a country's autarky price by drawing a line tangent to the offer curve at the origin.) Explain which country benefits the most from a more favorable movement in its terms of trade when it abandons its autarky position.
(d)   "The Guatemalan offer curve is likely to be less elastic than the US offer curve." Justify this claim by explaining what factors determine the elasticity of an offer curve.

11 Suppose labor is the only cost of production and labor productivities (output per unit of labor input) in Japan and India are as follows:

Country	Nails (kg)	Oranges (kg)	Rice (kg)
Japan	10	10	30
India	1	2	5

(a) If these are the only two nations who trade, and consumers in both countries demand all three goods (the only ones that are available), explain what you can conclude about the comparative advantage of each country.

(b) Within what limits must the ratio of Japanese wages to Indian wages settle when trade is possible? If that ratio turns out to be 5.5, what goods will each country export and import?

Suggested further reading

In addition to the original works cited in the chapter, authors who put the contributions of the classical writers in perspective are:

- Allen, William R., *International Trade Theory: Hume to Ohlin*, New York: Random House, 1965.
- Chipman, John, "A Survey of the Theory of International Trade, Part I: The Classical Theory," *Econometrica* 33, no. 3 (July 1965), pp. 477–519.
- Heilbroner, Robert, *The Worldly Philosophers*, New York: Simon and Schuster, 1953.

Additional sources that present analytical tools developed in this chapter are:

- Meade, James E., *Trade and Welfare*, London: Oxford University Press, 1955.
- Samuelson, P.A., "Social Indifference Curves," *Quarterly Journal of Economics*, February 1956, pp. 1–22.
- Viner, Jacob, *Studies in the Theory of International Trade*, New York: Harper, 1937.

Appendix: the role of money prices

In the modern world traders actually place their orders and strike bargains on the basis of money prices, not the barter ratios that we have examined thus far. Traders buy a foreign good when its price is lower than it is at home. (For the sake of simplicity we are still ignoring transport costs, but traders must allow for them and for all other costs – tariffs, insurance, commissions, legal costs, and so on – in comparing domestic and foreign prices.) German wheat importers pay no attention to the barter ratio between steel and wheat, and they may be oblivious to opportunity cost as we have used it earlier. Nevertheless, the basic principles on which trade is based, principles laid bare in our simple barter examples, will still apply when we bring in money prices. In this discussion, the determination of an equilibrium exchange rate between two currencies plays a key role, in a very similar way to the determination of relative wage rates across countries in the many-good model of comparative advantage. Because countries often find it more acceptable politically to talk of changing exchange rates rather than wage rates, and because exchange rates apply to all costs of production, not just wages, we develop the current explanation in terms of exchange rates.

A barter exchange ratio, such as the one we have used in our example of trade between France and Germany, implies a ratio of money prices. For example, if one apple exchanges for two oranges, the price of an apple is twice the price of an orange. (If an apple costs €0.50 and an orange costs €0.25, then one apple is equal in value to two oranges.) Therefore, if barter exchange ratios differ in two countries, relative money prices will also differ.

We can use the French–German constant-cost example to illustrate this point, but in discussing the money value of trade we shall use the separate national currencies that existed prior to the creation of the euro. Before trade, the domestic (barter) exchange ratios were:

> France: 1 ton of steel for 3 tons of wheat
> Germany: 1 ton of steel for 1 ton of wheat

The money price in France of 1 ton of steel is therefore equal to the money price of three tons of wheat. That is, 1 ton of steel costs 3 times as much as 1 ton of wheat. In Germany, the money price of 1 ton of steel is equal to the money price of 1 ton of wheat. We assume the following actual money prices in the two countries:

	France	*Germany*
Steel (per ton)	Fr 300	DM 400
Wheat (per ton)	Fr 100	DM 400
Ratio (P_s / P_w)	3:1	1:1

The relative ratios based on money prices mirror the differences in opportunity cost ratios in our barter example, and they tell us that an opportunity for gainful trade exists.

These are the money prices prevailing before trade begins. When trade opens up, how can traders compare prices? Will German buyers wish to buy French steel at Fr 300 per ton? Or will French buyers find German steel a bargain at DM 400 per ton? Since the currencies used are different, we must know the exchange rate between francs and marks before meaningful price comparisons can be made. The exchange rate is a price, a rate at which we can convert one currency into another. If the exchange rate is Fr 1 = DM 2, French buyers can compare German prices with their own: German steel will cost them Fr 200 per ton (Fr 200 = DM 400) compared to Fr 300 at home; German wheat will cost Fr 200 per ton compared to Fr 100 at home. French traders will therefore import steel and export wheat. At the same time, German traders will find French wheat cheaper (Fr 100 × DM 2/Fr = DM 200) than domestic wheat. Thus a two-way trade, profitable to both sides, will spring up: German steel will exchange for French wheat, although each trader is simply pursuing his or her own individual interest in buying at the cheapest possible price.

Although we examine in detail the determination of exchange rates in the second half of this book, here we consider the simple case where only merchandise trade between these two countries is possible. Therefore, we ask, will the money value of French imports of steel be equal to that of German imports of wheat? If so, we will have balanced trade; if not, the imbalance in trade will cause the exchange rate to shift. In our preceding barter example, we had France import 45 million tons of steel and export 90 million tons of wheat. The money value of its trade, at the prices we have used above, would therefore be:

> Wheat exports, 90 million tons @ Fr 100 = Fr 9 billion
> Steel imports, 45 million tons @ Fr 200 = Fr 9 billion

Thus we have a position of balanced trade in money value, just as we did in barter terms.

If French exports did not equal imports in money value, the exchange rate would change. For example, if German traders wanted to buy 100 million tons of French wheat when the exchange rate was Fr 1 = DM 2, they would try to buy Fr 10 billion in the foreign exchange market, but French traders would be offering only Fr 9 billion for German steel. The excess demand for francs would drive up their price – that is, 1 franc would exchange for somewhat more than 2 marks, for example, Fr 1 = DM 2.5. If domestic money prices were kept unchanged in the two countries, the higher exchange value of the franc would make French wheat more expensive to German buyers (1 ton of wheat now costs DM 250 instead of DM 200), and German steel would now be cheaper to French buyers (1 ton of steel now costs Fr 160 (400/2.5 = 160) instead of Fr 200). These price changes will tend to reduce German purchases of French wheat and increase French purchases of German steel. When exports become equal to imports in money value, the exchange rate will stop moving and equilibrium will exist. With fixed money prices in the two countries, the exchange rate thus plays the same role as the barter exchange ratio in our previous examples.

Are there any limits on the movement of the exchange rate? Profitable two-way trade can take place only at an exchange rate that makes wheat cheaper in France than in Germany. If *both* commodities were cheaper in Germany, trade would flow in only one direction: from Germany to France. The reader should consider the consequences of exchange rates such as Fr 1 = DM 5 (all goods cheaper in Germany), or Fr 1 = DM 1 (all goods cheaper in France) to see why the exchange rate must lie between the limits set by the money price ratios of steel and wheat in the two countries: Fr 1 = DM 1 1/3 and Fr 1 = DM 4. These exchange rate limits are analogous to the limits on the barter terms of trade noted earlier. Again, if the ratio of the two money prices in the two countries is identical, then no basis for trade would exist.

Notes

1 Adam Smith, *The Wealth of Nations*, Modern Library Edition (New York: Random House, 1937). Smith's work was first published in 1776.

2 David Ricardo, *Principles of Political Economy* (London: J.M. Dent, 1911). Ricardo's work was first published in 1817. Scholars have disputed the origin of Ricardo's contribution, with some giving credit to Henry Torrens and others to James Mill. See Jacob Viner, *Studies in the Theory of International Trade* (New York: Harper, 1937).

3 Such monopolies existed in the sixteenth, seventeenth, and eighteenth centuries as European governments gave corporations, such as the British East India Company, the sole right to trade between the home country and a foreign area or colony. The resulting profits were typically shared with the government through taxes, although such tax payments were in part compensation for the government's use of its navy to provide security for the corporation's ships.

4 Ricardo, op. cit., p. 83.

5 Gottfried Haberler, *The Theory of International Trade* (New York: Macmillan, 1936), ch. 12.

6 John Stuart Mill, *Principles of Political Economy* (Ashley edition, London: Longman, Green, 1921), book 3, ch. 18. Originally published in 1848.

7 The slope at a given point along the indifference curve, rather than over a discrete interval between two points along the curve, is represented as $-dF/dC = MU_c/MU_f$. The left-hand side of this expression is the slope of the indifference curve, where dF and dC represent infinitesimally small changes in food and clothing, respectively.

8 For a useful diagrammatic treatment of community indifference curves, see H. Robert Heller, *International Trade, Theory and Empirical Evidence* (Englewood Cliffs, NJ: Prentice Hall, 1968), ch. 4.

9 J. Richard Huber, "Effect on Prices of Japan's Entry into World Commerce after 1858," *Journal of Political Economy* 79, no. 3, 1971, pp. 614–28.

10 The relevant elasticity, η, along a straight-line demand curve is given by the standard formula

$$\eta = \frac{\Delta Q}{Q} \bigg/ \frac{\Delta P}{P} = \frac{\Delta Q}{\Delta P} \frac{P}{Q}$$

The second expression shows the inverse of the slope of the demand curve (-2) multiplied by price divided by quantity at any point chosen along the demand curve. By substituting the corresponding price and quantity values along the curve into the formula, you find that at point a the elasticity is -3.0, at point b it is -1.0 and at point c it is -0.33.

11 For the development of a formal model to show these results, see R. Dornbusch, S. Fischer, and P. Samuelson, "Comparative Advantage, Trade, and Payments in a Ricardian Model with a Continuum of Goods," *American Economic Review* 67, no. 5, December 1977, pp. 823–39.

12 G.D.A. MacDougall, "British and American Exports: A Study Suggested by the Theory of Comparative Costs," *The Economic Journal* 61, no. 244, December 1951, pp. 697–724, reprinted in R. Caves and H.G. Johnson, eds, *Readings in International Economics* (Homewood, IL: Richard D. Irwin, 1968). For later studies that support MacDougall's findings, see Robert M. Stern, "British and American Productivity and Comparative Costs in International Trade," *Oxford Economic Papers* 14, no. 3, October 1962, pp. 275–96, and Bela Balassa, "An Empirical Demonstration of Classical Comparative Cost Theory," *Review of Economics and Statistics* 45, no. 3, August 1963, pp. 231–8.

3 Trade between dissimilar countries

Insights from the factor proportions theory

Learning objectives

By the end of this chapter you should be able to understand:

- how differences in factor endowments across countries create differences in costs of production and create a basis for trade – the basic model from this chapter predicts that a country will export goods that use intensively the factors in which it is relatively abundant;
- why an increase in the price of a country's export good will have the long-run effect of benefiting the abundant factor used intensively in its production and hurting the scarce factor used intensively in the production of import-competing goods;
- why an increase in the price of a country's export good will have the short-run effect of benefiting all factors employed in that industry and hurting all factors employed in the import-competing industry;
- why economists have obtained mixed, and sometimes paradoxical, results from their tests of the factor endowments theory's ability to predict patterns of trade.

In the preceding chapter we saw that if relative prices differ in two isolated countries, the introduction of trade between them will be mutually beneficial. Different relative prices of commodities reflect the fact that relative opportunity costs differ in the two countries. In the simple two-good model, each country has a comparative advantage in one commodity and a comparative disadvantage in the other. Given the opportunity to trade, each country will increase production of the commodity in which it has a comparative advantage, exporting it in exchange for the commodity in which it has a comparative disadvantage.

Why do relative prices and costs differ in the first place? Classical theory did not ask this question: Ricardo simply took it for granted that labor cost ratios (and hence prices) differed in the two countries before trade. In fact, Ricardo probably surprised his readers by assuming in his original example that Portugal had an absolute advantage in the production of both wine and cloth. He never bothered to explain why the British were unable to figure out how the Portuguese achieved this superior performance. Apparently, technology could be transmitted extremely well within Portugal, but it could remain a secret inaccessible to the British. Such extreme assumptions may have seemed plausible in the case of Britain and Portugal, because here were two countries with different languages, different legal systems, and different religions and cultural traditions. Ricardo explicitly encouraged that interpretation by pointing to the "financial or real insecurity of capital" in operating abroad and "the natural disinclination which every man has to quit the country of his birth and connections."[1]

Classical writers did envision technology and factors of production crossing borders, but Adam Smith included this possibility in his discussion of colonies. He noted that colonists carried with them "a knowledge of agriculture and other useful arts," as well as important understandings of commercial law and government structure. John Stuart Mill recognized that movements of capital to the colonies kept its return from declining in England.

The discussion in this chapter rests on yet another characterization of economies throughout the world, one where ideas and technology have diffused across countries to become equally accessible everywhere. Labor, capital, and other factors of production, however, are fixed in supply in each country. Differences across countries in these factor endowments provide a basis for explaining why opportunity cost ratios differ across countries. Thus, differences in factor endowments allow us to predict patterns of trade across countries.

Factor proportions as a determinant of trade

The factor proportions theory of trade is attributed to two Swedish economists, Eli Heckscher and Bertil Ohlin. Their initial contributions appeared in Swedish and received little attention among English speaking economists until the publication of Ohlin's book *Interregional and International Trade* in 1933.[2] Let us begin with one of the examples suggested there by Ohlin: why is it that Denmark exports cheese to the United States and imports wheat from the United States? The Heckscher–Ohlin model (hereafter referred to as the H–O model) that answers this question rests upon two key ideas that differ from the classical approach. First, rather than focus on the single input labor, the H–O model allows for additional inputs and recognizes that different goods require these inputs in different proportions. For example, both land and labor are necessary to produce either cheese or wheat, but cheese production requires relatively more labor and wheat production requires relatively more land. In fact, we assume that cheese is always the more labor-intensive good, regardless of what the relative costs of land and labor happen to be in a country. Second, differences across countries in technology are no longer assumed, but the H–O model distinguishes countries by the availability of factors of production, that is, by their factor endowments. Although the United States has both more land and more labor than Denmark, it has relatively much more land than labor. Therefore, Ohlin reached the conclusion that the United States will have a comparative advantage in producing wheat, the good that requires relatively more land in production.

In the next section of this chapter, we demonstrate more formally why this line of reasoning holds. The classical model of two countries and two goods provided a simple but powerful analytical framework that also lent itself easily to subsequent diagrammatic representations. In a similar vein we will initially devote our attention to a model with two countries, two goods, and two factor inputs (the $2 \times 2 \times 2$ case). We then go on to consider other applications of the model. It has proven very useful in addressing questions about growth and the changing patterns of trade over time, as well as the implications of trade for the distribution of income within a country. In the classical model with a single factor input, distributional issues were irrelevant: either all individuals gained from trade or all individuals lost, but there was no divergence of interests within the country. In the H–O model it is possible to consider the conflicting interests of different factors of production when prices change internationally. This approach does not predict that some factors gain a little and some gain a lot. Rather, the real income of some factors rises but for others it falls. Understanding the reasons for this outcome is quite relevant to our discussion in future chapters of the political economy of changing international trade policy.

Another modification of the H–O model we consider is what happens in the short run when not all factor inputs can be shifted immediately to their long-run desired uses. In many respects, such a model yields results that are less of a departure from more simple partial equilibrium analysis of supply and demand conditions in a single market. Recognizing why results differ in the short run and the long run help to reinforce our understanding of the general equilibrium H–O model.

Just as we considered implications of the classical model in a many-good world as a way to understand how the theory might be tested in the real world, we follow the same procedure for the H–O model. The mixed results that economists have reported from various empirical tests suggest why the H–O model, useful as it is, does not reign as the only explanation of the observed patterns of international trade.

Formulating a model

We retain the seven assumptions listed in Chapter 2 when we discussed ways in which the ideas of the classical economists were formalized and extended. That list was not exhaustive and we must add to it here. Even in our discussion of increasing opportunity costs, we did not make specific enough assumptions to determine why the production-possibilities curve is bowed outward, as shown in Figure 3.1. We did suggest two possibilities, however, that are particularly relevant to the H–O theory.

First, specialized inputs may be needed to produce different goods. In the extreme, that may mean an input is productive in one industry only and adds nothing to output in another industry if it is employed there. A less extreme situation exists when there are differences in the labor skills necessary to produce cheese from those needed to produce wheat. If firms have hired the most efficient workers in each industry initially, what happens as workers are transferred out of cheese production into wheat production? Those newly hired to grow

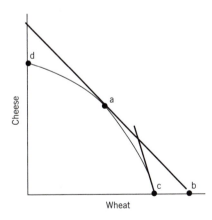

Figure 3.1 Production with different factor intensities. One reason the production-possibility curve may have increasing opportunity costs is that factor intensities are not the same in wheat and cheese production. Reducing cheese output does not make land and labor available in the same proportions as they are currently used in wheat production. Note the rising cost of wheat as the economy moves from *a* to *c*.

wheat are likely to be progressively less productive than current employees who already have a practiced eye to know when to plant and harvest. As a further example, pasture land on mountainsides may sustain cattle but yield very little additional output of wheat if it is transferred to that use. These various possibilities are elaborated later in the chapter when we discuss fixed factors of production in the short run.

Second, we suggested that even if there are not differences in the two industries' requirements of specific labor skills or land fertility, homogeneous land and labor nevertheless may be required in different proportions. To see the importance of this condition, assume instead that land and labor are required in the same proportion in each sector. Also, assume that production in each sector is characterized by constant returns to scale, where doubling each input leads to double the output being produced. Then, if the economy shifts away from production at point a in Figure 3.1 and chooses to produce more wheat, it will move along the line segment ab, which denotes constant opportunity cost.

Now assume that the optimal land/labor ratio required in wheat production is greater than the land/labor ratio in cheese production. Reducing cheese output does not free up land and labor in the same proportions as they are currently being used in wheat production. Rather, too little land is available and too much labor. With this new, smaller ratio of land to labor being used in wheat production, output expands less than in the constant opportunity cost case. Because this new land/labor mix is less suited to producing wheat, less wheat is gained for a given amount of cheese forgone, and the opportunity cost of wheat rises.

At point c, where all of the economy's resources are devoted to wheat production, observe the slope of the production-possibility curve. The tangent drawn in Figure 3.1 denotes the price of wheat in terms of cheese. The steeper this line, the more cheese must be given up to produce wheat. Consider how that price line will change if this economy all of a sudden has twice the land available to be worked with the same labor force. We expect the production-possibility curve to be affected, but not in a symmetric way. Because the economy has more of the factor that is used intensively in producing wheat, we expect point c, where only wheat is produced, to shift to the right by a greater proportion than the position that indicates complete specialization in cheese, point d, shifts upward along the vertical axis. In addition, the line tangent to point c becomes flatter: the relative price of wheat need not be as high to induce the country to become specialized in wheat production now that it has relatively more of the factor best suited to producing wheat. We can also state this relationship in terms of relative factor prices in this closed economy. Because land has become relatively more abundant, it becomes less expensive, which reduces the relative cost of the land-intensive good. Alternatively, because labor is relatively more scarce, it becomes more expensive, which increases the cost of the labor-intensive good.

That reasoning allows us to attach the correct country labels to the two production-possibility curves shown in Figure 3.2. At the outset we characterized the United States as having a higher land/labor endowment than Denmark. Stated in terms traditionally used to express the factor proportions theory of trade, the United States is relatively abundant in land and Denmark is relatively abundant in labor. Because of these differences in factor abundance, the right panel should be labeled United States and the left panel Denmark. The land-abundant country will have a lower relative price of wheat when it is completely specialized in wheat production. In fact, for any comparison of the slopes of the two production-possibility curves at points that represent the same ratio of wheat to cheese production, the US curve has a lower relative cost of wheat.

Figure 3.2 incorporates another important assumption to guarantee that the United States exports wheat. Our discussion thus far has focused on differences in production costs when

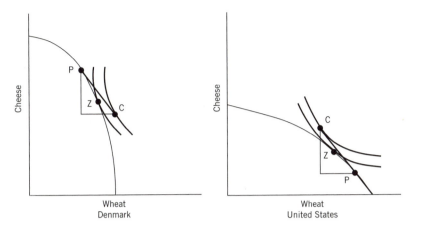

Figure 3.2 Patterns of trade given by the factor proportions theory. Trade according to the factor endowments theory results in the relatively land-abundant country, shown in the right panel, exporting the land-intensive good (wheat) and importing the labor-intensive good (cheese) from the relatively labor-abundant country shown in the left panel. Trade causes each country to become more specialized in production at P and allows it to reach a higher indifference curve at C.

the two countries produce wheat and cheese in the same proportions. We also must rule out certain types of country preferences that otherwise may offset the US cost advantage in producing wheat. If the United States has a particularly strong preference for wheat, it is possible that US consumers will demand so much wheat that its pre-trade price exceeds the price in Denmark. In that case the United States will import wheat to satisfy its strong preference for wheat. While such a case may seem unlikely, Figure 3.2 rules out such a possibility by imposing the condition that preferences in each country are identical. Confront Danes and Americans with the same prices and give them the same income, and they will choose to buy the same bundle of goods. Furthermore, if income levels differ across the two countries, or income is distributed differently within the two countries, that does not affect the outcome because all individuals are assumed to spend their income on available goods in the same proportions, regardless of whether they are rich or poor. These strong demand assumptions guarantee an unambiguous result, although small deviations from these conditions are unlikely to be significant enough to overturn the importance of differences in supply conditions in determining autarky prices.

Given the demand and supply conditions specified above, the $2 \times 2 \times 2$ model yields the **Heckscher–Ohlin theorem**: *A country will export the good that uses intensively the factor in which it is relatively abundant.* Figure 3.2 shows that the land-abundant United States exports the land-intensive good, wheat, and labor-abundant Denmark exports the labor-intensive good, cheese.

Implications of the factor proportions theory

Trade and changing factor endowments

One of the attractions of the H–O model is that several testable predictions can be derived from it. One such prediction is based on a change in **relative factor endowments** and the consequent implications for the changing patterns of production and international trade.

Box 3.1 How different are factor endowments?

There are obvious differences in factor endowments across countries, but documenting them in a systematic way is difficult. One data set compiled by Daniel Trefler for 1982 provides the basis for the endowment shares shown in Table 3.1. Each entry shows a country's percentage share of the endowment of a given factor of production, where the calculation is based on the total endowment of the factor observed in a sample of 33 countries.

Table 3.1 Differences in factor endowments by country, 1982

| Country | Capital | Labor | | | | | Land | | GDP | Labor cost |
		Professional technical	Sales	Service	Agriculture	Production	Crop	Pasture		
Bangladesh	0.1	1.3	5.8	3.9	14.1	3.0	2.2	0.1	0.2	—
Canada	4.0	4.0	2.5	3.3	0.6	2.5	11.1	5.9	3.7	10.45
France	8.0	7.1	4.0	5.6	1.8	5.4	4.5	3.1	6.8	7.85
Germany	9.0	5.5	5.1	5.6	2.1	7.0	1.8	1.1	8.2	10.25
Hong Kong	0.4	0.3	0.6	0.9	0.1	0.9	0.0	0.0	0.4	1.66
Indonesia	2.8	3.4	15.2	5.1	29.5	7.6	4.7	2.9	1.1	—
Italy	7.0	5.4	3.6	4.5	2.1	5.9	3.0	1.3	5.0	7.44
Japan	16.0	10.2	17.8	10.3	6.0	15.1	1.2	0.1	14.4	5.60
Pakistan	0.5	1.9	4.1	2.1	11.5	4.3	4.9	1.2	0.4	—
Singapore	0.4	0.2	0.3	0.3	0.0	0.3	0.0	0.0	0.2	1.96
Sri Lanka	0.3	0.5	0.7	0.5	1.8	0.8	0.5	0.1	0.1	.24
UK	5.1	8.6	3.0	6.7	0.3	5.8	1.7	2.8	6.1	6.92
USA	28.7	32.2	21.6	28.3	2.8	22.9	45.9	58.0	39.9	11.68

Source: Daniel Trefler, "The Case of the Missing Trade and Other Mysteries," *The American Economic Review*, 85, no. 5, December 1995, pp. 1029–46, available from http://www.nber.org/pub/trefler/HOV/hov_pub.dat and ftp://ftp.bls.gov/pub/special.requests/ForeignLabor/supptab.txt

Note: The numbers reported are percentage shares of a 33-country total, where this set of countries includes all those market economies for which comparable data were available. In addition to countries shown in the table, the remainder are Austria, Belgium, Columbia, Denmark, Finland, Greece, Ireland, Israel, the Netherlands, New Zealand, Norway, Panama, Portugal, Spain, Sweden, Switzerland, Thailand, Trinidad, Uruguay, and Yugoslavia. The final column gives the hourly compensation cost for production workers in US dollars for 1982.

If there were just two factors, then simply comparing a country's capital share to its labor share would show it was capital-abundant if a ratio greater than one were observed. Because there are many factors and many potentially conflicting ratios could be calculated, a different comparison is more appropriate. The GDP column of the table gives the country's share of income calculated across the same set of countries. One way of interpreting the income share is as a weighted average of the country's shares of each of the individual factors. If factor prices are equalized across all countries, that interpretation is accurate. We also may interpret the income share as an approximation of domestic demand for the factor, given the H–O assumption that all countries spend their incomes in the same proportions. Therefore, if the country's endowment share for a factor exceeds the country's income share, the country is relatively abundant in that factor and will export goods that require it intensively. For example, Germany is abundant in capital but scarce in labor and land. Therefore, we expect the bundle of goods Germany exports to require above-average amounts of capital, but its imports to require labor and land-intensively. If factor prices are equalized, we cannot predict precisely which goods will be traded; Germany will not necessarily import the most labor-intensive good. We know on average, however, that when trade is balanced, Germany's imports will require more labor than its exports.

The H–O model implies that countries with a relatively greater abundance of a factor will have a lower autarky cost of using that factor. An indication of that intermediate relationship is shown in the final column of Table 3.1 for production workers. Any comparison is imprecise, in part because the exchange rates used to convert all entries into US dollars may not reflect equilibrium purchasing power parity values (a topic addressed in Chapter 13). Nevertheless, it is generally true that countries where the share of production workers relative to the share of GDP is high will have a lower cost of hourly compensation. For example, in Sri Lanka the production labor endowment share is eight times the GDP share, and the hourly compensation cost is $0.24, whereas in the USA the corresponding ratio of production labor to GDP is only 0.57, and the hourly compensation cost is $11.68.

While the issue of changing factor endowments and economic growth will be addressed more fully in Chapters 9 and 10, consider a very specific case that applies the H–O assumptions about supply and demand conditions to a small country unable to affect world prices. Let the labor force in this country grow. As shown in Figure 3.3 the shift in the production-possibility curve is biased toward cheese, the labor-intensive good. In fact, note that for the same relative price of cheese and wheat, shown by the initial tangency of the international terms of trade line to the production-possibility curve at P, the corresponding point of tangency along the new curve occurs at P^1. Output of cheese has increased substantially, while the output of wheat has fallen. This effect, known as the **Rybczynski theorem,**[3] holds because at unchanged terms of trade and unchanged returns to land and labor, producers of cheese and wheat choose to use exactly the same factor proportions as at P. How can the same proportions of land to labor be maintained if there is no additional land available to the economy as a whole? Such an outcome is possible only if less of the land-intensive good, wheat, is produced. All of the extra labor is used to produce cheese. The same ratio of land to labor can be maintained in cheese production by reducing wheat output, which makes land (and some more labor) available to the expanding cheese sector. Without that reduction in wheat output, adding all the extra labor to the same amount of land in the cheese sector would drive up the return to land in that sector, a disequilibrium situation and a signal to shift land away from wheat production. Note that for a small country, this expansion of output of cheese is not large enough to affect world prices, and producers of cheese continue to receive the fixed world price for however many units they produce.

A more general observation from the Denmark–US example is that growth in the US labor force makes the US relative factor endowment more similar to Denmark's and consequently reduces the amount of trade predicted by the H–O model. Conversely, if factor endowments become less similar across countries, the H–O model predicts that more trade will occur. In accord with this theory, the choice of China and India to join the world trading system over the past 20 years will lead to an expansion of trade between industrialized

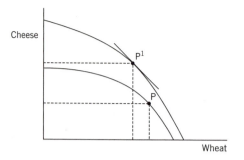

Figure 3.3 Growth in the labor force. When more labor becomes available, with constant output prices, the same factor proportions used in each industry at point P will now be used at point P¹.

and developing countries, because the addition of two very labor-abundant countries to the latter group has increased the disparity in relative factor endowments between the two groups.

In the H–O model a nation's comparative advantage position is not permanently fixed, but changes as factor supplies change both within the country and in its trading partners. For example, a nation's labor supply depends on its growth in population, and the proportion that is of working age. Labor-force participation rates among women and older workers also have changed substantially in many countries in recent decades. Distinctions between skilled and unskilled workers often are relevant, and creating a more skilled labor force depends on educational policy and other socioeconomic circumstances that can change through time. Capital can be accumulated through domestic saving. As an illustration of such influences, during the 1950s and 1960s Taiwan was a labor-abundant country and exported inexpensive garments and shoes. During the 1970s and 1980s, however, large expenditures on education and high rates of savings and investment produced a highly skilled labor force and a larger physical capital stock. During that period, Taiwan's exports started to shift toward products that required higher skills and more capital. By 2000, Taiwan was the fourth largest recipient of patents in the United States, behind Japan and Germany, a reflection of its further shift toward goods requiring more advanced technology, and a topic we pursue in Chapter 4.[4]

The distribution of income and factor price changes

The gains from trade identified by classical economists continue to exist in the H–O model. This is demonstrated in Figure 3.2 where both countries move to higher indifference curves in the free-trade equilibrium. The H–O model allows us to address an additional question: how are those gains from trade distributed across different factors? The application of the H–O framework to this issue by Wolfgang Stolper and Paul Samuelson resulted in remarkably strong predictions:[5] a rise in the price of the good a country exports causes the real return to the relatively abundant factor, which is used intensively in producing the export good, to rise and the real return to the scarce factor to fall. In this section we demonstrate why the **Stolper–Samuelson theorem** holds.

We first review some important aspects of production in the H–O model. As demonstrated more thoroughly in the appendix to this chapter, producers of cheese and wheat typically can choose between many alternative combinations of land and labor to determine the most

Box 3.2 How different are factor intensities?

The H–O theory requires that different goods use factor inputs in different proportions. Theoretically, this distinction is important, because the greater the differences in factor intensities, the greater the extent to which we will observe increasing opportunity costs of production and the more significant will factor endowments be in explaining autarky prices. Empirically, measuring these differences is not so straightforward.

One approach is to consider the value-added in an industry (the value of its output minus the value of intermediate inputs it buys from other industries) and to observe how it is divided among different factors. A useful category from national income accounts is compensation to employees. Even this measure is problematic in sectors such as farming where much production is accounted for by farms owned and operated by a single family, but in manufacturing over 97 percent of the labor input is provided by employees, not by the owners of the business. We attribute the rest of the value-added to factors such as land, tangible capital (plant and equipment), and intangible capital (patented ideas, trade secrets, brand image). The value-added generated by such factors represents a flow of factor services, not a stock of machines or ideas allocated to a particular industry. Not measuring the stock of capital avoids some problems, because machines and buildings are bought at different times at different prices and they wear out at different rates. Land varies tremendously in its fertility, and intangible ideas are even more difficult to measure. Looking at the income factors receive avoids those problems, but introduces others. Profits may vary considerably over the business cycle, and some industries may be more sensitive to the business cycle than others. No single measure is ideal.

Column two of Table 3.2 gives labor's share of value-added in several US manufacturing industries in 1997. They are ordered by the relative importance of labor. Note that industries such as textiles, apparel, and furniture are relatively labor-intensive, while chemicals, petroleum refining, and tobacco products are not. When material inputs can be freely traded internationally, we expect relatively more of these more labor-intensive activities to be located in more labor-abundant countries.

Can we infer anything else from the information in Table 3.2? Column three shows the average compensation per employee in the industry, which may indicate a difference with respect to labor skills. If labor is paid on the basis of its productivity, and if wage rates for labor of a given skill are equal in all industries, then we could infer that industries with higher average wages have higher skill requirements. In fact, economists find that there are systematic differences in wages across industries that cannot be explained by years of experience or education of the workers, and therefore, skill differences are not the only factors that influence the figures in column three. Workers in some industries may receive a wage premium based on high profits earned in the industry. Nevertheless, it is instructive to note that industries such as apparel and textiles are quite labor-intensive, but their lower wages suggest lower skill requirements. Scientific instruments are quite labor-intensive, too, but their higher wages suggest higher skill requirements. Countries relatively abundant in skilled labor are more likely to produce and export scientific instruments, and countries relatively abundant in unskilled labor are more likely to produce and export apparel.

Table 3.2 Differences in factor input requirements by industry

Industry	Employee compensation/ value-added	Employee compensation/full-time equivalent worker
Other transportation equipment	0.998	$59,564
Instruments and related products	0.901	$59,298
Textile mill products	0.763	$31,897
Furniture and fixtures	0.760	$33,509
Rubber and miscellaneous plastic	0.743	$39,368
Primary metal industries	0.728	$54,925
Industrial machinery and equipment	0.720	$53,452
Apparel and other textile products	0.715	$25,290
Stone, clay and glass products	0.711	$44,042
Motor vehicles and equipment	0.696	$61,387
Printing and publishing	0.670	$45,083
Fabricated metal products	0.639	$43,398
Paper and allied products	0.633	$51,644
Lumber and wood products	0.613	$33,115
Leather and leather products	0.566	$30,528
Miscellaneous manufacturing	0.566	$36,253
Electronic equipment	0.555	$52,230
Food and kindred products	0.545	$39,105
Chemicals and allied products	0.451	$70,242
Petroleum and coal products	0.313	$81,674
Tobacco products	0.165	$75,750

Source: US Department of Commerce, *Survey of Current Business*, November 19, 1997.

efficient form of production. The lower the wage rate, the more likely producers are to use more labor and less land, thereby reducing their costs of production. As the wage ratio rises, producers will give up labor-using forms of production and use more land. This incentive to use more land exists both in wheat production and in cheese production. The extent to which production of cheese or wheat will become more land-intensive, however, depends upon how easy it is to substitute one input for the other.

A second important relationship is the one between factor productivity and factor returns. Given the assumption of constant returns to scale, we know that if a wheat producer is able to double the inputs of both land and labor, output of wheat will double. If the producer is unable to rent more land and can only hire more labor, each extra unit of labor will add progressively less to total output, a demonstration of the law of diminishing returns. In fact, returns will diminish more rapidly when it is more difficult to substitute labor for land. Hiring more labor that is available does not provide much advantage if it cannot serve as a good substitute for the factor, land, whose quantity cannot be increased. If it is simply impossible to substitute labor for land, then additional labor adds nothing to wheat output.

The wheat producer will continue to hire extra labor as long as the extra output produced (labor's marginal product) is greater than the wage rate. Once labor's marginal product declines to the point where it equals the wage rate, the producer will hire no more labor. Note that as the producer continues to add more labor to a fixed amount of land, the land/labor ratio becomes smaller and labor's marginal product declines. Because labor productivity declines as the land/labor ratio declines, the wage that producers are willing to pay for labor also falls.

We have discussed these concepts of factor productivity and factor substitution as they apply to each industry in isolation. To derive the Stolper–Samuelson results cited above, we must evaluate how production in the two industries changes at the same time. Consider the situation in Denmark where the opportunity to trade improves the Danish terms of trade and causes the price of cheese to increase. The increase in the price of cheese provides an incentive for cheese producers to expand output. As they try to hire more labor and rent more land, however, they must bid these inputs away from wheat production. Because wheat production is land-intensive, a cutback in wheat production releases more land relative to labor than cheese producers want to use at the current wage rate and rental rate for land. Too little labor is available and too much land, which causes the wage rate to rise relative to land's rental rate.

The same outcome arises if we think of this adjustment to greater trade resulting in greater competition for producers of the import-competing good, wheat. Again, a decline in wheat production results in a big reduction in demand for land that is not offset by the greater demand for land in the expanding cheese sector. Conversely, the reduction in demand for labor in wheat production is not great enough to satisfy the extra demand for labor in the cheese sector. Thus, wages must increase relative to land rental rates in order that both land and labor remain fully employed. The lower rental rate for land gives both cheese producers and wheat producers an incentive to substitute land for labor and to increase their demand for land enough to keep it fully utilized. Because producers in both sectors see this incentive to substitute land in place of labor, the land/labor ratio rises in both sectors.

At first glance, this result may seem curious. The total amounts of labor and land in the economy are fixed, yet we claim that the land/labor ratio rises in each sector. How is that possible? Consider a simple numerical example where initially wheat production accounts for 16 hectares of land and eight workers, while cheese production accounts for 8 hectares of land and 16 workers. Let the price of cheese rise in Denmark as a result of trade. Suppose we transfer one hectare of land and one worker out of wheat production into cheese production. In the new equilibrium 15 hectares of land and seven workers are utilized in wheat production, while 9 hectares of land and 17 workers produce cheese. The ratio of land to labor rises in each sector. The ratio can rise, even though total quantities of land and labor are fixed, because the labor-intensive cheese sector now accounts for a larger share of national output.

We dwell on the change in the land/labor ratio because the fact that it increases indicates labor productivity rises in both sectors. As a consequence, labor's wage rises. This represents an increase in real income, because an hour's work now produces more kilograms of wheat, and also more kilos of cheese, the good whose price has risen. Even if workers spend all of their income on cheese, they can buy more cheese than in the pre-trade equilibrium, because their output of cheese per hour has risen. At the same time, the return to land declines because the land/labor ratio rises in both sectors and production per hectare declines in both sectors. Rental rates for land decline, and Danish landowners now are worse off than they were before trade. Even if the landowners spend all their income on wheat, the good whose price is held constant in this barter world, and avoid cheese entirely, they receive less wheat per hectare than they did previously.

We have now arrived at the strong Stolper–Samuelson result: *Liberalization of trade causes the abundant factor, which is used intensively in the export industry, to gain, and the scarce factor, which is used intensively in the import-competing industry, to lose.* In Denmark, labor does not simply gain at a faster rate than land gains. Rather, labor gains and land loses.

In the United States, trade liberalization causes the relative price of wheat to rise compared to its autarky level. As US output of wheat rises, the land/labor ratio falls in each sector; the contracting cheese sector does not release enough land relative to labor to meet the rising demand created by land-intensive wheat production. A declining land/labor ratio means labor productivity falls, and as a result, US wages fall. Land rents rise because more labor is available to work each hectare in both sectors. Again, the opportunity to trade has resulted in an increase in the real return to the abundant factor (land) used intensively in the production of the export good and a decline in the real return to the scarce factor (labor) used intensively in import-competing production.

Let us summarize these results from the two countries together. Originally, in the pre-trade situation, the United States had low returns to land and high wages, due to the relative scarcity of labor and abundance of land. Conversely, Denmark had high returns to land and low wages, due to the relative scarcity of land and abundance of labor. Trade creates more demand for each country's abundant factor and less demand for each country's scarce factor. In the United States land prices rise while in Denmark they fall. Wages fall in the United States and rise in Denmark. Thus, the pre-trade gap in factor returns declines as a result of trade.

Does the reduction in factor price differences across countries continue until they have been entirely eliminated and we reach a point of **factor-price equalization** across countries? The formal logic of the H–O model indicates that will be the equilibrium outcome, as long as both Denmark and the United States continue to produce both wheat and cheese. Because wheat producers in each country, for example, face the same price of output, and have available the same technology to use in production, they will use exactly the same proportions of land to labor at a given ratio of wages and rental rates of land. A bigger share of the world's wheat production will be located in the United States than in Denmark, in comparison with cheese production, because the United States is relatively land-abundant. But, there will be no difference in the way wheat is produced in the two countries, nor in the way cheese is produced in the two countries. With producers of a given good in each country using factor inputs in exactly the same proportions, the productivity of those factors is the same in both countries, and consequently there will be no difference in factor rewards.

In the real world we do not observe that factor prices have actually equalized, but we can quickly recognize that the stringent assumptions of the H–O model often fail to hold. For example, trade is not free, and producers in all countries are not responding to the same prices of output. In our $2 \times 2 \times 2$ example, if the United States limits imports of cheese from Denmark, then Danish wages will not rise sufficiently to equal US wages. Also, technology does not appear to move costlessly from country to country, and consequently producers do not all have the same choices in how to produce. Our examples from the classical economists demonstrated that economies with more productive technologies could pay higher wages, and that same principle applies in the more complicated H–O model if the same quantities of labor and land inputs yield greater output in one country than another. Furthermore, our assumption that the two countries remain incompletely specialized is an important one, because once Denmark becomes completely specialized in cheese production, a higher price of cheese will no longer tend to benefit labor and harm landowners. The price rise no longer causes the land/labor ratio to rise, because no further reduction in wheat production is possible. Instead, higher cheese prices benefit Denmark, which already is producing as much cheese as possible, and we expect both labor and land to gain, as in the classical model.

There are many qualifications to the prospects for factor price equalization. Nevertheless, the basic insight from the Stolper–Samuelson theorem, that a rise in the price of exports will benefit the abundant factor and harm the scarce factor, is remarkably relevant in interpreting current controversies over the consequences of trade and closer integration of the world economy. Owners of the relatively scarce factor of production (land in Denmark, labor in the United States) can be expected to oppose free trade in favor of severe barriers to imports, while the owners of relatively abundant factors (labor in Denmark, land in the United States) will be free-traders. This prediction is borne out in many political disputes over trade policy. This alignment was particularly apparent in the United States during the 1993 debate over the establishment of the **North American Free Trade Agreement** (NAFTA) with Canada and Mexico. The AFL-CIO, the broadest representative of organized labor, waged a fierce battle against Congressional approval of the agreement. The unions lost that battle, but their continued dissatisfaction with this decision resulted in the president being unable to gain Congressional approval to negotiate other trade agreements until 2002.

Box 3.3 The widening income gap: is trade to blame?

Changes in the distribution of income in the United States and in Europe since 1980 have favored skilled labor and hurt unskilled labor. Can this be attributed to increased international trade, especially with countries abundant in unskilled labor, such as China and India, turning away from policies of economic self-sufficiency and instead playing a larger role in international trade? That remains a controversial issue among trade and labor economists. Many trade economists approach the topic by examining two important links in the Stolper–Samuelson line of reasoning:[6] (1) have the relative prices of goods that require unskilled labor intensively actually fallen over this same period? and (2) has the expansion of output in industries that use skilled labor intensively caused the ratio of skilled labor to unskilled labor to decline in all sectors, as would be predicted for the United States and Europe? Evidence does not suggest that relative prices of unskilled labor-intensive goods have fallen. Nor do we observe that producers have shifted to production techniques that require relatively more unskilled labor in response to the rising relative cost of skilled labor, a result we would predict if the incentives identified by the Stolper–Samuelson theorem were the major determinant of wage movements.

   The most widely accepted alternative explanation for the decline in wages of unskilled labor is that changes in technology have played a dominant role, especially changes that have resulted in less demand for unskilled labor. This role of technology also seems relevant in explaining the experience of developing countries, where we would expect a rise in the price of goods that use unskilled labor intensively to result in higher relative wages for unskilled labor. In many of those countries, too, we observe that demand for skilled labor is rising more rapidly than the demand for unskilled labor. Again, such a result appears attributable to significant changes in technology that reduce the demand for unskilled labor.

   Others warn against too ready acceptance of this line of reasoning. Robert Feenstra notes that industries in developed countries have been able to increase their utilization of skilled labor relative to unskilled labor by breaking previously integrated production processes into separate steps.[7] They then outsource the most unskilled-labor-intensive steps to low-wage countries. As this upgrading in the skill content of what is done domestically occurs within exporting and importing industries, relative prices of goods need not change as posited in the Stolper–Samuelson example. Yet, demand for skilled labor rises and demand for unskilled labor falls.

In developing countries, those same outsourced jobs may create demand for relatively more skilled workers, which is an additional force for divergence in wages within those countries, beyond the influence of any changes in technology. Apparently, this outsourcing strategy does not make use of the least skilled workers in developing countries, because their current wages relative to those of more skilled workers are unattractive. Because direct observation of either the impacts of technical change or the significance of outsourcing is limited, economists have not resolved this issue.

Is North–South trade likely to accelerate in the future and create larger competitive pressure on unskilled wages than it does at present? Certainly the decline in trade barriers negotiated in the **Uruguay Round** of multilateral trade negotiations completed in 1994 (a topic addressed in Chapter 8) may give Southern exporters greater access to currently protected sectors such as apparel, which use unskilled labor intensively. On the other hand, Northern production of some unskilled-labor-intensive goods may cease. Further declines in their prices no longer would create pressure for divergent shifts in skilled and unskilled wages, because the assumption of incomplete specialization in production no longer would be met. Instead, both skilled and unskilled labor would gain from the lower price of a good that neither of them produces.[8]

Income redistribution and the welfare economics of trade

The income redistribution effect of international trade presents some serious problems for the earlier conclusion that free trade must increase economic welfare in both countries. Although total income (real GNP) in each country clearly rises with trade, some groups in society gain a great deal, whereas other groups lose. The relatively abundant factor of production wins, but the scarce factor loses. What happens to total welfare depends on how the gains of one group of people are evaluated relative to the losses of others.

Because total income rises, the winners must gain more income than the losers give up. If everyone can be assumed to have the same marginal utility for income (personal valuation of an extra dollar in income), and society attaches the same value to an extra dollar of income received by A as it does to a dollar received by B, then the earlier conclusion is maintained. The winners must have received more additional utility than the losers gave up. It is unfortunate that there are losers, but because total utility rises with the increase in income, society is still better off. The problem is in making the assumption that everyone puts the same value on extra income.

Suppose half the people in society gain $100 each, but each person in the other half loses $50. We cannot be certain that total utility rose just because average income rose by $25. What if each of those losing $50 happens to care much more about extra income than do the winners? What if they care three times as much about an extra dollar than do those gaining $100 each? Even though total income rises, utility or welfare falls. Because we cannot know how different groups evaluate income gains or losses, we can make no certain conclusion as to what happens to national welfare when free trade increases total income but redistributes enough income from the scarce to the abundant factor to leave owners of the scarce factor poorer than they were without trade.

One attempt to deal with this problem is known as the "compensation principle"; it argues that because the winners gain more income than the losers lose, the winners can fully compensate the losers and still retain net gains. In the example of the preceding paragraph, if each of those who gained $100 spent $50 to compensate the losers, they would still have a gain of $50 left and the previous losers would have returned to their original incomes. (If each winner spent $55 on compensation, everyone would gain something.) The problem is how to gather political support for, and then institutionalize, such compensation, particularly if those on the losing side of free trade are politically weak or do not trust the winners to continue the compensation payments after free trade is instituted.

Owners of the scarce factor (or factors) of production in any country tend to oppose free trade and to support protectionism. This problem is particularly relevant in the United States and the European Union where the relatively scarce factor is unskilled labor. The winners from free trade are owners of human capital (highly educated people), and those with financial capital invested in export industries. The losers are unskilled or semi-skilled workers. Those who would gain from free trade are primarily people whose incomes are already above average, whereas the group being harmed consists overwhelmingly of those with below-average incomes. Free trade would increase total incomes in the United States and Europe but would make the distribution of income more unequal than it now is. Those who represent the interests of unskilled labor are opposed to reducing barriers to more imports of labor-intensive products such as textiles, garments, and shoes. If some form of wage insurance was offered, and if workers were confident that it would be maintained after trade was liberalized, opposition to freer trade might decline. Although steps in this direction were taken in the law that granted President Bush trade negotiating authority in 2002, protectionist sentiment in the US labor movement is likely to remain strong.[9]

Who would we expect to be hurt by trade liberalization in labor-abundant countries? When unskilled labor is relatively abundant but available land, capital, and skilled labor are scarce, we predict unskilled labor will gain, while skilled workers and owners of capital and land will lose. In many cases, those potential losers are successful in maintaining a protectionist policy because politically they have special access to influence government trade policy. Unskilled workers may be too poorly organized to lobby effectively for a more open trade policy. Calls for workers of the world to unite in their opposition to more open trade appear to be consistent with the interests of labor in labor-scarce industrialized countries but are a disservice to those in most developing countries.

How are these theoretical predictions about income distribution borne out in practice? As Korea, Taiwan, and Singapore increased their labor-intensive exports of apparel and footwear products in the 1960s and 1970s, economists noted that the wages of unskilled workers rose relative to those of more skilled workers in those countries. That result is what we would predict on the basis of the Stolper–Samuelson theorem. When Latin American countries adopted more liberal trade policies in the 1980s, however, wage inequality increased in Colombia, Costa Rica, Mexico, and Uruguay. What reasons might explain this different outcome? In Adrian Wood's review of this situation, one possibility he suggests is that as Latin American countries reduced trade barriers, they faced greater import competition from even more labor-abundant countries, such as China, Indonesia, India, Bangladesh, and Pakistan, as well as more industrialized countries.[10] This situation would imply that in Latin America the least skill-intensive and the most skill-intensive industries contracted, while those with intermediate skill requirements expanded. That result is consistent with the Stolper–Samuelson framework. An alternative possibility already raised in the case of industrialized countries is that technical change creates more demand for skilled workers and reduces demand for unskilled labor, which explains the fall in unskilled labor's wage.

Fixed factors of production in the short run

The conclusion that the abundant factor of production gains from free trade and that the relatively scarce factor loses is based on the assumption that the adjustment to free trade is complete – that is, that both factors of production have moved from the import-competing to the export industry and that full employment has been reestablished. In the short run, before this new equilibrium is reached, the results can be quite different. During the contraction of the import-competing industry, both capital and labor employed in that sector will experience declines in income, whereas both factors in the export sector are likely to be better off during its expansion.

For example, consider a capital-abundant, labor-scarce country. If free trade means that the labor-intensive apparel industry contracts while the capital-intensive steel industry expands, we do not immediately observe the Stolper–Samuelson result that all labor loses and all capital gains. While the apparel sector is shrinking, both capital and labor in that sector will suffer as jobs are lost and factories are shut down. In the expanding steel industry both labor and capital will benefit as sales, employment, and profits all grow. In fact, these short-run, industry-specific interests often dominate the political debate over trade policy, a topic we address in Chapter 6. The longer-run outcome, that a factor experiences the same change in income regardless of the industry where it is employed, only emerges gradually. As labor laid off in the apparel industry seeks employment in the steel industry, wages paid in the steel industry are driven down, too. Similarly, capital will leave the apparel industry until its return there is as high as can be earned in the steel industry.

Trade: A substitute for factor movements

Another important implication of factor proportions theory is that international trade can serve as a substitute for the movement of productive factors from one country to another.[11] The actual distribution of productive factors among the nations of the world is obviously very unequal. One possible market response would be movements of labor and capital from countries where they are abundant and cheap to countries where they are scarce and more expensive, thus reducing the differences in factor rewards and making factor endowments more equal throughout the world.

The factor proportions theory suggests that international factor movements may not be necessary in any case, because the movement of goods in world trade can accomplish essentially the same purpose. Countries that have abundant labor can specialize in labor intensive goods and ship these goods to countries where labor is scarce. Labor is embodied in goods and redistributed through trade. The same point applies to capital, land, and other factors. The economic effects of international factor movements can be achieved without the factors themselves actually having to move.

The major economic effect of an international factor outflow is to alter the relative abundance or scarcity of that factor and thus to affect its price, that is, to raise the prices of abundant factors by making them less abundant relative to other factors. Thus, when Polish workers migrate to Germany, wage rates tend to rise in Poland because labor is made somewhat less abundant there, whereas wage rates in Germany tend to fall (or at least to rise less rapidly than they otherwise would) because the relative scarcity of labor is reduced. The

---

Box 3.4 An intermediate case: a specific factors model

Economists recognize that in some cases labor and capital may not be equally mobile. Rather, labor may be mobile between industries, while capital is unable to move and remains specific to a given industry.[12] Of course, there are circumstances where labor adjustment may be protracted, too; an industry contraction may be so large that it results in layoffs of older workers, who have less incentive or interest to relocate or retrain. We disregard that situation here and refer to the case of industry-specific capital as a **specific factors model**.

Consider the consequences of trade liberalization when capital is assumed to be industry-specific and labor is mobile. Output in the import-competing industry falls. Not only does the relative price of the import-competing good fall, but labor shifts out of the industry, which causes the fixed capital stock to be less productive. Because output per machine falls, as occurs if only one shift a day is employed rather than two, then capital invested in the import-competing industry clearly loses. At the same time, output in the export industry rises, and more labor is now working in the export industry. Therefore, output per machine rises in the exports sector, and the return to that capital increases.

While the implications for capital in each sector are clear, the impact on labor is ambiguous. As more labor is used with a fixed amount of capital in the export industry, labor's productivity declines in that sector. Because labor's wage is based on its productivity, it will now receive a wage that buys less of the export good. The relative price of the imported good declines, however, and if a large enough share of labor's budget is spent on the imported good, labor becomes better off. This ambiguous result suggests that labor may have less incentive to lobby for changes in trade policy than owners of industry-specific factors do.

---

same result is achieved when Germans buy Polish goods that are produced by relatively labor-intensive methods. More labor is demanded by Polish export industries, and Polish wage rates tend to rise.

The fact that free trade and factor mobility are driven by parallel causes and have the same effects on the distribution of income has implications for the politics of immigration laws. In a labor-scarce country either free trade or liberal immigration policies will threaten the incomes of labor, whereas the opposite will be true in a labor-abundant country. Labor unions in relatively labor-scarce countries tend to oppose free trade or immigration for the same reason. Either policy will reduce the incomes of workers and increase those of owners of land and capital. Nevertheless, countries worried about the clash of cultures posed by immigration have seen trade liberalization as a preferred way for incomes in the labor-abundant countries to rise, rather than through emigration.

Trade and factor movements can be regarded as substitutes in the situation where trade barriers exist and factor flows occur in response to the differences in factor rewards created by those barriers. In other circumstances, however, trade and factor flows can be regarded as complements. For example, James Markusen presents a case where the H–O model is modified to rule out differences in factor endowments and to allow one country to have a technical advantage in producing the labor-intensive good.[13] That country will have a comparative advantage in producing the labor-intensive good and also will pay a higher wage rate after trade occurs. Therefore, there is still an incentive for labor to immigrate to this country, and that will further reinforce its comparative advantage in producing the labor-intensive good. Trade and factor flows are complements in those circumstances.

Empirical verification in a world with many goods

As in the case of the classical model, formulating an appropriate empirical test of the stylized $2 \times 2 \times 2$ model is difficult because actual data come from a world where there are many goods and many factors of production. Also, we cannot observe autarky or pre-trade costs, and therefore we must infer what they would be, based on characteristics such as factor endowments or factor intensities. Two basic approaches have been developed by past researchers: one attempts to predict trade in particular goods, as was the case for the classical model, and another predicts the factor content of trade. They both give useful insights into relationships implied by the H–O model, but they generally do not constitute complete tests of the theory, either. Because the second approach emerged first, and is more consistent with the full H–O model with factor price equalization, we consider it.

Wassily Leontief framed the question by asking how much labor and capital were necessary to produce $1 million of US exports and how much labor and capital would be required to produce domestically $1 million worth of imports.[14] Leontief was uniquely positioned to make such a calculation because he had led the development of an input–output table that broke the US economy into 200 different sectors and showed what any one sector bought from all the others. Besides showing demands for intermediate inputs, the table indicated how much of the primary factors, labor and capital, were employed in an industry. Therefore, Leontief could determine how much labor and capital were required, directly and indirectly through intermediate inputs, to produce a dollar's worth of output in any industry. To derive his final answer, he simply weighted each industry's input requirements by that industry's importance in total exports or total imports in 1947, although for imports he was forced to exclude goods such as tin and coffee that were not produced in the United States.

From all these calculations, Leontief ended up with four numbers: capital and labor inputs required to produce $1 million of exports, and capital and labor inputs required to produce $1 million of import-competing goods. It was generally believed (indeed, Leontief took it for granted) that the United States was a capital-rich country and that it had a greater abundance of capital relative to labor than did its trade partners. Consequently, the Heckscher–Ohlin theory predicted that US exports would be more capital-intensive than its import-competing goods – that is, that:

$$[K/L] \text{ export goods} > [K/L] \text{import-competing goods}$$

To Leontief's great surprise, his results showed the opposite, namely that US exports were more labor-intensive than its import-competing goods. The following table shows Leontief's actual figures on inputs required to produce $1 million of exports and $1 million of import-competing goods. The capital/labor ratio in export industries ($14,011) was lower than the capital/labor ratio in import-competing industries ($18,182).

This result, which contradicted the Heckscher–Ohlin thesis, came to be known as the **Leontief paradox**. It stimulated many further studies, and a large number of books and articles have since been published on the subject. Edward Leamer noted that the wrong standard was being applied to test the theory for a country whose trade was not balanced, and in fact no paradox exists in Leontief's data when the appropriate test is applied: US production is capital-intensive relative to US consumption.[15] Aside from any resolution of

Leontief's paradox, the substantial prior and subsequent effort to test the H–O theory has been instructive in demonstrating whether the theory is sensitive to changes in underlying assumptions and in developing more complete tests of the theory. We mention a few of the main results of this work.[16]

Modifying the basic assumptions

Several economists have suggested that considering only two productive factors, capital and labor, may give biased projections. With more than two factors, however, it becomes less straightforward to decide what we mean by factor abundance: is labor scarcity indicated by the capital/labor ratio or by some other ratio? Vanek suggests a useful framework to resolve that ambiguity, and we review that approach because it adds to our understanding of how to draw inferences from the H–O model in a many-good, many-factor model.[17]

First, based on observed input requirements in each industry, determine what demand for a factor is created by the country's net trade position in each industry. That is, exports create more demand for a factor while imports reduce demand for it. Sum across all industries to obtain the net factor demand created by trade. According to the H–O theory, this net foreign demand for a factor should be equal to the endowment of the factor available in the country minus the amount of that factor used to satisfy demand by home consumers. For each factor considered, we expect the following:

$$\text{Net factor demand from international trade} = \text{Factor endowment} - \text{Factor demand from domestic expenditure}$$

We can be more precise about home demand, because of the H–O assumption that all individuals spend their income the same way, regardless of the level of income. What residents of a country consume is simply a bundle of goods that represents a claim on factor services equal to the country's share of world income. If a country accounts for 20 percent of the world's income, then its demand for goods represents a demand for 20 percent of the world's capital stock, 20 percent of the world's labor force, etc. Given that simplification, then, we can say that a country is relatively abundant in a factor when its share of the world endowment is greater than its share of world income. Thus, if a country accounts for 25 percent of the world's capital stock, and earns 20 percent of the world's income, it is relatively abundant in capital.

Although attention to additional factors of production did not resolve the paradox in Leontief's numbers, it has been particularly fruitful in economists' thinking about the roles of human capital and trade. We have already distinguished between unskilled labor and skilled labor in discussing the consequences of trade on income distribution; that distinction is empirically grounded on the work of researchers who found that the United States tends to export goods that require skilled labor intensively and to import goods that require unskilled labor intensively.[18] Or, in the factor content framework, the United States is a net exporter of skilled labor and a net importer of unskilled labor. For a US share of the world stock of skilled labor that exceeds the US share of world income, and a US share of the world stock of unskilled labor that is less than the US share of world income, those observations support the H–O predictions that a country that is relatively abundant (scarce) in skilled labor (unskilled labor) will be a net exporter (importer) of skilled labor (unskilled labor).

A more comprehensive analysis of the factor content of trade for 12 different factors and 27 different countries by Harry Bowen, Edward Leamer, and Leo Sveikauskas gives a less encouraging message regarding the generality of the H–O theory.[19] The sign of the factor content of trade (surplus or deficit) is predicted correctly by relative factor abundance in merely half of the cases considered. Two responses to that work give a more encouraging assessment. One, by Adrian Wood, notes that if we restrict attention to trade between industrialized and developing countries, the H–O theory explains such trade fairly well: developed countries export skilled-labor-intensive goods to and import unskilled-labor-intensive goods from developing countries.[20] Wood also notes that capital has become sufficiently mobile internationally that returns to capital are roughly equal across countries. Predicting commodity trade on the basis of differences in capital endowments mistakenly assumes that cost differences exist where none should be expected. Rather, attention should be restricted to endowments of immobile factors, like land and labor.

A second perspective is provided by the work of Daniel Trefler.[21] He pursues a line of reasoning suggested by Leontief: if US labor is more productive than foreign labor, due to a US technological advantage, then the United States will appear labor-abundant if we are able to measure labor units of comparable productivity everywhere. Trefler also points to the importance of differences in technology to explain observed patterns of trade. The basic problem he observed was that H–O predictions systematically perform poorly. Poor countries appear to be abundant in most factors, but export much too little, while rich countries appear to be scarce in most factors, but import much too little. To account for this missing trade, Trefler allows for differences across countries in technology. Just as in Leontief's formulation, this changes the measure of relative factor abundance. Making that adjustment results in much less predicted trade than when technology is assumed to be the same everywhere. Subsequent work suggests that the failure of factor prices to be equalized, even among industrialized countries, alters the measured factor content of production and trade, and reduces the extent of missing trade. In addition, taking into account the costliness of trade helps explain its observed factor content.[22]

Can any conclusions be drawn regarding the overall validity of the H–O theory? In its unaltered form, the H–O model frequently does not perform well. It appears to do the best in predicting trade where a country's factor endowments differ most from the worldwide endowment pattern, as in trade between industrialized and developing countries. Explicitly recognizing the importance of differences in technology, the quality of factor inputs, or impediments to trade all improve the model's predictive ability. Because the H–O model provides a coherent framework for addressing questions of trade patterns, income distribution, and economic growth, it will be an important building block for any hybrid approach that emerges.

Summary of key concepts

1 When goods require factor inputs in different proportions, differences in relative endowments of these factors across countries can explain why autarky prices of goods will differ across countries. The two-good H–O model predicts that a country will have a lower autarky price and therefore export the good that uses intensively the factor in which it is relatively abundant. As a country becomes more similar to the rest of the world, it will trade less.

2 Although trade gives a country an incentive to produce more of its export good, it is less likely to lead to complete specialization in production than in the classical model with constant opportunity costs. In the H–O model, complete specialization only results

when a country's factor endowments are quite different from the endowments of other countries.

3   Trade benefits both countries, as in the classical model, when the equilibrium price ratio lies between the autarky price ratios of the two countries. As trade equalizes prices of goods internationally, however, those price changes alter the distribution of income within each country. In the short run, trade benefits those resources employed in the country's export industry and hurts those employed in the import industry. In the long run, trade benefits the abundant factor used intensively in producing the country's export good and hurts the scarce factor used intensively in producing the import-competing good.

4   Tests of the factor proportions hypothesis have given unexpected results. Leontief found US imports required more capital relative to labor than did US exports, even though he expected a capital-abundant country like the United States to export capital-intensive goods. More complete tests of the theory suggest that it works best in predicting trade between dissimilar countries but that some trade is not well explained by differences in factor endowments.

Questions for study and review

1   Based on the factor proportions theory, how will the opportunity to trade affect relative factor prices compared to a no-trade position? Explain why.

2   What does the factor proportions theory imply about the composition of a nation's exports and imports? Why?

3   "Alpha, a country with abundant labor and scarce capital, initially has completely free trade with the outside world. If Alpha imposes a tariff on imports, its ratio of wages to return on capital will rise." Do you agree? Why or why not?

4   What role do factor intensities of production play in the factor proportions theory of trade? If there were no differences in the factor intensities of the goods produced, how could that affect the predicted pattern of trade?

5   Suppose that Argentina has abundant capital and scarce labor compared with Brazil, and assume that wheat is capital-intensive relative to cloth and that other Heckscher– Ohlin assumptions of the 2 × 2 × 2 case apply.

   (a)   Using appropriate diagrams, show that mutually beneficial trade between the two countries is possible. Label the diagrams clearly to indicate the pattern of trade that occurs, and explain in words the sequence of changes that occur as the two economies move from no trade to free trade.

   (b)   Once a free-trade equilibrium is reached, if Brazil imposes a tariff on imports, what will be the effect on its ratio of wages to return on capital? Explain why.

6   When trade begins, Country Z imports cloth, the labor-intensive commodity. What does this imply about Z's own factor endowment? Why? What is likely to be the effect of trade on wages in Z? Why?

7   What group in Country Z would you expect to support free trade? Why? Who would oppose it? How would you evaluate the claims by opponents that free trade reduced national welfare?

8   If the United States restricts imports from Mexico, what is the probable effect of such restrictions on the number of Mexican workers attempting to enter the United States? Explain why.

9   Why might those opposing free trade in the short run differ from those opposing it over a longer period? What groups in an industrialized country might feel a conflict on this issue, because they realize that the short- and long-run impacts of free trade on them are quite different?

10   What exactly is paradoxical about the so-called Leontief paradox? What explanations have been offered to account for it or to resolve it?

11   You are given the following information about each country's share of the world endowment of a factor and about each country's share of world income (GNP). Explain how this information allows you to predict differences in the trade patterns of the countries shown.

Country	Physical capital	R&D scientists	Skilled labor	Semi-skilled labor	Unskilled labor	Arable land	GNP
US	33.6%	50.7%	27.7%	19.1%	0.2%	29.3%	28.6%
Japan	15.5%	23.0%	8.7%	11.5%	0.3%	0.8%	11.2%

Entries represent the percentage of the world endowment of a factor accounted for by each country.

Suggested further reading

Several of the original articles cited in this chapter have been reprinted in volumes of collected works that will make locating them easier:

• Bhagwati, Jagdish, ed., *International Trade*, Baltimore: Penguin, 1969.
• Caves, Richard and Harry G. Johnson, eds, *Readings in International Economics*, Homewood, IL: Richard D. Irwin, 1967.
• Ellis, Howard and Lloyd Metzler, eds, *Readings in the Theory of International Trade*, Philadelphia: Blakiston, 1949.

A particularly useful algebraic presentation of the H–O model is in:

• Jones, Ronald, "The Structure of Simple General Equilibrium Models," *Journal of Political Economy* 73, 1965, pp. 557–72.

Surveys of empirical work that tests trade theories appear in:

• Deardorff, Alan, "Testing Trade Theories and Predicting Trade Flows," in Ronald Jones and Peter Kenen (eds) *Handbook of International Economics*, Vol. I, Amsterdam: North-Holland, 1984.
• Leamer, Edward and James Levinsohn, "International Trade Theory: The Evidence," in Gene Grossman and Kenneth Rogoff (eds), *Handbook of International Economics*, Vol. III, Amsterdam: North-Holland, 1995.

For extensions of the basic H-O framework, see:

• Findlay, R. and L. Jeung, and M. Lundhall, eds, *Bertil Ohlin: A Centennial Celebration*, Cambridge, MA: MIT Press, 2002.

Appendix: a more formal presentation of the Heckscher–Ohlin model with two countries, two commodities, and two factors

In the text we have already specified the assumptions under which the Heckscher–Ohlin theorem will hold in a two-country, two-good, two-factor world. This appendix demonstrates more precisely the economic relationships that hold in such a world, making use of some analytical tools from beyond the introductory level.

The production function

A **production function** defines the relationship between inputs of productive factors and the resulting output of a commodity. A commodity such as wheat can be produced with many different combinations, or proportions, of land and labor. For example, a given quantity of wheat, say 160 metric tons, might be produced with 80 hectares of land and 1 man-year of labor, or with 8 hectares of land and 20 man-years of labor, or with many other combinations of land and labor.

This relationship can be illustrated by a production **isoquant**, such as the curve W_1 in Figure 3.4. Points on W_1, such as E and F, represent a constant, given output of wheat (160 metric tons). The coordinates of each point (40 hectares of land and 2 man-years of labor for point E) show the inputs of land and labor required to produce that amount of wheat. As we move down and to the right on W_1, for example from E to F, the proportion of land to labor decreases. The slope of the vector OF (20 hectares/4 man-years) is smaller than the slope of OE (40 hectares/2 man-years).

To show the input requirements for a larger output of wheat, we can draw another isoquant above and to the right of W_1. Thus W_2 in Figure 3.4 shows the alternative combinations of land and labor required to produce 320 metric tons of wheat. Other isoquants can be drawn to represent other quantities of wheat production.

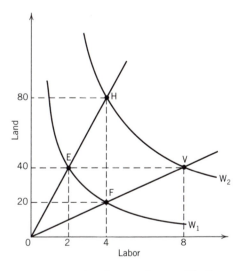

Figure 3.4 Isoquants for wheat production. W_1 illustrates all of the combinations of land and labor that are sufficient to produce a given amount of wheat. W_2 then represents the land and labor requirements for a considerably larger volume of wheat. The curvature in these lines results from the law of diminishing returns.

Our assumption that the two countries have identical production functions means that this entire set of isoquants is the same for countries A and B. Note carefully, however, that it does not say that countries A and B will actually use the same combination of land and labor to produce wheat. They are in fact likely to choose different points on the production function. For example, in India wheat is produced on tiny plots of land with highly labor-intensive methods, whereas in Australia a 500-hectare farm may be cultivated by a single farmer. Nevertheless, these facts are consistent with the assumption that production functions are everywhere the same; producers in India have an incentive to choose more labor-intensive methods because relative wages are much lower in India.

Constant returns to scale can also be demonstrated with the aid of Figure 3.4. Suppose a given combination, or proportion, of factors is being used, as at point E. These inputs yield the output indicated by the isoquant W_1, namely 160 metric tons. Constant returns to scale mean that if the inputs of land and labor are both increased by a given proportion, then the output also increases by that same proportion. For example, if the inputs at point E are doubled, the output of wheat doubles, as at point H, which lies on the isoquant W_2 representing an output of 320 metric tons.

Thus far we have concentrated on the production function for wheat. The production function for cheese is constructed in a similar way, but the position and shape of the isoquants will be different from those for wheat, reflecting our assumption that cheese is labor-intensive relative to wheat.

Production isoquants also help explain how a firm chooses the particular combinations of land and labor used to produce its output. In making this decision the firm takes into account the prices it must pay for the services of land and labor (factor prices) and the technological data embodied in the production function. Its objective is to maximize production for a given level of expenditure.

Geometrically, we can show the factor-price and budget information in a budget line such as MN in Figure 3.5. The firm's budget is just sufficient to rent OM of land or ON of labor

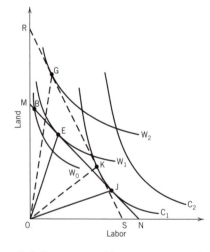

Figure 3.5 Comparison of factor intensity in cheese and wheat. The two sets of isoquants indicate that cheese is far more labor-intensive than is wheat. With relative land and labor costs represented by the line MN, an amount of wheat represented by W_1 or an amount of cheese represented by C_1 can be produced. If, however, land becomes cheaper as represented by isocost line SR, the same amount of money can produce either C_1 or W_2, wheat production rises because wheat is land-intensive.

inputs, or any combination of land and labor inputs indicated by points lying on MN. The slope of MN represents the factor-price ratio. Given the budget constraint and the factor-price ratio represented by MN, a wheat-producing firm will maximize its output by producing at point E, the point of tangency between MN and W_1. Hence the firm will choose the land-labor ratio indicated by the vector OE. If it uses any other input ratio, such as at B, it will find itself on a lower isoquant, W_0, meaning that it obtains a smaller output for the same expenditure.

Also, the assumptions of perfect competition and perfect mobility of factors within the economy guarantee that producers of both wheat and cheese must pay the same wage rate and land rent. In Figure 3.5 at the common factor-price ratio given by the slope of MN, firms would choose factor proportions OE in wheat and OJ in cheese. If wages were higher, giving a common factor-price ratio as indicated by the slope of RS, firms would choose the factor proportions OG in wheat and OK in cheese. Note that in both cases the ratio of land to labor is higher in wheat than in cheese. We impose the condition that within each country, for any given factor-price ratio, wheat will always be land-intensive relative to cheese. This assumption rules out a factor intensity reversal, which potentially could occur if wheat producers were able to substitute labor for land much more easily in response to a fall in wages than cheese producers could; in those circumstances, wheat might become the labor-intensive good at a lower wage rate.

Derivation of the production-possibility curve

Given production functions for wheat and cheese, then, once we know a country's resource endowment we can derive its production-possibility curve. To do so, we use one more geometric device, the Edgeworth box.

Let us first consider Country A, with an initial endowment of land and labor. The availability of these resources obviously limits the volume of output in Country A. Our task is to show how the choices made by producers of wheat and cheese, as they hire the available labor and rent the available land, determine the corresponding combinations of outputs of wheat and cheese that lie along the production-possibility curve.

We return to the isoquants shown in Figure 3.5, which demonstrate that wheat is land-intensive relative to cheese. To place these two industries in competition with each other for the given production resources available in Country A, construct a rectangular box diagram as in Figure 3.6a. Its dimensions represent Country A's total endowment of land and labor; the country's total labor supply is measured by the horizontal dimension of the box, and its total land endowment by the vertical dimension. Measure the amount of land and labor used in the cheese sector from the origin labeled O_{cheese}, and draw the set of isoquants for cheese producers just as in Figure 3.5. Measure the amount of land and labor used in wheat production from the origin labeled O_{wheat} and draw a set of isoquants for wheat production measured from that origin. We can think of taking the wheat isoquants shown in Figure 3.5 and rotating them in a counterclockwise direction up to the upper right corner of the box diagram.

Every point within the box represents a possible allocation of resources between wheat and cheese, but we are primarily interested in the "efficiency locus," the points at which the output of wheat is maximized, given the output of cheese. These efficient points turn out to be the points of tangency between wheat isoquants and cheese isoquants, such as points P, Q, and R in Figure 3.6a. The reason for this result can be seen as follows. Consider a point that is not on the efficiency locus, such as point Z. Cheese output is indicated by isoquant

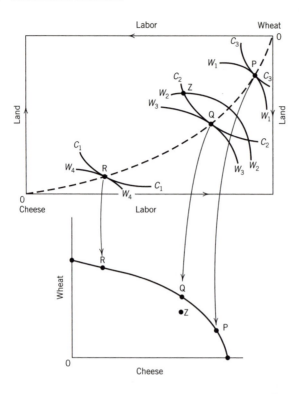

Figure 3.6 (a) Box diagrams for Country A (input space). (b) Production-possibility curve for Country A (output space). Country A has an endowment of labor represented by the horizontal length of the box and an endowment of land represented by its vertical height. This country's production possibilities are derived from the two isoquant sets C and W. The country maximizes efficiency and therefore output at tangencies between C and W isoquants, and those tangencies generate a dashed contract curve that goes from one origin to the other. The combinations of wheat and cheese produced at points R, Q, and P in the box diagram then provide points R, Q and P along the lower production-possibility curve. Point Z in the box diagram is not at a tangency and is therefore off the contract line. It is inefficient, as shown by point Z inside the production curve.

C_2, and wheat output by isoquant W_2. However, we can hold cheese output constant, move along isoquant C_2 to point Q (i.e. produce the same amount of cheese with less land and slightly more labor), and thereby release resources that make it possible to produce more wheat. At point Q we have the same output of cheese, but we have increased the output of wheat by moving from isoquant W_2 to W_3. At point Q, however, we have maximized wheat production for the level of cheese output indicated by isoquant C_2. Point Q represents a combination of wheat and cheese outputs that lies on the production-possibility curve. P, R, and other points on the efficiency locus also correspond to points on the production-possibility curve.

Another way of seeing this point is to recall that firms in each industry have minimized costs when the factor-price ratio equals the slope of the production isoquant. But at Z the slopes of the isoquants are different in wheat and cheese; this condition implies that wages and rents are not equal in the two industries. That situation indicates a disequilibrium situation in the market for productive factors, because under perfect competition factor prices are the same in both industries. Only when the isoquants for wheat and cheese are tangent to each other will factor prices be the same in both industries. This equality is a necessary condition to maximize output.

To construct Country A's production-possibility curve, note the wheat and cheese outputs indicated by the production isoquants for each point on the efficiency locus. Move along the efficiency locus from O_{cheese} to O_{wheat}, and record the output levels for wheat and cheese in the output space of Figure 3.6. For example, point R in Figure 3.6a represents a small output of cheese but a large output of wheat for Country A; it appears as point R in Figure 3.6b. Point P represents a large output of cheese but a small output of wheat, whereas point Q is an intermediate position. (We also show point Z in Figure 3.6b; it lies within the production-possibility curve.)

The slope of the production-possibility curve depends upon differences in the factor intensities of wheat and cheese. If the two goods had identical intensities and used land and labor in the same proportions, then the contract curve would be a diagonal line from one origin to the other. The corresponding production-possibility curve would be a straight line indicating constant opportunity cost, because any expansion of cheese production could be achieved by maintaining the same factor proportions as at the original point. The factors the cheese industry needs to expand output at the same cost are exactly those released by the wheat industry.

When factor intensities in the two sectors differ, an expansion of cheese output, for example, causes its opportunity cost of production to rise; the contracting wheat industry releases less labor and more land than the cheese industry finds it efficient to use at initial prices, and the extra cheese produced per ton of wheat given up declines. The greater the difference in factor intensities, the more the contract curve in the box diagram will differ from the diagonal, and the greater the degree of increasing opportunity cost observed along the production-possibility curve.

We can also see how a country's resource endowment influences the shape and size of its production-possibility curve. If Country B has a relative abundance of labor compared to Country A, its box diagram will be elongated horizontally. The dimensions of the box diagram for each country reflect its resource endowment. Then, with identical production functions, the resources available in each country determine its production-possibility curve. Figure 3.7 shows a box diagram for each country. Country A clearly has more land relative to labor than does Country B. In Heckscher–Ohlin terms, Country A has a relative abundance of land, and Country B has a relative abundance of labor. These differences in resource endowment are reflected in the production-possibility curves for the two countries. Because wheat requires a higher proportion of land to labor than does cheese, Country A's relative abundance of land causes its production-possibility curve to be elongated, or biased, along the wheat axis. Country B's relative abundance of labor is similarly reflected in a greater relative capacity to produce cheese.

If these two countries do not engage in trade, but operate as closed economies, then their relative commodity prices will differ: cheese will be cheaper in Country B than in Country A, relative to the price of wheat, as may be seen by the price lines (tangents to production-possibility curves) in Figure 3.7. This analysis mirrors that in Chapter 2, where we showed that, given different production-possibility curves and similar demand patterns, relative prices in the two countries will be different and each country will have a comparative advantage in the commodity it produces more cheaply.

What the Heckscher–Ohlin theory has added is an explanation of the cause of the relative price differences, a basic reason for the existence of comparative advantage. In particular,

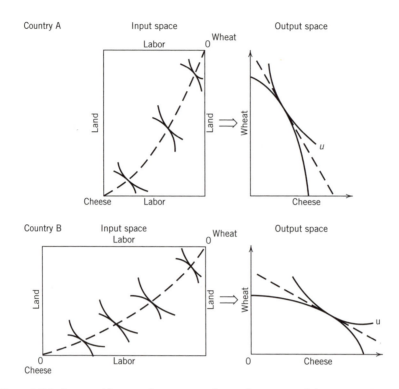

Figure 3.7 Influence of factor endowments on the production-possibility curves. Country A has a large
endowment of land, which results in a production-possibility curve that is biased toward
wheat, meaning that country can produce either a large volume of wheat or a small volume
of cheese. Country B has a far larger relative endowment of land and therefore has a
production-possibility curve that is biased toward cheese.

we can now say that in each country the price will be relatively lower for the commodity
that uses relatively more of that country's abundant factor of production. Hence the
difference in relative factor endowments is the underlying basis of comparative advantage
and the fundamental determinant of the pattern and composition of international trade.

The Stolper–Samuelson theorem and factor price equalization

Figure 3.6a shows several alternative efficient production points along the contract curve in
the box diagram for Country A. We can demonstrate how factor productivities are changing
as we move from one point to another and thereby confirm the Stolper–Samuelson theorem,
which predicts that an increase in the price of a good will benefit the factor used intensively
in its production and harm the other factor.

For example, if the relative price of wheat rises and wheat production expands from point
Q to point R, the land/labor ratio in both sectors falls. We can confirm that by drawing a ray
from each origin to points Q and R. The ray O_cQ indicates a higher land/labor ratio than
O_cR, just as O_wQ indicates a higher land/labor ratio than O_wR. Because the land/labor ratio
falls, labor is less productive and its wage must fall. Conversely, because more labor is used
with each hectare of land, the productivity of land rises and its return rises. As noted in the
text, because labor's productivity falls in both sectors, and land's productivity rises in both

sectors, labor's real income must fall irrespective of how much of the relatively cheaper cheese it consumes, and land's real income must rise irrespective of how much wheat it consumes. An alternative statement of these relationships is that a relative increase in the price of a good will result in a proportionally large or magnified increase in the return to the factor used intensively in its production. This magnification effect, identified by Ronald Jones,[23] is what ensures that in the example above the return to land rises even if landowners only buy wheat.

This relationship that holds as the economy moves along the efficiency locus described above can be summarized in another form that clarifies the likelihood of factor prices being equalized in two countries.[24] As shown in the left panel of Figure 3.8, over the range of prices where a country produces both goods, an increase in the relative price of wheat will increase the rental return to land and decrease the wage rate. Note, however, that a higher price of wheat eventually will cause a country to specialize in producing wheat; at that point the wage-rental ratio will fall no further, because no further decline in the land-labor ratio is possible. In the right panel of Figure 3.8 two loci show the choices producers of cheese and wheat will make in selecting the best combination of capital and labor to use at a given wage-rental ratio. The loci simply summarize the implication of a movement around an isoquant, from point Z to point Q in Figure 3.6a, say, as the wage-rental ratio falls and the firm uses more labor relative to land. The wheat locus lies further to the right, because wheat is the more land-intensive good. The two loci do not intersect because of the assumption that no factor intensity reversal occurs, and wheat always is the more land-intensive good regardless of the wage-rental ratio considered.

For the price ratio at A to be an equilibrium that results in factor price equalization, the endowments of the two countries must be similar enough that they lie between the range given by points B and C. If Denmark's land-labor endowment were smaller, say at D, it would be completely specialized in cheese production, because that sector does not require much land. The downward sloping curve in the left panel would no longer apply in Denmark. Rather, for the relative price of wheat shown at A, there would be a lower wage-rental ratio in Denmark than in the United States. While the H–O prediction of the pattern of trade still holds even though Denmark is completely specialized, factor price equalization does not.

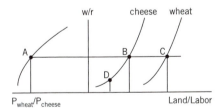

Figure 3.8 Factor price equalization. If a given world price of wheat relative to cheese represents an equilibrium where both countries will produce both goods, the same wage-rental ratio will be established in each country.

The Rybczynski theorem and another application of the box diagram

The box diagram allows a convenient demonstration of the reason why an increase in a country's endowment of a factor will cause the output of one good to rise and the other good to fall. Consider the initial production point A, in Figure 3.9, where the cheese and wheat

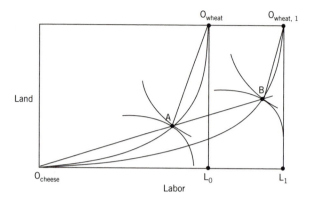

Figure 3.9 The Rybczynski theorem. An increase in the labor force from L_0 to L_1 results in an expansion of cheese output from O_cA to O_cB, while wheat output falls from O_wA to $O_{w1}B$.

isoquants are tangent. If world prices remain constant, then the wage-rental ratio that corresponds to the equilibrium at A will be the same wage-rental ratio that applies when the country's labor force grows from L_0 to L_1. Correspondingly, the land-labor ratios chosen by cheese and wheat producers at A will be the same ratios chosen in the new equilibrium at B. At that new point, output of the labor-intensive good, cheese, has increased, and output of wheat has fallen.

We can make a stronger statement about the increase in cheese output: a given percentage increase in the labor force will result in a greater percentage increase in cheese production, another magnification effect identified by Jones. As noted in the text, not only is all of the additional labor in the economy allocated to cheese production, but labor and land are released by the contraction of wheat production necessary to maintain the land-labor ratio in cheese production. The percentage increase in the amount of labor used in cheese production is greater than the percentage increase in the labor force. Both labor and capital used in cheese production have grown by the same percentage as the economy moves from A to B, and because of the assumption of constant returns to scale, cheese production increases by that same percentage. Consequently, the percentage growth in cheese production exceeds the percentage growth in the labor force.

Notes

1 David Ricardo, *Principles of Political Economy* (London: J.M. Dent, 1911), p. 95.
2 Bertil Ohlin, *Interregional and International Trade* (Cambridge, MA: Harvard University Press, 1933). Also see Eli Heckscher, "The Effect of Foreign Trade on the Distribution of Income," in H. Ellis and L. Metzler, eds, *Readings in the Theory of International Trade* (Philadelphia: Blakiston, 1949).
3 T. M. Rybczynski, "Factor Endowments and Relative Commodity Prices," *Economica* 22, no. 84, November 1955, pp. 336–41, reprinted in R. Caves and H. Johnson, *Readings in International Economics* (Homewood, IL: Irwin, 1968), pp. 72–7.
4 Jason Dean and Terho Ulmonen "Long Adept at Copying Taiwan Takes to Patents," *Wall Street Journal*, January 11, 2002, p. A8.
5 Wolfgang Stolper and Paul Samuelson, "Protective and Real Wages," *Review of Economic Studies* 9, 1941, pp. 58–73.
6 Paul Krugman and Robert Lawrence, "Trade, Jobs and Wages," *Scientific American* 270, no. 4, 1994, pp. 44–9.

7   Robert Feenstra, "Integration of Trade and Disintegration of Production in the Global Economy," *Journal of Economic Perspectives* 12, no. 4, 1998, pp. 31–50.

8   Adrian Wood, "Openness and Wage Inequality in Developing Countries: The Latin American Challenge to East Asian Conventional Wisdom," *The World Bank Review* 11, no. 1, January 1997, pp. 233–57.

9   For an econometric study that supports the conclusion that both international trade and immigration are reducing US wages for less skilled workers, see George J. Borjas, Richard B. Freeman, and Lawrence F. Katz, "On the Labor Market Effects of Immigration and Trade," in George J. Borjas and Richard B. Freeman, *Immigration and the Work Force* (Chicago: University of Chicago Press, 1992), pp. 213–44. Also see Adrian Wood, "How Trade Hurt Unskilled Workers," *Journal of Economic Perspectives* 9, no. 3, Summer 1995, pp. 57–80, and the survey by G. Burtless, "International Trade and the Rise in Earning Inequality," *Journal of Economic Literature*, June 1995, pp. 800–16. For discussion of the wage impacts on trade impacted workers, see Lori Kletzer, *Job Loss from Imports: Measuring the Costs* (Washington, DC: Institute for International Economics, 2001).

10 Wood, "Openness and Wage Inequality," op. cit.

11 See Robert Mundell, "International Trade and Factor Mobility," *American Economic Review* 47, no. 3, June 1957, pp. 321–35, for an early version of this argument.

12 For a more formal but tractable presentation of this approach, see Ronald Jones, "A Three-Factor Model in Theory, Trade and History," in J. Bhagwati, Ronald Jones, Robert Mundell, and Jaroslav Vanek, eds, *Trade, Balance of Payments and Growth* (Amsterdam: North-Holland, 1971), pp. 3–20.

13 James Markusen, "Factor Movements and Commodity Trade as Complements," *Journal of International Economics* 13, 1983, pp. 341–56.

14 Wassily Leontief, "Domestic Production and Foreign Trade," *Economia Internazionale* 7, no. 1, February 1954, pp. 3–32. Reprinted in R. Caves and H.G. Johnson, eds, *Readings in International Economics*, (Homewood, IL: Irwin, 1968), pp. 503–27.

15 E.E. Leamer, "The Leontief Paradox Reconsidered," *Journal of Political Economy* 88, 1980, pp. 495–503.

16 Alan Deardorff, "Testing Trade Theories and Predicting Trade Flows," in Ronald Jones and Peter Kenen, eds, *Handbook of International Economics*, vol. 1 (Amsterdam: North-Holland, 1984) gives an excellent survey of this work. For a more recent study supportive of the H–O theory, see E.E. Leamer, "The Heckscher–Ohlin Model in Theory and Practice," *Princeton Studies in International Finance*, no. 77, 1995.

17 Jaroslav Vanek, "The Factor Proportions Theory: The *N*-factor Case," *Kyklos* 21, no. 4, 1968, pp. 749–56.

18 See Robert Baldwin, "Determinants of the Commodity Structure of US Trade," *American Economic Review* 61, no. 1, March 1971, pp. 126–46, and Robert Stern and Keith Maskus, "Determinants of the Structure of US Foreign Trade, 1958–76," *Journal of International Economics*, 1981, pp. 207–24.

19 Harry Bowen, Edward Leamer, and Leo Sveikauskas, "Multicountry, Multifactor Tests of the Factor Abundance Theory," *American Economic Review* 77, no. 5, 1987, pp. 791–801.

20 Adrian Wood, "Give Heckscher and Ohlin a Chance!," *Weltwirtschaftliches Archiv* 130, no. 1, 1994, pp. 20–49.

21 Daniel Trefler, "The Case of the Missing Trade and Other Mysteries," *American Economic Review* 85, no. 5, 1995, pp. 1029–46.

22 Donald Davis and David Weinstein, "An Account of Global Factor Trade," *American Economic Review* 91, no.5, pp. 1423–1453.

23 Ronald Jones, "The Structure of Simple General Equilibrium Models," *Journal of Political Economy* 73, pp. 557–72.

24 For a complete explanation of this line of reasoning, see P.A. Samuelson, "International Factor-Price Equalization Once Again," *Economic Journal*, Vol. 59, no. 234 (June 1949) pp. 181–97.

4   Trade between similar countries
Implications of decreasing costs and imperfect competition

Learning objectives

By the end of this chapter you should be able to understand:

- that average costs for all firms in an industry may fall as its output expands, creating a basis for trade even in the absence of different autarky prices;
- why monopolistically competitive firms that produce differentiated products will face more competition when trade is possible, and gains arise from their charging lower prices and achieving greater economies of scale;
- how competition between oligopolistic firms may allow another type of national gain to a country if above-normal economic profits are shifted to its own producers;
- how collusion between producers internationally to form a cartel and restrict output may drive up price at least temporarily;
- why trade that results in the contraction of output in industries where above-average profits are earned may leave a country worse off.

The factor proportions or Heckscher–Ohlin theorem, which was presented in the previous chapter, implies that trade should occur primarily between pairs of countries with very different relative factor endowments. As noted earlier, that theory is most successful in explaining trade between many industrialized and developing countries: the industrialized countries import unskilled labor and tropical land-intensive products from less developed countries (LDCs), and export skilled labor and temperate-climate land-intensive goods to them.

A far larger volume of trade is not between industrialized and developing countries, however, but among industrialized countries that often have similar relative factor endowments. The H–O theorem is far less applicable in explaining these trade flows, because the factor content of what is traded turns out to be quite similar. One type of machinery may be imported and another type exported, but both machines have similar capital and labor input requirements.

Such trade is more difficult to relate to our familiar principles of comparative advantage and differences in opportunity costs of production. Even when two countries have the same factor endowments and use the same production technologies, two sources of comparative advantage or cost differences as described in earlier chapters, there still may be a basis for gains from trade due to economies of scale in production. Specialization in production may allow a country to achieve lower costs per unit of output, a sign of decreasing opportunity cost. The more of one good a country produces, the lower its cost of producing it becomes. Expanding output to serve a world market rather than a national market allows costs per unit to fall. Depending upon how prices are set in relation to costs, both countries can gain from trade in these circumstances. The actual pattern of trade, and the determination of what goods a country imports and what goods it exports, may reflect a created comparative advantage attributable to historical accident or government intervention.

Some economies of scale exist that are external to an individual firm. A single firm may continue to face rising marginal costs of production as it expands output, just as in the H–O world with perfectly competitive producers. If all firms in the industry expand output, however, costs for all of the firms as a group may fall. Such economies may be particularly common if an industry is concentrated in a region. Examples of such concentrations are producers of semiconductors in Silicon Valley of California, international financial services in London, watches in Switzerland, and software in Bangalore, India. The possibility of such economies can alter our conclusions about patterns of trade and gains from trade, as we show in the first section of this chapter even when we retain the assumption of perfectly competitive markets.

More often, economies of scale are internal to the firm. As an individual firm expands output, its cost per unit declines. As a result it may gain an advantage over other firms, both domestic and foreign, in producing a particular good or variety of good. To develop this line of reasoning, we begin by considering two contributions that provide useful insights but provide a much less comprehensive framework for analysis than the H–O model. One examines a firm's introduction of a new product, a case where firms in all countries no longer are assumed to use the same technology to produce the same products. While the innovating firm gains at least a temporary competitive advantage over others, that advantage may erode over time. A country that initially exports the product eventually may come to import it instead. For the United States, TVs are an example of such a product cycle. A second theory places more attention on product variety and the tendency for similar countries to trade different varieties of the same product. For example, a country may produce and export some types of automobiles but nevertheless import others. Such **intra-industry trade** of manufactured products is particularly noticeable among high-income countries.

Economists have tried to explain such trade more formally in models that pay more explicit attention to industry structure and the number of firms in an industry and to general equilibrium concerns over the allocation of resources across industries. Yet, economists have no single unified theory to predict how markets function between the extremes of perfect competition and monopoly. Therefore, theories of international trade that recognize the importance of internal economies of scale depend critically on what economists assume about a particular market. Are there many producers or only a few? To answer that question, it is often useful to know the importance of a firm's fixed costs, which must be borne even if the firm produces nothing at all, relative to its variable costs. When fixed costs are relatively unimportant, it is easier for new competitors to enter an industry when prices rise, and they are most likely to leave the industry when prices fall. In those circumstances, models of monopolistic competition and product differentiation provide important insights. For example, if Ireland imports Heineken beer from the Netherlands but exports Guinness beer to the Netherlands, this trade in similar products implies that the availability of different varieties of a product is important to consumers. Economists have developed increasingly more complete models to analyze trade under these circumstances. We consider such models later in this chapter, and assess how this approach affects our predictions about patterns of trade, the gains from trade, and the implications of trade for income distribution.

In other markets, fixed costs may be large relative to variable costs, and a new firm may face major obstacles in entering an industry. Economists use the term "oligopoly market" to describe such a situation where few firms produce. Because of the high barriers to entry in such markets, firms may earn economic profits that are not competed away by others. Prices are not determined simply by costs of production but also by the producers' ability to charge more than the average cost of production. In the final section of this chapter we consider how such models give different predictions about the patterns of trade and gains from trade.

External economies of scale

When several firms in the same industry expand output, they all may achieve lower costs of production. This situation characterizes **external economies of scale** and it is particularly likely to arise when the firms operate in the same region. The source of these lower costs may be gains from the emergence of specialized input suppliers, benefits from a common pool of skilled workers, or the spillover of knowledge among firms which allows new technologies to diffuse and develop more quickly. Let us consider these possibilities in turn and note the importance of proximity of firms when it arises.

Specialized machinery to serve the needs of a specific industry can allow productivity to rise and costs of production to fall. However, a firm in that industry may find it quite time-consuming and inefficient to try to design and make such machinery itself. If the firm is part of an industry where several producers face similar production bottlenecks and limitations, they may all benefit if a new firm specializes in the task of developing more efficient equipment that all of them can buy. The gain will be even greater if there are enough producers of the final good to entice several new entrants into this specialization in input production, thereby resulting in more competition among them.

An example of this development is American agriculture as the country moved westward. A pioneer family had to be jacks-of-all trades, able to do all of the myriad tasks of clearing land, building a house, planting and harvesting a crop, and tending livestock. Self-sufficiency was a more common goal than specialization. An individual farmer might figure out how to plow the ground, harvest and thresh grain more efficiently, or save the best seed from one harvest to plant next year, but such knowledge simply made that farm more efficient. It was the eventual concentration of many farmers in particularly fertile regions, all producing the same crops, that helped make specialization more worthwhile. Clever individuals who came up with successful innovations that worked for them became full-time producers of plows and threshers to sell to others. Although better communication and transportation eventually allowed those ideas and products to spread to farmers in more isolated areas, producers of implements or hybrid seeds had an incentive to locate in the fertile regions where the concentration of potential customers was greater.

Not only may equipment become highly specialized to serve an industry, but labor skills specific to an industry also are likely to develop. To meet that need, one solution is for each firm to train the labor it requires. While that certainly may occur, proximity to other firms offers an additional advantage. Random good luck may cause the demand faced by one producer to rise, while random bad luck causes demand faced by another to contract. When the two firms are located in the same region, the expanding firm can hire the labor laid off by the contracting firm, without having to experience the delay of training newcomers. Thus, production costs for the industry will be lower.

Finally, spillovers of knowledge may spread new technology quickly among firms. When firms are geographically close to each other, that process occurs more easily and improvements are introduced at a faster pace. Of course, firms often have an incentive to keep new technology a secret. In the eighteenth and nineteenth centuries, immigrants to the United States arrived, not carrying a purloined set of blueprints for a machine, but having memorized how such a machine was built in Europe. What are the consequences of this transfer of technology? If firms reap no benefit from developing a new product or production process, their incentive to innovate is reduced. But, once an idea is developed, society benefits if it is shared widely. In Chapter 9 we consider the trade-off that exists between rigorous enforcement of the rights of the inventor and the social gains from others' gaining access to new technology. That issue has been particularly important in recent international negotiations over **intellectual property rights** and patents.

In industries where technology is changing very quickly, and one idea is quickly superseded by another, even innovating firms may benefit from rapid diffusion. The gain from access to new ideas offsets the loss from not being able to prevent spillovers to others. Under those circumstances, the innovator is less worried about competitors being free-riders on its research and development efforts.

Are external economies likely to be limited to a country or even some region within a country? Some barriers to diffusion are geographic because ideas spread more rapidly when those who work in the same industry move from company to company and socialize together. The spread of Internet usage, however, may reduce the role of proximity or national boundaries in some industries. Sometimes the barriers to diffusion are cultural. If American engineers do not read Japanese, they will not learn about the latest Japanese research and development in semiconductor design and production as rapidly. Sometimes the barriers to diffusion are legal. For example, legal scholars have attributed part of the success of the electronic revolution in California, and its retreat in Massachusetts, to different interpretations of what information an individual hopping from one firm to another can pass on without violating stipulations that they must not compete with their former employers.[1] For the current discussion, we assume that there are settings where the potential sources of external economies within a country that we have mentioned here are significant.

Decreasing opportunity cost

The existence of external economies affects the shape of the production-possibility curve. To demonstrate why that is true, we begin by restating the effect of these economies of scale in a slightly different form: an industry that doubles the inputs it hires will more than double the output it produces. Expansion of output by a greater proportion than inputs used in production is what allows costs per unit to fall.

The importance of this condition is shown in Figure 4.1, which represents an economy's ability to produce semiconductors and soybeans. To simplify our diagram, we assume there are no differences in factor intensities in the production of these two goods. If we imposed the assumption of constant returns to scale, we would be right back to the classical model of constant opportunity cost in Chapter 2. In a more complete analysis, we could assess how differences in factor intensities create a tendency toward increasing opportunity costs, as demonstrated in Chapter 3, which in turn may be offset by increasing returns to scale and a tendency toward decreasing opportunity cost. Our more modest goal here is to show why increasing returns to scale result in decreasing opportunity cost.

The production-possibility curve is bowed inward (convex to the origin) in contrast to the curve that bowed outward (concave to the origin) in the case of increasing opportunity cost. Start at point A, which represents the case where just half of the country's resources

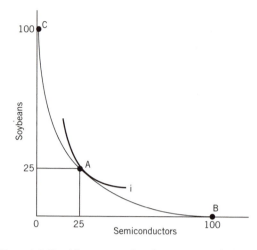

Figure 4.1 Equilibrium in a closed economy with decreasing opportunity cost. External economies of scale allow industry output to expand by a greater proportion than the expansion of inputs used in production. Compare production at point A where half of the economy's resources are devoted to producing each good with points B and C where all resources are devoted to the production of a single good. Inputs double and output more than doubles.

are devoted to the production of each good. As drawn in Figure 4.1, that corresponds to being able to produce 25 units of each good. Suppose now that the economy allocates all resources to semiconductor production. Inputs into semiconductor production have just doubled. Due to economies of scale, however, output of semiconductors more than doubles to 100 units. A comparable result is shown if all resources are allocated to soybean production: doubling inputs leads to more than double the output.

We can interpret those changes in terms of opportunity cost, too. As the economy moves from point C to point A, it gives up 75 tons of soybeans in return for 25 semiconductors, which implies a relative price of 3 tons of soybeans per semiconductor. Now move the economy from point A to point B. It has given up 25 tons of soybeans in return for 75 additional semiconductors, which implies a relative price of 0.33 tons of soybeans per semiconductor. The marginal rate of transformation is declining as more semiconductors are produced, which also represents decreasing opportunity cost.

In a closed economy the equilibrium level of production of the two goods again is given by the tangency of the community indifference curve i with the production-possibility curve. All firms still act as price takers and each one expands its output of a good until its marginal cost of production equals the market price. Because that condition will not be met in the imperfectly competitive models that follow later in this chapter, we note it here. Thus far, the autarky solution for this economy appears no different from that in our previous models.

When we consider the possibility of trade, this similarity no longer automatically holds. To demonstrate these differences most clearly, consider two economies that are identical in all respects. In autarky they both choose the same consumption point A along the production-possibility curve in Figure 4.1, and they both face the same relative prices at that point. By the principles of comparative advantage developed in the preceding two chapters, there would appear to be no basis for trade. Yet both economies could gain if one were to specialize in semiconductors and the other in soybeans. In Figure 4.2 we show the special case of symmetric demand and production conditions, where each economy can trade along the barter line CDB. One economy specializes in semiconductors. It produces at point B, consumes at point D, and trades BE of semiconductors for ED of soybeans. The other economy specializes in soybeans. It produces at point C, consumes at point D, and trades CF soybeans for FD semiconductors. The two trade triangles are identical at this equilibrium price. Also, both economies move to a higher indifference curve, from i_1 to i_2. Two countries can gain from trade by having each exhaust the available external economies in producing one good rather than each trying to be self-sufficient and unable to achieve those same economies.

The possibility of gains from trade is familiar, but we cannot rely upon differences in autarky prices to explain why this pattern of trade emerges. In this example of perfectly identical economies, the pattern of trade is indeterminate; it could be assigned by a master planner or settled by the flip of a coin but it would not matter, because both countries experience the same gains from trade. In a more realistic setting, the equilibrium price ratio is not likely to be one that results in both countries moving to the same higher indifference curve. For example, suppose consumers in both countries have a stronger preference for semiconductors than for soybeans. Let trade again result in the same specialized production pattern, but now observe that a higher price of semiconductors and a steeper barter line drawn from point B would allow the country that specializes in their production to reach a higher indifference curve. Correspondingly, the country that specializes in producing soybeans now finds that the barter line drawn from point C gives it a smaller gain in welfare than in the symmetric case of Figure 4.2. Although both countries start from identical circumstances, the pattern of production that emerges rewards one more than the other. Such an outcome fuels policy debates over the potential role of governments to pick successful industries that allow larger gains from trade and to avoid those that may even leave a country worse off. We return to this topic in Chapter 6.

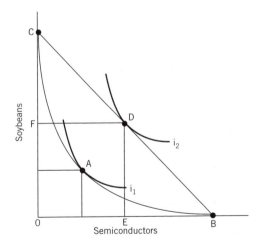

Figure 4.2 Equilibrium with foreign trade and decreasing opportunity cost. This special case of trade under conditions of decreasing opportunity cost shows identical countries gaining equally from the opportunity to trade. One country specializes in semiconductors and trades EB semiconductors for 0F soybeans. The other country specializes in soybean production and trades CF soybeans for 0E semiconductors. Both countries move to the higher indifference curve i_2.

This indeterminacy of the actual pattern of trade can be demonstrated in another way. One country may have greater potential to achieve low per-unit costs of production, perhaps due to a difference in endowments that favors the factor used intensively in producing the good where scale economies exist. The other country, however, may have a head-start in producing the good. Because of that head-start and higher volume of output, the country achieves economies of scale that allow it to sell at a lower price than the prospective competitor. We represent such a situation in Figure 4.3, which shows average cost curves that correspond to Chinese and Japanese production of automobiles. At any level of output, the Chinese industry's cost curve lies below the Japanese industry's curve. Yet, because of Japan's head-start, its industry produces a much greater quantity of cars and achieves a lower average cost than China does based on its smaller volume of output.

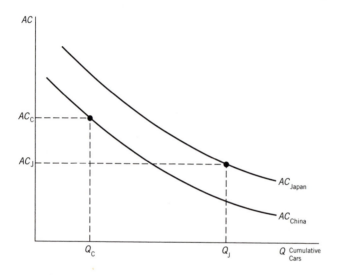

Figure 4.3 The advantage of a long-established industry where scale economies are important. China has the potential to be a more efficient producer of this good than Japan, but the Japanese industry is already large, operating at Q_J, and therefore enjoys large-scale economies. The far smaller Chinese industry, operating at Q_C, cannot compete successfully against the Japanese industry because the Chinese lack the large-scale economies that Japan enjoys.

The existence of scale economies can offset the importance of differences in factor intensities and relative factor abundance, which may otherwise account for China's projected cost advantage. Japan may export a labor-intensive good, even though labor is a scarce factor in Japan, because large external economies of scale exist in its production. If the Japanese industry expands aggressively, as its initial success and profitability allow it to do, it may maintain this advantage over China. The Chinese projected cost advantage never is observed in the market.

The Japanese advantage may rest not only on external economies of scale but also on economies of scale internal to the firm. To consider their role, however, we need to specify more fully what determines industry structure in each country and how firms set prices in relation to their costs. Those are topics we pursue later in this chapter.

The product cycle

When economies of scale are internal to a firm and not all firms share the same technology, the perfectly competitive markets assumed above are not appropriate. On the other hand, when new products and technology are developed, the innovator is unlikely to gain a permanent monopoly position as the producer of such a product. Raymond Vernon proposed the hypothesis that new products pass through a series of stages in the course of their development,[2] and the comparative advantage of the producers in the innovating country will change as products move through this product cycle. The theory, often referred to as the "**Vernon product cycle**," applies best to trade in manufactured, as opposed to primary, products.

Looking at the 1950s and 1960s, Vernon noted that many new products were initially developed in the United States. To some extent that was a function of US scientific and innovative capacity, and indeed subsequent research has shown that US exports used the skills of R&D scientists and engineers intensively.[3] Yet some inventions that occurred outside the United States, such as television, were first commercialized in the United States. That aspect of the cycle was attributable to the US position after World War II as a nation that did not have to use scarce resources to rebuild a war-torn economy. Rather, the United States could devote more of its resources to production and consumption of new goods that were not simply essentials for survival but often luxuries that only those with more discretionary income could afford to buy. Also, in some circumstances it was the relatively higher cost of labor in the United States that provided an incentive to develop new products and processes that economized on the use of that scarce input.

Thus, many new products initially were developed in the United States, with production and sales first occurring in the domestic market. Locating production close to buyers was important, so that problems identified by consumers could be communicated immediately to producers, and changes could be made without long delays or the build-up of defective, unsatisfactory inventory. After a new product caught on in the United States, however, the US producer might send a sales force abroad to cultivate foreign markets among consumers with similar preferences and income levels. Or, foreign merchants and trading companies attentive to developments in the United States might place orders for the product. Thus, the United States began to export the product.

As foreign demand grew, sales in some countries might eventually reach a threshold level large enough to tempt foreign firms to undertake production for themselves. Foreign firms might acquire the technology necessary to manufacture the product or the US producer might find it profitable to establish a subsidiary abroad to produce the good. In either case, a certain degree of standardization presumably had occurred with respect to the product's features and reliability, which meant that immediate contact between the producer and consumer was no longer so important. Production of the standardized good no longer required large inputs from scientists and engineers but instead relied upon assembly operations performed by less skilled workers. As production in other countries rose, US exports to those markets fell, as well as to third-country markets.

Finally, as foreign firms mastered the production process and as their costs fell with the increased scale of production, they might begin to export the product to the United States itself. This sequence of events completes the cycle: the United States began as the exclusive exporter, then competed with foreign producers for export sales, and finally became a net importer of the new product. In terms of the US trade position, the product cycle implies a change through time as illustrated in Figure 4.4 with the following four stages:

   I Product development and sale in US market.
   II Growth in US exports as foreign demand cultivated.
   III Decline in US exports as production abroad begins to serve foreign markets.
   IV United States becomes a net importer as foreign prices fall.

This scenario seems to fit very well the observed experience with a number of new products in recent decades, such as radio, television, synthetic fibers, transistors, and pocket calculators. There is some evidence that the time span between stages I and IV may be getting shorter, although the length of the cycle varies from one product to another. A particular product might even move directly from stage I to stage IV, skipping stages II and III altogether, as cheaper foreign production sites are immediately used to supply all markets.

The product cycle hypothesis can be adapted and modified to take account of a variety of circumstances and explanatory factors. This gives it great flexibility but also weakens its predictive power as a theory. For example, the unique role of the United States as a high income market fertile for new product innovation no longer holds with such force. Rapid growth in Japan and economic integration in Europe have resulted in other large markets where economies of scale can be achieved and new product innovation will be profitable. Differences in factor endowments are smaller and the distribution of scientists and engineers engaged in research and development is wider now than in the 1950s. Other countries now have higher wage costs and an incentive to develop labor-saving innovations.

Even if it is now less certain where a new product cycle may begin, the innovating country will find that its lead is temporary. As demand grows for a product, as the new technology is learned and assimilated in other countries, and as the productive process is standardized, then the basic determinants of comparative advantage begin once again to dominate the location of production. Thus, this theory is essentially short-run, and it is explicitly dynamic. If the United States is a leader in innovation, it has a temporary comparative advantage in the latest products, but it steadily loses that advantage and must continually develop other new products to replace those that are maturing and being lost to competitors. The United States benefits from a favorable terms-of-trade shift and the monopoly power of its firms that introduce new products, but its terms of trade decline as competition from new producers and products occurs.

We emphasize again that the product cycle theory is not directly in conflict with comparative advantage and factor proportions theory. The United States has a relative

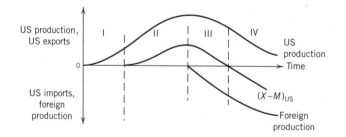

Figure 4.4 The product cycle. The United States has a monopoly on the knowledge necessary to produce this good through stages I and II, and therefore has growing output and exports. At the beginning of stage III, however, production in other countries begins, pulling the original innovating country's output and exports down. In stage IV, this country imports the product that it had previously invented and exported.

abundance of scientific and technical personnel, which gives it a comparative advantage in innovation. However, once a breakthrough is accomplished and a learning period has elapsed, production will gravitate toward the countries that have a relative abundance of factors required for routine production of the new product.

The compression of the product cycle, which leaves fewer years between stages I and IV, may be partly the result of an acceleration in the rate of technical change, so that product monopolies are more short-lived than they were in the past. Products can be "reverse-engineered" and successfully imitated and even improved by those able to apply the new idea developed by another. More countries have that imitative capability than in the past. Industrial espionage and theft of intellectual property also are current concerns of those who innovate. In addition, the product cycle may be compressed because multinational firms move production abroad. The company may retain a monopoly position but the inventing country does not. The fact that many US firms carry on research and development activities abroad further complicates the product cycle model, which initially was interpreted in terms of a unidirectional flow of ideas and goods. Texas Instruments, for example, does much of its scientific programming in Bangalore, India, and the results of these efforts are applied to US production.

It has also become more common to license technology to foreign firms, particularly for inventions that are expected to have a short period of profitability. Allowing foreign firms to use technology in exchange for a fee is often the preferred way of maximizing profits over a brief lifetime. It is too expensive to build factories abroad which may only be needed for a few years, and domestic capacity may be inadequate to meet export demand. A recently invented computer chip, for example, may only be marketable for a few years before it is replaced by a newly developed competitor. Understanding the short expected lifetime of such a product encourages its inventors to license it for foreign production quickly in order to extract as much revenue from it as possible before improved competitors arrive.

This process is further complicated by the fact that research and development costs have risen so rapidly that many companies have concluded that they can no longer finance new products by themselves. Consequently, companies in different countries often share the costs of developing a new product, with each of them using the new technology in their home markets. For example, Toyota and General Motors have formed one alliance, and Daimler-Chrysler, Ford and Ballard Power Systems of Canada another to develop alternatives to the internal combustion engine.[4]

In summary, the product cycle hypothesis provides important insights into the ways the process of new product innovation and production affects the mix of products a country trades internationally and the country's gains from that trade. Anecdotally, it explains why innovators may initiate production but subsequently cease production altogether. As a predictive theory it is difficult to apply in a systematic way, though, because we are less able to claim where a product cycle will begin or how long it will last.

Preference similarities and intra-industry trade

Staffan Burenstam Linder formulated the **preference similarity hypothesis**, which starts with the proposition that as a rule a nation will export products for which it has a large and active domestic market.[5] The reason is simply that production for the domestic market must be large enough to enable firms to achieve economies of scale and thus to reduce costs enough to break into foreign markets. Linder argues that the most promising and receptive markets for exports will be found in other countries whose income levels and tastes are generally comparable to those of the exporting country. This is why the term preference similarity is relevant. Linder contends that countries with similar income levels will have similar tastes. Each country will produce primarily for its home market, but part of the output will be exported to other countries where a receptive market exists.

An interesting aspect of this theory is its implication that trade in manufactured products will take place largely between countries with similar income levels and demand patterns. The theory also implies that the commodities entering into trade will be similar, though in some way differentiated. These two implications accord well with recent experience: the great majority of international trade in manufactured goods takes place among the relatively high-income countries: the United States, Canada, Japan, and European countries. Furthermore, a great deal of this trade involves the exchange of similar products. Each country imports products that are very much like the products it exports. Germany exports BMWs to Italy while importing Fiats. France imports both car brands, and exports Peugeots and Renaults to Germany and Italy.

Linder emphasized that his theory was applicable only to trade in manufactured goods, in which tastes and economies of scale were deemed to be especially important. In his view, trade in primary products can be adequately explained by the traditional theory, with its emphasis on the supply of productive factors, including climate and natural resources.

The Linder model does not explain why one country originates particular products or why particular firms enter the industry, and so these origins might be viewed as accidental. BMW happened to start producing cars in Bavaria, whereas Fiat began in Milan, and Peugeot entered the car business from Paris. Each local economy had to be large enough to support a firm that was big enough to gain economies of scale, thus making competitive exports possible. Otherwise, there is no particular explanation of why various types of cars were produced in each country.

The Linder trade argument, like those discussed earlier, also depends on economies of scale and implies imperfectly competitive markets. If there were no economies of scale, intra-industry trade would be unlikely because each model or type of product could be efficiently produced in each country, thereby saving transport costs. BMW would have factories in France and Italy, while Fiat would produce in France and Germany. Sizable economies of scale in automobile assembly, however, would make it very inefficient for these companies to maintain factories in each country, and large savings would become available by concentrating production of each type of car in one factory and exporting cars to the two foreign markets.

The examples of trade in cars demonstrate that consumers value product variety. Producers also gain from product variety, as implied by our earlier discussion of the gains from specialized inputs that enable the firm to be more productive and produce at lower cost. Specialized intermediate inputs are a significant source of trade. Steel alloys can differ in their tensile strength, corrosion resistance, and malleability, or semiconductors can differ in

---

Box 4.1 Intra-industry trade: how general is it?

Although intra-industry trade is important for a variety of high-income countries, this is not a universal pattern. Figures in Table 4.1 indicate a substantial discrepancy between the values observed for the United States and Europe on the one hand, and for Japan on the other hand.

Table 4.1 calculations are based on the following formula for intra-industry trade in industry i: $IIT_i = \{1 - [\,|\,X_i - M_i\,|\,/\,(X_i + M_i)]\} \times 100$, where the numerator is the absolute value of the trade balance in that good and IIT ranges in value from zero to 100. A value of zero denotes no intra-industry trade and will occur when the product is either imported or exported, but exports and imports do not occur simultaneously. A value of 100 denotes exports equal to imports. The values for each industry are weighted by their share of trade to give a country average value. The 1970 entry for Japan of 32 represents much less intra-industry trade than the French value of 78 does.

Table 4.1 Average intra-industry trade in manufactured products

Country	1970	1975	1980	1985
Japan	32	26	28	26
United States	57	62	62	61
France	78	78	82	82
West Germany	60	58	66	67
South Korea	19	36	40	49

Source: Edward Lincoln, *Japan's Unequal Trade* (The Brookings Institution, 1990), p. 47. Calculations based on three-digit SIC categories.

Such calculations are always subject to imprecise interpretations because they may reflect two contrasting cases: (1) imported inputs of intermediate goods and exports of final goods categorized in the same industry, which may be quite consistent with the H–O model's explanation of trade, and (2) trade in different varieties of final goods, which represents the type of trade predicted by Linder. More significantly, such calculations have fueled debate over the openness of the Japanese economy, the protective effect of private business practices, and the ease of distributing products within the current inefficient system. Critics claim the lack of intra-industry trade is clear evidence of a Japanese mercantilistic philosophy that tries to eliminate any reliance on foreign production for goods that can be produced domestically. Defenders of Japanese practice note that Japan's pattern of trade differs from that of other countries due to its much greater dependence on imports of raw materials and consequent need to export a larger volume of manufactured exports. As a result, less intra-industry trade will occur.

Such calculations have caused economists more recently to estimate whether a country's manufactured imports, or imports from a particular country, differ significantly from what we would predict after controlling for the country's domestic production or factor endowments. A study by James Harrigan calculates that Japan's ratio of imports to expenditure is only 28 percent of the US value,[6] but the US value is much smaller than comparable European ratios. On a bilateral basis, he finds the United States is more open to trade in manufactures than any of its **Organization for Economic Cooperation and Development (OECD)** partners.

An appeal to numbers alone is unlikely to resolve this debate. In years of depressed Japanese economic growth and burgeoning Japanese trade surpluses, the issue is certain to attract western attention.

their performance at extreme temperatures or power requirements. Different final uses require different specialized characteristics, and a single supplier will seldom find it efficient to try to produce all these different varieties. Thus, intra-industry trade can be motivated by a variety of reasons. The theories that we have discussed thus far, however, do not develop that reasoning very rigorously. In the next section we examine work that looks at product variety and imperfect competition more systematically.

Economies of scale and monopolistic competition

The previous examples of individual firms specializing in different varieties of a product rest upon the existence of economies of scale internal to the firm: a firm's average cost of production falls as its own output rises. We begin by considering two possible sources of such economies of scale and the implication that a firm will find it efficient to specialize in particular products rather than produce an entire range of products itself. We then examine the sources of gains from trade in the case of monopolistic competition in two countries, where firms find it easy enough to enter this industry that any economic profits are eliminated.

One of the most common sources of economies of scale is fixed costs of production. To enter an industry, before it even starts to produce any output at all, a firm typically must buy equipment, set up a distribution network, engage in research and development, or launch an advertising campaign. These costs are then recovered through subsequent sales of the good it produces. The average fixed cost per unit declines the more units are sold, and the firm will be able to cover those costs at a lower price.

Simply setting up a production line to produce a different product can have a high opportunity cost, because production of one good must cease while machinery is recalibrated to produce another product. This down-time to produce very small quantities of a different good represents a fixed cost of production. Short production runs can only be justified if prices are sufficiently high to recover those fixed costs. Studies of the Canadian economy in the 1960s indicated the disadvantage of a policy to protect domestic producers and produce small amounts of a broad range of goods: few economies of scale were achieved in comparison with producers in the United States, and consequently average costs of production were 20 percent higher for many household appliances.[7]

Economies of scale also exist when there are increasing returns to scale, and a doubling of variable inputs leads to more than a doubling of output. A set of industries where firms experience these economies of scale includes beer brewing, flour milling, oil refining, and chemical processing. Production in these industries often requires vats, tanks, silos, or warehouses where the material necessary to make them depends upon their surface area, but the output obtained from them depends upon the volume they hold. Because the surface area of a sphere, for example, increases with the square of the radius, while the volume it holds is a function of the radius cubed, increasing returns to scale occur over an important range of output as the radius is increased.

Increasing returns to scale apply to cases such as the early automobile production lines of Henry Ford, who used much more capital equipment than the craft shops that initially dominated the auto industry. This much larger scale of plant allowed Ford to obtain a more than proportional increase in output. His ability to achieve these economies of scale as he produced large volumes of automobiles allowed his average cost per unit to fall below that of his competitors.

Although we treat other sources of economies of scale in this chapter, the two concepts covered thus far give us a basis for expecting to observe an initial range of output where the firm is able to reduce average cost per unit by producing more units. If fixed costs are particularly large relative to total costs or increasing returns continue to exist as output expands, these economies of scale give a firm an incentive to expand output. If the firm does not encounter other constraints in expanding output, potentially it may take over the entire market. While some industries do become monopolies, with only a single producer, more often a firm's choice to expand output is limited by the demand conditions that it faces, especially the possibility that other firms may enter the industry and lure customers away from the original producer. In this section of the chapter, we consider the model of monopolistic competition to explain what firms will produce.

Figure 4.5 shows a firm that faces a downward-sloping demand curve. The firm has market power to set prices, but it will not exercise that power arbitrarily. Rather, the firm will determine its optimal level of output where the extra revenue from producing another unit just equals the extra cost, that is, where marginal revenue equals marginal cost. The extra revenue from selling another unit of output no longer equals the price of that unit, as in a perfectly competitive market, because the firm must take into account the reduction in price necessary to expand the quantity sold. Additional revenue is raised only when the gain from more units sold offsets the loss from offering existing customers a lower price. Marginal revenue will be positive only if demand for the product is elastic, and the positive quantity effect offsets the negative price effect. Based on the profit-maximizing rule that the firm produces where marginal revenue equals marginal cost, the firm chooses to produce at Q*. The price that customers are willing to pay for this much output is P*. This price represents a mark-up above marginal cost, which will be larger when customers have fewer options and demand is less elastic. In spite of being able to charge a price greater than marginal cost, however, the firm only makes an average rate of return. There are no economic or above-average returns. That result is shown by the tangency of the average total cost (ATC) curve to the demand curve at P*, where ATC includes an average rate of return to capital used by the firm. If the ATC curve had been lower and positive economic profits had been earned, those profits would have attracted new entrants into the industry. In that case the demand curve for the existing firm shifts inward until this tangency condition is established.

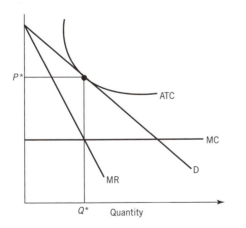

Figure 4.5 Production under monopolistic competition. The firm produces at Q* where marginal revenue, MR, equals marginal cost, MC. The firm charges the price P*, which represents a mark-up above marginal cost, which will be greater the less elastic is demand. The firm makes an average rate of return, because P equals ATC.

When trade is possible between two countries that each have monopolistically competitive industries, what results can we predict regarding the pattern of trade and the gains from trade? If both countries have the same preferences and factor endowments, as well as the same technical capabilities, then firms from one country are just as likely to be successful producers in an integrated market as are firms from the other country. For identical countries, we expect the same number of producers of a good to exist in autarky in each country. Nevertheless, integration of the market does offer gains to both countries, because we expect industry rationalization to occur. As a result of the opportunity to serve a larger market, some firms will expand and achieve greater economies of scale, which allows them to underprice those which continue to produce the same level of output for the domestic market only. Some firms will be driven out of business as this process of industry rationalization occurs. There will be fewer total firms in each country, but the average output of each one will be greater than before trade. Average costs of production fall as the demand curves for the remaining firms shift outward in Figure 4.5. Even when the marginal cost of production is constant, and does not fall as output expands, average cost per unit falls and the economy as a whole gains, because there is less duplication from separate firms meeting the fixed costs of entering this industry. If there are increasing returns to scale, which results in both average cost and marginal cost falling as each firm's output expands, the gain from rationalization is even easier to see. Trade results in competition between more firms and ensures that these cost savings are passed on to consumers. Because consumers now can buy from both domestic and foreign producers when trade is possible, available foreign product variety increases too. Consumers gain from trade on two counts: a lower price and greater variety.

We might summarize this relationship between trade and competitiveness as shown in Figure 4.6. PP represents the relationship between the number of firms and the ability of competition to lower costs and prices. The larger the number of firms, the more vigorous the competitive climate. CC represents the impact of economies of scale on average costs within a closed national economy; as the number of firms increases, and therefore the size of the typical firm declines, average costs rise. With a small number of firms, however, each enterprise will be larger. It will more fully exploit economies of scale, thereby driving down costs. With a closed national market, the equilibrium average cost is AC. If the market is instead defined as the world, because imports and exports are allowed, the relationship between the number of firms and average costs shifts to CC' because far more firms can exist without losing economies of scale in the much larger world market. Free trade then helps lower the equilibrium average cost to AC' because the world market has both larger firms and more vigorous competition than were possible in an isolated national market.

Where scale economies are important, international trade can also offer consumers a far more diverse set of product choices than would be possible with only domestic sourcing. Economies of scale may mean that only a few models or product types can be produced within a nation, but if imports are allowed, far more product types can be made available without the loss of economies of scale. The Canadian automobile market provides a useful example of this impact of trade. Before the 1965 US–Canada auto pact, Canada maintained tariffs on US cars. All of the major US auto companies operated plants in Canada, but the market was so constrained that only a limited range of cars could be produced, and even with this limitation costs and prices were high. In the mid-1960s the United States and Canada agreed on free trade in cars and parts, with side agreements between the car companies and the Canadian government guaranteeing the maintenance of Canadian production and employment. Through this arrangement all of the car models and types available in the

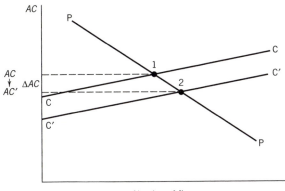

Figure 4.6   The impact of free trade on prices: increased competitiveness despite economies of scale. The PP line indicates that the more firms in a market, the more vigorous the competition and the lower the average costs. The CC line represents economies of scale in the domestic industry and shows that the more firms, the smaller each must be and the fewer scale economies they will enjoy. As a result, more firms means higher average costs. If free trade exists, so that the relevant market includes foreign producers and markets, CC shifts to C'C' because there can be both more firms and bigger firms in a world market. A combination of larger firms and more vigorous competition is therefore possible at point 2 than was true in a solely domestic market at point 1. The impact of trade then is to lower average costs.

United States became available in Canada. Moreover, the Canadian plants could sharply reduce costs by concentrating on the production of one or two models, with the vast majority of the output being shipped to the United States. Canadian car-buyers were able to choose from a far wider range of models and no longer had to pay the high prices that resulted when Canadian factories produced at a less-than-optimal scale.

The implications of this trade for changes in the distribution of income differ from the H–O model too. Because the basis for trade does not rest upon different factor intensities in production, there is no change in relative factor demands. While some firms will cease production, industry output expands in the case of symmetric countries as presented above. That expansion results from greater sales at the lower prices now necessary to cover lower costs of production. When trade is liberalized among countries that primarily produce differentiated manufactured goods with similar input requirements, necessary adjustments may be much less contentious than in the potential conflict between skilled labor and unskilled labor described in Chapter 3.

Trade with other forms of imperfect competition

Our analysis in the preceding section was simplified by the assumption that entry of new firms into the industry allowed any above-average profits to be competed away. The smaller are fixed costs relative to variable costs, the smaller the barriers to entry in the industry, and the more likely that a surge in demand and higher profits will attract new entrants into the industry. On the other hand, some industries are not well described by those conditions. Barriers to entry are significant enough that some firms can earn above-average profits and no new entrant competes them away. What part of any cost savings is passed on to consumers in the form of lower prices is less certain. A further contrast to models of

Box 4.2　Further reasons for economies of scale: the learning curve

Fixed costs and increasing returns to scale are not the only reasons why average costs of production fall as output rises. Another important factor in some industries has been the **learning curve**, which relates the firm's average cost of production to its cumulative output. An example of the way we might express such economies is that every time a company doubles its output, costs per unit fall by 25 percent. Such reductions in cost may occur due to better organization and scheduling of complex production processes, such as the assembly of aircraft. In the production of semiconductors they result from the ability to eliminate flaws in the production process. Initial production runs may yield as few as five usable chips out of 100 produced; after more experience is gained, the yield of usable chips may rise as high as 95 percent.

An important aspect of learning is whether it can be transferred from one plant to another within a company or whether it easily spills over to other firms in the same country or even to other countries. A steep learning curve where costs fall rapidly as output expands is likely to result in an industry with fewer firms, because learning represents a barrier to entry similar to fixed costs or increasing returns. Learning is less of a barrier to entry if it easily spills over to domestic competitors. In fact, that possibility is what creates external economies of scale in an industry. If the learning of one firm spills over to another, and vice versa, then expansion of industry output allows all firms to produce more cheaply. Correspondingly, if learning spills over internationally to firms in other countries, then external economies do not create a competitive advantage for producers of just one nation.

A study by Douglas Irwin and Peter Klenow of the worldwide semiconductor industry provides empirical evidence on several of the points raised above.[8] Based on analysis of seven successive generations of dynamic random-access memory chips (DRAMs) from 1972 to 1992, they report an average learning rate of 20 percent. This figure holds for both US and Japanese firms. With respect to spillovers within the industry, they find that firms learn three times more from an additional unit of their own cumulative output than from another firm's cumulative output. Thus, firms appear able to appropriate a large share of the benefits from their learning, but because world output is far more than three times the output of any one firm, spillovers play a major role in allowing firm production costs to fall. Spillovers that do occur are just as large across firms in different countries as they are across firms in the same country, and therefore policies to promote national production end up providing a benefit to others. Also, spillovers across different generations of chips generally are not observed, specifically not in the two most recent generations. Thus, fears that government measures will create successful firms in one generation and thereby develop a competitive advantage over other firms in subsequent generations do not appear well founded.

monopolistic competition is that there are few enough firms in the industry that the action of one will not be ignored by the others.

There is even more diversity among models that economists have applied to represent the variety of circumstances that may apply. One extreme is the case where a single domestic producer would not find it attractive to produce for the domestic market alone, but the opportunity to trade and serve the larger world market would warrant the entry of one firm.

High research and development costs to develop a drug that very few people in any one country ever require represents such a case. In the absence of trade, the drug simply would not exist, a clear loss of world welfare. Similarly, the high cost of developing a wide-bodied long-range aircraft to seat 600 passengers would never be warranted if sales were limited to airlines based in a single-country market, and even with access to the world market, no more than one producer appears likely to produce such a plane.

Consider a less extreme case where two firms producing an identical product do exist to serve the world market. We begin by applying a duopoly model that shows how one firm alters its output in response to output decisions of the other firm.[9] Such a model, developed by Augustin Cournot,[10] can be summarized in two reaction curves as shown in Figure 4.7. Let the two curves correspond to a Dutch firm and to an English firm. If the Dutch firm held a monopoly it would produce at point D_M along the vertical axis; if the English firm held a monopoly it would produce at point E_M along the horizontal axis. The English firm's reaction function shows that as Dutch output rises, English production will fall. Because two firms find it profitable to operate in this industry, the English firm will not be able to operate as a monopolist at point E_M. If English output initially were at that level, the Dutch response would be to produce at D_1, as given by the Dutch reaction function. At that level of output, the English firm would then choose to produce E_1. In turn, the Dutch firm would respond by producing D_2. This process converges to the equilibrium shown at Z where the two reaction curves intersect. Point Z does not lie along a straight line connecting D_M and E_M, and therefore this solution shows that more total output will be produced than when a monopoly controls the market. Because more output is sold, a lower price must be charged. Thus, gains from competition are possible in a duopoly setting.

Douglas Irwin applied this duopoly framework to explain the rivalry between the English East India Company and the Dutch United East India Company for the spice trade with Southeast Asia from 1600 to 1630.[11] Because land transportation was such an expensive alternative, competition between sea-faring traders provided the main check on the market power of any one firm. Furthermore, Queen Elizabeth I granted a 15-year exclusive monopoly

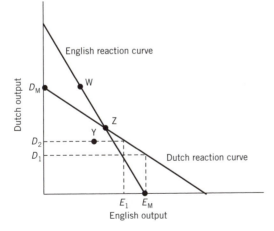

Figure 4.7 Reaction curves and duopoly trade. An English monopolist chooses to produce E_M. If a Dutch firm enters the market, it offers the quantity D_1 as indicated by its reaction curve. The English firm reacts by producing E_1, as indicated by its reaction curve, which results in a further Dutch response to offer D_2. This sequential adjustment leads to equilibrium at point Z.

to the English East India Company, and the Dutch similarly granted the Dutch United East India Company monopoly rights to trade with Asia. No other country had comparable maritime power, and thus, a duopoly setting describes this trading situation quite accurately.

The Cournot model implies that the basic decision each firm must make is how large a quantity of goods to bring to market, which is an appropriate description of the spice trade. Each trading company determined the number of ships to send to Asia and then auctioned off the pepper brought back to Europe. The symmetric diagram shown in Figure 4.7 also appears appropriate because the Dutch and English each sold pepper in the same European market, they both had access to the Asian markets to acquire pepper, and they had comparable costs to transport it back to Europe. We would expect each firm to gain half of the market.

That outcome, however, did not emerge. The Dutch accounted for nearly 60 percent of the market. Irwin suggests that the Dutch East India Company followed a strategy other than the profit maximization assumed in the Cournot model. Stockholders could not check the actions of company agents in the field, whose remuneration depended upon total turn-over and growth. Such agents had no incentive to cut back their efforts when British sales expanded, and the Dutch produced more than called for by the Cournot model. Nevertheless, this strategy was beneficial to the Dutch, giving them 20 percent higher profits than in the Cournot case, because it in effect implemented a leadership strategy later identified by Heinrich von Stackelberg.[12] The success of the strategy arises due to the reduction in the competitor's (British) output, given the leader's (Dutch) decision to expand so much. The outcome is comparable to Dutch maximization of profits assuming it could count on a subsequent British reduction in output. In terms of Figure 4.7, the strategy represents a point such as W, where total industry output (British plus Dutch) is greater than at Z, and prices are lower. Dutch profits are greater due to their larger share of this expanded market. Even though prices are lower, they still exceed the cost of production and contribute to higher profits when sales expand sufficiently.

In Chapter 6 we return to this topic because it has arisen in current debates over **strategic trade policy**. The Dutch gain was not the result of a carefully implemented government strategy, and Irwin demonstrates that an even larger gain was possible. Could modern-day governments achieve similar gains with more purposeful intervention? Although any historical example is subject to multiple interpretations, Irwin raises the cautionary note that aggressive Dutch expansion in the Indonesian spice trade relegated Britain to greater trade with India. The subsequent British opportunity to develop trade in cotton and cotton textiles is viewed by some economic historians as an important ingredient in the birth of the Industrial Revolution.[13]

The model presented above applies when two firms compete to serve a single market as in the case of the seventeenth-century pepper trade. An advantage of that situation is that drawing any conclusions about the welfare of the two supplying countries is more straight-forward. When the consumption primarily occurs in some third-country market, only the change in profits earned by the supplying firms must be examined. However, we can also apply this framework to consider two identical countries that initially are each served by a domestic monopoly. If trade becomes possible and the two firms compete as Cournot oligopolists, with the same cost of serving either market, the solution in Figure 4.7 applies to any one country's market. The English producer, for example, no longer holds a monopoly in the English market. Competition with the Dutch firm leads to the solution at point Z, where more of the product is sold to consumers at a lower price. In the Dutch market, the Dutch monopolist likewise must compete with the English firm, which results in a greater quantity and a lower price being charged. The possibility of trade has a pro-competitive effect that benefits each country, as the market price comes closer to marginal cost, the optimal condition from a competitive market. Although monopoly profits fall, that represents a benefit to consumers, and in the symmetric case assumed here, any loss in English (Dutch) profits is more than offset by gains to English (Dutch) consumers.

Cartels

If the Dutch and English firms represented above could reach an agreement not to compete against each other, they could increase their profitability. In Irwin's example of the world pepper trade, he estimated that their combined profits would have been 12 percent greater with collusion than in the Cournot solution. Such collusion simply represented both firms producing half the amount that a monopolist would choose, at point Y in Figure 4.7. As long as this market sharing arrangement can be enforced, the two firms can each earn higher profits and gain at the expense of the world's consumers.

Real-world examples of cartels do not exhibit the symmetries assumed in the example above, and it is worth examining more realistic cases to understand why collusion and cartel agreements often are fragile. The most significant case of the past three decades has been the Organization of Petroleum Exporting Countries (OPEC). Its success in the 1970s appeared to be a role model for exporters of other primary products, who envisioned a new world order emerging.[14]

These hopes have been disappointed and even OPEC's ability to influence prices has been uneven over time. The requirements for creating a successful cartel are rather stringent, and cartels have a tendency to weaken the longer they are in operation. For a cartel to be successful in raising prices well above marginal costs, the following conditions must exist:

1   The price elasticity of demand for the product must be low, which means that it has no close substitutes. Otherwise the volume sold will shrink dramatically when prices are raised.
2   The elasticity of supply for the product from outside the cartel membership must be low, which means that new firms or countries are not able to enter the market easily in response to the higher price. If this condition does not hold, the cartel will discover that higher prices result in a sharp reduction in its sales as new entrants crowd into the business.
3   At least a few members of the cartel must be able and willing to reduce production and sales to hold the price up. If all members insist on producing at previous levels despite the higher price, there will almost certainly be an excess supply of the product, resulting in a price decline. Such increases in production often follow secret price cuts by members competing for sales despite promises not to do so. Production and sales cutbacks are easier to maintain if a product is durable and can be stored. Failure to sell perishable crops results in large losses.
4   The membership of the cartel must be congenial and small enough to allow successful negotiations over prices, production quotas, and a variety of other matters. Cartels are more difficult to maintain as the number of members rises, particularly if some of them were historic adversaries.

From this list of conditions a reader can see why OPEC was temporarily successful and why this kind of success has been so rare in other markets. Most products do have substitutes and/or can be produced by new firms or countries if prices are increased sharply. Cartels have frequently failed when the market available to the members shrank, but none of them was willing to cut production sufficiently to support the price. Cheating in the form of secret price cuts to gain new customers followed, and the intended monopoly collapsed. De Beers Consolidated Mines can be viewed as a successful cartel in the diamond business. Through its own mines and marketing contracts with other producers in Africa and elsewhere, it controls the vast majority of the gem-quality diamonds arriving on the market, and it is able to manage, if not quite control, prices. Nevertheless, the European Commission has favorably ruled on De Beers' distribution system, something the United States has not done.[15]

OPEC was successful in the 1970s because all four of the above conditions held for oil, but the longer high prices remained in effect, the weaker OPEC became. Efforts to conserve energy and the increased use of alternative energy sources reduced the demand for oil. NonOPEC countries such as Mexico and the United Kingdom increased production sharply in the late 1970s. The results were a sharp reduction in the volume of oil that OPEC members could sell, unsuccessful attempts to get members to curtail production sufficiently, and an eventual decline in the price, as can be seen in Figure 4.8.

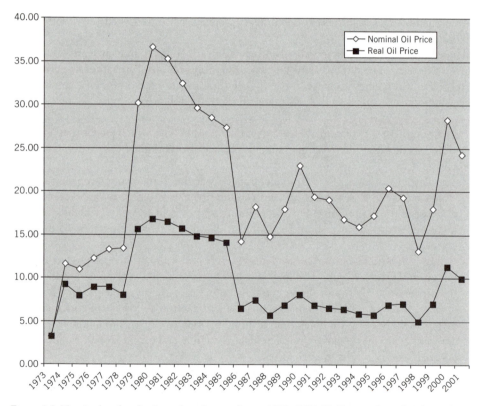

Figure 4.8 Nominal and real prices of crude petroleum, 1973–2001 (dollars per barrel). The real price of oil was not much higher in the 1990s than prior to OPEC. Price increases in the twenty-first century demonstrate renewed market power.

Source: IMF, *International Financial Statistics*. The real price is based on the average price of crude oil divided by the export unit value index for industrial countries which was set equal to 1.0 for 1973.

Predicting whether OPEC is permanently weak is problematic. The low oil prices of the 1980s encouraged consumption and discouraged exploration, thus increasing world reliance on OPEC sources. Iraq's invasion of Kuwait in 1990 led to a temporary increase in the price of oil. The Asian financial crises of the late 1990s, however, led to a period of slow growth and less demand for oil; at the same time economically distressed oil-producing countries were unwilling to reduce output. The terms of trade of oil producers in 1998 fell to a level nearly as low as before OPEC's formation. Subsequently, economic recovery and coordinated reductions in output by OPEC and nonOPEC oil producers allowed oil prices to rise.

Further aspects of trade with imperfect competition

Another element of trade with imperfect competition that warrants further attention is the effect of competition when we no longer start from symmetric situations in the two countries. Previously, we considered the potential gains from trade when an equal number of monopolistically competitive firms operate in each country in autarky, or when a monopolist in the home market becomes a duopolist in an integrated world market. What if the symmetric expansion of production and consumption does not hold?

Regarding the gains from trade, no simple answer emerges, because two offsetting factors operate. Allowing trade to lower prices internationally represents a gain to consumers. If this price reduction leads to less production in a monopoly industry where price exceeds marginal cost, however, the country may not benefit from trade. This outcome demonstrates the **principle of second best**: removing one distortion in an economy where other distortions exist may not raise welfare. Here we simply show one application of that theory.

Figure 4.9 represents an economy whose autarky production and consumption point is A.[16] To avoid any confusion over the role of monopoly power versus economies of scale, we present the case where opportunity costs are increasing. Note that at point A the slope of the production-possibility curve, which gives the relative marginal costs of producing the

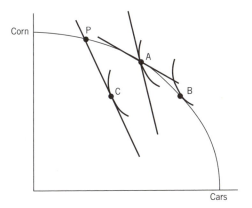

Figure 4.9 A possible decline in welfare from trade with domestic monopoly. In autarky the economy produces and consumes at point A. The price of cars that faces consumers, given by the line tangent to the indifference curve at A, is steeper than the marginal cost of production, given by the line tangent to the production-possibility curve, due to the monopoly power of the car producer. When trade occurs, the firm's monopoly power declines, and the gap between price and marginal cost falls, as shown at production point P. In this example, domestic output of cars falls enough, however, for the economy to move to a lower indifference at point C.

two goods, is not the same as the slope of the community indifference curve, which corresponds to the price at which consumers substitute one good for another. The steeper slope of the indifference curve indicates that the relative price of cars is greater than the relative cost of producing cars. The gap between those two lines represents the mark-up of the domestic monopolist in car production. Indeed, the existence of the monopoly leaves the country worse off than it would be at point B with competitive markets, where more cars would be produced and sold at a lower price.

Now introduce trade into this situation. The exact solution will depend upon whether the monopolist competes with just one other firm or with several additional firms and whether it is a relatively high-cost producer. If the monopolist is forced to operate as a perfect competitor, where price equals marginal cost and the international price line is tangent to the production-possibility curve, the country gains from trade. Under some conditions, however, the new equilibrium price may result in a situation shown by production at point P and consumption at point C. Additional competition has reduced the gap between price and marginal cost, but production of cars has fallen so much that the country becomes worse off, shown by the movement to a lower indifference curve. When fewer cars are produced, the economy saves the marginal cost of producing them, but simply loses the monopoly profit it earned from charging a higher price for cars. That margin cannot be earned as resources are shifted into corn production. This outcome contrasts with the earlier symmetric case, where the domestic monopoly became an exporter and increased its sales in the foreign market at the same time as it was subject to more competition at home. If there is little or no potential to increase sales abroad, a large country with a high-cost producer is more likely to lose from this shift in monopoly output to foreign producers. We return to this topic in Chapter 6 where alternative trade policies and potential profit-shifting are evaluated.

Summary of key concepts

1 External economies of scale allow average costs in an industry to fall as its output expands. Potential gains from specialization and trade can be considerable, even when there are no differences in autarky prices. The actual pattern of trade, however, is indeterminate. Historical accident or government intervention to give a country a head-start may explain the pattern of trade observed.

2 Internal economies of scale allow average costs of a firm to fall as its output expands. When these economies of scale are not so great that they create a major barrier to entry in an industry, there are likely to be many producers of differentiated products in the industry. When trade is possible, producers in just one country are unlikely to become the sole exporters. In the absence of other cost advantages, there will be intra-industry trade with firms in both countries exporting. The gains from trade come from a greater variety of products becoming available in an open world market. Also, lower prices are achieved because of greater competition internationally, while within any single country the smaller number of producers exhaust more economies of scale.

3 Internal economies of scale may be so great that only a few firms produce in an industry. Predicting trade in oligopoly industries requires predicting how a firm responds to the output or price decisions of another firm. Gains from trade include greater competition and lower prices, but the opportunity to shift oligopoly profits from one country to another makes net benefits less certain.

4   Oligopolistic firms may collude by forming cartels to reduce competition among themselves. Such collusion is difficult to enforce, not only because new entrants may be attracted by higher profits, but also because members of the cartel have an incentive to cheat on any agreement reached.

Questions for study and review

1   If the production of athletic shoes is an industry where external economies of scale are important determinants of costs of production, how would that make it more difficult for China to replace Korea as the world's leading producer? If China nevertheless were able to become the top producer, would you expect all production to take place in a single province? What role does proximity among producers play in determining whether external economies of scale are achieved?

2   What assumptions of the factor proportions model does the product cycle model relax or violate? To what extent are predictions of the product cycle model consistent with the factor proportions model? Does the product cycle model help explain the Leontief paradox?

3   Why does Linder's theory of trade in manufactured products predict that more trade will take place between similar countries? Trade in services is becoming increasingly important to the United States; would you predict that this US trade is more likely to be conducted with similar countries or with dissimilar countries?

4   Explain what the index of intra-industry trade shows, and suggest why the values of this index for Japan and Germany are so different.

5   Assume the fashion industry represents a monopolistically competitive industry, and explain what types of economies of scale exist that keep it from being a perfectly competitive industry. How is the opportunity to trade likely to change the structure of the fashion industry and the output of each designer in the industry?

6   Suppose two firms serve an integrated world market, and their reaction curves are given by

$$q_1 = 30 - 0.5\, q_2$$
$$q_2 = 30 - 0.5\, q_1$$

where q_1 is the output of firm 1 and q_2 is the output of firm 2. If firm 1 were guaranteed a monopoly in this market, what would it choose to produce? What will each duopolist produce in the equilibrium given by the intersection of these curves? Comparing the duopoly solution to the monopoly solution, how has total output changed and how will the price charged be affected? If these two firms were to collude, what would they produce instead?

7   Trade increases competition in previously closed markets. What economic conditions discussed in this chapter suggest such competition nevertheless can leave a country worse off?

Suggested further reading

For greater attention to the case of external economies of scale, see:
- Kemp, Murray, *The Pure Theory of International Trade*, Englewood Cliffs, NJ: Prentice Hall, 1964, Chapter 8.

For an early presentation on intra-industry trade, see:
- Grubel, Herbert and Peter Lloyd, *Intra-Industry Trade: The Theory and Measurement of International Trade in Differentiated Products*, New York: Wiley, 1975.

For a more advanced presentation of trade with imperfect competition, see:
- Helpman, Elhanan and Paul Krugman, *Market Structure and Foreign Trade*, Cambridge, MA: MIT Press, 1985.
- Helpman, Elhanan, "Increasing Returns, Imperfect Markets, and Trade Theory," in R. Jones and P. Kenen, eds, *Handbook of International Economics*, Vol. I, Amsterdam: North-Holland, 1984, Chapter 7.
- Jones, Ronald and Peter Neary, "The Positive Theory of International Trade," in R. Jones and P. Kenen, eds, *Handbook of International Economics*, Vol. I, Amsterdam: North-Holland, 1984, Chapter 1, pp. 48–53.

Appendix: derivation of a reaction curve

In this appendix we present the mechanics of deriving the reaction curves used in analyzing oligopoly markets. Our goal is to be able to explain which points lie along each country's curve. Begin by supposing that we know the profits of the English producer at all possible combinations of English and Dutch output. If we connect all points that represent the same level of profit (an isoprofit curve) we obtain the sort of curves shown in Figure 4.10. For English output of a_1, a_2, or a_3, English profits are the same. We already know that E_M represents the English monopoly solution, and we recognize that producing a smaller amount at

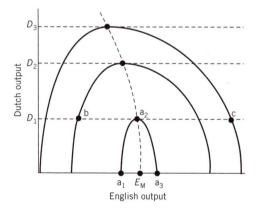

Figure 4.10 Isoprofit curves and the derivation of a reaction curve. An isoprofit curve for England connects all combinations of Dutch and English output that yield the same level of English profit. If Dutch output is given at D_1, English profits are higher at a_2 than at b or c, and therefore a_2 is the English firm's profit-maximizing level of output. The English reaction curve is given by finding the English profit-maximizing output, which occurs at the peak of an isoprofit curve, for each level of Dutch output.

a_1 or a larger amount at a_3 implies a lower level of profits. That level of profits is also what the English firm earns at a_2, where it is no longer a monopolist. In fact, if Dutch output is given by D_1, then a_2 represents the English firm's best output choice. Any other level of English output, such as at point b or point c, lies on a lower isoprofit curve further away from the maximum attained at E_M. Other points along the English reaction curve are derived by this same process of determining the highest isoprofit curve that can be attained for a given level of Dutch output. If the English firm expects Dutch output to remain constant irrespective of its own choice of output, its profit-maximizing output choice will be given by a point along its reaction curve. Note, however, that as Dutch output rises, the English firm does not reduce output by a comparable amount to restore the initial price. That response would not maximize the firm's own profits because it would not be the sole beneficiary of a price increase. The Dutch firm also would reap part of the benefit from a higher price. Therefore, any rise in Dutch output exceeds the reduction in English output, as indicated by the steeper slope of the English reaction curve and the smaller English response. As we noted in the text, total output of the duopolists exceeds the output of a monopolist.

Economists also have analyzed the competition between duopolists when they compete on the basis of the prices they set, not the quantities they produce. If one firm sets its price assuming that the price of the other firm will remain constant, we can derive a reaction curve similar to the situation shown for quantity choices. If the two firms produce identical goods, competition based on prices will result in a perfectly competitive solution where price equals marginal cost. In such a setting the implications for potential government policy intervention can be quite different from in the Cournot case of quantity competition.

Notes

1 Ronald Gilson, "The Legal Infrastructure of High Technology Industrial Districts: Silicon Valley, Route 128, and Covenants Not to Compete," unpublished paper (Columbia University, 1998).
2 Raymond Vernon, "International Investment and International Trade in the Product Cycle," *Quarterly Journal of Economics* 80, May 1966, pp. 190–207.
3 See William Gruber, Dileep Mehta, and Raymond Vernon, "The R and D Factor in International Trade and Investment of United States Industries," *Journal of Political Economy* 75, February 1967, pp. 20–37, and Robert Baldwin, "Determinants of the Commodity Structure of US Trade," *American Economic Review* 61, no. 1, March 1971, pp. 126–46.
4 "Fuel Cells Hit the Road," *The Economist*, April 24, 1999, p. 77.
5 Staffan B. Linder, *An Essay on Trade and Transformation* (New York: Wiley, 1961).
6 James Harrigan, "Openness to Trade in Manufactures in the OECD," *Journal of International Economics* 40, 1996, pp. 23–39.
7 D.J. Daly, B.A. Keys, and E.J. Spence, *Scale and Specialization in Canadian Manufacturing*, Economic Council of Canada, Staff Study No. 21 (Ottawa: Queen's Printer, 1968).
8 Douglas Irwin and Peter Klenow, "Learning-by-Doing Spillovers in the Semiconductor Industry," *Journal of Political Economy* 102, no. 6, 1994, pp. 1200–27.
9 See Hal Varian, *Intermediate Microeconomics* (New York: W.W. Norton, 1987), for a thorough treatment of alternative oligopoly models.
10 Augustin Cournot, *Researches into the Mathematical Principles of the Theory of Wealth* (New York: Macmillan, 1838).
11 Douglas Irwin, "Mercantilism as Strategic Trade Policy: The Anglo–Dutch Rivalry for the East India Trade," *Journal of Political Economy* 99, no. 6, 1991, pp. 1296–314.
12 Heinrich von Stackelberg, *Marktform und Gleichgewicht* (Vienna and Berlin: J. Springer, 1934).
13 David Landes, *The Wealth and Poverty of Nations* (New York: W.W. Norton, 1998).

14 For a more detailed discussion of the rise of OPEC, see Raymond Vernon, ed., *The Oil Crisis* (New York: W.W. Norton, 1976). The World Bank's World Development Report 1986 (Washington, DC: World Bank, 1986) deals extensively with problems of agricultural cartels.
15 David Lawsky, "De Beers: Ok'd for Diamond Sale Overhaul," *Reuters*, 11 November 2002.
16 J.R. Melvin and R.D. Warne, "Monopoly and the Theory of International Trade," *Journal of International Economics* 3, 1973, pp. 17–134.

5 The theory of protection
Tariffs and other barriers to trade

Learning objectives

By the end of this chapter you should be able to understand:

- how tariffs reduce economic efficiency by promoting output where a country has a comparative disadvantage and discouraging consumption of goods that consumers prefer;
- why quotas can result in larger efficiency losses than tariffs for a country that no longer gains the tariff-equivalent revenue of a quota;
- how the goal of greater domestic production generally can be achieved more efficiently through subsidies than trade barriers;
- how a large country may gain at the expense of others when it imposes a tariff and improves its terms of trade;
- how the nominal tariff rate may understate the protection provided to an industry;
- why export taxes have effects comparable to import tariffs.

In our exposition of the theory of international trade, we started with countries that were initially operating as closed economies. We threw open these isolated countries and allowed them to trade freely with each other, and then we examined and analyzed the economic effects of trade. An important conclusion of this analysis was that countries, if not all individuals in the countries, generally gain from trade. When each country specializes in products in which it has a comparative advantage, exporting them in exchange for imports of other products in which it has a comparative disadvantage, the result is a gain in economic welfare. Even when comparative advantage and autarky differences in costs of production do not provide a basis for trade, gains are possible as economies of scale are attained and competition results in greater production and lower prices.

That countries gain from free trade has long been a major tenet of trade theory. One of Adam Smith's principal objectives in his *Wealth of Nations* was to overturn and destroy the mass of mercantilist regulations that limited international trade. He argued that elimination of artificial barriers to trade and specialization would lead to an increase in real national income. David Ricardo shared this belief, as have most economists in subsequent generations.

This view has always been debated, however. Even if some trade is better than no trade, it does not necessarily follow that free trade is the best of all. Therefore we now need to turn the question around the other way: starting from a position of full free trade, what is the effect of introducing an obstacle to, or restriction on, trade? Can a nation's welfare be improved by imposing tariffs or other barriers to trade, not necessarily to eliminate trade but at least to reduce it below the free-trade level?

Administrative issues in imposing tariffs

In the past, tariffs (taxes on imports) were the dominant form of government regulation of trade, but that has changed. Average tariff levels have fallen, in part due to the successful completion of several rounds of multilateral negotiations under the GATT. Governments, however, have sought ways to restrict trade without violating commitments to lower tariffs. As a result, **nontariff trade barriers**, widely known as NTBs, have proliferated and have become the most active means of interference with trade. A nontariff trade barrier is any government policy, other than a tariff, which reduces imports but does not similarly restrict domestic production of import substitutes. Quotas, which are limits on the physical volume of a product that may be imported during a period of time, are the most important NTB, but there are many others. Their range is limited only by the imagination of government officials seeking ways to restrict imports without violating GATT commitments. The following discussion deals first with tariffs, and then with quotas and other NTBs.

Import tariffs may be *ad valorem* (a percentage of the value of the imported article), specific (a given amount of money per unit, such as $0.50 per yard of cloth), or compound (a combination of *ad valorem* and specific, such as 10 percent *ad valorem* plus $0.20 per yard of cloth). **Ad valorem tariffs** have the administrative advantage of rising automatically with inflation and of taxing different qualities of products at the same percentage rate. A tariff of 10 percent on wine produces proportionally more revenue as the price and quality of imported wine rise. A **specific tariff** will not have this effect. Its protective effect will decline in periods of inflation. The very high level of protection of US agricultural output established in the 1930s has subsequently fallen a great deal, not due to multilateral trade negotiations, but rather due to a rising price level that reduces the protective effect of specific tariffs. A specific tariff also will severely restrict imports of lower priced items within a product category while having little effect on expensive items. A tariff of $2 per bottle on wine would be prohibitive for inexpensive wines, but would have very little impact on imports of high-priced wines. Such a tariff discriminates against producers and consumers of the cheaper wines.

A disadvantage of an *ad valorem* tariff is that it creates opportunities for cheating through what is called false invoicing or **transfer pricing**. If a misleading low price is shown on the shipping invoice, part of the tariff can be avoided. A 10 percent tariff on cars, for example, might encourage both car exporters and their customers to invoice the cars $1000 below their true value, thus saving $100, with a fictitious transaction being used to move the $1000 as well as part of the $100 back to the exporter. A specific tariff of $500 per car would avoid this problem, because the customs official would simply collect $500 times the number of cars driven off the ship and have no interest in the value of each car.

Some countries that believe they have been victimized by under invoicing of imports refuse to accept normal documents showing the price of products being imported, and use their own customs valuation procedures to set the prices to which *ad valorem* tariffs will be applied. In some cases, this may allow greater administrative consistency, given the uneven results that emerge where there are high incentives to bribe customs officials in countries with high tariffs and other licensing requirements. To avoid such corruption some countries have relied upon outside administrators, such as the Swiss firm SGS (Société Générale de Surveillance), who independently compile information on world prices of traded goods which can be used in establishing appropriate valuations. In other cases, revaluation procedures are arbitrary and result in tariff rates that are much higher than those that would be appropriate. If the customs officials can simply decide that products are worth three times their actual value, a seemingly low tariff rate becomes very high. Customs valuation procedures are frequently a source of conflict in international trade.

Tariffs in a partial equilibrium framework

Begin by considering the effects of a tariff imposed on a single commodity. Assume that the industry involved is a very small part of the total economy. It is so small, in fact, that changes in this industry have negligible effects on the rest of the economy, and these effects can be ignored. We call this framework partial equilibrium analysis. Also, we consider the case of a competitive market, where an industry supply curve represents the aggregate response of many individual firms to the market price. No single firm is big enough to affect the market price by its own decision to increase or decrease output. The fortunes of one farmer lucky enough to produce 90 bushels of oats per acre under perfect weather conditions or unlucky enough to have a hail storm reduce the farm's output to 10 bushels per acre will be too small to affect the market price of oats. In Chapter 6 we consider situations where there are fewer firms in an industry and each one has some power to influence the market price.

The small-country case

In the left panel of Figure 5.1, we show Country A's domestic demand (D) and supply (S) curves for a particular commodity, say, oats. If trade is free, oats will be imported into Country A at the prevailing world price, P_w. At that price, Country A's total consumption will be 100, its production will be 60, and imports will make up the difference, 40. Total supply (60 of domestic output plus 40 of imports) equals total demand (100) at that price. Alternatively, we can show this same situation in the right panel of Figure 5.1, where we use the residual import demand curve first presented in Chapter 2. Note that there is no demand for imports at a price of oats greater than the autarky price, P_A. At a price lower than P_R where the domestic supply curve cuts the vertical axis and the quantity supplied equals zero, then the import demand curve is the same as the market demand curve. At prices between P_A and P_R the quantity of imports demanded is simply the difference between the quantity demanded and the quantity supplied domestically. At the world price P_W the import quantity is 40.

Now suppose that Country A imposes a tariff, equal to T or \$.50 per bushel, on imports of oats. The immediate result of the tariff is that the price of oats in Country A will rise by the amount of the tariff to P_T. In this section of the chapter we assume that the world price of oats remains unchanged when Country A imposes its tariff. That is, we assume that Country A is a small country whose actions will not affect the world market. The increase in price has a number of effects that can conveniently be examined in Figure 5.1. The first effect is that the consumption of oats is reduced from 100 to 95. The second effect is that domestic output rises from 60 to 70. Domestic producers do not pay the import tariff, of course, and the higher domestic price gives them an incentive to increase their output, as indicated by a movement along the supply curve. The third effect is that imports fall from 40 to 25. Both the fall in consumption and the rise in production cut into the previous level

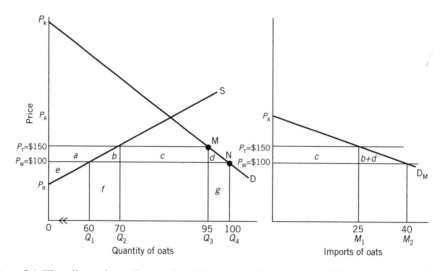

Figure 5.1 The effects of a tariff: partial equilibrium, small-country case. The imposition of a $50 per ton tariff shifts the world supply price from P_W at $100 to P_T at $150, reducing the volume of imports from 40 tons to 25. The lost consumers' surplus, $a + b + c + d$, is divided between the government, which takes in tariff revenues of area c, and the domestic industry, which receives additional producers' surplus of area a. Triangles b and d are deadweight losses.

of imports of oats. Note that if the tariff were large enough to raise the price to P_A imports would fall to zero. Domestic producers would supply the entire demand. This would be a prohibitive tariff.

We can also use Figure 5.1 to show the welfare gains and losses that result from the tariff. To show these gains and losses, we use the concepts of **consumers' surplus** and **producers' surplus**. First, we recognize that the area under the demand curve shows what consumers are willing to pay for a product. Consumers are willing to pay a lot for the first bushel of oats fed to a champion race horse, but because consumers value each succeeding bushel less they offer a progressively lower price shown as we move downward along the demand curve. Another way of interpreting this downward slope is that many consumers are likely to require a reduction in price to convince them to switch from a breakfast of bacon and eggs or bagels and cream cheese to oatmeal. When consumers pay the market price for all of the bushels purchased, they receive a benefit given by the difference between the price they are willing to pay and the price they actually have to pay for each of the bushels bought. At the world price P_W this measure of consumers' surplus is the triangle $P_K N P_W$, which is the total area under the demand curve, $P_K N Q_4 O$, less the amount spent on oats, $P_W N Q_4 O$. Imposition of the tariff reduces the consumers' surplus to $P_K M P_T$, a reduction equal to the area of the trapezoid $P_W P_T M N$. That trapezoid includes the separate areas a, b, c, and d. For those who like to confirm such calculations numerically, the area is $4,875 for the values show in the diagram.

Although consumers lose from the imposition of the tariff, domestic producers gain. They are now able to charge a higher price and sell a larger quantity, which causes their revenues to rise by areas a, b, and f. Not all of that additional revenue represents higher profits, though, because domestic costs of production rise too. In a competitive industry where the supply curve is based upon the marginal cost of output of the firms in the industry, the extra cost of producing $Q_1 Q_2$ of output is areas $b + f$. Therefore, the change in producers' surplus is the change in revenue minus the change in cost, area a, which equals \$3,250 for the numerical values shown. Alternatively, area a can be interpreted as a windfall gain to domestic producers. Previously, they were willing to sell Q_1 of output at P_W, and now they receive P_T, a gain of \$.50 per bushel. Also, as they expand output from Q_1 to Q_2, P_T exceeds the extra cost of producing that output for all bushels except the very last one at Q_2. The gain on existing output plus additional output motivated by the tariff is represented by area a. A final way to think of this change in producers' surplus is to calculate the value of producers' surplus before the tariff is imposed and then calculate it after the tariff is imposed. We define producers' surplus as the difference between the price that a supplier is willing to accept compared to the price actually received in the market. Because the price a firm is willing to accept is given by the supply curve, area e represents the initial value of producers' surplus. When price rises to P_T, then the producers' surplus triangle becomes $e + a$, and the change in producers' surplus is represented by the trapezoid a.

Not only do domestic producers gain, but the government also gains tariff revenue equal to area c. The tariff revenue is equal to the tariff, T, times the imports on which the tariff is collected, Q_2Q_3, which equals \$1,250 for the numerical values shown. It is a transfer from consumers to the government.

From a national point of view, therefore, areas a and c are not net losses; they are transfers from consumers to producers and to the government, respectively. But the situation is different for the remaining pieces of the decreased consumer surplus. Areas b and d are lost to consumers, but they are not gained by any other sector. These areas therefore represent the net welfare loss resulting from the tariff, sometimes called the **deadweight loss**. Area b can be thought of as a loss resulting from inefficiency in production, as resources are drawn into oats production and paid more than would be needed to buy imported oats through free trade. Similarly, area d is a loss from a less favorable consumption choice. Consumers are willing to pay areas $d + g$ for Q_3Q_4 of oats, but when the tariff causes them to buy other products they only get satisfaction equivalent to g and lose area d. The numerical values of areas b and d are \$250 and \$125, respectively, giving a total deadweight loss of \$375.

The net effects of a tariff that we have identified in the left panel of Figure 5.1 can also be derived in the right panel. The apparent loss in consumers' surplus that we infer from the import demand curve is given by areas $c + b + d$. Because this is a residual demand curve, however, it represents the loss to consumers net of the gain to producers. Thus, area a does not appear, and looking at the import market alone misses important distributional effects within the country that imposes the tariff. Nevertheless, we can observe the same gain in tariff revenue, given by T times the quantity of imports, or area c. The same deadweight loss, areas $b + d$, arises as the quantity of imports falls. We know the single deadweight loss triangle in the import market must equal the two deadweight loss triangles in the domestic market; the change in price is identical and the two quantities that serve as the bases of triangles b and d (the change in domestic production and the change in consumption) are exactly equal to the change in the quantity of imports that serves as the base of the triangle in the import market. For the numerical values shown in Figure 5.1, the deadweight loss triangle shown in the import market is \$375, which is identical to what we reported earlier based on the left panel of the figure. The import market representation is particularly useful when we consider other policies and relax the small country assumption of a horizontal foreign supply curve, and therefore we introduce it here.

Calculations of deadweight losses from tariffs often turn out to be quite small when expressed as a share of GDP, which causes some critics to say there is no reason to worry about the loss in efficiency from current tariffs. Nevertheless, that may not be the most

---

Box 5.1   How do economists measure welfare changes?

Economists often predict the size of the deadweight loss for a proposed tariff, but they usually are not given a diagram like Figure 5.1. Instead, they know how much is spent on the imported good, PM. An econometrician may have estimated the elasticity of demand for imports, α, which tells how large a percentage reduction in the quantity of imports will result from a 1 percent increase in the price of imports. How can we use those two pieces of information? First, we recognize that when demand and supply curves are approximately straight lines in the relevant range, then the deadweight loss triangle is equal to one-half times the reduction in imports times the increase in price, which, for a small country, is the tariff, T. Economists project the percentage reduction in imports, $(\Delta M/M)$, on the basis of the estimated value of the elasticity of demand for imports, α, and the predicted percentage change in price, $\Delta P/P$:

$$(\Delta M/M) = \alpha\ (\Delta P/P) = \alpha\ (T/P)$$

where the percentage change in price equals (T/P). Therefore, we can derive the following expression for the deadweight loss to the economy:

$$\text{Welfare loss} = 0.5\ \Delta M \Delta P = 0.5\ (\Delta M/M)\ (T/P)\ PM = 0.5\ \alpha(T/P)^2\ PM$$

The equation shows that the welfare loss will be larger when the import elasticity of demand is larger in absolute value, when the tariff is larger, and when initial spending on imports is larger. A larger elasticity of demand means that a bigger change in imports will occur, which represents a bigger distortion of consumer choices and production patterns. Note that the tariff term is squared, which indicates that high tariff rates are particularly costly to an economy; in an economy with a 100 percent tariff compared to an economy with a 5 percent tariff, all else equal, the welfare loss will be 400 times as great. For that reason the World Bank often recommends in its structural adjustment programs that countries reduce high tariff rates.[1] The loss in efficiency is so large because a progressively higher tariff rate not only distorts consumer choices but also leads to a loss in tariff revenue as the quantity of imports falls.

---

appropriate comparison. If the goal of tariff policy is to preserve output, profits or jobs in the domestic sector, then the change in one of those variables is a more appropriate denominator by which to judge the tariff's effectiveness.

In fact, the political debate is more likely to revolve around the costs imposed on consumers or users of a product from a tariff that generates higher profits for producers. Those distributional effects typically are much larger than the deadweight losses. Some analysts pay less attention to the losses to capital from a change in trade policy, because capitalists can diversify their holdings across expanding and contracting industries. Workers do not have that same opportunity. Estimates of consumer losses per job saved in trade-impacted industries, however, have far exceeded what a worker would earn in the industry.[2]

Box 5.2 World steel trade – a case of permanent intervention?

President Bush's intervention to protect the US steel industry in 2002 raised severe doubts about US leadership of any movement toward a more open trading system, a policy US officials advocated for other countries. Yet, government intervention in the steel market has a long history. Unfair trade cases filed in the United States in 1968, and the subsequent adoption of voluntary export restraints, represented a pattern that was repeated several times over the following decades.

The significant government role arises for several reasons. Large integrated steel producers have very high fixed costs of plant and equipment. In many countries worker layoffs are unacceptable, and labor costs become fixed regardless of the amount of steel produced. Even in the United States, where layoffs are more common, health and pension benefits to retired union workers represent a significant fixed cost that must be met regardless of actual output. Under such cost conditions, firms are likely to continue producing even when prices fall substantially, a sign of inelastic supply. Falling profits create a strong incentive to lobby for government intervention.

For many countries, a successful steel industry has been seen as a necessary step for economic development and the expansion of the manufacturing sector. In some cases governments established state-owned enterprises with little consideration of their economic profitability, while in others they provided favorable financing and adopted other policies to promote a national champion. Those policies contributed to a major expansion in world steel capacity, and even when state-owned enterprises were subsequently privatized, that additional capacity remained in production.

The issue of firms selling at pries below costs of production has led to a plethora of antidumping cases (a topic addressed in Chapter 6). Similarly, producers have brought countervailing duty cases to offset government subsidies. As noted by Hufbauer and Goodrich, the fundamental problem is that demand for steel has not grown nearly as rapidly as the world economy as a whole in this electronic age.[3] Rising labor productivity has reduced the demand for steel workers worldwide, as shown in Table 5.1.

Table 5.1 Employment in the steel industry

Country	1974	1990	1999
EU	998	434	280
Brazil	118	115	59
Japan	459	305	208
US	521	204	153

Source: International Iron and Steel Institute, as reported in Hufbauer and Goodrich, Institute for International Economics, July 2001.

The US industry has further changed with the growth of mini-mills that employ nonunion workers and use scrap steel inputs to produce in electrical furnaces. These producers have much lower fixed costs but higher variable costs. They actually expanded capacity from 1995 to 2000. Thus, the industry does not speak with a single voice on the appropriate solution to the challenges it faces.

The Asian financial crises of 1997–8 (a topic discussed in Chapter 20) resulted in an economic recession in that part of the world and the diversion of steel to the US market. This surge of imports, shown in Table 5.2, led to trade restrictions being imposed on steel wire rod under President Clinton, and a broader set of restrictions under President Bush. Tariffs up to 30 percent were imposed on 13 million tons of imported steel. The relief was temporary, for a 3-year period, and theoretically contingent on the industry developing a plan to become economically viable by the end of this protection.

Table 5.2 The US market for steel mill products

	1997	1998	1999	2000	2001
US imports	13,617	16,434	12,749	15,026	11,630
US domestic shipments	68,700	65,500	59,200	60,30	51,074
Imports/Consumption	17.6	21.3	18.8	21.3	20.1
Producer price index, steel	112.0	110.0	102.3	104.4	98.4

Source: ftp://ftp.usitc.gov/pub/reports/studies/PUB3525A.pdf and http://www.bls.gov

What economic and political consequences followed? From the US perspective, Hufbauer and Goodrich predict quite negative downstream effects on users of steel, who will face lower sales and reduced profits as they try to pass on higher costs of production. Due to those losses, they project the cost of every job saved in the steel industry to be $360,000 per year. As an indication of the cost disadvantage US steel users faced, in October of 2002 the US price of hot rolled steel was $350 per ton, while in the EU it was $270 per ton.[4]

Other countries such as the EU and Malaysia responded by imposing trade restrictions to avoid a surge of imports into their markets. Also, the EU announced a possible set of US industries against which it might impose retaliatory tariffs. Their targets were industries whose production was concentrated in swing states critical to Republican election prospects.[5] The Japanese sought compensation through tariff reductions on other items. The Bush Administration subsequently provided extensive exemptions for the EU and Japan, which forestalled retaliatory action. US producers reported substantial improvements in profits for the third quarter of 2002. Part of the adverse effect of US restrictions on other countries may have been offset by strong Chinese demand, as it became the world's leading importer of steel.[6] Nevertheless, claims for government intervention are unlikely to disappear.

Quotas and other nontariff trade barriers

As was noted earlier, barriers to trade other than tariffs have become far more important in recent years as governments have looked for ways to restrict imports without raising tariffs that were reduced in GATT negotiations. Quotas, which are limits on the physical volume of a product that may be imported per period of time, are the most transparent NTB, but there are many others. The mere fact that a policy reduces imports does not make it a trade barrier, however; it must discriminate against imports relative to domestic alternatives.

Higher gasoline taxes would reduce imports of gasoline, but would equally discourage consumption of domestic gasoline and would therefore not be a trade barrier.

Most NTBs are decidedly intentional, but they are sometimes disguised to look like a policy directed at another goal. Product quality standards are a particularly common way to keep foreign products out while appearing to have another purpose. Such standards are often written by domestic producer groups, and they often focus on aspects of product design that only local producers meet, in contrast to standards of performance attained regardless of design. For years foreign producers were frustrated by Japanese product standards that found US baseball bats, European skis and Canadian lumber unacceptable. While the European ban on approving the sale of additional genetically modified foods in the late 1900s raised important scientific issues over what constituted convincing evidence of food safety, the policy had a substantial protective effect as well.

Countries sometimes use administrative procedures to slow the passage of goods through customs. France, for example, unhappy about the volume of Japanese VCRs coming into its market, simply required that they all pass through a single customs post, which was located far from any airport or seaport and was open for only part of the week. The extra cost of shipping the VCRs to this customs post and the delay in clearing the machines into France effectively kept the Japanese products out of France for a number of months until GATT ruled against the French procedures. When the products being imported are perishable or directed at a seasonal market, delays in clearing customs can be very effective in keeping foreign products out of a national market. Japanese restrictions on leather imports reflect a similar ingenuity, as licenses could only be obtained on a single day of the year.

Governmental procurement rules are probably the most important NTB other than quotas. Such rules usually require that whenever government money is being spent domestic products must be purchased even if they are more expensive or less useful than imported alternatives. Many governments have such rules, although Europeans hope to eliminate them within the European Union, which would mean that a French firm would be able to compete equally with German firms in bidding on German government contracts.

The highly desirable goal of cleaning up the environment can become an excuse for supporting what actually amount to barriers to imports. The Canadian province of Ontario, for example, levies a high tax on beer sold in cans. US brewers faced a higher cost of transporting empty bottles and therefore relied on cans. Because the Canadian tax immediately followed an unfavorable GATT ruling about other provincial beer restrictions, and because it only applied to aluminum beer cans and not to other aluminum cans, Ontario's main interest appeared to be keeping out US beer rather than protecting the environment. In Chapter 11 we consider environmentally-motivated production standards imposed by the United States that limited imports of tuna from Mexico and shrimp from several developing countries. The **World Trade Organization** ruled that these restrictions were not justified.

Quantitative restrictions on imports

Quotas or limits on the quantity of allowable imports have some effects that are similar to a tariff but others that are quite different. Agricultural products often are protected by quotas, in many cases seasonal ones, although a major accomplishment of the Uruguay Round of trade negotiations is to require the conversion of these quotas into tariffs. Much of the world trade in textile and apparel products has been governed by quotas, but these protectionist regimes also are to be phased out under Uruguay Round agreements. Another form of quantitative restrictions to limit trade in manufactured goods became quite prevalent during the 1980s, a **voluntary export restraint** (VER). While the importing country does not restrict the quantity imported by some regulation or statute, the exporting country agrees to limit the volume being exported to some agreed upon-level. These, too, have been prohibited by the Uruguay Round agreements.

The effects of an import quota are shown in Figure 5.2. The same situation is depicted as in the tariff analysis of Figure 5.1. Imports are cut back from 40 to 25 and the price rises from $100 to $150. Producers gain area *a* in producers' surplus, but consumers lose areas *a* + *b* + *c* + *d* in consumers' surplus. Areas *b* and *d* again are deadweight losses.

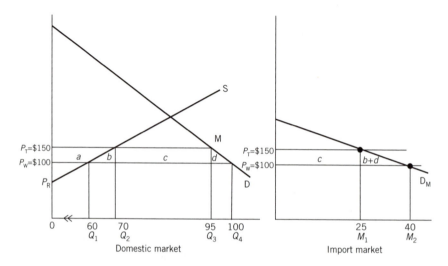

Figure 5.2 The effect of an import quota. If an import quota of 25 tons is imposed, the domestic price rises to P_T as imports fall by 15 tons; the same price effect occurs as in Figure 5.1. Consumers lose areas *a* + *b* + *c* + *d*, domestic producers gain area *a*, and areas *b* + *d* are deadweight losses. Who receives the tariff-equivalent rent created by the quota, area *c*?

Area *c*, however, is different. If a tariff is maintained, that area is government revenue that can be used to make public expenditures or to allow a reduction of other taxes. Under a quota, however, this tariff-equivalent revenue goes to whomever is fortunate enough to have the right to ship the product from the exporting to the importing country. If quota rights are allocated to importers, they receive the windfall profit. Suppose oil can be purchased on the world market at $1.50 per barrel and shipped to the East Coast of the United States for $0.75 per barrel for a total landed cost of $2.25 at the same time a US quota is being used to protect an internal price of approximately $3.50. Those allowed to bring oil into the United States receive a gift of $1.25 per barrel. They land oil here at a cost of $2.25, and it is immediately worth $3.50. This example represents the situation prevailing from the 1950s into the 1960s in the United States. It produced enormous monopoly rents for the major oil companies that were allocated quota rights by Washington.

Note that a key assumption of the example above is that US importers are able to buy foreign goods at a world price that does not rise as a result of US actions. This outcome is particularly likely when there are many foreign producers who are not organized in any way to take advantage of the scarcity of the product in the US market. US importers can seek competitive bids to fulfill the available quota of goods that can be imported, and they gain area *c* as a result. In the case of apparel trade, however, exporting nations such as Hong Kong established a system of export quota tickets that had to be acquired for goods to leave the country. These tickets were freely bought and sold among apparel producers, and their value increased when the demand for items rose. Even though there were many producers who could not easily be organized into a group to bargain with American or European buyers, the trade in quota tickets ensured that part of area c was captured by Hong Kong producers who no longer would be willing to sell at the world price P_W.

In the case of a VER, the exporting country explicitly limits the volume shipped, and it can allocate the quota rights and determine who gets the windfall profits. In this case the bonanza goes to exporting firms rather than to importers. As a result, exporting countries often accept VERs. The VER on Japanese cars that limited sales in the United States to 1.85 million cars per year during the early 1980s had the effect of raising US car prices by almost $1,000 per car.[7] That meant an additional profit of about $1.85 billion per year for the Japanese car companies. They were forced to reduce sales but were compensated through a gift of almost $2 billion per year. Because the Japanese government told each firm how much it would export, there was no reason for Japanese producers to compete against each other to try to win a bigger share of the restricted US market. An implication of this large windfall for Japanese producers was that the competitive position of US producers may not have improved much as a result of the VER. While a VER allows domestic profits to rise and provides a source of finance for retooling efforts, the foreign producer may receive an even larger boost in profits and be better positioned to introduce new products.

If the US government had auctioned the quota rights to the highest bidder, the Treasury would have recaptured the monopoly rents through the auction revenues. If there was a competitive market to distribute cars and therefore the auction as competitive, dealers would bid approximately the area of the windfall profit rectangle for the right to bring cars into this market. Such an outcome was observed in Australia, which auctioned a portion of its quota rights to importers of apparel and footwear. Of course, foreign producers are less likely to accept such a system, because they no longer capture area c. Rather than voluntarily agree to a cutback in their exports under a VER, they are more likely to demand compensation under GATT provisions ruling out actions that impair the value of prior concessions those countries have made.

It is much more common for governments to allocate quota rights arbitrarily, which creates obvious opportunities for graft and corruption. The allocation of quotas can be a source of bribery if importers offer money to government officials in charge of deciding who gets the rights. In the case of VERs the executive branch of government may readily accept the loss of a potential source of revenue from a tariff or quota auction because it gains flexibility in administering trade policy. Specific markets can be protected without having to submit a bill to Congress that would quickly attract protectionist interests from many more industries. VERs can be negotiated country-by-country, rather than applied across the board to all suppliers, which allows allies to receive more favorable treatment or exploits the weak bargaining position of countries with access to few alternative markets.

The variations discussed above, which determine whether the importer, the foreign exporter, or the government gains the tariff-equivalent of the quota, are important from the perspective of economic efficiency. The cost that quantitative restrictions imposes on the importing country obviously is greater if it loses not only the deadweight loss triangles $b + d$ but also area c. Irrespective of this efficiency question, however, there are other aspects of quantitative restrictions that help explain why domestic industries are likely to prefer them over tariff protection, and we now turn to those issues.

Domestic producers enjoy the stability created by a quota. If a foreign innovation allows foreign producers to supply goods at a much lower cost, domestic producers are insulated from the competitive advantage that foreigners would otherwise gain. The foreign supply curve may shift downward, but foreigners cannot gain a larger share of the market by selling at a lower price. Similarly, in a world with volatile exchange rates, if the home currency rises in value internationally, foreigners can charge a lower price in the currency of the importing country and still cover their costs of production. In the first half of the 1980s when the US dollar rose sharply in value, the enhanced competitive position of foreign producers was blunted by VERs negotiated to protect US producers from what many saw as an unpredictable and unexpected change in market conditions. The **US Trade Representative** (USTR) often negotiated VERs with exporting countries under the perceived threat that the US Congress might enact even more severe measures.

Domestic producers also gain from a quota when market demand is expanding. From Figure 5.2 note the outcome of an outward shift in the demand curve when the quantity of imports is fixed. Prices rise and the tariff-equivalent effect of the quantitative restrictions rises. Without a separate legislative vote or executive review, the protective effect of the quantity restriction rises over time.

A further distinction between a tariff and a quota arises if the domestic industry is not perfectly competitive, and producers have market power. Think of the extreme case where demand can be met by imports or by a domestic monopoly. A tariff, unless it is extremely high, provides only limited protection for the local monopoly because the maximum price it can charge is the world price plus the tariff. Any attempt to charge more than that will result in a flood of imports that will decimate its sales volume. A quota, however, offers much more protection for the monopolist. Once the quota amount has been imported, the monopolist has nothing more to fear from foreign suppliers. The monopolist sells less than it would in autarky by the amount of the quota, but once that volume has arrived from abroad, it has an incentive to restrict output to the level at which marginal cost equals marginal revenue and still to charge more than a competitive price. In this way it can maximize profits without regard to further competition from abroad. With the same level of imports, a quota will allow higher prices and monopoly profits than will a tariff. Tariffs are clearly preferable to quotas, then, if elements of monopoly exist in the domestic import-competing industry.

Foreigners may respond to quantitative restrictions by upgrading the product exported to the protected market. Recall the earlier distinction between an *ad valorem* tariff and a specific tariff; the specific tariff has a bigger effect deterring imports of low-cost goods than high-cost goods. Quantitative restrictions have this same effect, comparable to a quota ticket price of a fixed amount per unit imported. The consequent percentage increase in the price of low-cost goods is much greater than the percentage increase in the price of high-cost goods. During the period in which Japanese firms were limited to selling 1.85 million cars per year in the United States, virtually all of the cars exported to the United States were top of the line models and had a variety of expensive options. Japanese producers moved beyond their market niche for small fuel-efficient cars and began to compete in the market for larger sedans, where US producers previously held a more dominant market share. The deadweight loss to the economy also is larger, because of the disproportionally large price increase in the price of low-end goods; recall our earlier demonstration that the loss in efficiency rises as a function of the price increase squared.

Not only may the effectiveness of quotas be weakened for reasons of product upgrading, but country-specific quotas may suffer another defect. When a country's producers have filled the quota allocated to them, as occurs under the Multi-Fibre Agreement (MFA), those

Box 5.3 Super sleuths: assessing the protectiveness of Japanese NTBS

Measuring the effect of nontariff barriers is difficult, because economists cannot simply consult a tariff schedule or compile a list of the maximum allowable quantities of imports. Many restrictions on trade are not based on such formal and clearly stated limitations. In the case of Japan, especially, foreign exporters have complained of informal government and business practices that reduce market access. To assess the importance of such claims, economists have calculated the difference between world prices and domestic prices: the greater the gap by which domestic prices exceed world prices, the more closed to trade the economy must be.

Some studies compare retail prices of identical products in different countries. Because finding identical products often limits the comparisons that are possible, here we consider some examples from work by Sazanami, Urata and Kawai,[8] which compare prices of imports when they arrive at a Japanese port to prices of Japanese products at the factory. While differences in the characteristics of the goods being compared may account for a portion of the observed difference in price, consider some of the price differences they report for 1989. The figures suggest that tariffs account for little of the observed difference. The highest NTB rates of protection are found for agricultural goods, which suggests the Japanese trade regime shifts resources into agriculture and away from more efficient uses such as manufacturing. Significant differences do exist for some manufactures products, but not particularly the most high-tech items that critics might suspect if Japanese restrictions single mindedly targeted those sectors. The absence of significant price gaps between import and domestic prices in the vast majority of industries (for 90 percent of industries, the gap did not exceed 5 percent), makes the exceptions reported here even more striking.

Table 5.3 The Japanese price gap: domestic production versus imports

Sector and product category	In percentage terms		
	Unit value differential	Tariff rate	Implied NTB rate
Food and beverage	280.7	8.2	272.5
Citrus fruits	128.5	14.1	114.4
Milled rice	737.1	0.0	737.1
Beer	143.0	1.7	141.3
Tobacco products	143.0	1.7	141.3
Textiles and light industries	102.5	11.0	91.5
Knit fabrics	8.1	8.1	0.0
Clothing	292.6	10.4	282.2
Plywood	30.7	11.6	19.1
Machinery			
Electric computing equipment	75.8	0.0	75.8
Communication equipment	236.6	0.1	236.5
Semiconductor devices	106.6	0.0	106.6

Source: Yoko Sazanami, Shujiro Urata, and Hiroki Kawai, *Measuring the Costs of Protection in Japan* (Washington, DC: Institute for International Economics, 1995), pp. 6–7.

producers may ship finished products, or almost-finished products, through another country. By changing the country of origin through some minor change in the product, the items no longer count against the quota assigned to the producing country. Chinese shipments through Hong Kong long confounded those enforcing the MFA. Indian shipments through Nepal or Mauritius have raised similar concerns. Establishing the country of origin of a product, and enforcing such rules, has proven increasingly difficult.

Production subsidies

If a government objective is to increase output in a particular industry, economists claim that a first-best solution is to provide a subsidy to producers rather than to impose a tariff. Figure 5.3, shows this case, based on exactly the same initial situation as in Figure 5.1. If a subsidy equal to s (per unit) is paid to producers in Country A, their supply curve shifts from S to S′ because the subsidy reduces average and marginal costs of production. They will expand output to OQ_2. Since the price of oats in Country A remains at P_W consumers continue to purchase OQ_4, and imports are Q_2Q_4. Because the price of oats remains unchanged at P_W, the loss of consumers' surplus does not occur. The subsidy to domestic producers must be included in government expenditures, however, and represents a transfer payment to producers from the rest of the economy. The amount of the subsidy appears in Figure 5.3 as area a plus area b. Taxes in that amount must be levied to pay it. Area a is a pure transfer from taxpayers to producers, but area b involves the same inefficiency in resource use as before and can therefore be regarded as a deadweight loss. Since the subsidy does not reduce consumption, however, we avoid the other part of deadweight loss (area d in Figure 5.1). The conclusion is that a production subsidy is preferable to a tariff on welfare grounds: It has a smaller deadweight loss, and it leaves consumption unchanged.[9]

Although subsidies are a less inefficient means of increasing domestic output, they are relatively uncommon because they are politically unpopular. A tariff raises money for the government, and a quota appears to be costless, but the taxpayers have to provide the funds

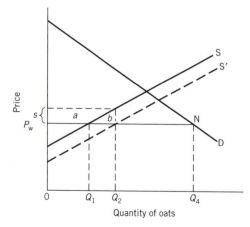

Figure 5.3 The effect of a subsidy: partial equilibrium, small-country case. The domestic supply function shifts down by the amount of the subsidy s, that is, from S to S′. Domestic production rises by Q_1Q_2. The cost of the subsidy to the government is the rectangle consisting of areas a and b. Area a is increased producers' surplus for the domestic industry, and triangle b is a deadweight loss of productive efficiency.

for a subsidy. The domestic industry does not want to be seen as the recipient of a public handout, which must be approved annually in government budget deliberations. Instead, it prefers a tariff or quota (particularly if it is allocated the import rights), which is a more indirect and less obvious form of public support. Subsidies are the least inefficient method of encouraging domestic output, but they are also the least common.

Tariffs in the large-country case

Returning to the subject of tariffs, we can extend the earlier partial equilibrium analysis to deal with the case in which Country A is large enough to influence the world price when it changes the amount of a given commodity it imports, such as oats. We continue to ignore the effects of any change outside of the oats industry.

In Figure 5.4 we simply modify the right panel depicting the import market to show that the foreign supply curve is no longer horizontal at the free trade world price, P_{W0}. If a country imposes a specific tariff of T on imports of oats, the new foreign supply curve shifts up parallel to the original foreign supply curve by the amount of the tariff. The new equilibrium price faced by consumers, P_1, however, does not rise by the amount of the tariff, because at that price consumers are unwilling to buy the quantity M_0 of imports. At P_1, we can subtract the tariff T to see the price net of the tariff that foreign producers receive, P_{W1}. Because the price falls from P_{W0} to P_{W1}, foreigners supply a smaller quantity of imports. Because the price consumers face rises from P_0 to P_1, they only wish to demand this smaller quantity of imports.

What determines whether the tariff primarily is reflected by a rise in price seen by consumers or a fall in price seen by foreign producers? The size of the elasticity of foreign export supply, ϵ, and the elasticity of demand for imports, η, determine this outcome. As derived in the note,[10] we can show the percentage increase in price to consumers more formally as

$$\frac{\Delta P}{P} = \frac{\epsilon}{\epsilon - \eta} \cdot \frac{T}{P}$$

which indicates that a larger elasticity of foreign export supply and a smaller import elasticity of demand (in absolute value) cause a bigger price increase. For example, if ϵ equals 4 and η equals –2, then the fraction $\epsilon / (\epsilon - \eta)$ equals two-thirds, and two-thirds of the tariff is passed forward to consumers and one-third is passed backward to foreign suppliers.

What causes the elasticity of foreign export supply to be larger? In our discussion of the small country case, where ϵ is so large that the supply curve is a horizontal line, we noted that foreign producers have many good options or alternative markets where they can sell this product. If the net-of-tariff price offered by Country A falls, foreign suppliers divert their sales to other markets. A high foreign export supply elasticity also may indicate that a small drop in price will lead to a large increase in sales in its domestic market. Or, the inputs used in producing this good may easily be transferred to other uses; producers of oats may plant wheat instead, use the same machinery to harvest it and store it in the same grain bins.

Why may the demand for imports be less elastic? Consumers in Country A may not switch easily to substitutes when the price of oats rises, if alternative products do not taste as good or offer less nutrition. Domestic production of oats may be very unresponsive to the price if the limited amount of available land already is devoted to growing oats. Thus, the consumer has few alternatives other than buying from the foreign supplier.

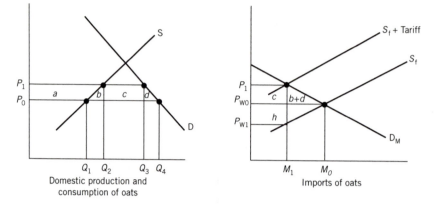

Figure 5.4 The effect of a tariff: partial equilibrium, large-country case. When a large country imposes a tariff, a portion of it results in higher domestic prices, a loss to consumers of $a + b + c + d$ and a gain to domestic producers of a. Some portion of the tariff is borne by foreign producers who now receive a lower price, P_{w1}, for their exports. The government gains tariff revenue of $c + h$. The net efficiency effect is $h - b - d$.

The extent to which the tariff drives up the price faced in Country A is important in determining who within Country A benefits and who loses from the tariff and whether the country as a whole may benefit. As shown in the left panel of Figure 5.4, the rise in price causes consumers to lose areas $a + b + c + d$, and producers to gain area a. The tariff revenue gained by the government is no longer just equal to area c. Rather, in the right panel of Figure 5.4 we can see tariff revenue collected is $c + h$. Adding these three effects together shows that the net economic efficiency effect on Country A is $h - b - d$. Areas b and d still represent deadweight losses from less efficient production and consumption choices, but Country A now gains area h at the expense of producers in the rest of the world. We can refer to area h as a terms of trade gain, because Country A is now able to pay foreigners a lower net-of-tariff price for the goods that it imports. For a given import demand elasticity, this terms of trade gain is likely to be greater the less elastic is the foreign export supply curve, that is, the more dependent foreigners are on sales to Country A.

Whether a country gains from imposing a tariff depends upon whether its trading partners retaliate and impose tariffs of their own. A trade war that leaves all countries worse off is a likely outcome, such as the world experienced during the 1930s. Nevertheless, the economic power of individual countries is not symmetric, and some may be able to gain at the expense of others. The world as a whole loses, though, and that is one of the key motivations for establishing international rules that limit the ability of individual countries to exploit that power.

General equilibrium analysis

Although the foregoing analysis has enabled us to reach many useful conclusions about the nature and effects of tariffs, it does leave out some potentially significant repercussions. For example, when a tariff causes the output of a particular commodity to rise in Country A, resources must be drawn into that industry, but we do not see what happens in other industries from which those resources must be taken. Assuming full employment, output of other commodities must fall. Similarly, when Country A's imports decline, other countries will themselves have less money to spend on imports; therefore Country A's exports will also decline. Import tariffs have many such effects that reverberate through the economy. To deal with these in a comprehensive way we must utilize a form of general equilibrium analysis.

One approach is to use the tools of analysis that we developed in Chapter 2, the production-possibility curve and community indifference map. These tools bring us back to the abstract world of two countries, two commodities, two factors, and perfect competition. Also, assume that the tariff revenue is redistributed to consumers, which means we do not need to introduce a separate set of preferences for the government.

The small-country case

It is convenient to start with a small country, where the world terms of trade remain unchanged. The reader will recall that we reached the conclusion in Chapter 2 that in free-trade equilibrium, assuming only two commodities, food and cloth, Country A will maximize its welfare by producing at the point where its domestic ratio of marginal costs equals the world exchange ratio, and then by engaging in trade in order to reach the highest possible indifference curve. Such a free-trade equilibrium is shown in Figure 5.5, with the world price ratio shown by the slope of TT, production at point P_1, and consumption at point C_1, where TT is tangent to the indifference curve i_2. Country A exports cloth and imports food.

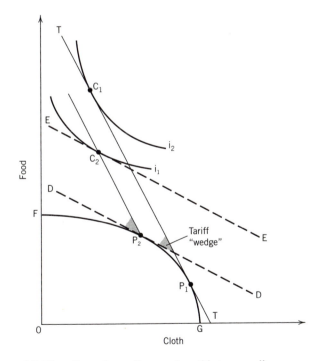

Figure 5.5 The effects of a tariff: general equilibrium, small-country case. With free trade this country produces at P_1 and consumes at C_1. The slope of TT is the price ratio between the two goods. The tariff shifts the internal price ratio to the slope of DD and EE, while the world price ratio remains the slope of TT and the line parallel to it on the left. This country now produces at P_2 and consumes at C_2, the volume of trade being sharply reduced by the tariff. The "tariff wedge" refers to the difference between the two price ratios, represented by the differences between the slopes of the lines where the wedge appears.

Now if Country A imposes a tariff on its imports of food, the first effect will be to increase the domestic price of food, thus causing a divergence between the domestic exchange ratio and the world exchange ratio. We show this effect in Figure 5.5; the domestic exchange ratio becomes equal to the slope of DD, which is flatter than TT, indicating a higher relative price of food. The tariff drives a wedge between the domestic and external price ratios; geometrically, that wedge can be seen as the angle between the two price lines. The higher price of food induces firms to expand food production and to reduce cloth production. The production point moves to P_2, where the domestic price line (DD) is tangent to the production-possibility curve.

Because we are assuming that the world price ratio remains unchanged, international trade takes place along the line P_2C_2 (parallel to TT). A new equilibrium in consumption is reached when two conditions are satisfied: (1) a domestic price line, EE, whose slope is equal to the tariff-distorted domestic price ratio, is tangent to a community indifference curve; and (2) the world price line, P_2C_2, intersects the community indifference curve at its point of tangency with the domestic price line, EE. These two conditions are both satisfied at the point C_2 in Figure 5.5. Technically, the first condition guarantees that the marginal rate of substitution in consumption equals the domestic price ratio facing consumers; the second condition satisfies the requirement that the domestic price ratio diverges from the world price ratio exactly in proportion to the tariff.

In the new equilibrium, Country A continues to export cloth and import food but in smaller quantities than before. The tariff has stimulated domestic production of food, reducing Country A's dependence on food imports. It has also reduced domestic output and exports of cloth and reduced welfare, as indicated by the movement to the lower indifference curve, from i_2 to i_1. Thus we reach the same conclusion in both general and partial equilibrium analysis: in the small-country case a tariff reduces national welfare.

The large-country case

When the country imposing a tariff is large enough to influence the world price of what it buys, we must consider what effect a tariff will have on the world price ratio. To continue the same example, when Country A levies a tariff on food, the result may be that the world price of food falls relative to the price of cloth. In that event, for a given *ad valorem* tariff, the domestic price of food will not rise as much as before. Thus the shift in production will be somewhat smaller. We illustrate this outcome in Figure 5.6, where conditions are the same as in the case just described except that the tariff now causes the world price ratio to change from the slope of the line TT to the slope of the line P_3C_3. Production takes place at P_3. (Note that the tariff is the same proportion as before, as measured by the size of the wedge.)

International trade now takes place at the world price ratio (i.e. along the line P_3C_3). A new equilibrium in consumption is reached at point C_3, where the tariff-distorted domestic price line is tangent to a community indifference curve, and the world price line also passes through this point of tangency. As drawn in Figure 5.6, Country A reaches a higher indifference curve as a result of the tariff. This result is not inevitable, however. It depends on the magnitude of the change in the world exchange ratio. Intuitively, one can see that country A benefits from the tariff when its gain from the improved terms of trade outweighs its loss from a less efficient use of domestic resources. How much its terms of trade will improve depends in turn on domestic and foreign elasticities of demand and supply.

Any gain, however, is at the expense of the rest of the world. If other countries act in concert, they can retaliate by imposing tariffs of their own, thus causing the terms of trade

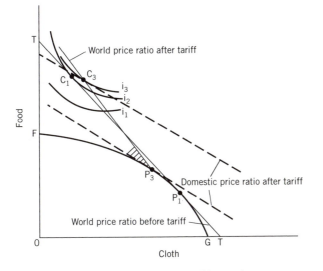

Figure 5.6 The effects of a tariff: general equilibrium, large-country case. This graph is similar to the previous figure except for the fact that this country is large enough to impose some of the tariff on the rest of the world in the form of worsened terms of trade. The country imposing the tariff enjoys improved terms of trade, as the slope of the world trading line changes from that of TT to that of P_3C_3. This country produces at P_3 and consumes at C_3, which is a slight welfare improvement from the free-trade outcome, because of the terms-of-trade improvement.

to shift back the other way. The terms of trade may return to the free-trade ratio (not a necessary result), but world trade is greatly reduced and so is world welfare. A trade agreement for the mutual, reciprocal reduction of tariffs would be beneficial to both countries.

The effective rate of protection

Thus far we have assumed that a given commodity is wholly produced in one country. For example, a yard of cloth is the output that results from using a certain combination of inputs of primary factors of production (land, labor, capital) in that country. We have ignored the case in which some of the inputs, or some parts of the commodity, are imported. Thus we have ignored the large and important trade in intermediate products.

For many purposes, this omission is harmless. For analyzing the protective effect of tariffs, the treatment of intermediate products makes a great deal of difference. The key point is that when a producer has the option of importing some of the material inputs required for the production of a given product, the *ad valorem* tariff on that product may not accurately indicate the protection being provided to the producer. A distinction needs to be drawn between the nominal tariff rate, which is just the usual *ad valorem* tariff or its equivalent, and the effective rate of protection (ERP).[11]

The ERP refers to the level of protection being provided to a particular process of production by the given nominal tariffs on a product and on material inputs used in its production. We are particularly interested in how a set of tariffs affects the firm's value-added or what is available to cover primary factor costs, such as payments for the services of labor and capital, and also the net profit of the firm. We define the ERP as the percentage increase

Box 5.4   Tariff escalation and other complications

The tendency for countries to levy higher tariffs on fully processed goods than on raw materials is a fairly general characteristic of current trade policy. The WTO provides the following summary of tariff escalation in several countries for the textile and leather sector.

Table 5.4 Tariff escalation in the textile and leather sector

	Initial processing	*Semi-processed*	*Fully processed*
EU	0.9	6.7	9.7
US	2.2	9.8	10.3
Japan	9.8	6.8	12.0
Argentina	11.4	18.8	22.4
Brazil	10.6	18.7	22.2
Mexico	12.7	17.9	31.4
Korea	5.2	8.8	11.4
India	25.1	28.5	34.2
South Africa	5.4	20.7	29.1

Source: WTO, *Overview of Developments in the International Trade Environment, Annual Report* by the Director General, WT/TPR/OV/8, November 2002, pp. 44–6.

Such escalation can be expected to yield high effective rates of protection in fully-processed goods, in this case apparel and footwear.

Tariff escalation plays a role in a variety of policy debates. In the United States, lobbying over tuna tariffs pit one company, Bumble Bee Seafoods, against Charlie the Tuna of Starkist (or Con-Agra Foods versus H.J. Heinz).[12] Bumble Bee wanted to retain a tariff of 12.5 percent on canned tuna from Ecuador. That would adversely affect Starkist. Although Bumble Bee also operates in Ecuador, it simply guts, clean, and cooks the tuna, to ship them as fillets that will be canned in Puerto Rico or California. The US tariff on fillets is 1.5 percent. Such tariff escalation gives substantial protection to the US canning operations of Bumble Bee.

The tuna tiff raises other issues regarding preferential trade agreements that we examine in Chapter 7. While Ecuador sought treatment comparable to Mexico and Trinidad–Tobago under the special agreements applied to those countries, Philippine and Thai tuna exporters feared that Ecuador would claim a large share of the US market at their expense. These Asian producers already complained of the EU tariff of 24 percent that they faced, while suppliers from former European colonies had duty-free access to the EU market. In addition, Chicken of the Sea brand tuna is owned by a Thai company, and it currently benefits from processing tuna in American Samoa, which has tariff-free access to the US market. Without high tariffs levied on products elsewhere in the world, processing in American Samoa could become uneconomical. Congress addressed this situation in 2002 by leaving the tariff on canned tuna unchanged, but it eliminated the tariff on tuna in foil pouches, the product Starkist produces in Ecuador.

A final complication to note with respect to tuna policy is that the US restriction actually is a **tariff rate quota**, a policy combination particularly common for agricultural commodities in most countries. In this case, foreign suppliers are subject to a 6 percent tariff on imports up to 20 percent of the previous year's US production of canned tuna. For imports beyond that amount, the tariff becomes 12.5 percent (if packed in water). Given that US imports substantially exceed the quota, we predict that the price in the US market will be determined by the 12.5 percent tariff, but not the 6.25 percent tariff. The lower tariff provides a windfall gain, either to foreign exporters or to US importers, as discussed in the case of quotas generally.

in an industry's value added per unit of output that results from a country's tariff structure. The standard of comparison is value added under free trade.

An example will help to explain the meaning of this definition. Suppose the world price of shoes is $20 and that it takes $12 worth of leather at the free-trade world price to make a pair of shoes. In the manufacture of shoes, then, value added at world prices is $8. Now suppose Country A levies a nominal tariff of 30 percent on shoe imports but allows leather to be imported duty free. The price of shoes in Country A would rise to $26 (i.e. the world price plus the tariff), and consequently the value-added of domestic shoe producers would become $14. In other words, they could incur factor costs of $14 and still be competitive with a foreign firm whose factor costs were $8. Value added in Country A can be 75 percent larger than value-added at the free-trade price [($14 − $8)/$8 = 75 percent]. Thus the ERP is 75 percent, while the nominal tariff is only 30 percent. Compare a shoe-producing firm in Country A and its free-trade competitor:

	Firm in Country A	*Free-trade competitor*
Shoe price	$26	$20
Leather input	$12	$12
Value-added	$14	$8

We expect that high effective rates of protection will attract resources into industries where a country has production costs much higher than abroad, ie where it has a comparative disadvantage. As a result, the country's economic efficiency falls.

Note that a tariff on leather would reduce the effective rate of protection for shoes. The reason is obvious: a tariff on leather increases the price of leather in Country A and raises A firms' costs of production, which means value-added must be smaller for A firms still to sell shoes at $26. In our example, a 20 percent nominal tariff on leather would lead to the following result:

	Firm in Country A	*Free-trade competitor*
Shoe price	$26.00	$20.00
Leather input	$14.40	$12.00
Value-added	$11.60	$8.00

The **effective tariff** rate on shoes has fallen from 75 percent to 45 percent [($11.60 – $8) / $8 = 45 percent] as a result of the tariff on leather. Shoe producers in Country A will tend to favor tariffs on shoes but oppose tariffs on leather.

A formula for calculating the effective tariff rate follows from the above discussion:

$$e_j = \frac{t_j - \sum_i a_{ij} \cdot t_i}{1 - \sum_i a_{ij}}$$

where we define the terms above and apply them to the shoe example:

e_j = the effective rate of protection in industry j, shoe production
t_j = the nominal tariff rate in industry j = 30 percent tariff on shoes
t_i = the nominal tariff rate in industry i = 20 percent tariff on leather
a_{ij} = the share of inputs from industry i in the value of output of industry j at free-trade prices = ($12/20) = 0.60

and the sigma term, Σ, represents summation over all the necessary intermediate inputs i. Therefore the effective rate of protection for shoes is

$$e_j = \frac{30\% - 0.60(20\%)}{1 - 0.60} = \frac{18\%}{0.40} = \frac{0.18}{0.40} = 45\%$$

In this example we had only a single intermediate input, leather. In actual practice, a given product has many intermediate inputs, each with its own nominal tariff rate. The formula uses the share of each such input (a_{ij}) to weight the nominal tariff rates in forming the sum ($\Sigma a_{ij} t_i$).

The tariff structures of many countries show a systematic pattern in which nominal tariff rates increase as the stage of production advances – that is, tariff rates are low (or zero) on raw materials, higher on semi-finished products, and highest on finished manufactures. Such a pattern in nominal tariff rates produces an even greater escalation in effective tariff rates, with very high protection being accorded the higher stages of manufacture. Industrial countries have been accused of using such a tariff structure to preserve their lead in manufacturing and to keep the less-developed countries from developing exports of finished manufactures.

Although ERPs are higher than nominal rates in the examples above, they can also be lower and may even be negative. In our shoe industry example, if the nominal rate on leather were increased to 60 percent, then the ERP for shoes would be –15 percent. The economic meaning of such a rate is that a firm must pay such high nominal tariffs on its imported inputs that it is actually at a disadvantage in comparison to its free-trade competitors in the outside world. That is, its value-added margin must be less than that of a free-trade competitor. The disadvantage of the domestic firm is shown in the following comparison:

	Firm in Country A	Free-trade competitor
Shoe price	$26.00	$20.00
Leather input	$19.20	$12.00
Value-added	$6.80	$8.00

To compete with a foreign firm whose factor costs are $8.00, the firm in Country A must hold its factor costs to $6.80.

Negative effective tariff rates often turn up among a nation's export products. The nominal tariff applicable for an export product is zero because it is being sold in foreign countries at the world market price. Therefore, if firms producing the export item use any imported inputs at all that are subject to tariffs, their effective tariff rate is negative, which means that there is an implicit tax on exports. Suppose, for example, that Thailand exports rice at the world market price, whereas rice production uses imported inputs such as fertilizer, water pumps, and tractors, on which nominal tariffs are levied. The result is that the value-added margin of Thai rice producers is lower, because of the nation's tariff structure, than it would be under full free trade. The effective tariff on rice is negative.

Box 5.5 Effective rates of protection and the Indonesian bicycle boom

In the late 1980s and early 1990s, Indonesian bicycle exports grew rapidly, fostered by special tariff preferences on sales in the European market. This expansion occurred without major promotional efforts by the government, and it certainly raised hopes that Indonesian sales to the US market might take off. In that market, however, Indonesian bicycles were granted no special preferences in competition with Chinese bicycles. What factors might affect the competitive positions of these two producers?

The concept of effective rate of protection provides important insights. The cost of an $80 bicycle is accounted for by $25 of imported parts (gears, chain wheels, and hubs), $40 of domestically produced parts, and $15 of value-added in the bicycle sector. Indonesia imposes a tariff of 40 percent on bicycles and 30 percent on bicycle parts. Also, domestically produced parts are $4 higher than free-trade prices due to protection provided to the domestic monopoly producer of steel.

We can organize this information to reflect three situations: production when no tariffs are imposed, traditional production for a protected home market, and modern production for the European export market.

Table 5.5 The economics of Indonesian bicycle assembly

	No tariffs	Home market	Exporter
Price of bicycle	$80.00	$80 + 40% tariff = $112	$80.00
Price of imported parts	$25.00	$25 + 30% tariff = $32.50	$32.50
Price of domestic parts	$36.00	$36 + $4* = $40.00	$40.00
Value added	$19.00	$39.50	$7.50
Effective rate of protection		108%	–60%

*Protection of the domestic steel industry causes the price of domestic parts to rise by $4.

The traditional producer serving a protected home market can have costs 108 percent greater than European producers (39.50 / 19.00 – 1) × 100, a high effective rate of protection that results from an escalating tariff structure. Is that market situation still relevant, though? Only if there are restrictions on which firms can sell in the domestic market do we expect the domestic price to be as high as $112, because some

Indonesian producers (often with Japanese or Taiwanese partners) now are efficient enough to produce for the export market.

What return do those producing for the European export market receive? If exporters are unable to receive a rebate for the $7.50 tariff paid on imported parts, the effective rate of protection for exporters is –60 percent; their costs must be only 40 percent of European producers' costs. If Indonesian exporters in fact receive prompt payment of such a rebate for bicycles that are exported, their value-added can rise to $15 and the effective rate of protection is –21 percent. The higher cost of domestic parts still imposes a significant penalty on Indonesian exporters.[13]

Many developing countries have strong comparative advantages in final products which nevertheless are not exported, because they impose a tariff or otherwise restrict imports of inputs where they have a comparative disadvantage. A partial response to this problem is the establishment of free trade zones, which allow producers to claim a rebate for duties paid on imported inputs if the producers export their final output.

A potential problem in calculating ERPs is the assumption, made in all input–output analyses, that the input coefficients are fixed constants, unaffected by changes in prices. We know that international trade causes changes in relative prices and shifts in the allocation of resources. It seems likely that these changes will also affect the amounts of various inputs used to produce a particular product, but ERP calculations do not allow for this influence.

Export subsidies

The issues presented thus far suggest that government regulation of international trade is intended solely to restrict imports. Although that remains the dominant form of intervention, governments sometimes attempt to encourage exports through subsidies. This may occur because of a desire to improve a country's trade account, aid a politically powerful industry, or help a depressed region in which an export industry is located. The subsidy may be a simple cash payment to exporters, but frequently is more indirect or subtle. Research and development grants, favorable financing or tax treatment, or a variety of other government benefits may be provided to encourage exports. In order to simplify this discussion, however, assume that the subsidy takes the form of a fixed cash payment for each unit of a product which is exported.

Figure 5.8 illustrates the effects of an export subsidy in a competitive market, where we allow the country to be large enough to affect the world price of the good. Just as we derived the import demand curve as a residual from domestic demand less domestic supply, here we show the export supply curve in the right panel, a residual from domestic supply less domestic demand. The free-trade world price P_0 is given by the intersection of country A's export supply curve with the demand curve for the rest of the world. Exports are equal to domestic production of Q_3 minus consumption of Q_2.

We show the effect of the export subsidy by a downward shift in the export supply curve; exporters will accept a lower price in foreign markets than they do in the domestic market, because the difference is made up by the government payment. The result of the subsidy is that the quantity of exports rises, as foreign consumers respond to the drop in price from P_0 to P_{w1}. In the domestic market, however, the price rises to P_1. The higher price discourages

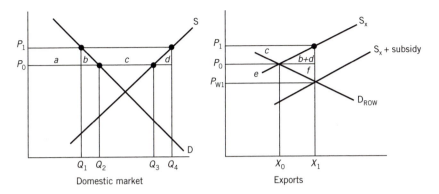

Figure 5.7 The effect of an export subsidy. Introducing an export subsidy results in producers
expanding output from Q_3 to Q_4 and diverting sales from the domestic market to the
foreign market, Q_2 minus Q_1. Foreign buyers benefit from a lower world price, P_{W1}, but
domestic consumers face a higher price, P_1, as exports rise from X_0 to X_1.

domestic consumption, which falls from Q_2 to Q_1, and encourages domestic production,
which rises from Q_3 to Q_4. These change in domestic production and consumption are what
make more of the good available to export.

The distributional effects of the subsidy within Country A are that domestic consumers
lose areas $a + b$, while domestic producers gain areas $a + b + c$. In addition, the cost of the
subsidy to the government is $c + b + d + e + f$, shown in the right panel. A key effect of the
subsidy is to drive down the price Country A receives on foreign markets, and areas $e + f$
represent this terms of trade loss to A. Part of the subsidy is a transfer from the government
to its own producers, given by areas $c + b + d$. Area d is a deadweight loss because it represents
the rising marginal cost of A's production, which exceeds what is paid by customers in the
rest of the world. Area b is also a deadweight loss; it represents not only a loss to consumers
and a gain to producers, but also a loss to the government. The net effect is that Country A
loses $e + f + b + d$. The drop in price internationally provides an obvious benefit to customers
in the rest of the world, but producers in the rest of the world will be worse off. Direct
government subsidies of manufactured products are regarded as an unfair trade practice under
the GATT, and countervailing duties can be imposed on subsidized exports if producers in
the importing country are injured.[14]

Determining what government assistance constitutes an unfair subsidy has proven quite
contentious in practice. Typically, those who lodge a complaint must distinguish between
practices that provide a benefit to a specific industry, in contrast to practices that are
available to all industries. For example, a lower corporate tax rate or a lower interest rate
that benefits all industries does not represent a countervailable subsidy. The subsidies code
adopted in the Tokyo Round of international trade negotiations, however, suggests that
subsidies need not benefit only exported goods to be countervailable. In the early 1980s US
steelmakers' complaints about European subsidization of state-owned enterprises represented
an early test of this new clause, but the negotiated resolution of those cases did not clarify
the applicability of limits on state assistance.

Another key issue to be negotiated multilaterally is any limitation on the favorable
financing provided on export sales. Such financing is especially important in the sale of large
capital goods, such as airplanes or power plants. An agreement among OECD countries sets
conditions on the maximum length and minimum interest rates on commercial terms for

---

Box 5.6 EU sugar subsidies and export displacement

An important example of the effects of export subsidies is provided by the EU Common Agricultural Policy (CAP). Sugar is a commodity where export subsidies have been particularly large. High EU target or intervention prices domestically mean that producers have an incentive to produce more than they would at world prices. For given national quotas the EU is obligated to purchase sugar. To reduce the need for such purchases, imports (aside from preferential trade agreements) were eliminated by a variable levy on foreign sugar that made it noncompetitive. In addition, the EU subsidizes the exportation of sugar. This complex scheme allows the domestic price to be two to three times the world price. For example, in 1999 the world price was €200 per ton while the intervention price was €631. Of most relevance in this discussion is the fact that the EU no longer is a net importer of sugar. Rather, it now is the second largest exporter of sugar in the world, accounting for 20 percent of all exports.

Why does such a policy attract world attention? Many developing countries with a comparative advantage in sugar production are highly dependent on sugar exports as a source of foreign exchange. Because the price elasticities of supply and demand in world markets are low, the large increase in quantity supplied by the EU has a severe depressing effect on the world price. Although not all of these exports are subsidized, economists estimate that eliminating the subsidies would allow world sugar prices to rise by 20 percent, a major boon to developing countries.[15]

---

such loans. Negotiations under the Doha Development agenda discussed in Chapter 8 are intended to extend such discipline to a wider set of countries.

A long-running conflict between Canada and the United States demonstrates other difficulties that exist in interpreting subsidy provisions. In the case of softwood lumber production, British Columbia allows local firms to harvest lumber on provincially owned land in exchange for stumpage fees which are considerably lower than those prevailing in the United States. These cost savings are available on all lumber cut on this land, including that which is sold to Canadian buyers. Canadians argue that such a benefit is a windfall gain that does not alter the marginal cost of production or optimal level of output. The US lumber industry, however, views the lower Canadian stumpage fees as an unfair cost advantage for British Columbia, and argues that a subsidy exists which calls for a **countervailing duty**. This situation has given rise to several countervailing duty cases in the 1980s and 1990s. At one point the US Department of Commerce ruled that a 15 percent subsidy margin existed, but the case was resolved by Canada levying a 15 percent export tax. Subsequent rulings by the GATT and by a binational trade dispute settlement panel set up under the 1989 US–Canada Free Trade Agreement both favored the Canadian position. Further WTO action still has not resolved this case.

Subsidies also are viewed as an important tool of strategic trade policy in industries where economies of scale exist. We return to that topic in the following chapter.

Export Tariffs

Although governments usually design trade policies to reduce imports or encourage exports, some countries have applied tariffs to exports.[16] Less developed countries sometimes do so

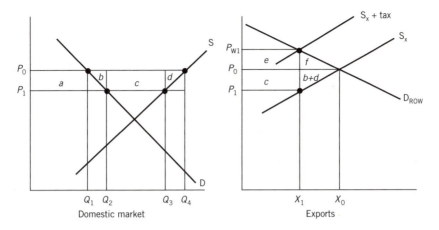

Figure 5.8 The effect of an export tax. Introducing an export tax results in producers contracting output from Q_4 to Q_3 and domestic consumers purchasing Q_2 rather than Q_1. Exports fall from X_0 to X_1 as domestic producers respond to the lower domestic price P_1 and foreign purchasers to the higher world price P_{w1}.

in order to raise revenues. Export taxes may be less costly to collect than other taxes, and they often are perceived as falling on wealthy landowners in the case of agricultural exports. **Export tariffs** may also be used to protect consumers from increases in world prices of an export commodity. In the early 1970s, President Nixon imposed an **embargo** on US soybean exports to keep US food prices low. In the late 1970s, and again in the 1980s, India used an export tax on tea to hold down prices to domestic consumers when world tea prices increased sharply. Sometimes the favored domestic purchasers are processors, who are being encouraged to create more value-added at home rather than export raw materials. For example, an Argentine tax on the export of soybeans was intended to keep prices of beans low for crushers of soybean oil and meal, and an Indonesian ban on rattan exports promoted production of furniture domestically.

Some of these effects of an export tax can be shown in Figure 5.8. In contrast to the case of an export subsidy, now the export supply curve shifts upward by the amount of the tax. As shown in the right panel exports fall from X to X_1 as world price rises from P_0 to P_W, and the domestic falls to price P_1. In the left panel this price decline causes consumers to expand purchases from Q_1 to Q_2 and to gain area a. Producers reduce output from Q_4 to Q_3 and lose areas $a + b + c + d$. The government collects tax revenue of $c + e$, as shown in the right panel. Area e represents a terms of trade gain, and as demand in the rest of the world becomes less elastic relative to export supply, this gain will be larger. Areas b and d are deadweight losses: lower domestic production releases resources that produce a lower value of output elsewhere in the economy, area d, and greater domestic consumption shifts output to those who value it less than it is worth in foreign markets, area b. The net effect on Country A is $e - b - d$. An export tax may allow a country to exploit its dominant position in an export market. Because the tax applies to all of the country's exporters, the terms of trade improvement can be achieved without forming a cartel among all producers. The distributional effects differ from those with a successful cartel, though, because with an export tax the government gains while producers lose. As in the case of a tariff, the gain comes at the expense of other countries, and the world as a whole is less efficient, by areas $b + d + f$.

Summary of key concepts

1   A tariff is a tax levied on imported goods. For a small country that cannot affect international prices, levying a tariff will reduce its national income or welfare by encouraging too much domestic production and discouraging domestic consumption. While producers' surplus and government tariff revenue rise, the loss in consumers' surplus from the rise in domestic prices is even greater.

2   A quota limits the amount of goods that can be imported. Imposing a quota also drives up the domestic price, which benefits domestic producers and reduces consumers' surplus. The net loss to the economy will be greater than with a tariff that yields the same reduction in imports if foreigners are able to claim the tariff-equivalent rent or revenue created by the quota.

3   The same expansion in domestic production achieved by a tariff or a quota can be accomplished at lower cost with a production subsidy that does not distort consumption choices. Production subsidies are less common because they must be financed with tax revenues and are subject to closer and more frequent political scrutiny than trade measures.

4   A country large enough to affect international prices may improve its terms of trade by levying a tariff. This gain from a lower world price of imports will be larger when the elasticity of demand for imports is large relative to the foreign export elasticity of supply; the market power of the importing country that levies the tariff is greater when importers have more alternatives than exporters. Foreign retaliation may reduce or eliminate such gains. The world as a whole loses.

5   The nominal tariff rate may be a misleading indication of how much a set of tariffs encourages an industry, once we recognize the role of intermediate inputs. The effective rate of protection indicates how much higher value added in an industry can be compared to free trade. While the effective rate of protection often exceeds the nominal rate of protection for many finished manufactured goods, it is likely to be negative for export goods.

6   Export subsidies hurt domestic consumers and help domestic producers. In the case of a competitive industry, the export subsidy unambiguously reduces national welfare, especially when the additional exports reduce the world price of the product.

7   Export taxes help domestic consumers and hurt domestic producers. In the case of a competitive industry large enough to affect world prices, the export tax may raise national welfare if improved terms of trade are sufficient to offset deadweight losses from less efficient production and consumption choices. The world as a whole loses.

Questions for study and review

1   Explain how import restrictions affect domestic producers and consumers. How are the concepts of producers' surplus and consumers' surplus useful in demonstrating these effects?

2   You are given the following information about copper in the European Union:

	Situation with tariff	Situation without tariff
World price	1.50 euros per kg	1.50 euros per kg
Tariff (specific)	0.15 euros per kg	0
EU domestic price	1.65 euros per kg	1.50 euros per kg
EU consumption	200 million kg	230 million kg
EU production	160 million kg	100 million kg

Draw a supply–demand diagram on the basis of these data and indicate imports with and without the tariff. Calculate:

(a) The gain to EU consumers from removing the tariff.
(b) The loss to EU producers from removing the tariff.
(c) The loss of tariff revenue to government when the tariff is removed.
(d) The net gain or loss to the EU economy as a whole.

Explain briefly the meaning of each calculation. In the case of (d), what implicit assumptions do you make in reporting a net result?

3   Problem 2 assumes that the EU acts as a small country in the world copper market, because the world price remains constant at 1.50 euros per kilo. Assume instead that with the 0.15 euro tariff the world price becomes 1.45 euros per kilo, EU consumption falls to 210 million kilos and EU production rises to 140 million kilos. Show that new situation diagrammatically and calculate the effect of the tariff on EU consumers, EU producers, government, and the economy as a whole.

4   Suppose the electronic calculator industry faces severe foreign competition, and asks you to prepare a position paper its lobbyist can use to seek government assistance. Contrast the consequences of imposing a quota, negotiating a VER, and providing a production subsidy.

5   At free-trade prices, a widget sells for $20 and contains $8 worth of tin and $6 worth of rubber. In Country A nominal tariff rates are:

Widgets   40 percent
Tin   20 percent
Rubber   10 percent

What is the effective rate of protection on widgets in Country A? Explain briefly the economic meaning of your result. If this country were a large exporter of widgets, how would that affect your interpretation of the effective rate of protection received by this industry?

6   Draw the supply-and-demand graph for a product for which there is both a tariff and a quota, a situation that applies to many agricultural and textile/apparel

products. (Hint: this graph can be derived from Figures 5.1 and 5.2 in this chapter.) Explain what effect the tariff has on the quantity of imports, the price of imports, and the welfare effects of these trade restrictions.

7　Given your understanding of the different effects of tariffs and quotas, why has the World Trade Organization attempted to reduce sharply the current reliance on quotas and other quantitative restrictions?

8　Who gains and who loses from the imposition of an export tax? For countries that have constitutional prohibitions against imposing export taxes, have they lost an effective trade policy tool? Explain.

Suggested further reading

For government reports that you can access from the US International Trade Commission's internet site, see the following overviews that include many case studies and general assessments of the effects of trade barriers:

- US International Trade Commission, *The Economic Effects of Significant U.S. Import Restraints: Third Biannual Update 2002*, Investigation No. 332–225, Publication 3519, June 2002.
- US International Trade Commission, *The Economic Effects of Antidumping and Countervailing Duty Orders and Suspension Agreements*, Investigation No. 332–344, Publication 2900, June 1995.

http://www.usitc.gov/332s/332index.htm#SECTION%20332
http://www.usitc.gov/wais/reports/arc/w2900.htm

Notes

1　See Arnold Harberger, "Reflections on Uniform Taxation," in R. Jones and A. Krueger, eds, *The Political Economy of International Trade, Essays in Honour of Robert E. Baldwin* (Oxford: Basil Blackwell, 1990), pp. 75–89, and Arvind Panagariya and Dani Rodrik, "Political-Economy Arguments for a Uniform Tariff," *International Economic Review*, 1993.
2　See G. Hufbauer and K. Elliott, *Measuring the Costs of Protection in the United States.* (Washington, DC: Institute for International Economics, 1994), D. Tarr and M. Morkre, *Aggregate Costs to the United States of Tariffs and Quotas on Imports* (Washington, DC: Federal Trade Commission, 1984), and J. Mutti, "Aspects of Unilateral Trade Policy and Factor Adjustment Costs," *Review of Economics and Statistics*, 60 no. 1, February 1978, pp. 102–10. These studies apply a somewhat different framework from that given in the text, because they do not assume that imports and domestic goods are perfect substitutes. For a recent application of the imperfect substitutes framework to European trade barriers, see Patrick Messerlin, *Measuring the Cost of Protection in Europe* (Washington, DC: Institute for International Economics, 2001).
3　Gary Hufbauer and Ben Goodrich, "Steel: Big Problems, Better Solutions," Institute for International Economics, Policy Brief PB01–9, July 2001.
4　Robert Matthews, "Foreign Steelmakers' Prices Rise," *The Wall Street Journal*, October 8, 2002, p. A8.
5　Geoff Winestock and Neil Kring, Jr., "EU Aims at White House in Retaliation to Steel Tariff," *The Wall Street Journal*, March 22, 2002, p. A2.
6　Robert Matthews, "China Could Spur Steel Production," *The Wall Street Journal*, Nov. 25, 2002, p. A2.
7　Robert Crandall, "Import Quotas and the Automobile Industry: The Cost of Protectionism," *Brookings Review*, Summer 1984.

8 Yoko Sazanami, Shujiro Urata, and Hiroki Kawai, *Measuring the Costs of Protection in Japan* (Washington DC: Institute for International Economics, 1995).

9 This judgment assumes that tax revenues can be raised without imposing some deadweight loss on the economy. Public finance economists typically challenge this assumption and in the United States suggest that for every dollar of tax revenue raised, the cost to the economy is $1.23. See Charles Ballard, Don Fullerton, John Shoven and John Whalley, *A General Equilibrium Model for Tax Policy Evaluation* (The University of Chicago Press, 1985).

10 The expression for the change in price that results from the imposition of the tariff can be derived from a linear demand curve, $m - nP$, and a linear supply curve, $u + vP$. Setting quantity demanded equal to quantity supplied gives the initial equilibrium price as $P_0 = (m - u) / (v + n)$. When the tariff is imposed the supply curve becomes $u + v(P - T)$ and the new price faced by consumers is $P_1 = (m - u) / (v + n) + Tv / (v + n)$. The change in price, ΔP, equals $Tv / (v + n)$, or in percentage terms $\Delta P / P = [v / (v + n)] T / P$. The expression $v / (v + n)$ is written in terms of the slopes of the supply and demand curves, but if the numerator and denominator of the fraction are each multiplied by P / Q, then $Pv / Q = \epsilon$, the elasticity of supply and $Pn / Q = -\eta$, the elasticity of demand, and $\Delta P / P = [\epsilon / (\epsilon - \eta)] T / P$.

11 For estimates of nominal and effective rates of protection for the United States, Japan, and the European Community both before and after the effects of the Tokyo GATT Round tariff cuts, see Alan Deardorff and Robert M. Stern, "The Effects of the Tokyo Round on the Structure of Protection," in R. E. Baldwin and Anne O. Krueger, eds, *The Structure and Evolution of Recent U.S. Trade Policy* (Chicago: University of Chicago Press, 1984), pp. 370–75.

12 See Gene Rushford, "Tuna Tiff," *The Rushford Report*, March 2002 and USITC, *The Economic Effects of Significant US Import Restraints*, Third Update, 2002, Investigation No. 332–325, June 2002, Publication 3519, pp. 98–100.

13 W.E. Morgan and Bambang Wahjudi, "The Indonesian Bicycle Industry: A Boom Export Sector," (University of Wyoming, 1992).

14 For a more detailed treatment of trade subsidies, see G. C. Hufbauer and J. S. Erb, *Subsidies in International Trade* (Washington, DC: Institute for International Economics, 1984).

15 Netherlands Economic Institute, *Evaluation of the Common Organization of the Markets in the Sugar Sector*, Sept. 2000 and Roger Thurow and Geoff Winestock, "How an Addiction to Sugar Subsidies Hurts Development," *Wall Street Journal*, Sept. 16, 2002, p. A1.

16 Section 9 of Article I of the U.S. Constitution prohibits taxes on exports. This provision was included at the insistence of southern states which feared that northern states would attempt to tax their exports of agricultural commodities.

6 Arguments for protection and the political economy of trade policy

Learning objectives

By the end of this chapter you should be able to understand:

- why tariffs are an ineffective way of addressing macroeconomic goals regarding employment or the balance of trade;
- why scarce factors of production have reason to seek protection if they are unlikely to be compensated for losses attributable to freer trade;
- that a large country whose restrictions do not provoke retaliation may levy an optimum tariff that allows it to gain at the expense of others;
- how targeting industries may allow national gains if the policy creates positive spillovers for other firms or shifts profits to domestic producers;
- how democratically elected governments may choose protectionist policies that reduce economic efficiency.

Although the basic presumption that countries gain from trade is accepted by most economists, this has not consistently translated into comparable political support for an open trading system. Individual industries and labor unions adversely affected by foreign competition frequently lobby for protection, often going to great lengths to demonstrate why they represent a special case or national interest that warrants government intervention.

Some industries argue that protection is necessary to maintain a way of life. Farm groups in Europe and the United States frequently make this claim, as do those in developing countries who appeal for the preservation of indigenous cultures and a halt to the inroads of modernization. Or domestic production may be defended as vital to national security and a nation's ability to feed, clothe, and defend its people, as in the case of Japanese and Korean bans on imported rice or US restrictions on coastal shipping. Fear of dependence on outside suppliers may be an argument raised not only in the case of traditional goods such as food but also in the case of innovations at the forefront of technological advance. Governments may intervene to promote national champions in high-technology industries, as the French have done in the computer industry or a group of European countries did to launch Airbus. Producers in developing countries often claim that protection is necessary because free trade will leave them producing primary products with limited opportunities to develop their own industrial capability.

In spite of such claims, many countries unilaterally reduced trade barriers in the 1980s and 1990s. Some countries designed those reforms on their own initiative and proceeded energetically in implementing them. Others made changes only as necessary concessions to receive assistance from international financial institutions such as the World Bank. A recipient's lack of enthusiasm in administering such reforms often results in less change than public pronouncements might suggest.

These various developments may cause us to ask why any country ends up with the trade policy it has. Have economists simply ignored those adversely affected by these trends and failed to respond to weak or self-serving arguments against free trade? Are there more sophisticated economic arguments in favor of government intervention that we have not addressed thus far? Does the political process mean that net economic efficiency and aggregate gains to the economy as a whole – standards we have relied upon in our economic analysis – provide a poor basis by which to judge the attractiveness of a policy? This chapter attempts to address those questions.

Arguments for restricting imports

Increasing output and employment

It is often argued that protectionism is a desirable way of increasing output, incomes, and employment because of the multiplier effect of reduced imports. If imports can be cut by $10 billion, it is argued, the resulting $10 billion increase in production of import substitutes will start a Keynesian multiplier process that will ultimately increase domestic output and incomes by far more than $10 billion. If the multiplier were 4, the ultimate increase in GNP would be $40 billion. This superficially attractive argument is simply wrong.

First, domestic output of import-competing goods does not increase by the amount imports decline. In our graphical representations of tariffs and quotas presented in the previous chapter, such protectionism produced only a partial increase in domestic output; the remainder of the import decline was caused by reduced consumption, with the associated deadweight loss of consumer surplus. If imports decline by $10 billion, domestic production may only rise by $5 billion as consumption falls by the other $5 billion.

Furthermore, such a multiplier effect assumes that there is sufficient idle plant and equipment to allow output to expand without driving up costs of production. In a business downturn this might be temporarily true, but few advocates of tariffs seek their imposition for only a short-run time-frame until the cyclical demand for investment goods and consumer durables recovers. Politically, tariffs are extremely difficult to remove once they are imposed, and therefore they are poorly suited to deal with temporary macroeconomic problems. Even if domestic prices were not to rise, estimates of the multiplier for a country the size of the United States are not in the range of 4, but less than half that figure. For countries that spend a bigger share of their extra income on imports the multiplier would tend to be even smaller. Consequently, the increase in output in the above example would be much less than $40 billion.

In addition, this argument assumes no retaliation by countries that lose export sales and output. Protectionism does not increase employment; rather, it merely shifts it from one country to another, and the country on the losing end of the process is very likely to respond by reclaiming the output and employment with protection of its own. If the United States were to adopt protectionist policies that did serious damage to production and employment in Europe, for example, it is unlikely that officials of the European Union would remain passive. Retaliation in the form of protectionist policies directed at US exports would follow, with the net result that neither economy would gain any output or employment, and both would become less efficient. This sort of protectionism is often referred to as a "beggar my neighbor" policy, and the neighbor can be expected to react strongly to the losses imposed on it.

Finally, this argument for protection ignores the availability of alternative policies to increase output and employment. If a country's level of aggregate demand is insufficient to support acceptable levels of output and employment, expansionary fiscal and/or monetary policies provide a better remedy. It might be argued that such policies are inflationary, but protection is even more so. The first impact of a tariff or quota, as demonstrated in the previous chapter, is to raise prices of the imported good and of import substitutes. Expansionary domestic macroeconomic policies normally become inflationary only when capacity constraints are approached, but the first effect of a tariff or quota is to increase prices.

Under the regime of flexible exchange rates that currently prevails for most industrialized countries, protectionism is even less likely to increase domestic output than if exchange rates were fixed. Under flexible exchange rates, protectionist policies cannot be expected to significantly increase output and employment in the domestic economy because the exchange rate adjusts to largely cancel such an impact. This subject will be discussed in greater detail in the chapter on floating exchange rates in Part Two of the book (Chapter 19).

To preview it briefly here, assume that the United States adopts a tariff that cuts domestic demand for European goods by $50 billion. That means a reduction in the supply of dollars in the exchange market of $50 billion and a parallel reduction in the demand for the euro. The euro will then depreciate and the dollar appreciate. US goods will become more expensive in Europe and European goods cheaper in the US. European residents will buy fewer US products, and American purchases of European goods will recover. This response of trade flows to the exchange rate should leave the trade balance and the level of output and employment in the United States where they were before the tariff was adopted. Creating jobs and incomes is among the weakest of arguments for protection, but it remains surprisingly popular.

Closing a trade deficit

Countries with large balance-of-payments deficits sometimes view import restraints as a means of reducing or eliminating such problems. The causes and possible solutions for balance-of-trade problems will be discussed in Part Two, but for now it is sufficient to note that such deficits are normally macroeconomic in cause, the result of less domestic saving than domestic investment. Solutions are typically to be found in exchange rate changes and other macroeconomic policies. When a deficit is large enough to threaten foreign exchange reserves, however, governments often seek any short-term policy available, and limits on nonessential imports are sometimes adopted as a stopgap measure.

Pauper labor

One of the oldest arguments against free trade is based on a simple comparison between foreign wages and those prevailing in the home country. Employers in industrialized countries argue that it is impossible for their employees to compete against the pauper labor (i.e. low-wage labor) available abroad. Those employers often object that minimum wage laws make it illegal for domestic firms to pay wages that would match those that prevail in developing countries from which competing products are imported. If apparel manufacturers must pay wages that are ten times as high as in India or China, not surprisingly those firms feel that they are at an unreasonable competitive disadvantage. They are likely to argue for tariffs that offset these cost differences, thus putting them on a level playing field in competing with imports.

Despite its initial attractions, this is not a sound argument. First, it implicitly assumes that labor is the only cost of production. Capital, raw materials, and a variety of other inputs may be cheaper in the industrialized country, largely offsetting the differences in wage costs. Despite their high wages, industrialized countries actually export many textile products, particularly those using artificial fibers. Low US prices for natural gas, which is the feedstock for these fibers, give US firms a competitive advantage in this market compared to EU producers who face higher input costs.

Second, this argument implicitly assumes that there are no differences in labor productivity among nations, and that differences in wage rates are fully reflected in parallel differences in unit labor costs. Wage rates in industrialized countries have historically been higher than those in developing countries precisely because labor productivity is higher in the former countries than the latter. Lower productivity in industrialized countries would require lower wage rates or a lower value of the currencies of those countries. As shown in Chapter 2, a high-wage country should export goods where its productivity advantage offsets its higher wage rate, and import goods where the productivity advantage is lower. Applying the pauper labor argument to all sectors of the economy would imply the country should not import any products at all.

Avoid adverse effects on income distribution

Recall from Chapter 3 that relatively scarce factors of production are likely to seek protection. For unskilled and semi-skilled laborers in industrialized countries, the fact that free trade would increase total national income is irrelevant. In Europe reductions in existing trade barriers would likely add to the already high unemployment rate of unskilled workers, while in the United States such a policy would likely reduce the real wage rate of unskilled workers. Labor unions and others representing the interests of labor are understandably determined to restrict imports of labor-intensive products in order to preclude the effects of the factor-price equalization process. In industrialized countries labor-intensive products generally are more heavily protected than other goods. The particularly stringent limits on imports of textiles and garments under the Multi-Fibre Arrangement are a prime example. Could a policy to compensate unskilled workers for their losses through taxes and transfer payments shift part of the gains from trade from skilled labor, capital and land? In that way a country could enjoy the benefits of freer trade without having to accept an undesired shift in the distribution of income.

How such compensation might be provided is not a straightforward question, however. **Trade Adjustment Assistance** (TAA) is a US program intended to provide payments to individuals who lose their jobs as a result of trade. It was initially created in 1962 with the proviso that assistance be provided to those who could demonstrate that they lost their jobs because of a change in trade policy agreed to under the Kennedy Round negotiations. So few workers qualified under that standard that the link between greater imports and a change in trade policy was dropped in 1974. The provision of extended unemployment compensation benefits may encourage workers to search more carefully for a new job and thereby suffer a smaller reduction in wages. Because the benefits are available only as long as the worker remains unemployed, however, they may prolong the adjustment process. Primary recipients of assistance in the 1970s turned out to be auto workers affected by imports of fuel-efficient cars; little adjustment in helping those workers move to other industries occurred, because their high wages in the auto industry made it more logical for them to await recall in that industry.[1] The payments did represent a form of compensation. Nevertheless, retraining programs were of little benefit to older workers, and an early sample of workers who received TAA benefits showed that 40 percent never found another job.[2] While trade economists generally viewed such programs as necessary steps to support a more open trade policy, labor economists have been perplexed by the attention given to just one group of workers, when a better adjustments program for all the unemployed would be desirable. The higher cost of a comprehensive program makes it less likely to be adopted, however. Some new features of the program adopted in 2002 were limited to workers older than 50, although benefits were extended to workers who supply trade impacted industries.

If compensation is not provided, protection is warranted from a national perspective when a sufficiently high value is placed on income earned by unskilled workers compared to the income received by skilled workers and owners of capital and land. Such a calculation only includes national incomes, however. In the developing world, which is relatively abundant in unskilled labor, a decision by the industrialized countries to move to free trade would increase wages and therefore the incomes of low-income workers. Free trade would increase the total incomes of all workers across the world, but it would reduce the incomes of unskilled workers in industrialized countries. Because labor unions in industrial countries represent their members, and not workers of the developing world, their support of tariffs and other restrictions on imports of labor-intensive goods is not surprising.

The terms-of-trade argument

As we found in Chapter 5, by imposing a tariff a large country may be able to turn the terms of trade in its favor. This gain may be large enough to outweigh the loss from a reduced volume of trade. So runs the terms-of-trade argument, which is also known as the "**optimum tariff**" case, although it is optimal only for the country imposing the tariff and not for the world.

We use the partial equilibrium diagram of the import market from Chapter 5 to show this effect in the left-hand panel of Figure 6.1. The tariff causes the price of domestic purchases to rise to P_c but the price received by foreign suppliers falls to P_f. A portion of the tariff revenue raised is not simply a transfer from domestic purchasers, but comes from foreign producers, as shown by the area m. When imports decline from M_0 to M_1, however, economic efficiency declines by area n, which represents the combined effect of less efficient domestic producers expanding their output and of domestic consumers shifting to less desirable substitutes. The tariff that results in the largest value of area m minus area n is the optimum tariff.

We show a comparable effect from imposing an export tax in the right-hand panel of Figure 6.1. In that situation, the tax results in foreign buyers paying a higher price for the export good, P_f, but domestic consumers now pay P_d. The exporting country gains part of the export tax revenue at the expense of foreign buyers, which is shown by area m. That gain may offset the efficiency loss, shown by area n, that results from less production of a good where the country has a comparative advantage and from greater domestic consumption of it. The optimal export tax maximizes the difference between area m and area n.

Regardless of whether Country A levies an import tariff or export tax, its gain comes at the expense of the rest of the world. In fact, because the tariff reduces the degree of specialization in the world economy, world welfare is reduced. This effect matches what we

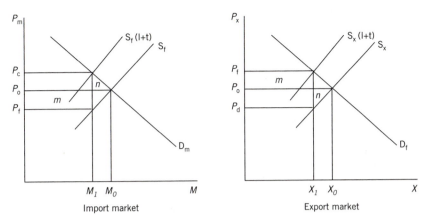

Figure 6.1 An optimum tariff in a partial equilibrium model. In the import market, an optimum tariff maximizes the difference between the terms-of-trade gain at the expense of foreign suppliers, area *m*, and the loss in economic efficiency from reducing the quantity of imports, area *n*. In the export market, the optimum export tax maximizes the difference between the terms-of-trade gain at the expense of foreign buyers, area *m*, and the loss in economic efficiency from reducing the quantity of exports, area *n*.

observed in the case of cartels in Chapter 4; the world as a whole loses, but the export tax considered here ensures that all firms will raise the price at which they sell. The terms-of-trade argument takes a national perspective: it suggests that a nation may be able to use a tariff to take for itself a larger share of the gains from trade, thereby improving its welfare. This argument is logically correct, but it is irrelevant for most nations of the world that exert little influence on world prices.

Even for large countries, the benefit obtained through improved terms of trade may be lost if other countries retaliate by imposing tariffs of their own. Any benefits also may erode if the higher relative price of Country A's export good attracts greater entry and competition from producers in other countries. We expect the optimum tariff to decline over time.

The infant-industry argument

When production of a commodity first begins in a country, the firms producing it are often small, inexperienced, and unfamiliar with the technology they are using. Workers are also inexperienced and less efficient than they will become in time. During this breaking-in stage, costs are higher than they will be later on, and infant firms in the new industry may need temporary protection from older, established firms in other countries. So runs the infant-industry argument for tariff protection.

Thus stated, the infant-industry argument is analytically persuasive. It does not conflict with the principle of comparative advantage. In terms of our earlier analysis of trade, the argument is that the country's present production-possibility curve does not reflect its true potential. Given time to develop an industry that is now in its infancy, the production-possibility curve will shift and a potential comparative advantage will be realized. Also, note that the infant-industry argument takes a global perspective: in the long run, world economic welfare is improved because tariff protection enables a potential comparative advantage to become realized and a more efficient utilization of resources to be achieved. Thus world output is increased.

Box 6.1 Optimum tariffs: did Britain give a gift to the world?

British debate over repeal of the Corn Laws and other tariffs in the 1840s was not simply a controversy between landowners and industrialists about the division of national income. Robert Torrens was the most outspoken of classical economists who claimed that the net effect on the country as a whole from unilateral removal of tariffs would be negative. The loss would occur due to an adverse shift in the terms of trade, a point we encountered in Chapter 5. British terms-of-trade would fall, but to determine whether that decline would be large enough to offset other efficiency gains from tariff removal requires that we calculate the relative size of these effects.

The likelihood that Britain could lose from unilaterally reducing its trade barriers exists because it certainly was not a small country in the sense that it faced a fixed world price for its imports and exports. As the birthplace of the Industrial Revolution, it was the primary source of manufactured goods on world markets. A tariff on food diverted resources away from the production of manufactured goods, and the consequent reduction in the quantity of British exports supplied resulted in improved British terms-of-trade. By repealing the Corn Laws did Britain give up some of its monopoly gains?

Douglas Irwin estimates relevant demand and supply elasticities for Britain in that era, and he applies them in assessing the effect of a reduction in the average British tariff rate from 35 percent to 31 percent.[3] He finds that British terms of trade would worsen by 3.5 percent and result in a loss in national income of 0.4 percent. Although Irwin does not calculate whether 35 percent represents an optimum British tariff, his result indicates that Britain was moving away from an optimum tariff, because its welfare fell.

How should we judge the actual repeal of the Corn Laws? Irwin notes that Britain probably did not lose from this policy because other European nations happened to reduce trade barriers shortly after the British action. Furthermore, as Britain's share of world industrial production declined and more alternatives to British goods became available, its optimum tariff would have been lower, even in the absence of tariff reductions by others.

This argument has great appeal for countries in an early stage of industrialization who are eager to develop a modern industrial sector. They fear that their attempts to develop new industries will be defeated by vigorous price competition from already established firms in advanced industrial countries such as the United States, Germany, and Japan. Early in American history Alexander Hamilton forcefully advocated the infant-industry argument in his Report on Manufactures.[5] It served as a rationale for the protective tariffs imposed in 1815 after Britain lifted the blockade of the United States that it had imposed during the war of 1812. Industries that had sprung up during the war feared the ravages of competition with the more advanced industries of Europe. Friedrich List made similar arguments in favor of a protective tariff in the United States and in Germany; later in the century, as Bismarck unified the separate German states and sought to expand their industrial capacity, he granted protection to the iron, steel, coal, and textile industries.

The infant-industry argument also has a strong intuitive appeal. It seems to accord with common sense. Everyone knows that even a gifted beginner has trouble competing with a mature, experienced person, whether in sport, profession, or business. Societies acknowledge

Box 6.2 Another view of the optimum tariff: offer curve analysis

The opportunity for a country to improve its terms of trade by levying a tariff can also be shown with offer curves. If Country A imposes a tariff on imports of food, for example, that will shift its offer curve inward from OA to OA´, and A's terms of trade improve as the relative price of cloth rises from OE to OE´. The potential for Country A to gain depends importantly upon the elasticity of the foreign offer curve. In Figure 6.2, note that the initial equilibrium occurs along the inelastic range of Country B's offer curve. Just as a monopolist in a domestic market wants to restrict output to find an optimal solution along the elastic portion of the industry demand curve, a country seeking to impose an optimal tariff will want to reach a solution along the elastic range of Country B's offer curve. At the equilibrium shown at point E´, Country A offers much less cloth in return for a greater amount of food than it received in the initial equilibrium. Given that no retaliation will occur, Country A's choice of an optimal tariff is intended to maximize its welfare by allowing it to reach the highest possible community indifference curve. James Meade developed the related concept of a trade indifference curve, such as TT in Figure 6.2, and demonstrated that Country A should set the tariff that allows it to reach the point where the highest possible trade indifference curve is tangent to Country B's offer curve.[4]

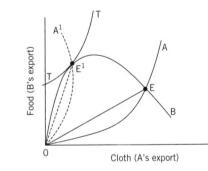

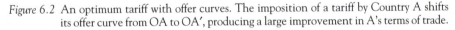

Figure 6.2 An optimum tariff with offer curves. The imposition of a tariff by Country A shifts its offer curve from OA to OA´, producing a large improvement in A's terms of trade.

this disparity and deal with it in various ways: schools, training programs, apprenticeships, and others. Shielding infant firms from foreign competition during their most vulnerable stages seems to be an eminently fair and sensible thing to do.

Despite its analytical validity and its appeal to common sense, **infant-industry protection** encounters severe difficulties in actual practice.[6] It is difficult to determine in advance just which industries possess a potential comparative advantage. If protection is extended to the wrong industry, the cost to society can be heavy. Firms will expand their capacity, but costs per unit will remain high and continued protection will be necessary for their survival. Tariff protection involves a social cost in that consumers have to pay higher prices for the protected commodity than would be necessary with free trade. Higher prices reflect the greater amount of scarce resources required to produce the commodity at home. If the industry eventually develops a comparative advantage, the extra costs incurred during its infancy may be recovered during its maturity. If a mistake is made, however, the nation is saddled with a continuing burden. The record is mixed, but infant industries have shown a distressing tendency to remain dependent on protection. A mistake, once made, is not easily corrected. Owners and workers in the new industry have a vested interest in it, and they will fight to preserve it.

Many economists argue that a country should let the market decide which industries have the greatest potential to perform well. They doubt that government officials, no matter how dedicated, honest, and intelligent, can have the wisdom and foresight to pick out, in advance, exactly those industries in which a potential comparative advantage exists. If an industry is potentially profitable, private entrepreneurs will discover it, and they will bear the cost of its learning stage just as they bear the cost of construction, capital equipment, and training labor in any new venture. Also, some of the distortions that an infant industry must overcome are related to externalities we considered in Chapter 4. For example, a firm may develop a more efficient method of production that can then be copied by others or it may train workers who are then hired away by competitors. A direct subsidy to that firm encourages the activity that otherwise goes unrewarded in the market and will be underproduced. In contrast, a tariff encourages firms that copy a good idea or lure away trained workers just as much as it favors the firm that is the initial innovator or trainer.

As we noted in Chapter 5, a direct subsidy can provide the same protective effect as a tariff, but without distorting prices and causing a loss of consumers' surplus. Also, subsidies can be used to address other distortions, such as an inadequate capital market or banking system to finance the plant, equipment, or training necessary to enter an industry. Borrowers with inadequate collateral to offer may appear to be poor credit risks who are passed over by private lenders in spite of promising ideas. While economists generally advocate policies to deal directly with capital market distortions, a trade barrier that provides some assurance of high future profitability nevertheless may be the only tool available to promote such an industry. In spite of the fact that it is an inefficient tool, a tariff may appear desirable in countries that have great difficulty collecting tax revenue. Eliminating distortions directly often requires scarce tax revenues, a drawback that does not exist in the case of the tariff.

With respect to the difficulty of identifying potential comparative advantage industries, one useful rule is that infant-industry protection should be extended only when the country possesses an ample supply of the basic resources required in that industry. With no coal or iron ore, Costa Rica would be unwise to impose a tariff on steel imports in the hope that an efficient, low-cost steel industry would spring up in response. Possession of an adequate supply of raw materials and natural resources thus seems to be a necessary condition for infant-industry protection, but it may not be enough to assure efficient production and prices low enough to compete in world markets. When the protected home market is so small that it can support only one modern plant, there may be little competitive pressure for that firm to produce efficiently behind a tariff wall. Applying the infant-industry argument in practice is problematic.

Industrial strategy or strategic trade

Industrial targeting may appear to be an attractive policy when one country attempts to catch up with others and follows their blueprint for development. Such a plan may provide infant-industry protection for successively more complex industries. A different motivation for targeting arises, however, when the government identifies an industry where above-average profits can be earned and finds that it can strengthen the strategic position of its national producer to capture those profits. For example, in the 1980s some US commentators faulted the US government for its failure to pursue a more active trade policy that would have kept American industry from falling behind Japanese producers of high-technology products.[7] They predicted that without protection and the opportunity to exploit economies of scale at home, US producers would be ill-prepared to compete internationally. They also felt Japanese firms had been able to earn high profits in a closed domestic market, which allowed them to exhaust economies of scale and to make additional sales at lower prices in foreign markets where demand was more elastic. By this line of reasoning, full trade was an outmoded policy that was no longer relevant in a world of imperfect competition.

Consider the case where a government can identify new product areas that require large research expenditures but promise large future profits (and therefore tax receipts). An activist strategy calls for protection to guarantee the home market for domestic firms while this research is done and paid for and until these firms become large and experienced enough to bring costs down. Once the research and development costs are recovered and large-scale production is under way, protection will no longer be needed and exports may be possible. As in the infant-industry argument, to leave the home market open to foreign firms during this start-up period would make it impossible for domestic firms to earn enough revenue to pay for expensive research or to become large enough to enjoy lower costs. Temporary protection is advocated during the period necessary to accomplish these goals.

The ability to produce high-technology goods may be an end in itself, if a country is concerned about its international status as a technology leader and if it seeks a national champion to maintain this position. By the standard of economic efficiency that we have applied to other policy questions, however, we need to demonstrate that there is an economic advantage from a country producing more of these goods. We consider two potentially important reasons why a country may gain from such strategic intervention: (i) it may shift economic profits to its own firms rather than let them be captured by other producers; and (ii) it may benefit from the chance to reduce costs of production or otherwise reap spillovers that occur if more of the production takes place within its borders rather than somewhere else in the world.

With respect to the opportunity to shift profits, we can recognize the relevance of this argument to imperfectly competitive industries, particularly oligopolies where significant barriers to entry exist and a firm can permanently earn economic profits without their being competed away by another. If we apply this reasoning to the Chapter 4 model of oligopoly competition in a third-country export market, we can demonstrate how government action to ensure that its own firms earn those profits creates a gain for the country as a whole.

An example may indicate how a country might gain from such a protectionist policy. If Sony and RCA were both considering undertaking large research and development efforts to enter the high-definition television market, each would have greater sales and profits if the other did not compete. If either company, or its government, could somehow discourage the other firm from undertaking the research to develop such a television system, it would receive larger profits, or tax revenues. The "payoff matrix" facing the two firms might be as shown in the matrix on page 150.

In this matrix, p stands for Sony producing, n stands for Sony not producing, P stands for RCA producing, and N stands for RCA not producing. In each box, the number at the lower left is RCA's profits and the number to the upper right is Sony's profits. If both produce, each absorbs a loss of $5 million, because each would have a relatively low sales volume across which to spread large research costs. If only one firm produces, it earns $100 million because it will have a much larger volume of sales across which to spread these costs, thus bringing average costs down. In this case, whichever firm commits itself to a research effort first is

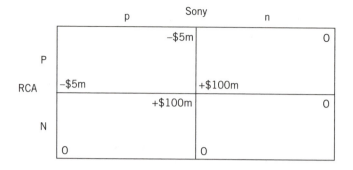

likely to remain dominant: the other firm will recognize that it faces a loss if it enters the business and therefore it will not choose to enter.[8]

The US government, however, could adopt a policy that would shift this matrix in favor of RCA and make it very unlikely that Sony would enter the industry. If the United States provides a subsidy large enough to ensure that RCA makes a profit even if Sony enters the market, the payoff matrix could become as follows:

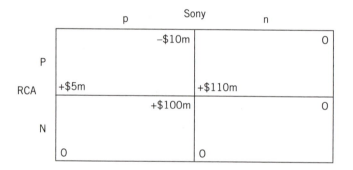

The US subsidy means that if both firms enter the market, Sony will lose $10 million, whereas RCA will receive profits of $5 million. This means that RCA will enter the market without regard to what Sony decides. Once the management of Sony understands this situation, it will be strongly discouraged from entering a market in which it faces certain losses of $10 million. Without competition from Sony, RCA earns profits of $110 million, some part of which accrues to the US government as tax revenues.[9] The large benefit to a small subsidy arises because RCA now is the sole supplier and earns monopoly profits.

A slightly modified situation can be represented with the reaction curves framework from Chapter 4, as is presented in Figure 6.3. A subsidy per unit of export sold shifts RCA's reaction curve to the right and results in greater production at W than at Z. The benefit from extra production is particularly large if the firm's marginal cost of production falls as output rises, which occurs with increasing return to scale. Even without that gain, the United States benefits from the expansion of sales at a lower price, something that did not hold true in the case of an export subsidy under perfect competition, which was shown in Figure 5.8. The difference here is that for these extra sales marginal revenue exceeds marginal cost, and monopoly profits are transferred to the country that offers the subsidy. The situation in Figure 6.3 also suggests a gain even if the competitor is not driven out of the market. In the absence of a subsidy, RCA would not expand output to such an extent, if it knew Sony's

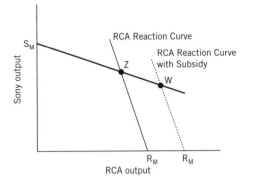

Figure 6.3 Subsidization of an oligopoly producer. A US subsidy to RCA shifts its reaction curve to the right and results in greater industry sales and a lower price. Because the lower price results in a decline in Sony's output and an expansion of RCA's output, the United States gains even taking into account the payment of the subsidy.

output would remain at the same level given at Z. The government subsidy, however, reduces the market price and makes Sony production less profitable. Thus, Sony does not maintain the same level of output, and government intervention has assisted RCA in pursuing the leadership strategy discussed in Chapter 4, where expansion of the Dutch United East India Company came at the expense of the British East India Company.

More realistic examples of government intervention are not restricted to competition in export markets alone, where the interests of domestic consumers can be ignored. An early example by Richard Baldwin and Paul Krugman of a more complete analysis that includes effects in the domestic market is their numerical simulation of the competition between Airbus and Boeing in the market for medium-range, wide-bodied jet aircraft.[10] In that case Airbus subsidized the entry of the A300 but did not deter Boeing from producing the 767 too. Baldwin and Krugman found that European subsidies clearly benefited consumers of aircraft everywhere, as more competition reduced prices faced by airlines. Also, European subsidies clearly reduced the profitability of Boeing, because it could not charge a monopoly price for the 767. In addition, because Boeing sold fewer airplanes, its cost of production per plane rose as it earned less from its smaller cumulative output. Although US consumers benefited, the United States is a net exporter of aircraft, and therefore Boeing's losses more than offset those consumer gains.

With respect to Europe itself, the outcome is more ambiguous. Consumers gained but taxpayers had to provide the subsidy that allowed Airbus to enter the market. Baldwin and Krugman found that Europe either had a small gain or a small loss as a result of its intervention, depending upon the way future consumer gains were calculated. Similarly, for the world as a whole, the gain from EC intervention is ambiguous. Entry reduces the distortion caused by Boeing's monopoly pricing, but entry requires the additional outlay for research and development and other fixed costs of a second competitor. The Baldwin–Krugman calculation indicates the world as a whole lost from European intervention, although by looking at a single generation of products, they ignore potential gains from more rapid introduction of innovations that is likely to occur under a duopoly in comparison with a monopoly.

The discussion thus far has focused on the gains from government intervention when profit shifting is possible. As suggested above, a second reason for intervention may exist if production at home generates positive spillovers. For example, additional output by one firm, and the learning it acquires, may spill over to other firms, an example of external economies of scale discussed in Chapter 4. When such learning is symmetric, and the problem of innovators versus copiers is not a concern, then promoting output by any firm results in a gain that an individual firm will not take into account. Tariff protection is not as disadvantageous relative to a production subsidy under those circumstances, and identifying which firm is most likely to innovate is not necessary. All firms may find it easier to gain financing if protection is provided. Recognize, however, that we must be assuming that the learning only spills over to other home producers and not to competing producers in other countries. Evidence from the semiconductor industry suggests that the gains from learning are not so easily confined. Therefore, the source of external economies must be considered carefully in claiming that large competitive gains will result from trade protection.

Spillovers may exist between industries. Advances in one industry may benefit another industry. For example, new semiconductors may allow more efficient computers to be designed and produced. If the new semiconductor becomes available to all producers at the same time, then computer producers everywhere benefit. If the new semiconductor is only available in the country where it is developed, and at least in the initial stages of production is a nontraded good, then computer producers in that country with access to the new semiconductor will have an advantage over producers elsewhere. During the 1980s US producers of supercomputers were worried about their access to fast chips produced by their Japanese competitor, Fujitsu. In the semiconductor example the advantage may be only temporary, but when products change rapidly this advantage nevertheless may be significant. If this spillover is particularly important, we might expect a semiconductor producer and a computer producer to merge, irrespective of trade policy.

Although plausible cases may exist for trade intervention in some industries, who is going to pick the "winners" and distinguish them from the "losers" who should not be protected? If this task falls to an elected legislature, politics and the desire of powerful elected officials to protect their constituents are likely to dominate the outcome. And since there is no reason to believe that the executive branch of the government would be any better than the legislature in picking winners, the question remains: who makes the choices? In the past, it was assumed that Tokyo had this problem solved, and that all of its choices had paid off. A closer look at Japan's experience, however, suggests this presumption of uniform success is unwarranted.[11] The past growth of the Japanese economy can better be attributed to a very high savings and investment rate and the development of a huge stock of human capital, rather than to any **industrial strategy**. Many of the "winners" that Tokyo supported have recently performed poorly, and Japanese resources may have been wasted through protection. The expensive Japanese effort in the area of high-definition television, for example, has been overtaken by US technology, which was developed with very little help from the US government. Steel was a major beneficiary of Tokyo's help, and that industry is having serious trouble competing with firms in newly industrialized countries, such as South Korea, and with low-cost US mini-mills.

Although Japan's macroeconomic downturn in the 1990s and its prolonged banking crisis have diverted attention away from the alleged virtues of government targeting, the historical record may be interpreted by some as a demonstration that the Japanese economy prospered in spite of, rather than because of, Tokyo's efforts to target future winners. Europeans have tried the same strategic trade approach by supporting what they viewed as critical industries. The French computer industry has been a huge recipient of aid from Paris, but it continues to perform poorly in competition with US and Japanese firms. Airbus's technological success

Box 6.3 Semiconductors and strategic trade policy

What effects are important in evaluating policies that restrict access to the domestic market and rely upon import protection as a form of export promotion? As suggested in general terms above, such a strategy may be successful as a result of allowing domestic producers to achieve economies of scale or reduce costs through learning by doing. The profits that can be earned in a protected home market may allow domestic producers to expand capacity and deter competitors from expanding. Because the significance of these factors cannot be demonstrated in the abstract, we again turn to a numerical calculation that takes into account these various effects.

In another early example of such analysis, Baldwin and Krugman present a simulation model to assess whether closure of the Japanese semiconductor market to US competitors was a critical step in allowing their ascendancy in the industry.[12] In contrast to the previous examples of an integrated world market, here segmented markets are central to the analysis. Baldwin and Krugman ignore the extent to which the learning from output by one firm spills over to benefit other firms, and therefore they may overstate the benefits from a closed market if the international spillovers subsequently reported by Irwin and Klenow are recognized.[13] In any event, Baldwin and Krugman conclude that restricted entry into the Japanese market for 16K DRAMs was critical to the success of Japanese producers in achieving sufficient economies of scale to be competitive with US producers.

They project that Japanese entry, however, resulted in higher prices both in the United States and in Japan than would have occurred under a policy of free trade, because the market would not have been split among as many firms. Potential gains from protection are dissipated by the entry of more firms, which duplicates fixed costs of entry and results in less output and learning by each firm. If the United States had reacted by closing its market, and no trade were possible, Japan would have become even worse off by being confined to its own limited market. The United States would have become worse off, too, because its firms would have become smaller, benefited from less learning, and had higher marginal costs. A trade war becomes more expensive to both countries than in the case of constant costs of production because both countries lose economies of scale.

Any verdict on actual trade policy has been even more complicated than the simulation models described above. Restrictions in the semiconductor market negotiated in 1986 by Japan and the United States demonstrate some of the complexities. Japanese producers were forced to raise prices to avoid charges of dumping. The higher price resulted in a major transfer of profits to Japanese firms, because they already controlled over 80 percent of the US market for DRAMs. That benefit left them even better prepared to finance production of the next generation of memory chips. Their continued domination of this segment of the market would have been even more likely, if not for the entry of Korean producers who may have benefited from their own government's targeting strategy. In the case of another type of memory chips, EPROMs, Japanese producers accounted for less than 40 percent of the market. US producers had sufficient capacity to meet additional demand generated by the agreement, and Japanese firms had less incentive to act collusively when demand recovered.[14]

and ability to command a sizable part of the market for commercial aircraft are clear, but its privatization and successful operation on commercial terms are still uncertain. Even assuming its eventual profitability, the use of scarce tax resources to create a viable competitor may have benefited European taxpayers less than alternative uses of those funds. The superficial logic behind the industrial strategy argument for protection may be attractive, but the track record of countries that have pursued it is not convincing.

Dumping

Another claim for protection is that imported goods benefit from unfair trade practices. These allegations include products that are dumped at unfairly low prices in foreign markets and those that benefit from government subsidies. In fact, the World Trade Organization recognizes that actions to offset such unfair practices can be entirely consistent with a member's WTO commitments. Each of these areas raises important intellectual questions with respect to the circumstances when they will be consistent with a set of principles that maximize world welfare. Complaints about dumping are far more prevalent than complaints about subsidies, however, as illustrated by the fact that in 2001, 347 antidumping cases were initiated worldwide, compared to 27 countervailing duty cases to address foreign subsidies.[15] Therefore, we do not elaborate the comments on subsidization presented in Chapter 5, and we focus on dumping.

Because transport costs and border regulations do separate national markets, firms may choose to discriminate across markets and charge different prices in different countries. When the firm chooses to charge a higher price in the home market and a lower price in the foreign market, economists refer to the practice as dumping. We first demonstrate how dumping represents a profit-maximizing strategy for the firm and then consider the effects of dumping on the importing country.

The firm will distinguish between markets because the elasticity of demand is not the same in each market. The firm often benefits from protection in the home market, due either to high transport costs or various tariff and nontariff barriers that keep out foreign competitors. In the category of nontariff barriers, we include tradition and business practices that limit competition from firms outside established business groups. Because foreign substitutes are not available, demand is less elastic than in foreign markets where the firm's product must compete with producers from many other countries.

Figure 6.4 presents an extreme example of this situation. The firm faces a downward sloping demand curve, denoted D, in the home market but must act as a perfectly competitive firm in the foreign market and face a horizontal demand curve, denoted D'. If there is no foreign trade, the firm will produce Q_1 of output and charge the price P_1. Now suppose the firm has the opportunity to export its output at the fixed world price P_2. If it can prevent the exported output from being brought back into the domestic market, to maximize its profit the firm will now raise its domestic price to P_3 and reduce its domestic sales to Q_3 and export the quantity Q_2–Q_3 at the world price P_2. At first glance it may seem paradoxical that the firm would reduce its sales in the higher-priced market, but it turns out that the firm is simply following the general rule of profit maximization: it equates marginal revenue and marginal cost, and does so in each market. The marginal revenue curve for sales in the domestic market is downward-sloping, but it becomes horizontal at P_2 for export sales at D' = MR'. Therefore no output will be sold in the home market that yields a marginal revenue less than P_2. On the other hand, exports are profitable out to the point at which MR = MC. The opportunity to sell in foreign markets at the lower world price increases the firm's profits by

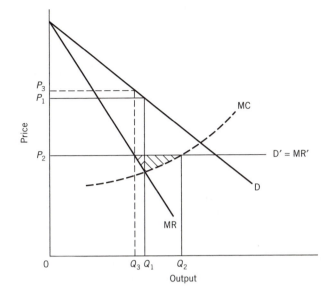

Figure 6.4 Dumping can increase profits – an example of price discrimination. This firm charges a price of P_3 and sells a volume Q_3 in the home market. It then exports volume $Q_2 - Q_3$ at a price of P_2, thereby maximizing total profits from the two separate markets.

the amounts indicated by the shaded areas in Figure 6.4 – the difference between MR' and MC for the output that is exported. Again, this whole argument depends on the assumption that the two markets can be kept separated: the exported output cannot be returned to the home market. If it could be returned, the domestic price would fall to P_2 and the country would become a net importer.

This result is a special case of a general proposition about price discrimination. A firm that sells its output in two or more distinct and separate markets will maximize its profits by equating MC and MR in each market. For the given MC, the price will be higher the smaller the elasticity of demand in each market.

The WTO recognizes dumping as an unfair trade practice and allows action to be taken against it. In the United States, for example, legal action follows a two-step procedure. If a charge of dumping is formally made, the Department of Commerce is required to investigate. If dumping is found to exist, the International Trade Commission (ITC) determines whether the domestic industry is being injured by the dumping. If it is, an antidumping duty equal to the margin of dumping is imposed.

One might think that importing countries would welcome the opportunity to obtain imports at bargain prices and that the exporting countries would be the ones to object. After all, trade improves consumer welfare by reducing the price of imported goods. However, it is usually the importing country that protests against dumping. Competing firms in the importing country recognize that low-priced imports are adversely affecting their sales and profits, and they are quick to claim that foreigners are engaging in unfair competition. Governments do have a valid interest in preventing **predatory dumping**. This occurs when foreign firms cut prices temporarily in order to drive domestic firms out of business, after which they will raise prices to exploit a monopoly advantage. Predatory dumping is more likely in industries in which start-up costs are high or in which other barriers to entry of new firms exist. Although national antitrust or competition laws are intended to address such practices, enforcing them against foreign firms may not always be feasible. In the vast majority of dumping cases, however, offending foreign producers account for small shares of the relevant market, which makes the predatory outcome unlikely.

Firms are likely to find dumping an attractive strategy even when they have no likelihood of driving foreign competitors out of the market. Rather, when markets can be separated within a country, domestic firms are likely to follow the same practice. A firm that has many gasoline stations in one part of the country, but hopes to enter the market in another part of the country, is unlikely to charge the same price for gasoline in each market. Instead, the firm will charge a lower price in the new market, to attract customers away from existing firms which already dominate the market. Lowering the price in the market where it makes few sales initially is a successful strategy, because the percentage reduction in price to existing customers represents a small loss in revenue compared to the large percentage gain in sales it will achieve when demand is quite elastic. In the market where it already is well established, a comparable price reduction represents a loss of revenue from a much larger number of customers, and the prospective percentage increase in sales is smaller given the less elastic demand. This line of reasoning implies that dumping makes sense as a domestic competitive strategy, and by extension as an international competitive strategy, too. Within a country, a domestic firm cannot be restricted from competing in any region, but internationally, competitors may not have a comparable ability to dump in each other's markets.

A further controversial aspect of antidumping laws is that in many countries they prohibit sales below the average cost of production. As a result foreign firms can be found guilty of dumping even when they charge the same price in all markets. Because average cost of production is interpreted to include an average rate of return to capital, this rules out sales below a full-cost price, which commonly take place during business downturns. The domestic practice of holding a sale to clear out overstocked merchandise is not legal by this standard. This form of dumping can be observed in competitive markets where individual firms have no power to set prices and discriminate against some buyers and favor others; both foreign and domestic firms sell at a lower price, which still covers their variable costs of production, and hope for more favorable conditions in the future that will allow them to earn an average rate of return. Yet, the dumping law says this strategy is legal for the domestic firm and illegal for the foreign firm.

Aside from these qualifications regarding the theory of dumping determinations, the actual practice of calculating dumping margins raises further concerns. Foreign firms are required to provide enormous amounts of accounting data in computer-readable form to defend themselves against such charges. If they cannot do so within a brief period of time, administrators use the "best information available," which often means figures submitted by those who bring the complaint, to determine the existence of dumping. Given those circumstances, negative decisions in the United States typically do not rest on a finding of no dumping but instead on the ITC finding that serious injury to the US industry has not resulted.

Even when cases are rejected by either the Department of Commerce or the ITC, the firm accused of dumping must cover the high legal costs of a defense, which may deter it or other foreign firms from competing aggressively in the US market. Thomas Prusa provides another insight for interpreting this process.[16] He cites US evidence from the early 1980s which shows industries that win dumping cases (roughly one-third) do much better than industries that lose dumping cases (roughly one-third); imports fall roughly 36 percent for the former but rise 9 percent for the latter. When cases are withdrawn (roughly one-third), however, industries do roughly as well as when they win. Withdrawal often results from successful private negotiations, which may come closer to approximating the monopoly cartel solution identified above. Thus, some dumping actions appear to serve as a signal to foreign competitors to collude.

During the 1980s, Australia, Canada, the European Union, and the United States accounted for 96 percent of all dumping cases filed. The larger the country, the more likely that measures to prevent dumping will benefit domestic producers rather than other foreign producers. Table 6.1 summarizes the US and EU experience. In both cases the steel and chemical industries have been the primary users of these provisions. The column labeled "number successful" includes cases where antidumping duties were imposed and also where cases were withdrawn. Average dumping margins were much higher than the roughly 7 percent tariff rates for trade in manufactured goods as bound under international agreements by the European Union and the United States. Because EU practice allows for a duty smaller than the dumping margin, where the protection granted is proportional to the injury caused, the EU actions were less restrictive than implied by the average margin reported in the final column. Nevertheless, these barriers still are significant, and not surprisingly, Patrick Messerlin found that EU imports fell 36 percent 3 years after antidumping protection was granted.[17]

Table 6.1 Dumping cases in the United States and European Community, 1979–89

Industries	United States			European Community		
	Number initiated	Number successful	Average margin	Number initiated	Number successful	Average margin
Chemical	69	40	34.0	155	121	38.1
Metal	224	162	29.5	57	37	31.4
Nonelectrical machinery	27	21	26.4	34	24	52.7
Electrical equipment	24	17	24.4	33	24	29.2
Four industry total	344	240	28.6	279	206	37.8
All industries	451	275	33.2	385	270	37.4

Source: Patrick Messerlin and Geoffrey Reed, "Antidumping Policies in the United States and the European Community," *The Economic Journal*, 1995, pp. 1565–75.

The popularity of this policy tool is spreading. In the 1990s, many more countries came to rely on antidumping duties to protect domestic industries. The WTO secretariat reports that from 1995 to 2001 the four largest initiators of antidumping cases were the United States (257), India (248), the European Community (247) and Argentina (166). The countries most often named in such complaints were China (261), Korea (139), the United States (103) and Taiwan (96).[18] Some commentators regard dumping cases as a substitute for tariffs and alternative trade barriers now constrained by the WTO. Others consider a country's reliance on dumping actions as part of a broader approach to trade and competition policy; some countries may effectively limit imports through collusive business practices rather than resort to dumping laws. Therefore, progress in negotiating tighter limits on the way antidumping restrictions are used is likely to require simultaneous attention to other uncompetitive practices.

Secondary arguments for protectionism

A variety of other arguments has been advanced in support of protection on the grounds that it will enable a country to achieve some desirable social or economic objective. In nearly all these cases, an economist would argue that if society does indeed desire the stated objective, it can achieve it more efficiently in some other way. In other words, the economist would argue that a tariff is a second-best policy. In fact, we have already made this point regarding the infant-industry argument. We have observed that if a given industry were identified as a potential comparative-advantage industry worthy of being assisted in its infancy, a subsidy would be a better method than a tariff to provide that assistance. Nevertheless, the argument that a tariff is a second-best policy may be irrelevant because no first-best policy can be used. It may be beyond the administrative capacity of the country, or the country may be unable to collect enough taxes to pay subsidies. That same reasoning may apply to the arguments raised here.

National defense

A particular industry may be considered essential to maintain a nation's military strength. In order to preserve some capacity to produce in this industry, the nation may choose to protect it. Economists have always recognized this exception to the case for free trade, and even Adam Smith observed that "defense is more important than opulence." However, it is quite difficult to prove how much the gains from domestic production contribute to national defense.

If the product requires use of a depletable natural resource, tariffs will accelerate exhaustion of the national reserves. National security would seem to call for importing as much as possible to supply current consumption, thereby saving domestic reserves for future needs. It is curious that the United States imposed quotas on oil imports during much of the post-World War II period on the ground that these restrictions were necessary to national defense. Import quotas do encourage domestic exploration, but they also increase production and thus use up domestic reserves. The US quota policy was sometimes referred to as the "pump America dry first" approach. In fact, US purchases of imported oil for its Strategic Petroleum Reserve in the 1980s represent a more economically efficient policy for a product that can be stored.

The real issue concerning national security is maintenance of a domestic capacity to produce certain essential items. If that capacity is not maintained, skills and technological expertise may be lost, and the nation becomes dependent on foreign sources of supply. We know that trade means specialization. The other side of that coin is interdependence. The only real escape is to become self-sufficient, but self-sufficiency is extremely inefficient and its pursuit could weaken the nation by impoverishing it. Consequently, any serious use of the national defense argument for protection requires a careful calculation of the tradeoff between efficiency and defense essentiality.

The market for launching communications satellites in orbit provides an interesting example of this argument for protection. The role of historical accident and created comparative advantage arises here, for the United States became dependent on foreign launch services with the disastrous loss of the Challenger Shuttle in 1986. Some replacement for that means of launching military and communications satellites was necessary. France held the dominant position in this market, accounting for half of satellite launches in 1994 and 1995. The US government negotiated a quota system of agreements with both China and Russia regarding the number of launches and the price to be charged; under the original agreement Russian prices were to be no less than 15 percent below US prices, and under the 1993 extension Russian prices were to be no less than 7.5 percent below US prices. The high price provided an incentive for Lockheed Martin and Boeing/McDonnell Douglas to add to the capacity and capabilities of the Atlas and the Delta rockets, respectively. The US goal was not to drive foreigners out of the business, however, as national security objectives were judged to be met by building sufficient launchers for military programs. The National Security Adviser under President Bush felt a more important goal than claiming a large share of the commercial launch market was to maintain the dominant US share of the market for making satellites. Nevertheless, the satellite market has been characterized as highly competitive, with very small profit margins.[19]

Cultural or social values

The specialization that results from international trade may also be opposed for cultural and social reasons. Countries may wish to protect a way of life: small-scale agriculture, a village system, a diversified structure of production. Some of the so-called romantic movements in the nineteenth century included attempts to prevent, or at least slow, the growth of industrialization, the migration from farm to city, and other manifestations of economic progress. Similar motives have been at work in many countries in more recent times, as traditional societies have been exposed to international trade and have seen its effects on resource allocation. Imports of manufactured goods, mass-produced in large-scale factories, have often led to a decline in traditional small-scale handicraft industries, a decline that is resisted on cultural as well as economic grounds. In such cases trade restrictions are advocated precisely because the effects of trade are unwelcome. The society chooses to forgo the gains from trade in order to retain its traditional way of life.

Correcting distortions in the domestic market

When some imperfection in the market causes a divergence between private and social costs, a case can be made for government intervention to offset or compensate for that divergence. We have already discussed this rationale regarding the benefits from increasing output in industries where external economies of scale exist or in imperfectly competitive industries where price exceeds marginal cost. The same reasoning applies if union workers receive a wage premium in an industry, or if a given industry is subject to a higher tax rate than other industries.

Figure 6.5 illustrates this basic idea. For a particular commodity it shows the domestic demand curve (D) and the domestic supply curve as perceived by private producers (S_p). The foreign supply curve is perfectly elastic at the world price, P_W. Consequently, with free trade, domestic production will be OA, domestic demand OF, and imports will make up the difference, AF.

Now let us suppose that the private supply curve (S_p) does not reflect certain external economies involved in the production of this commodity. When these are allowed for, the supply curve becomes Ss. That is, private marginal cost exceeds social marginal cost for any output by the vertical distance between these two curves. Given the world price, P_W, domestic production would be equal to OB if the social marginal cost were being equated to price. However, because of the domestic divergence between private and social costs, output is actually OA.

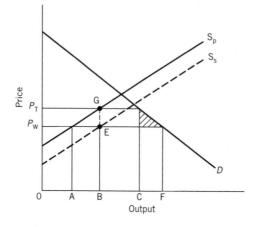

Figure 6.5 Use of a tariff to correct a domestic distortion. If the private supply curve is S_p, while society views the relevant supply function as S_s due to positive production externalities, the lack of government intervention will mean domestic production of only OA and imports of AF at the world price of P_W. A tariff that increases the domestic price to P_T increases domestic production to AB, which is where the supply curve that accounts for costs to society suggests it should be. Consumption falls from OF to OC due to the higher price, however, imposing a loss of consumer surplus of the shaded triangle.

To correct this divergence and encourage private producers to expand output to OB, a government may levy a tariff to raise the domestic price to P_T. That form of intervention represents a second-best policy, however. Although it does correct the distortion in production, it introduces another distortion in consumption. That is, at the tariff-distorted price, P_T, consumption is reduced from OF to OC, and there is a deadweight loss in consumer welfare (the shaded area in Figure 6.4). Recall from Chapter 5 that this consumption effect could be avoided if a subsidy were used instead of a tariff. A subsidy of EG per unit of output would induce domestic producers to expand output from OA to OB but would leave the price unchanged at P_W. Consumption would remain the same. Thus, domestic distortions, when they do exist, may constitute a basis for protection, but a subsidy is a better option than a tariff or a quota.

Revenues

Thus far, we have viewed government restrictions on imports solely as a means of protecting domestic producers, but tariffs are frequently a major source of revenue for governments. Tariffs on necessities that cannot be produced domestically can raise large sums of money without creating large distortions in the economy. In the late nineteenth century, the British tariff structure was designed exclusively to collect revenue from imports of tobacco, tea, spirits, and wine, goods which either were not produced at home or were subject to a comparable excise tax. Thus, the tariff did not create a deadweight loss by attracting resources into domestic production. In the United States tariffs accounted for 95 percent of federal government receipts at the onset of the Civil War in 1860, and even after subsequent growth in alcohol and tobacco taxes, tariffs still accounted for nearly half of federal government receipts in 1913. US tariffs, however, were not designed to avoid an expansion of output by competing domestic producers. Much of the developing world is simply following the US pattern.

Tariffs are attractive as a source of revenues for a developing country because of the lack of alternative ways to tax efficiently. If much of an economy is subsistence farming or is based on barter, domestic taxes are difficult to impose. Even in that part of the economy that is monetized, most transactions may be through paper currency rather than checks; therefore accurate records of transactions may be unavailable, making consistent taxation impossible. International trade may be the only large sector of the economy for which good records of transactions are available, so it becomes an obvious target for taxation. Goods entering through a single port or a few border checkpoints can be monitored relatively easily. If tariffs on imports (or exports) are high, however, smuggling becomes an attractive route for tax avoidance and revenues decline.

Ideally, better taxation systems would be developed in such countries, and considerable efforts are being made in this area by international agencies such as the International Monetary Fund and the International Bank for Reconstruction and Development (also known as the World Bank). This is a slow process, however, and it is not surprising that governments of developing countries are resistant to reducing tariffs that have been a dominant source of operating revenues. Unless those countries have been particularly success-ful in imposing high tariffs on goods with less elastic demands, however, they can gain from imposing one single tariff rate and avoiding the large efficiency losses from exceptionally high rates on some goods.

The political economy of trade policy

The attention that economists have focused on the way trade barriers affect national income and world welfare certainly gives useful insights into the types of ideal policies and international rules appropriate to achieve greater world efficiency. Nevertheless, those perspectives may be of limited relevance in explaining what domestic policy makers try to accomplish or what voters seek through trade policy. Therefore, we consider other factors that determine the policies actually adopted.

One common model applied in the analysis of public decision-making or public choice is the median voter model. If people were ordered by their preference on a given issue, such as the appropriate tariff to levy on imported cars, then the median voter would play a key role: half of the group would desire a higher tariff, and half would desire a lower tariff. The preference of the median voter would determine the outcome of a referendum in which everyone voted, because any lower value could be defeated by a majority of voters and similarly any higher value could be defeated by a majority of voters.

Such a model suggests that the outcome may deviate substantially from the economically efficient outcome. In particular, if we predict the consequence of the tariff on the basis of the Stolper–Samuelson theorem presented in Chapter 3, we expect in a labor-scarce country that labor gains and capital loses. If there are many more workers than capitalists, then the median voter is likely to be a worker who supports a high tariff, regardless of whether this tariff results in a terms-of-trade gain, targets a promising growth industry, or reduces economic efficiency.

Although this outcome appears plausible, it nevertheless may be a misleading prediction. For example, if voters consider more than one issue at a time or if not everyone votes, the outcome may be different. Also, although we expect Stolper–Samuelson-type adjustments to occur over the long run, individuals may perceive their interests on a more short-run basis and may demand a different type of trade policy. Furthermore, given that most decisions are not made by direct democracy or referendum, the role of government decision-makers, or the suppliers of trade policy, can be relevant too.

An implication from the median voter model is that the intensity of voter preferences does not matter. Capitalists with a very strong interest in free trade due to the gains they receive have no way to make their preference felt. If other votes can be considered at the same time, however, logrolling or trading of votes may occur. Capitalists may be willing to vote for training programs, regional development programs, urban renewal, or any other issue that labor regards as important enough to modify its vote on trade policy. In some cases, a direct form of compensation paid to those who lose as a result of a lower tariff may occur. But, if capitalists can identify some other issue that is sufficiently important to a large enough group of workers to win their agreement to a lower tariff, then a trade-related compensation program may not be adopted.

Is the Stolper–Samuelson theorem a good basis for predicting voting behavior? Stephen Magee suggests that such a long-run view where all labor perceives its interests to be the same and all capital likewise votes as a bloc does not describe the US political process well.[20] He noted whether Congressional testimony on the 1974 Trade Act by unions and manufacturers' associations within the same industry advocated the same position, as we expect from a short-run, specific-factors model of trade, or whether their testimony supported different positions, as we expect from the Stolper–Samuelson theorem. Magee reports that in 19 of 21 industries, labor and capital took the same position, a result that supports a short-run interpretation of interest-group participation.

The specific factors model seems particularly relevant when a decision in a single industry is under consideration, for then the effect on labor and capital outside the industry will be felt primarily in their role as consumers. Often that effect can be small. For example, the United States has a highly restrictive sugar policy that in the mid-1980s resulted in a domestic price more than twice the world price. Nevertheless, it cost the typical individual $11 per year. Such a small effect may result in many individuals not being concerned enough to vote. Rather, voters may remain rationally ignorant on many issues, concluding that the time and effort necessary to become informed exceed the cost likely to be imposed on them by an adverse vote. This lack of participation may be a positive factor in the case of intra-industry trade in differentiated products, for neither gainers nor losers may perceive a large enough stake to motivate intense lobbying for an activist trade policy.

Even when the cost of protection is more substantial, as in the case of the Japanese auto VER, which at its peak cost consumers over $1,000 per car, individuals still may not be motivated to vote. With so many individuals adversely affected, any one person may suspect that his or her vote is unlikely to influence the outcome. Rather, each individual expects to free-ride on the efforts of others. Likewise, an individual is unlikely to contribute to a lobbying effort to mobilize other voters. If all consumers make the same probabilistic calculation, they are unlikely to vote even though the individual and aggregate losses are substantial. When benefits are more highly concentrated than costs, then the expected return to special-interest voters is greater. And, because there are fewer beneficiaries to organize into a force to lobby for a trade restriction, free-riding will be less common. Generally, the expressed demand for restrictive trade policy appears likely to exceed the expressed demand for a more open policy, although distributors of imported goods or downstream users of protected goods have sometimes been effective lobbies for freer trade.

The role of politicians elected or appointed to carry out trade policy also is an important influence. In the United States the president potentially may be swayed by campaign contributions to impose trade restrictions in certain sectors. At the same time, the inefficiencies created by trade restrictions may slow economic growth and limit the growth of jobs in export sectors of the economy. While individual representatives in Congress may ignore these national effects, the president is less likely to do so. Rightly or wrongly, the president is likely to be held responsible for the economy's macroeconomic performance, international political stability, and the country's international standing. Imposing trade restrictions can damage any of these objectives. For this reason, we may find that an administration generally is more willing to impose trade barriers in sectors where the economic distortions created are smaller, but it nevertheless will be more attentive to domestic producers that are well organized. While each special-interest lobby recognizes that its campaign contribution is unlikely to be the one that determines an election outcome, it nevertheless expects to influence administrative decisions, such as an administration's aggressiveness in negotiating import cutbacks, in initiating dumping cases, or in changing customs classifications of imports to benefit domestic producers.[21]

Although trade barriers may be less efficient than other transfers to benefit a particular sector, they appear to represent a more credible commitment of assistance than alternative policies. Trade restrictions are likely to retain adherents long after they have outgrown their importance as a source of revenue to the government, met a national security need, or encouraged a new industry to emerge. Ignoring their distributive effects limits our ability to understand the limited commitments to free trade that we observe worldwide.

Summary of key concepts

1   Economists' arguments in favor of an open trading system have been opposed for a variety of reasons, some quite misdirected and some more plausible.

2   Claims that protection will raise domestic employment or eliminate a trade deficit ignore important macroeconomic relationships in the economy, especially one that operates under flexible exchange rates.

3   When trade is determined by relative factor endowments, protection will raise the real income of scarce factors even when it reduces national income. Because there are net gains to trade, those who gain can compensate those who lose and still themselves be better off. Actual payments of compensation have been unpredictable.

4   A country large enough to affect international prices may improve its terms of trade by imposing a tariff or an export tax. Retaliation by trading partners may leave all countries worse off.

5   Protection to benefit an infant industry may allow it to cover fixed costs of entry and learn enough to become competitive internationally. Such protection is intended to make production profitable enough to offset distortions in the economy that raise the industry's costs of production. Other measures to deal with these distortions directly, as in the case of a production subsidy, are generally more efficient.

6   Strategic trade policy to subsidize exports or to impose a tariff on imports may allow a country to shift monopoly profits to its own producers or to benefit from lower costs and larger spillovers from higher domestic production. Not only is identifying appropriate industries to target difficult, but designing effective policy will depend upon how oligopoly firms respond to the actions of each other. Gains from trade restrictions may be dissipated by the entry of additional firms into the industry.

7   Predicting what trade policy a country will adopt requires attention to how individuals are affected by the policy, how concentrated those benefits and costs are, and what incentive individuals have to vote. Because a tariff reduction tends to have a large negative effect on a few and a small positive effect on many, those adversely affected are more likely to mobilize to influence policy.

Questions for study and review

1 If the United States raises tariffs enough to reduce its imports by $10 billion, what are likely to be the employment effects of this action? Discuss, considering as many aspects of this issue as you can.

2 "Higher tariffs don't increase employment; they just redistribute the unemployed." Do you agree? Explain.

3 "To show its support for underpaid workers in poor countries who are exploited in sweatshops and made to work in unsatisfactory conditions, the European Union should restrict imports from countries where such conditions are allowed to exist." Critically evaluate this statement.

4 Why will eliminating a tariff on clothing have a different effect on income distribution from eliminating a tariff on computers? In which case are the predictions of the Stolper–Samuelson theorem more relevant?

5 Under what circumstances is the terms-of-trade argument for a tariff valid for a single nation? Does the world as a whole gain? Why or why not?

6 "A tariff is an attractive form of taxation because the tax burden falls on the foreigner." Do you agree? Explain.

7 India argues that infant-industry protection of its automobile industry is necessary. What factors support this claim? How would you assess the benefits and the costs from targeting this industry?

8 "Russian wages are so low that European producers will require additional protection to maintain current wages and generous welfare state benefits." Evaluate the economic basis for this statement.

9 If West Virginia became a separate nation, would it be better able to solve its economic problems (high unemployment, depressed industries, etc:) through tariffs? Discuss, using economic analysis.

10 Under what circumstances might US protectionist policies be intended to discourage foreign research and development efforts?

11 Why can external economies from an industry's growth justify support for protection? Is this an argument for permanent or temporary protection?

12 How can subsidizing exports and accepting a decline in a country's terms of trade make a country better off?

13 "Dumping will be observed most often in imperfectly competitive markets where above-average profits can be earned." Explain whether you agree or disagree with this statement. How does the imposition of anti-dumping duties affect producers in the importing country? Why may your answer depend upon their market share?

14 If large financial contributions by political action committees and other special-interest groups account for most of a candidate's campaign financing, what keeps a country's trade policy from being highly protectionistic? Why do we not observe a political action committee representing consumers of cars? Where do you expect the highest trade barriers to be imposed?

Suggested further reading

For two collections of accessible articles on trade policy and debate over the gains from government strategic actions, see:

- Krugman, Paul, ed., *Strategic Trade Policy and the New International Economics*, Cambridge, MA: MIT Press, 1986.
- Stern, Robert, ed., *US Trade Policies in a Changing World Economy*, Cambridge, MA: MIT Press, 1987.

For a more direct application to debates over trade policy, see:

- Tyson, Laura, *Who's Bashing Whom: Trade Conflict in High Technology Industries*, Washington DC: Institute for International Economics, 1992.

More advanced examples of numerical analysis of trade policy in imperfectly competitive markets are included in:

- Feenstra, Robert, ed., *Trade Policies for International Competitiveness*, Chicago: University of Chicago Press, 1989.
- Krugman, Paul and Alisdair Smith, eds, *Empirical Studies of Strategic Trade Policy*, Chicago: University of Chicago Press, 1994.

Two examples of economists presenting the case for an open trading system are

- Bhagwati, Jadish, *Free Trade Today*, Princeton: Princeton University Press, 2002.
- Irwin, Douglas, *Free Trade Under Fire*, Princeton: Princeton University Press, 2002.

Notes

1 The number of TAA recipients reached a peak in 1980 at nearly 600,000; the number in the 1990s varied between 60,000 and 90,000 workers. For a summary of the program's operation, see: http://aspe.os.dhhs.gov/96gb/07TAA.TXT

2 Malcolm Bale, "Adjustment Assistance under the Trade Expansion Act of 1962" *Journal of International Law and Economics* 4, 1974, p. 49.

3 Douglas Irwin, "Welfare Effects of British Free Trade: Debate and Evidence from the 1840s," *Journal of Political Economy* 96, no. 6 , 1988, pp. 1142–64.

4 Economists formally show that this will be an optimum tariff when Country A's trade indifference curve is tangent to Country B's offer curve. James Meade, *A Geometry of International Trade* (London: George Allen and Unwin, 1952), shows the derivation of a trade indifference curve, which corresponds to all combinations of goods to be traded that leave a country equally well off.

5 Alexander Hamilton, *Report on Manufactures*, 1791.

6 For a careful critique of the infant-industry argument, see Robert E. Baldwin, "The Case against Infant-Industry Protection," *Journal of Political Economy* 77, 1969, pp. 295–305.

7 See Paul Krugman, "Is Free Trade Passé?," *Journal of Economic Perspectives*, Fall 1987, pp. 131–41, for a general statement of these issues. The example in the text follows his presentation. The original contribution in this area appears in J. Brander and B. Spencer, "Export Subsidies and International Market Share Rivalry," *Journal of International Economics* 16, 1985, pp. 83–100.

8 Krugman, op. cit.

9 This example ignores the possibility that RCA and Sony could decide to collaborate on the research for high-definition television (HTV), sharing the costs and then producing sets for their home markets while competing in the rest of the world. Also, the example overlooks the question of how a national champion is to be selected. Because RCA is owned by the French company Thomson, the US government may see less reason to support it, even if some of its production would be located in the United States. Finally, the example represents the happy, but far from automatic, outcome where the government already has identified the most efficient firm to subsidize and need not worry about its squandering the subsidy without being able to match the production costs of the foreign competitor.

10 Richard Baldwin and Paul Krugman, "Industrial Political and International Competition in Wide-bodied Jet Aircraft," in R. Baldwin, ed., *Trade Policy Issues and Empirical Analysis* (Chicago: University of Chicago Press, 1988), pp. 45–71.
11 See Michael Porter, *The Competitive Advantage of Nations* (New York: Free Press, 1990), for examples of successful and unsuccessful government intervention in a variety of industries and countries.
12 Richard Baldwin and Paul Krugman, "Market Access and Competition: A Simulation Study of 16K Random Access Memories," in Robert Feenstra, ed., *Empirical Research in Industrial Trade* (Cambridge, MA: MIT Press, 1988).
13 Douglas Irwin and Peter Klenow, "Learning-by-Doing Spillovers in the Semiconductor Industry," *Journal of Political Economy* 102, no. 6, 1994, pp. 1200–27.
14 L. Tyson, *Who's Bashing Whom: Trade Conflict in High Technology Industries* (Washington DC: Institute for International Economics, 1992).
15 World Trade Organization, *Overview of Developments in the International Trading Environment*, Annual Report by the Director General, Nov. 15, 2002 (WT/TPR/OV/8).
16 Thomas Prusa, "Why Are so Many Antidumping Petitions Withdrawn?," *Journal of International Economics* 33, no. 1–2, 1992, pp. 1–20.
17 Patrick Messerlin, "The EC Antidumping Regulations: A First Economic Appraisal," *Weltwirtschaftliches Archiv* 125, 1995, pp. 563–87.
18 WTO, op. cit.
19 See *The Financial Times*, May 25, 1996, and *The Washington Post*, July 15, 1998, for discussion of the satellite launch agreements and the *Wall Street Journal* February 1, 2001 for commentary on consolidation in the satellite industry. For a more comprehensive treatment of the national defense argument for protection, see T.N. Srinivasan, "The National Defense Argument for Intervention in Foreign Trade," in Robert M. Stern, ed., *US Trade Policy in a Changing World Economy* (Cambridge, MA: MIT Press, 1987), pp. 337–76.
20 Stephen Magee, "Three Simple Tests of the Stolper–Samuelson Theorem," in Peter Oppenheimer, ed., *Issues in International Economics* (London: Oriel Press, 1980), pp. 138–53.
21 Gene Grossman and Elhanan Helpman, "Protection for Sale," *American Economics Review* 84, no. 4, September 1994, pp. 833–50.

7 Regional blocs

Preferential trade liberalization

Learning objectives

By the end of this chapter you should be able to understand:

- why various degrees of economic integration within preferential trade blocs exist;
- how trade blocs result in gains from trade creation and losses from trade diversion, as well as potential gains from economies of scale and greater capital formation;
- how the European Union has successfully created trade in manufactured goods, but diverted trade in agricultural goods;

To this point we have assumed that restrictions on imports are nondiscriminatory; that is, all trading partners are treated equally in terms of market access. Such nondiscriminatory trade is a major goal of the GATT/WTO system, which we examine in Chapter 8, but it is far from universal. Most countries have different levels of protection, maintaining the lowest level for partners in trade blocs or friends, and less favorable circumstances for others. The GATT allows such trading blocs when their preferential treatment applies to substantially all trade among the partners. There has been an explosion of over 130 such arrangements since 1995. Whether their members regard them as substitutes for multilateral agreements is not yet clear.

In this chapter we pay primary attention to the European Union (EU), the most ambitious trade bloc with regard to the extent of economic integration it has fostered among its members. We also consider the North American Free Trade Agreement (NAFTA), a more recent and less comprehensive agreement which nevertheless creates an internal market nearly as large as the EU market.

Preferential trading is not a new concept. Colonial empires, such as those that existed in the nineteenth and early twentieth centuries, can be viewed as discriminatory trading blocs, because the colonial power frequently maintained a highly favorable situation for itself selling in the colonies and for the colonies selling in its markets. One reason for creating such empires was to guarantee export markets and sources of imports that could not be produced at home. Such an example may cause us to question who gains from such discriminatory trade blocs: just some members, all members, or the world as a whole? If the bloc gains at the expense of nonmember countries, does this GATT exception make sense, or do trade blocs represent an important step toward a more liberal trading order that ought to be encouraged? We begin this chapter by considering alternative structures for preferential trade areas, and we consider what factors are especially relevant in assessing the gains and losses from their establishment.

Alternative forms of regional liberalization

Regional trading blocs can be categorized at different levels according to how extensive the integration of national economies becomes. The first and easiest to negotiate is a free-trade area, under which tariffs and other barriers to trade among the members are removed (sometimes only for manufactured goods, owing to differing agricultural support programs). To the extent that each country retains its own antidumping procedures, national restrictions can still influence trade among members. Also, each country maintains its own tariff schedule and other commercial policies with regard to goods coming from nonmember countries. Such arrangements encourage the importation of goods into whichever member has the lowest tariffs and their subsequent reshipment to member countries with higher external tariffs. Certificates of origin are supposed to guarantee that products coming tariff-free from a member country really were produced there, but enforcing such a system effectively to prohibit transshipments is far from automatic.

This problem can be avoided with the adoption of a **customs union** arrangement. A customs union is a free-trade area in which external tariffs and other barriers to imports coming from nonmembers are unified; that is, all member countries maintain the same restrictions on imports from nonmembers. A **common market**, the next step in regional integration, is a customs union that allows the free mobility of capital and labor among the member countries. A final step is **economic union**, a customs union where countries have agreed to common tax and expenditure policies and a jointly managed monetary policy. The European Economic Community (EEC), established by the Treaty of Rome in 1957, created a customs union. Subsequent progress in removing remaining barriers to the free movement of goods, services, labor, and capital in a single market and in achieving greater coordination of economic and social policies has been reflected in the establishment of the European Union in 1993.

Efficiency gains and losses: the general case

The creation of a regional bloc or other form of discriminatory trading arrangement would appear to be a movement toward free trade and therefore toward greater economic efficiency. Because some barriers to trade are being eliminated and others are being left in place, the average tariff level for the world declines. This appearance of liberalization and of greater efficiency can be deceiving, however. Some regional blocs do increase efficiency, but others can represent a movement away from the allocation of resources that would occur under free trade and can therefore reduce world efficiency. The fact that the tariff cutting is discriminatory creates this possibility. There is no general rule to establish whether discriminatory trade blocs increase or decrease efficiency; instead, each must be evaluated separately.[1] We begin by considering factors relevant in the general case with competitive markets and then consider additional insights when imperfect competition and economies of scale are important. In the general case, early analysis of preferential trade agreements rested on two effects: trade creation and trade diversion.

- *Trade creation.* This is the beneficial effect of a discriminatory trading arrangement. For the case of constant costs of production in two countries, we observe it when a member country was not previously importing the product and was instead consuming local goods that were produced inefficiently. As a result of the creation of the trading bloc, the product is imported from more efficient firms in another member country. Inefficient local production is displaced by more efficient output in another member country. Since the product was not being imported from a nonmember before the beginning of the arrangement, outsiders lose no exports and are unaffected.

- *Trade diversion.* This is the undesirable or efficiency-reducing effect of such a bloc. It occurs when a member country was previously importing a product from a country that does not become a member of the bloc. When the discriminatory tariff-cutting occurs, other members have an advantage over nonmembers; as a result, a member country takes export sales away from a nonmember. Discriminatory tariff cuts mean that the more efficient nonmember country loses sales to less efficient producers in a member country, thus reducing world efficiency. Trade is diverted from low-cost to higher-cost sources.

A simple modification to the Chapter 5 treatment of a tariff in a small country illustrates these two points. Consider French production and imports from two potential sources, Germany and Japan. If the French supply curve is upward-sloping, while supply curves for Germany and Japan remain horizontal, it is possible to show both trade creation and trade diversion in the same market. This situation can be seen in Figure 7.1. Prior to the creation of the customs union, France maintained a uniform tariff, which is shown as the vertical distance between S_J and $S_J + T$. German costs were higher, as shown by S_G, so with the uniform tariff, Germany sold no bicycles in France. The elimination of the French tariff on German bikes makes S_G the relevant import supply function; thus Japan loses export sales of Q_3Q_2, with a resulting efficiency loss of rectangle e, which represents the difference between German and Japanese costs times the number of bicycles whose production is diverted. Since the French price of bicycles declines from P to P', however, consumption expands from Q_3 to Q_4 and French production declines from Q_2 to Q_1, thus increasing total imports from Q_3Q_2 to Q_4Q_1. The efficiency gains from this expansion of trade consist of the areas of triangles b and d. Whether efficiency increases or declines in this market depends

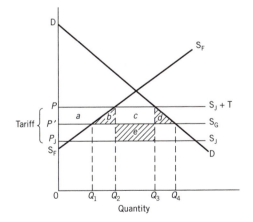

Figure 7.1 Effects of a customs union between France and Germany. Before the customs union is formed, Japan, which is the lowest-cost producer, exports a volume of Q_2Q_3 to France. Germany, with higher costs and no discriminatory advantage, has no sales in France. The customs union, however, gives Germany a discriminatory advantage, and its supply curve to France becomes S_G, while the Japanese supply curve remains at $S_J + T$. All French imports now shift to German sources, and imports rise to Q_1Q_4. The trade creation gains are triangle b and d, but the trade distortion loss is rectangle e. The French government loses tariff revenues of rectangles c plus e.

on the relationship between the area of rectangle e (loss) and the sum of triangles b and d (gain). This net effect can be derived from the increase in consumers' surplus of area a + b + c + d, while French manufacturers lose producers' surplus of area a and the French government loses tariff revenue of area c + e.

Although the government loses revenues and manufacturers lose profits, French consumers gain a large amount of consumer surplus, and German firms gain sales. The only clear loser is Japan: it loses export revenues, and its firms lose sales to firms that are less efficient. Except for the impact on government revenues, regional blocs are generally beneficial to the members, but they can be decidedly harmful to nonmembers who find themselves on the losing side of a discriminatory trade arrangement. If a member of a **free-trade area** found that it did not gain, because its losses from trade diversion exceeded its gains from trade creation, it could simply reduce its tariff sufficiently to eliminate the loss from diversion. A member of a customs union with a common external tariff, however, does not have this same opportunity.

We can add another possible effect to the situation shown in Figure 7.1: the French terms of trade may improve when the foreign supply curves it faces are not horizontal. Preferential treatment of imports from Germany is less likely to displace Japanese exports completely, as Japanese exporters are willing to accept a decline in the before-tariff price they receive. This price reduction represents a potential gain to France.[2] We discussed a similar effect in Chapter 6 regarding the optimum tariff a large country might levy. As countries join together in regional trading blocs, their market power and potential to shift the terms of trade in their favor increases.

Panagariya suggests another modification of Figure 7.1. Suppose France produces none of the imported product, and the upward sloping supply curve instead represents German production. An initial tariff on imports from Germany would shift that supply curve to the left, implying a smaller German share of the market and a larger Japanese share. Removing the tariff on German goods only does not affect the price seen by consumers, which is determined by the tariff-laden Japanese goods, but German production expands while French imports from Japan fall. Thus, France gets no benefit from trade creation, but experiences a big trade diversion loss captured by Germany. Panagariya suggests such asymmetric outcomes are likely when a high-tariff, small developing country joins with a low-tariff, more developed country, such as Mexico and the United States in NAFTA or the EU in its southern expansion to include Greece, Spain, and Portugal in the 1980s.[3]

That a country may gain from joining a regional trade bloc represents another example of the theory of second best; the first-best solution of multilateral trade liberalization is not adopted, but choosing a policy of free trade with just some partners may increase a nation's welfare compared to the case of uniformly-applied trade barriers. From Figure 7.1 we might conclude that if two countries initially account for a large share of each other's trade, their union is more likely to raise welfare. Presumably, they are each other's cheapest source of supply when nondiscriminatory trade barriers exist, and therefore shifting to a system of preferences that benefits the low-cost partner does not result in trade diversion. When foreign supply curves are not horizontal and the entire import market for a product is not claimed by a single country, however, this simple benchmark is less useful, because the most elastic supply may be from a nonpartner. From the standpoint of potential trade creation, if countries have overlapping production structures, then a reduction of trade barriers that results in lower prices and greater imports from the partner is more likely to displace inefficient domestic production. If members of a customs union set a lower common external tariff, then less trade diversion will occur.

Efficiency gains and losses with economies of scale

When economies of scale and imperfect competition exist, additional efficiency effects from trade liberalization exist. We identified these concepts in Chapter 6 and find them relevant when we discuss preferential trade liberalization, too. We list them separately:

1   a shift in output, where price exceeds average cost and economic profits are received;
2   a scale effect, where firms' average costs of production fall as output expands;
3   a variety effect, where trade allows a greater variety of final goods and intermediate inputs to be purchased.

An expansion of output that shifts profits from one country to another is most relevant in those industries where high barriers to entry ensure that above-average profits continue to be earned in the long run. Such a strategy may have been a plausible motivation for the colonial empires mentioned above, but modern-day preferential trade agreements where members voluntarily assent to membership imply that such profit-shifting more likely must come at the expense of nonmembers. Empirical analysis of preferential trade blocs has not identified this as a major benefit extracted from others.

In contrast, scale effects have been found to be a significant source of additional gain. Recall that internal economies of scale depend upon a firm's output, not the industry's output. Therefore, an important determinant of these potential gains is what happens to the number of firms in an industry. If the formation of a European customs union results in greater competition between previously protected French and German producers, they each perceive a more elastic demand for their output and the profit margins they charge will be reduced. Output per firm rises, which results in lower average costs of production. This benefit from greater competition will be greater among countries that have overlapping industry structures.

Based on our reasoning developed in Chapter 4, we expect the total number of producers in France and Germany to fall, which means fewer resources need be devoted to the fixed costs of a firm entering the industry. The remaining firms producing this particular product achieve greater economies of scale. When producers who do cease production of this product can easily shift inputs into producing other products and exhaust economies of scale available there, the economic and social costs of adjustment are likely to be much smaller than we predict from trade motivated by differences in factor endowments.

An alternative reason for scale economies to be observed is the decline in average costs of production possible when external economies of scale exist. In Chapter 4 we considered how a concentration of output in one country might lower costs of production by promoting the introduction of specialized intermediate-input suppliers, by creating a pool of trained labor, and by encouraging the spread of information about new technologies. A larger market created within the preferential trade bloc may make it more likely that these externalities or benefits from agglomeration are realized.[4]

A major concern within trading blocs has been where these more efficient producers will tend to be located. Are they likely to be spread across all countries, with some locations gaining the benefits from agglomeration in one industry and other locations gaining a comparable benefit in other industries? Or, is this activity likely to be concentrated in the center or core of the market, with peripheral areas either forced to accept much lower wages or to be left out of this opportunity to produce goods where external economies exist? Some economists have suggested this latter outcome is likely when transportation costs make it cheaper to serve the mass of customers in the core by locating in that core. That choice to produce where there are many consumers will be reinforced by subsequent production externalities. Other economists note that this explanation ignores the role of transportation costs for goods where externalities do not exist.[5] Although the issue is unresolved among economists, it has been a serious concern of members of the European Union.

Dynamic effects and other sources of gain

In addition to the efficiency effects summarized thus far, another rationale for expecting a gain from a regional trade agreement is a potential increase in capital formation. In Chapter 9 we consider the contribution of more capital to a country's growth rate and a higher level of output. Here we note whether formation of a trade bloc is likely to have such an effect.

If investors believe that locating inside a trading bloc offers the best way to serve a protected market, there may be a surge of investment from both domestic and foreign sources. For example, the accession of Spain and Portugal to the European Community in 1986 and Mexico's entry into the newly created NAFTA in 1994 were both preceded by a boom of investment by firms that anticipated labor-intensive products could be produced more competitively in these newly available locations with access to a large market within the trading blocs. Such investment may have an immediate positive effect on the growth of the host country, although it may represent diversion of investment away from more efficient locations outside of the bloc.

If capital is not so mobile internationally, formation of the bloc still may lead to an increase in output, either from a more efficient use of resources or from activity diverted to it from nonmembers. Out of that additional output, incomes rise and saving from that income is likely to rise. In addition, if demand for capital-intensive goods rises, the rate of return to capital will rise and generate more savings, assuming the amount of saving is responsive to higher returns. Finally, if the price of capital equipment falls within the bloc due to trade liberalization, a given dollar of saving will result in a larger increase in the capital stock. If a larger capital stock created for any of these reasons allows external economies of scale to be achieved, then there is an extra benefit to those who join the trade bloc.[6]

The conceptual framework presented thus far assumes that prior to the formation of the preferential trading bloc, firms are operating efficiently given the limited national markets they face and the market power they possess. A more fundamental possibility is that firms have grown complacent in sheltered national markets. Competition from rivals in other member countries is a powerful stimulus to managerial efficiency. Firms become acutely cost-conscious and much more receptive to technological improvements than before. Some commentators claim that one of the main reasons for the United Kingdom's belated decision to join the European Community in 1973 was its hope that competition would stimulate labor and management to increase productivity and generally shake them out of their lethargy. The European Commission identified this as an expected source of gain from the 1992 single market program.

Reduced international tensions and an increased likelihood of peace may be another benefit from a regional trading bloc. One of the reasons why the United States supported the formation of the European Economic Community was a desire to tie Germany and France as closely together as possible after World War II. On both sides of the Atlantic integration of the two economies was viewed as a way to make it difficult or even impossible for them to be disentangled.

Can any of these effects be measured, especially the various efficiency effects that are familiar from previous chapters? Economists have addressed this issue in two different ways.

One approach develops numerical simulation models that attempt to represent demand and cost conditions and the way firms interact in determining industry output. Changes in policy can be entered as exogenous changes in these models, and the consequent impacts on prices and output can be assessed. We reported examples of this approach in our consideration of trade policy in general in Chapters 5 and 6. This approach is particularly useful in predicting what the future effect of a policy will be. A second approach is to observe what changes in trade patterns have occurred during a period when there were policy changes, and to project what trade patterns would have been in the absence of the policy change. We comment on results from both of these approaches applied to the two preferential trade agreements we discuss, the EU and NAFTA.

The European Union

European political and economic cooperation over the past 50 years demonstrates remarkable progress in achieving deeper economic integration and in expanding to include more countries. In 1948 Belgium, Luxembourg and the Netherlands formed a customs union known as Benelux. Those countries, plus France, Germany, and Italy, created the European Coal and Steel Community in 1951. The Treaty of Rome in 1957 established the European Economic Community of those same six nations, and by 1968 a customs union with a common external tariff had been implemented. Also in 1967 the EEC joined with the European Coal and Steel Community and Euratom to form the European Community (EC).[7] Denmark, Ireland and the United Kingdom joined in 1973, Greece in 1981, Spain and Portugal in 1986, and Austria, Sweden, and Finland in 1995. In addition, EC members began a major initiative in 1987 to establish a single European market by 1992. The Maastricht Treaty, ratified in 1993, marked the creation of the European Union and established a plan to introduce a common currency in 1999; the latter topic is addressed in Chapter 20. The decision in December 2002 to offer admission to ten new members and the deliberations of the constitutional convention begun in 2002 under Valerie Giscard d'Estaing both point to further evolution in the union's goals and operations. We do not attempt to provide a comprehensive treatment of each of these steps in European unification. Instead, we present some of the more significant issues that have arisen in measuring the economic effects of the Community's formation and expansion, and then briefly consider major economic challenges confronting the EU.

Empirical assessments and interpretations

With respect to the initial formation of the EEC, the most systematic analyses have addressed trade in manufactured goods. For example, between 1958 and 1970, Balassa reports that imports from members as a share of domestic consumption rose from 4.8 percent to 12.4 percent, while the comparable figure for imports from nonmembers rose from 6.4 percent to 8.7 percent.[8] To interpret these figures, he examines the way growth in income affected imports from both sources in the 1953–9 base period and in the 1959–70 period. He concludes that trade creation exceeded trade diversion by $11.4 billion. In terms of the welfare triangles shown in Figure 7.1, he calculates the gain from this trade creation represents 0.15 percent of GNP. In the case of agricultural trade, he reports a loss from trade diversion equal to half that amount. He further applies a very general procedure to project that gains from economies of scale equal 0.5 percent of GNP. Because much of the EEC expansion in trade was intra-industry, the social tensions involved in the adjustment process were much lower than if large industry contractions had been necessary.

Although the United Kingdom had originally chosen to remain outside of the EEC, due to its concerns over a federalist European structure and its own ties to nonEuropean countries, it negotiated an accession agreement in 1971. A significant economic and political factor was the projected higher cost of food and the transfer of tariff revenue from the UK to the EC. Because higher food prices have the greatest impact on low-income families, the Labour Party opposed British membership, and as late as 1983 waged an unsuccessful general election campaign to withdraw from the EEC. Aside from these distributional implications, by one elegant analysis British acceptance of import restrictions under the Common Agricultural Policy, the loss of the previous subsidy benefit on food imports from the EC, and the required transfer of 90 percent of tariff revenue to the Community were projected to result in a loss of 1.9 percent of GDP. This effect more than offset gains of 0.13 percent of GDP from trade creation/diversion effects on manufactured trade.[9]

The issue of British support of the EC budget was a point of contention from the outset. For example, in 1979 the United Kingdom contributed over 21 percent of the budget but received less than 13 percent of expenditures. On an ability-to-pay principle such a financial burden would not seem warranted because the UK is far from the highest-income country within the Community. The UK was able to renegotiate those terms, but still remained a net contributor because its small agricultural sector benefited less from the high internal commodity prices advocated by the French, Danes, and Irish and financed by the EC budget.[10]

The single market program begun in 1987 was not completed by 1992, but that date still has provided a focal point for economic analysis. Tariffs had long since been removed on intra-EC trade, but several other barriers kept national markets segmented rather than unified. These included differing industrial product standards, government procurement policies that favor national producers, professional licensing requirements that limit labor mobility, capital controls, border regulations, and restrictions on trade in services such as banking, insurance, and transportation. To achieve the goals of free movement of people, capital, goods, and services requires changes in thousands of national laws, regulations, and procedures. The positive economic implications were projected by the European Commission to be quite large. Reasons for its strong advocacy are summarized in Table 7.2 from initial estimates in the Cecchini Report,[11] which projects that forming a single market will raise GDP by 4 to 6 percent.

Subsequent analysis by economists using more comprehensive analytical models, which at the same time do not purport to measure as many separate influences, put this gain in a smaller range. Baldwin and Venables' survey of five different studies breaks their effects into the three sources of gain identified earlier: general trade-creation effects raise GDP by 0.5 percent of GDP; including economies of scale raises that figure to 0.40–1.18 percent of GDP; and adding effects of capital accumulation raises it to 0.8–2.60 percent.[12] Attention to factors beyond trade creation and trade diversion clearly is important.

Important challenges

The EU commitment to accept ten new members by 2004 is a bold move to ensure stable democracies in those countries and to promote economic development in an expanded European market. It also creates a certain urgency to address very broad issues of EU governance. With so many voting members, can countries agree to qualified majority voting to determine more issues in the Council of Ministers, or will each country retain the right to veto issues of critical importance to it? What will be the power of national governments

Box 7.1 Fortress Europe?

The ambitious EU program to establish a single internal market by 1992 raised fears among outsiders that this policy would result in a more insular Europe that would be less likely to trade with those who were not members of the Union. Are those fears justified? Consider the figures in Table 7.1 that show European trade patterns in 1988, at the outset of the initiative, and in 1994, the final year before the EU enlargement to include Austria, Finland, and Sweden. The values for exports and imports are simply derived by summing the trade of individual EU members.

Table 7.1 European Union trade, 1988 and 1994 (US$ million)

| | Total | Exports to | | | |
		US	Japan	European Union	Developing
1988	1,065	84.6	19.9	633.2	179.4
1994	1,465	113.1	30.3	827.4	310.6
Change:	37.6%	33.7%	52.3%	30.7%	73.1%

| | Total | Imports from | | | |
		US	Japan	European Union	Developing
1988	1,083	79.4	50.2	624.5	193.2
1994	1,455	119.4	61.4	792.8	302.7
Change:	34.3%	50.4%	22.3%	27.0%	56.7%

Source: International Monetary Fund, *Direction of Trade Statistics Yearbook*, 1988–1994.

Any interpretation with respect to changing trade patterns is clouded by changes in the real exchange rate that occurred over this time period and by the European recession that affected its growth relative to other nations. In Part Two of this book we address such issues more carefully. Nevertheless, a few generalizations are worth noting.

Trade among member countries, both exports and imports, grew more slowly than the total trade of members, a contrast to the pattern Balassa reported in the 1950s. Although a simplistic prediction might be that European recession will affect all suppliers proportionally, that outcome does not occur. Rather, above-average increases in imports occur from developing countries and from the United States. Economists sometimes adjust the figures in Table 7.1 to control, say, for the fact that US exports to the world as a whole rose over the period, but the corresponding intensity ratio (US share of EU imports/US share of world trade) still rises, an indication of greater intensity of US trade with the EU in spite of the single market. A continued outward orientation of EU exporters is suggested by above-average increases in exports to developing countries and to Japan. While a more thorough analysis would consider exports and imports disaggregated by product category, where greater attention can be paid to differential growth and price effects, an overview of EU trade based on these 2 years does not appear to justify the "Fortress Europe" label.

Table 7.2 Projected gains from completion of the internal market

	Percentage of GDP
Gain from removal of trade barriers	0.2–0.3
Gain from removal of barriers affecting overall production	2.0–2.4
Gains from exploiting economies of scale more fully	2.1
Gains from intensified competition reducing business efficiencies and monopoly profits	1.6
Total	4.3–6.2

Source: Commission of EC, Study of Directorate-General for Economic and Financial Affairs, in Paulo Cecchini, *The European Challenge 1992*, Table 9.2.

relative to EU institutions? Answers to those questions are beyond the scope of this book. We mention them by way of noting why the attention of European leaders and the public will not be focused on economic aspects of the enlargement alone. Nevertheless, there are significant economic issues to be addressed in this process.

One provocative issue has been the operation of the Common Agricultural Policy (CAP), a set of policies to guarantee high farm incomes within Europe. The CAP accounted for three-fourths of the EU budget in the 1980s and for half of it in the 1990s. The EU stands ready to buy surplus production of several commodities, because domestic output at target prices exceeds domestic demand. Until 1995 imports of agricultural commodities were limited by a variable levy that raised the price of foreign commodities to the European target price level, and the subsequently chosen bound tariff rates have not allowed greater access to the EU market, either. To avoid buying and storing surplus production the EU subsidizes export sales. As noted in Chapter 5, that has resulted in lower food prices in international markets, a benefit to nonmembers who are net importers of food and a loss to net exporters.

Within the EU, an initial effect of the CAP was to redistribute income from Germany to France. The accession of Greece, Spain and Portugal added other net recipients of funds. The enlargement of the EU will bring in other countries with large agricultural sectors. A key point of the eastern accession agreements rested on newcomers receiving less than half of the direct subsidy rate available to current farmers. A 10-year phase-in period before full benefits become available is intended to allow time for restructuring of their agricultural sectors. Also, Poland requested a 7-year delay before foreigners could buy Polish farmland.

Regional assistance represents a second important issue. The potential concentration of economic activity in core countries, leaving peripheral countries with fewer prospects for growth, has required EU attention even before enlargement. Transfers to governments to deal with lagging or stagnant regions represent over 30 percent of the EU budget. Because total budget expenditures are not to exceed 1.27 percent of GNP, additional expenditures to benefit new members will imply restraint on payments to current recipients. The new entrants will reduce GNP per capita in the EU by about 13 percent. Therefore the standard of providing development funds to regions with income per capita less than 75 percent of the EU average will result in a substantial reallocation, once the ability of the new entrants to absorb a higher level of transfers is reached. Pre-accession aid also has been provided to new entrants.

Table 7.3 presents the net budgetary positions of EU members for 2001. Although the calculations cannot be made with a high degree of precision, the table does suggest why

Table 7.3 EU operational budgetary balance, 2000

Country	Millions of euros	% of GNP
Germany	–9,273	–0.47
United Kingdom	–3,775	–0.25
Netherlands	–1,738	–0.44
France	–1.415	–0.10
Sweden	–1,177	–0.50
Austria	–544	–0.13
Luxembourg	–65	–0.35
Denmark	169	0.10
Finland	217	0.17
Italy	713	0.06
Ireland	1,675	1.83
Portugal	2,112	1.93
Greece	4,374	3.61
Spain	5,056	0.86

Source: Allocation of 2000 EU Operating Expenditure by Member State, p. 126, http://europa.eu.int/comm/budget/agenda2000/reports_enhtm

Germany, the Netherlands, and the UK have been most concerned over the need for fiscal discipline and CAP reform.

A further issue of importance within the EU is the goal of harmonization of government policies, such as social programs, taxes, and environmental standards. In a market where fewer barriers to the movement of goods, services, people, and capital remain, the influence of government programs designed to address national problems or preferences now account for more of the differences in relative prices across suppliers in different countries. Whereas those price differences made less impact when other prohibitions and regulations limited entry of outsiders, now capital is more free to move within the EU to locations where higher returns can be earned. Some fear a race to the bottom in providing social services if economic activity and the tax base of more generous states is eroded by these new freedoms. We discuss that issue in more detail in Chapter 11, particularly the harmonization of corporate income taxation.

NAFTA

A precursor to NAFTA was the Canada–US Free Trade Agreement, initiated in 1989.[13] The trade flow between the two countries was already the largest bilateral flow in the world (about $220 billion per year). Given this large amount of trade initially, and the prospect of gains in efficiency from greater competition among overlapping industries, the agreement appeared to be overwhelmingly trade creating. From the perspective of trade policy, the United States viewed this agreement, and later NAFTA, as a demonstration that like-minded countries could move ahead with more comprehensive agreements and have less concern over countries free-riding on the concessions of others, which seemed to be the case in stalled multilateral negotiations. Because the Canadian market was only one-tenth the size of the US market and similar wages were paid in both countries, much of US industry anticipated neither major gains nor losses from the agreement.

Within Canada the agreement was controversial. The western provinces specialized in natural-resource-based products exported to the United States, such as lumber, metals, oil, and gas, and they stood to benefit from cheaper imports. Ontario had a large manufacturing sector, much of which was of relatively small scale and high cost. Many Ontario residents, fearing that their manufacturing jobs would be lost as US products arrived on a free-trade basis, strongly opposed the pact. Cox and Harris projected that Canadian producers could realize substantial economies of scale by exporting to the much larger US market, and their work pioneered academic efforts to include scale economies in such analyses.[14] On that account they indicated there were significant gains to Canada from approving the free-trade agreement. On the other hand, other economists noted that Canada was making larger tariff reductions than the United States and would likely experience an offsetting loss in its terms of trade.[15]

Were there other convincing points raised in the public debate? An important gain to Canada, in spite of low US tariffs prior to the agreement, was a binational dispute resolution mechanism that provided a check on the arbitrary application of US antidumping and countervailing duty laws against Canadian exporters. These panels give producers in either country the opportunity to appeal decisions where they feel the local law is misapplied, a major innovation relative to weak dispute resolution procedures available multilaterally under the GATT at that time.

Debate in the United States over the North American Free Trade Agreement, which extended the free-trade area to include Mexico, was much more contentious than for the Canada–US agreement. It was negotiated and signed in 1992, passed by the Congress in late 1993, and began operation in 1994.[16] To gain Congressional approval, however, the Clinton administration added side-agreements to address fears that US firms would shift production to Mexico to take advantage of lax enforcement of pollution control laws and guarantees of workers' rights. Although a 10-year phase-in period was specified for the movement to free trade, many tariffs have been reduced more quickly. The treaty liberalizes investment rules in Mexico, although a few sectors such as petroleum are excluded. Banks and other financial institutions from one member country are able to operate in other member countries.

The dominant reason for the controversy over NAFTA was discussed in Chapter 3: the H–O model of factor-price equalization. The relative abundance of low-wage labor in Mexico made the agreement threatening to unskilled union workers in the United States and Canada. Owners of firms that produced labor-intensive goods also opposed the agreement, as would be predicted by the specific factors model of Chapter 3. Although most US farmers supported NAFTA, those in California and Florida who produced fruit and vegetables that are grown in Mexico opposed it. The strongest US support for NAFTA came from the management of firms such as IBM, Kodak, and others in high-tech or capital-intensive industries. Human and physical capital are more abundant in the United States than in Mexico, and firms that produce items that use those factors intensively expect to have rapidly expanding sales in Mexico.

Some trade diversion from NAFTA is likely. Asian newly industrialized countries (NICs) and other Caribbean and Latin American countries are likely to lose sales of apparel and electronic goods in the United States as Mexico displaces them, while Japan and Europe will lose some Mexican sales to the United States. In 1996 Mexico moved ahead of China to become the largest foreign supplier of apparel to the United States, which suggests that such diversion is occurring. Politically, trade diversion is attractive to NAFTA members in all three countries, because the trade displacements described above will improve member trade balances (export receipts minus import expenditures) at the expense of nonmembers.

A major US motive in negotiating NAFTA was to encourage rapid economic growth in Mexico and to promote the continuation of policy reforms initiated in the late 1980s. The formal treaty structure of NAFTA gives more confidence to prospective foreign investors that Mexican policy will not revert to the more restrictive environment pursued during Mexico's years of inward-oriented development policies. More rapid job creation in Mexico also would reduce the incentive for immigration into the United States.

Consider projections that economists made before the implementation of the agreement regarding the three major categories of benefits: general trade-creation effects increase GDP in Mexico by 0.3 percent; including economies of scale raises that figure to 1.6–3.4 percent; and adding the effect of capital accumulation raises it to 4.6–5.0 percent.[17] The gain to the United States is roughly 0.1 percent of GDP, an indication of the relatively small size of the Mexican market and the more limited change in US trade policy.

Box 7.2 A NAFTA scorecard

Although the analysis of export and import flows before and after the creation of a trade bloc is an important economic yardstick for evaluating its effects, another perspective on NAFTA is quite relevant politically in the United States. Because the Mexican economy was one-twentieth the size of the US economy, both positive and negative trade effects were likely to be small. Nevertheless, if these marginal effects added to an already difficult process of adjustment for US industries, the demands for government intervention would be magnified.

Table 7.4 shows a breakdown by all 20 US manufacturing industries of post-NAFTA trade, consumption, and employment performance, from 1993 to 1998. In 17 of the 20 industries, exports to Mexico rose more rapidly than total shipments. Other patterns emerged that suggest generally manageable impacts:

1   In spite of the deterioration of the overall bilateral trade balance with Mexico, in some industries improvement actually occurred – textiles, paper, chemicals, petroleum products, and rubber and plastic products.
2   Imports from Mexico grew more slowly than imports from the rest of the world in the case of petroleum products and lumber and wooden products.
3   In nine industries, the initial Mexican share of total imports was less than 3 percent, the de minimis standard applied in dumping cases to determine if imports are a cause of serious injury; in addition to four already mentioned, these are tobacco products, leather products, industrial machinery, transportation equipment other than motor vehicles, and miscellaneous manufactures.
4   In four industries the increase in the Mexican share of imports was less than 3 percentage points, and generally less than half a percentage point of US apparent consumption.
5   In the remaining six industries, employment rose in four – fabricated metal products, printing and publishing, electrical machinery, and motor vehicles.
6   Employment fell by 2 percent in instruments and related products and 23 percent in apparel.

The sharp decline in apparel sector employment suggests why US trade negotiators have been reluctant to make concessions in this sector in multilateral negotiations. Overall, and in spite of the Mexican peso crisis in 1994–5 that slowed growth in US exports, the phase-in of NAFTA occurred during a major US economic expansion, a favorable macroeconomic position to reduce industry adjustment pressures.

Table 7.4 US trade and employment by SIC industries

Description	Change in bilateral trade balance	Mexican share of all imports		Total import share of US market		Ratio, US apparent consumption	Ratio, US employment
	93–98	1993	1998	1993	1998	1998/1993	1998/1993
Food And kindred prod.	−235	0.053	0.079	0.042	0.053	1.165	1.010
Tobacco prod.	−17	0.006	0.022	0.025	0.013	1.507	0.889
Textile Mill prod.	420	0.019	0.080	0.087	0.112	1.090	0.881
Apparel and other textile prod.	−3,498	0.066	0.134	0.354	0.453	1.207	0.772
Lumber and wood prod.	−203	0.034	0.028	0.099	0.123	1.252	1.148
Furniture and fixtures	−1,288	0.136	0.164	0.133	0.184	1.497	1.092
Paper and allied prod.	685	0.010	0.019	0.085	0.099	1.243	0.981
Printing and publishing	−74	0.032	0.071	0.014	0.017	1.248	1.036
Chemicals and allied prod.	2,197	0.028	0.030	0.097	0.140	1.264	0.970
Petroleum and coal prod.	990	0.056	0.028	0.075	0.078	1.013	0.913
Rubber and plastic prod.	1,495	0.026	0.051	0.109	0.127	1.280	1.114
Leather and leather prod.	−98	0.028	0.036	0.598	0.718	1.102	0.719
Stone, clay, and glass prod.	−440	0.089	0.109	0.102	0.118	1.497	1.088
Primary metal industries	−372	0.054	0.078	0.163	0.222	1.375	1.050
Fabricated metal prod.	−469	0.068	0.115	0.080	0.092	1.378	1.128
Industrial machinery	−1,968	0.027	0.063	0.274	0.298	1.665	1.143
Electronic and electric equip.	−6,115	0.139	0.196	0.319	0.325	1.576	1.112
Motor vehicles and equip.	−8,307	0.071	0.140	0.280	0.300	1.375	1.191
Other transportation equip.	−28	0.015	0.023	0.126	0.206	1.136	0.978
Instruments and related prod.	−1,554	0.065	0.106	0.173	0.212	1.217	0.979
Miscellaneous manuf.	−510	0.025	0.036	0.430	0.465	1.415	1.038
Total, all manuf.	−19,389	0.062	0.100	0.159	0.193	1.318	1.042

Calculated from http://www.bea.doc.gov/bea/uguide.htm for industry shipments and employment, http://dataweb.usitc.gov for exports and imports.

Other regional groups

There has been a rapid proliferation of preferential trade arrangements. EC agreements with former colonies through the Lomé Convention, and the successor Cotonou Agreement, demonstrate that such arrangements are not limited to neighboring countries. We limit comments here to MERCOSUR, an example of a trade bloc among developing countries. It was first thought that developing countries would be especially likely to benefit from regional economic integration, because they could then overcome limitations imposed by the small size of national markets. Those hopes have not been widely realized. Regional economic integration among developing countries has not been very successful. When member countries export primary products such as coffee or cocoa, their major markets are in the industrial countries, and regional integration does nothing to expand the market. When it is a matter of developing a new industry, conflicts arise about its location within the customs union. Which country will get the new industry? Member countries do not like to pay a higher price to import the commodity from a partner country than they would have to pay in the world market. They correctly see this as a welfare loss from trade diversion.

MERCOSUR, formed in 1991 and consisting of Brazil, Argentina, Paraguay, and Uruguay, may be an exception to this pattern. Trade among members expanded much more rapidly than would be predicted on the basis of geographic proximity and the size of their economies. Over the 1990–6 period MERCOSUR imports from members rose 314 percent to $17.1 billion, imports from nonmembers rose 185 percent to $66.7 billion, and exports to nonmembers rose 37 percent to $57.9 billion.[18] Skeptics suggest that this rapid pace of intraregional integration is the result of trade diversion. The product items where the exports of MERCOSUR members have grown most rapidly are those where trade within the region has grown most rapidly and where trade barriers against nonmember producers are the greatest. In addition these industries tend to be capital-intensive, and they tend not to be industries where members have a revealed comparative advantage.[19] This evidence indicates that trade diversion may be substantial. Also, MERCOSUR terms of trade improved at the expense of nonmembers.[20] Hopes to become a customs union were set back by Argentine financial crises in 2001 and its decision to unilaterally raise tariffs.

Summary of key concepts

1 Discriminatory trade liberalization may or may not increase the welfare of a group's members or the efficiency of the world trading system.

2 Trade creation arises when prices of imports fall and consumption of the protected good increases. It benefits both the importing country and world efficiency. Trade diversion arises when imports from more efficient nonmembers decline. World efficiency falls and the importing country loses tariff revenue.

3 Preferential trade blocs may alter the terms of trade in their favor, a benefit that comes at the expense of nonmembers and therefore does not improve world efficiency.

4 Achieving economies of scale in larger, more competitive markets may benefit members. Projections of these effects from simulation models indicate they are quite large relative to trade creation gains for small countries.

5 The European Union, composed of 15 countries, imposes a common external tariff and promotes the free movement of goods, services, capital, and people among its members. Although the EU has successfully expanded from six original members, its expansion into Eastern Europe will require considerable political and economic resources.

6   NAFTA is a free-trade agreement between Canada, Mexico, and the United States that also promotes free investment flows. Because more trade with Mexico is based on differences in factor endowments, potential effects on US income distribution have been more prominent than in EU debates over expansion.

Questions for study and review

1   Free-trade areas are far more common than customs unions. Why is it much easier to negotiate a free-trade area than it is to arrange for a customs union or a common market?

2   How can both trade creation and trade diversion effects occur in the same product market when a regional bloc is created?

3   The European Economic Community was widely viewed as predominantly trade creating rather than diverting, except in the area of agriculture. What aspects of the European economies led to that conclusion? What happens to the trade creation and diversion effects of the EEC as more members, such as Poland and Hungary, are added?

4   Why was NAFTA so difficult to pass through the US Congress when the US–Canada arrangement went through so easily? Why is the proposed entry of Chile likely to be far less controversial? What if Brazilian membership were proposed?

5   What would have happened to Canada's gains from its free-trade arrangement with the United States if a US–Mexico free-trade deal had been negotiated that did not include Canada?

Suggested further reading

In addition to the readings cited in the endnotes, for empirical analysis of several trade blocs in one unified framework, see:

- Frankel, Jeffrey, *Regional Trading Blocs in the World Economic System*, Washington, DC: Institute for International Economics, 1997.

For a skeptical view of the current proliferation of trade blocs, see:

- Panagariya, Arvind and Jagdish Bhagwati, eds, *Free Trade Area or Free Trade? The Economics of Preferential Trade Agreements*, Washington, DC: American Enterprise Institute, 1996.

Notes

1   See Jacob Viner, *The Customs Union Issue* (New York: Carnegie Endowment for International Peace, 1953), for an early discussion of this topic. See also R.G. Lipsey, "The Theory of Customs Unions: A General Survey," *Economic Journal*, September 1960, and Richard Baldwin and Anthony Venables, "Regional Economic Integration," in Gene Grossman and Kenneth Rogof, eds, *Handbook of International Economics*, Vol. III (Amsterdam: Elsevier Science, 1995), pp. 1598–640, for surveys on this topic.

2   In this example, France's terms of trade with Germany may worsen, as greater French demand for German bicycles drives up their price. If German gains turned out to be greater than comparable French terms-of-trade gains on items exported to Germany, further negotiation within the union

might be necessary to ensure that all members gain. As we will see in the case of British entry into the EEC, the division of gains can be an important issue.

3   A. Panagariya, "The Regionalism Debate: An Overview," *The World Economy*, June 1999, pp. 477–511.

4   For econometric estimates of possible external economies of scale in Europe, see R. Caballero and R. Lyons, "Internal versus External Economies in European Manufacturing," *European Economic Review* 34, June 1990, pp. 805–30.

5   See H. Helpman and P. Krugman, *Market Structure and Foreign Trade* (Cambridge, MA: MIT Press, 1985), and Donald R. Davis, "The Home Market, Trade, and Industrial Structure," *The American Economic Review*, December 1998, for development of these ideas.

6   Richard Baldwin, "The Growth Effects of 1992," *Economic Policy*, 9 October, 1989.

7   For discussion of issues addressed here see Baldwin and Venables, op. cit.; Michael Calingaert, *European Integration Revisited: Progress, Prospects, and US Interests* (Boulder, CO: Westview Press, 1996); and Jeffrey Frankel, *Regional Trading Blocs in the World Economic System* (Washington, DC: Institute for International Economics, 1997).

8   Bela Balassa, "Trade Creation and Diversion in the European Common Market," *European Economic Integration* (Amsterdam: North-Holland, 1975). For a projection that focuses on the EC terms of trade gain at the expense of nonmembers, see Howard Petith, "European Integration and the Terms of Trade," *The Economic Journal*, June 1977, pp. 262–72.

9   Marcus Miller and John Spencer, "The Static Economic Effects of the UK Joining the EEC: A General Equilibrium Approach," *Review of Economic Studies*, February 1977, pp. 71–94. Economists have also made after-the-fact assessments of the UK accession, as summarized by Alan Winters, "Britain in Europe: A Survey of Quantitative Trade Studies," *Journal of Common Market Studies* 25, 1987, pp. 315–53.

10 See Alan Winters, *International Economics* (London: George Allen and Unwin, 1985), pp. 124–31, for further elaboration of this situation.

11 The Cecchini Report, *The European Challenge* 1992 (Aldershot, UK: Wildwood House, 1988).

12 Baldwin and Venables, op. cit.

13 Chapter 4 of the 1988 Economic Report of the President contains a discussion of the US–Canada free-trade arrangement. See also J. Schott and M. Smith, eds, *The Canada–United States Free Trade Agreement: The Global Impact* (Washington, DC: Institute for International Economics, 1988), and Peter Morici, ed., *Making Free Trade Work: The Canada–US Agreement* (New York: Council on Foreign Relations Press, 1990).

14 David Cox and Richard Harris, "Trade Liberalization and Industrial Organization: Some Estimates for Canada," *Journal of Political Economy*, 1995, pp. 115–45.

15 Drusilla Brown and Robert Stern, "A Modeling Perspective," in Robert Stern, Philip Trezise, and John Whally, eds, *Perspectives on a US–Canadian Free Trade Agreement* (Washington, DC: The Brookings Institution, 1987), pp. 155–87.

16 For a discussion of the details of NAFTA and an analysis supporting it, see G. Hufbauer and J. Schott, *NAFTA: An Assessment* (Washington, DC: Institute for International Economics, 1993). See also D. Brown, A. Deardorff, and R. Stern, "North American Integration," *Economic Journal*, November 1992, pp. 1507–18, and J. Mutti, *NAFTA: The Economic Consequences for Mexico and the United States*, Economic Strategy Institute, 2001.

17 Baldwin and Venables, op. cit., pp. 1630–1. They note particularly wide variation in the predicted effects on Canada, and due to that uncertainty, we omit them from the summary comments in the text.

18 US International Trade Commission, *Market Developments in Mercosur Countries Affecting Leading US Exporter* (Washington, DC: USITC, 1997).

19 Alexander Yeats, "Does Mercosur's Trade Performance Raise Concerns about the Effects of Regional Trade Arrangements?," *The World Bank Economic Review* 12, no. 1, January 1998, pp. 1–28. Revealed comparative advantage is calculated by considering how important a member's exports are in the shoe industry, say, relative to its total exports, compared to the importance of world trade in shoes relative to world trade in all goods. If Brazil's exports of shoes account for 5 percent of its total exports, while shoes as a group account for 3 percent of world trade, then Brazil has a revealed comparative advantage in shoes.

20 W. Chang and A. Winters, "Preferential Trading Arrangements and Excluded Countries: Ex Poste Estimates of the Effects on Prices," *The World Economy*, June 2001, pp. 797–807.

8 Commercial policy
History and recent controversies

Learning objectives

By the end of this chapter you should be able to understand:

- that by the middle of the nineteenth century Britain was a leader in promoting free-trade policies;
- why during the late nineteenth century and up to the onset of the worldwide depression of the 1930s, trade policy became more restrictive internationally;
- why in 1934 the United States embarked on a reciprocal trade agreements program to negotiate reductions in tariffs bilaterally;
- how the formation of the GATT in 1947 established a set of trading principles to be applied multilaterally and led to several subsequent rounds of trade negotiations;
- how the Uruguay Round, completed in 1994, established the WTO and extended international rules to many new or ignored areas of international trade;
- what areas of dissatisfaction, particularly among developing countries, the Doha Round is intended to address.

Regulation of external trade through tariffs, quotas, and other means has long been a prominent aspect of national sovereignty. In Chapters 5 and 6 we indicated how the policy choices made by one country affect not only its own production, consumption, and trade, but also conditions in other countries. Relaxation of those trade barriers on a joint but discriminatory basis in preferential trading agreements was the topic of Chapter 7. In this chapter we consider another basis for joint action in establishing rules for trade in goods and services, one which has come to rely upon multilateral cooperation.

British leadership in commercial policy

Taking a long historical perspective, we can observe recurrent swings in **commercial policy** from protection toward free trade and then back again toward protection. The rise of nationalism in the Western world (c. 1500–1800) was associated with **mercantilism** and the close and detailed regulation of economic activity, foreign trade included. Under mercantilism, a national goal was to export much, import little, and thus acquire specie (gold and silver) through a favorable balance of trade. During the mercantilist period, all nations pursued highly restrictive commercial policies. They used tariffs, quotas, embargoes, state monopolies, and a variety of other measures to control and regulate their foreign trade.

The classical economists (such as Smith and Ricardo) were essentially attacking the whole edifice of mercantilist thought when they developed the theory of trade and comparative advantage. They stood mercantilist policy on its head: according to classical theory, imports are desirable, whereas exports are merely the necessary cost of obtaining them. As this theory gained ascendancy, the response in commercial policy was a swing from protection toward free trade. It did not go all the way and it was not universal, but there was a pronounced movement in the direction of free trade in the middle decades of the nineteenth century.

Great Britain was unmistakably the leader in this movement. As recounted in Chapter 6, the Corn Laws (which placed restrictions on grain imports) were repealed in 1846, and by 1850 virtually all British tariffs and other restrictions on imports had been swept away. Thus Great Britain, the leader in the Industrial Revolution, had unilaterally adopted a policy of free trade. Other nations were influenced by the British example. Denmark, the Netherlands, and Turkey accepted virtually full free trade, and many other European nations substantially reduced their tariff rates. Thus, Britain did not suffer as large a terms-of-trade decline as we otherwise might predict for unilateral action by a country large enough to affect international prices. Although there was no international organization to oversee this process, multilateral trade liberalization meant that the volume of trade expanded more rapidly and relative prices internationally changed less than if Britain alone had changed policy.

For their part, the British pushed the cause of free trade with an almost evangelical fervor. Commercial treaties providing for tariff reductions and other measures to liberalize trade were negotiated with many European countries. Most of these treaties included a clause requiring **most-favored-nation status**: the signatory countries agreed to extend to each other, automatically, the lowest tariff rates that might be granted to any third country in the future. The resulting network of commercial treaties accomplished a substantial reduction in the level of protection in European trade.

British diplomacy also pushed the cause of free trade in other parts of the world. British colonies were required to eliminate protective tariffs, keeping only a few revenue duties. British diplomacy and power combined to persuade a number of other countries to sign commercial treaties in which these countries agreed to open their economies to foreign trade and to fix very low tariff rates on such trade. In some of these "unequal treaties," as they came to be called, the concessions were made almost entirely by the weaker country. Of course, it is true that Britain had already removed its trade restrictions, so it could claim that parity prevailed, but other Western powers quickly followed the British lead and asked for similar concessions, even though they made none themselves.

For example, after Britain negotiated a treaty with Thailand in 1855 in which Thailand agreed to limit its import tariffs to 3 percent *ad valorem*, the same terms were obtained by other Western powers, including some nations that retained high protective tariffs themselves (notably, the United States).[1] After the infamous Opium War (1839–42) in which Britain forced China to allow the importation of opium, China signed treaties that committed it to open certain port cities to foreign trade and fixed tariff rates at low levels. Other Western powers demanded and obtained the same terms.

The free-trade tide reached its peak in about 1870 but then began to ebb. In Germany, France, Italy, and other European countries, emerging industries called for protection against the established industries in the UK. The rapid expansion of American grain exports after 1870 led European agrarian interests to join with the industrialists in support of higher tariffs. As a result, tariff increases were frequent in the last quarter of the nineteenth century. Of the major nations, only Britain and Holland clung to free trade.

This swing toward protection was accompanied by a competitive scramble for colonies. Between 1875 and 1914, the entire continent of Africa was swallowed up, with the sole exceptions of Liberia and Ethiopia. In Asia and the Middle East, Western imperialism extended its sway over areas that had previously escaped. Colonies were seen as potential markets, as outlets for the new industrial capacity being created in the mother countries, and as sources of raw materials to supply the new industries. In many cases, preferential trading arrangements were set up between colony and mother country. Even Britain was not immune to this element of neomercantilism, and the dominions (such as Canada) began giving preferential treatment to imports from Great Britain in 1898. The protectionist tide continued to swell after World War I, reaching its peak in the depression years of the 1930s. By that time, world trade was severely restricted by tariffs and other barriers to trade. Even in Britain, the citadel of free trade, protectionist tariffs were installed in the aftermath of World War I, with preferential rates for dominions and colonies of the British Empire.

The United States did not participate in the free-trade movement during the nineteenth century. From 1789 to 1934, tariff rates were set by acts of Congress, and the levels fixed in successive tariff acts reflected Congressional preoccupation with domestic political and economic concerns. Rates rose and fell several times, sometimes sharply, between 1820 and 1930, but for most of the period, tariffs were quite high. An important distinction is that by the end of this period US actions had a significant impact on other countries. **The Smoot–Hawley Tariff** Act of 1930 imposed an average rate exceeding 50 percent, which represented a higher level than existed at the previous peak in 1828. The United States, however, had emerged from World War I as a major market. Other countries had borrowed heavily from it both during and after the war. To pay their debts, other nations had to sell the United States their goods and services, but the Smoot–Hawley Tariff seriously impaired their ability to do so.

Other countries soon retaliated with increases in their tariffs, and world trade steadily shrank as the world sank into depression. No one can say exactly how much the Smoot–Hawley Tariff Act was responsible for the economic woes of the 1930s, but it seems clear that it had a substantial effect. US trade dropped 70 percent in value (50 percent in volume) from 1929 to 1932, and declining world trade contributed to the spread of depression throughout the world. It was under those circumstances that another swing toward free trade got under way.

A US initiative: the Reciprocal Trade Agreements program

As trade barriers rose after 1930 and the world slipped more deeply into depression, it became clear that something needed to be done to revive world trade and restore the gains from trade and specialization. In 1934 the US President Franklin D. Roosevelt persuaded Congress to authorize a new approach to tariff policy that promised to help achieve two important goals: revival of trade and expansion of employment.

In that year Congress passed the Reciprocal Trade Agreements Act, authorizing the president to negotiate bilateral trade agreements in which each signatory country would agree to reduce its tariff rates on specific commodities. The act authorized the president to reduce existing tariff rates by up to 50 percent. One of the remarkable features of this legislation was that Congress delegated to the executive the power to fix tax rates (i.e. tariffs), perhaps its most jealously guarded prerogative. There were restrictions and limitations, of course, and Congress could rescind the delegation any time it chose, but the fact is that since 1934 US tariff rates in effect have been determined by the president.

From 1934 to 1947, the United States negotiated bilateral trade agreements with 29 nations. These agreements provided for tariff concessions on 69 percent of all dutiable imports into the United States and reduced the average tariff by about one-third.[2] Two important principles were embodied in these trade agreements. First, every one of them included the unconditional most-favored-nation (MFN) clause. As noted earlier, this means that each of the signatory countries agreed to extend the tariff reductions covered in the agreement to all other countries that have MFN status, even though these other countries made no concessions themselves. For example, if France and the United States conclude an agreement in which France reduces its tariff on electrical machinery, the reduced tariff automatically applies to French imports from all MFN countries, even though the other countries give France no concession in return. Similarly, the US concession to France, for example a reduction in its tariff on wine, would automatically be extended to all other countries with MFN status.

The effect of the most-favored-nation clause is to keep a given country's tariff rates uniform and equal to all countries. Without it, bilateral trade agreements would produce a situation in which imports into a given country would be charged different tariff rates, depending on where the imports came from. Such tariff differentials are difficult to administer and economically inefficient from a world perspective, although a large country with market power might exploit that power by imposing higher tariffs on countries with less elastic supply and few alternative markets. The purpose of the most-favored-nation clause is to achieve a nondiscriminatory tariff structure that promotes worldwide efficiency.

The second negotiating principle, the "chief supplier" rule, was used to lessen the sense people had that third countries were getting something for nothing as a result of the most-favored-nation principle. The United States sought to bargain with the chief supplier of a given imported commodity. When the United States offered a tariff reduction on that commodity, it obtained, in return, tariff reductions on certain of its export commodities. That is the sense in which the agreements were reciprocal. By negotiating with the chief supplier of each commodity, the United States minimized the unearned benefit accruing to third countries to which its tariff reductions were extended without any concession on their part.[3]

By negotiating trade agreements with a large number of countries, the United States was able to achieve a significant reduction in the level of world tariffs. Even though each agreement was bilateral, the concessions they contained were generalized through the most-favored-nation clause. On the other hand, small countries that were not chief suppliers of products had little power to ensure that items of interest to them became the subject of negotiations.

The shift to multilateralism under the GATT

During and after World War II, plans were drawn up for an International Trade Organization through which nations could regulate and coordinate their commercial policies. In 1945 the United States presented a draft charter for such an organization that would serve as a counterpart, in the field of trade and commercial policy, to the International Monetary Fund in the monetary field. However, this proposed charter ran into heavy opposition. When the US Congress declined to approve it, it was quietly dropped.

Under the authority contained in the Reciprocal Trade Agreements Act, the United States invited other nations to participate in multilateral negotiations for the reduction of tariffs and other trade barriers. At a conference held in 1947, a General Agreement on

Tariffs and Trade was adopted. From this unlikely beginning an international organization by that name, which is frequently known by its acronym, GATT, also emerged. In 1995 the newly created World Trade Organization replaced the GATT organization and established a stronger multilateral decision-making structure. The WTO administers an amended GATT agreement that governs trade in goods, along with new agreements that cover trade in services (the General Agreement on Trade in Services, or GATS) and intellectual property (the Agreement on Trade-Related Aspects of Intellectual Property Rights).

The GATT articles of agreement constitute a code of conduct for international trade and a basis for multilateral negotiation of trade agreements. They seek to reduce tariffs and other barriers to trade, and to place all countries on an equal footing in their trade relationships. The principle of nondiscrimination in trade is central. Article One incorporates the unconditional most-favored-nation clause, and all contracting parties are bound to grant to each other treatment as favorable as they give to any other country. This clause, which guarantees equality of treatment and rules out discriminatory trade barriers, is the most important single feature of GATT.

There are two important exceptions to Article One. First, when a group of countries forms a customs union or free-trade area, they may eliminate tariffs among themselves but retain tariffs against outside countries. Second, countries may apply lower tariff rates to imports coming from developing countries than they apply to imports from other countries. That exception was adopted in 1971 in response to demands of developing countries to encourage their export industries.

Article Three is another central principle of the agreement. It calls for national treatment of foreign and domestic goods. Once foreign goods enter a country and clear customs, they must be treated no less favorably than domestically produced goods. An explicit intent of this provision is to keep discriminatory domestic taxes and regulations from protecting domestic producers, because those measures otherwise could be used to offset the effect of tariff concessions.

The agreement also opposes quantitative restrictions (quotas) on trade. The general position is that if trade barriers are to exist, they should take the form of explicit tariffs so that everyone can judge their severity and determine that they are being applied in a non-discriminatory manner. Quantitative restrictions are almost unavoidably discriminatory, and their true protective effect is difficult to judge. Despite the general prohibition against quantitative restrictions, however, they continue to be widely used. One rather open-ended exception provides that quantitative restrictions can be applied by a country in order to safeguard its balance of payments. Another exception allows such restrictions if they are needed because of a country's economic development policies. Such provisions do not set any standard to judge when a country's balance of payments again is satisfactory or whether a country has graduated from the need to impose barriers for development purposes. In practice, it was the GATT's consultative machinery that enabled these loosely worded exceptions to remain manageable.

The United States initially insisted that members could impose quantitative restrictions on agricultural products when needed to permit the operation and enforcement of domestic agricultural support programs. Japan and the EU have been the strongest advocates of this provision in more recent years. The price support schemes of those economies have the effect of holding the domestic price above the world level, which requires that imports be restricted. Only in the 1990s was there much success in bringing agricultural trade into conformity with general GATT principles, but the conversion of quotas to tariffs resulted in extremely high *ad valorem* equivalent rates, for example, greater than 1000 percent in Japan.[4]

The GATT organization's most important activity was its sponsorship of a series of negotiations in which member countries bargained to reduce their tariffs and other trade barriers. Each country prepared lists of concessions it was willing to offer and of concessions it wanted to obtain from other countries. Although these offers and requests were initially bilateral, they acquired a multilateral aspect because they were circulated to all other participating countries. Through the operation of the most-favored-nation clause, a concession to one country is a concession to all members. By having all countries negotiating simultaneously, each country is able to evaluate the benefits it may obtain because of concessions made between any two other countries.

This negotiating process is complicated, cumbersome, and lengthy; some negotiations have taken four or five years to complete. However, it has distinct advantages over the traditional bilateral negotiation, as the following passage makes clear:

> The multilateral procedure for tariff negotiations, by contrast with the traditional methods, has the advantage of enabling participating countries to assess the value of concessions granted by other countries over and above the direct concessions negotiated. In traditional bilateral negotiations these indirect benefits could not be assessed with any accuracy and were generally disregarded. With the new approach the tendency is to strike a balance, not between direct concessions but between the aggregate of direct and indirect benefits; this enables negotiating countries to go much further in the way of tariff negotiation than would otherwise be possible.[5]

Five rounds of multilateral negotiations took place between 1947 and 1961. They varied in scope and in the size of the tariff reductions accomplished, but their cumulative effect was a substantial reduction in tariff levels for manufactured goods, especially those levied by industrial countries. The average US tariff on dutiable goods declined from 53 percent in 1933 (the peak level reached after the Smoot–Hawley Tariff Act) to about 10 percent in the 1960s. A substantial part of that decline, however, appears to be due to inflation in the 1940s which eroded the protective effect of specific tariffs,[6] and therefore we should not overstate the role of negotiations. Furthermore, tariff averages conceal large disparities in tariff rates on individual items and much room remained for further moves toward trade liberalization. We describe the four most recent GATT rounds in greater detail.

The Kennedy Round

The first five rounds of tariff negotiations conducted under GATT auspices led to progressively smaller reductions in trade barriers. Bilateral bargaining for tariff cuts on specific commodities seemed to be running out of steam. Consequently, in the sixth session, known as the Kennedy Round, a new approach was used.

The Trade Expansion Act of 1962 authorized the United States to engage in negotiations for across-the-board tariff reduction. After protracted bargaining, countries taking part in the Kennedy Round of GATT negotiations reached an agreement in 1967 providing for average tariff cuts of about 35 percent, with most reductions occurring across the board. Many exceptions were made, as each country had its list of sensitive items requiring special treatment, but for the great majority of specific tariff lines, existing tariffs were reduced by a uniform percentage.

One reason why this method was used was that the European Economic Community had just agreed on a common external tariff schedule for its six member nations. The EEC was bargaining as a single unit in the GATT negotiations, and agreement on across-the-board tariff cuts was much easier to achieve than tariff reductions of varying size on different commodities. The latter procedure threatened to disturb the delicate balance of interests established among the member nations when the common external tariff had itself been negotiated.

A difficulty that arose in the negotiations was the treatment of a US practice of imposing a variable levy on certain chemical and footwear products. Because the United States needed separate Congressional approval to address those issues, they were handled in a separate protocol agreement, with concessions by other countries contingent on their adoption.[7] When the US Congress failed to approve that side-agreement, one portion of the negotiations was simply lost.

Most countries retained an "**escape clause**": a provision to allow the country to assist an industry injured by tariff reductions. Under US procedures to invoke the escape clause, the industry filed a petition with the US Tariff Commission. The USTC investigated and reported its findings to the President, who then weighted foreign policy interests and consumer impacts in determining an appropriate response.

In contrast to the unfair trade claims against foreign subsidization or dumping, no allegation of unfair trade is made in escape clause actions. The petitioner simply claims that some period of relief from import competition is necessary to allow retooling, retraining, or implementing some other strategy to adjust. The standard of injury to be met is higher than in unfair trade cases, and the automatic imposition of a remedy without presidential review in those cases contrasts to the more political nature of escape-clause relief cases. Economists have noted that large industries with a high political profile were more likely to be successful in gaining protection from escape-clause relief actions, whereas smaller, less politically powerful industries found the unfair trade laws more likely to benefit them.[8] Also, industries with political power have been more successful in getting the president to negotiate voluntary export agreements with foreign suppliers.

The Tokyo Round

A seventh round of GATT negotiations got under way in 1973. This negotiation, popularly known as the "Tokyo Round" was finally completed in 1979. The final Tokyo Round agreement entailed a reduction of tariffs by the major industrialized countries of about 33 percent on items included, although again each country excluded certain sensitive items. The agreed-upon formula for tariff reductions had the effect of reducing high tariff rates more than low ones, thus tending to harmonize tariff levels around the world.[9] Similarly, tariff cuts on finished goods were deeper than those on raw materials, thereby tending to reduce the degree of tariff escalation; this lowered the effective rate of protection on finished goods. This was an impressive achievement in such a troubled period of oil price shocks and poor macroeconomic performance. The magnitude of the cuts made, and the resulting low levels of average tariffs in industrial countries after the Tokyo Round, can be seen in Table 8.1. After the Tokyo Round, tariffs were so low that they did not constitute a major barrier to trade in industrial countries. Indeed, one study found that total elimination of all remaining tariffs would have minuscule effects on the world economy, an increase in welfare of only 0.1 percent.[10] However, as tariffs have come down, other forms of protection have come into greater use.

Bargaining for the reduction of nontariff barriers (NTBs) was a prominent feature of the Tokyo Round. Achieving such reductions is difficult, however, because they often involve

Table 8.1 Average tariff rates in selected economies

	Tariffs on industrial products (percent)		
	Before Tokyo Round	After Tokyo Round	Reduction
European Community	6.6	4.7	29
Japan	5.5	2.8	49
US	6.4	4.4	31
All industrial countries	7.1	4.7	34

Source: International Monetary Fund, *Developments in International Trade Policy*, Occasional Paper no. 16, 1982.

elements of domestic policy that national legislatures have typically controlled. In order to avoid the experience of the unsuccessful side-agreement in the Kennedy Round, drafters of the US 1974 Trade Act devised a procedure called "fast track." This procedure specified that a bill to approve agreements on nontariff measures could not be amended once introduced, that it would be reported out of committee within a specified time limit, and that floor debate would be limited. This procedure worked remarkably well in 1979 for the bill implementing the Tokyo Round. Given that successful precedent, Canada insisted that the fast-track procedure apply to the Canada–US Free Trade Agreement.[11]

The Tokyo Round addressed NTBs through separate codes and agreements in several areas: subsidies, technical barriers to trade; import licensing procedures; government procurement; customs valuation; and dumping. Not all countries signed these codes, and they were not automatically administered through the same dispute resolution mechanism as the tariff agreement. The reliance on codes and their potentially limited applicability across countries raised the fear of a GATT à la carte, where countries could pick and choose what provisions to accept. The subsequent Uruguay Round sought to avoid that outcome.

The principle of preferential tariff treatment for imports from developing countries was adopted in the Tokyo Round. The rationale for this approach is a variant of the infant-industry argument. The US **Generalized System of Preferences** (GSP) grants duty-free entry for imports of goods on an approved list, but it imposes a number of restrictions and qualifications on developing countries. Many commodities were excluded from the list, especially where imports already threatened to injure domestic producers (eg. textiles, steel, footwear, glass, and watches). Also, the tariff preference was denied to any developing country that supplied 50 percent or more of total US imports of a given article, or that supplied more than $30 million worth of the article. As a result, only about 12 percent of the exports of developing countries to the United States qualified for GSP treatment. European coverage under the Lomé Convention was similar in magnitude.

The Uruguay Round

This round, which took over 7 years to complete, was by far the most difficult to conclude and almost failed. Negotiations began in 1986, were suspended in 1990 and 1992 due to an impasse over agricultural provisions, and finally were completed on 15 December 1993, the day that US fast-track negotiating authority was to end. The round was more difficult than its predecessors because tariffs had already been reduced to very low levels. Nontariff barriers were the dominant remaining issue, but these were less easily quantified and it was much harder to reach an acceptable balance of concessions. Although further tariff cuts were a goal of this round, other important issues included:

1   *Agricultural trade and subsidies.* Most developed countries subsidize agricultural prices, making free trade very improbable. The European Union maintains very high support prices under the Common Agricultural Policy and produces large surpluses. These commodities are sold at very low prices in export markets, reducing prices received by Australia, Canada, and other countries with a comparative advantage in farm products. The United States and other agricultural exporters wanted tight limits on the ability of the European Union to subsidize production and exports, a goal that France strongly opposed.

2   *Textiles and garments.* The Multi-Fibre Agreement had become an exceedingly complex web of product- and country-specific quotas that limit sales of products where developing countries have a comparative advantage. It discriminated against countries that received small quotas (such as India) and provided large monopoly rents to the large-quota holders (such as Hong Kong and Korea). Garment and textile producers in industrialized countries strongly opposed a move away from quotas to tariffs.

3   *Intellectual property.* Several industrialized countries wanted stronger protection for patents, copyrights, and trademarks.

4   *Services.* Purchases by foreigners of banking, insurance, medical care, education, telecommunications, tourism, and other services have grown rapidly in recent years. The United States, which tends to have a comparative advantage in many of these services, wanted barriers to its exports of such services to be reduced, although it was much less anxious to liberalize construction or transportation.

5   *Dispute resolution and US unilateralism.* During the 1980s the United States became increasingly frustrated with the GATT dispute resolution mechanism. The GATT procedures had evolved over time and reflected two different motivations, one that they provide a clear basis for rule-based trade, and another that they facilitate negotiation between disputing members. Referring a dispute to a panel of three or five experts to rule on the compatibility of a country's practices with its GATT obligations addresses the first view. Requiring that contracting parties adopt any report by consensus (a unanimous vote) reflects the second view. The European Union particularly felt that some issues were of such central importance, such as the operation of its Common Agricultural Policy, that entrusting the outcome to a panel of outsiders was unsatisfactory. In spite of considerable US delay in bringing some of its own practices into compliance after unfavorable GATT rulings, the United States sought a dispute resolution mechanism with more teeth in it.

The United States unilaterally initiated actions under its own trade laws against foreign trade practices it regarded as unfair but which were not adequately addressed by the GATT. These **Section 301** proceedings (a reference to the section of the Trade Act of 1974 under which they were taken), together with US administration of its dumping and countervailing duty laws, were sources of considerable dissatisfaction among US trading partners. Foreign countries, including allies such as Canada, viewed the US procedures as biased toward a finding of guilt, extremely expensive to defend against for foreign firms, and generally threatening to open trade. These countries wanted GATT-enforced rules that would limit the ability of the US government to unilaterally determine appropriate trade remedies.

This agenda was a challenging one, almost too challenging, as demonstrated by the breakdown of talks at various points. Regional trade groupings looked more and more attractive to stymied negotiators. With the deadline for the US government's loss of its negotiating authority approaching, the participants produced an agreement at almost the last possible moment. Although not all goals were met, it was a surprisingly successful outcome, given the difficulty of the issues.[12] The major accomplishments of the Uruguay Round can be summarized as follows:

1   *Tariffs.* Industrialized countries reduced tariffs on manufactured goods by over one-third, with over 40 percent of such goods to enter without tariff.
2   *Agriculture.* Subsidies of exports and import barriers were cut significantly over 6 years. Domestic farm supports, which generate the surpluses that become a problem, were decreased by 20 percent. Subsidized exports were cut by 36 percent in value. Japan and Korea agreed to some opening of their rice markets. Countries converted their

---

Box 8.1 Tariff bindings and applied tariffs

Agreements to reduce tariff rates multilaterally have been central to GATT negotiations since 1947. Also important has been the effort to encourage each country to bind its existing tariffs at maximum rates that cannot be exceeded without consulting with its trading partners, should a country choose to alter its trade policy in the future. Binding creates predictability in the world trading system and warrants greater investment to serve the world market. The Uruguay Round resulted in a substantial increase in the extent to which countries bound their tariffs, especially developing countries.

Table 8.2 Tariff bindings and applied tariffs

	Share of bound lines	Simple average bound rates		Simple average applied rates	
		Agricultural	Industrial	Agricultural	Industrial
European Union (2002)	100.0	16.3	4.0	16.3	4.1
Japan (FY 2002)	98.7	26.5	3.8	26.5	3.9
United States (2001)	100.0	8.1	4.0	8.1	4.4
South Africa (2001)	95.7	46.8	18.1	11.3	10.9
Brazil (2000)	100.0	35.9	29.6	12.9	13.8
Bangladesh (1999)	0.9	195.2	50.0	25.1	21.9
India (2001)	68.2	115.7	36.2	41.7	31.0

Source: WTO, 2002, p. 7–8.

The figures shown demonstrate that tariffs in industrialized countries generally are much lower than in developing countries, but many developing countries have accepted the rationale for making tariff bindings. Those countries illustrate the pattern of binding tariffs at rates much higher than the rates actually applied. (More generally, for industrial goods, Latin American bindings were three times the applied rates, and in South-East Asia the corresponding ratio was 2.5.) Nevertheless, bindings represent a useful step in ensuring that trade liberalization is permanent.

quantitative restrictions to tariffs and guaranteed at least as much market access as existed prior to the agreement; this gave rise to the tariff rate quotas discussed in Chapter 5. Tariffs on tropical agricultural products, which largely come from developing countries, were cut by 40 percent.

3 *Textiles and garments.* The Multi-Fibre Arrangement quotas were to be phased out over 10 years and tariffs to be reduced. The phase-out of quotas, however, is "back-end loaded," so an important part of the liberalization does not occur until 2005.

4 *Intellectual property.* The Agreement on Trade Related Aspects of Intellectual Property Rights (TRIPS) was established as part of the WTO. Developing countries agreed to much stricter protection for intellectual property. Patents for products and processes are to be provided for 20 years from the filing of an application. Copyright protection of music, literature, computer programs, and computer chip designs, among other items, is to be provided. Even geographic indications are protected: thus, if a cheese carries the name of a French region, it must come from that region of France.

5 *Services.* The General Agreement on Trade in Services (GATS) was established as part of the WTO. Less was accomplished in the services area, particularly financial services and telecommunications. Subsequently, in 1997, agreements were reached in these two areas, a somewhat surprising result because any potential disadvantages arising from these concessions were not balanced by favorable benefits in some other agreement. Perhaps the important role played by an adequate financial and communications infrastructure in producing other goods provided enough incentive for progress to be made.

6 *Dispute resolution and US unilateralism.* The World Trade Organization was established as the successor to the GATT, and a stronger basis for dispute resolution procedures was established. Panel reports are automatically approved unless appealed to a newly created Appellate Body. Its findings are adopted automatically unless there is consensus not to do so. Although offending countries cannot be forced by the WTO to bring their practices into compliance, the complaining country may be granted the right to retaliate. Voluntary export restraints are now illegal, but any limits on antidumping actions were minor.

7 *Limitations on trade-related investment measures (TRIMs).* Many multinational corporations that operate in developing countries are required by host governments to export a minimum percentage of their production or to refrain from importing parts and components. Such laws distort trade flows away from efficient patterns and harm the trade performance of developed countries. The Uruguay Round resulted in domestic content requirements or trade balance requirements being prohibited, but export performance requirements still are allowed. The United States was disappointed over the lack of progress with respect to other TRIMs, such as technology transfer requirements and the right to repatriate profits. Negotiations under the auspices of the Organization for Economic Cooperation and Development, a group of largely higher-income countries, were initiated in 1995 under the label Multilateral Agreement on Investment (MAI). An agreement seemed more likely among countries with similar interests. Nevertheless, these talks broke down in 1998, due to objections raised over potential infringement of an individual country's ability to deal with environmental degradation, food safety, cultural diversity, and social cohesion.[13]

A key aspect of the Uruguay Round was its treatment of the various agreements under the World Trade Organization as a single package. Countries did not have the opportunity to pick and choose what sections to accept. Because countries did not expect a favorable balance of concessions in every group, but rather gains in one area could offset losses in another, a much more ambitious agreement was reached. After almost collapsing, the Uruguay Round turned out to be a far greater success than had been expected.

Box 8.2 WTO dispute resolution and the banana war

In 1999 the European Union and the United States had severe disagreements over several trade issues, including bananas, beef, and biotechnology. The value of trade involved did not seem to explain very well the intensity of the rhetoric from each side, and the difficulty in resolving the least significant one, the banana dispute, was not a good omen for the future operation of the dispute resolution mechanism.

The EU banana regime adopted in 1993 extended to the EU market prior British and French preferences for bananas from former colonies in Africa, the Caribbean, and the Pacific. Those sources were to be guaranteed 30 percent of the EU market. Europeans were reluctant to reopen this issue, which effectively passed the cost of supporting high banana prices on to other European partners. The change in policy harmed more efficient Latin American producers who previously supplied the EU market, as well as US distributors who handled those bananas. The World Bank judged the policy to be a highly inefficient way of aiding the Caribbean states and recommended a more generous development program.

In May 1993 a GATT panel ruled against the EC banana regime, but under GATT rules that required panel reports to be adopted by consensus, the EC was able to block adoption of the report. The EC issued new regulations in July, which it claimed met its GATT obligations. In January 1994 a GATT panel ruled against this regime as well, and the EC again blocked the adoption of the report by the GATT council. With the formation of the WTO, panel reports could no longer be blocked by the offending party. A 1997 panel found that the EU banana regime violated both the GATT and the GATS. The EU appealed against these findings to the WTO Appellate Body, which upheld the panel ruling. Efforts to negotiate a settlement were not fruitful, and in 1998 the EU announced modifications to the banana regime that it claimed were WTO-consistent. The EU blocked reconvening the WTO panel in the fall of 1998 and the US announced retaliatory steps. Eventually, the panel was reconvened, and yet again it ruled against the EU program.

In April 1999 WTO arbitrators ruled that the US could impose retaliatory trade measures that affected $191 million of imports from the EU. Items selected by the US included handbags, paper, bed linen, and coffee makers, although some lawmakers favored a rotating retaliation list, to create maximum political pressure for a settlement.[14]

In fact, a successful compromise between the US and the EU was reached in April 2001 to resolve this dispute. At the time observers hoped that was a good omen for more amiable trade relations between the two. The goodwill seemed to evaporate quickly, however, as additional disputes arose over US export subsidies and steel safeguards. Latin-American banana exporters conditioned their acceptance of a WTO waiver for an EU–Africa, Caribbean and Pacific Economic Partnership upon good faith implementation of the banana accord.

Nevertheless, the success of the agreement will depend upon the way individual countries implement their commitments and the way they use WTO procedures. If member countries treat WTO procedures as a forum to handle minor disputes, but rely on bilateral negotiations to deal with major issues, the tension between rule of law and rule of negotiating power will remain.

There has been considerable use of the WTO dispute resolution procedures. As of July 2002 the number of requests for consultation had been 261. The major complainants were the United States (71) and the EU (57), although developing countries brought 93 complaints. Early examples of panel rulings favorable to developing countries, as were made in the case of US restrictions on underwear imports from Costa Rica, wool shirts from India and reformulated gasoline from Brazil and Venezuela, demonstrate the advantages of a rule-based system to smaller countries. The goal of dispute resolution is that countries bring their practices into conformity with WTO obligations, but in cases where insufficient adjustments were made, retaliation was authorized: the EU ban on hormone-treated beef imports, the EU banana import regime, Brazilian export financing of aircraft, and US export subsidies provided through its tax code.[15] Table 8.3 lists dispute settlement cases initiated in 2002 to indicate the breadth of complaints brought to the WTO.

Table 8.3 Cases brought for WTO dispute resolution in 2002

Respondent	Issue	Complainant
Canada	Exports of wheat and treatment of imported grain	US
Venezuela	Import licensing on certain agricultural products	US
US	Safeguards on imports of steel products	Chinese Taipei
Korea	Trade in commercial vessels	EC
Peru	Antidumping duties on vegetable oils	Argentina
Australia	Importation of fresh pineapple	Philippines
Australia	Importation of fresh fruit and vegetables	Philippines
EC	Customs classification of frozen boneless chicken	Brazil
US	Antidumping measures, oil country tubular goods	Argentina
US	Subsidies on upland cotton	Brazil
EC	Export subsidies on sugar	Brazil, Australia
US	Antidumping measures, softwood lumber	Canada
EC	Imports of wine	Argentina
US	Antidumping and countervailing duties, steel products	France, Germany
Uruguay	Tax treatment on certain products	Chile
EC	Safeguards on imports of steel products	US
US	Safeguards on imports of steel products	Brazil, New Zealand
US	Countervailing duties, softwood lumber	Canada
Turkey	Import ban on pet food	Hungary
Peru	Tax treatment on certain imported products	Chile
US	Safeguards on imports of steel products	Norway, Switzerland, China, Korea
US	Excise taxes by Florida on orange and grapefruit products	Brazil
US	Safeguards on imports of steel products	Japan, EC
US	Antidumping duties, softwood lumber	Canada
EC	Conditions for granting tariff preferences to developing countries	India
Japan	Importation of apples	US
US	Antidumping duties, carbon steel flat products	Japan
US	Rules of origin for textiles and apparel products	India

Source: www.wto.org/english/tratop_e/dispu_e/dispu_status_e.htm (January 1, 2003).

Intellectual property

The treatment of intellectual property rights under the WTO has proven particularly contentious. Developed countries have a comparative advantage in research-and-development intensive industries, and they benefit from the monopoly profits earned before their technology becomes widely available in other countries. As a consequence, developed countries were strong advocates of the TRIPs agreement. Prior to the step, the United States had taken action unilaterally under provisions of the 1988 Omnibus Trade Act to retaliate against the exports of countries whose governments did not make reasonable efforts to enforce US patents and copyrights within their borders. China particularly was seen as a flagrant violator.

Box 8.3 Pharmaceutical flip flops and the TRIPS agreement

The Uruguay Round TRIPs Agreement stipulated that members provide patent protection for pharmaceutical products, among its various provisions. While copyrights and patents for other products were important, the economic value of pharmaceutical patents is particularly high. At the same time, poor countries reliant on foreign technology are concerned that their failure to gain access to patented medicines at low prices will cost human lives. The tension between these two points of view explains some ambiguities in the agreement over the flexibility of countries to take measures to protect public health.

Just as the textile agreement phased in slowly over time, developing and transition economies were given 5 years, and least developed countries 11 years, to fulfill this commitment. Over that time-frame, however, discussion changed substantially due to the AIDS epidemic and high rates of HIV infection in many developing countries, who could not afford to pay the high price of treatment in industrialized countries. Protests in favor of compulsory licensing for HIV drugs occurred in Thailand and South Africa. An Indian generic drug producer offered to sell HIV drugs at a 90 percent discount from prices in industrialized countries. Brazil produced its own copies of several of these drugs, and its expenditures per AIDS patient were roughly one-third of the $12,000 annual expense in the United States. As Brazil succeeded in containing the spread of the virus and cutting its AIDS-related deaths by 50 percent, its program was viewed as a model for other middle-income countries to follow.[16] For countries that had no indigenous generic producers, that raised a further trade issue regarding the rights of such countries to import drugs from producers that had no assent from the patent holders.

Yet, if pharmaceuticals could be freely exported and imported by any country, including the United States, what would happen to the ability of drug firms to price discriminate and charge high prices in the US market where there was a higher ability and willingness to pay? Without these high-priced sales, the return to innovation of new drugs would be much lower, and many fewer life-saving remedies would be developed.

Discourse on this topic further changed with the terrorist attacks on the United States and a subsequent scare over an anthrax epidemic in 2001. The US Secretary for Health and Welfare demanded a lower price from the makers of Cipro, a powerful antibiotic, to be able to address this emergency. Many developing countries noted that

AIDS, tuberculosis, and malaria constituted public health emergencies in their countries, and their demands for lower prices or compulsory licensing agreements were comparable. The issue became a major element of the Doha Development Agenda established at the November 2001 ministerial meeting to launch a new round of trade talks. Least developed countries were given until 2016 to provide patents for pharmaceutical products. The Doha Round will attempt to clarify what circumstances constitute national emergencies that warrant compulsory licensing or under what conditions the initial producer can control trade in drugs after their original sale. (The latter issue covers "**parallel imports**"; to be effective, price discrimination strategies rely upon control over parallel imports.) Related issues to address include the treatment of traditional knowledge and folklore.

Although the loss of profits to firms that innovate makes the issue of copying appear to be just a matter of transferring funds from the North to the South, the world as a whole has a wider interest in ensuring that innovation continues to occur in the future. Stricter enforcement of patents and copyrights allows higher returns to be earned by the creators of existing literary and musical innovative works, new products, and more efficient production processes. Those profits also provide an incentive for future innovation and result in greater willingness to finance current research and creative activity. Thus, intellectual property protection affects the speed at which science and technology advance.

Developing countries often have weak regimes to protect intellectual property, because that effort drains funds and skilled personnel away from alternative uses that directly benefit their residents rather than foreign copyright and patent holders. Charles Dickens complained of weak US copyright protection in the nineteenth century, and in a similar vein developing countries see little direct benefit from stricter enforcement today. Rather they expect to gain from free riding on the efforts of others to promote innovation. While that strategy may mean that few products are developed that primarily benefit developing countries, in the case of products aimed at a worldwide market developing countries may take little action in the absence of external pressure.

What is the effect on world welfare of enforcing rules to extract greater payments for innovators of new products? To answer that question economists need to know whether too little research is carried on presently, a likely outcome when much of the benefit from an innovation spills over to others. They also must judge whether granting monopoly power to an innovator for a 20-year period, the patent life agreed to in the Uruguay Round, is a reasonable rule of thumb. Does it appropriately balance the payoff from future innovation against the welfare loss that comes from charging monopoly prices that far exceed marginal costs of production? In turn, that requires assessing how productive is another dollar spent on research in generating new ideas, and how great will the incentive be for a monopolist to introduce a new product that undercuts demand for one of its existing products.

The Uruguay Round agreement represents a judgment that the world is underinvesting in research and development, and that promoting more research effort will lead to higher standards of living. Not all countries necessarily gain from stricter enforcement of intellectual property rights, which suggests why trying to reach agreement on this issue outside of a round where several other items are considered at the same time is unlikely to be successful. From a world perspective, even coming up with an ideally designed policy may founder because of difficulties in enforcing any agreement.

The rocky road to further multilateral agreements

Although the Uruguay Round broke ground in many new areas, it merely marked the status quo in some of them and therefore most countries anticipated a subsequent round of negotiations to address this unfinished business. For example, the commitment to convert quotas on agricultural imports into tariffs resulted in countries imposing extremely high tariffs, over 1000 percent in the case of rice in Japan. The Uruguay Round mandated that negotiations start no later than 2000 to ensure that improved agricultural market access was accomplished. Similarly, in the service area countries made commitments in some sectors, but the Uruguay Round more nearly represented a stand still on further restrictions, not a major opening.

The expectations of initiating another round were not met at the ministerial meeting at Seattle in November 1999. Prior to the meeting wide gaps in country positions still existed, and further pressures were created by the protests of industrial country labor unions, environmental activists, and other antiglobalization forces. Complaints were raised over secrecy and the decision-making processes within the WTO. US and EU representatives talked of the need to incorporate labor rights and environmental protection into the WTO, while many developing countries saw these as code words to limit their potential exports. Subsequent bilateral agreements, such as the Canadian–Chilean or US–Jordanian free trade agreements, have addressed those topics, but no clear basis for broader action exists.

In 1998 the International Labor Organization declared that all 175 members had an obligation to promote four fundamental rights by guaranteeing: (1) freedom of association and the right to collective bargaining; (2) elimination of all forms of forced labor; (3) effective abolition of child labor; and (4) elimination of discrimination in employment.[17] Yet, there is little agreement on what these provisions reasonably require, or whether they necessarily make workers better off in a world with imperfect capital markets and the inability to borrow against future earnings. Labor interests in industrialized countries have seen the ILO as ineffective in ensuring adherence to these standards, and therefore they have pushed for inclusion of this issue in trade agreements where a stronger dispute resolution mechanism is available.

Various European and North American groups have promoted "fair trade" movements to ensure that production in developing countries does not exploit workers or the environment. For example, some attempt to certify that rugs are produced without child labor or that a higher price is paid to small, organic producers of cocoa or coffee. Anti-sweatshop activists object to working conditions in the apparel and footwear industries, and they attempt to pressure brand name producers like Nike to subcontract only with companies that meet basic health, safety, and human rights standards. Advocates of these changes claim that few jobs will be lost, because any increase in costs will come primarily at the expense of profits, especially in quota-constrained apparel markets. Many developing countries, however, fear that their jobs are at risk, and correspondingly that their opportunity to take the first step toward industrialization and away from low productivity agriculture or undesirable activities such as prostitution will be blocked.

In the case of environmental issues, activists are particularly alarmed that the WTO dispute resolution bodies will allow trade rules to dominate the provisions of domestic legislation and international environmental agreements. Examples of those concerns are discussed in Chapter 11.

The Doha Development Agenda

After the pronounced failure of WTO members to agree upon an agenda for further multi-lateral trade negotiations at the Seattle ministerial meeting of 1999, a new round of multi-lateral trade negotiations was initiated at the WTO's fourth ministerial conference in Doha, Qatar in November 2001. Developing countries were skeptical of participating in such a round, because they claimed that few concrete benefits to them had emerged from the Uruguay Round. Therefore, industrialized nations made a major effort to ensure that concerns of developing countries would be addressed more directly through the Doha Development Agenda. Again, the goal is to establish a single agreement covering several areas.

Because 70 percent of poor country exports are in agriculture and textiles and apparel, progress in these two areas is a priority.[18] Continued negotiations in agriculture were mandated by the Uruguay Round Agreement to begin in 2000, but the political sensitivity of agricultural tariff rates, export subsidies and domestic supports in the EU may limit progress here. Japanese and European negotiators sought a broader agenda including environmental issues and competition policy, perhaps to be able to demonstrate new areas where their interests were addressed or perhaps to slow down the entire negotiating process. With respect to textiles and apparel, the United States found this a particularly sensitive area, especially given promises made by the Bush Administration to gain fast-track trade negotiating authority. Many peak rates in the US tariff schedule occur in this sector, and therefore major reductions in these barriers may be difficult to achieve.

Several important items are to be addressed which include the following:

- implementation of WTO commitments by developing countries;
- tariffs on nonagricultural goods, including the peak rates mentioned above;
- TRIPs, especially public health concerns as discussed in Box 8.2;
- antidumping and subsidies disciplines, with particular reference to fisheries;
- regional trade agreements and determination of their compatibility with WTO standards;
- the relationship between multilateral environmental agreements and WTO rules; and
- services, an area where further negotiations also were mandated by the Uruguay Round to begin in 2000.

Working groups were to develop proposals that might be included in the single package, as determined at the fifth ministerial conference in 2003: TRIMs; the interaction of trade and competition policy; and transparency in government procurement.

Expanding the World Trade Organization

Chinese Taipei (Taiwan) became the 144th member of the WTO on 1 January 2002. Several additional countries are in the process of negotiating accession to the WTO, and their entry will require further attention to the unwieldy nature of decision-making in such a large organization. The entry of China and the prospective entry of Russia and other former communist states pose a particular challenge, due to their limited historical reliance on market institutions.

Other nonmarket economies are WTO members, but their smaller size means that their actions have limited impact on producers in other countries or on international prices. In the case of Russia and China that is far from true. Determining whether the prices of goods

---

Box 8.4 Who's afraid of China?

After a lengthy process of negotiating to join the World Trade Organization, China became a member on 1 December 2001. Although all countries had to approve China's membership, some of the most contentious bilateral talks occurred with the EU and with the US. In addition to the access they sought to Chinese markets for goods and services, both were concerned about a potential flood of products from China. In particular, worries abounded that in sectors where state-owned enterprises still dominated production, trade would be determined by government preferences and priorities, not by comparative advantage or market forces. Organized labor in the United States vehemently opposed Chinese entry, as it feared that competition with such a labor-abundant country would drive down US wages.

On the one hand, developing countries expected some benefit from having the strong voice of a powerful developing country in the WTO. On the other hand, developing countries were worried because they saw themselves competing much more directly with Chinese goods. Other Asian countries particularly feared China as an alternative site for foreign direct investment in export-oriented industries. As country-specific quotas on textiles and apparel are removed, will countries such as Bangladesh be able to export as many pants and shirts as in 2000? Will ASEAN countries find that nearly all foreign investment in the region now flows to China?

Even a country as seemingly removed from the scene as Mexico was affected, and in fact Mexico was the last country to assent to Chinese entry into the WTO. Was such concern warranted? The rapid growth of the assembly industry in Mexico under NAFTA was adversely affected by the US economic slowdown in 2001, as was US trade with China. In 2002, however, after China's accession to the WTO, US imports from China rose by $20 billion or 20 percent, while imports from Mexico only rose 2 percent. The two countries do not compete head to head in all categories, but Chinese expansion and Mexican contraction in several key assembly operations are evident. In the three tariff categories for computers, office machinery, and calculators, Chinese sales rose by $3.8 billion, or 40 percent, while Mexican sales fell by $1.4 billion or 15 percent. A less dramatic pattern shows up in apparel, where Chinese sales rose by $0.5 billion or 7 percent, while Mexican sales fell $0.5 billion or 6 percent. Although this record also may reflect minor influences from exchange rate changes, the Mexican forecast of trouble ahead appears to be accurate.

Furthermore, the difference in performance across different industry categories does not seem to be related to the level of US tariff protection or the difference between the most-favored-nation rate granted to WTO members and the rate applied to nonmembers. The attraction of Chinese-based assembly seems to have risen due to the greater perceived predictability and consistency of Chinese policy, now that it is a WTO member.

---

they export reflect opportunity costs of production or government subsidies is not possible. Judging whether imports can freely enter a country and then benefit from national treatment is difficult when purchasers and competitors are state enterprises that do not face budget constraints. The swelling Chinese trade surplus overstates its general acceptance of a market-oriented economic system, because such production typically occurs in export-processing zones where any output must be exported rather than sold in domestic markets. Pervasive reliance on quantitative controls to restrict the growth of imports and limited efforts to enforce intellectual property rights suggests that substantial changes in Chinese trade practices will be necessary to meet WTO standards. Similarly thorny issues arise in the case of Russian accession.

Summary of key concepts

1   During the nineteenth century, Great Britain unilaterally adopted a policy of free trade, which many other countries subsequently followed. This stance was a major contrast to the state control of trade pursued in earlier centuries under mercantilism.
2   High tariffs adopted by the United States in 1930 contributed to a major reduction in trade and production worldwide. In 1934, the United States began negotiating bilateral trade agreements that reduced tariffs on a most-favored-nation basis.
3   The General Agreement on Tariffs and Trade, founded in 1947, established a set of rules for international trade. It encouraged negotiations to reduce trade barriers on a nondiscriminatory basis.
4   The Kennedy Round of trade negotiations, concluded in 1967, reduced tariffs under a multilateral approach, which in general made across-the-board cuts.
5   The Tokyo Round, concluded in 1979, applied a formula to cut tariffs further, and in separate codes it addressed several nontariff barriers to trade. Developing-country participation in the round was limited.
6   The Uruguay Round, completed in 1994, covered several items that had escaped GATT discipline (agriculture and textiles) and extended the agreement to include several new areas (services, intellectual property, and investment requirements). The World Trade Organization was established, and a more rigorous dispute resolution mechanism was created. The agreement was treated as a single package that all members accepted without the opportunity to make exceptions.
7   A major goal of the Doha Development Agenda initiated in 2001 is to ensure that greater market access to highly protected sectors promised in the Uruguay Round actually is achieved.

Questions for study and review

1   How is the objective of nondiscrimination achieved in GATT tariff agreements? What are the two major exceptions that have been formally agreed on by GATT?
2   Does the growth of regional trading blocs warrant WTO encouragement? If groups had an open membership policy would that be more desirable from a world standpoint?
3   What is the most-favored-nation clause? How exactly does it work, and why is it used in tariff agreements? How is it related to the concept of reciprocity?
4   If trade agreements consisted of several independent sections or codes that only applied to countries that signed each code, how would that likely affect the extent of liberalization of world trade?

5   The United States has encouraged foreign producers to adopt voluntary export restraints and orderly marketing arrangements to reduce US imports and protect domestic industries. Why has the WTO outlawed such agreements?

6   Why did the Uruguay Round almost fail in late 1990? Why was the United States so forceful on the subject of EU agricultural subsidies? What countries might you have expected to have been allied with the United States on this subject? Allied with the EU on this subject? Why?

7   What countries would you expect to support the US position on intellectual property within the WTO? Why?

8   How are trade disputes resolved within the WTO? If this rule-based approach to trade policy were to break down, which countries would be most adversely affected?

9   Should the WTO attempt to govern trade by nonmarket economies, or should a different organization with a different set of rules be established to do that?

Suggested further reading

For an excellent overview of GATT/WTO principles, see:
- Jackson, John H., *The World Trading System, Law and Policy of International Economic Relations*, 2nd edn, Cambridge, MA: MIT Press, 1997.

For a contrasting overviews of the prospects for current multilateral trade negotiations and ongoing globalization, see:
- Schott, Jeffrey, ed., *The World Trading System: Challenges Ahead*, Washington, DC: Institute for International Economics, 1996.
- Raghavan, Chakravarthi, *Recolonization: GATT, the Uruguay Round and the Third World*, Atlantic Highlands, NJ: Zed Books, 1990.

Notes

1   It should be added that the United States took the initiative in revising this treaty 75 years later. The first revision graciously allowed Thailand to increase tariffs to 5 percent.
2   US Tariff Commission, *Trade Barriers*, Vol. 3 (Washington, DC: USTC, April 1974), Chapter 5.
3   Some observers claim this approach reflects an inappropriate mercantilistic focus, because it implies that exports are a good thing and should be encouraged, whereas imports are harmful to a country. See K. Bagwell and R. Staiger, "An Economic Theory of GATT," *American Economic Review* 89, no. 1, March 1999, pp. 215–48, for a defense of the focus on reciprocity as a means of offsetting the incentive a country has to restrict trade in order to improve its terms of trade.
4   WTO, "Overview of Developments in the International Trading Environment," (November 15, 2002), WT/TPR/OV/8 p. 10.
5   GATT, *GATT in Action* (Geneva, January 1952), pp. 20–1.
6   Douglas Irwin, "Changes in US Tariffs: The Role of Import Prices and Commercial Policies," *American Economic Review* 88, no. 4, September 1998, pp. 1015–26.
7   John Howard Jackson, *The World Trading System: Law and Policy of International Economic Relations* (Cambridge, MA: MIT Press, 1989), pp. 131–41.
8   J.M. Finger, H. Keith Hall, and D. Nelson, "The Political Economy of Administered Protection," *American Economic Review* 72, 1982, pp. 452–66.
9   The actual formula used was proposed by the Swiss. It is:

> Tariff reduction = $t/(t + 0.14)$, where t = the existing tariff rate. Thus a 40 percent existing tariff would be cut by $0.40/(0.40 + 0.14) = 74$ percent, whereas a 10 percent existing tariff would be cut by $0.10/(0.10 + 0.14) = 42$ percent.

10 Alan Deardorff and Robert Stern, "The Economic Effects of Complete Elimination of Post-Tokyo Round Tariffs," in William Cline, ed., *Trade Policy in the 80s* (Cambridge, MA: MIT Press, 1983).

11 Jackson, op. cit.

12 For a discussion of the contents of the Uruguay Round agreement, see the *Economic Report of the President: 1994* (Washington, DC: US Government Printing Office, 1994). For a more detailed treatment of the agreement, see Jeffrey Schott, *The Uruguay Round: An Assessment* (Washington, DC: Institute for International Economics, 1994).

13 See E. Graham, *Fighting the Wrong Enemy* (Washington, DC: Institute for International Economics, 2000).

14 See Guy de Jonquières, "WTO Puts Skids under Banana Regime," *The Financial Times*, March 20, 1997, p. 7, and "Trade Goes Bananas," *The Financial Times*, January 26, 1999, p. 15, as well as WTO, "Overview of the State-of-Play of WTO Disputes," (May 5, 1999), http://www.wto.org/wto/dispute/bulletin/htm (May 25, 1997), and "At Daggers Drawn," *The Economist*, May 8, 1999, pp. 17–19.

15 WTO, op. cit., p. 38.

16 Miriam Jordan, "Brazil May Flout Trade Laws to keep AIDS Drugs Free for Patients," *Wall Street Journal*, February 12, 2001, p. B1, and United Nations, *Human Development Report 2002*, p. 106.

17 See Drusilla Brown, "Labor Standards: Where Do They Belong on the International Trade Agenda?" *Journal of Economic Perspectives* 15 (Summer 2001) pp. 89–112, for further discussion of these issues.

18 WTO, op. cit., p. 2

9 International mobility of labor and capital

Learning objectives

By the end of this chapter you should be able to understand:

- how international capital flows reduce differences in returns across countries and raise world output;
- how international flows of labor reduce differences in wages across countries but may reduce per capita income in the host country;
- that a firm may have special expertise that it finds more profitable to exploit by producing abroad (as a multinational corporation) rather than export from the home country.

The previous chapters assume that goods are internationally mobile (i.e. that merchandise trade occurs) but that factors of production are not mobile. The basis of Heckscher–Ohlin trade is precisely that large differences in relative factor endowments produce parallel differences in factor prices; these in turn lead to differences in relative goods prices, which makes trade based on comparative advantage possible. A country with a relative abundance of labor, for example, will have low wages, which will give it a comparative advantage in labor-intensive goods such as apparel and shoes. The fact that differences in factor prices exist prior to trade implies that labor and capital are internationally immobile; otherwise the abundant factor in each country simply moves elsewhere to earn higher returns. Labor will migrate to capital-abundant countries, and capital will move in the opposite direction, roughly equalizing relative factor endowments and prices, thus eliminating the basis for Heckscher–Ohlin trade.

Although the theory of international trade presented thus far assumes that factors of production are immobile, in reality some labor and capital movement occurs between countries. Labor migrates, legally or otherwise, from low- to higher-wage countries. International capital flows seeking higher returns are a major element of international finance. Of course, labor mobility is limited by immigration laws, transportation costs, lack of information about job opportunities, and language differences. International investors are deterred by different legal and regulatory environments, discriminatory taxes, potential expropriation, incomplete information, and a variety of risks, including a decline in the value of assets it holds that are denominated in foreign currencies. That latter topic is addressed in Part Two of this book.

Nevertheless, there is sufficient mobility of capital and labor to warrant our attention. In fact, some economists believe that migration of labor has had a bigger effect on the earnings of low-skilled workers within developed countries than has imports of goods that use unskilled labor intensively.[1] As shown in Table 9.1, immigrants, as a share of the population and particularly as a share of the work force, have risen in most of Europe and the United States. While the peak rate of population growth due to immigration occurred in the United States in 1900, at 1.2 percent annually, that rate has risen steadily since World War II from less than 0.1 percent to 0.3 percent. Within Europe, Germany experienced rates greater than 1.0 percent in the early 1990s due to the opening up of Eastern Europe.[2] With respect to capital mobility, private capital flows to LDCs as a group are far larger than official aid or multilateral assistance. Their distribution across countries is quite uneven, though, and their volatility often raises concerns over the benefits they confer. Investment by multinational corporations often is linked to the flow of capital between countries, but generally it has even more to do with the flow of ideas and technology between countries. Analyzing the motivation for these various factor flows and assessing their consequences is the focus of this chapter.

Table 9.1 The role of immigrants as a share of the population or work force

Country	Share of population		Share of labor force	
	1982	1993	1991	1999
Australia[8]	20.6	[3]22.7	[3]24.8	24.6
Austria	4.0	[4]7.1	[4]8.9	9.5
Belgium	9.0	[4]9.0	7.4	8.7
Canada[9]	16.1	15.6	[4]18.5	
Denmark	2.0	3.6	2.5	2.5
Finland	0.3	1.1		1.2
France[9]	6.8	[2]6.3	6.2	6.1
Germany	7.6	8.5	[5]8.9	8.7
Italy	0.6	1.7		3.6
Japan[7]	0.7	1.1	[4]0.9	1.0
Luxembourg	26.2	[4]30.3	33.3	57.3
Netherlands	3.8	[4]5.0	3.9	3.4
Norway	2.2	3.8	[4]4.4	2.9
Spain	0.5	[4]1.0	0.4	1.0
Sweden	4.9	[4]5.7	[4]5.5	4.1
Switzerland	14.4	18.1	[4]20.1	18.1
United Kingdom[8]	2.8	3.5	3.3	3.9
United States[9]	[1]4.7	[2]7.9	[2]9.3	11.7

[1]1980 data. [2]1990 data. [3]1994 data. [4]1992 data. [5]Western Germany only. [6]Excludes unemployed. [7]Residence permits. [8]Labor force survey. [9]Census data.

Source: Organization for Economic Cooperation and Development, Paris, *OECD Observer*, no. 192, February/March 1995; *Trends in International Migration*, Paris, OECD, 2001.

Arbitrage in labor and capital markets

The international migration of capital and labor can be viewed as an arbitraging process that is similar to the movement that occurs between regions of a country. People living in low-wage or high-unemployment areas of the United States, for example, move to states where wages and job opportunities are better. This movement reduces wage differentials by reducing the supply of labor where wages are low and by increasing the number of people seeking work in high-wage areas. Transportation costs, preferences for remaining in one's home region, and lack of information about job availability mean that this arbitraging process is not perfect, for it does not produce a single wage across all parts of the United States. It does, however, limit the range of wage differentials, because low-wage states consistently lose working-age residents and higher-wage states gain them.

The international movement of workers reflects the same arbitraging process, except that the barriers to migration are higher than in the case of domestic migration. Transportation is more costly, information about job availability is harder to obtain, and differences in language, culture, and even climate make preferences for remaining in one's home country stronger. These distinctions apply even within the European Union, in spite of the absence of legal restrictions on movement within the EU. More generally, international migration is restrained by national laws that limit entry to those the country chooses to accept.

In Chapter 3 the Heckscher–Ohlin framework led to the prediction that if free trade prevailed, factor prices would become sufficiently similar to greatly reduce the pressure for labor or capital migration. It is largely because merchandise trade is not costless or free of restrictions that international differences in factor prices persist and thus create incentives for migration. Heckscher–Ohlin trade and international factor mobility can then be viewed as close substitutes in terms of both causes and effects. Both result from differences in factor prices that reflect differences in relative factor endowments, and both would reduce or eliminate those price differences. Either process would sharply narrow international differentials in wage rates. If industrialized countries either had free trade or imposed no barriers to people immigrating from abroad, domestic wage rates would fall and returns to capital and land would rise.[3]

This parallelism between Heckscher–Ohlin trade and factor mobility extends to politics. Because the relatively scarce factor of production absorbs income losses from either free trade or factor mobility, it tends to support both protectionism and strict limits on factor movements, whereas the abundant factor of production gains from both processes, and therefore favors free trade and more factor mobility. Within the United States the AFL-CIO favors strict immigration laws and firm enforcement efforts for the same reason that it supports protection. Both will maintain or increase US wage rates for less skilled workers. In the early 1970s, American labor favored limits on the ability of US firms to move capital abroad, and in the debate over NAFTA, labor predicted that runaway plants would be attracted to Mexico by low wages and thereby reduce employment within the United States. US farmers and owners of businesses, who want readily available low-wage labor, tend to favor much less strict limits on immigration.

Formulating a model

To indicate the consequences of factor movements we consider a somewhat simpler model than the H–O approach, which nevertheless yields many of the same insights. In Figure 9.1 we represent the utilization of capital in two economies that produce the same good. Therefore, we cannot use this framework to show how trade is affected by factor flows. The approach is quite useful, however, to show how factor mobility increases efficiency and total output, which occurs because scarce productive assets move from less productive to more productive locations and uses. Output should rise by the difference in marginal products times the amount of the factor that moves. Rates of return, and therefore marginal products,

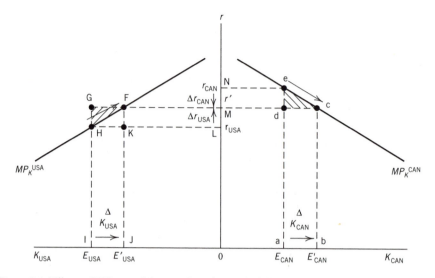

Figure 9.1 Effects of US capital flow to Canada. With differing interest rates of r_{CAN} in Canada and r_{USA} in the United States, an amount of capital E_{USA} minus E'_{USA} moves from the United States to Canada, bringing the interest rates of the two countries into equality at r' and increasing the Canadian capital stock to E'_{CAN}. Rectangle abcd is the payment of interest by Canada to US investors each year. Since Canadian output increases by area ecba, there is a net gain for Canada of triangle dce. The United States loses output of FHIJK, but gains interest income of IJFG, for a net gain of triangle FGH.

Source: Adapted from Peter B. Kenen, *The International Economy*, 2nd edn (Englewood Cliffs, NJ: Prentice Hall, 1989), p. 137.

are equated through arbitrage. The marginal product of capital (MP_k in the figure) is the increase in total output that results from adding one unit of capital while holding inputs of other factors unchanged. The marginal product lines slope down because of the law of diminishing returns. That is, adding more capital to unchanged amounts of labor and land reduces the marginal product of capital.

One way of thinking of capital mobility is in terms of an individual who owns a stock of machines and chooses to lease them to firms that will use them in production. Airplanes, railroad cars, and trucks are often leased in this way. When capital is mobile internationally, the equipment can be leased to operators on either side of the border, but with immobile capital, owners can only lease to operators on their own side of the border. Thus, in labeling the vertical axis of Figure 9.1, we can think of the price reflecting the rental rate received for the leased machines. Or we can express this return in percentage form as a share of the value of the machine. That form may seem more familiar when we think of financial flows across borders, which then allow borrowers to make investments in plant and equipment. Our model applies to both situations. In this graph, the difference in interest rates, which represent differences in the marginal productivity of capital, causes capital in the amount of IJ to flow from the United States to Canada, where the inflow is represented as *ab*. As a result, interest rates in Canada fall from r_{CAN} to r' while yields in the United States rise from r_{USA} to r'. Output in Canada rises by the area under the marginal product function, area ecbad, whereas output in the United States falls by area FHIJK. The increase in total output, which is the result of reallocating scarce capital to a more productive location, is the area of the two triangles, dce and FGH. Canadians make interest payments to Americans in the amount of the rectangle abcd per year, which means that the net gain in income for Canada is the triangle dce. The income received by American capitalists who invest in Canada, given by rectangle abcd, also equals rectangle IJFG. Given the loss of US output of area FHIJK when capital leaves the country, the net gain in income for the United States is triangle FGH. Capital moves from less to more efficient uses, interest rates are arbitraged together, and total income in both countries increases.

Sizable income redistribution effects exist, however. Canadian-owned capital (distance Oa) was earning an interest rate of r_{CAN} for a total income shown by the rectangle ONea. As a result of the inflow of US funds, this yield falls to r', which means total income of Canadian-owned capital is now rectangle OMda, giving a loss of area MdeN. This income is shifted to Canadian labor in the form of higher wages resulting from a higher capital-to-labor ratio in Canada and a higher marginal product of Canadian labor. Canadian-owned capital loses and labor gains. The same income redistribution process occurs in the United States but in the opposite direction. US-owned capital was previously earning r_{USA} for a total income of rectangle OLHI. The increase of US interest rates to r' means that American capital that does not go to Canada gains rectangle LMFK. This income is extracted from labor as US wages fall, due to a lower capital-to-labor ratio in the United States and a decline in the marginal product of US labor. US capital gains and labor loses.

International factor mobility produces the same dilemmas as does free trade. Total output and incomes clearly rise, but income is redistributed in ways that may be painful and politically controversial. From the perspective of Canadian labor and US capital, the process described here should be encouraged, but US workers and Canadian owners of capital will have the opposite view. Political conflicts over immigration laws and policies affecting international capital movements are likely to reflect these differing interests.

The influence of taxes and risk

Taxes can affect the conclusion that total incomes in both countries rise as a result of these factor movements. The example above assumes that US capitalists lend money to Canadian borrowers, and that the interest income is not subject to any Canadian tax. If instead a Canadian tax is imposed, and as a result the Canadian government rather than the US government taxes this income, the United States as a whole may lose from the capital outflow.

Consider a situation where both countries impose a 40 percent income tax. If a US firm invests domestically, let the pre-tax return be 10 percent. The net return to its investors is only 6 percent, but the US Treasury gets 4 percent, which can be used for public purposes. Suppose the pre-tax return in Canada is 12 percent. The after-tax return to a US investor in Canada is 7.2 percent, but the US Treasury gets nothing because the 4.8 percent collected in taxes goes to Ottawa, presuming that the United States offers a credit for the Canadian tax paid. The total return to the United States is 7.2 percent, meaning a loss of 2.8 percent. World output rises by the 2 percent difference in gross yields, and the Canadian government and US private investors certainly gain. However, the US government loses 4 percent of the investment income per year, and the American economy as a whole loses 2.8 percent. International capital flows do increase efficiency, as does a system of granting foreign tax credits, but it is not clear that the flows benefit both the investing and the host country.

The model above also has the implication that the flow of capital is in just one direction, from a capital-abundant to a capital-scarce country. In reality, we often observe two-way capital flows. When savers in one country choose to lend to borrowers in another country, as when they buy a government or corporate bond, they clearly do respond to differences in real rates of return across countries, all else being equal. They are most interested, however, in the way a purchase of a bond in another country will affect the return to their total savings or portfolio. Buying a bond that offers a lower rate of return can still make sense when it reduces the riskiness of the portfolio, or the volatility of all returns received. If returns in Japan rise exactly when returns in the United States fall, and vice versa, a Japanese saver's portfolio can yield the same return at a lower level of risk if it is diversified and includes US bonds. Even though both the United States and Japan are capital-abundant countries, capital may flow from Japan to the United States, and vice versa, as a result of these gains from diversification. That topic is covered in Part Two. The model assumed in Figure 9.1 best applies to net flows of capital.

Our capital flow model abstracts from another aspect of capital mobility that was a feature of the 1990s: financial instability. If lenders reassess the attractiveness of providing capital to foreigners, the adjustment in the case of financial flows is not as simple as a leasing company bringing its equipment home. Rather, the desire of lenders to withdraw funds may require borrowers to sell assets that have few alternative uses. Over-reliance on short-term debt to finance long-lived assets results in the borrower becoming particularly vulnerable to unexpected bad news. Determining a firm's appropriate financial strategy to avoid such problems is another important topic in international finance.

Additional issues raised by labor mobility

The one-good model with capital flows represented in Figure 9.1 can be applied to the case of labor mobility, too, if we assume that labor moves while capital remains fixed. Due to changes in immigration laws in Australia, Canada, and the United States, the proportion of immigrants from developing countries rose from 20 percent in 1960 to over 80 percent in the 1990s. A less pronounced but similar trend has occurred in Europe.[4] Although recent immigrants have more education than earlier immigrants, the level of education in host countries has risen even faster. Thus, the gap between immigrant and native wages has risen.[5] Nevertheless, higher wages in industrialized countries create a huge incentive to move, legally or otherwise. It is becoming increasingly difficult for authorities in industrialized countries to control their national borders. Many governments in developing countries view emigration to industrialized countries as a safety valve for excess population pressures, and therefore oppose attempts of the industrialized countries to tighten immigration controls. A UN study estimates that restriction on migration from developing countries reduces their income by $250 billion a year.[6] Even among developing countries, migration occurs, as Indonesians migrate to Malaysia and Guatemalans migrate to Mexico. If high rates of population growth continue in the developing world, this problem could prove extremely difficult for industrialized countries and newly industrialized countries.

Although immigration into a labor-scarce country increases total income in the nation, it does not necessarily increase per capita income, because the population grows. If the immigrants are unskilled and bring little or no capital with them, they are likely to lower US or European per capita output. Only if we do not count the new arrivals as part of the population, and focus only on the original residents, is that issue avoided. While some defend such a view on the grounds that the new arrivals must be better off or they would not have come, most governments have to be concerned about the standard of living and eventual integration of all who live within their borders.

The effect of such immigration on host-country output per person can be seen most easily through a standard growth model:

$$Y = F(K, LB, LN)$$

where Y is gross domestic product, K is capital stock, LB is labor force, and LN is the stock of land. This equation states that potential output is a positive function of the size of the capital stock, the labor force and the availability of land. Technology determines the nature of this function. Capital is defined as including education and training, which is often referred to as "human capital."

If the labor force is a constant proportion, a, of the population, then output per capita, Y/c, can be expressed as:

$$Y/c = a F(K / LB, LN / LB)$$

where we have assumed constant returns to scale in production. This equation says that output per capita is positively related to the capital-to-labor ratio and the land-to-labor ratio. Output per capita will grow if the amount of capital per worker rises or if the amount of land per worker increases. Improvements in technology also allow output per capita to rise. Increases in the population of a country, without corresponding increases in the stocks of capital and land, will cause GDP per capita to fall. This would not be true if a country were underpopulated to the extent that useful land was idle or markets were too small to achieve economies of scale, conditions we have excluded from the model. The United States may have faced this situation during much of the nineteenth century, but certainly not today.

The arrival of large numbers of immigrants without significant amounts of financial or human capital in Europe or the United States will reduce the capital-to-labor ratio and the land-to-labor ratio, thereby decreasing wages and potential per capita GDP. In Europe, where wages have been less flexible, the fear has been that immigrants will contribute to a rising unemployment rate, and more people over whom to spread the same output. European nations particularly have worried about the large influx of immigrants seeking political asylum. The effects of emigration from labor-abundant countries such as Mexico or Morocco are, of course, exactly opposite when unskilled labor leaves. Potential GDP per capita increases with the reduced population and the increased capital-to-labor and land-to-labor ratios. This explains the unavoidable conflict between the government of the United States and the governments in Mexico City, Kingston, and San Salvador, or between EU capitals and Algiers or Rabat. Developing countries want their citizens to have the opportunity to seek employment in industrialized countries, and they may even view such emigration as crucial for economic development. While total output would rise in the industrialized countries, output per capita would not, and therefore it is not in their interest to allow unlimited entry.

This prediction from the simple one-good model is more extreme than what the H–O model suggests. In the latter case, an influx of unskilled labor leads to a shift in output toward goods that require unskilled labor intensively, such as apparel. At unchanged prices, there is no reason for wages to fall, because capital can be attracted out of capital-intensive sectors, whose output will fall, to be reallocated to the expanding apparel sector; with no decline in the capital-to-labor ratio, wages are not driven down. Because labor is more productive in industrialized countries, however, the increase in their output of apparel will exceed the decline in apparel output in the country the immigrants have left. Total apparel output will rise and therefore we expect its price to decline. The wages of unskilled workers will fall, just as we observed in the one-good model, because the value of their output declines. But, as net importers of apparel, the industrialized countries will benefit from a decline in the price of apparel. To determine the effect on income per capita we need more information to predict how large this terms-of-trade gain may be.

In any case, an influx of immigrants can further affect welfare in the host country when it leads to congestion in the use of public goods and services, such as roads, parks, and schools, or greater demand for transfer payments to cover expenses of housing, food, and medical care. The net fiscal balance from immigration depends upon taxes paid versus the extra demands for services and transfers created.

When immigrants arrive with significant amounts of capital (financial or human), the situation described above changes because the capital-to-labor ratio can rise rather than fall with their arrival. That is why countries such as Canada maintain immigration preferences for people who arrive with sufficient capital to start new businesses. Education and training constitute the more typical form of capital that makes immigrants a potentially important source of economic growth. The United States benefited enormously from the arrival of large numbers of scientists and engineers fleeing Europe before World War II, as it is benefiting today from the talented people migrating from a variety of developing countries. Scientists from East and South Asia have become a major force in US high-technology industries. In fact, gains to industrialized host countries pose a problem for many developing countries similar to the example above, where capital moved from the United States to Canada and US tax collections and US welfare fell even as world welfare rose. In this case, developing countries lose significant tax revenue when a **brain drain** of highly skilled individuals occurs. For example, nearly one-third of skilled Africans had moved to Europe as of 1987.[7] The problem is compounded because much of the education of these individuals is paid for with public funds. The benefits of providing more education simply spill over to the rest of the world. Although some countries have imposed exit taxes on those emigrating, some commentators instead call for payments by the wealthy host countries to compensate for this loss of revenue. More recent trends suggest a circular flow of trained individuals, with some acquiring experience and savings in industrialized host countries. Then they return home and become successful entrepreneurs. Under those circumstances developing countries suffer a short-run loss that may be offset by a long-run gain.

The unavoidable, if unpleasant, conclusion is that it is in the economic interest of industrialized countries to allow highly educated and talented immigrants to enter, but not to allow large numbers of unskilled people to immigrate. Only if a corresponding inflow of capital is attracted by the higher returns possible with greater availability of unskilled labor does this argument lose some of its force.

Multinational corporations

A multinational corporation (MNC) is a firm that operates in several countries through branches or subsidiaries that it effectively controls. Because MNCs are not equally likely to be observed in all industries, and not necessarily in capital-intensive sectors, we should recognize that they are not particularly a conduit for transferring capital from countries where it is abundant to countries where it is scarce. Rather, they are much more likely to be in industries where superior technology or unique products provide an important competitive advantage to the firm.

Although US MNCs were most prevalent in the 1950s and 1960s, recovery from World War II in Europe and Japan led to the expansion of MNCs headquartered in many countries. UN figures show that the US share of all foreign direct investment fell from 50 percent in

1967 to 25 percent in 1995. In fact, a feature of the 1990s was that MNCs from developing countries began to emerge and in 1995 accounted for 8 percent of the stock of investment[8] The shrill rhetoric directed at US MNCs and US imperialism in the 1960s and 1970s has declined.[9] Direct investment has become characterized by two-way flows between industrialized countries, which in 1995 were the source of over 90 percent of the stock of foreign investment and the destination of over 70 percent. Countries everywhere recognize the advantages of gaining access to the production and marketing networks of MNCs; roughly one-third of manufactured goods traded internationally are accounted for by MNC sales, particularly sales from one affiliate to another as intra-company shipments. MNCs have played a significant role in integrating the world economy.[10]

Another important perspective on MNCs is given by Table 9.2, which presents the top 25 global corporations ordered on the basis of sales from *Fortune* magazine. A variety of industries is represented, but many of the largest industrial corporations operate in mature industries, such as automobiles and petroleum, not in newly emerging industries where technological breakthroughs are most critical to success. Also, note that large Japanese trading companies rank high in terms of sales, although they have relatively fewer employees and less equity than the other giants. The US firm Enron shows up in this listing prior to its collapse in 2002, and in many respects it appears similar to the Japanese trading companies, with reported high revenues but relatively few employees or equity. Actual rankings across years are likely to show some variation, because competition within an industry, or the decline of an entire industry, contributes to changes in this list, as will the variation in growth rates observed across countries in which the MNCs operate. While a conglomerate that operated in every industry and in every country would be more immune to such variation, such conglomerates do not tend to be the most successful MNCs.

Given that there are many disadvantages of operating in a foreign country where local firms have the advantage of a better understanding of local culture, customs, and contacts, why does a firm become an MNC? J.H. Dunning provides a useful framework to answer that question.[11] He considers three factors: ownership, location, and internalization. We shall define these terms and show how they help determine a firm's decision to become an MNC. We then consider how both the host and the home country are affected by the operations of MNCs and how they try to influence those operations.

The decision to become an MNC

An MNC typically has some special expertise that it has developed and now hopes to exploit in a larger market. Such expertise may include technological know-how that it has acquired through research and development or learned from its past experience. This may include a particular new product innovation or a process to produce a product. Advertising that creates a brand image and an organizational strategy that coordinates complex production and distribution systems also qualify as ownership advantages. A common characteristic of many of these items is that they represent intangible knowledge that can be provided to one operation without leaving less for others to use. The firm that owns these intangible assets can spread the costs of developing this knowledge over more customers by selling in foreign as well as domestic markets. Yet we have not demonstrated why such sales could not simply occur as exports from the innovating country. Therefore, we need to consider the other categories proposed by Dunning.

Location includes a variety of factors that make production abroad, rather than in the MNC's home country, attractive. In many service industries, the MNC must be located in

Table 9.2 The top 25 global corporations (in US$ million)

Rank	Company	Country	Revenues	Profits	Assets	Stock-holders' equity	Employees
1	Wal-Mart Stores	US	219,812.00	6,671	83,375	35,102	1,383,000
2	Exxon Mobil	US	191,581.00	15,320	143,174	73,161	97,900
3	General Motors	US	177,260.00	601	323,969	19,707	365,000
4	BP	Britain	174,218.00	8,010	141,158	74,367	110,150
5	Ford Motor	US	162,412.00	−5,453	276,543	7,786	352,748
6	Enron	US	138,718.00	NA	NA	NA	15,388
7	DaimlerChrysler	Germany	136,897.30	−593	184,671	34,728	372,470
8	Royal Dutch/Shell	Neth/Brit	135,211.00	10,582	111,543	56,160	91,000
9	General Electric	US	125,913.00	13,684	495,023	54,824	310,000
10	Toyota Motor	Japan	120,814.40	4,925	150,064	55,268	246,702
11	Citigroup	US	112,022.00	14,126	1,051,450	81,247	268,000
12	Mitsubishi	Japan	105,813.90	482	61,455	7,761	43,000
13	Mitsui	Japan	101,205.60	443	50,314	6,904	36,116
14	ChevronTexaco	US	99,699.00	3,288	77,572	33,958	67,569
15	Total Fina Elf	France	94,311.90	6,858	78,887	30,212	122,025
16	Nippon Telegraph & Telephone	Japan	93,424.80	−6,496	157,551	44,564	213,000
17	Itochu	Japan	91,176.60	242	35,857	3,000	36,529
18	Allianz	Germany	85,929.20	1,453	839,551	28,193	179,946
19	IBM	US	85,866.00	7,723	88,313	23,614	319,876
20	ING Group	Neth.	82,999.10	4,099	627,816	19,155	113,143
21	Volkswagen	Germany	79,287.30	2,610	92,976	21,364	322,070
22	Siemens	Germany	77,358.90	1,857	82,070	21,686	484,000
23	Sumitomo	Japan	77,140.10	362	36,613	4,907	30,264
24	Philip Morris	US	72,944.00	8,560	84,968	19,620	175,000
25	Marubeni	Japan	71,756.60	−931	36,259	1,991	31,000

Source: Fortune, July 22, 2002, p. F-1.

the same country as the customer in order to provide the service. McDonald's can satisfy Muscovite demand for a Big Mac only by locating in Moscow. In other industries high transportation costs may preclude exports from one country to another. A French firm that has special expertise in producing cement nevertheless will not find it economical to export cement to the United States. Instead the firm will produce cement in the United States, where it can serve US customers without incurring high transport costs. As we discussed in the case of the product cycle, some MNCs may find that standardized production processes are carried out most economically in countries that are well endowed with unskilled labor. A shoe that is designed by Nike in the United States but produced in China takes advantage of differences in factor endowments in the two locations according to their requirements in two different stages of the production process. Location becomes an especially important factor to MNCs when trade barriers are imposed or threatened, and MNCs find that the protected markets can best be served by producing within a country rather than exporting to it. For example, the common external tariff of the **European Economic Community** was a major stimulus to the large direct investments made by US firms in Europe during the 1960s. US and European restrictions on imports of Japanese automobiles in the 1980s gave Japanese firms an incentive to locate assembly plants in those countries.

The examples above are particularly relevant in identifying likely differences in the marginal cost of serving a market from different locations. MNCs, however, are concerned about fixed costs as well. A particularly useful way of recognizing the role of fixed costs is to distinguish those that are specific to a plant and those that are specific to the firm as a whole.[12] A firm's research and development which generates ideas applicable in all locations is a fixed cost specific to the firm as a whole, while the fixed cost of building a factory and installing machinery is specific to a plant. The existence of high firm-specific fixed costs makes it more likely the firm will try to serve foreign markets to exploit its unique knowledge, but high plant-specific costs make it more likely the firm will do so by exporting rather than by producing abroad. Separate plants in many separate locations result in the duplication of expenditures for plant-specific costs and raise the average total cost of serving the market that way. Conversely, when plant-specific fixed costs are low but transportation costs and trade barriers are high and the host country's factor endowments are well matched to the inputs necessary to produce the good, the MNC is more likely to locate a plant abroad.

If the MNC has decided that production abroad is more efficient than exporting, we still must consider the final criterion mentioned above, internalization, to assess why the MNC chooses to operate its own plant rather than license someone else to produce the good. An advantage of licensing is that the firm need not raise capital itself or tie up its own management resources in learning how to produce in a foreign setting. Yet, by licensing technology to others, the innovator takes the risk that this information may leak out to others or be used to compete directly with it. Production abroad also raises the possibility that employees will defect and start their own competing firm, but at least the MNC can control that process better through the incentives and wages it pays its employees. When the pace of technological change is rapid in an industry, the firm may find licensing is the best way to earn an additional return on its innovation before that product is superseded by another. In the semiconductor industry, for example, companies have chosen to use licensing agreements to exploit their technological advances quickly. Licensees are more likely to become competitors when high tariff creates high profit potential and when plant-specific costs are low and entry of new firms is easy.[13]

Licensing may not be feasible if the innovator and prospective foreign producer cannot agree on an acceptable royalty rate and means of enforcing the contract. Such agreements will be easier to reach when both parties have a good basis for judging the success of the technology being transferred. If those conditions hold, we expect to observe large royalty payments between unrelated parties. For the United States, that outcome is not common: over three-fourths of royalties received by US companies from abroad come from related affiliates. Reaching and enforcing international agreements to transfer technology is far from straightforward.

Box 9.1 Mergers, acquisitions and takeovers: hold the phone

In 2001 there was a substantial decline in foreign direct investment internationally, most of it accounted for by fewer mergers and acquisitions among firms in industrialized countries. What explains merger activity, and the decision of one group of investors to offer a higher price for the assets held by another group? We can think of the value of an asset being determined by the stream of income it will yield into the future and by the cost of obtaining the funds to buy the asset. One rationale for an acquisition is that the new owner expects to use the assets in a way that will yield more income than they do to the current owner. This may be possible because the new owner has the opportunity to enter new markets and to utilize expertise it already has developed. Thus, it can spread that fixed cost over greater sales. Also, the new firm may be able to reduce the duplication of costs incurred by two separate firms. When the merging firms already control major shares of the market, their combination may allow higher prices to be charged, a likely concern to competition authorities in the market where they sell. Finally, the new owner may have a lower cost of obtaining funds than the current owner, and therefore be willing to offer a higher price. A firm may be more creditworthy and able to borrow at a lower interest rate, or in a booming stock market, a firm may be able to issue more of its own shares to finance acquisitions.

While these economic factors are relevant in domestic and international mergers, national interests often affect international mergers. For example, in 2000 Vodafone of the UK acquired Mannesmann of Germany in the first hostile takeover of a German company. During the height of the telecom boom, Vodafone was the most valuable publicly traded company in the UK. Even with the worldwide decline in prices in that sector, it still remains the world's largest wireless telephone company, serving 28 countries across five continents. At the end of 2002, Sir Christopher Gent notified stockholders that he was stepping down as chief executive officer, given the shift in company emphasis away from expansion through acquisition. Instead, it sought more effective integration of its many separate operations to take full advantage of potential economies of scale.

The Vodafone strategy may well prove successful, although in past mergers stockholders of the acquired firm more typically gain while stockholders of the acquiring firm lose. Additional fall out from this merger has been renewed EU debate over financial regulation and the extent to which it allows hostile takeovers.

Effects of MNC operations in the home country

The discussion thus far indicates how an MNC determines the most profitable way to exploit its specialized expertise and expand into foreign markets. By making location choices that allow it to produce more output at lower cost, and by transferring technology to and mobilizing productive resources in locations where they were scarce, the MNC generally contributes toward a more efficient world pattern of production. Whether the home country and the host country both share in those benefits is an issue that has proven to be the source of contentious debate.

Early treatments of MNC investment focused on flows of capital from the home country to the host country. With a smaller capital stock at home, labor receives a lower wage. More consistent with the rationale for MNCs discussed above, however, is the situation where the MNC does not bring capital from the home country, but instead raises capital in the host country by borrowing locally. Thus, a negative distributional effect in the home country does not arise due to a falling capital-to-labor ratio.

The shift in production to the host country may displace previous exports from the home country and thereby reduce demand for factors used intensively in their production. US evidence suggests that the majority of MNC investment is intended to serve the host-country market, and that the ratio of affiliate sales to parent-company exports is higher in markets where transport costs and trade barriers are high. On the other hand, many economists find that firms that produce more abroad also export more. The apparent complementary relationship may arise due to investment abroad in distribution, sales, and service networks that benefit sales of goods produced in the host country but also other goods in a firm's product line that are produced in the home country. Or, goods produced in the home country may be important inputs in what is produced abroad. Thus, measures that encourage investment in a host country, such as a low tax rate, may also result in increased home-country exports that are complementary to this foreign output. Whether the choice of an MNC to produce abroad necessarily reduces output at home remains a question that has yet to be resolved by the available evidence.[14]

Higher MNC profits may result in a general benefit to the home-country government if it shares in this gain through higher tax revenue. For countries that tax the worldwide income of their residents and corporations, as do Japan, the United Kingdom, and the United States, a gain in tax revenue is possible. As we noted in the case of portfolio capital, though, these countries grant a credit for foreign income tax paid, up to the tax liability due in the home country. The host country gets the first opportunity to tax this income, and the home country collects a residual tax. In reality most of the tax revenue from active business income of affiliates is collected by the host-country government.

Domestic labor interests have been even more concerned by another provision of US tax law that allows this residual tax liability to be deferred until the income actually is repatriated to the United States. The same issue arises to an even greater extent in countries such as Canada, France, and Germany that entirely exempt from tax the active foreign income earned by affiliates of their MNCs. Suppose the rate of return from a foreign investment is 10 percent and the host-country tax rate is 10 percent, while the rate of return from a domestic investment is 15 percent and the home-country tax rate is 50 percent. The MNC comparing the after-tax return from these alternative investments will choose the foreign investment, because it yields 9.0 percent while the home-country return is 7.5 percent. Even though the home-country investment is more productive and adds more to world output, it will not be selected.

Tax competition between host countries can result in less activity in high tax countries, especially when it occurs between neighboring states which serve the same market. As barriers to trade have fallen within the EU politicians in high-tax countries such as France and Germany have sought greater harmonization of member-country corporate tax rates, preferably at rates close to their own. They are opposed by countries such as Ireland and the United Kingdom that impose lower taxes. These differences and the general reduction in tax rates over the past decade are discussed more fully in Chapter 11.

Effects of MNC operations in the host country

Various sources of gain to host countries are the introduction of new technology and management, training of labor, and access to capital markets and sales networks that MNCs bring. More productive use of resources in the country causes income to rise. There may be spillovers from the activity of MNCs to the rest of the economy, much as we outlined in Chapter 4 regarding external economies of scale, due to its creation of a pool of trained labor and the spread of ideas from the MNC to suppliers of inputs and to potential competitors. Nevertheless, there are circumstances where host countries question whether they share in the gains from MNC operations.

When MNCs raise capital locally rather than bring additional funds into countries with limited savings and few links to world capital markets, host countries voice the concern that this competition for funds with local producers simply displaces local producers and reduces the base of local entrepreneurs. This argument is not particularly convincing, if inefficient producers are being replaced by more efficient producers who can produce more output with the same inputs. The argument is more relevant if the domestic industry initially earns monopoly profits in a protected market, and the entry of an MNC transfers those profits from domestic producers to foreign owners.[15]

From the perspective of the home country, we raised the concern that host countries have the opportunity to tax MNC income first, which reduces the tax benefit to the home country. For many developing countries, there is a benefit from being able to impose a corporate tax on enterprises that keep books and are subject to financial audits, conditions that may not hold for domestic enterprises. Nevertheless, host countries complain that MNCs are able to shift income out of their jurisdiction to avoid taxation, too. For example, suppose a US MNC finances the expansion of an affiliate by borrowing from a subsidiary in the Cayman Islands rather than selling shares of stock to pension funds in New York. The affiliate's reliance on debt financing means that it deducts the interest payments from its income to be taxed in the host country. The interest payment is received in a tax-haven country where that subsidiary pays no tax, and in some circumstances the parent MNC may even avoid paying a residual tax to its home government. Neither the home country nor the host country gains a share of the MNC profits. The loss of tax revenue to the host country is one reason why it may not recognize interest paid on loans from a related party as a deductible cost of doing business.

Transfer-pricing represents another strategy to shift income from a high-tax to a low-tax jurisdiction. If MNCs operating in high-tax countries pay higher prices for goods they buy from related parties and charge lower prices for goods they sell to related parties, they will have less income to declare in the high-tax jurisdiction. Even though the MNC still has a factory in the high-tax location, the tax base can be shifted out of the country more easily than the plant and equipment. A study of income-shifting by US MNCs suggests that in a host country with a tax rate of 40 percent they will declare a before-tax return on sales of 9.3 percent but in a host country with a tax rate of 20 percent this margin rises to 15.8 percent.[16]

With respect to inward foreign investment in the United States, politicians have promised to greatly increase tax collections from the affiliates of foreign firms which have declared much lower rates of profitability than their US counterparts. While the empirical evidence continues to evolve, an important part of the difference observed in the early 1990s could be attributed to the recent entry of many affiliates of foreign firms; younger firms typically have lower rates of profitability. More recent evidence of US corporations that have a foreign ownership share of only 25 to 50 percent indicates they also are less profitable than domestic firms, even though their potential to shift profits out of the United States presumably is less than when foreigners control the corporation.

The transfer of technology to host countries has tax implications that are worth noting here, too. If the costs of developing the new technology are deducted against the MNC's income tax in the home country, but the income from exploiting that new technology is earned by affiliates abroad, then the home country loses tax revenue, and the tax base in the host country will expand. Countries that tax worldwide income have adopted rules to require some allocation of research and development expense to affiliate operations and an expectation that affiliates pay appropriate royalties to the parent. Some host countries remain suspicious of royalty payments that transfer taxable income out of their jurisdiction, and they impose high withholding taxes on those payments. This is another example of the natural conflict between home and host countries in determining how the benefits from new technology are to be divided.

Host countries are often concerned over the balance-of-payments implications of MNC investment. We consider that topic more fully in Part Two, but a few points are directly relevant to the trade and factor mobility issues raised here. MNCs often are a vehicle for increasing the host country's exports, and many countries that previously pursued an inward-oriented development strategy and tightly limited MNC participation in their economies now have adopted a much more open attitude. Also, in contrast to the short-run horizon of portfolio capital flows discussed earlier in this chapter, MNC operations generally are motivated by longer-run assessments of market opportunities, and therefore foreign direct investment tends to be less volatile than portfolio investment.

Regulating MNC operations raises several quasi-political issues that touch on sovereignty, political control, legal jurisdictions, and the fairness of contracts. Since direct investment implies managerial control by the parent company over the foreign affiliate, there is ample scope for jurisdictional conflicts between the source country, whose laws govern the parent company, and the host country, whose laws govern the affiliate.

One such jurisdictional conflict has involved the US insistence that foreign subsidiaries of US firms are subject to certain US laws and regulations. These laws may run into conflict with the laws of the host country. For example, in the 1970s the United States required Canadian subsidiaries of US firms to abide by a US ban on exports to Cuba. Canada had no such ban, and Canadians were incensed about the infringement on their sovereignty when this US law was applied to firms incorporated in Canada.

These conflicts are difficult to resolve. From the US point of view, its laws would be made ineffective if US firms could evade them simply by setting up a foreign subsidiary. But from the host-country point of view, the extension of US laws into its geographical domain is an unacceptable violation of national sovereignty. The word "extraterritoriality" is often applied to this issue because it involves attempts by the United States to enforce its laws outside its territory.

Attitudes toward MNCs in developing countries appear to have gone through a full cycle. During the 1950s and early 1960s, they were viewed as engines of development and therefore as highly desirable. During the latter half of the 1960s and throughout the 1970s, they were widely viewed as agents of capitalism, imperialism, and of every ill to afflict an LDC other than bad weather. During the 1980s, however, opinions appeared to have come back to the center. Most leaders in developing countries now view MNCs as desirable elements in their economies but want to bargain over how the benefits of their activities will be divided. MNC investments are actively sought, but governments want promises that the firms will export guaranteed proportions of their output, employ and train at least so many local people, pay taxes in reasonable proportion to the local business they do, and so on. Host countries appear to be in a stronger bargaining position now than in the past, because of the great expansion in the number of MNCs which compete against each other to win contracts, make sales, or locate plants abroad. On the other hand, there are many more potential locations from which to choose, because many countries are more receptive to MNCs and have chosen to participate in an integrated world economy.

Summary of key concepts

1   Mobility of labor and capital internationally reduces differences in wages and rates of return across countries. By shifting resources from where they are less productive to where they are more productive, world output expands.

2   Factor flows redistribute income within countries, just as trade based on factor endowments does. For example, an inflow of capital into a capital-scarce country raises labor productivity and wage rates, while returns to capital decline.

3   An inflow of labor may raise national income but reduce income per capita in the host country. This outcome is particularly likely if immigrants bring little human or financial capital. A further factor affecting the welfare of the host country is the balance between the demand for public services created by immigrants and their payments to finance such services.

4   An important motive for firms to become multinational corporations is the opportunity to exploit their special expertise through expanding sales internationally. Firms are more likely to produce abroad when the costs of establishing a plant in a new location are a small share of total costs and when transport costs and trade barriers are high. The MNC may produce abroad itself, rather than license another firm, when it is difficult to reach an enforceable agreement over the value of the technology being transferred.

5   MNC operations generally increase world production by introducing technology and managerial expertise that allow greater output from the same inputs. How the gains from higher production are divided between home and host countries has been a continuing source of controversy internationally, particularly when the home country is industrialized and the host country is less developed. LDC host countries have tended to gain most from MNC investments that inject additional capital, train labor, raise tax collections, and increase exports.

Questions for study and review

1   What is the relationship between Heckscher–Ohlin trade and free factor mobility? Explain.
2   What groups in Europe benefit from the rising immigration of Africans and Asians? What groups are harmed?
3   As the United States implements a free-trade arrangement with Mexico, what do you expect to happen to the number of Mexican residents trying to come to the United States? What will be the impact of this agreement on those Mexicans who have already come to this country?
4   If the goal of Canadian policy is to increase real GDP per capita, what type of immigration should it encourage? Why might some developing countries feel that they would be harmed by this Canadian immigration policy?
5   Is a producer of salt, a producer of medical imaging equipment, or a producer of automobiles more likely to become a multinational corporation? What differences in demand and cost conditions are relevant to each example?
6   What is transfer pricing? Why is it a problem for national tax authorities? Who is harmed by this practice?
7.   What advantages are gained by a home country when its MNCs claim a bigger share of world markets? Are there groups in the home country that nevertheless would be adversely affected? What happens to domestic employment and wages?
8   Why can host countries gain from an inflow of investment by MNCs? What sorts of distortions in host countries may make such an inflow less advantageous? Do host countries need special policies to regulate the operations of MNCs?

Suggested further reading

For an overview of immigration issues see:
- Borjas, George, "The Economics of Immigration," *Journal of Economic Literature* 32, no. 4, December 1994, pp. 1667–717.

For a broader discussion of MNC operations see:
- Bergsten, C.F., T. Horst, and T. Moran, *American Multinationals and American Interests*, Washington, DC: Brookings, 1978.
- Graham, E. and P. Krugman, *Foreign Direct Investment in the United States*, 3rd edn, Washington, DC: Institute for International Economics, 1995.
- Porter, M., *Competitive Advantage: Creating and Sustaining Superior Performance*, New York: Free Press, 1985.

Notes

1   See George J. Borjas, Richard B. Freeman, and Lawrence F. Katz, "On the Labor Market Effects of Immigration and Trade," in George J. Borjas and Richard B. Freeman, *Immigration and the Work Force* (National Bureau of Economic Research, Chicago: University of Chicago Press, 1992), pp. 213–44, and the survey by R.M. Friedberg and J. Hunt in "The Impact of Immigrants on Host Country Wages, Employment and Growth," *Journal of Economic Perspectives* 9, no. 2, Spring 1995, pp. 23–44.

2 Klaus Zimmerman, "Tackling the European Migration Problem," *Journal of Economic Perspectives* 9, no. 2, Spring 1995, pp. 45–62.

3 For a collection of recent research papers on US immigration, see Borjas and Freeman, op. cit., and the symposium of articles in the *Journal of Economic Perspectives*, Spring 1995. An early discussion of the similarity of Heckscher–Ohlin trade and factor mobility can be found in Robert Mundell, "International Trade and Factor Mobility," *American Economic Review* 47, no. 3, June 1957, pp. 321–35.

4 United Nations Development Program, *Human Development Report* (New York: UN, 1992), p. 54.

5 George Borjas, "The Economics of Immigration," *Journal of Economic Literature* 32, no. 4, December 1994, pp. 1667–717.

6 UN Development Program, op. cit., p. 58.

7 UN Development Program, op. cit., p. 57.

8 United Nations, *World Investment Report* (New York, 1997).

9 Some of the origins of the debate over multinational firms can be found in R. Vernon, *Sovereignty at Bay* (New York: Basic Books, 1971), and R. Barnet and R. Muller, *Global Reach* (New York: Simon and Schuster, 1974). A European view of US-based MNCs can be found in J. Servan-Schreiber, *The American Challenge* (New York: Atheneum, 1968).

10 For an example of this newer view of the role of MNCs internationally, see J. Dunning and K. Hamdani, eds, *The New Globalism and the Developing Countries* (New York: United Nations University Press, 1997).

11 J.H. Dunning, *Economic Analysis and the Multinational Enterprise* (London: Allen and Unwin, 1974).

12 See I.J. Horstman and J.R. Markusen, "Endogenous Market Structures in International Trade," *Journal of International Economics*, 1986, pp. 109–30, for this development.

13 See Wilfred Ethier and James Markusen, "Multinational Firms, Technology Diffusion and Trade," *Journal of International Economics*, 1996, pp. 1–28, for a theoretical treatment of these issues.

14 See S. Lael Brainard, "An Empirical Assessment of the Proximity–Concentration Tradeoff between Multinational Sales and Trade," NBER Working Paper No. 4583, December 1993, for evidence of substitution between exports and affiliate production. C. Fred Bergsten, Thomas Horst, and Theodore Moran, *American Multinationals and American Interests* (Washington, DC: The Brookings Institution, 1978); Robert Lipsey and Merle Weiss, "Foreign Production and Exports in Manufacturing Industries," *Review of Economics and Statistics*, November 1982, pp. 488–94; Robert Lipsey and Merle Weiss, "Foreign Production and Exports of Individual Firms," *Review of Economics and Statistics*, May 1984, pp. 304–7; and Harry Grubert and John Mutti, "Taxes, Tariffs and Transfer Pricing in Multinational Corporate Decision Making," *Review of Economics and Statistics* 73, 1991, pp. 285–93, report a complementary relationship.

15 See J. Bhagwati and R. Brecher, "National Welfare in an Open Economy in the Presence of Foreign-owned Factors of Production," *Journal of International Economics*, 1980, p. 103, for discussion of the potential loss to host countries from attracting foreign direct investment into protected industries.

16 Grubert and Mutti, op. cit.

10 Trade and growth

Learning objectives

By the end of this chapter you should be able to understand:

- how the effect of growth on trade depends upon the relative increase in productive capacity of exports and imports, and on the preferences of consumers as income rises;
- why a large country may find that some of the benefits of growth are offset by a decline in its terms of trade;
- why developing countries that rely upon primary product exports have experienced volatility in export earnings and a decline in their terms of trade;
- how import substitution policies attempt to avoid such terms-of-trade declines but risk creating permanent inefficiencies;
- why policies to promote export diversification appear to have promoted growth more successfully than import-substitution industrialization.

As economies grow over time, their patterns of trade are unlikely to remain the same. For example, while the United States primarily exported tobacco, cotton, and foodstuffs in the eighteenth and nineteenth centuries, by the twentieth century it had become a major exporter of manufactured goods. At the start of the twenty-first century it had further shifted toward the exportation of services. In the post-war period alone, Korea has shifted from being an exporter of primary materials to a dominant provider of apparel and footwear, and most recently to goods such as steel, electronics, and semiconductors.

Reasons for these changing patterns of trade can be traced to the basis for trade sketched out in Chapters 2, 3, and 4. Changing factor endowments as a country acquires capital and trains workers can move it away from natural-resource-based trade. Better diets, improved health standards, and the availability of education lead to a more productive labor force, and these investments in human capital further alter the goods where its comparative advantage lies. Improvements in technology through the Green Revolution in agriculture have converted many Asian nations from being food importers to food exporters and also allowed those countries to shift labor into the manufacturing sector. New production processes have allowed Europe and America to maintain their production of manufactured goods with far fewer workers. While the classical theory recognized that differences in technology could explain patterns of comparative advantage, more recently economists have considered how new technologies are created, what incentives affect that process, and how those advances diffuse across countries, thereby influencing patterns of trade. In the first half of this chapter, we consider these varied influences of growth on trade.

Not only do we expect growth to affect trade, but we also expect trade to affect a country's growth prospects. We discussed the gains from an open trading policy in Chapters 5 and 6, but noted they were subject to some exceptions. Many developing countries have taken the opposite perspective, claiming that the international trading system is largely to be distrusted and likely to impoverish developing countries further. In fact, in the 1950s and 1960s many newly independent countries rejected linkages to their colonial past and the market system. Instead, they aimed for less dependency and more self-sufficiency. They felt that prices for the primary products (raw materials and agricultural goods) they exported were unfairly low, and protection in the developed world made it impossible for them to export manufactured goods from which they could earn higher incomes.

Many supporters of the developing countries argued for a radical transformation of the trading system under the rubric of the **New International Economic Order**, with the **United Nations Conference on Trade and Development (UNCTAD)** being the primary forum for the advancement of these ideas during the 1970s. Primary-product prices were to be increased and stabilized, special trade preferences were to be created for developing countries, foreign aid was to be sharply increased, and a variety of other reforms were to be put in place to help poor countries.

Two decades later very little was heard of this agenda, although the Generalized System of Preferences did emerge from its goals. The sense of pessimism that permeated much of the earlier discussion (i.e. developing countries face such poor prospects that they have no chance of growing under existing market mechanisms) no longer dominates because many previously underdeveloped countries have experienced rapid economic growth without a remaking of the international economic order. Nevertheless, many countries have failed to share in this progress.

In the second half of this chapter we consider the variety of trade policies developing countries have chosen since the 1950s. Problems faced by primary-product exporters still remain for many developing countries, and we briefly review those. We then trace the reasoning that led many developing countries to adopt an import-substitution industrial-ization strategy, and we assess its successes and failures. Finally, we turn to the experience of several developing countries that were so successful in implementing an export-led growth strategy that they have been labeled **newly industrialized countries (NICs)**.

The effects of economic growth on trade

Changes in factor supplies

With a given endowment of resources and a given technology, a country's production-possibility curve depicts its capacity to produce various combinations of commodities. However, if its resources are growing over time (e.g. the labor force is increasing through population growth, or the stock of physical capital is being augmented by net investment from year to year), then the production-possibility curve shifts up and to the right, indicating that the country's capacity to produce is expanding.

Many different patterns of growth can occur, depending on the rates at which different factors of production are growing and on the pace of technological change in various industries. These changes in supply conditions, in turn, will interact with demand conditions at home and abroad to determine the final effects on output, the quantities of exports and imports, and the terms of trade. Because many outcomes are possible, we do not attempt an exhaustive discussion. Rather, we discuss a few examples in order to illustrate how various cases can be analyzed.

Neutral growth and the role of demand

Perhaps the simplest case is one in which all of Country A's factors of production grow at the same rate over a certain time interval, while constant returns to scale exist in all industries and technology remains unchanged.

In such a case of neutral growth in capacity, the production-possibility curve simply shifts outward in the same proportion throughout its length, as illustrated in Figure 10.1. The new curve, F_2C_2, is just a radial extension of F_1C_1, expanded outward in proportion to the growth in resources that has occurred. If Country A is small relative to the rest of the world, the terms of trade will remain unchanged, and Country A will continue to produce the two commodities in the same proportions as before, as indicated by the points P and P' on the vector OP'.

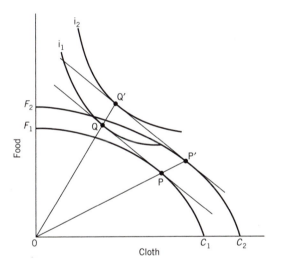

Figure 10.1 Neutral growth in a small country. With equal growth in its ability to produce both goods and with no change in its terms of trade, this country (Country A) enjoys all of the benefits of its growing productive capacity by shifting its consumption set from point Q to Q'.

The effects on Country A's consumption and its volume of trade will then depend on its pattern of demand, as shown by its community indifference curves. Country A may choose to consume food and cloth in the same proportions as before, in which case both its imports of food and its exports of cloth will rise in proportion to the increase in output. In this case, where Country A's income elasticity of demand for both goods is unity, its consumption points (Q and Q') will lie on the vector OQ', as shown in Figure 10.1, and consumption of both goods increases in proportion to economic growth. This case of income elasticities equal to one gives a linear expansion path, because the two goods are always consumed in the same proportions. However, if Country A's demand for food (the imported commodity) rises more than proportionately to income, then its exports and imports will also increase by a larger proportion than does output. Growth is biased toward trade. On the other hand, if

Country A's demand for food rises less than proportionately to income (i.e. it is income-inelastic), then trade will increase by a smaller percentage than output. Growth is biased against trade. The volume of trade could even shrink if Country A's demand for food had very low income elasticity.

Figure 10.2 summarizes possible outcomes for this case of equiproportionate growth in factor supplies, holding world prices constant. Before growth, production occurs at P, consumption at Q, and the trade triangle SPQ represents cloth exports, SP, and food imports, SQ. If the terms of trade remain unchanged when growth occurs (slope of P'Q' = slope of PQ), the production of both commodities will rise in the same proportion and the outcome will depend on demand conditions in Country A. The various possibilities can be seen by considering the expansion path of consumption from point Q. The neutral path, with income elasticity of unity for both goods, is along the vector OQ': consumption of both goods rises in proportion to income growth. If the demand for food rises more than in proportion to income (income elasticity of demand for food is greater than one), then the expansion path will be steeper than QQ', falling in the angle GQQ', and exports will increase by a greater proportion than output. If the demand for food rises less than in proportion to income (income elasticity less than one), then the expansion path will be less steep than QQ', falling in the angle Q'QH, and exports will increase by a smaller proportion than output, or they may even decline. (We exclude the case of inferior goods, in which consumption of one of the two goods actually declines when income rises.)

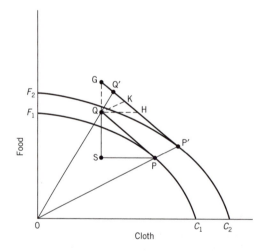

Figure 10.2 Effect of demand conditions on the volume of trade. With unbiased growth and unchanged terms of trade, Country A shifts its production from point P to P'. It can then consume anywhere between points H and G on the barter line P'G. If the income elasticity of demand for food exceeds one, the country will consume between points Q' and G, while a low-income elasticity of demand for food would put it between points Q' and H.

If we drop the assumption that the terms of trade remain unchanged, we expect that increased exports from Country A will tend to reduce export prices and thus turn the terms of trade against Country A. In our example, we can show that exports will rise for any expansion path steeper than QK. (We have drawn QK parallel to PP', so QP = KP'.) In general, the larger the income elasticity of demand for imports, the steeper the expansion path and the greater the adverse movement in the terms of trade.

Biased production and growth

In Chapter 3 we considered the case for a small country where the supply of only one factor increased. In the factor proportions model the outward shift in the production-possibility frontier is biased toward the commodity that uses intensively the factor whose supply has increased. An increase in a country's relatively abundant factor yields export-biased growth and a potentially unfavorable reduction in its terms of trade if the country is large enough to affect world prices. Growth in a country's relatively scarce factor makes the country more similar to the rest of the world. If a labor-abundant country experiences a large enough expansion of its capital stock, it can become a capital-abundant country, and its comparative advantage will shift from labor-intensive goods to capital-intensive goods. Comparative advantages change over time as circumstances change.

Shifts in the production-possibility curve occur not only because of changes in factor endowments, but also because of changes in technology. Economists often describe this process in terms of the ability to produce more output with the same amount of inputs, or to produce the same output with fewer inputs. If both labor and capital requirements can be reduced by the same proportion in both cloth and food production, then the analysis of neutral growth applies to this situation, too. If instead the technical progress leads to a larger reduction in factor requirements in the production of just one good, say cloth, then there will be a biased shift in the production-possibility curve. If the country is labor-abundant and exports cloth, then the increase in trade will be greater than in the case of neutral growth. If instead the country is capital-abundant and exports food, then the country will trade less and be more self-sufficient.

Box 10.1 Malaysia's changing pattern of trade

Malaysia is one of the countries that grew so rapidly in the 1970s and 1980s that it qualifies as part of the second wave of NICs, after the first wave of Hong Kong, Korea, Singapore, and Taiwan. This rapid growth has been characterized by a changing pattern of trade, which is shown in Table 10.1. In 1965 Malaysian exports primarily reflected its bountiful endowment of natural resources: rubber, tin, lumber, iron ore, petroleum, and food products. By 1995 those natural resources were still important, but even more of Malaysia's export earnings came from a variety of electronic products. Its exports had become much more diversified. A well-trained, English-speaking labor force has been an attraction for multinational corporations who in turn have added to the available capital stock and technology base; recall from Chapter 1 that for Malaysia the stock of foreign direct investment relative to GDP exceeded 50 percent in 1995. Attracting that amount of foreign investment also has allowed external economies of scale to be achieved, when the emergence of pools of specialized labor and input suppliers allows costs for all producers to decline. Thus, a combination of changes in factor supplies, factor productivity, and available technology appears important in explaining Malaysia's changing pattern of trade. Other observers point to Malaysia's progression within a flying geese formation, led by Japan and then the Four Tigers. As the leaders produce successively more advanced products, and lose their comparative advantage in more standardized products, new opportunities become available to Malaysia, provided that it keeps up with the leaders by increasing its capital stock and the education of its work force.

Table 10.1 Leading Malaysian exports, 1965 and 1995 (US$ million)

1965			1995		
SITC code	Commodity	Value	SITC code	Commodity	Value
231.1	Rubber	477.7	776	Transistors, valves, etc.	13240.0
687.1	Tin and alloys unwrought	282.4	759	Office, ADP mchpts., acce	4767.8
242.3	Saw logs and veneer logs	85.8	424	Fixed veg. oil, nonsoft	3833.6
281.3	Iron ore and concentrates	52.7	764	Telecom eqpt., pts., access	3784.4
332.0	Petroleum products	52.4	762	Radio broadcast receivers	3485.1
422.2	Fixed vegetable oil	39.5	763	Sound recorders, phonogr.	2792.0
243.3	Lumber (nonconifer)	31.6	333	Crude petroleum	2684.6
75.1	Pepper and pimento	13.6	761	Television receivers	2239.1
53.0	Fruit, prepared or preserve	13.4	752	Automatic data proc. equip.	2185.1
			248	Wood shaped sleepers	1833.2
			634	Veneers, plywood, etc.	1687.3
			232	Natural rubber gums	1612.9
Items shown as a percent of total exports		28%			24%

Source: United Nations, *International Trade Statistics Yearbook.*

To complete our analysis, consider the combined production and consumption effects. The key question we ask is whether Country A offers more or fewer exports, at constant terms of trade, allowing for both production and consumption effects, as a result of factor growth or improved technology. If the outcome is that exports increase and Country A is large enough to influence world prices, then its increased offer of exports will tend to cause a fall in their price.

Box 10.2 Sustaining growth and economic miracles

Increases in the capital stock, made possible by greater saving and investment within an economy or by foreign investment or foreign aid from outside the economy, traditionally have been viewed as a key to economic growth. More recently, economists have paid greater attention to human capital, which creates the opportunity to raise worker productivity by education and training and to adjust more effectively to changing technology. This ability to increase factor inputs other than unskilled labor will continue to be an important determinant of economic growth and rising standards of living.

The growth record of some Asian countries seems to be well accounted for by their high saving rates and expenditures on education, as well as an increase in the share of the population in the work force. In that sense their story may not seem so miraculous.[1] Rather, they sacrificed considerable current consumption in order to build up their productive capacity, and their successful growth says the resources were allocated efficiently; in other high-saving economies such as the USSR that was not necessarily true.

Economists have noted that the growth of output in some economies, however, has been far faster than can be accounted for by the growth in their inputs alone. In a sense, their record may seem more miraculous. To explain those improvements in output, and their sustainability over time, economists have often attributed the result to technological improvement. Recent interest has focused on the extent to which such change appears to be a gift determined by outside forces, or whether the incentives to innovate and imitate, and the resources necessary to do either, can be considered more explicitly.

Trade appears to lead to higher growth rates, perhaps because of the access it provides to more productive imported machinery, more specialized intermediate inputs, or the transmission of ideas. If the gap between best-practice techniques and those actually used can be reduced and thereby provide growth, trade may contribute to that process. Economists still have several unresolved issues to address in this area.

Worsening terms of trade and immiserizing growth

If growth leads to a decline in the country's terms of trade, this price effect counteracts the benefits derived from economic growth. It is even possible that the loss from an adverse change in the terms of trade will exceed the gain from increased capacity, thus leaving the country worse off than before. This rather extreme case, called "**immiserizing growth**," has attracted much attention, especially in connection with complaints of developing countries over their prospects in world trade.

Consider the changes in production and consumption for Country A shown in Figure 10.4. Because this argument has most often been raised in the context of developing-country exports of primary products to industrialized countries for manufactured products, we have labeled the axes accordingly. Initially, A is producing at P_0 and exporting primary products in exchange for manufactures at the terms-of-trade ratio indicated by the slope of P_0C_0. Through trade it can reach the welfare level represented by indifference curve i_0. Consumption is at C_0.

As a result of growth in the supply of factors used in the production of primary products, A's production-possibility curve shifts to the right, from AB to HK. It now offers larger quantities of exports, and its terms of trade decline as shown by the flatter slope of P_1C_1. At this exchange ratio, A continues to export primary products, but it can only reach the lower indifference curve, i_1. Thus, growth in capacity has reduced economic welfare. This outcome is more likely when an export-biased production effect is combined with a strong preference in Country A to spend additional income on manufactured goods. Growth results in a large increase in the quantity of exports supplied, and because import demand in the rest of the world is inelastic, there is a substantial decline in the relative price of primary goods. In fact, Country A receives a smaller quantity of manufactured goods in exchange for a larger quantity of primary-product exports.

Although the theoretical possibility clearly exists, actual cases of immiserizing growth are especially hard to prove. It requires a country large enough to have a significant effect on the world price of its export, and one whose growth is strongly biased toward exports. For example, the demand for imports of sugar may be inelastic, but the import demand for sugar from Mexico is likely to be elastic; Mexican sugar is a very good substitute for sugar from other countries, and because Mexico accounts for a small share of the market it can attract

Box 10.3 The terms-of-trade effects of growth: offer curve analysis

Analysis of change in the terms of trade can usefully be put in terms of the offer curves described in Chapter 2. Suppose Country A's original offer curve is OA, as in Figure 10.3. At the initial equilibrium, with terms of trade OT, Country A exports OC_1 of cloth and imports OF_1 of food. Then, as a result of growth in its labor force, Country A's offer curve shifts from OA to OA', indicating its willingness to export a larger quantity of cloth at each terms of trade. This is export-biased growth.

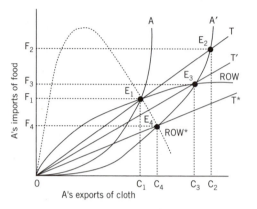

Figure 10.3 Effect of growth on the terms of trade. Rapid expansion in Country A's export capacity results in its offer curve shifting from OA to OA'. The effect on Country A's terms of trade depends upon the elasticity of demand in the rest of the world: when foreign demand is infinitely elastic, the relative price of cloth remains OT; when foreign demand is elastic, the relative price of cloth falls to OT'; and when foreign demand is inelastic, the relative price of cloth falls to OT*.

How are Country A's terms of trade affected? In Figure 10.3 we show three possible outcomes:

1 If Country A is a small country, too small to affect the world price, then the offer curve for the rest of the world (ROW) will be the straight line OT and the new equilibrium will be at E_2, where Country A exports OC_2 of cloth and imports OF_2 of food.
2 If Country A is large enough to influence the world price and the ROW offer curve is elastic, as indicated by the offer curve labeled ROW in Figure 10.3, the shift in Country A's offer curve will now cause a fall in the price of cloth relative to the price of food. The new equilibrium is at E_3, where A's offer of cloth has increased by a bigger proportion (from OC_1 to OC_3) than has the amount of food it receives in return (from OF_1 to OF_3). Country A's terms of trade have fallen, because a unit of cloth now buys less food, shown by the flatter terms-of-trade line OT'.
3 If the initial equilibrium occurs on the inelastic range of the ROW offer curve, as shown by the offer curve ROW*, the new equilibrium will be at E_4. Country A offers more of its export good, OC_4, as a result of growth, but it receives back less of the good it imports, OF_4, compared to the original solution at E_1. An inelastic foreign demand, which contributes to a large terms-of-trade deterioration, is one of the conditions that makes immiserizing growth more likely.

customers away from other suppliers. Some economists believe that groups of developing countries have sometimes suffered losses as a result of their joint expansion of capacity to produce certain export commodities. In that case, a single country no longer increases its market share at the expense of others, and all face a lower price. The policy implication of that possibility is that developing countries with highly concentrated exports – that is, countries that export very large volumes of one or two commodities – should diversify exports into new product areas. This is particularly important if a country's exports of one commodity represent a large part of world consumption and if the prospects for rapid growth of world demand for that commodity are weak. Brazil, for example, would not want to base its export strategy on increasing production of coffee, and Bangladesh would not be well advised to orient its growth plans toward vast increases in plantings of jute.

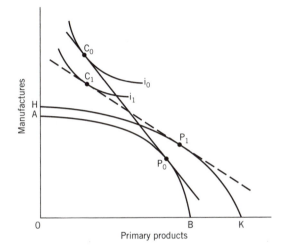

Figure 10.4 The case of immiserizing growth. Economic growth has left this country worse off because of a terms-of-trade deterioration. It was producing P_0 and consuming at C_0. Now it produces at P_1 and consumes at C_1, which is on a lower indifference curve.

Trade policies in developing countries

Public debate often lumps developing countries into a single category, implies they have a common interest in the way the trading system evolves, and claims they should adopt a common policy stance to increase their negotiating power versus industrialized countries. Such perceptions were at their peak in the 1970s but still exist today. We avoid that oversimplification here, but suggest a two-way categorization of developing countries that also is subject to the complaint that it ignores large differences between countries. The two groupings are:

1   Certain countries export primary products and import manufactured goods. Therefore, they depend vitally on the ratio of prices of primary products to prices of manufactured goods. A few of these countries, such as Botswana, which exports diamonds, have done well, but most of them have been through a very difficult period. The terms of trade of these countries peaked in the 1970s and are now well below levels that prevailed then. Economic growth in these countries has typically been slow, and in a few cases it has

been insufficient to keep up with population growth, producing declining real per capita incomes. This category includes almost all of the OPEC members, all of sub-Saharan Africa except South Africa, and countries such as Ecuador and Bolivia in Latin America. Some Asian countries, such as Cambodia, Myanmar (Burma), and the Asian republics of the former Soviet Union, are in this category, but most of Asia has become much less dependent on primary-product production.

2   Other countries have broken away from exclusive reliance on primary-product exports and now export a range of manufactured goods, most of which are labor-intensive. The countries that have most thoroughly completed this transition are now moving toward exports of more skill- and capital-intensive goods, although they maintain some labor-intensive exports such as textiles, garments, and shoes, especially where they earn **quota rents** in protected markets of industrialized countries. These countries have experienced rapid economic growth, much of which has been encouraged by a particularly strong export performance. The original "Four Tigers" – Taiwan, South Korea, Hong Kong, and Singapore – began this process, but they have recently been joined by a second wave of newly industrialized countries (NICs), including Thailand, Indonesia, Malaysia, and, of course, China. Although the Asian financial crises of the late 1990s has reduced the frenetic growth, rapid expansion of capacity, and speculative activity of earlier in the decade, most of these countries are recovering from that shock. In the western hemisphere growth has been less consistent, but Chile, Mexico, and Brazil are no longer dependent on primary exports alone.

Box 10.4 An overview of developing-country trade

The overview of trade and investment in Chapter 1 demonstrated that trade grew more rapidly than output in most countries over the past 30 years. The pattern of trade has also changed, and Table 10.2 shows some of those changes for developing countries.

Table 10.2 Trade of developing countries (US$ million)

Exports to	1965	1980	1995	Growth rate 1965–95
Developed economies	26,020	392,576	772,088	12.0
Europe	14,770	182,289	270,272	10.2
US	6,861	116,762	313,074	13.6
Japan	2,745	77,709	146,017	14.2
Developing economies	7,904	138,558	583,956	15.4
Africa	1,133	13,386	23,796	10.7
America	2,502	43,678	77,613	12.1
Asia	4,826	84,781	477,318	16.5
Centrally planned (European)	2,006	15,894	24,277	8.7
Total	37,661	558,602	1,408,085	12.8

Source: United Nations, *Yearbook of International Trade Statistics*, 1982 and 1996, Special Table B.

While 69 percent of developing-country exports in 1965 went to developed countries, by 1995 that figure had fallen to 55 percent. Shipments to other developing countries grew more rapidly than shipments to developed countries, but that aggregate comparison hides the fact that exports to Africa and Latin America grew at below-average rates, while exports to Asian developing countries grew particularly rapidly. Among developed countries, European markets were the most significant in 1965, but by 1995 the United States was the largest buyer from developing countries. The centrally planned European economies played a small role in trade initially, and that share had shrunk even further by 1995 to account for less than 2 percent of developing-country exports. While rising primary-product prices were an important cause of the change from 1965 to 1980, the 1980–95 period demonstrates the importance of growth in developing-country exports of manufactures.

Primary-product exporters

The developing countries that are in the first category described above typically export large amounts of a small number of products, which makes their export revenues quite volatile. Many OPEC members derive more than 80 percent of their export revenues from oil and gas. As a result, the decline in oil prices from the early 1980s to 2000 reduced export receipts. A country with highly concentrated exports is analogous to a family with all of its net worth invested in the common stocks of one or two companies in a single industry: the family's investment income is likely to be very unstable. For a sample of the least developed countries Table 10.3 reports the large role played by their top three exports, and their consequent vulnerability to volatility and declines in those prices. Various World Bank and UNCTAD studies document greater volatility of primary product prices than prices of manufactures.[2] Why should that be the case? One reason may be that the prices of such products are determined in highly competitive auction markets, such as the London Metal Exchange, whereas manufactured-goods prices are determined in more oligopolistic markets. Highly competitive markets are known to have more price variability than do oligopolistic markets. Another explanation is that elasticities of supply and demand are lower for primary products than for manufactured goods. A developing country that has grown a certain amount of a perishable commodity is willing to sell it for whatever price is available, because in the short run it has few alternatives; its supply is very inelastic. If the price elasticity of demand for these products is also very low, because they have relatively few substitutes, the likelihood of large price swings is greater. A shift of either the supply or the demand curve causes a far larger price change than will occur when the demand and supply curves are more elastic.

Price volatility does not necessarily mean export earnings will change to the same extent. Lower prices may be offset by a greater quantity sold. In the case of the least developed countries, the purchasing power of exports was slightly higher in 1999 than it was in 1986.[3] For several intervening years, however, purchasing power was up to 20 percent lower. Recognize, furthermore, that 1986 was a year of low oil prices and not a particularly favorable starting point of comparison.

Why is the volatility of export earnings particularly problematic? The ability of countries to maintain their standard of living suffers. Countries are even more likely to reduce their investment as incomes and foreign exchange earnings decline. Not only does that adversely affect long-run growth, but an inability to import spare parts results in reduced capacity

Table 10.3 Concentration of merchandise exports for least developed countries

Country	Products	Share (three leading exports)/ (total merchandise exports)	
		1981–3	1997–9
Afghanistan	Grapes, furs and skins, wool carpets	67.7	43.5
Angola	Petroleum and diamonds	96.5	97.6
Bangladesh	Men's and women's clothing	60.3	53.2
Cambodia	Garments, footwear, wood	64.4	61.3
Ethiopia	Coffee, sesame seed, leather	80.2	81.1
Liberia	Diamonds, rubber, timber	84.6	92.2
Madagascar	Garments, shellfish, coffee	70.7	40.5
Malawi	Tobacco, sugar, tea/coffee	82.9	78.8
Nepal	Carpets, garments	39.6	61.7
Tanzania	Coffee, cashew nuts	54.9	51.3
Uganda	Coffee, fish	97.5	69.9
Zambia	Copper, cobalt	93.8	89.3
Weighted average, LDCs		78.2	76.0

Source: UNCTAD, *The Least Developed Countries Report 2002*, p. 110.

utilization and more immediate downward pressure on income. Volatility of a few prices is especially critical for countries that are overly reliant on exports of those goods. Some even talk of a curse of natural resource wealth. While natural resource extraction may be capital-intensive and have a less favorable effect on income distribution, the dangers of price volatility have more to do with the likelihood that high earnings in boom-years will be used effectively to cushion periods of price decline. The lure of natural resource rents may attract opportunistic politicians who gain considerable personal wealth while in office. Democratic succession becomes less likely and armed conflict more likely in those circumstances as well.

International commodity-price stabilization programs are often suggested as a solution to this problem of price volatility. If both importers and exporters agree on a target or "normal" price and if the industrialized consuming countries are willing to provide initial financing, the stabilization fund purchases and stores the commodity whenever the market price falls below the target, thereby pushing it back up. When market prices rise above the target, the program sells the commodity from previously accumulated stocks, pushing the price back down.[4]

This approach sounds attractive, but such programs have a very poor track record. Consumers and producers seldom agree on the target price, and when such prices have been set, they are almost always too high. The fund has to continually purchase the commodity and soon runs out of money. Production quotas are frequently proposed as a way to support prices without continual commodity purchases by the fund, but every exporting country wants a large quota. If quotas are agreed upon, countries frequently cheat by producing above their quotas and trying to sell this output secretly. Programs in coffee, coca, tin, and sugar proved unsuccessful. Nevertheless, in 2002 Thailand took the initiative in forming the International Rubber Corporation with Malaysia and Indonesia to regulate rubber prices. Together they account for 80 percent of the world's output.[5]

Stabilizing commodity prices is not synonymous with stabilizing export revenues. If price shocks primarily originate on the demand side, that may be true, but if supply shocks (weather, crop diseases) are more typical, stabilizing prices with a buffer stock program such as that described above is actually likely to destabilize export incomes. In years of small harvests, an offsetting rise in prices is not allowed, while in years of large harvests, a high price is paid anyway.

Commodity futures markets offer some potential to reduce export revenue volatility. Futures markets allow the sale of a commodity at a price that is set now for delivery at a fixed date in the future. If a country is worried that prices may decline before the crop is ready for delivery, the sale of a future contract, the maturity of which matches the commodity's availability for delivery, has the effect of locking in its export prices and revenues. Futures markets exist for many, but by no means all, commodities; they can therefore ease the price volatility problems of only some developing countries.

The long-term answer to the problem of revenue volatility is product diversification. Countries should actively pursue new or nontraditional export markets rather than make all of their revenues dependent on one or two commodity prices. This prescription is easier for a large country such as Brazil to follow, but quite difficult for small countries such as Togo or Benin. Nevertheless, many small countries, including Sri Lanka, Cyprus, and Morocco, have sharply reduced their export concentration, thereby reducing revenue volatility.

Deteriorating terms of trade

The larger problem for primary-product exporters has been not price volatility, but price declines. Since 1980 prices of nonfuel commodities relative to manufactured goods exported by developed countries have fallen by 45 percent.[6]

Is this evidence of a long-run relationship that affects developing countries negatively, as predicted by Raul Prebisch and Hans Singer 50 years ago? The **Prebisch–Singer hypothesis** suggests that the terms of trade for primary-product producers will continue to fall over time. Based on the change in Britain's terms of trade from 1876 to 1947 they concluded that technical progress in manufacturing had not created an expected benefit for primary-product producers in the form of improved terms of trade. Rather, the opposite had occurred.

One possible explanation was that technological improvements in manufacturing simply allowed unionized workers in those countries to receive higher wages, or monopolists to increase profit margins, without passing this benefit on as lower prices to buyers. In contrast, workers who produced primary products could not avoid pressure to accept wage cuts in cyclical downturns.

Another concern was that demand for primary commodities tended not to be income elastic. Foods and beverage markets have always been threatened by Engel's law, which states that the income elasticity of demand for such products is less than one. This idea is named after Ernst Engel, a nineteenth-century economist who found data supporting this conclusion. Poor people spend a high percentage of their incomes on food, but this percentage steadily declines as incomes rise. This means that markets for food and beverage items do not expand as rapidly as the world economy unless the distribution of income shifts to lower income groups.

Technical progress in manufacturing also has tended to reduce demand for raw materials. That scenario is particularly relevant in explaining experience in the 1980s. Prices of metals, fuels, and fibers might have been expected to decline in the early 1980s when virtually all of the industrialized world was in a recession that sharply reduced the demand for these products. However, the lack of price increases during the strong macroeconomic recovery of the mid- and late 1980s came as something of a surprise. Technical breakthroughs, which produced substitutes for some primary products, were one cause of this outcome. Fiber optics replaced copper in the telephone industry. Steel was replaced by plastic, aluminum, and other products in various uses. Natural fibers were supplanted by artificial fibers, and technical changes reduced the amount of oil consumed in many industries.

Over the longer run, the situation is more difficult to characterize. Economists have progressively assembled better data to carry out such analysis. Also, they have more carefully tested whether the pattern of prices represents random variation without a clear trend and whether there have been clear breaks in any trend. A tentative summary of the evidence for the twentieth century is that no clear trend exists, and a break in the series likely occurred in 1921.[7] Further research may well yield different conclusions.

Alternative trade policies for developing countries

The governments of many developing countries concluded some time ago that reliance on growing exports of primary products was not a promising development strategy. This realization led to a search for alternatives. Two broad policy trends that have emerged are commonly referred to as import substitution and export-led growth.

Import substitution

During the 1950–70 period, the governments of many developing countries, encouraged by some academic economists, concluded that international trade was unlikely to benefit poor countries and that they should therefore design policies to minimize their reliance on trade. Instead of stressing export growth, tariffs and other trade barriers were used to encourage the growth of local industries in order to produce substitutes for products that had previously been imported. This inward-looking, or autarkic, approach was designed to sharply reduce the role of trade in a nation's economy. If substitutes for most imports could be produced, declining primary-product prices would be less threatening because large export revenues were no longer needed to pay for imports. The export sector could be ignored or even taxed, a strategy that promoted the shift of resources out of primary production. For countries where adverse terms-of-trade movements were feared, a policy to reduce primary production was advisable if a large enough group of producers pursued it to drive up primary prices in world markets. In world grain markets, however, the United States has found that such supply cutbacks are largely offset by other producers claiming a larger share of the market, and developing countries have seen that pattern in many other markets.

Based on the material presented in Chapters 2 and 3 of this book, the reader would likely conclude that this approach is exactly the opposite of the one that will maximize its welfare. Scarce resources are being invested precisely where they will be least efficiently used. Labor-abundant countries, with very limited investment budgets, are putting large amounts of money in capital-intensive industries that provide very little employment. Labor-abundant countries, as Chapter 3 would suggest, should be doing the opposite: spreading their limited capital stocks thinly across labor-intensive industries, where comparative advantages exist, thereby maximizing employment opportunities for an abundant labor force and generating export revenues. The extremes of this policy are reflected in Balassa's measures of the effective rate of protection for consumer durables in several developing countries during the early 1960s: Brazil 285 percent, Chile 123 percent, Mexico 85 percent, Malaysia –5 percent, Pakistan 510 percent, and the Philippines 81 percent.[8]

Although most economists have rejected extensive reliance on import substitution, the historical record indicates that this approach can succeed if it is pursued for a limited period of time in carefully chosen sectors. The infant-industry argument for protection, discussed in Chapter 6, suggested that if a country had a clear potential comparative advantage in a product, protection might be justified for a brief period while that industry could expand, learn, and bring its costs down. South Korea and Taiwan, for example, pursued such infant-industry protection with considerable success. It was critical, however, that protection be provided only in those sectors in which firms could clearly become competitive in world markets, and that this protection not be permanent. Providing protection for only a limited time avoids the danger of perpetuating mistakes if the infant industry never matures. Most of the industries for which protection was provided were relatively labor-intensive. Both Korea and Taiwan used this approach for a limited number of years and then moved away from it when the potential comparative-advantage industries had been developed.

Import substitution was an expensive failure in countries such as India that relied upon it for decades and extended it to capital-intensive industries. This policy is particularly disastrous if applied to industries whose products are inputs for sectors that should export. As a consequence, many negative effective rates of protection are created in the export sector. A country may have a comparative advantage, for example in textiles, but a comparative disadvantage in dyestuffs and textile machinery. If such a country protects inefficient manufacturers of dyestuffs and textile machinery, it will destroy its export potential in cloth. The prices of dyestuffs and machinery will be so high that the country cannot compete in world textile markets, despite an abundance of inexpensive labor. Many developing countries protect inefficient steel industries, and thereby lose the opportunity to export products that use steel; recall the example of the Indonesian bicycle industry in Chapter 5. For many years Brazil was determined to develop a local computer industry and therefore prohibited the importation of foreign computers. Because the local computers that were available in Brazil were expensive and of poor quality, that harmed every export industry that needed computers. Although Brazil now allows foreign computers to be imported, it still maintains a high tariff that harms the country's export potential in other sectors.[9]

Free-trade zones

A free-trade zone may help a country develop export industries that require inputs that it produces inefficiently. The country does not need to completely eliminate protection for such inefficient sectors, but instead can create a free-trade zone at a seaport or airport. Although inputs can be imported into the zone without facing a tariff or other barrier, they must be used to produce goods that are then exported. If the finished goods are sold locally, tariffs apply.

Sri Lanka, for example, has maintained such a zone at the Colombo airport with considerable success. Textiles can be brought without tariff into the zone, where garments are cut and sewn for export to the United States or Europe.

As another example, India maintains such a zone for the electronics industry near Bombay. Electronic components, which tend to be capital-intensive, are imported without restrictions into the zone, where labor-intensive assembly is completed, and the finished products are then exported. In this way, the Indian government can maintain protection for an inefficient component industry for the local market, while still pursuing electronics exports that require inexpensive components.

A sounder long-run approach is to eliminate protection for industries that produce key inputs for other sectors, and thereby to pursue exports across the entire economy rather than only in a small free-trade zone. Nevertheless, this may be difficult if inefficient input industries are long established and politically powerful.

Export-led growth

Despite the success of some temporary import substitution policies in carefully chosen infant industries, economists have reached a consensus that the export-led growth approach to trade policy is more promising.[10] Very few economists would now support the common argument of the 1950–70 period that international trade is bad for developing countries and that inward-looking or autarkic policies ought to be followed.

As early as the 1970s, studies were published showing that developing countries that pursued an export-led approach experienced far more rapid economic growth than did countries with protectionist policies.[11] The original Four Tigers (Hong Kong, Taiwan, Singapore, and South Korea) were the subject of most of this early research, but the second wave of Asian NICs (Indonesia, Thailand, Malaysia, and China) has also been very successful in pursuing export markets. As a result, these countries have grown rapidly. India, Mexico, and Brazil could be added as recent converts to this approach. All of these countries export labor-intensive manufactured goods, as Heckscher–Ohlin would predict, but more capital- and skill-intensive industries are beginning to prosper in these markets. Better education has proven to be an important prerequisite to benefit from the spillovers of technology from more advanced countries. India has a strong technical labor force and is now exporting computer software, primarily from Bangalore which is the Silicon Valley of South Asia.

Note that this export promotion strategy rests upon diversification and expansion of nontraditional exports. Countries blessed with fertile land are not to exit from agricultural industries but to consider alternatives to single-commodity economies. For example, Malaysia successfully reduced its dependence on rubber production by shifting to palm-oil production.

An export-led policy still requires supportive government policies. Governments need to promote physical infrastructure, such as ports, roads, electricity and telephone service. Basic health and education ensure a more capable labor force. A clear set of legal rights and its consistent application and enforcement encourages long-term investments. Our discussion of effective rates of protection demonstrates why tariffs on key imports are counter-productive. When such tariffs are in place, some countries have successfully provided offsetting benefits, such as favorable financing or direct subsidies to potential export industries. Yet, the cost of these measures limit their feasibility for many countries, and they may conflict with a country's WTO obligations, as well. Government tax and regulatory policies also can deter production in areas of comparative advantage, topics that we treat more fully in Chapter 11.

A particularly significant problem facing developing countries is one that is beyond their control: protection provided by industrialized countries for their labor-intensive manufacturing industries. One reason for Taiwan's success in overcoming those restrictions, without resort to false certificates of origin and other strategies discussed earlier, was the ability of its producers to shift from producing goods where quotas were binding to producing other items that still were not restricted. Future NICs may not find this strategy so easy to carry out if industrial countries have more effectively protected all labor-intensive sectors.

In sectors where NICs already command a large share of the market in industrial countries, the new wave of developing-country exporters may largely displace sales by NICs. Thus,

---

Box 10.5 Measuring economic development: the Nike index

Production of shoes is a labor-intensive process. Not surprisingly, US footwear companies have found it attractive to produce abroad, or license others to produce footwear that they design, in locations where wages are sufficiently low to offset low labor productivity. Nike is an example of a company that has relied on offshore production to stitch shoes. Its choice of where to locate production abroad is not a one-time decision, however. Rather, Nike has progressively altered these locations to take into account the pace of economic development in the countries concerned. In particular, because economic development results in new opportunities in sectors where labor productivity is greater and employers are willing to pay higher wages, workers may have more attractive alternatives outside of the footwear industry. To retain workers, footwear producers must raise wages. Yet, if they pass on these higher labor costs to consumers, they may lose most of their sales; demand facing a given location is likely to be quite elastic because there are many potential sources of footwear supply.

Over time, Nike initiated Japanese production in 1972, switched to Korean and Taiwanese production in 1975, and then to Indonesian, Chinese, and Thai production in 1987. Nike's decision where to produce is quite consistent with the progressive economic development in these countries. Its arrival, however, is not simply a matter of finding where the greatest wage advantage can be obtained. Rather, it signifies that the country has sufficient political stability, infrastructure, and an open trade climate to promote the quality and volume of production needed to serve international markets. Nike's cutback in Indonesian production in 2002 appears to correspond to a decline in political stability. When a country is able to maintain an attractive production environment, but also acquires more human and physical capital, it is likely to climb the ladder of development that allows wages to rise across the economy. That eventually destroys its comparative advantage in footwear production.[12]

---

expansion of Chinese and Indonesian shoe production has largely displaced Korean and Taiwanese exports. In the apparel and textile sector, however, industrial countries still have substantial domestic production which will face further competitive pressure if more developing countries adopt export-led growth strategies. It was not easy for the industrialized countries to adapt to the export prowess of the original Gang of Four, but at least they were small, their export potential was limited, and they were likely to face higher wage rates as industrial growth advanced. The new entrants in the export-led approach are another story: Thailand has over 60 million people, Indonesia 200 million, and China 1.2 billion. Export growth in labor-intensive products can proceed for a long time in these countries before labor shortages will be encountered.

Summary of key concepts

1   Neutral growth, where production of all goods rises by the same percentage, will result in the same percentage increase in export supply if consumers continue to consume all goods in the same proportion.

2   If growth at constant prices results in a disproportionately large increase in output of the export good, and consumers wish to spend the extra income primarily on the import good, then the increase in the country's export supply will be especially large.

3   If a country is large enough to affect world prices, growth that results in a large increase in the supply of exports may result in a sufficiently large decline in the relative price of the export good to leave the country worse off. This special case of immiserizing growth is more likely to occur when foreign import demand for this good is quite inelastic.

4   Many developing countries remain highly dependent on the exportation of one or two primary products. Producers of primary products have been especially concerned over the declining prices of these goods compared to manufactures.

5   To avoid over-reliance on primary exports, many countries in the 1950s and 1960s adopted a policy of import substitution to shift resources into manufactures. Although this policy promoted industrialization, it became quite costly when countries chose to permanently protect capital-intensive industries that produced key inputs into other goods where the country had a comparative advantage.

6   Export-led growth has been a successful strategy for countries that diversify into nontraditional exports where they have a long-run comparative advantage in production and where they face a more elastic foreign demand. Although these exports were labor-intensive initially, as countries have acquired more physical and human capital, their pattern of comparative advantage has shifted to more technologically advanced goods.

Questions for study and review

1   Volatile prices of primary export products result in unstable export earnings for many LDCs. How will earnings be affected by price stabilization pacts?

2   Falling computer prices do not seem to be a source of hardship in the United States. Why are falling prices of primary commodities in LDCs a serious problem?

3   Nominal tariff rates in industrial countries commonly increase with the stage of processing. Why exactly do LDCs object to such a tariff structure?

4   In a country with tariffs on a wide range of imported products, what can be said about the effective rate of protection in the country's export industries? Explain.

5   Discuss the issues (pros and cons) in the debate over import substitution and export promotion as a strategy for LDCs to follow. Which strategy do you favor? What factors are likely to limit the success of import substitution and of export promotion?

6   "LDC tariffs intended to promote industry may in fact inhibit development of the LDCs' most efficient industries." Do you agree? Explain how this could happen.

7   What interest groups within the United States would you expect to support a US policy of allowing more products to be imported from emerging industrialized countries such as Thailand, Taiwan, and China? Why? Who within the US political system would oppose such a liberal trade policy? Why?

8   Why is the completion of the Doha Round of multilateral trade negotiations important to the likely future success of export-led development strategies for LDCs?

Suggested further reading

In addition to the studies cited in the text, consider two monographs by Nobel-prize-winning economists cited for their contributions to economic development:

- Lewis, Arthur William, *The Evolution of the International Economic Order*, Princeton, NJ: Princeton University Press, 1978.
- Schultz, Theodore William, *Investing in People: The Economics of Population Quality*, Berkeley, CA: University of California Press, 1981.

Notes

1 Alwyn Young, "The Tyranny of Numbers: Confronting the Statistical Realities of the East Asian Growth Experience," *Quarterly Journal of Economics* 110, no. 3, August 1995, pp. 641–80.
2 World Bank, *Global Economic Prospects and the Developing Countries* (Washington, DC: World Bank, 1994), pp. 52, and UNCTAD, *Least Developed Countries Report 2002*, p. 142.
3 UNCTAD, op. cit., p. 140.
4 For a thorough analysis of commodity-price stabilization programs, see J. Behrman, *Development, the International Economic Order, and Commodity Agreements* (Reading, MA: Addison-Wesley, 1978).
5 Shawn Crispin, "Thailand Initiates Plan for Commodity Cartels," *Wall Street Journal*, Dec. 5, 2002, discusses Thai efforts in rice as well as rubber to create a cartel arrangement.
6 UNCTAD, op. cit., p. 138.
7 J. Cuddington, R.Ludema and S. Jayasuriya, "Prebisch-Singer Redux," US International Trade Commission, Working Paper, June 2002.
8 Bela Balassa, *The Structure of Protection in Developing Countries* (Baltimore: Johns Hopkins University Press, 1971).
9 For a summary of Brazilian trade policy measures that have concerned US policy-makers, see the USTR's *National Trade Estimate Report on Foreign Trade Barriers* at http://www.ustr.gov/reports/nte/1999/contents.html
10 See World Bank, *The East Asian Miracle: Economic Growth and Public Policy* (New York: Oxford University Press, 1993), ch. 3; P. Chow, "Causality between Export Growth and Industrial Development: Empirical Evidence for the NICs," *Journal of Development Economics* 26, no. 1, June 1987, pp. 55–63; and S. Edwards, "Openness, Trade Liberalization, and Growth in Developing Countries," *Journal of Economic Literature*, September 1993, pp. 1358–93.
11 In addition to numerous country studies, there are three volumes that synthesize and summarize the overall results of this research: Ian Little, T. Scitovsky, and M. Scott, *Industry and Trade in Some Developing Countries: A Comparative Study* (Oxford: Oxford University Press, 1970); Jagdish Bhagwati, *Foreign Trade Regimes and Economic Development: Anatomy and Consequences of Exchange Control Regimes* (New York: Columbia University Press, 1976); and Anne Krueger, *Foreign Trade Regimes and Economic Development: Liberalization Attempts and Consequences* (New York: Columbia University Press, 1976). A later survey of the literature on trade policy and development can be found in Oli Havrylyshyn, "Trade Policy and Productivity Gains in Developing Countries," *World Bank Research Observer*, January 1990, pp. 1–24.
12 "Nike's Trainers Track Fitness of Asian Tigers," *The Financial Times*, April 2, 1997, p. 15., and "Footwear is Fleeing Indonesia," *Wall Street Journal*, September 9, 2002, p. A12.

11 Issues of international public economics

Learning objectives

By the end of this chapter you should be able to understand:

- how production may create a negative externality such as pollution, and national measures to reduce pollution can affect the location of production internationally;
- why negative externalities that extend across borders are especially difficult to address because property rights are not well established and individual countries may free-ride on the clean-up efforts of others;
- why, when governments impose taxes on mobile factors of production, they are likely to affect the location of production internationally.

In previous chapters we have seen that free trade may not make a country better off if other distortions exist in the economy, such as monopoly power. Another important distortion is an **externality**, that is, an effect from the production or consumption of a good that is not taken into account in its market price. An example of a positive externality that we considered in Chapter 4 was an external economy of scale: costs for all firms fall when one firm expands output. While the individual firm ignores this benefit to others, the economy as a whole gains as industry output expands. When this externality exists in the production of the export good, trade creates an additional gain by allowing output to increase and more of the external economy of scale to be achieved. When this externality exists in an import-competing good, however, trade reduces domestic output and the benefits from this externality. A trade barrier might improve the country's welfare by promoting an expansion of industry output.

In this chapter a major topic we address is the implications of negative externalities, and we particularly focus on environmental externalities. Expanding output in a polluting industry imposes a cost on the economy that an individual producer need not consider in the absence of some corrective action by the government or others. Our expectations are just the reverse of what we reported above for a positive externality. With a negative externality in the production of the export good, overproduction of the good is aggravated by trade. In the case of an import-competing good, trade may reduce its output domestically and thereby provide an additional benefit to the economy.

When economies adopt policies to reduce pollution, their primary concern typically is not with the effects on trade. Nevertheless, they do affect trade. Especially when different countries adopt different pollution control standards, the location of production is more likely to be affected. Fears of US companies that they would face competition from producers located in Mexico who were subject to more lenient environmental standards was one of the major points of opposition in the United States to Congressional approval of NAFTA. We examine that issue in this chapter.

Many types of pollution spill over from one country to another, and therefore reducing pollution may not be a matter of a country forcing its own polluters to clean up. The number of countries affected by cross-border pollution affects what type of solution might be adopted, because in general the more parties involved the more difficult it will be to reach agreement. We begin by considering effects on regional air sheds or water basins, where European efforts to clean up the River Rhine and to deal with acid rain provide instructive examples.

Some countries have taken action to limit imports of goods that generate negative production externalities, because the standards that they impose on their own producers otherwise could be undercut by foreign competitors free of such requirements. These actions have resulted in contentious GATT or WTO cases, because the importing country appears to be imposing its own production standards on an extraterritorial basis to other countries. We examine cases where trade measures taken by the United States against foreign producers to require fishing methods that protect marine mammals and endangered species have been ruled inconsistent with its GATT obligations.

In some cases the negative effects of a country's production may affect others worldwide. Two relevant examples are using chlorofluorocarbons (CFCs) in refrigerants, which depletes the ozone layer, or burning of carbon fuels, which adds to greenhouse gases and affects global warming. Economists refer to the ozone layer or the condition of the atmosphere generally as **common property resources**. No one can be excluded from their benefits. Yet, individual countries can take actions that deplete the ozone layer or add to the accumulation of greenhouse gases in the atmosphere, and thereby reduce the benefits that others receive from these common resources. Countries have an incentive to free-ride on the efforts of others to preserve the common property resource, because they cannot be excluded from the benefits of conservation or clean-up by others. Therefore, multilateral agreements to take action may be particularly difficult to reach.

Another aspect of addressing externalities and adopting policies to achieve other domestic goals is the ability to finance them. In the immediate post-World War II period, trade, capital mobility and immigration were all near their lowest points of the century. As a result, the implications of tax policy were largely limited to the home economy. Over the last 50 years, however, trade in goods and flows of factors have expanded more rapidly than output. A country's tax structure now is more likely to affect its competitive position and the location of production internationally. In some cases countries have the opportunity to shift a portion of their tax burden to foreigners, as we saw in Chapter 6 for an optimum export tax. Higher taxes on domestic production may improve the country's terms of trade, but they do not necessarily increase the country's output or welfare. Low-tax countries may attract a larger tax base and a greater amount of economic activity.

Many countries are concerned that the operation of tax haven countries reduces their own tax collections and their ability to fund social programs that have long been expected by the electorate. Within geographic blocs such as the European Union, where efforts to establish a single market have progressed the furthest, countries are especially concerned over their ability to pursue policies that impose higher taxes or adopt more redistributive social welfare policies than their neighbors. Irish success in attracting foreign investment by levying a lower corporate income tax rate has caused other countries to call for a policy of tax harmonizing to reduce such competitive effects. Would it be desirable for formal directives to require some minimum rate closer to the average imposed by member countries, as a means of reducing tax competition among countries and preserving a greater common role for the government sector?

Environmental externalities

We begin by considering a negative externality that just affects environmental conditions in a single country. Thus, we rule out pollution that crosses a national border, and only consider the way residents of a single country are affected by the pollution. Economists are unlikely to suggest a general goal of eliminating all pollution, because they think in terms of an optimal level of pollution, which occurs where the extra benefit of reducing pollution just equals the extra cost of reducing pollution. As shown in Figure 11.1, the intersection of the marginal benefit and marginal cost curves indicates along the horizontal axis how much abatement is warranted from the perspective of economic efficiency. Controls that are too stringent add more to the cost of compliance than they do to the benefits from a cleaner environment. Conversely, ignoring pollution entirely is likely to leave the nation worse off, because when little effort is made the extra benefits of a cleaner environment exceed the cost of additional abatement expenditures.

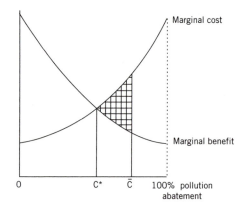

Figure 11.1 Marginal benefits and marginal costs of pollution abatement. The optimal amount of environmental clean-up is given at C* where the marginal benefits of clean-up just equal the marginal costs. Imposing a more stringent standard at C̄, say, results in additional costs greater than additional benefits and a loss in economic efficiency given by the shaded triangle.

If all countries placed the same value on a cleaner environment and faced the same clean-up costs, which would be shown by identical marginal benefit and marginal cost curves for all countries, then unilateral action by each country would result in the same clean-up standards everywhere. In that situation, there would be no tendency for runaway plants to leave a country that imposed its own optimal pollution control standard, because the plant would be subject to the same controls in any alternative location. The existence of the externality, and the government's effort to make the offending plant recognize the cost it imposes on others, would not alter trade patterns, because relative costs of production would be affected identically in all countries.

More typically, there are differences in the way countries value a cleaner environment, or there are differences in the clean-up costs they face. The marginal benefit and marginal cost curves will not be identical in each country, and on economic grounds it is then in the interest of countries to choose different pollution control standards. The value that countries place on environmental clean-up is especially likely to diverge when one of the countries is an industrialized country and the other is a developing country, as in the case of the United States and Mexico. Environmental quality tends to be a luxury good; as income rises, demand for environmental quality rises to a greater extent. Based on this relationship we predict that richer countries will impose stricter standards and enforce them more stringently. Also, richer countries may demand goods and services that generate less pollution per unit of output. At the same time, though, production per person is much greater in high-income countries, which tends to generate more pollution and raise the cost of maintaining a given level of environmental quality. Rather than examine this cost effect separately from the benefit effect, economists have looked at their combined influences, and that of any other factors that might vary as income varies across countries, by asking the following question: as a country's income rises, does its environmental quality rise?

Grossman and Krueger examine this relationship for several measures of pollution and find that in most cases an inverted U-shaped relationship exists.[1] Pollution rises as output rises up to a certain threshold, and then declines as shown in Figure 11.2. That threshold is about $5,000 per capita in their work, and in subsequent studies appears to be somewhat lower. Although an implication of these findings is that convergence in income levels among neighbors will create more similar demands for environmental quality, there is still a significant gap between income levels in Western Europe and Eastern Europe or in the US and Mexico. Even if Mexico reaches the threshold where its demand for environmental quality rises rapidly, a difference in willingness to pay for a clean environment may continue to exist, and thus actual practice on each side of the border is likely to differ.

From a normative perspective, some environmentalists argue that mobile corporations should not be able to take advantage of the lower level of concern for environmental quality in developing countries. The most disturbing cases of developing countries accepting shipments of toxic waste after bribes are paid to key officials offends most observers' sense of propriety. Those who bear the cost of poor health and birth defects receive none of the benefits when corrupt officials accept such risks on their behalf. Demands that such shipments be prohibited are similar in nature to the rationale for laws that prevent individuals from selling themselves into slavery. The ability of individuals or countries to act in their own self interest and live with those consequences is questioned.

In the less extreme case, developing countries simply recognize that in order to meet pressing demands to feed and cloth their own growing population, as well as satisfy

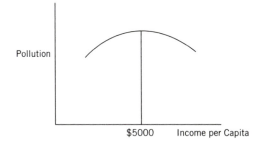

Figure 11.2 The pollution-income relationship. For many pollutants, pollution rises as economic development occurs, but after a certain threshold is reached, pollution declines.

Box 11.1 Trade in toxic waste

The fear that developing countries would end up as a dumping ground for the most dangerous waste products generated by the industrialized world was one of the motivations for the 1989 Basel Convention to control such trade. Over 90 percent of the world's annual production of toxic waste such as chlorine, lead, and cadmium comes from OECD countries, and advocates of the agreement believed those countries should be responsible for disposing of their own waste or, better yet, avoiding its creation in the first place. In 1994, the convention passed a resolution to ban shipments from industrialized OECD countries to developing countries, and in 1995 a treaty to bar such shipments was signed. The European Union has been a strong advocate of the treaty, and EU members were the first to ratify it. However, three-fourths of the members of the convention must ratify it for it to enter into force, and the United States has not ratified it.

Although the United States has favored looser language to allow trade for purposes of recycling, opponents claim that would gut the agreement and allow continued abuse. Major efforts are now directed at training personnel in developing countries to enforce bans on the importation of toxic waste that they have imposed and at transferring cleaner technologies and production methods to those countries.[2]

---

aspirations for industrial products and progress, they will accept worsened environmental quality. Accepting dirtier water or air is simply using up a national resource, similar to using up a deposit of oil or cutting a forest, which allows an increase in current output. Dirtier industries will locate in poorer countries.

Intuitively, such an outcome is plausible, but in fact are pollution abatement costs significant enough to cause major relocations of activity? In the case of the United States, expressing these abatement costs as a share of value-added in manufacturing industries gives an average figure of 1.38 percent. For Mexican–US trade and the operation of maquiladora assembly plants in the border zone, Grossman and Krueger report that the operations located in Mexico are well explained by their high labor intensity and low requirements of capital and skilled labor. Industries where there are high US costs of complying with environmental protection standards do not represent a significant portion of those located in Mexico. Other recipients of major amounts of foreign investment, such as China and Brazil, have shown major improvements in air quality.

Cross-border pollution

The situation sketched above becomes more complicated if the reduction in air or water quality is not confined to a single country. If plants were to locate in the country with the most lax environmental standards, say Mexico, but the pollution were to cross the border, say the United States, not only would the issue of a potential loss of competitiveness and employment in the United States arise, as in the situation above, but no compensating improvement in environmental quality would occur either. Indeed, Americans have been concerned over Mexican producers dumping chemicals in the Rio Grande river, which affects US users of that water, too. Similarly, Canadians have objected to power plants in the US midwest burning high-sulfur coal that contributes to the acidification of lakes in

Ontario, and Austrians protested the construction and eventual activation of a Russian-designed nuclear reactor in the Czech Republic.

When only a small number of countries is involved, prospects for some resolution of these conflicts are better. The pattern assumed above where each nation acted independently in imposing standards, however, may not apply. In those cases we assumed that the polluter paid the price of meeting the standards. That cost could represent the installation of new pollution-abatement equipment, redesign of a production process to reduce the pollution generated, or payment of an emissions tax set by the government. In reality, most countries have relied upon the use of uniformly mandated technologies and have only introduced market mechanisms such as taxes or auctions of pollution rights very gradually. The cost of mandating a single technological fix to reduce pollution often is much more expensive, but that distinction is not the focus of our discussion.

Rather, we consider alternative approaches besides those based on the polluter pays principle. We no longer start from the presumption that individuals have a right to clean air or clean water. Instead, consider the case where producers have the right to use rivers and air sheds for the disposal of waste. In that case individuals interested in clean air and clean water must bribe the polluters to clean up. As demonstrated by Ronald Coase, when negotiating costs are low we expect to arrive at the same agreed-upon level of pollution regardless of who is awarded the right to control the use of the air and water.[3] In fact, it should conform to our earlier statement about extra benefits from tighter control matching the extra costs of that control. But, the distribution of the costs of reaching that level of pollution are much different. From the standpoint of negotiating an agreement, generally it is difficult to organize all those hurt by pollution, for some of the same political economy reasons we raised in Chapter 6: small costs are imposed on a large number of individuals and each one sees little benefit from acting individually to make a contribution to bribe the polluter to clean up. Therefore, any resolution generally rests upon a government acting on behalf of those adversely affected.

An example of this type of solution is given by the agreement to clean up the River Rhine. Because the Rhine originates in Switzerland and passes through France, Germany and the Netherlands, those four countries were involved in the solution. Industrial growth and disposal of waste in the river in the 1950s and 1960s led to ever lower levels of dissolved oxygen in the Rhine and the death of the salmon fishery, while high levels of salt affected vegetable production and drinking water in the Netherlands. A third of the salt was attributable to dumping by French potassium mines. Although the four countries signed the Bonn Salt Treaty in 1976, not until 1987 did France agree to measures to reduce the discharge of salt. The allocation of costs to deal with this situation were estimated to be: France 30 percent; Germany 30 percent; the Netherlands 34 percent; and Switzerland 6 percent. In the interest of achieving some form of clean-up, the four countries found it desirable to deviate from the expectation of polluter pays that the OECD articulated in 1972. Other concerns remain over the concentration of heavy metals and agricultural run off that also affect water quality.

European efforts to deal with acid rain demonstrate a somewhat different strategy. In 1985 twenty-one countries signed the Helsinki Protocol to reduce emissions of sulfur dioxide by 30 percent from 1980 levels.[4] Thirteen countries chose not to sign, including Poland, Spain, and the United Kingdom. The latter countries happen to be large net exporters of SO_2 who, given European wind patterns, would benefit relatively less from an effective agreement. Even in their case, however, some clean-up appears desirable because SO_2 emissions do not travel far and a large share are deposited in the emitting country. It still would be a remarkable coincidence if the extra benefits to Europe as a whole from a 30 percent reduction in emissions just matched the extra costs from achieving that cutback in every country. The World Bank cites a study that suggested a more efficient strategy would be for five countries to make cuts of more than 60 percent, and other countries to make cuts of less than 10 percent.[5] The Oslo Protocol of 1994 incorporated some of those insights by setting different adjustment goals for different countries, taking into account their different degrees of dependence on fossil fuels and costs of clean-up.

Unilateral action and extraterritoriality

In some cases, international agreement over the need for action to improve or preserve environmental quality may not be reached. Individual countries who have been unable to convince others of the urgency of their cause have then taken action unilaterally. When those actions include imposing trade sanctions or embargoes on other countries, however, the GATT and the WTO have often ruled against such practices. A 1991 decision that fanned the conflict between environmentalists and trade policy-makers dealt with a US embargo of tuna imported from Mexico.[6] The US action was taken under its 1976 Marine Mammal Protection Act, which outlawed the practice of catching tuna by using nets that entrapped dolphins feeding on the tuna; the dolphins generally did not escape and died in the process. US fishing fleets could be controlled by this law, but the goal of protecting dolphins would be defeated if a reduced US catch was replaced by greater numbers of tuna caught by foreign ships. While the United States could not force others to adopt this same standard, it called for an embargo on tuna caught by those who did not meet it.

The GATT ruled against the US position. Only in the case of goods produced by prison labor does the GATT specifically allow countries to take into account the process by which a good is produced. In the absence of an international treaty establishing a different standard, foreign goods must be treated the same as domestic goods, regardless of how they are produced. Furthermore, the GATT ruled that the US restrictions were imposed in a discriminatory way, applying to tuna caught in only one part of the world. Mexico also challenged the scientific basis for the policy, which did not apply to an endangered species.

Again in 1998 the WTO ruled against US restrictions on imports of shrimp caught in nets without devices to exclude sea turtles. The appellate body did rule that endangered species could be regarded as exhaustible resources and that measures to protect them were compatible with Article XX(g) of the GATT. Nevertheless, it found that the US ban was imposed in an arbitrary and discriminatory fashion; the United States negotiated agreements with some countries, but not others, gave some countries a 3-year phase-in period and others a 4-month period, and unilaterally presumed there was only one acceptable way to protect sea turtles. In 2001, however, the Appellate Body ruled that subsequent US efforts to negotiate a memorandum of understanding with South-East Asian countries and to draft a conservation and management plan did represent a sufficient good faith effort to pursue a no discriminating policy. In addition, the US approach allowed flexibility in how comparably effective measures were achieved, which thereby avoided the charge that it unilaterally imposed an inflexible standard on others.

Internationally, there appears to be substantial agreement that unilateral action is inappropriate. There is much less agreement over what consensus is necessary to provide a multilateral basis for action, and whether multilateral environmental agreements can rely upon trade remedies to enforce their provisions. While no case of action under a multilateral environmental agreement had been challenged under WTO dispute resolution by 2002, the

WTO has a standing Committee on Trade and the Environment that is mandated to consider the relationship between these two different types of agreements. A particular problem arises when some countries are not members of the environmental agreement. Therefore, while the committee has fostered useful discussions, to date no clear solutions have emerged.

The tragedy of the commons

Compared to the environmental externalities we have considered thus far, some actions have more than a local or regional effect. Instead, they alter conditions globally. In the introductory comments to this chapter, we noted that two situations where such global effects occur are depletion of the ozone layer and global warming. Because the beneficiaries of any actions to address these situations are spread so widely, no single country sees a strong incentive to take action individually. There typically will be inadequate protection of global common property resources in the absence of multilateral agreement. The disincentive to take action results in the tragedy of the commons, as summarized by the following example from Garret Hardin.[7]

While we expect privately owned property to be maintained and preserved because it is in the interests of the owner to do so, commonly owned property will be badly overused because no individual has an incentive to protect it. If, for example, 1,000 people are grazing excessive numbers of sheep on land that is commonly owned, a single farmer has no incentive to reduce the number of animals he puts on the land. All of the sheep owners may understand that the land is being badly overgrazed, but if any single farmer reduces the number of his sheep, nothing will be accomplished because 999 farmers are still overgrazing. As a result, nobody acts to protect the commonly owned grazing land, which may ultimately be ruined.

The oceans and the air mass can be viewed as an international commons to which the same problems apply. It is widely understood that the oceans have been overfished for decades and that the stock of fish is now badly depleted. A sharp reduction in fishing activity, which would allow the fish population to recover, would ultimately produce more fish for everyone, but no single country has an incentive to reduce its fishing activity unless it is confident that all other countries will do so. Since such confidence is lacking, the stock of fish continues to be depleted.

In spite of the incentive for each country to refuse to conserve itself, and to free-ride on the actions of those who do choose to conserve, international agreements have been successfully reached in some cases. Sandler identifies several key factors that contributed to the success of the Montreal Protocol of 1987 to phase out the use of chlorofluorocarbons (CFCs).[8] First, the United States was both the leading consumer and producer of CFCs. Although few countries followed US action in 1978 to ban CFCs as aerosol propellants, scientific study and monitoring proceeded. As evidence accumulated on the thinning of the ozone layer at the poles and its spread to the whole world, countries had less reason to question the scientific rationale for taking action against CFCs. Also, the US Environmental Protection Agency calculated that the benefits from reduced cancer risks were large. Therefore, the United States was prepared to act unilaterally. Within the United States, production was entirely accounted for by five large, diversified firms who were not highly reliant on CFC sales. The fortuitous development of effective substitutes for CFCs further reduced domestic opposition. That situation reduced the costs of immediate action and also made it easier to reach an agreement multilaterally with the other major producers. Japan, the USSR and the United States accounted for 46 percent of world production in 1986, and over three-fourths of production occurred in just 12 countries. Thus, free riding by non-participants was less of an issue as well. Subsequent tightening of the protocol through amendments adopted in London in 1990 and again in Copenhagen in 1992 sped up the agreed-upon reduction in production of CFCs and also extended it to other ozone-depleting chemicals. Several countries were granted 10-year exemptions in the original protocol due to their low initial levels of production; eventually greater attention will have to be directed at achieving reductions in their emissions and providing financial assistance to promote that outcome. Nevertheless, the agreement has functioned remarkably well thus far.

In the case of global warming, progress has been more difficult, because no single country can claim that the local gains from unilateral action to reduce its own greenhouse gas emissions will exceed the costs. The EU has taken a leadership role in advocating that action be taken to curb emissions of greenhouse gases under the precautionary principle: although all the scientific relationships that explain global warming still are not as clearly understood as in the case of ozone depletion, to fail to take action now would be imprudent and likely cause even higher costs of environmental clean-up or adaptation in the future. The greatest benefits globally from avoiding further warming will be felt by countries that are more dependent on agriculture, forestry, and economic activity in coastal plains. Small countries with only a single climate zone are particularly vulnerable, as are islands with little elevation above sea level. Some countries such as Canada and Russia may gain from global warming that unlocks frozen northlands and opens new navigation routes.

Because greenhouse gases result from so many different types of activity that are spread over a far greater number of countries, adjustment would not be limited to one small sector of the economy. A more fundamental problem is that requiring reductions in greenhouse gas emissions, and a consequent sacrifice in GDP, is resisted by developing countries. They regard the build-up of greenhouse gases in the atmosphere as the responsibility of developed countries that accounted for much of that accumulation through their industrialization and progressively higher energy usage over the past two centuries. Denying developing countries their opportunity to industrialize on the grounds of modern environmental aware-ness and eco-imperialism is rejected as the basis of an agreement that will lead to an unjust distribution of benefits and costs.

The opportunity for developing countries to free-ride on the clean-up efforts of the indus-trialized countries might be regarded as a major source of assistance from the industrialized countries to developing countries, particularly if measured relative to the small amount of official aid provided. Such behavior may not be an optimal transfer if reductions in CO_2 emissions can be achieved in less costly ways, however. The agreement allows developed countries to meet a portion of their commitment to reduce emissions by jointly implement-ing projects with former communist transition economies and by carrying out clean development projects in developing countries. Many worry that this flexibility may allow some countries to avoid action at home, and therefore the agreement specifies that these mechanisms supplement domestic action, which must be a significant element of their effort.

The Kyoto Protocol to the Climate Change Convention agreed to in December 1997 called for industrialized countries to reduce greenhouse gas emissions from their 1990 levels by the year 2012. Reductions were to be 8 percent in Europe, 7 percent in the United States, and 6 percent in Japan and Canada, while Russia was to stabilize its emissions. No targets were set for developing countries. In December 2002 Canada became the 100th country to ratify the Kyoto Protocol. The expected ratification by Russia in 2003 will satisfy the remaining trigger condition (that developed countries representing at least 55 percent of the group's carbon dioxide emissions in 1990 must join the agreement) for it to enter into force. The United States, which accounts for 36 percent of the group's emissions, has stated it will not join the accord and neither will Australia.[9]

Taxation in an open economy

In previous chapters, we have noted the role of tariffs and export taxes, both as important sources of government revenue in many developing countries and as distortions to international trade. As a country becomes more developed, taxes imposed on sales of goods, income, and property typically become more important. Here we consider the effects of such taxes when goods are traded internationally and factors of production can move across borders. How do these taxes affect the location of economic activity, and to what extent do they cause distortions in the world economy?

We begin with an overview of how revenue is raised by industrialized countries. Table 11.1 shows the relative importance of different tax sources to OECD member countries in 1995. Note some major distinctions between the United States and members of the European Union: (1) EU members raise revenue to finance a larger public sector; (2) EU members rely upon **indirect taxes**, that is taxes on goods rather than income, to a greater extent than the United States, which is accounted for by their reliance on value-added tax collections; (3) although direct taxes on income account for a larger share of public sector revenue in the United States than in Europe, as a share of GDP US reliance on these taxes is comparable to the EU figure. Compared to figures 30 years earlier in both the US and the EU, the public sector has grown, with the biggest increase accounted for by social security contributions and a more modest increases in personal income taxes. We rely upon these stylized facts in discussing tax policy of each group.

Table 11.1 Tax revenue as a percentage of GDP, 2000

	Income and profits	Social security	Payroll	Property	Goods and services	Other	Total
Canada	17.5	5.1	0.7	3.5	8.7	0.2	35.8
United States	15.1	6.9	—	3.0	4.7	—	29.6
Australia	18.0	—	2.0	2.8	8.7	—	31.5
Japan	9.2	9.9	—	2.8	5.1	0.1	27.1
France .	11.3	16.4	1.1	3.1	11.7	1.7	45.3
Germany	11.4	14.8	—	0.9	10.6	0	37.9
Italy	13.9	11.9	—	1.8	11.9	2.2	42.0
Netherlands	10.4	16.1	—	2.2	12.0	0.3	41.4
Spain	9.8	12.4	—	2.3	10.5	0.1	35.2
Sweden	23.4	15.2	2.3	1.9	11.2	0	54.2
United Kingdom	14.6	6.1	—	4.4	12.1	0	37.4
OECD Total	13.6	9.5	0.4	1.9	11.6	0.4	37.4
EU 15	14.9	11.4	0.4	2.0	12.3	0.3	41.6

Source: OECD, *Revenue Statistics of OECD Member Countries*, 2002, Table 6.

Taxes on goods

The two most common forms of taxing goods are a retail sales tax and a value-added tax (VAT). Although their economic effects are essentially the same, the VAT is by far the more popular. All European countries and all Latin American countries impose a VAT. Therefore, we briefly review the mechanics of value-added taxation.

Suppose an auto producer buys intermediate inputs worth $8,000 from suppliers, hires labor and pays capital owners $5,000 in the assembly of the auto, and sells the auto for $13,000. Value-added is $5,000 and a 20 percent value-added tax rate would result in the payment of $1,000 in tax. Most countries do not rely on each firm to determine its value-added and then pay the corresponding tax due on it. Rather, they administer the VAT by imposing it on the total value of the firm's sales but allow a credit to be claimed for VAT paid by suppliers. For example, suppliers of intermediate inputs pay a VAT of $1,600 on their sales to the auto assembler, whose intermediate inputs now have an invoiced cost of $9,600. In turn, the auto assembler collects a VAT of $2,600 from the sale of an auto. The auto assembler can claim a credit for the $1,600 paid by input suppliers, and therefore the auto assembler's net payment is $1,000, the same as above. However, to claim this credit, the assembler must present an invoice demonstrating that the supplier has in fact paid the VAT. Therefore, the system provides a major advantage in terms of tax administration by deterring tax avoidance.

If the auto is exported, the assembler can claim a rebate for the $1,600 VAT paid by suppliers, and no VAT is charged on the export sale. Conversely, if a $13,000 auto is imported, the value-added tax of $2,600 is imposed. That procedure, which applies the **destination principle**, ensures that goods sold in the taxing country are subject to the same tax burden, whether they are imported or produced domestically. While the exported good is free of tax where it is produced, it will be subject to the same taxes that are imposed on goods in the country that consumes it.

Although US businessmen have often regarded this border tax adjustment mandated by the GATT for indirect taxes as creating an unfair advantage for European producers, US adoption of a VAT by itself would not improve US competitiveness. The tax would be paid by US firms on sales in the United States, just as it would be imposed on imports into the United States; this would not create some competitive disadvantage for foreign goods because domestic goods suffer from the same tax. Although exports do not have the burden of the VAT imposed on them, neither do competing goods produced in other countries, and no gain in competitiveness occurs here, either.

If the United States were to adopt a VAT and use the revenue raised to reduce its corporate income tax rate, that would create an incentive to locate more activity in the United States. Although the VAT has a neutral effect, the corporate income tax creates a distortion in the choice where to locate production, and reducing that tax reduces the disincentive to locate in the United States.[10] We return to that topic in a few pages.

Within Europe, the VAT system was a particular improvement over prior systems of taxation that imposed a tax on transactions each time a good changed hands. Rather than allow credits to be claimed for taxes paid at an earlier stage of production, the system resulted in the tax burden compounding the more times a good changed hands. Applying the VAT based on the destination principle led to much less distortion of trade within Europe. A further change in the application of the VAT may result from the move toward a single market, where no further border checks occur once goods enter the EU market. In 1987 the European Commission proposed that for trade among members the VAT be levied based on the **origin principle**. In that case, the VAT would be imposed in the producing country. For sales elsewhere within Europe the home tax would not be rebated, nor would a VAT be imposed by the consuming country.

Under the origin principle, what are the competitive implications of differences in the tax rates across countries? If the standard VAT rate is 15 percent in Germany and Spain but 25 percent in Denmark and Sweden, then rents and other factor returns must decline enough in Denmark and Sweden to offset the disadvantage of a higher tax rate. As we will find in Part Two of this book, that same adjustment in relative prices could occur through a fall in the value of their currency relative to other member countries; the establishment of a single currency in Europe, however, rules that out as an avenue of adjustment to future tax changes. In the absence of such relative price adjustments, countries with higher VAT rates will suffer a fall in output and employment, and as a consequence there will be some pressure for countries to harmonize their tax rates. Nevertheless, in the United States retail sales tax rates of individual states vary from zero to 7 percent, a possible indication that the sensitivity of cross-border shoppers to different rates may not force explicit harmonization around some lower rate.

Aside from this question of relative prices, total tax revenue collected may be different under the origin principle and the destination principle. A country that exports more goods to EU partners than it imports from them will collect more revenue under the origin principle, whereas a country that imports more goods from EU partners than it exports will collect less revenue. For example, in 1995 Greece, Portugal, and Spain were net importers from their EU partners, whereas France, Germany, and the Netherlands, among others, were net exporters.

The decision to set a lower tax rate may result in greater exports, fewer imports, and an inflow of cross-border shoppers. How are tax collections affected? Figure 11.3 shows the initial situation with respect to a country's sales to foreigners when it imposes the higher tax rate t_2. When the country reduces that tax rate to t_1, then the value of sales to foreigners rises if their demand is elastic. Diagrammatically, areas $b + c$ exceed area a. Area a represents a loss in the country's terms of trade, because it now sells to others at a lower price. The government collects area b in revenue from its expansion in sales to foreigners. Area c represents the opportunity cost of resources used in producing those goods. If demand is sufficiently elastic, area b will exceed area a, tax revenue will rise, and the loss in the country's terms of trade will be offset by its opportunity to charge more foreigners a price that exceeds the cost of producing the good.

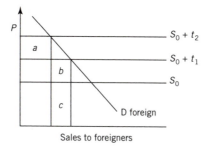

Sales to foreigners

Figure 11.3 Tax collections and the terms of trade. A reduction in country's tax rate from t_2 to t_1 means that foreign purchases benefit from a lower price. If enough additional foreign demand results at the lower price, then area b, the tax revenue collected on those additional sales, will exceed the tax revenue lost from the reduced tax rate, area a.

Taxes on factor income

In the post-World War II period when the GATT was founded, most public finance economists viewed taxes on incomes to be taxes that would not be shifted. A uniform tax on labor
income, for example, simply results in lower after-tax income for workers, but does not affect
the supply of labor or the pattern of production in the economy. Similarly, when capital is
immobile internationally and savings do not respond to changes in interest rates (so the
capital stock is fixed), a tax on all capital income simply results in lower after-tax income
for capitalists. Because the before-tax returns to labor or capital are unchanged, no change
in relative prices occurs as a result of variation in the income tax rate and no change in the
international competitiveness of a country's producers occurs. Therefore, applying the origin
principle to these direct taxes would not create an initial incentive to buy more goods from
the low-tax country, as we discussed above when the origin principle was applied to indirect
taxes.

More recently, economists have looked at the way factor suppliers respond to changes in
returns. When higher taxes cause workers to leave the work force, then costs of production
rise. Taxes cause the cost of domestic output to rise relative to imported goods, and therefore,
we no longer observe the neutral effect achieved when the destination principle was applied
to indirect taxes.

A more significant adjustment to taxes than changing labor-force participation has been
labor migration, especially by highly skilled workers. A higher tax in Country A results in a
loss of skilled workers in Country A. Their wages rise and the cost of producing skill-
intensive products rises. The less ability the country has to affect the prices of goods traded
internationally, the greater the reduction in its output of these goods. If the country produces
goods that have few substitutes internationally, it may benefit from an increase in the price
of its exports. Such an improvement in its terms of trade results in the exportation of some
of its tax burden to foreigners. Again, terms-of-trade gains transfer income from one country
to another, but the world as a whole ends up with a less efficient allocation of resources.

We expect the pattern of production and world efficiency to be affected as long as the
individuals who migrate can escape the higher tax in their home country; the difference in
tax rates can affect the pattern of production and world efficiency. Only if Country A
workers were taxed on their income wherever in the world they earned it (a standard referred
to as the **residence principle** of taxation) would the efficiency loss from divergent tax rates
be avoided. Even then we must assume individuals cannot change their country of residence
and become citizens elsewhere.

A country that has a progressive income tax system that imposes a higher tax rate on those
with higher incomes is more likely to lose skilled workers who earn high incomes. Of course,
some tax revenue may be used in ways that confer more benefits on high-income individuals;
subsidizing a state opera company or providing free university tuition might represent
expenditures whose benefits primarily accrue to high-income families, if they are more likely
to attend the opera or to adequately prepare their children to pass college entrance exams.
The greater the reliance on public revenues to redistribute income within the economy, the
less likely high-income individuals are to regard income taxes as benefit taxes. High taxes
on labor income in Scandinavian countries, for example, gives skilled workers an incentive
to seek jobs in Britain.

Portfolio capital

Many economists regard capital as more mobile internationally than labor. In the case of portfolio capital flows, where no monopoly profits from special expertise are expected, economists have suggested that tax competition to attract more capital to a host country may drive a country's optimal tax rate to zero.[11] Again, if tax revenues are not used in a way that creates benefits to capital owners, a country that levies a higher tax on capital than its competitors will experience a capital outflow. The outflow continues until the before-tax return to capital is high enough to yield the same after-tax return available elsewhere in the world. The higher before-tax payment to capital comes at the expense of labor and land that cannot relocate to another country and are left bearing the burden of the tax imposed on capital. If the country imposing the tax were to recognize that the same distributional effect would result from taxing labor and land directly, then it could avoid the capital outflow and loss of production that follows from taxing highly mobile capital. In fact, many countries impose low tax rates on inflows of portfolio capital. An inflow of capital that results in payments of interest income to foreign lenders, for example, typically is subject to low withholding tax rates, and many countries such as the United States, France, Germany, and the United Kingdom, impose no tax at all.

Figure 11.4 shows the effect of a tax levied by a country too small to affect the rate of return internationally. Therefore, the supply of capital to it from the rest of the world is horizontal at the world rate of return, r_w. Imposing a tax on all capital used in Country A, both the portion raised from domestic saving and the portion that flows in from abroad shifts both of those supply curves upward. (This practice applies the **source principle** of taxation to income earned in the country, regardless of the country of residence of the recipient.) One result of the tax is a smaller capital stock in Country A, K_1 rather than K_0. Note that the domestically provided capital, K_d, has remained unchanged, while all the loss in the capital stock is accounted for by a smaller inflow from the rest of the world.

Again, we can use this diagram to demonstrate distributional effects of the tax on capital used in the country. The demand curve for capital is based upon the extra output produced by an additional unit of capital. The output of the economy for the capital stock of K_0 is given by the area under the demand curve, r^*aK_0O. Total payments to capital are

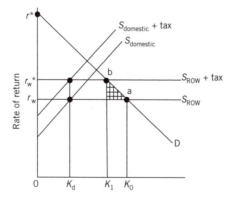

Figure 11.4 A tax on capital in a small country. A tax on capital in Country A results in a decline in its capital stock from K_0 to K_1, which causes the return on capital to rise by the amount of tax. The return to immobile land and labor falls by the amount of the tax revenue collected and also by the loss in efficiency given by the shaded triangle.

represented by the rectangle given by r_w times K_0. The portion left over for the immobile factors of production, labor and land, is the triangle given by r^*ar_w. Now note what happens to this area when the tax is levied. Because the before-tax return to capital rises, the triangle representing the return to labor and land declines to $r^*br_w^*$. The burden of the tax on capital has been shifted entirely to the immobile factors of production.[12] In fact, the loss to labor and land is greater than the gain to the government due to the loss of the shaded triangle in Figure 11.4. The less efficient allocation of resources leaves less capital to work with labor and land. For a country that is too small to affect prices of goods or returns to mobile capital internationally, taxing portfolio capital reduces national income and is less desirable than taxing land and labor directly.

Foreign direct investment

The assumption of a horizontal supply of capital relevant for analyzing portfolio capital flows into a small country is less relevant for foreign direct investment. If the MNC investing abroad is motivated primarily by the opportunity to serve a host-country market, then the host country is less likely to be forced by tax competition to offer a zero tax rate to attract investment. Those who buy what the MNC produces must pay a higher price to cover the MNC's higher cost of capital. But, if the MNC is making monopoly profits, then the host country can gain some share of those profits. The MNC will reduce output by less than a competitive firm would, because it does not want to lose as many customers who will still be paying it a price greater than the marginal cost of production.

As more MNC investment becomes geared to production for export markets, a higher host-country tax that raises the cost of capital to the firm is more likely to deter investment in the country. The MNC will consider alternative locations that let it serve the same market without being subject to a high tax. Countries relying upon MNC investment to promote an export-led growth strategy will find that low-tax rates are an important part of the policy mix it pursues. Indeed, some economists have found that host-country tax rates have significant effects on the location of real investment and production, especially so when a country pursues an open trade policy.[13]

Because a substantial share of MNC activity is not so footloose, countries have not been driven to repeal their corporate income taxes. The first, second, and third columns of Table 11.2 show the statutory tax rates that various countries levy on manufacturing activity, where the 2 years shown bracket a major US tax reduction in 1986. Not all countries followed the US cut, although some effects of tax competition can be seen. The effects are more pronounced in the fourth and fifth columns, which show the average effective tax rate paid by the affiliates of US MNCs. The average across all foreign locations fell from 40 percent to 27 percent. The more substantial reductions may be due to special tax rates applied in export processing zones or to other provisions, such as investment tax credits, that allow firms to pay less than the statutory rate would suggest. A lower effective rate may apply to new investment, while countries do not want to reduce the statutory tax rate applied to income from existing operations.

Several EU members have advocated the harmonization of corporate tax rates to avoid a competitive race downward to ever lower levels of social spending. Has the ability to tax corporate income eroded? Although tax rates have fallen, countries also broadened the base of income to be taxed. For this, or possibly other reasons, there does not appear to be a commensurate decline in revenue collected. Figures in Table 11.3, which show corporate tax revenues as a share of GDP, suggest that any declaration of the demise of the corporate

Table 11.2 Corporate income tax rates on US manufacturing affiliates

	Statutory tax rate		Effective tax rate	
	1984	1992	1984	1992
Canada	0.44	0.39	0.37	0.35
Mexico	0.42	0.35	0.36	0.28
Costa Rica	0.50	0.30	0.42	0.12
Brazil	0.39	0.35	0.31	0.13
Chile	0.37	0.15	0.38	0.10
France	0.50	0.34	0.44	0.23
Ireland	0.10	0.10	0.03	0.06
Italy	0.47	0.48	0.37	0.33
United Kingdom	0.52	0.33	0.32	0.19
Germany	0.61	0.59	0.50	0.29
Sweden	0.52	0.30	0.57	0.17
Switzerland	0.16	0.17	0.21	0.14
India	0.58	0.52	0.58	0.44
Indonesia	0.35	0.35	0.37	0.35
Malaysia	0.50	0.35	0.17	0.08
Singapore	0.15	0.10	0.08	0.06
China	0.50	0.33	0.16	0.06
Hong Kong	0.17	0.17	0.20	0.10
Japan	0.63	0.57	0.53	0.50
Australia	0.50	0.39	0.41	0.32

Source: Harry Grubert, "Taxes and the Division of Foreign Operating Income among Royalties, Interest, Dividends, and Retained Earning," *Journal of Public Economics* 68 (12), May 1998.

Table 11.3 Taxes on corporate income as a percentage of GDP, 1965–2000

Country	1965	1970	1975	1980	1985	1990	1995	2000
Australia	3.6	3.8	3.3	3.3	2.7	4.1	4.4	6.5
Canada	3.8	3.5	4.3	3.6	2.7	2.5	2.9	4.0
France	1.8	2.1	1.9	2.1	1.9	2.3	2.1	3.2
Germany	2.5	1.8	1.6	2.0	2.3	1.7	1.1	1.8
Ireland	2.3	2.5	1.4	1.4	1.1	1.7	2.8	3.8
Italy	1.8	1.7	1.6	2.4	3.2	3.9	3.6	3.2
Japan	4.1	5.2	4.4	5.5	5.7	6.5	4.2	3.6
Luxembourg	3.1	5.2	5.8	6.6	7.9	6.4	7.4	7.4
Netherlands	2.6	2.4	3.2	2.9	3.0	3.2	3.1	4.2
Sweden	2.1	1.7	1.8	1.2	1.7	1.7	2.9	4.1
Switzerland	1.4	1.7	2.2	1.7	1.8	2.1	1.9	2.8
United Kingdom	1.3	3.2	2.2	2.9	4.7	4.1	3.3	3.7
United States	4.0	3.7	3.1	2.9	2.0	2.1	2.6	2.5
Weighted average	3.3	3.3	2.9	3.1	3.0	3.2	2.8	2.9
All OECD average	2.2	2.4	2.2	2.4	2.7	2.7	2.9	3.6
EU 15	1.9	2.1	2.1	2.1	2.6	2.6	2.7	3.8

Source: OECD, *Revenue Statistics of OECD Member Countries* (Paris: OECD, 2002) Table 12.

income tax as a source of revenue is premature. Although the figure for any given year is influenced by a country's position in the business cycle, due to the pro-cyclical movement of corporate profits, the weighted average figure for the OECD countries shown has remained fairly stable over time and the unweighted average reported by the OECD has even risen. Countries appear to have the ability to tax capital income, in spite of the potential for their own domestic producers or foreign-controlled companies to shift income to low-tax countries or to relocate production abroad.

A further point to note from Table 11.3 is that US reliance on corporate income taxes does not differ much from the average for all OECD countries; if anything, it appears less than for Japan or its European trading partners. Thus, any shift toward a system of rebating corporate income taxes paid in the case of exported goods and applying those taxes to imports (the destination principle applied to direct taxes on income) would not appear to offer any competitive advantage to the United States. Not only would such a system be difficult to administer, but for many key trading partners, current corporate income taxes appear to place their producers at a disadvantage relative to US producers.

Box 11.2 Wealth of the Irish

St Patrick's Day brings back nostalgic and romanticized stereotypes of Ireland – poor but saintly farm families, often forced to emigrate to find work, ever contending with a rich and resented ex-colonial power that insists on maintaining control of the only prosperous part of the island – the six counties of Ulster.

Now for the reality. The Republic of Ireland has enjoyed almost two decades of rapid economic growth and now has a real GNP per capita that is tied with that of the United Kingdom. If recent trends continue, incomes in Ireland will soon be far higher than in Britain.

A variety of social welfare indicators in the Republic are now as good or better than in Britain. The two countries have the same infant mortality rate, which is lower than in the United States. Life expectancy is about the same. Ireland spends a higher percentage of its GDP on public education than does the Untied Kingdom and has a higher percentage of its teenagers enrolled in secondary schools. Six out of 10 citizens of the Republic live not on farms or even in villages or towns but in urban areas. Ireland's fertility rate has plummeted and is now below that required for a stable population. Emigration has been replaced by immigration as thousands of new residents arrive in the country each year seeking better jobs.

How was all of this accomplished in less than 20 years? Through a combination of pre-existing strengths and sound economic policies, Irish entry into the European Union in the mid-1970s was critical, but it was also helped by the presence of a well-educated, English-speaking labor force. The European Union Common Agricultural Policy and regional grant programs provided money from Brussels, and tough controls on government costs were used to move the budget from deficit to sizable surpluses. Most important, low-corporate tax rates were aggressively used to attract foreign investors, who were also drawn by the labor force, a relatively central location and free access to markets in Europe.

The corporate profits tax rate for foreign financial or manufacturing firms in the Republic is only 12.5 percent. Personal income tax rates have also been cut, the top rate being 42 percent, which is below that faced by Americans in states with high local tax rates, and far lower than in most European countries. Ireland has made itself a magnet for foreign capital and highly productive individuals.

The six counties of Ireland that make up Ulster, in contrast, now constitute one of the poorest regions of the United Kingdom, which means that area is far poorer than the Republic. Output per person in Ulster is 20 percent below that of the Republic.

Ireland now has no economic interest in Ulster's being transferred to its control. To the contrary, it would be a disaster for the Republic, where the core of a successful development strategy has been low taxes. If 3.7 million citizens of Ireland had to pay welfare and police costs for 1.6 million poor and frequently violent people in Ulster, a large tax increase would be needed. Why would the people of Ireland accept such an increase, which would reverse the growth strategy that has succeeded so brilliantly?

Besides, there are serious problems facing Dublin, most of which will cost money. First, the economic growth of the past two decades has overstretched the transportation system and other elements of the country's infrastructure. The government just announced a $2.2 billion project to build a new railroad to connect Dublin with the airport and a number of suburbs. More such projects will be needed.

Second, when Ireland was one of the poorer countries in the EU, it received sizable payments from Brussels. Now that it is more prosperous, those payments will disappear and Dublin gets to send money to Brussels. When Eastern European countries, all of which are poor, enter the EU, Ireland will no longer be a priority for regional development funds. If the EU Common Agricultural Policy is reformed, as is widely discussed, that will cost Ireland more money.

Finally as is usually the case when an economy grows rapidly, benefits go disproportionately to the young, the highly educated and the energetic, most of whom live in cities. Those lacking some or all of these characteristics, particularly if they live in rural areas, have received fewer benefits from the Irish boom, leaving questions as to how the gains from growth might be spread more widely.

But these are all problems of success, which certainly is an improvement over the circumstances faced by Ireland a mere two decades ago.

Source: *Washington Post*, Robert M. Dunn, Jr., @2002, Op-ed page, March 16, 2002. Reprinted with permission.

Summary of key concepts

1   If production creates a negative externality such as pollution, government regulations to reduce pollution will raise the cost of the good produced. If other countries impose less stringent pollution control standards, production of pollution-intensive goods may shift to those countries. That factor does not appear to explain much US investment in Mexico, however.

2   When pollution crosses international borders, the affected countries must negotiate how much to reduce pollution and how to allocate the costs of clean-up. Because there is no internationally recognized right to clean air or clean water, the principle of polluter pays may not always be followed.

3   WTO rulings have limited the ability of nations to act unilaterally in imposing trade sanctions if foreign goods are not produced in a way that the country regards as environmentally acceptable.

4   A multilateral agreement to protect the ozone layer was easier to achieve than one to deal with global warming. Developing countries contend that industrialized countries have the responsibility to solve the global warming problem because they have caused most of the accumulation of greenhouse gasses.

5   European countries raise more of their government revenues from indirect taxes on goods than the United States does. When goods cross national borders, the WTO calls for a border tax adjustment for indirect taxes on the basis of the destination principle: indirect taxes are rebated on exports and imposed on imports.

6   A general tax on labor income does not affect the international competitiveness of a country's goods if the labor force remains constant. If income taxes cause less work effort or labor migration, output in the taxing nation will fall. For a large country the price of its exports will rise.

7   A tax on portfolio capital will raise a country's cost of capital. For a small country, the after-tax return remains constant and the burden of the tax is shifted to less mobile factors of production such as labor and land. Economic efficiency falls.

8   Foreign direct investment by MNCs to produce for export markets is much more sensitive to taxation than is production for domestic markets.

Questions for study and review

1   Are there economic reasons for a country to reject a policy of eliminating all pollution? If a country does nothing to eliminate pollution, why does that usually result in a loss in economic efficiency? Is there a correct level of pollution to allow?

2   As a country's GDP rises, how do you expect that to affect the country's air quality? As a country's GDP rises, what offsetting factors exist regarding the benefits from lower concentrations of SO_2 in the air and the costs of reducing those concentrations?

3   If two countries adopt different pollution control standards, under what circumstances will this have little influence on the location of production internationally?

4   "Transborder pollution should be solved by making the polluter clean it up." Discuss the advantages and disadvantages of a country insisting upon this policy approach.

5   If Europe were to act unilaterally in imposing a carbon tax to reduce emissions of CO_2, how successful would that strategy be in preventing global warming? In what sense is the earth's atmosphere a common property resource?

6   Why does making border tax adjustments according to the destination principle avoid giving a competitive advantage to countries that impose high value-added taxes?

7   Countries are to follow the origin principle regarding border tax adjustments for corporate income taxes paid. How does this principle affect the competitiveness of the goods that country produces compared to a situation where the destination principle is applied?

8   If all European countries agree to levy an identical tax on the income earned by foreign capital, what are the consequences of the policy likely to be?

9   Why has competition among countries over the taxation of corporate income increased in the past 20 years? Which countries are less likely to engage in competitive tax reductions?

Suggested further reading

In addition to the studies cited in the text, for further treatment of international environmental externalities, see:

- Pearce, David and Jeremy Warford, *World without End: Economics, Environment and Sustainable Development*, New York: Oxford, 1993.

For a broad discussion of issues in international taxation, see:

- Tanzi, Vito, *Taxation in an Integrating World*, Washington, DC: Brookings, 1995.

Notes

1   Gene Grossman and Alan Krueger, "Environmental Impacts of a North American Free Trade Agreement," in Peter M. Garber, ed., *The Mexico–US Free Trade Agreement* (Cambridge, MA: MIT Press, 199), pp. 13–56. Gene Grossman and Alan Kruger, "Economic Growth and the Environment," *Quarterly Journal of Economics* 110, no. 2, pp. 353–77. For more recent estimates, see S. Dasgupta, B. Laplante, H. Wang and D. Wheeler, "Confronting the Environmental Kuznets curve," *Journal of Economic Perspectives*, Winter 2002, pp. 147–68.

2   See the Associated Press, "Global Treaty Bars Toxic Waste Dumping in the 3rd World," September 22, 1995, and the United Nations Environmental Programme's site that describes the convention and tracks its ratification, http://www.basel.int/pub/basics.html (January 19, 2003).

3   R. Coase, "The Problem of Social Cost," *Journal of Law and Economics*, 1961, pp. 1–44.

4   Todd Sandler, *Global Challenges: An Approach to Environmental, Political and Economic Problems* (Cambridge: Cambridge University Press, 1997) for an overview of this situation.

5   World Bank, *World Development Report 1992: Development and the Environment* (New York: Oxford University Press, 1992) p. 155.

6   Hilary French, *Costly Tradeoffs: Reconciling Trade and the Environment* (Washington DC: Worldwatch Institute, 1993).

7   Garrett Hardin, "The Tragedy of the Commons," *Science*, December 1968.

8   Sandler, 1997, op.cit.

9   For an accessible discussion of the potential costs of global warming, the costs of reducing greenhouse gas emissions, and various tax policy implications, see the papers in the *Journal of Economic Perspectives* 1993 symposium on global climate change. For more complete information on the UN Framework Convention on Climate Change and its Kyoto Protocol, see the guide released by the Climate Change Secretariat in 2002, as well as updates from http://unfccc.int.

10   The effect on the US capital stock is clear when all investment is financed by equity; it is more ambiguous in reality, because the incentive to increase equity-financed investment may be offset by less debt-financed investment. For a related discussion of the effect of various consumption tax proposals as an alternative to the current income tax, see Harry Grubert and Scott Newlon, "The International Implications of Consumption Tax Proposals," *National Tax Journal* 48, no. 4, December 1995, pp. 619–47.

11   R.H. Gordon, "Taxation of Investment and Savings in a World Economy," *American Economic Review* 76, no. 5, December 1986, pp. 1086–102.

12   In a model with more than one sector, economists have noted how the burden shifted to labor may be even greater than the tax revenue collected. See A. Harberger, "Corporate Tax Incidence in Closed and Open Economies," Paper presented to NBER Summer Institute in Taxation, 1983, and

John Mutti and Harry Grubert, "The Taxation of Capital Income in an Open Economy: The Importance of Resident-Nonresident Tax Treatment," *Journal of Public Economics*, 1995, pp. 291–309.

13 See Harry Grubert and John Mutti, "Taxes, Tariffs and Transfer Pricing in Multinational Corporate Decision Making," *The Review of Economics and Statistics*, LXXIII, 1991, pp. 285–93, James Hines and Eric Rice, "Fiscal Paradise: Foreign Tax Havens and American Business," *Quarterly Journal of Economics* 109, no. 1, 1994, and John Mutti and Harry Grubert, "Empirical Asymmetries in Foreign Direct Investment and Taxation," *Journal of International Economics*, 2003, for studies that suggest a decline in the country's tax rate that reduces the cost of capital by 1 percent can increase the MNC affiliates stock of capital in the country by 2 to 3 percent. This outcome appears to depend upon the country pursuing an open trade policy.

Part Two

International finance and open economy macroeconomics

The first half of this book dealt overwhelmingly with aspects of the international economy which were "real" and was microeconomic in nature. Monetary or financial issues, or macroeconomics, seldom intruded. Now this all changes. The second half of the book, which you are about to begin, covers the macroeconomic part of international economics and deals extensively with monetary and financial concerns.

This half of the book deals primarily with two related issues: the balance of payments position of a country, in terms of how it is determined and how it can be improved when it performs badly; and macroeconomics in an economy which is open to both trade and financial transactions with the rest of the world under alternative exchange rate regimes, namely a fixed parity or a floating rate. A chapter at the end of the book deals with the history of international monetary relations and with current policy problems, such as the Asian debt crisis of 1997–9, and the more recent crisis in Argentina.

Chapter 12 deals with balance-of-payments accounting. These accounts play the same role in international finance as national income accounts play in domestic macroeconomics. They must be understood before the following theory can make sense. This chapter includes a discussion of how a country's balance-of-payments accounts might be expected to perform as it went through the development process; that is, as it moved from being an under-developed country to being prosperous and industrialized.

Chapter 13 deals with markets in which foreign exchange is bought and sold. A considerable emphasis is placed on the parallel relationship between a disequilibrium in the payments accounts, as discussed in the previous chapter, and the mirror-image disequilibrium in the exchange market. The role of central bank intervention in the exchange market is discussed under alternative legal arrangements. The institutional arrangements through which foreign exchange is traded are discussed, along with nominal and real effective exchange rates, later in the chapter.

Chapter 14 introduces international derivatives, with a particular emphasis on forward exchange markets, that is, on contractual arrangements in which firms buy or sell foreign exchange today at an agreed-upon price, with payment and delivery at a fixed date in the future. These contracts are very important as a way to cover or hedge exchange rate risks arising from export/import business and international capital flows, and can also be used for speculative purposes, that is, to take on risk rather than avoid it. This chapter also includes a brief discussion of foreign exchange futures contracts and a somewhat more lengthy coverage of foreign exchange options, that is, puts and calls for foreign currencies.

Chapter 15 returns to the balance of payments by discussing alternative models of how it is determined, that is, why countries often move from payments equilibrium to serious and unsustainable deficit, or why payments results improve through time. It is noted in this chapter that the same forces that cause a country to go into payments deficit if it maintains a fixed exchange rate would cause its currency to depreciate if it had a floating exchange rate. There is no single view as to what drives the balance of payments or the exchange rate, and alternative models are presented.

Chapter 16 presents alternative routes for the adjustment, or improvement, of a serious balance-of-payments disequilibrium under the assumption that a change in the exchange rate is not to occur. The text of this chapter presents the alternative theories without the use of theoretical tools that would normally be learned in an intermediate macroeconomics course. Boxes in the chapter, however, teach the IS/LM/BP graph in some detail and then use this tool to illustrate how alternative adjustment mechanisms function. If teachers and students wish, these boxes can be avoided without the loss of critical concepts, but understanding of the theory will be much more complete if the effort is made to learn these graphs and use them in this and the following three chapters.

Chapter 17 is about balance-of-payments adjustment through changes in an otherwise fixed exchange rate; that is, it deals with devaluations as a means of eliminating an unsustainable payments deficit. Such devaluations frequently fail, in the sense that the payments deficit returns and subsequent devaluations become necessary. Some countries devalue the way some people quit smoking – sequentially. These failures are typically the result of poor fiscal and monetary policies, which leads to a discussion of the policies that the IMF encourages deficit countries to adopt to increase the likelihood that a devaluation will succeed and not have to be repeated.

Chapter 18 leaves balance-of-payments problems and adjustment, and turns to macroeconomics in an open economy, in this case under a fixed exchange rate. First, international trade is introduced into a simple Keynesian model of national income determination. The model works quite differently with this alteration. Then capital flows and macroeconomic policies are added, which complicates the model considerably. The effectiveness (or lack thereof) of both fiscal and monetary policy in a world of internationally integrated capital as well as goods markets is discussed at some length. This topic can be pursued in the main text without reference to the IS/LM/BP graphs, but reading the boxes which use these graphs will add significantly to a student's understanding of this theory. At the end of this chapter a graph developed by Trevor Swann is used to indicate why exchange rate adjustments often have to be accompanied by changes in domestic macroeconomic policies to reach a combination of payments equilibrium and an acceptable level of aggregate demand.

Chapter 19 covers the same topics as those in Chapter 18 under the assumption of a floating or flexible exchange rate, which is the actual arrangement for the United States, the United Kingdom, and Canada. The euro, the currency of the countries which are members of the European Monetary Union (EMU) also floats relative to most of the rest of the world. Again, it is possible to follow the theory in the regular text alone, but using the boxes where the IS/LM/BP graphs are employed will add considerably to a reader's level of understanding. This chapter also deals briefly with other aspects of floating exchange rates, such as their impact on trade volumes and the distinction between a "clean" or pure float and a managed or "dirty" float. The major industrialized countries typically maintain the latter arrangement.

The last chapter of the book (Chapter 20) deals both with the history of the international financial system, and with recent problems and crises. The failure of flexible exchange rates to perform as expected is covered, along with the failure of models based on economic or financial fundamentals to explain exchange rate behavior. The European Monetary Union, which began formal operation in January 1999, is discussed at some length. The discussion of EMU is followed by a more extensive coverage of developing debt crises. Virtually all of

Latin America was in crisis in the early 1980s, and Mexico encountered serious problems in 1994–5. The Asian debt crisis of 1997–9 was quite different from those of Latin America because institutional problems in financial markets played a far larger role in Asia than in Latin America. The IMF has had relatively little experience with circumstances such as those in the Asian crisis countries, and its response was something of a work in progress. Argentina's collapse of 2002, which threatens to spread to Brazil at the time of this writing, is also discussed. The chapter, and the book, then concludes with a prospective look at the next decade, by trying to suggest what the major issues and problems in international trade and finance are likely to be in the first decade or 15 years of this new century.

12 Balance-of-payments accounting

Learning objectives

By the end of this chapter you should be able to understand:

- the nature of the entries in a country's balance-of-payments accounts, and how whether each is a credit (+) or a debit (–) is determined;
- the analogy between a country's balance-of-payments accounts and a cash-flow statement that might be prepared for a family;
- the source of the "net errors and omissions" item in the accounts, and how it is calculated;
- the organization of the accounts for a country on a fixed exchange rate, and the meaning of a payments disequilibrium in that circumstance;
- why the existence of a floating or flexible exchange rate can affect the format of the accounts; how they are now organized for the United States;
- the linkage between a country's current account performance and the resulting changes in its international investment position;
- how the balance-of-payments behavior of a country might be expected to change as it moves through the development process;
- how the concept of intertemporal trade provides a new view of current account disequilibria.

The **balance-of-payments** accounts discussed in this chapter form the basic accounting system for all international commercial and financial transactions. Their relationship to international economics is analogous to that of national income accounts to domestic macroeconomics.

Balance-of-payments accounting is, to be candid, a less than fascinating topic, but it must be understood if the more interesting parts of international finance are to make any sense. Just as domestic macroeconomics would mean very little without an understanding of gross domestic product and related accounting concepts, international finance requires an understanding of the payments accounts. In addition, people who work in the area of international economics are usually assumed to understand balance-of-payments accounting, and they often spend significant amounts of time interpreting these accounts for countries in which their employers have an interest. Although these accounts are hardly fascinating, they are very important.

A nation's balance of payments is a summary statement of all economic transactions between residents of that nation and residents of the outside world which have taken place during a given period of time. Several aspects of this definition require further comment and emphasis. First, "resident" is interpreted to include individuals, business firms, and government agencies. Second, the balance of payments is supposed to include all economic transactions with the outside world, whether they involve merchandise, services, assets, financial claims, or gifts. Whenever a transaction is between a resident and a nonresident, it is to be included. Third, the balance of payments measures the volume of transactions that occur during a certain period of time, usually a year, or a quarter. Thus it measures flows, not stocks. In the case of transactions in assets, the balance of payments for a given year shows the changes that have occurred in, for example, domestic assets held abroad, but it does not show the stock of such assets.

The term "balance of payments" is itself a misnomer, because some of the transactions included do not involve any actual payment of money. For example, when an American firm ships a drill press to Canada for installation in its branch plant or subsidiary, no money payment will be made, but an economic transaction with the outside world has taken place and should be included in the balance of payments. Similarly, if the United States donates wheat to India, no payment will be made, but the shipment should be included in the balance of payments. Most transactions do involve a money payment, but whether or not a transaction involves payment, it is included in the balance of payments. A more appropriate name for this account might therefore be "statement of international economic transactions," but we will use the conventional name, which has the sanction of long-established usage.

A nation's balance of payments is of interest to economists and policy-makers because it provides much useful information about the nation's international economic position and its relationships with the rest of the world. In particular, the accounts may indicate whether the nation's external economic position is in a healthy state, or whether problems exist which may be signaling a need for corrective action of some kind. An examination of the balance of payments for a period of time should enable us to determine whether a nation is approximately in external balance, or whether it suffers from a disequilibrium in its balance of payments. Much of international monetary economics is concerned with diagnosis of deficits or surpluses in balance of payments for countries with fixed exchange rates, and especially with analysis of the mechanisms or processes through which such disequilibria may be corrected or removed.

Balance-of-payments accounts are not analogous to a balance sheet, because they represent flows of transactions during a year, whereas the balance sheet represents stocks of assets and liabilities at a moment of time, such as the close of business on 31 December. This might suggest that balance-of-payments accounts are somehow similar to a corporate profit-and-loss statement, but this is also a poor analogy. A sources-and-uses-of-funds account for a business, which can be found in some corporate annual reports, would be a closer fit because the balance-of-payments accounts show flows of payments in and out of a country during a given time period.

Distinguishing debits and credits in the accounts

Items in the balance-of-payments accounts are given positive or negative signs, and they are therefore labeled credits or debits, respectively, depending on whether the particular transaction causes a resident of a country to receive a payment from a foreigner or to make a payment to a foreign resident. If a payment is received, the transaction is a credit and carries a positive sign, and vice versa. Because every transaction that is a payment into one country is a payment out of another, each transaction should sum to zero for the world. The world's **trade balance**, for example, should be zero. In fact, the published data total to a negative number, in part because imports are normally valued on a basis that includes shipping (**c.i.f.**, cost, insurance, and freight), whereas exports are shown without these costs (**f.o.b.**, free on board, or **f.a.s.**, free alongside ship). In addition, many sources of errors in the numbers (discussed later in this chapter) result in the published data not totaling zero.[1]

The assignment of pluses and minuses is fairly straightforward for trade and other **current account** transactions; exports are a plus and imports are a minus. Foreign tourist expenditures in this country are a plus in our accounts, whereas our payments of dividends or interest to foreigners is a minus. When a good or service is being exchanged for money, ascertaining what is a credit and what is a debit is fairly obvious.

International capital flows can be more difficult, because what is being exchanged for what is sometimes not clear. If an American deposits funds in a Canadian bank, that transaction is a minus for the United States and a plus for Canada. If the American later writes a check on that account to pay for imports from Canada, there are two transactions of opposite sign. The American is withdrawing short-term capital from Canada, which is a plus for the United States and a minus for Canada, and the merchandise imports are a minus for the United States and a plus for Canada. When the American wrote the check on the Canadian bank to pay for the imports, the process was shortened, but actually two offsetting accounting transactions occurred.

Long-term capital flows, such as the purchase of foreign bonds or the movement of direct investment funds, are less complicated. If an American purchases German bonds, that is a minus for the United States and a plus for Germany, because it is clear which way the money moves. If a British firm purchases a US business, that is a plus for the US and a minus for the United Kingdom, and again the direction in which funds move is clear.

Matters can become more confusing for movements of **foreign exchange reserves**, which are funds held by central banks (or occasionally, but rarely, by finance ministries). These funds are used to finance deficits in the remainder of the accounts, and payments are made into these reserves when there is a surplus in the other items.

Foreign exchange reserves can be held in a number of forms. Financial claims on foreign governments or central banks constitute one particularly important form, but gold and financial claims on the **International Monetary Fund (IMF)** are alternatives. Many countries hold US dollars as their primary reserve currency, and their central banks have accounts at the New York Federal Reserve Bank, as well as holdings of US Treasury securities, for which the New York Fed typically acts as custodian. The United States holds reserves in the form of financial claims on the governments or central bank of the European Monetary Union, Japan, and other industrialized countries, as well as in the form of gold and the US reserve position at the IMF.

Some countries hold part of their reserves in the form of deposits at the Bank for International Settlements (BIS) in Basle, Switzerland. This institution, which was founded in the 1920s to handle German reparations payments, is a sort of central bank for the central banks of industrialized countries. It can, with privacy and discretion, undertake a variety of transactions on behalf of member central banks, and also acts as a forum at which monetary policies and other matters of interest to those institutions are discussed.

According to the 2002 Annual Report of the IMF, foreign exchange reserves for all countries totaled $2,463 billion as of March 2002.[2] Eighty-four percent of these funds were

---

Box 12.1 Gold as a reserve asset

Foreign exchange reserves are supposed to be held in forms which are safe, that is, on which large capital losses will not be taken. This raises a question as to the desirability of gold in such reserves. Gold was a strong investment from 1971 to 1980, increasing in price from $35 to $850, which produced enormous capital gains for central banks that held it in large volumes. Since then, however, things have been different. At the time of this writing gold was selling for $350 per ounce, which represents a 59 percent loss from its 1980 high. Allowing for the fact that gold earns no interest, while exchange reserves in the form of dollars or DM earn market interest rates in the United States or Germany, the losses incurred by holding gold over the two decades since 1980 have been even larger. Some central banks have been quiet but sizable sellers. The Dutch sold 9.6 million ounces in 1997, which brought in about $3.4 billion at the $350 price prevailing then, and the Belgians have reportedly sold 15 million ounces in recent years.

Countries holding really large amounts of gold, such as the United States, Germany, Switzerland, and France, have been discouraged from selling by the fear that they will push the price down even further. If the Dutch and Belgians quietly sell a few million ounces, the market may be unaffected, but if Germany, which holds almost 100 million ounces, sold off its holding, the price could collapse. The United States, with about 260 million ounces, would have an even larger problem if it decided to sell.

Gold's value as an investment is only as a hedge against inflation. It has done well precisely in periods such as the 1970s when inflation was severe. Since the central banks of the major industrialized countries have apparently concluded that serious inflation really is a thing of the past, they look for additional opportunities to sell.

The Bank of England announced on 9 May 1999 that it intends to sell 58 percent of its gold holdings, or 415 tons, during the next few years. This announcement drove the price of gold down by almost $7 to about $283. Another report suggests that Switzerland, which has enormous holdings, also intends to sell. Gold may be in the process of becoming just another commodity.

Source: Adapted from the *Financial Times*, January 21, 1997, p. 14, and the *New York Times*, May 8, 1999, p. B–1.

---

held in the form of foreign exchange, 11 percent was gold, and the remainder was IMF-related assets, meaning **Special Drawing Rights (SDRs)** and countries reserve position within their IMF quotas. These reserves had grown by 42 percent in the 1996–2002 period, with virtually all of the growth being in foreign exchange. The value of reserve holding of gold actually declined slightly during these 6 years. Almost 70 percent of the world's holdings of reserves in the form of foreign exchange represented US dollars, with most of the remainder being euros, followed by smaller holdings of sterling, yen, and Swiss francs.

It was originally thought that SDR allocations would be the major source of reserve growth, but there have been only six SDR allocations, totaling 21.4 billion SDRs, with the last allocation being made in the early 1980s. SDRs now constitute only 1.4 percent of the world reserves.

As was suggested above, the foreign currency part of a country's reserves are normally held in the form of a deposit at a foreign central bank or as short-term securities issued by a foreign government (such as US Treasury bills), with a clear emphasis on the avoidance of risk. Occasionally, however, central banks will take large risks while seeking higher returns, frequently with unhappy results. It was reported in late 1998, for example, that the Bank of Italy invested $250 million of that country's reserves in a US hedge fund, Long Term Capital Management, a large part of which was lost when that fund almost went bankrupt.

Data on a country's foreign exchange reserves are sometimes less than fully accurate because governments and central banks find ways of making their reserves appear to be larger or smaller than they are. If a developing country wishes to inflate the size of its reserves, it might have a state-owned firm borrow large sums in New York and then sell the dollars to the central bank. A forward contract would be used to protect the firm from possible losses if the exchange rate moves before its loan must be repaid. The central bank adds the dollars to its reserve assets, but does not have to enter the forward contract on its balance sheet. If, on the other hand a central bank wishes to conceal the fact that its reserves have increased, perhaps because it is maintaining a managed floating exchange rate which it is holding down for mercantilist purposes, it might instruct domestic commercial banks to buy the dollars from it and invest them in New York, and then offer those banks slightly better than market forward contracts to get them back into the local currency in 90 or 180 days. It is widely thought that the Bank of Japan has used such techniques to disguise the extent to which it is holding the yen down to encourage a large trade account surplus. Some care and a bit of cynicism are sometimes necessary in interpreting a country's published foreign exchange reserve position.

Foreign exchange reserves are analogous to an individual's holdings of cash: they increase when the individual has a surplus in his or her other transactions, and they decrease when he or she has a deficit. If a country's foreign exchange reserves rise, that transaction has a minus in that country's payments accounts because money is being sent out of the country to purchase a foreign financial asset. If, for example, British holdings of such reserves in the form of Swiss francs increased, the Bank of England would purchase those francs in the London foreign exchange market, and then send them to Switzerland in exchange for a financial claim on the Swiss government or central bank. Money would leave Britain, and the ownership of a financial claim on foreigners would return in exchange.

Many foreign governments and central banks hold their reserves in the form of dollar claims on the US Treasury or the New York Federal Reserve Bank. If Canada reduces its holdings of such dollars, thereby reducing US official reserve liabilities to foreigners, that transaction is a minus for the United States and a plus for Canada, because funds flow out of the United States. Counter-intuitive as it seems, increases in a country's reserve assets or reductions in its reserve liabilities are a minus, whereas reductions in its assets or increases in its liabilities are a plus.

Analogy to a family's cash-flow accounts

The balance-of-payments accounts can be viewed as analogous to a cash statement that might be maintained to keep track of a family's financial affairs. In such an account, any transaction that brought money into the family would be a plus, and vice versa. Items would normally be separated into current and capital account classifications, with the current segment including all current income (+) and all current living costs (–), with the balance in that account representing the change in the family's financial net worth. The **capital account** would include all purchases of financial assets, such as common stocks or bonds, and repayments of previous borrowing as debits, because they result in money flowing out of the family. Sales of assets or new borrowing by the family would be credits because they bring money in. The monthly mortgage payment would have to be split between current and capital accounts, with interest costs being current, and repayment of the principal being put in the capital account. Because the current and capital accounts together represent all transactions bringing money into or out of the family, the number at the bottom of the account should equal the change in the family's holdings of cash during the period.

If cash balances were checked at the beginning and end of the period, and if the change in cash did not match the total in the account, it would be clear that errors or omissions existed. Since offsetting errors could occur, the gross errors can never be known. Therefore the difference between the change in cash predicted by the account and what actually happened to cash holdings would be the net error. Such errors would probably be the result of cash expenditures for current living costs. Hence an error and omission item would be put in the current account with an entry that would make the number at the bottom of the account match actual changes in cash holdings.

This family account is analogous to the balance-of-payments account of a country, with foreign exchange reserves playing the role of cash. The current account includes all international purchases and sales of goods and services (including the services of capital, since dividend and interest payments are included), and its net balance represents the change in a country's net investment position relative to the rest of the world. A current account surplus means that the country either increased its net creditor position or reduced its net indebtedness by that amount during the year, which makes it quite analogous to the current account in the family account discussed above. The capital account includes all purchases and sales of financial claims (except foreign exchange reserves), in which one participant in the transactions is a local resident and the other is not. This account is frequently divided into long-term and short-term segments on the basis of whether asset maturities are more or less than 1 year. Long-term capital flows include direct investments by multinational firms, purchases or sales of bonds and common stocks, as well as loans with maturities of over 1 year.

Short-term capital includes money coming into or going out of asset forms such as Treasury bills, commercial paper, and bank accounts, as well as the short-term financing of export sales. If, for example, Rolls-Royce exports automobiles to France in November with 90-day payments terms, the British balance-of-payments accounts for that year will show an export (+) in the current account and a short-term outflow (–) in the capital account. During the following year, when payment is received from France for the automobiles, the British capital account will show an inflow (+), thus completing the earlier transaction.

If a country's current and capital accounts sum to a positive number, its foreign exchange reserve assets should increase (or its reserve liabilities decrease) by that amount. Thus, if the items are measured correctly, the following must hold:

$$CA + KA = \Delta FXR$$

Therefore,

$$CA + KA - \Delta FXR = 0$$

where CA is the current account, KA is the capital account, and ΔFXR is the change in the country's foreign exchange reserve position (i.e. an increase in reserve assets or a decline in liabilities).

Since increases in reserve assets (or reductions in liabilities) represent a minus in the payments accounts, the total for all items in the balance-of-payments accounts must sum to zero. This is an important point in understanding balance-of-payments accounting; the accounts must sum to zero because foreign exchange reserve movements just offset or cancel the total of the rest of the items. (Algebraic statements such as those above are sometimes presented with a three-line equals sign, which means that the statement is true as an identity. The identity may result from a definition, such as the velocity of money equals nominal GDP divided by the money supply, or from an accounting format, such as assets equal liabilities plus net worth.)

Calculation of errors and omissions

The fact that the accounts must total zero provides the basis for calculating net errors and omissions, or the **statistical discrepancy**, as it is sometimes known. All the items in the current and capital accounts are estimates, and they are subject to sizable mistakes, usually because actual transactions are not recorded for some reason. Some of the omissions are innocent, as when an American travels to Canada with currency, spends it there on vacation services, and the records for the transactions are incomplete. Often, however, the omissions are not innocent. Illegal drug traffic is the source of sizable errors (e.g. unrecorded exports for Colombia and imports for other countries), as is the international movement of funds that results from terrorist or other criminal activities. Gross errors and omissions are unknown, because offsetting errors occur; the number reported in the accounts represents net errors and omissions.

The errors and omissions entry is calculated by adding up everything in the current and capital accounts and comparing the total to the known change in a country's foreign exchange reserve position. The errors and omissions number is whatever figure is necessary to make the two totals match. If, for example, the current and capital accounts total +$3,155 million, whereas foreign exchange reserve assets actually increased by $2,955 million, the net error and omission number must be –$200 million. That entry frequently appears in the short-term capital accounts, because it is thought that most of the unrecorded transactions are of that type. If –$200 is entered in the capital account for errors and omissions, the current and capital accounts will then total +$2,955, which matches what actually happened to foreign exchange reserves.

The fact that the balance-of-payments accounts must sum to zero means that they are a double-entry bookkeeping system: if one number changes, another number must change by the same amount in the opposite direction to maintain the total of all items in the accounts at zero. In some cases the offsetting transaction is quite clear; if General Electric sells jet engines to Airbus, which pays GE by drawing funds from a US dollar account in a New York bank, the US accounts show a debit in the form of a short-term capital outflow (funds withdrawn from the New York account by Airbus) to offset the export of the jet engines, which is a credit. If GE had accepted payment in euros, which it deposited in a Paris bank, the plus for the export of the jet engines would again be offset by a short-term capital outflow when GE deposited the funds in the French bank. Whenever a single firm (in this case GE) is simultaneously involved in two international transactions of the same size and opposite sign, it is relatively easy to see how the double-entry aspect of the payments accounts operates. This becomes a bit more complicated, however, if the firm is involved in only a single balance-of-payments transaction. In that case, the foreign exchange market (an institution discussed in the next chapter) must be used, and the offsetting item in the payments accounts is provided by whoever is on the other side of the exchange market transaction.

Returning to the example of the exported jet engines, we observe that if GE wants to be paid in dollars, which Airbus does not have on deposit in the United States, Airbus must sell euros and purchase dollars in the foreign exchange market in order to pay GE. Whoever sells the dollars to Airbus would then provide the offsetting transaction in the balance-of-payments accounts. If, for example, in the United States Ford was importing automobile parts from France, it would sell dollars and purchase euros in order to complete payment for the parts. If Ford sold the dollars Airbus purchased, its imports of parts (a debit in the US accounts) would be the offset to GE's export of the jet engines to Airbus, which was a credit in the US accounts.

If any foreign firm purchases dollars in the exchange market in order to pay for US goods, services, or financial assets, the payments account offset to the resulting US payments account credit is provided by the individual or organization that sells the dollars to that foreign firm. The offset could have been provided by a US importer, or a US resident purchasing securities abroad, or anyone selling dollars and purchasing a foreign currency, in order to complete another transaction that would be a debit in the US payments accounts. Since there is no way to know who sold the dollars that Airbus purchased, there is no way to know exactly where in the US balance-of-payments accounts the offset to that US export of the jet engines was. All that is known is that somebody sold the dollars that Airbus purchased, so that there had to be an offset.

To summarize, the balancing of the payments accounts can occur in either of two ways. First, a single firm can simultaneously be involved in two offsetting transactions. In this case, no use is made of the exchange market; if GE accepted payment for the jet engines in euros which it deposited in Paris, such an automatic offset would occur. Alternatively, a firm may be involved in only one balance-of-payments transaction. This means that the exchange market must be used and that the offset is provided by the individual or firm that is on the other side of the exchange market transaction; if GE required payment for the jet engines in dollars which Airbus purchased in the exchange market, whoever sold the dollars to Airbus would provide the offset to the US jet engine export.

Organizing the accounts for a country with a fixed exchange rate

Exhibit 12.1 is designed for a country that maintains a fixed exchange rate; the balance-of-payments accounts were published in this form for the United States until the mid-1970s. Most countries still maintain fixed parities or exchange rates which fluctuate within a narrowly managed range, and publish payments accounts that are similar to this one. A somewhat different accounting format is appropriate for a country with a floating exchange rate; it will be discussed later in this chapter. (Readers may find it useful to make a photocopy of Exhibit 12.1 and have it at hand while reading the next few paragraphs.)

Readers may wonder why stress is being placed on a US accounting approach which has not been used for 25 years; there are two reasons for doing so. First, this account provides considerably more detail than the IMF format which will be discussed later. It therefore allows students to see more clearly the various items that appear in the current and capital accounts than would otherwise be possible. Second, this account makes a distinction between long- and short-term capital which does not appear in most other accounts. Short-term capital is debt with a maturity of a year or less, while long-term includes all equity capital and debt with a maturity of over a year. This distinction has not been widely viewed as important in recent years, but is returning to popularity because of the Asian debt crisis, a topic which is discussed in some detail in Chapter 20. One of the clear lessons of that crisis is that it is extremely dangerous for developing countries to rely upon short-term capital, which can be here today and gone tomorrow, to finance current account deficits. Long-term equity or debt capital provides a far more prudent means of financing current account deficits in developing countries, which makes it useful to discuss a payments accounting format which makes the distinction between the two forms of capital flows.

Turning to Exhibit 12.1, current account items are lines 1 through 14, with the total at line 15. Most of the items are self-explanatory, but remittances are payments by workers back to their families in another country, and US government grants represent foreign aid expenditures. The long-term capital account begins with line 16 and ends with line 25, with line 26 being the total of current and long-term capital transactions. Short-term capital flows begin with line 27 and continue through line 41, with line 42 being the total of all current and capital account transactions. Lines 43 through 46 represent movements of foreign exchange reserves, and the total of these lines exactly matches line 42 with the opposite sign, which means that the table then totals zero. Lines 43 through 45 represent changes in US foreign exchange reserve liabilities to foreign central banks and governments. These transactions exist because many foreign countries hold the US dollar as a reserve currency. These lines would not occur in the accounts of a country whose currency did not play this role. Line 46 is the change in US foreign exchange reserve assets.

Line 32 is net errors and omissions, and it was calculated by starting with the estimates for all the items totaled in line 42. That total was compared to the total for lines 43 through 46. Line 32 is whatever number is necessary to make a recalculated line 42 match the total for lines 43 through 46 so that the account can total zero. The memoranda items at the bottom are not part of the account and can be viewed as statistical footnotes.

Since the balance-of-payments accounts as a whole must total zero, surpluses or deficits obviously cannot be measured as the total of everything in the accounts. Rather, they are measured as the total of some items, with others being excluded. For countries that maintain fixed exchange rates, payment disequilibria are measured as the sum of the **autonomous transactions** in the accounts, with **accommodating transactions**, or residual items, being excluded. Autonomous transactions are those undertaken for ordinary commercial motives, without regard for their effect on the balance of payments. Accommodating transactions, on the other hand, occur in response to other transactions. They are not undertaken for their own sake, so to speak, but because other transactions leave a gap to be filled. Thus we may say that autonomous transactions are gap-making, and accommodating transactions are gap-filling.

Given this distinction, we place autonomous items above the line and accommodating items below, and we define a deficit in the overall balance of payments as a debit balance above the line. That is, a deficit exists when autonomous debits (payments) exceed autonomous credits (receipts), with the excess debits offset by accommodating credits. A surplus exists when the opposite condition holds true.

The most commonly used definition of a balance-of-payments disequilibrium is the total of lines 1 through 41 in Exhibit 12.1. All current and capital account items are viewed as autonomous, and only foreign exchange reserve flows (lines 43–6) are classified as accommodating. This is known as the **official reserve transactions balance** and is shown as line 42.

It is sometimes referred to as the "overall balance" or the "official settlements balance." If a country is described as having a "balance-of-payments deficit," without further comment, it can be assumed that the official reserve transactions or overall definition is being used.

EXHIBIT 12.1 US BALANCE OF PAYMENTS SUMMARY (MILLIONS OF DOLLARS, SEASONALLY ADJUSTED)

Line	(Credits +; debits −)	Reference lines (table 2)	1973	1974p	Change 1973-74	1973 I	1973 II	1973 III	1973 IV	1974 I	1974 II	1974 III	1974 IV	Change 1974 III-IV
1	Merchandise trade balance [1]		471	−5,881	−6,352	−954	−363	578	1,210	−175	−1,674	−2,474	−1,558	916
2	Exports	2	70,277	97,081	26,804	15,230	16,679	18,152	20,218	22,212	23,921	24,731	26,217	1,486
3	Imports	16	−69,805	−102,962	−33,156	−16,184	−17,042	−17,574	−19,006	−22,387	−25,595	−27,205	−27,775	−570
4	Military transactions, net	3, 17	−2,266	−2,099	167	−833	−763	−547	−123	−500	−658	−473	−458	15
5	Travel and transportation, net	4, 5, 6, 18, 19, 20	−2,710	−2,435	275	−686	−781	−613	−630	−531	−726	−566	−612	−46
6	Investment income, net [2]	11	5,291	9,679	4,388	1,447	1,206	1,257	1,378	3,104	1,870	2,282	2,422	140
7	U.S. direct investments abroad [3]	12, 13	9,415	18,240	8,825	2,194	2,210	2,323	2,688	4,650	4,546	4,824	4,220	−604
8	Other U.S. investments abroad	25, 26, 27	4,569	7,703	3,134	1,000	1,098	1,179	1,292	1,499	1,836	2,197	2,170	−27
9	Foreign investments in the United States [4]		−8,693	−16,265	−7,570	−1,747	−2,100	−2,245	−2,602	−3,045	−4,512	−4,739	−3,968	771
10	Other services, net [5]	7, 8, 9, 10, 21, 22, 23, 24	3,540	3,926	386	841	815	984	901	918	992	984	1,032	48
11	Balance on goods and services [6]	31, 32	4,327	3,191	−1,136	−186	116	1,659	2,736	2,816	−206	−247	826	1,073
12	Remittances, pensions and other transfers		−1,943	−1,775	168	−404	−411	−412	−717	−390	−467	−456	−463	−7
13	Balance on goods, services and remittances		2,383	1,416	−967	−589	−286	1,247	2,019	2,426	−673	−703	343	1,066
14	U.S. Government grants (excluding military grants of goods and services)	30	−1,933	−5,441	−3,508	−857	−645	−485	−447	⁷−2,561	−1,435	−772	−673	99
15	Balance on current account [7]		450	−4,025	−4,475	−946	−949	743	1,872	⁷−135	−2,108	−1,475	−310	1,165
16	U.S. Government capital flows excluding nonscheduled repayments, net [4]	34, 35, 36	−2,038	408	2,346	−699	−565	−606	−1,066	⁷1,297	311	−185	−1,014	−828
17	Nonscheduled repayments of U.S. Government assets	37	289	1	−288	111	174	4	(*)	(*)	......	(*)	119	(*)
18	U.S. Government nonliquid liabilities to other than foreign official reserve agencies	48	1,111	634	−477	217	485	205	204	53	273	189	119	−70
19	Long-term private capital flows, net	39	−4,872	−7,598	−7,660	309	−824	1,527	−1,451	504	−1,039	−2,402	−4,661	−2,259
20	U.S. direct investments abroad [3]	49	−4,801	−6,801	−1,229	−1,815	−973	−710	−1,374	−627	−1,527	−2,047	−2,600	−553
21	Foreign direct investments in the United States	40	2,537	2,306	−1,229	351	588	886	712	1,281	1,677	−89	−551	−472
22	Foreign securities	50	−807	−2,308	−1,144	51	−124	−200	−525	−646	−313	−206	−688	−380
23	U.S. securities other than Treasury issues	41, 53	4,051	1,190	−2,852	1,718	460	1,173	670	687	419	168	−75	243
24	Other, reported by U.S. banks	44, 51	−647	−1,185	−589	−120	−243	225	−504	−21	−902	68	−331	399
25	Other, reported by U.S. nonbanking concerns		−200	−1,157	−967	124	−56	162	−430	−170	−383	−196	−406	212

Line		Description	Ref.												
26		**Balance on current account and long-term capital †**		-1,025	-10,830	-9,554	-1,008	-1,170	1,861	-741	1,719	-2,543	-3,874	-5,846	-1,992
27		Nonliquid short-term private capital flows, net		-4,276	-12,955	-8,670	-1,668	-1,457	97	-1,253	-3,994	-5,296	-1,427	-2,238	-811
28		Claims reported by U.S. banks	42	-3,940	-12,228	-8,258	-1,644	-1,399	222	-1,119	-2,817	-5,311	-1,653	-2,442	-789
29		Claims reported by U.S. nonbanking concerns	45	-1,240	-2,453	-1,213	-57	-59	-460	-664	-1,591	-945	-207	40	247
30		Liabilities reported by U.S. nonbanking concerns	52	904	1,721	817	38	1	335	530	414	710	433	164	-269
31		Allocations of special drawing rights (SDR)	63												
32		Errors and omissions, net	64	-2,508	5,197	7,500	-8,943	850	-536	1,125	1,305	1,463	838	1,592	754
33		**Net liquidity balance †**		-7,606	-18,338	-10,732	-6,614	-1,777	1,642	-869	-970	-6,396	-4,463	-6,512	-2,049
34		Liquid private capital flows, net		2,302	10,268	7,966	-3,581	2,063	290	3,530	2,016	1,874	4,143	2,235	-1,908
35		Liquid claims	43	1,044	-5,464	-3,520	-1,853	923	-521	-493	-2,732	-1,197	133	-1,608	-1,801
36		Reported by U.S. banks		-1,103	-5,445	-4,342	-1,171	996	-456	-472	-2,368	-1,261	-431	-1,385	-954
37		Reported by U.S. nonbanking concerns	46	-841	-19	822	682	-73	-65	-21	-364	64	564	-283	-847
38		Liquid liabilities	54	4,246	15,732	11,486	-1,728	1,140	811	4,023	4,748	3,071	4,010	3,903	-107
39		To foreign commercial banks		2,982	12,655	9,673	-1,673	729	699	3,227	4,643	2,161	2,896	2,935	39
40		To international and regional organizations		377	151	-226	11	32	-50	384	-530	297	221	163	-58
41		To other foreigners		887	2,926	2,039	-66	379	162	412	615	613	893	905	-88
42		**Official reserve transactions balance †**		-5,304	-8,070	-2,766	-10,195	286	1,942	2,661	1,046	-4,522	-320	-4,277	-3,957
		Financed by changes in:													
43		Liquid liabilities to foreign official agencies	55	4,452	8,253	3,801	8,816	-729	-1,488	-2,145	-557	4,255	1,263	3,295	2,032
44		Other readily marketable liabilities to foreign official agencies †	56	1,118	596	-522	1,202	259	11	-354	-277	182	61	630	569
45		Nonliquid liabilities to foreign official reserve agencies reported by U.S. Government	57	-475	655	1,130	-43	167	-452	-147	-2	443	-1	215	216
46		U.S. official reserve assets, net	58	209	-1,434	-1,643	220	17	-13	-15	-210	-358	-1,003	137	1,140
		Memoranda:													
47		Transfers under military grant programs (excluded from lines 2, 4, and 14)	14,28	2,772	1,790	-982	693	833	755	487	393	542	352	504	152
48		Reinvested earnings of foreign incorporated affiliates of U.S. firms (excluded from lines 7 and 20)		8,124	n.a.	n.a.	n.a.	n.a.	n.a.	n.a.	n.a.	n.a.	n.a.	n.a.	n.a.
49		Reinvested earnings of U.S. incorporated affiliates of foreign firms (excluded from lines 9 and 21)		945	n.a.	n.a.	n.a.	n.a.	n.a.	n.a.	n.a.	n.a.	n.a.	n.a.	n.a.
50		Gross liquidity balance, excluding allocations of SDR	54,55,56, 57,58, 63.	-9,550	-23,802	-14,252	-8,467	-854	1,131	-1,362	-3,702	-7,593	-4,330	-8,180	-3,850

Not seasonally adjusted

Line	Description	Ref.									
51	Balance on goods and services		------	------	------	404	228	-195	3,800	3,948	-45	-3,030	2,317	5,347
52	Balance on goods, services and remittances		------	------	------	116	-187	-623	3,077	3,584	-514	-3,502	1,848	5,350
53	Balance on current account		------	------	------	-259	-872	-1,071	2,653	1,005	-1,990	-4,239	1,199	5,438
54	Balance on current account and long-term capital †		------	------	------	-1,054	-1,193	222	999	2,120	-2,539	-5,441	3,719	2,722
55	Net liquidity balance †		------	------	------	-6,050	-2,104	637	-89	-144	-6,784	-5,773	5,637	2,136
56	Official reserve transactions balance †		------	------	------	-9,994	700	939	2,982	1,495	-4,105	-1,609	3,851	-2,242

Source: US Department of Commerce, Bureau of Economic Analysis.

It has sometimes been argued, however, that some short-term capital transactions are accommodating in nature. If a British company purchases German goods and pays for them by drawing down a pre-existing euro account in Frankfurt, the short-term capital flow into the United Kingdom could reasonably be viewed as accommodating to the merchandise import. In addition, as was noted earlier, the short-term capital account is volatile and unpredictable, so it might be excluded from a long-term view of a country's fundamental payments position. The **"basic balance"** approach measures surpluses or deficits as the sum of the current account and the long-term capital account, and both foreign exchange reserve flows and the short-term capital account are put "below the line" as accommodating items. The basic balance of payments is the sum of lines 1 through 25, totaled as line 26, in Exhibit 12.1. The "basic" format has become less popular in recent years, but, as was argued earlier, can be expected to be used more widely for developing countries due to the Asian debt crisis which made it clear how dangerous it can be for a country to rely on short-term capital inflows to finance a sizable current account deficit.

The IMF International Financial Statistics accounts

Many readers who are seeking payments data on various countries will find the country pages of the *International Financial Statistics*, which is published by the International Monetary Fund, to be the most convenient source.[3] Recent IFS accounts for the United Kingdom will be found in Exhibit 12.2.

The IMF now uses somewhat different terminology for the accounts from that used previously in this chapter. The Fund uses the phrase "Financial Account" for what has been referred to here as the capital account. The phrase "Capital Account" is used for what the IMF calls transfers linked to the acquisition or disposal of a fixed asset, and the disposal or acquisition of nonproduced nonfinancial assets. Some of this involves situations in which a foreign company has put in place a "build and run" factory or power plant, which is then transferred to the host government at the end of a fixed period. That transfer would be in the newly defined capital account.

After the change from capital to account to financial account is made, the format of the International Financial Statistics payments accounts, as presented in Exhibit 12.2, roughly corresponds to the form introduced earlier for the United States. There is, however, no distinction between long- and short-term capital. Errors and omissions appear where they do in the US accounts, and the "overall" payments outcome resembles the "Official Reserve Balance" in the earlier account. There is, however, one important difference in the treatment of foreign exchange reserve flow. The US accounts view changes if both reserve assets and liabilities are below the line items. The IMF accounts put changes in reserve assets and funds borrowed from the IMF below the line, but treat changes in other central bank liabilities to foreigners (other than the IMF) as an above the line item. The rationale for the IMF's placement of this item is not clear, but it is usually important only for reserve currency countries such as the United States. If, for example, the United States has an Official Reserve Transactions deficit, which is financed by other countries increasing their dollar foreign exchange reserves, it would not have an overall deficit in the IMF accounts. For nonreserve currency countries, whose central banks borrow abroad only from the IMF, there should be little or no difference between the two formats.

The IMF publishes its accounts in the same format both for countries on fixed and on floating exchange rates. For the remainder of this book the phrase "Financial Account" will not be used, and "Capital Account" will have its traditional non-IMF meaning.

EXHIBIT 12.2   UK BALANCE OF PAYMENTS IN THE IMF FORMAT

United Kingdom
112

		1995	1996	1997	1998	1999	2000	2001
International Transactions								
Exports....................................	70	153,353	167,764	171,595	164,066	165,739	186,171	185,673
Imports, c.i.f.	71	168,055	184,113	187,135	189,532	196,504	221,027	222,944
Volume of Exports...................	72	100.0	108.2	116.5	118.4	123.8	137.8	140.2
Volume of Imports...................	73	100.0	110.1	120.4	132.0	142.1	158.9	164.4
Export Prices	76	100.0	100.7	95.3	90.3	89.5	92.9	93.0
Import Prices	76.x	100.0	99.8	93.2	87.6	86.4	90.1	89.8
Balance of Payments								
Current Account, n.i.e...................	78ald	-14.29	-13.44	-2.85	-7.96	-31.94	-28.82	-29.37
Goods: Exports f.o.b.	78aad	242.32	261.25	281.54	271.72	268.88	284.38	275.95
Goods: Imports f.o.b...................	78abd	-261.32	-282.48	-301.74	-307.85	-313.18	-330.27	-324.20
Trade Balance	78acd	-19.01	-21.23	-20.20	-36.13	-44.29	-45.89	-48.25
Services: Credit.........................	78add	78.78	87.34	97.72	107.23	113.94	116.81	110.55
Services: Debit..........................	78aed	-65.41	-72.28	-77.20	-86.26	-94.84	-98.71	-94.60
Balance on Goods & Services....	78afd	-5.64	-6.17	.32	-15.15	-25.19	-27.80	-32.29
Income: Credit..........................	78agd	138.87	144.49	157.74	171.92	163.10	204.36	201.40
Income: Debit...........................	78ahd	-135.59	-142.72	-151.40	-151.09	-159.04	-190.25	-188.18
Balance on Gds, Serv. & Inc......	78aid	-2.35	-4.39	6.66	5.68	-21.13	-13.68	-19.07
Current Transfers, n.i.e.: Credit ...	78ajd	19.70	29.46	21.44	20.59	22.70	18.66	23.30
Current Transfers: Debit..............	78akd	-31.64	-38.51	-30.95	-34.23	-33.51	-33.80	-33.60
Capital Account, n.i.e.	78bcd	.84	1.14	1.32	.79	1.52	2.76	2.15
Capital Account, n.i.e.: Credit.....	78bad	1.84	2.18	2.77	2.44	2.91	4.36	4.06
Capital Account: Debit	78bbd	-.99	-1.04	-1.45	-1.65	-1.38	-1.60	-1.91
Financial Account, n.i.e..............	78bjd	7.47	7.98	-12.16	.23	30.97	26.17	23.30
Direct Investment Abroad...........	78bdd	-45.31	-34.82	-62.44	-122.06	-201.57	-266.25	-34.24
Dir. Invest. in Rep. Econ., n.i.e..	78bed	21.73	27.39	37.38	74.65	89.53	119.93	63.11
Portfolio Investment Assets	78bfd	-61.69	-93.13	-84.99	-52.98	-33.09	-99.89	-134.34
Equity Securities	78bkd	-13.15	-16.30	7.04	-4.65	-23.37	-28.66	-68.34
Debt Securities	78bld	-48.55	-76.83	-92.03	-48.33	-9.72	-71.23	-66.00
Portfolio Investment Liab., n.i.e..	78bgd	58.79	67.98	43.46	35.28	186.06	258.34	63.88
Equity Securities	78bmd	8.07	9.40	7.85	63.09	116.04	179.17	25.99
Debt Securities	78bnd	50.72	58.58	35.61	-27.82	70.02	79.17	37.89
Financial Derivatives Assets.......	78bwd	....	....	....	....	....	....	....
Financial Derivatives Liabilities..	78bxd	2.63	1.52	1.90	-5.07	4.41	2.26	12.20
Other Investment Assets	78bhd	-74.90	-215.31	-275.87	-26.84	-94.07	-411.53	-259.02
Monetary Authorities................	78bod	....	....	....	....	....	....	....
General Government..................	78bpd	-.74	-.53	-.07	.25	-1.93	-.42	.02
Banks	78bqd	-34.91	-102.10	-241.01	-28.36	19.99	-291.77	-125.86
Other Sectors	78brd	-39.25	-112.68	-34.79	1.28	-112.14	-119.34	-133.18
Other Investment Liab., n.i.e.	78bid	106.22	254.36	328.40	97.24	79.70	423.31	311.71
Monetary Authorities	78bsd	—	—	—	—	—	—	—
General Government	78btd	.59	-1.06	-1.74	.42	.54	—	.12
Banks	78bud	41.95	111.45	243.06	78.16	16.41	308.92	183.58
Other Sectors	78bvd	63.68	143.97	87.09	18.66	62.75	114.39	128.01
Net Errors and Omissions	78cad	5.13'	3.66	9.79	6.68	-1.58	5.19	-.54
Overall Balance........................	78cbd	-.85	-.65	-3.90	-.26	-1.04	5.30	-4.45
Reserves and Related Items	79dad	.85	.65	3.90	.26	1.04	-5.30	4.45
Reserve Assets.............................	79dbd	.90	.65	3.90	.26	1.04	-5.30	4.45
Use of Fund Credit and Loans ...	79dcd	—	—	—	—	—	—	—
Exceptional Financing	79ded	-.04	—	—	—	—	—	—

Source: IMF, *International Financial Statistics.*

Balance-of-payments accounting with flexible exchange rates

The United States publishes its balance-of-payments accounts in a format which is designed specifically for a country on a **floating exchange rate**. Such an exchange rate regime would suggest that the concept of a payments deficit ceases to have much meaning. If a country maintains a **clean floating exchange rate**, no transactions occur that involve foreign exchange reserve movements, so the official reserve transactions account is zero by definition. If the account must total zero and there are no movements of reserves, then the current and capital accounts must total zero. The balance of payments is kept in equilibrium in the same way that the market for Microsoft common stock is kept in balance: through constant and occasionally large price changes. In this case it is the foreign price of the domestic currency that changes when payments shocks occur. If clean floats were in operation, the payments accounts could be published with only the current and capital accounts, and these would sum to zero. The actual world of floating exchange rates, however, is more complicated.

The United States and a number of other countries maintain what are commonly called "dirty" or **managed floating exchange rates**. No parity is maintained, but foreign exchange reserves do move when central banks engage in foreign exchange transactions because they are displeased with the direction or speed of exchange rate movements. If, for example, a currency is declining in the exchange market, that country's central bank may sell foreign exchange and purchase the local currency to stop or slow its fall. As a result, foreign exchange reserves decline despite the existence of a floating exchange rate. Some developing countries claim to be maintaining a floating exchange rate, but actually manage it so aggressively as to produce something very similar to a fixed parity.

The US balance-of-payments accounts have been published since 1976 in a format that reflects this situation of managed floating exchange rates[4] (see Exhibit 12.3). Again, readers may find it useful to make a photocopy of the exhibit and have it available while reading the next paragraph.

Fixed exchange rate	*Floating exchange rate*

Current account
  (balance shown)
	Current account
	  (no balance shown)

Capital account
Long-term capital
	Capital account
	  Changes in US assets abroad
	    Changes in US reserve assets
	    Other changes in US claims on
	      foreigners

Basic payments balance	

Short-term capital
  (including errors and omissions)
	Changes in foreign assets in United
	  States

Official reserve transactions balance	Changes in dollar FXR claims
	  Other changes in claims on United
	    States

Changes in foreign exchange reserves
  Changes in foreign holdings
    of US dollar reserves
  Changes in US Foreign Exchange
  Reserve Assets
	Statistical discrepancy (E&O)

Current account items appear in more detail (lines 1 through 38) than in the earlier format. No current account balance is shown in the table, although it does appear in the memoranda at the bottom (line 76). The capital account, which for the first time in 2001 used the IMF nomenclature, appears as line 39. It primarily represents transfers of productive facilities at the end of "build and run" contracts. The financial account which begins with line 40, is reorganized into two broad categories: changes in US assets abroad (lines 40 through 54) and changes in foreign assets in the United States (lines 55 through 69). Changes in US foreign exchange reserve assets (lines 41 through 45) appear as a subcategory of changes in US assets abroad. Changes in foreign holdings of reserves in the form of US dollars are treated similarly and appear as lines 56 through 62 minus line 60. No official reserve transactions or basic balances appear, and the accounts end with the statistical discrepancy (line 70) which is merely a new name for errors and omissions. The structure of the accounts published by the United States is quite different under the two exchange rate regimes and is summarized in the accompanying listing. Despite the US Department of Commerce's decision to adopt the phrase "financial account," the remainder of the book will retain the phrase "capital account" in its historic use, because almost all economists have chosen that route.

The international investment position table

In addition to the balance-of-payments accounts discussed earlier in this chapter, many countries publish tables showing their net creditor or debtor situation relative to the rest of the world. This account is analogous to a balance sheet, in that stocks of foreign assets are shown along with stocks of liabilities to foreigners to reach a net international investment position, which is similar to the concept of net worth. A country's net investment position should change each year by the amount of its current account balance. A current account surplus of $1 billion means an increase in that country's net investment position of that amount. Consequently, either its foreign assets increase and/or its liabilities to foreigners fall by that amount. A recently published table for the United States is presented in Exhibit 12.4.

The deterioration of the US net investment position in recent decades is rather striking. At the end of 1985 (not shown in this table) the United States was a net creditor relative to the rest of the world in the amount of about $500 billion. At the end of 2001, it was a net debtor by $2,309 billion. This decline of over $2.6 trillion was the result of a series of enormous US current account deficits, the causes of which will be discussed later in this book.

The way in which real assets in the form of direct investments are valued in this table creates a problem for the earlier conclusion that the change in a country's net investment position should equal its current account balance for that year. If direct investments were carried at purchase price or book value, the earlier conclusion would hold, but allowing for inflation and unrealized capital gains (or losses) introduces a complication. Until 1990 direct investments were entered in this table at purchase price, but in recent years the Bureau of Economic Analysis of the US Department of Commerce, which is responsible for these tables, has decided to value direct investments alternatively at market or replacement value.

Because the effects of inflation on the value of foreign assets and unrealized capital gains are not included as investment income in the current account of the balance of payments, the previous linkage between the net investment table and the current account no longer holds. The US current account deficit during 1992, for example, was only about $57 billion,

EXHIBIT 12.3 US INTERNATIONAL TRANSACTIONS 1993–2001 (MILLIONS OF DOLLARS)

Line	(Credits +; debits –)[1]	1993	1994	1995	1996	1997	1998	1999	2000	2001	Line
	Current account										
1	Exports of goods and services and income receipts	777,044	869,328	1,005,935	1,077,966	1,195,538	1,192,045	1,247,682	1,417,236	1,281,793	1
2	Exports of goods and services	642,884	703,890	794,433	852,120	934,980	932,679	957,146	1,064,239	998,022	2
3	Goods, balance of payments basis[2]	456,943	502,859	575,204	612,113	678,366	670,416	683,965	771,994	718,762	3
4	Services[3]	185,941	201,031	219,229	240,007	256,614	262,263	273,181	292,245	279,260	4
5	Transfers under U.S. military agency sales contracts[4]	13,471	12,787	14,643	16,446	16,675	17,405	15,804	13,981	12,220	5
6	Travel	57,875	58,417	63,395	69,809	73,426	71,286	74,731	82,267	73,119	6
7	Passenger fares	16,528	16,997	18,909	20,422	20,868	20,098	19,785	20,760	18,007	7
8	Other transportation	21,958	23,754	26,081	26,074	27,006	25,604	26,916	30,137	28,306	8
9	Royalties and license fees[5]	21,695	26,712	30,289	32,470	33,228	35,626	36,902	39,607	38,668	9
10	Other private services[5]	53,532	61,477	65,094	73,858	84,456	91,318	98,158	104,707	108,109	10
11	U.S. Government miscellaneous services	883	887	818	928	955	926	885	786	831	11
12	Income receipts	134,159	165,438	211,502	225,846	260,558	259,366	290,536	352,997	283,771	12
13	Income receipts on U.S.-owned assets abroad	132,725	163,895	209,741	224,090	258,756	257,432	288,326	350,656	281,389	13
14	Direct investment receipts	67,246	77,344	95,260	102,505	115,323	103,963	128,456	149,677	125,996	14
15	Other private receipts	60,353	82,423	109,768	116,994	139,874	149,868	156,673	197,133	151,832	15
16	U.S. Government receipts	5,126	4,128	4,713	4,591	3,559	3,601	3,197	3,846	3,561	16
17	Compensation of employees	1,434	1,543	1,761	1,756	1,802	1,934	2,210	2,341	2,382	17
18	Imports of goods and services and income payments	-821,930	-949,312	-1,077,701	-1,155,706	-1,283,116	-1,351,363	-1,491,781	-1,774,135	-1,625,701	18
19	Imports of goods and services	-711,675	-800,568	-890,821	-953,963	-1,042,745	-1,099,612	-1,219,383	-1,442,920	-1,356,312	19
20	Goods, balance of payments basis[2]	-589,394	-668,690	-749,374	-803,113	-876,485	-917,112	-1,029,987	-1,224,417	-1,145,927	20
21	Services[3]	-122,281	-131,878	-141,447	-150,850	-166,260	-182,500	-189,396	-218,503	-210,385	21
22	Direct defense expenditures	-12,086	-10,217	-10,043	-11,061	-11,707	-12,185	-13,334	-13,560	-15,198	22
23	Travel	-40,713	-43,782	-44,916	-48,078	-52,051	-56,509	-58,865	-64,788	-60,117	23
24	Passenger fares	-11,410	-13,062	-14,663	-15,809	-18,138	-19,971	-21,315	-24,306	-22,418	24
25	Other transportation	-24,524	-26,019	-27,034	-27,403	-28,959	-30,363	-34,139	-41,598	-38,823	25
26	Royalties and license fees[5]	-5,032	-5,852	-6,919	-7,837	-9,161	-11,235	-12,609	-16,115	-16,359	26
27	Other private services[5]	-26,261	-30,386	-35,249	-37,975	-43,482	-49,388	-46,313	-55,253	-54,588	27
28	U.S. Government miscellaneous services	-2,255	-2,560	-2,623	-2,687	-2,762	-2,849	-2,821	-2,883	-2,882	28
29	Income payments	-110,255	-148,744	-186,880	-201,743	-240,371	-251,751	-272,398	-331,215	-269,389	29
30	Income payments on foreign-owned assets in the United States	-105,123	-142,792	-180,617	-195,443	-233,705	-244,757	-264,449	-323,005	-260,850	30
31	Direct investment payments	-7,943	-22,150	-30,318	-33,093	-42,950	-38,418	-53,447	-60,815	-23,401	31
32	Other private payments	-57,804	-76,450	-96,490	-97,079	-112,117	-127,052	-136,455	-179,217	-156,784	32
33	U.S. Government payments	-39,376	-44,192	-53,809	-65,271	-78,638	-79,287	-74,547	-82,973	-80,665	33
34	Compensation of employees	-5,132	-5,952	-6,263	-6,300	-6,666	-6,994	-7,949	-8,210	-8,539	34
35	Unilateral current transfers, net	-37,637	-38,260	-34,057	-40,081	-40,794	-44,509	-48,757	-53,442	-49,463	35
36	U.S. Government grants[4]	-17,036	-14,978	-11,190	-15,401	-12,472	-13,270	-13,774	-16,821	-11,628	36
37	U.S. Government pensions and other transfers	-4,104	-4,556	-3,451	-4,466	-4,191	-4,305	-4,406	-4,705	-5,798	37
38	Private remittances and other transfers[6]	-16,497	-18,726	-19,416	-20,214	-24,131	-26,934	-30,577	-31,916	-32,037	38

	Line	-88	-469	372	693	350	704	-3,340	837	826
Capital and financial account										
Capital account										
Capital account transactions, net	39	-88	-469	372	693	350	704	-3,340	837	826
Financial account										
U.S.-owned assets abroad, net (increase/financial outflow (–))	40	-200,552	-176,056	-352,376	-413,923	-487,599	-359,760	-477,569	-606,489	-370,982
U.S. official reserve assets, net	41	-1,379	5,346	-9,742	6,668	-1,010	-6,783	8,747	-290	-4,911
Gold [7]	42									
Special drawing rights	43	-537	-441	-808	370	-350	-147	10	-722	-630
Reserve position in the International Monetary Fund	44	-44	494	-2,466	-1,280	-3,575	-5,119	5,484	2,308	-3,600
Foreign currencies	45	-797	5,293	-6,468	7,578	2,915	-1,517	3,253	-1,876	-681
U.S. Government assets, other than official reserve assets, net	46	-351	-390	-984	-989	68	-422	2,750	-941	-486
U.S. credits and other long-term assets	47	-6,311	-5,383	-4,859	-5,025	-5,417	-4,678	-6,175	-5,182	-4,431
Repayments on U.S. credits and other long-term assets [8]	48	6,270	5,088	4,125	3,930	5,438	4,111	9,559	4,265	3,873
U.S. foreign currency holdings and U.S. short-term assets, net	49	-310	-95	-250	106	47	145	-634	-24	72
U.S. private assets, net	50	-198,822	-181,012	-341,650	-419,602	-486,657	-352,555	-489,066	-605,258	-365,565
Direct investment	51	-83,950	-80,167	-98,750	-91,885	-104,803	-142,644	-188,901	-178,294	-127,840
Foreign securities	52	-146,253	-60,309	-122,506	-149,829	-118,976	-136,135	-128,436	-127,502	-94,662
U.S. claims on unaffiliated foreigners reported by U.S. nonbanking concerns	53	766	-36,336	-45,286	-86,333	-121,760	-38,204	-95,466	-150,805	-14,358
U.S. claims reported by U.S. banks, not included elsewhere	54	30,615	-4,200	-75,108	-91,555	-141,118	-35,572	-76,263	-148,657	-128,705
Foreign-owned assets in the United States, net (increase/financial inflow (+))	55	282,040	305,989	438,562	551,096	706,809	423,569	742,479	1,015,986	752,806
Foreign official assets in the United States, net	56	71,753	39,583	109,880	126,724	19,036	-19,903	43,666	37,640	5,224
U.S. Government securities [9]	57	53,014	36,827	72,712	120,679	-2,161	-3,589	32,527	30,676	31,665
U.S. Treasury securities	58	48,952	30,750	68,977	115,671	-6,690	-9,921	12,177	-10,233	10,745
Other [10]	59	4,062	6,077	3,735	5,008	4,529	6,332	20,350	40,909	20,920
Other U.S. Government liabilities [11]	60	1,313	1,564	-105	-982	-881	-3,326	-2,740	-1,909	-1,882
U.S. liabilities reported by U.S. banks, not included elsewhere	61	14,841	3,665	34,008	5,704	22,286	-9,501	12,964	5,746	-30,278
Other foreign official assets [12]	62	2,585	-2,473	3,265	1,323	-208	-3,487	915	3,127	5,719
Other foreign assets in the United States, net	63	210,282	266,406	328,682	424,372	687,773	443,472	698,813	978,346	747,582
Direct investment	64	51,362	46,121	57,776	86,502	105,603	179,045	289,454	307,747	130,796
U.S. Treasury securities	65	24,381	34,274	91,544	147,022	130,435	28,581	-44,497	-76,965	-7,670
U.S. securities other than U.S. Treasury securities	66	80,092	56,971	77,249	103,272	161,409	156,315	298,834	453,213	407,653
U.S. currency	67	18,900	23,400	12,300	17,362	24,782	16,622	22,407	1,129	23,783
U.S. liabilities to unaffiliated foreigners reported by U.S. nonbanking concerns	68	10,489	1,302	59,637	53,736	116,518	23,140	78,383	174,251	82,353
U.S. liabilities reported by U.S. banks, not included elsewhere	69	25,063	104,338	30,176	16,478	149,026	39,769	54,232	116,971	110,667
Statistical discrepancy (sum of above items with sign reversed)	70	1,123	-11,220	19,265	-20,045	-91,188	139,314	31,286	7	10,701
Memoranda:										
Balance on goods (lines 3 and 20)	71	-132,451	-165,831	-174,170	-191,000	-198,119	-246,696	-346,022	-452,423	-427,165
Balance on services (lines 4 and 21)	72	63,660	69,153	77,782	89,157	90,354	79,763	83,785	73,742	68,875
Balance on goods and services (lines 2 and 19)	73	-68,791	-96,678	-96,388	-101,843	-107,765	-166,933	-262,237	-378,681	-358,290
Balance on income (lines 12 and 29)	74	23,904	16,694	24,622	24,103	20,187	7,615	18,138	21,782	14,382
Unilateral current transfers, net (line 35)	75	-37,637	-38,260	-34,057	-40,081	-40,794	-44,509	-48,757	-53,442	-49,463
Balance on current account (lines 1, 18 and 35 or lines 73, 74, and 75) [13]	76	-82,523	-118,244	-105,823	-117,821	-128,372	-203,827	-292,856	-410,341	-393,371

Source: US Department of Commerce, Bureau of Economic Analysis.

EXHIBIT 12.4 INTERNATIONAL INVESTMENT POSITION OF THE UNITED STATES AT YEAR-END

Line	Type of investment	1994[r]	1995[r]	1996[r]	1997[r]	1998[r]	1999[r]	2000[r]	2001[p]	Line
	Net international investment position of the United States:									
1	With direct investment positions at current cost (line 3 less line 24)	**-311,882**	**-495,966**	**-521,545**	**-833,158**	**-918,319**	**-784,094**	**-1,350,791**	**-1,948,134**	1
2	With direct investment positions at market value (line 4 less line 25)	**-123,736**	**-343,340**	**-386,514**	**-835,208**	**-1,094,156**	**-1,053,554**	**-1,583,153**	**-2,309,117**	2
	U.S.-owned assets abroad:									
3	With direct investment at current cost (lines 5-10+15)	**2,998,633**	**3,451,983**	**4,012,746**	**4,567,906**	**5,091,058**	**5,959,014**	**6,191,934**	**6,196,139**	3
4	With direct investment at market value (lines 5-10+16)	**3,326,650**	**3,930,269**	**4,631,276**	**5,379,128**	**6,174,452**	**7,386,970**	**7,350,862**	**6,862,943**	4
5	U.S. official reserve assets	163,394	176,061	160,739	134,836	146,006	136,418	128,400	129,961	5
6	Gold [1]	100,110	101,279	96,698	75,929	75,291	75,950	71,799	72,328	6
7	Special drawing rights	10,039	11,037	10,312	10,027	10,603	10,336	10,539	10,783	7
8	Reserve position in the International Monetary Fund	12,030	14,649	15,435	18,071	24,111	17,950	14,824	17,869	8
9	Foreign currencies	41,215	49,096	38,294	30,809	36,001	32,182	31,238	28,981	9
10	U.S. Government assets, other than official reserve assets	83,908	85,064	86,123	86,198	86,768	84,224	85,164	85,650	10
11	U.S. credits and other long-term assets [2]	81,884	82,802	83,999	84,130	84,850	81,654	82,570	83,128	11
12	Repayable in dollars	81,389	82,358	83,606	83,780	84,528	81,364	82,289	82,850	12
13	Other [3]	495	444	393	350	322	290	281	278	13
14	U.S. foreign currency holdings and U.S. short-term assets	2,024	2,262	2,124	2,068	1,918	2,570	2,594	2,522	14
	U.S. private assets:									
15	With direct investment at current cost (lines 17+19+22+23)	2,751,331	3,190,858	3,765,884	4,346,872	4,858,284	5,738,372	5,978,370	5,980,528	15
16	With direct investment at market value (lines 18+19+22+23)	3,079,348	3,669,144	4,384,414	5,158,094	5,941,678	7,166,328	7,137,298	6,647,332	16
	Direct investment abroad:									
17	At current cost [4]	786,565	885,506	989,810	1,068,063	1,196,207	1,377,263	1,515,279	1,623,122	17
18	At market value [5]	1,114,582	1,363,792	1,608,340	1,879,285	2,279,601	2,805,219	2,674,207	2,289,926	18
19	Foreign securities [5]	948,668	1,169,636	1,467,985	1,751,183	2,052,929	2,583,326	2,389,427	2,110,520	19
20	Bonds [5]	321,208	392,827	465,057	543,396	576,745	556,688	557,019	545,782	20
21	Corporate stocks [5]	627,460	776,809	1,002,928	1,207,787	1,476,184	2,026,638	1,832,408	1,564,738	21
22	U.S. claims on unaffiliated foreigners reported by U.S. nonbanking concerns [6]	322,980	367,567	450,578	545,524	588,322	677,498	821,564	830,111	22
23	U.S. claims reported by U.S. banks, not included elsewhere [7]	693,118	768,149	857,511	982,102	1,020,826	1,100,285	1,252,100	1,416,775	23
	Foreign-owned assets in the United States:									
24	With direct investment at current cost (lines 26-33)	**3,310,515**	**3,947,949**	**4,534,291**	**5,401,064**	**6,009,377**	**6,743,108**	**7,542,725**	**8,144,273**	24
25	With direct investment at market value (lines 26-34)	**3,450,386**	**4,273,609**	**5,017,790**	**6,214,336**	**7,268,608**	**8,440,524**	**8,934,015**	**9,172,060**	25
26	Foreign official assets in the United States	535,227	682,873	820,823	873,716	896,174	945,594	1,008,890	1,021,738	26
27	U.S. Government securities	407,152	507,460	631,088	648,188	669,768	693,781	749,904	798,844	27
28	U.S. Treasury securities [8]	396,887	489,952	606,427	615,076	622,921	617,680	625,161	650,703	28
29	Other	10,265	17,508	24,661	33,112	46,847	76,101	124,743	148,141	29
30	Other U.S. Government liabilities [8]	23,678	23,573	22,592	21,712	18,386	15,647	13,739	11,857	30
31	U.S. liabilities reported by U.S. banks, not included elsewhere [9]	73,386	107,394	113,098	135,384	125,883	138,847	153,403	123,125	31
32	Other foreign official assets [9]	31,011	44,446	54,045	68,432	82,137	97,319	91,844	87,912	32
	Other foreign assets in the United States:									
33	With direct investment at current cost (lines 35+37+38+41+42+43)	2,775,288	3,265,076	3,713,468	4,527,348	5,113,203	5,797,514	6,533,835	7,122,535	33
34	With direct investment at market value (lines 36+37+38+41+42+43)	2,915,159	3,590,736	4,196,967	5,340,620	6,372,434	7,494,930	7,925,125	8,150,322	34
	Direct investment in the United States:									
35	At current cost [10]	617,982	680,066	745,619	824,136	919,804	1,100,777	1,374,752	1,498,924	35
36	At market value [10]	757,853	1,005,726	1,229,318	1,637,408	2,179,035	2,498,193	2,766,042	2,528,711	36
37	U.S. Treasury securities [8]	235,684	330,210	440,832	550,613	562,036	492,781	400,966	440,966	37
38	U.S. securities other than U.S. Treasury securities [9]	739,695	969,849	1,165,113	1,512,725	1,903,443	2,351,291	2,673,608	2,356,654	38
39	Corporate and other bonds [9]	368,077	459,080	539,308	618,837	724,619	825,175	1,075,908	1,392,620	39
40	Corporate stocks [9]	371,618	510,769	625,805	893,888	1,178,824	1,526,116	1,547,640	1,464,034	40
41	U.S. currency	157,185	169,484	184,846	211,628	228,250	250,657	251,786	275,569	41
42	U.S. liabilities to unaffiliated foreigners reported by U.S nonbanking concerns [11]	239,817	300,424	346,810	459,407	485,675	564,873	729,340	804,417	42
43	U.S. liabilities reported by U.S. banks, not included elsewhere	784,925	815,043	828,248	968,839	1,013,995	1,067,155	1,153,363	1,298,197	43

while the US net debtor position increased by either $129 billion or $193 billion, depending on which valuation procedure is used for direct investments. In 1993, in contrast, the United States had a current account deficit of $91 billion, but its net debtor position actually improved, due to this valuation issue.

The IMF also publishes international investment position tables in the country pages of the International Financial Statistics. That table for the United Kingdom is presented as Exhibit 12.5. It is interesting to note that the UK is quite close to zero on a net basis; its assets abroad being only very slightly below its liabilities at the end of 2001.

EXHIBIT 12.5 UK INTERNATIONAL INVESTMENT POSITION

United Kingdom

International Investment Position		1995	1996	1997	1998	1999	2000	2001
Assets	79aad	2,391.34	2,764.53	3,247.52	3,546.24	3,901.19	4,449.02	4,606.31
Direct Investment Abroad	79abd	315.74	342.31	369.24	498.36	691.91	910.12	935.77
Portfolio Investment	79acd	773.94	930.84	1,076.56	1,172.18	1,333.57	1,343.62	1,304.04
Equity Securities	79add	336.30	404.67	466.94	505.15	664.31	635.34	558.38
Debt Securities	79aed	437.63	526.17	609.62	667.03	669.26	708.27	745.67
Financial Derivatives	79ald	—	—	—	—	—	—	—
Other Investment	79afd	1,252.52	1,444.99	1,763.93	1,836.86	1,839.84	2,152.31	2,329.26
Monetary Authorities	79agd	—	—	—	—	—	—	—
General Government	79ahd	14.71	16.69	16.33	16.17	15.87	14.66	13.79
Banks	79aid	979.78	1,063.88	1,367.33	1,457.48	1,364.00	1,579.68	1,641.21
Other Sectors	79ajd	258.04	364.42	380.28	363.20	459.97	557.96	674.26
Reserve Assets	79akd	49.15	46.39	37.79	38.84	35.86	42.97	37.24
Liabilities	79lad	2,426.47	2,882.36	3,372.31	3,771.20	4,031.36	4,504.30	4,664.12
Dir. Invest. in Rep. Economy	79lbd	226.63	259.17	287.31	355.40	404.51	457.47	503.96
Portfolio Investment	79lcd	629.75	815.00	964.63	1,155.19	1,343.40	1,493.50	1,420.03
Equity Securities	79ldd	267.66	383.89	499.23	668.90	824.10	901.93	793.68
Debt Securities	79led	362.09	431.10	465.40	486.29	519.31	591.58	626.35
Financial Derivatives	79lld	—	—	—	—	—	—	—
Other Investment	79lfd	1,570.09	1,808.19	2,120.36	2,260.62	2,283.45	2,553.33	2,740.13
Monetary Authorities	79lgd	—	—	—	—	—	—	—
General Government	79lhd	7.31	6.54	4.63	5.23	5.64	5.73	5.71
Banks	79lid	1,242.42	1,327.38	1,577.98	1,729.50	1,670.07	1,888.51	1,994.76
Other Sectors	79ljd	320.36	474.27	537.75	525.89	607.75	659.10	739.66

Source: IMF, *International Financial Statistics*.

Trade account imbalances through stages of development

The emphasis on balanced barter trade in the first half of this book may lead to the conclusion that it is normal or good for exports to equal imports so that the trade and current accounts are in balance. Trade and current account imbalances are actually more normal, and such disequilibria play a critical role in moving real capital from one country to another. For example, if a country has a current account deficit, then its domestic investment exceeds domestic saving, with the net inflow of real goods and services filling the gap. A current account surplus necessarily implies an excess of saving over investment, as can be seen through the standard national income accounting identities, first with the simplifying assumption of no government sector,

$$Y = C + I + (X - M)$$
$$Y = C + S_p$$

where Y is GNP, C is consumption, I is investment, S_p is private saving, X is exports, and M is imports. It then follows that

$$I + (X - M) = S_p$$

and that

$$I - S_p = M - X$$

A country must invest more than it saves if it has a current account deficit. Adding the government sector,

$$Y = C + I + G + (X - M)$$
$$Y = C + S_p + T$$

where G is government expenditures and T is taxes. It then follows that

$$I + (X - M) = S_p + (T - G)$$

and that

$$I - (S_p + (T - G)) = M - X$$

If

$$T - G = S_g$$

and

$$S_t = S_p + S_g$$

which simply says that total domestic savings equals private saving (S_p) plus government savings $(T - G)$, where the government can have negative savings. It then follows that

$$I - S_t = M - X$$

Investment will now exceed total domestic savings (including the government's) if the country has a current account deficit. Since world exports equal world imports, world investment equals world savings, so this is not a way of increasing the world's volume of investment above savings. Instead it is a way of allowing saving to take place in one country and the resulting investment to occur in another.

In the late 1990s, for example, the United States had gross private investment levels of about 18 percent of GNP despite gross savings (including depreciation charges) of only about 14 percent of GNP. The difference was made up through current account deficits of about 4 percent of GNP. Japan and Germany have been in a mirror-image situation, saving more than they invest and running current account surpluses. Savings originating in Japan, China, and Germany have financed a large volume of investment in the United States; current account imbalances have served as the mechanism through which real resources were moved from these three countries to the United States. German, Chinese, and Japanese lending to the United States provided the necessary financing for US current account deficits, allowing the overall balance of payments to be in approximate equilibrium.

The only unusual aspect of this situation is that a country as highly developed as the United States should be saving so little and therefore becoming dependent on large capital inflows. This is the more normal circumstance for a country that is beginning the development process.

An underdeveloped country typically has a small stock of capital relative to the size of its labor force; this situation implies a high marginal product of capital, which should be reflected as a high interest rate, high profit rates, or both. Such countries are natural magnets for external capital, unless the government adopts tax or other policies that destroy this underlying attractiveness for investors. As a result, well-governed developing countries have typically experienced large financial capital inflows that allowed parallel current account deficits and overall payments equilibrium. This situation allows domestic investment well in excess of savings levels, thus breaking the long-standing cycle-of-poverty argument that says that poor countries remain poor because they cannot save much, therefore cannot invest much, and can never increase their capital-to-labor ratios. As a result, labor productivity remains low, and poverty persists. With external capital inflows financing current account deficits, investment is no longer limited to the level of domestic savings, and the capital stock can grow more rapidly than would be possible with only domestic resources.

During the early decades of development, sometimes known as the "early debtor stage," countries normally run current account deficits to provide real resources so that they can invest more than they save, and they borrow the necessary funds abroad. During these years the country's net indebtedness to the rest of the world increases each year by the amount of its current account deficit.

This process is self-limiting or reversing, however. As the capital stock grows rapidly relative to the labor force (and relative to a fixed stock of land), the marginal product of capital falls and the marginal product of labor rises. As a result, interest and profit rates fall, but local labor incomes increase. The attractions for foreign capital decline, but local savings rates increase as incomes rise. Investment needs decline somewhat, because a large capital stock has already been put in place. The combination of rising savings rates and declining needs for massive investment levels allows the country to export more and import less, which is helpful because lower profit and interest rates mean that less foreign capital is flowing in.

When the trade and then the current account cease to be in deficit (the current account lags the trade account because it is necessary to make interest payments on previously accumulated indebtedness), and instead they become positive, net indebtedness reaches its peak and begins to decline.[5] This period is known as the "late debtor stage." Net indebtedness declines each year by the amount of the current account surplus, and eventually it reaches zero. The country then becomes a net creditor. This is known as the "early creditor stage." The current account remains in surplus, domestic savings exceed investment by the amount of this surplus, and the country accumulates net financial claims on the rest of the world. The only difference between the late debtor and early creditor stages is that the dividend and interest item within the current account should become positive in the early creditor stage. In theory, this stage could go on indefinitely, but economists do not like permanent disequilibria and seek ways to return to equilibrium.

The late creditor stage is a theoretical abstraction, but it could be considered the model for some OPEC countries after their oil reserves are depleted. In this situation, a country has accumulated large net financial claims on the rest of the world, from which it earns sizable dividend and interest payments. This income is used to pay for a trade deficit, so that both the current and capital accounts are in equilibrium. Such a country is analogous to a trust fund beneficiary who lives on income from capital. When countries such as Saudi Arabia and the United Arab Emirates have extracted all of their oil, or when oil becomes much less valuable due to the invention of inexpensive alternative energy sources, they may be in this situation. These countries do not appear to have other resources, and they now have high standards of living. When the oil is gone or is less valuable, the accumulated financial claims on the world will need to be sizable if the resulting income is to maintain current living standards.

The United States was an early debtor during much of the nineteenth century, and borrowed heavily in London and elsewhere to finance investments and a westward expansion. It became a late debtor near the end of the century, and it reduced its net indebtedness early in the twentieth century, becoming a net creditor sometime in the interwar period. It accumulated a sizable net creditor position after World War II and during the 1960s. It had an approximate balance in its current account in the 1970s and might be viewed as a mature creditor during that decade. Then, of course, this country turned the stages model of the balance of payments on its head by becoming a large debtor during the 1980s and early 1990s. The policies that caused this circumstance are discussed later in the book.

Intertemporal trade

The process through which countries borrow money abroad in order to finance current account deficits in one period, and later use current account surpluses to repay the loans (with interest) has recently been widely analyzed through models of intertemporal trade.[6] This concept begins with the idea that a current account deficit represents both an excess of investment over domestic saving, as was noted in the previous section, and a gap between total domestic absorption of resources (consumption plus investment plus government spending on goods and services) and what the country produces. Returning to the national income accounting identity on page 286:

$$Y = C + I + G + (X - M)$$

which can be reorganized as:

$$(X - M) = Y - (C + I + G) = Y - A$$

or as:

$$(M - X) = (C + I + G) - Y = A - Y$$

where A is total domestic absorption of goods and services.

In the intertemporal trade approach current account disequilibria are seen as a means of shifting the timing of absorption relative to national output, and the timing of investment relative to saving. A current account deficit allows a country to absorb more now than it produces and to invest more now than it saves, at the cost of having to be in the opposite circumstance, producing more than it absorbs and saving more than it invests, later. Since the current account of the world is zero, the world can only absorb what it produces and invest what it saves, meaning that current account deficits in one group of countries must be offset by parallel surpluses in the rest of the world. The surplus countries are shifting resource absorption in the opposite direction through time; that is, they are now absorbing less than they produce and investing less than they save, but will be able to absorb more than they produce and invest more than they save later when they are repaid. They are paid the real interest rate in addition to principle, so the real interest rate is their compensation for putting off current absorption, assuming that the real interest rate is positive. This means that they gain more in absorption later than they give up now.

There are a number of reasons for countries to shift the timing of absorption relative to output and of investment relative to saving. The most important is implicit in the previous discussion of the pattern of current account imbalances as countries go through the development process; nations in which the marginal product of capital is high, perhaps because they are underdeveloped and therefore have a low capital-to-labor ratio, attract capital inflows with high rates of return, and can thereby accelerate the development process by investing a great deal despite a low savings rate. This argument for current account imbalances and for offsetting capital flows is also implicit in the discussion of international factor mobility in Chapter 9.

There are, however, at least three other reasons for countries to run current account deficits now at the cost of repaying the necessary loans, with interest, later. First, such current account imbalances allow a country to maintain steady consumption levels in the face of sizable shocks to real output. Without the possibility of borrowing to finance a current account deficit, an agricultural country that experienced a drought, or any open economy whose terms of trade worsened badly, would have to severely reduce current consumption. A current account deficit allows a country to sustain consumption now, and then repay the necessary loans when the temporary negative shocks have been reversed. For a poor developing country, this may be the only way to avoid famines when crops fail. When OPEC increases in the price of oil sharply worsened the terms of trade of many poor oil importing countries in the 1970s, international capital flows, which financed current account deficits, made it less necessary to reduce consumption levels. Smoothing consumption in the face of such shocks is a vital role for current account imbalances and for the international capital flows which finance them, particularly for agricultural countries where bad weather can produce large output losses.

Another reason for international borrowing to finance current account deficits is to accommodate surges in government expenditures, particularly during a war. Great Britain simply could not produce enough to sustain its role in World Wars I or II, so it ran large current account deficits, which it financed by borrowing and by selling off previously accumulated foreign assets. Many countries in demanding military campaigns have relied on such financing. The problem, of course, is to repay the loans after the war is over. King Edward III of England borrowed large sums from Italian banks to finance his invasion of France in 1340. When he later defaulted on the loans, the two largest Florentine banks, those owned by the Bardi and Peruzzi families, failed.

A far more dangerous reason for current account deficits and for the required borrowing is because consumers in a country have a very high rate of time preference, that is, they greatly prefer current over future consumption. Such a country, which is likely to be very poor, borrows now to finance consumption in excess of its normal level of output, hoping to find a way of repaying the loans later.

The intertemporal trade approach, which views current account deficits and borrowing now as requiring current account surpluses and repayment (with interest) later, assumes that the loans will actually be repaid. An alternative "model," which occurs all too often, is that countries absorb more than they produce and invest more than they save in one period, borrowing money abroad to finance the current account deficits, and then simply fail to repay the loans. They never have to save more than they invest and produce more than they absorb, because foreign lenders have to write off the loans as uncollectable. As will be discussed at some length in Chapter 20, this has happened a number of times in Latin America and quite recently in Russia and Argentina. As was noted above, it also occurred in Europe in the fourteenth century. The history of international lending is littered with such defaults.

The large risks of default which exist when investors lend in foreign countries may explain something of an oddity in the historical data, namely that current account disequilibria are relatively small shares of GDP, and the correlation between national savings rates and national investment rates are very high. High savings countries typically invest a great deal in their domestic economies, and vice versa. This is known as "home bias," because investors and lenders seem to be biased toward their national capital markets. One study of cross-section data for 23 industrialized countries found that 69 percent of the variation in investment to GDP ratios could be explained by parallel variations in the saving to GDP.[7] This study was done with data from the 1970s and 1980s; the correlation could be slightly lower during the 1990s.

It might be expected that international capital flows would have sharply reduced this correlation, and that high savings countries would often invest primarily abroad where yields could be expected to be higher, but this has apparently not occurred yet. The concept of a globalized capital market is still an exaggeration. Capital markets are still significantly national or, in the case of the European Union, regional. Default risks, which become particularly dangerous when loans are made to developing or transition economies, may be a sizable reason for this outcome, but that problem will be discussed in more detail later in the book.

Summary of key concepts

1   The balance-of-payments accounts present a totaling by type of transactions between residents of one country and residents of the rest of the world, with transactions that result in a foreign payment made to a local resident being given a plus sign, and transactions that result in a local resident making a payment to a foreigner being given a negative sign.

2   Since the accounts, by definition, must sum to zero, the net errors and omissions entry is calculated as the sum of the estimates of all other items with the opposite sign.

3   For a country maintaining a fixed exchange rate, a payments surplus or deficit is calculated as the sum of the autonomous items, with the residual or accommodating items following. In the Official Reserve Transactions, or Overall, payments format, all items are viewed as autonomous except movements of foreign exchange reserves.

4   The concept of a payments surplus or deficit has little or no meaning for a country on a floating exchange rate, which leads to a quite different organization of the accounts for the United States.

5   A poor developing country would be expected to run a current account deficit, financed by capital inflows, so that it can invest more than it saves. As the development process proceeds, the current account moves to surplus and the earlier borrowings are repaid.

Questions for study and review

1 What sign would each of the following transactions have in the US balance-of-payments accounts, and in what section of the account (current, private capital, or foreign exchange reserves) would it appear?

   (a) IBM of Canada remits dividends to IBM of the United States.
   (b) The Bank of Japan purchases US dollars which are added to the foreign exchange reserves of Japan.
   (c) A Japanese corporation sells machinery to a US firm, with payment to be received 1 year after delivery. Delivery is this year.

2 "An increase in foreign-owned balances in US banks is equivalent to a short-term loan to the United States." True or false? Explain.

3 Distinguish between the reserve settlements balance and the current account balance.

4 Explain why both a foreign asset acquired and a foreign liability reduced give rise to a debit entry in a nation's balance of payments.

5 Distinguish between autonomous and accommodating transactions in the balance of payments. What is the purpose of the distinction?

6 If a country is an exporter of long-term capital, what do you expect its current account balance to be? Why?

7 What is the essential distinction between the current account and the capital account in the balance of payments?

8 Since the US net creditor/debtor table is now published on a market value rather than historic value basis, what changes would have to be made to the published version of the US current account to make it match changes in the new creditor/debtor table?

9 Organize the following items into a balance of payments account for a country on a fixed exchange rate. You must assign the pluses and minuses for all items except one and calculate net errors and omissions. What is the Official Reserve Transactions payments position of this country? Imports 80, domestic interest and dividend receipts from abroad 10, increase in short-term private claims on this country 25, increase in foreign exchange reserve assets of this country 30, exports 90, foreign purchases of domestic bonds 20, foreign direct investment abroad 30, decrease in domestic short-term private claims on foreigners 15, direct investment in this country by foreigners 25, and other services +25.

Suggested further reading

- Advisory Committee on the Presentation of the Balance of Payments Statistics, "Report," Survey of Current Business, June 1976, pp. 18–27.
- International Monetary Fund, *Balance of Payments Manual*, Washington, DC: IMF, 1993.
- International Monetary Fund, *Balance of Payments Yearbook*, Washington, DC: IMF, annual.
- International Monetary Fund, *International Financial Statistics*, monthly.
- Kemp, D., "Balance of Payments Concepts: What Do They Really Mean?," *Federal Reserve Bank of St Louis Review*, July 1975.

- Landefeld, J. Steven and Anne Lawson, "Valuation of the US Net International Investment Position," *Survey of Current Business*, May 1991, pp. 40–9.
- Obstfeld, M. and K. Rogoff, "The Intertemporal Approach to the Current Account," in G. Grossman and K. Rogoff, eds, *Handbook of International Economics*, Vol. III, Amsterdam: Elsevier, 1995, pp. 1731–800.
- Stern, R., Charles F. Schwartz, Robert Triffin, Edward M. Bernstein, and Walter Lederer, "The Presentation of the Balance of Payments: A Symposium," *Princeton Essays in International Finance*, no. 123, August 1977.

Notes

1 For a discussion of various sources of errors in the world's current account data, see Nawaz Shuja, "Why the World's Current Account Does Not Balance," *Finance and Development*, September 1987, pp. 43–5. A particularly large error typically occurs in the dividends and interest item because such payments are recorded as leaving one country, but not as arriving in another, where they would be taxable. Tax "avoidance" would appear to be an obvious reason for this anomaly.

2 For a detailed discussion of the volume and composition of foreign exchange reserves, see pp. 95–9 of the 2002 *IMF Annual Report*.

3 See the IMF *Balance of Payments Manual*, fifth edn, 1993 for a discussion of the new terminology which is used by the Fund. This volume also discusses other aspects of balance-of-payments accounting in some detail.

4 For the rationale for the mid-1970s reorganization of the US balance-of-payments accounts, see "The Report of the Advisory Committee on the Presentation on the Balance of Payments Statistics," *Survey of Current Business*, June 1976. See also: Robert Stern, Charles F. Schwartz, Robert Triffin, Edward M. Bernstein, and Walter Lederer, "The Presentation of the Balance of Payments: A Symposium," *Princeton Essays in International Finance*, no. 123, August 1977, and D. Kemp, "Balance of Payments Concepts: What Do They Really Mean?," *Federal Reserve Bank of St Louis Review*, July 1975, pp. 14–23. Detailed data can be found in the *Balance of Payments Yearbook*, which is published by the IMF. See the *Balance of Payments Manual*, fifth edn, 1993, which is another publication of the IMF, for a detailed discussion of how the accounts are put together, including definitions of the various components.

5 For one of the earlier discussions of the stages model of the balance of payments, see Dragaslav Avramovic, *Economic Growth and External Debt* (Baltimore: Johns Hopkins, 1994).

6 A review of the literature on the subject of intertemporal trade can be found in M. Obstfeld and K. Rogoff, "The Intertemporal Approach to the Current Account," ch. 34 in G. Grossman and K. Rogoff, eds, *Handbook of International Economics*, Vol. III (Amsterdam: Elsevier, 1995).

7 M. Obstfeld and K. Rogoff, "The Intertemporal Approach to the Currency Account," ch. 34 in G. Grossman and K. Rogoff, eds, *Handbook of International Trade*, Vol. III (Amsterdam: Elsevier, 1995) pp. 1176–84.

13 Markets for foreign exchange

Learning objectives

By the end of this chapter you should be able to understand:

- how those carrying on the transactions discussed in Chapter 12 use the exchange market to buy or sell foreign exchange, with credit (+) transactions in the payments account generating a supply of foreign exchange and a demand for the local currency, and the debit (−) items generating a demand for foreign exchange and a supply of local currency.
- the role of central bank intervention when private transactions in the exchange market are not balanced or in equilibrium;
- the mechanisms through which such intervention occurred under the gold standard, under the Bretton Woods system, and for countries with exchange or capital controls;
- the lack of any need for intervention for a country maintaining a floating exchange rate, but why countries now on floats intervene anyway;
- the institutional arrangements through which foreign exchange is traded in banking centers such as New York and London;
- the nominal effective exchange rate for a country, and the real effective exchange rate, with the latter being particularly important in determining the price and cost competitiveness of a country in world markets.

Foreign exchange markets appear to be rather exotic, but the basic idea behind them is simple. In order to complete the international transactions described in the previous chapter, people need to sell one currency and buy another. Foreign exchange markets are merely the institutional arrangements through which such purchases and sales are made.

If Americans purchase foreign goods or financial assets, they begin with dollars and need foreign exchange to complete the transactions. British exporters will expect to be paid in pounds sterling, so a US importer must sell dollars and purchase sterling to buy British goods. Even if the UK exporter were to accept payment in dollars, he or she would be selling them for sterling. Thus no matter which currency is used for payment, someone will be selling dollars and purchasing sterling. US purchases of British financial assets would result in the same requirement that someone sell dollars for sterling. Even an increase in US holdings of official foreign exchange reserves has this result. The New York Federal Reserve Bank sells dollars and purchases sterling to increase such reserves.

If foreigners purchase US goods or financial assets, they face a parallel need to sell their currencies and buy dollars. This also applies to foreign central banks that accumulate foreign exchange reserves in the form of dollars: they sell their currencies and purchase dollars in their exchange markets to add to such dollar reserves.

Balance-of-payments transactions that are debits and carry a minus sign in the US accounts cause sales of dollars and purchases of foreign exchange, whereas credits that carry a plus sign produce sales of foreign currencies and purchases of dollars. The only exception to this conclusion occurs when the same individual is simultaneously involved in two international transactions of the same size and the opposite sign. Such a set of transactions would be self-canceling in terms of its balance-of-payments effect. If, for example, a US newspaper purchased Canadian newsprint and paid for it with a Canadian dollar check drawn on the Bank of Montreal, there would be no purchase or sale of either currency in the exchange market. The US balance-of-payments accounts would show two entries: a short-term capital flow from Canada to the United States that would be a credit (+), and the importing of the newsprint which would be a debit (–). There would be no net impact on the US official reserve transactions balance and no use of the exchange market.

Except for such paired and offsetting transactions, there is a parallel or mirror-image relationship between what occurs in the balance-of-payments accounts and in the exchange market. Since credit (+) transactions represent demand for dollars, and vice versa, a balance-of-payments deficit means an excess supply of dollars in the exchange market, whereas a surplus would imply an excess demand for dollars. Disequilibria in the balance-of-payments accounts produce parallel disequilibria in the exchange market. In a regime of flexible exchange rates, a subject to be dealt with in detail later in this book, the price of foreign exchange adjusts to clear the market. Under fixed exchange rates, which will be discussed before flexible rates, it becomes the obligation of the central bank to intervene in the exchange market to absorb the excess demand or supply, so that the market can clear despite a lack of balance in the autonomous transactions. Foreign exchange reserves rise or fall through such intervention.

Supply and demand for foreign exchange

The operations of the exchange market can be represented by a standard supply-and-demand graph (see Figure 13.1). The demand for foreign exchange is derived from the domestic demand for foreign goods, services, and financial assets, whereas the supply of foreign exchange is similarly derived from the foreign demand for goods, services, and financial assets coming from the home country. Foreigners sell their currency in order to purchase US dollars for the purpose of completing purchases of US goods, services, or financial assets.

If the United States had a fixed exchange rate and a payments deficit, as shown in the figure, there would be an excess demand for foreign currencies in the exchange market. The New York Federal Reserve Bank and/or its counterparts abroad would then be obligated to buy up the excess dollars and sell the foreign currencies that were in excess demand. Such transactions would either reduce US foreign exchange assets (if the New York Fed acted) or increase foreign official holdings of dollar reserves (if foreign central banks intervened). If the central banks failed to intervene to purchase the excess dollars, the price of foreign exchange would rise to the equilibrium level shown in Figure 13.1, and a fixed exchange rate would no longer exist. It is the willingness of central banks to maintain a commitment to purchase or sell foreign currencies as needed to maintain unchanging exchange rates that differentiates a fixed parity system from a world of flexible exchange rates.

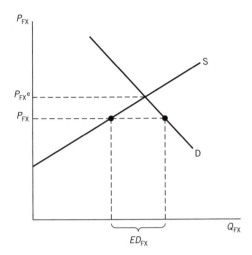

Figure 13.1 Supply and demand in the market for foreign exchange. A fixed price of foreign exchange of P_{FX} produces and excess demand for foreign exchange of ED_{FX} which the central bank must absorb through exchange market intervention. Allowing the price of foreign exchange to rise to $P_{FX}e$, which is the price that would prevail if floating exchange rates existed, eliminates this problem.

If the United States had a payments surplus, there would be an excess supply of foreign exchange (an excess demand for dollars), and central banks would need to provide the required dollars and absorb the excess foreign currencies. In this case, either US reserve assets would increase or foreign official reserve assets in the form of dollars would decline, depending again on which central bank acted. It is possible, of course, that both central banks would act and that the US surplus would be offset by a combination of an increase in US reserve assets and a decline in foreign official holdings of dollars, with the total intervention by the two sides equaling the US surplus.

Because all plus transactions (autonomous plus accommodating) represent purchases of dollars and all minus transactions are dollar sales, the balance-of-payments accounts including all transactions must total zero. For every dollar bought, one must be sold, or the transaction cannot be completed. Therefore the total of plus transactions must equal the total of the minuses, where foreign exchange reserve movements as well as autonomous transactions are included. **Exchange market intervention** by central banks fills the gap between imbalances in total autonomous transactions and the need for all transactions to total zero. It may be useful briefly to discuss different regimes or arrangements for such intervention, beginning with the pre-1914 gold standard.

Exchange market intervention regimes

The gold standard

Under the gold standard (discussed in more detail in Chapter 16), central banks set exchange rates indirectly by establishing relative prices of gold, and then by promising to buy and sell gold in unlimited amounts at those prices.[1] If, for example, the British government set the price of gold at £4 sterling per ounce while the US Treasury price was $20, as long as both governments or central banks maintained a willingness to buy and sell at those prices, the exchange rate would have to be about $5 equals £1. If, for example, sterling fell significantly below that value, British residents would be unwilling to sell in the exchange market because they had the obvious alternative of selling their sterling to the British government for gold, shipping the gold to New York, and selling it for dollars to the US Treasury. A British balance-of-payments deficit that produced an excess supply of sterling in the exchange market and downward pressure on the exchange value of sterling would automatically result in the loss of gold reserves by the UK and a gain in such reserves by the surplus country, in this case the United States.

If the United States had a payments deficit that produced an excess supply of dollars that drove the currency downward in the exchange market, Americans would not have to accept an unattractive price for their currency. The reason is that they would have the alternative of turning their dollars in for gold, sending the gold to London, and thereby transferring into sterling at an exchange rate of $5 for £1. If transportation costs were zero, the exchange rate could not diverge even slightly from the 5 to 1 parity. Because such costs were not zero, a narrow range (about 0.6 percent plus or minus for a total of about 1.2 percent) existed within which the exchange rate could move. When it hit the edge of that range, gold would start to flow between New York and London; the two edges of the range were therefore known as the "gold points." More will be said about this system later, but for now it is important to note that fixed exchange rates were maintained indirectly by a willingness of both central banks to buy and sell the same commodity at fixed prices. Gold had no particular significance in this arrangement. Any commodity (silver, wheat, or whatever) that could easily be shipped across the Atlantic could have been used.

The Bretton Woods arrangements

The Bretton Woods system, as described in the **Articles of Agreement of the International Monetary Fund**, emerged from a summer 1944 conference at a resort of that name near Mount Washington in New Hampshire. The World Bank, the International Monetary Fund, and a variety of other postwar economic and financial arrangements were agreed to at that conference. One of its results was the exchange market intervention system that prevailed from the late 1940s until August 1971. The dollar was tied to gold at $35 per ounce, and the US government promised to buy and sell at that price, doing business only with foreign central banks or governments. Other countries set fixed parities for their currencies in terms of the US dollar and intervened in their exchange markets to hold market rates within a narrow range around those parities.2 British sterling was, for example, $2.80 for many years, and the Bank of England (the British central bank) was committed to maintaining the market rate between $2.78 and $2.82. Whenever the United Kingdom had a payments deficit, the resulting downward pressure on sterling would drive the rate down toward $2.78. Before it got that low, the Bank of England would start selling dollars and buying sterling to slow its decline. If it fell significantly below $2.80, that is, if it approached $2.78, the sales of dollars/purchases of sterling would become sufficiently heavy to stop its decline.

If the UK had a payments surplus, the resulting upward pressure on the currency would take it above $2.80 and the Bank of England would purchase dollars and sell sterling in sufficient volume to guarantee that it did not reach $2.82. In the case of a British surplus, the dollars which the Bank of England bought in the London foreign exchange market would be deposited at the New York Federal Reserve Bank, thus adding to UK reserve assets and to US reserve liabilities. Any such reserves that would not soon be needed would normally be switched into an interest-bearing form such as US Treasury bills, with the New York Fed acting as custodian for the Bank of England. If the British accumulated more dollars than they wanted, they had the option of using them to purchase gold from the US government. If British payments deficits depleted their reserves of dollars, gold could be sold to the United States to replenish the dollar holdings of the Bank of England. Reserves were held both as dollars and as gold, with countries being free to switch back and forth, depending on their confidence in the ability of the United States to maintain the $35 fixed price of gold and the interest rates they could earn on US Treasury bills.

This arrangement placed the United States in a unique and somewhat disadvantageous situation because it had no control over its exchange rate. If there are N currencies in the world, there are $N - 1$ dollar exchange rates. If $N - 1$ countries peg their currencies to the dollar, the dollar exchange rate is automatically set relative to that of all other countries without US involvement or control. The United States could change its price of gold, which would be of interest to South African and Russian mines, but it could not change any **bilateral exchange rate**. This turned out to be a significant disadvantage for the US in the late 1960s and early 1970s, but that subject will be dealt with in greater detail later.

Payments arrangements in developing countries

Most developing countries had somewhat different arrangements throughout the Bretton Woods era. The system described above implies free currency convertibility; that is, private residents are free to buy and sell foreign exchange in order to carry out transactions in the current and capital accounts, although some industrialized countries did maintain restrictions on international capital flows. Many developing countries do not have free convertibility in that virtually all transactions are subject to government regulation.[3]

These legal arrangements are designed first to guarantee that foreign exchange revenues received by residents flow into official reserves immediately. Residents are required to sell any such funds, whether received from exports, tourism, or whatever, to the central bank promptly at the official exchange rate, inasmuch as the purpose of this system is to maximize foreign exchange reserve availability. Second, the government or central bank then licenses all transactions that require foreign exchange, granting approval only to those viewed as being important or at least useful. Investments abroad, imports of luxury goods, or foreign travel are not likely to receive permits and are therefore legally impossible. The goal of this part of the regulatory system is to allocate scarce foreign exchange to uses that the government considers vital for the country's development and to avoid use of such funds for less important expenditures.

The underlying reason for such exchange controls is the constant threat of balance-of-payments deficits and a resulting shortage of foreign exchange reserves. Facing such shortages, governments decide to control the use of available funds to guarantee the availability of vital imports such as food, oil, and medicines, and to avoid expenditures on non-necessities.

This approach to rationing scarce foreign exchange sounds reasonable, but it has a number of major disadvantages. Those residents who are denied legal access to foreign exchange will not only be displeased, but they will probably start looking for illegal sources of funds. In particular, they are likely to be willing to pay a premium for foreign exchange in an illegal or street market. If the legal exchange rate is 10 pesos per dollar, the street rate may be 15 or 20 pesos per dollar. The existence of this premium provides a strong incentive for exporters and other recipients of foreign exchange to divert their funds from the legal market at 10 pesos per dollar to the street market at 20 per dollar. Governments usually attempt to enforce the requirement that such funds be sold only to the central bank, but such efforts are seldom very successful. Foreign tourists are likely to be approached by large numbers of people offering very attractive rates for local money on the street. It is extremely difficult to stop people from arbitraging between the two rates. As a result, the flow of foreign exchange into legal reserves is likely to stagnate or decline as more business is diverted to the illegal market. Officials of the central bank or finance ministry may be offered bribes to allow the purchase of foreign exchange at the legal rate for what should be illegal transactions. Such systems of exchange market control are frequently the source of graft and corruption.

The illegal or street market sometimes becomes so important to commerce and finance that its exchange rate is viewed as the most accurate barometer of what is happening to the balance of payments. If, for example, the legal rate stayed fixed at 10 pesos per dollar, but the street rate suddenly fell from 20 to 30 per dollar, that would be taken as evidence of a deteriorating payments situation, and of a growing desire of local residents to move capital out of the country and into foreign currencies. Because fear of accelerating inflation or of political instability would produce such a desire, the street or illegal exchange rate is often viewed as a measure of confidence in the future of the price level and the political system. A sudden decline in the value of the local currency in that market indicates a deterioration of such confidence.

Often the difference between the official and the street exchange rates can be quite large. In Myanmar (Burma), for example, the legal rate has been about 6 kyats per dollar for years, while the street rate has varied between 30 and 100 kyats per dollar.

The alternative means of evading exchange controls are almost too many to list. Local currency can be used to purchase small valuable items (gold or gem diamonds) which are taken abroad and sold. A wealthy resident of India told one of the authors of this book that diamonds are favored for this purpose because a large amount of capital can be moved in a very small physical volume, and diamonds do not set off metal detectors at an airport.

Many developing countries have long borders and sea coasts which are poorly guarded. Any exportable commodity can be smuggled out of the country and sold without the normal paperwork, allowing the owner of the goods to secretly move capital. A country such as Indonesia, which consists of hundreds of islands, cannot stop small boats carrying lumber or other exportable items from sailing to nearby countries, where the goods are sold in "informal" transactions.

False invoicing or transfer pricing, which comes up again later in this book, is a particularly common way to move funds despite laws to the contrary. The value of an export shipment is understated on the invoice and other documents. The recorded amount is paid to the exporting country, and the remainder is deposited in an account in the importing country which is owned by the exporter. Over-invoicing of imports accomplishes the same purpose. A firm in India imports $1 million worth of steel from the United States, but the invoice and other documents show the steel as being worth $1,200,000. The latter amount is paid to the US exporter, who then deposits $200,000 in the New York bank account of the Indian importer, who can then sell checks drawn on that account at the unofficial exchange rate, thereby making a handsome profit. An official of a US steel company told one of the authors that it was impossible to sell steel in India unless his firm was willing to participate in such schemes.

What has become known as hawala banking is another means of evading exchange controls and also has more sinister possibilities. It is particularly relevant for remittance payments from foreign workers to their families. For example, there are large numbers of

Pakistanis employed in the United Kingdom who need to send money to their families. They earn sterling, but their families want rupees. If there are people in Pakistan with rupees who want sterling in the United Kingdom, the possibilities for an informal exchange system become apparent. Participants in the system gather sterling from the workers in the London, and promise to deliver rupees to their families in Karachi. The rupees of those desiring to get money out of Pakistan are used to pay the families, and the sterling gathered in London becomes available to them for whatever use they prefer.

All that is required is a communications route making it possible for those in Karachi to know which families are to be paid how many rupees. That might be done in coded form by phone, email, or courier. If the communications mechanism can be kept confidential and the exchange process in London and Karachi informal, there is no obvious way for the Pakistani or the British government to know what is going on. Hawala banking is not only a way to evade exchange controls, but is widely believed to be used by criminal enterprises and by terrorists to move funds from the Middle East and South Asia to industrialized countries. September 11 greatly increased the attention given to hawala banking by the US and European governments, and a few such operations have reportedly been closed.

The attractions of a regulated exchange market for a developing country facing payments deficits are obvious, but the record of such control systems is poor. Enforcement is difficult and frequently produces a decline in respect for law. Increasing volumes of export receipts (particularly from remittances and tourism) are diverted to an illegal market, so the availability of foreign exchange for important purposes stagnates or declines. Economics is about how rational economic agents maximize their self-interest, which means that it is about avarice and ingenuity. Few situations bring out the unattractive aspects of such maximizing behavior more quickly than a system of foreign exchange market controls that denies people the opportunity to purchase foreign exchange legally, thereby driving them to illegal alternatives. Such systems almost guarantee widespread lawbreaking and thereby undermine respect for the legal system. Despite the arguments of economists and a poor historical record, these systems of exchange market controls remain common in the developing world.

It ought to be noted that not just hawala banking, but all of the techniques for evading foreign exchange controls discussed above, are useful for criminals or terrorists seeking to move funds in forms that are difficult to trace in order to finance their activities. Since September 11, 2001 law enforcement agencies in many countries have become far more interested in finding ways to trace, and to stop, such transfers. This will not be an easy task.

Exchange market intervention with floating exchange rates

In theory, a flexible exchange rate system means that no central bank intervenes in the exchange market and that rates are determined the way prices of common stocks are settled: through shifts in supply and demand without official stabilization. In a clean or pure float, the exchange rate rises and falls with shifts in international payments flows, and these exchange rate movements keep the balance of payments in constant equilibrium (i.e. the official reserve transactions balance = 0). If the balance of payments and the exchange market were in equilibrium when a large surge of imports occurred, the local currency would depreciate to a level at which offsetting transactions were encouraged and the market again cleared, which is analogous to what happens to the price of General Motors stock if a sudden wave of selling hits the market. The price falls until enough buyers are attracted to clear the market. In a clean float, the exchange market operates in the same way, but countries do not maintain clean floats. Large or rapid exchange rate movements are seen as so disruptive that central banks instead operate dirty or managed flexible exchange rates.

There is no defense of a fixed parity, but instead discretionary intervention takes place whenever the market is moving in a direction or at a speed that the central bank or government wishes to avoid. If, for example, the yen were depreciating beyond the wishes of Tokyo, the Bank of Japan would purchase yen and sell foreign currencies in an attempt to slow that movement. Such purchases might be coordinated with similar actions by central banks in Europe and North America, creating a stronger effect on the market. Since the mid-1980s such intervention has increased, and more of it is being coordinated among the central banks of the major industrialized countries.

Many economists remain skeptical that such intervention can have more than temporary effects on exchange rates unless it is accompanied by changes in national monetary policies. Purchases of yen by the Bank of Japan may temporarily slow a depreciation, but a reduction in the total yen money supply, that is, a tighter Japanese monetary policy, would have a more lasting impact. Despite such doubts among economists, the central banks of countries with flexible exchange rates have become more active in exchange markets in recent years. The result seems to be some reduction in exchange rate volatility.[4]

Exchange market institutions

The foreign exchange market is maintained by major commercial banks in financial centers such as New York, London, Frankfurt, Singapore, and Tokyo. It is not like the New York Stock Exchange where trading occurs at a single location, but instead it is a "telephone market" in which traders are located in the various banks and trade electronically. Although trading occurs in other cities, the vast majority of the US market is in New York, where it includes New York banks, foreign banks with US subsidiaries or branches, and banks from other states that are allowed to do only international banking in New York. The banks typically maintain trading rooms that are staffed by at least one trader for each major currency.[5]

Orders come to the traders from large businesses that have established ties to that bank and from smaller banks around the country that have a correspondent banking relationship with that institution. The banks maintain inventories of each of the currencies which they trade in the form of deposits at foreign banks. If, for example, Citibank purchases yen from a customer, those funds will be placed in its account in Tokyo, and sales of yen by Citibank will come out of that account. Because these inventories rise and fall as trading proceeds, the banks take risks by frequently having net exposures in various currencies. If, for example, Citibank has sold yen heavily and consequently retains yen assets that are less than yen liabilities, the bank will have a **short position** in yen, and will lose if the yen appreciates and gain if it falls. Some banks try to impose strict limitations on such exposure by buying currencies to offset any emerging short or long positions, whereas others view such exposure as a way to seek speculative profits.

Currencies such as the Canadian dollar or the euro would normally be quoted in hundredths of a cent or basis points, with bid-asked spreads usually being about five basis points or one-twentieth of a cent for large transactions. The Canadian dollar, for example, might be quoted at 64.42–47 US cents, meaning that the banks are prepared to purchase it for 64.42 cents or sell it for 64.47 cents. Before the advent of flexible exchange rates in the early 1970s, bid-asked spreads were narrower, because exchange rate volatility and risk were smaller. The spreads widened to about ten basis points in the 1970s and narrowed to the current range of about five points in the 1980s. Spreads are sometimes narrower for sets of currencies that are very heavily traded and for which the bilateral exchange rate has been particularly stable.

These narrow spreads are for very large transactions for banks' best customers, and they widen when that circumstance does not prevail. When tourists exchange money at airport banks or similar institutions, the spreads are much wider because the institutions need to cover their costs and make a profit on small transactions.[6]

The spread of about five basis points also operates in what is known as the "interbank market," in which the banks trade among themselves. If, for example, Chase Manhattan had bought a large volume of Canadian dollars over a period of a few minutes and the traders became uncomfortable with the resulting **long position**, they would sell the excess Canadian funds in the interbank market, perhaps using a broker as an intermediary or perhaps dealing directly with another bank to save a brokerage fee. Information on interbank rates and spreads is provided electronically, primarily by Reuters, which supplies television monitors with the current rates for the major currencies. Reuters gathers information on current trades and on the willingness of banks to trade various currencies. The resulting spreads appear on its screens both in the major banks and in major industrial firms that have extensive international business dealings. As a result, everyone in the market should have the same information as to what rates are available. Bank traders have said, however, that Reuters and competing services can sometimes lag the market by 30 to 45 seconds when trading is particularly active, and that trading with customers at "screen rates" can therefore become risky. In such situations, traders are often in direct phone contact with other trading rooms to try to find out what the most current rates are.

Reduced cost and increased speed for international communications mean that during overlapping business hours, the European and New York markets are really a single market. Early in the day, New York banks can trade as easily in London or Frankfurt as in New York. Thus differences in exchange rates among these cities are arbitraged away almost instantly. Chicago and San Francisco continue trading after New York, and then Tokyo and Hong Kong open for business, so trading is going on somewhere in the world around the clock. Some New York banks are reportedly maintaining two shifts of traders, with one group arriving at 3 a.m. when London and Frankfurt open and the other group trading very late at night until Tokyo opens. The large New York banks have branches or subsidiaries in Tokyo, Frankfurt, and London; therefore these banks are trading somewhere all the time during business days.

Foreign exchange transactions in the **spot market** are typically completed or cleared with a 2-day lag, so that transactions agreed to on Monday will result in payments being made on Wednesday. This lag is partially the result of differences in time zones and is required to allow paperwork to be completed. Canadian/US dollar business is normally cleared in 1 day because New York and Toronto are in the same time zone.

Payment is made by electronic transfer through a "**cable transfer**," which is simply an electronic message to a bank instructing it to transfer funds from one account to another. If, for example, General Motors bought DM 2 million from Chase Manhattan on Tuesday, Chase would send such a cable transfer to its subsidiary or branch instructing it to transfer the funds from its account to that of General Motors on Thursday, and General Motors would transfer the required amount of dollars from its US account to Chase Manhattan. The transaction that had been arranged on Tuesday would then be complete. For the major industrialized countries, the cable transfers are handled through a system known as the **Society for Worldwide Interbank Financial Telecommunications (SWIFT)**, which began operations in 1987. The electronic system through which foreign exchange transfers are made in New York is known as the **Clearing House International Payments System (CHIPS)**, which was reportedly handling over $600 billion per day in the late 1990s, much of which was for trades made outside the United States. Worldwide foreign exchange trading was about $1,200 billion per day in 2002, with well in excess of 90 percent of the trading being for capital rather than current account transactions. Although most foreign exchange trading involves the dollar, London remains the largest foreign exchange market at about $500 billion per day, followed by New York ($250 billion), Tokyo ($150 billion), and Singapore ($140 billion).

The revolution that the Internet has introduced to common stock trading in the United States is beginning to extend to the foreign exchange market. Internet trading in foreign exchange has begun, and is expected to grow rapidly at the expense of the trading rooms in the large commercial banks. Internet and other electronic trading systems are particularly attractive for relatively small transactions, where bid/asked spreads are wider than those described above for large transactions. Some market participants expect 50 percent of foreign exchange transactions to be done without the involvement of a commercial bank trading room within a few years.

The major commercial banks have recently created a new transactions clearing system which will reduce or eliminate default risks in the case of a bank failure. This problem can arise because European banks are operating 6 hours ahead of US banks, so a transaction may be completed in Europe before New York is open for business. This means that a few hours have existed in which one half of the transaction is complete and the other is not. When a German bank, Herstatt, failed in 1974, a number of other commercial banks absorbed losses on transactions with Herstatt which were only half completed. The new system, operating under the name CLS (Continuous Linked Settlement) Bank first nets out transactions in the opposite between pairs of banks, so that only one net payment is made. It then schedules such payments during hours when both banks are open for the booking of transactions. The netting out of opposite transactions greatly reduces the volume of payments to be made. For one day in October 2002, for example, the gross transactions were $395 billion, but only $17 billion in net payments had to be made.

Alternative definitions of exchange rates

In the past, exchange rates were measured only bilaterally and as the local price of foreign money. The US exchange rate in terms of sterling might be $1.65 or whatever. This practice had two disadvantages: (1) it did not provide any way of measuring the average exchange rate for a currency relative to a number of its major trading partners; and (2) it meant that if a currency fell in value or depreciated, its exchange rate would rise. A decline of the dollar would mean an increased US cost of purchasing sterling and an increase in the US exchange rate. Because this practice was found to be confusing, informal usage has now changed. An exchange rate now means the foreign price of the currency in question, or the number of foreign currency units required to purchase the currency in question. The exchange rate for the US dollar in terms of sterling might be 0.6042. That is, just over one-half of a pound is required to purchase a dollar. The newspaper table shown in Exhibit 13.1 presents bilateral exchange rates in both forms. With the new usage, reading that the exchange rate for the dollar fell tells us that the dollar declined in value relative to foreign currencies. Thus less foreign money is required to purchase a dollar, but more US money is needed to buy foreign currencies.

The nominal effective exchange rate

We still have to resolve the problem of how to measure the exchange rate for the dollar relative to the currencies of a number of countries with which the United States trades extensively. The nominal effective exchange rate is an index number of the weighted average of bilateral exchange rates for a number of countries, where trade shares are typically used as the weights. An effective exchange rate might be calculated for the dollar, for example, using January 1973 as the base, by calculating how much the dollar had risen or fallen since that time relative to the currencies of a number of other countries, as can be seen in Figure 13.2. If 20 percent of US trade with that group was carried on with Canada, the Canadian dollar would get a 20 percent weight in that average; if 8 percent of that trade was with the UK, then sterling would get an 8 percent weight. Either US or world trade shares could be used as weights, and published indices sometimes appear in both forms. US trade shares would give the Canadian dollar the largest weight, whereas world trade shares would put the euro or the yen in that position.

EXHIBIT 13.1 EXCHANGE RATES

Exchange Rates

The foreign exchange mid-range rates below apply to trading among banks in amounts of $1 million and more, as quoted at 4 p.m. Eastern time by Reuters and other sources. Retail transactions provide fewer units of foreign currency per dollar.

Country	U.S. $ EQUIVALENT		CURRENCY PER U.S. $	
	Thu	Tue	Thu	Tue
Argentina (Peso)-y	.2994	.2972	3.3400	3.3647
Australia (Dollar)	.5634	.5612	1.7749	1.7819
Bahrain (Dinar)	2.6524	2.6524	.3770	.3770
Brazil (Real)	.2836	.2825	3.5261	3.5398
Canada (Dollar)	.6381	.6360	1.5672	1.5723
1-month forward	.6373	.6352	1.5691	1.5743
3-months forward	.6358	.6337	1.5728	1.5780
6-months forward	.6334	.6313	1.5788	1.5840
Chile (Peso)	.001392	.001388	718.39	720.46
China (Renminbi)	.1208	.1208	8.2781	8.2781
Colombia (Peso)	.0003524	.0003488	2837.68	2866.97
Czech. Rep. (Koruna)				
Commercial rate	.03309	.03326	30.221	30.066
Denmark (Krone)	.1395	.1414	7.1685	7.0721
Ecuador (US Dollar)	1.0000	1.0000	1.0000	1.0000
Hong Kong (Dollar)	.1282	.1282	7.8003	7.8003
Hungary (Forint)	.004390	.004451	227.79	224.67
India (Rupee)	.02083	.02086	48.008	47.939
Indonesia (Rupiah)	.0001121	.0001117	8921	8953
Israel (Shekel)	.2090	.2106	4.7847	4.7483
Japan (Yen)	.008331	.008420	120.03	118.76
1-month forward	.008340	.008430	119.90	118.62
3-months forward	.008359	.008448	119.63	118.37
6-months forward	.008388	.008476	119.22	117.98
Jordan (Dinar)	1.4092	1.4092	.7096	.7096
Kuwait (Dinar)	3.3320	3.3398	.3001	.2994
Lebanon (Pound)	.0006634	.0006634	1507.39	1507.39
Malaysia (Ringgit)-b	.2632	.2632	3.7994	3.7994
Malta (Lira)	2.4805	2.5089	.4031	.3986

Country	U.S. $ EQUIVALENT		CURRENCY PER U.S. $	
	Thu	Tue	Thu	Tue
Mexico (Peso)				
Floating rate	.0964	.0964	10.3767	10.3702
New Zealand (Dollar)	.5224	.5242	1.9142	1.9077
Norway (Krone)	.1427	.1444	7.0077	6.9252
Pakistan (Rupee)	.01720	.01717	58.140	58.241
Peru (new Sol)	.2856	.2855	3.5014	3.5026
Philippines (Peso)	.01870	.01873	53.476	53.390
Poland (Zloty)	.2606	.2612	3.8373	3.8285
Russia (Ruble)-a	.03130	.03130	31.949	31.949
Saudi Arabia (Riyal)	.2667	.2666	3.7495	3.7509
Singapore (Dollar)	.5734	.5765	1.7440	1.7346
Slovak Rep. (Koruna)	.02505	.02530	39.920	39.526
South Africa (Rand)	.1178	.1167	8.4890	8.5690
South Korea (Won)	.0008414	.0008431	1188.50	1186.10
Sweden (Krona)	.1136	.1152	8.8028	8.6806
Switzerland (Franc)	.7131	.7239	1.4023	1.3814
1-month forward	.7136	.7243	1.4013	1.3806
3-months forward	.7146	.7253	1.3994	1.3787
6-months forward	.7160	.7267	1.3966	1.3761
Taiwan (Dollar)	.02883	.02886	34.686	34.650
Thailand (Baht)	.02317	.02319	43.159	43.122
Turkey (Lira)	.00000060	.00000060	1666667	1666667
U.K. (Pound)	1.5939	1.6097	.6274	.6212
1-month forward	1.5904	1.6061	.6288	.6226
3-months forward	1.5837	1.5996	.6314	.6252
6-months forward	1.5740	1.5898	.6353	.6290
United Arab (Dirham)	.2723	.2723	3.6724	3.6724
Uruguay (Peso)				
Financial	.03690	.03700	27.100	27.027
Venezuela (Bolivar)	.000719	.000720	1390.82	1388.89
SDR	1.3546	1.3546	.7382	.7382
Euro	1.0361	1.0500	.9652	.9524

Special Drawing Rights (SDR) are based on exchange rates for the U.S., British, and Japanese currencies. Source: International Monetary Fund.

a-Russian Central Bank rate. b-Government rate. y-Floating rate.

Effective exchange rate indices can sometimes give an incomplete image of a currency's behavior if too few foreign currencies are included. Some of the early effective exchange rate indices for the dollar, for example, only included nine currencies of major industrialized countries. Although the majority of US trade is still with those countries, the role of a number of developing countries, particularly the NICs, has grown rapidly. A moderately representative index for the dollar would now have to include the currencies of China, South Korea, Taiwan, Hong Kong, Mexico, and Brazil, and an ideal index would include every country with which the United States has significant trade.

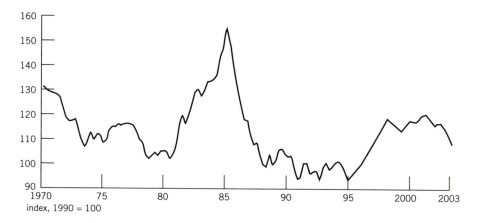

Figure 13.2 Nominal effective exchange rate for the dollar (1970–2003). The dollar experienced an enormous appreciation between 1981 and early 1985, followed by a slightly larger depreciation in the 1985–7 period. It traded in a narrow range through the early 1990s, and appreciated modestly late in the decade and at the beginning of the next decade, before declining moderately during 2002.

Source: Morgan Guaranty Trust Company of New York and the IMF, *International Financial Statistics*.

The real effective exchange rate

In the latter part of the twentieth century a new exchange rate index was developed which was designed to measure changes in a country's cost or price competitiveness in world markets. Such an index would begin with the nominal effective exchange rate but would be adjusted for inflation in the domestic economy and in the rest of the world. If, for example, a country's local rate of inflation was 8 percent whereas its trading partners had only 3 percent inflation, a fixed nominal effective exchange rate would imply a 5 percent real appreciation of its currency and a deterioration of its competitive position in world markets of that amount. If the currency depreciated by 5 percent in nominal terms, just offsetting the difference in rates of inflation, the competitive position of the country would remain unchanged. The index of the **real effective exchange rate** is constructed as follows:

$$XR_r = \frac{XR_n \times P_{dom}}{P_{row}}$$

where XR_r is the real effective exchange rate; XR_n is the nominal effective exchange rate, measured as the foreign price of local money; P_{dom} is the domestic price level, usually

EXHIBIT 13.2 REAL EFFECTIVE EXCHANGE RATE INDICES

(1995 = 100)

Industrial Countries

Based on Relative Unit Labor Costs (65um.110)

Country	Code	1996	1997	1998	1999	2000	2001	2001 I	2001 II	2001 III	2001 IV	2002 I	2002 II	2002 June	2002 July	2002 Aug
United States	111	102.6	109.2	112.9	110.9	118.5	132.0	127.8	134.0	132.8	133.4	137.2	131.8	...	...	...
Canada	156	103.9	106.2	102.8	102.1	105.4	98.1	99.7	98.5	98.0	96.1	96.0	97.4	...	...	...
Japan	158	83.8	79.4	76.4	85.9	90.2	81.4	82.5	81.5	81.4	80.0	75.4	77.3	...	...	...
Euro Area	163	99.2	89.9	86.4	82.5	75.4	74.7	76.2	73.7	74.3	74.4	73.7	74.8	...	...	...
Austria	122	95.8	90.6	89.3	87.5	87.0	87.4	87.2	87.0	86.7	87.1	87.1	87.3	...	...	...
Belgium	124	94.2	87.6	88.2	87.2	85.8	86.7	86.8	86.2	86.7	87.2	85.3	84.8	...	...	...
Finland	172	93.8	90.2	89.4	85.5	78.8	80.3	80.5	79.9	80.5	80.2	79.5	79.8	...	...	...
France	132	98.9	93.0	94.6	92.9	90.4	89.9	90.7	89.6	89.7	89.5	89.8	90.9	...	...	...
Germany *	134	98.1	91.6	87.0	84.9	79.2	77.8	78.9	77.5	77.5	77.5	77.1	77.3	...	...	...
Ireland	178	99.4	91.7	76.1	67.4	61.0	61.8	63.4	61.5	61.3	61.1	61.6	63.0	...	...	...
Italy	136	114.4	119.0	118.3	118.3	115.4	114.3	115.0	113.7	114.1	114.3	114.5	115.0	...	...	...
Netherlands	138	96.8	94.9	96.4	96.0	95.4	97.4	97.3	96.9	97.6	98.0	98.4	100.0	...	...	...
Spain	184	103.6	102.9	105.3	106.8	106.9	109.6	109.3	109.0	109.9	110.3	110.2	111.0	...	...	...
Denmark	128	104.9	99.3	100.2	101.7	96.2	98.2	97.9	97.4	98.4	99.0	98.7	99.4	...	...	...
Norway	142	101.3	107.6	108.2	114.5	119.2	125.4	122.1	124.6	126.6	128.4	130.8	137.6	...	...	...
Sweden	144	113.3	105.7	105.7	104.2	101.8	91.6	95.0	92.3	89.7	89.6	92.5	93.2	...	...	...
Switzerland	146	97.9	95.3	99.6	99.3	101.7	107.1	105.3	105.1	107.6	110.5	110.6	112.2	...	...	...
United Kingdom	112	106.0	130.4	141.2	141.7	147.6	143.6	141.9	144.0	143.9	144.7	146.5	144.8	...	...	...

Based on Relative Consumer Prices (.rec)

Country	Code	1996	1997	1998	1999	2000	2001	2001 I	2001 II	2001 III	2001 IV	2002 I	2002 II	2002 June	2002 July	2002 Aug
United States	111	104.3	112.0	120.0	119.3	125.2	134.5	131.3	135.7	135.0	135.9	138.6	134.9	132.1	129.1	131.1
Canada	156	101.7	103.2	98.6	97.6	99.5	98.7	98.7	100.0	99.3	96.7	97.5	99.0	99.4	97.5	96.6
Japan	158	84.5	80.2	78.9	89.3	95.5	85.5	87.5	85.5	85.3	83.5	77.8	78.9	79.8	82.1	81.9
Euro Area	163	99.9	90.8	93.0	88.5	79.1	82.2	82.4	80.6	82.3	83.4	82.8	85.0	87.0	88.4	87.9
Austria	122	98.0	94.6	94.6	92.8	90.3	91.1	91.2	90.7	91.2	91.3	91.1	91.8	92.4	92.6	92.5
Belgium	124	98.2	93.6	93.4	91.8	88.7	89.3	89.3	88.8	89.3	89.7	89.8	89.8	90.3	90.8	90.6
Finland	172	96.0	93.0	93.1	90.7	87.1	89.1	89.3	88.5	89.4	89.1	90.0	89.9	90.4	91.2	90.8
France	132	99.9	95.6	96.0	93.2	88.4	88.4	88.8	87.9	88.4	88.5	88.6	86.4	90.0	90.5	90.2
Germany *	134	96.8	92.0	92.5	89.5	84.6	85.6	86.2	85.1	85.5	85.7	85.9	84.4	87.1	87.4	87.1
Ireland	178	101.9	101.6	97.1	94.2	91.2	94.5	94.4	93.3	94.6	95.8	96.1	98.4	100.1	100.8	100.7
Italy	136	111.6	112.3	113.1	110.9	106.3	107.7	108.1	106.9	107.7	108.2	108.2	110.4	110.4	111.1	111.0
Netherlands	138	98.2	93.6	94.4	93.7	89.9	92.7	92.5	91.8	92.9	93.5	94.0	95.2	96.2	96.8	96.6
Spain	184	102.2	97.4	97.4	96.7	94.2	95.9	95.9	95.3	96.0	96.4	96.1	98.4	99.2	98.5	98.4
Denmark	128	99.3	96.5	98.3	97.5	93.5	94.9	94.9	94.1	94.9	95.5	95.5	96.3	97.1	97.7	97.4
Norway	142	99.8	101.1	98.2	97.9	96.1	99.6	98.0	99.6	99.8	101.0	102.0	106.8	109.3	110.2	109.7
Sweden	144	108.4	103.0	100.1	97.0	95.1	87.6	90.2	88.2	85.9	85.9	88.7	89.2	90.4	89.5	89.3
Switzerland	146	97.3	90.0	91.1	89.4	87.3	89.8	89.1	88.4	89.8	91.9	91.5	93.1	93.4	93.9	93.3
United Kingdom	112	102.4	120.5	128.0	127.6	131.9	129.5	128.4	129.9	129.9	129.8	130.9	129.0	127.3	129.3	129.3

* Data refer to the former
Federal Republic of Germany

Source: IMF, International Financial Statistics Yearbook (Washington, DC: IMF).

measured as consumer or wholesale prices. Unit labor costs may be used as an alternative to wholesale prices; P_{row} is the price level for the rest of the world, using the country's major trading partners as a proxy. Trade shares are used as weights. Unit labor costs may be used as an alternative to the price level.

Box 13.1 The Big Mac index

An amusing but insightful attempt to determine the extent to which market exchange rates misvalue currencies has been provided by *The Economist* magazine in the form of its Big Mac index. A problem in determining misvaluation has always been to find a basket of the same goods and services that are consumed in both, or all, countries through which to make the purchasing power parity comparison. *The Economist* begins by assuming that McDonald's sees to it that its Big Mac sandwich is exactly the same in all countries in which it is sold, and then allows the Big Mac to be its universal good for the purposes of determining under- or overvaluations of currencies relative to the dollar.

It is important that the raw materials and labor used for producing a Big Mac are locally produced, making a Big Mac a nontradable good. If the product being used for price comparison were a tradable, prices would be much more likely to be the same, or at least close to the same, in various countries despite many currencies being over or undervalued. Using a nontradable good for the comparison means that *The Economist* really is comparing the relative costs of doing business in each country through current exchange rates. Translating local currency prices of a Big Mac into dollars at the market exchange rate and comparing them to the average price of a Big Mac in the United States leads to the conclusion that, as of the end of 2002, most currencies were undervalued relative to the dollar, that is, that the dollar was overvalued. (See *The Economist*, January 18, 2003, p. 98.) A few currencies, however, were overvalued, relative to the dollar. The Swiss franc was the most overvalued, at 72 percent, followed by Sweden (31 percent, the United Kingdom (20 percent), and the euro area (8 percent). More currencies were undervalued, including Argentina (55 percent), all of the 1997–9 Asian debt crisis countries except South Korea, Russia (52 percent), China (55 percent), and Japan (16 percent). In the past *The Economist* has suggested that the Big Mac index has produced useful information as to how exchange rates are likely to move in the short- to medium-term future, with undervalued currencies rising relative to the dollar, and overvalued currencies falling, but no data were provided to support this conclusion. The dollar, which *The Economist* said was badly overvalued in early 2002 according to this index, did depreciate from spring 2002 to the end of the year and during the first half of 2003.

If the real exchange rate (XR_r) rises, the country's cost-competitive position has deteriorated because it has experienced more inflation than its trading partners after allowance for changes in the nominal exchange rate. Such a deterioration implies greater difficulty in selling exports and an increased volume of imports. Real exchange rate indices, calculated using prices and unit labor costs, can be found in the IMF, International Financial Statistics Yearbook. (See Exhibit 13.2.)

An alternative definition of the real effective exchange rate is the ratio of the domestic price of nontradable goods and services to the domestic price of tradables; that is:

$$\frac{P_{NT}}{P_T}$$

These two definitions of the real effective exchange rate look entirely different, but the second can be derived from the first with a few assumptions.[7] The common sense of the second definition of the real exchange rate is that when this ratio is too high domestic firms are encouraged to produce nontradables rather than tradables, whereas domestic consumers are encouraged to consume tradables rather than nontradables, thereby generating a trade deficit.

Different elements within the consumer price index are sometimes used as proxies for the prices of nontradables and tradables for the purpose of estimating the real effective exchange rate; services are used for non-tradables and goods are used for tradables. The wage rate might be used as the price of non-tradables, or an index of unit labor costs might be even better. Unit labor cost over the price of goods provides a clear index of the competitiveness of this economy as a place to produce for international markets; if that index rises, the country becomes an increasingly unattractive location for manufacturing, and vice versa.

Alternative views of equilibrium nominal exchange rates

Economists have had a variety of opinions as to how nominal exchange rates are determined, and the oldest of those views is implicit in the index of a real exchange rate. The **purchasing power parity** (PPP) view is that nominal rates should move to just offset differing rates of inflation, that is, that the real exchange rate ought to be constant.[8] In a regime of floating exchange rates it was widely expected that the workings of the exchange market would produce that result, in that nominal exchange rates would naturally follow differences in rates of inflation. That has not been the case since 1973, and changes in real exchange rates were quite large during the 1980s but were somewhat smaller in the 1990s.[9] The US dollar appreciated by approximately 40 percent in real terms between 1981 and 1985, and then depreciated by a similar amount in the following four years. Some developing countries have had modest success with a "purchasing power parity crawl" in that they have adjusted otherwise fixed exchange rates by small amounts every month or so to offset the difference between local and foreign inflation. If, for example, Brazil was experiencing 40 percent inflation when the rest of the world had 4 percent inflation, a 3 percent devaluation of the real per month would maintain the ability of Brazilian firms to compete in world markets.

The purchasing power parity view of equilibrium exchange rates is entirely tied to international trade in that it makes no allowance for capital account transactions as determinants of the exchange rate. In recent years exchange rates for the industrialized countries have frequently been modeled in an "asset market" context.[10] Since capital flow transactions have increasingly dominated the exchange markets in such countries, the equilibrium exchange rate is that which allows international markets for financial assets to clear. Borrowers and lenders are assumed to operate in both domestic and local markets, and therefore to move funds through the exchange market. The exchange rate then becomes an element in supply and demand functions for such assets, and the equilibrium exchange rate is determined by the clearing of these financial markets. This approach has the problem of ignoring trade. Although a majority of exchange market transactions is for capital accounts, it does seem a bit extreme to determine an equilibrium exchange rate without reference to differing rates of inflation or other factors affecting trade flows.

Finally, there is the somewhat tautological view that the equilibrium exchange rate is that which produces a zero official reserve transactions account balance. It is therefore the rate that would be observed in a regime of clean floating exchange rates. Such a view implies little permanence and instead a great deal of volatility. Large swings in short-term capital flows, in part driven by speculation, have produced large and frequently reversed changes in exchange rates during recent years. This approach therefore implies that the equilibrium exchange rate is likely to change from one month to another for reasons as ephemeral as speculative moods. As will be seen in Chapter 20, econometric attempts to explain short- to medium-term movements of floating exchange rates on the basis of economic or financial fundamentals, including purchasing power parity, have met with a decided lack of success.

Summary of key concepts

1   Minus transactions in a country's balance of payments accounts generate a domestic demand for foreign exchange, and vice versa. The exchange market is the institutional arrangement in which these supplies and demands are accommodated.

2   If private transactions are out of balance, the exchange market can clear only through official intervention, which is normally carried out by the central bank. A payments deficit requires that the central bank sell foreign exchange, thereby reducing its foreign exchange reserves, and buy its own currency in the exchange market.

3   Many developing countries try to protect scarce foreign exchange reserves from losses through such intervention by maintaining systems of exchange market control, particularly seeking to prohibit capital outflows from the country. Such control systems seldom succeed for long, because there are numerous ways to cheat on them, transfer pricing perhaps being the most important.

4   Although theoretically unnecessary, official intervention is quite common for countries that maintain floating exchange rates, with such intervention typically intended to produce a less volatile exchange rate than would otherwise exist.

5   The nominal effective exchange rate is a trade-weighted average of bilateral rates. The real effective exchange rate is the nominal effective rate, adjusted for inflation in the home country and abroad. It is therefore an index of this country's price and cost competitiveness in world markets.

Questions for study and review

1 Where does one look in a nation's balance of payments for items that give rise to a demand for foreign exchange? For a supply of foreign exchange?

2 When a nation chooses to peg its currency at a give exchange rate *vis-à-vis* another currency, what exactly must its central bank do if a gold standard exists? Under the Bretton Woods system?

3 Explain how the elasticity of demand for foreign exchange is influenced by the elasticity of home demand for imports and by the elasticity of home supply of import-competing goods.

4 Malaysia has just imposed exchange controls which are designed to make it impossible to move capital out of the country. What would you expect to happen to Malaysia's recorded current account results in the next year or so? Why?

5 If you are working in a developing country and only have access to local data, how would you estimate a "rough and ready" version of a real effective exchange rate time series for this country?

6 If the gold standard were again operating, why would you expect the "gold points" to be wider for the sterling/yen exchange rate than for the sterling/euro rate? If silver were substituted for gold in this fixed exchange rate regime, what would happen to the band within which exchange rates could move? Why?

Suggested further reading

- Aliber, Robert, *The New International Money Game*, 6th edn, Chicago: University of Chicago Press, 2002.
- Broadus, J. and M. Goodfriend, "Foreign Exchange Operations and the Federal Reserve," *Federal Reserve Bank of Richmond Quarterly*, Winter 1996, pp. 1–19.
- Campbell, T., and J. O'Brien, "Foreign Exchange Trading Practices: The Interbank Market," in A. George and I. Giddy, eds, *International Finance Handbook*, New York: John Wiley & Sons, 1983.
- Chrystal, K. Alec, "A Guide to Foreign Exchange Markets," *Federal Reserve Bank of St. Louis Review*, March 1984, pp. 5–18.
- Giddy, I., *Global Financial Markets*, Lexington, MA: D.C. Heath, 1994.
- Kubarych, Roger M., *Foreign Exchange Markets in the United States*, rev. edn, Federal Reserve Bank of New York, 1983.
- Pauls, B. Diane, "US Exchange Rate Policy: Bretton Woods to Present," *Federal Reserve Bulletin*, November 1990, pp. 891–908.
- Poniachek, Harvey, ed., *Cases in International Finance*, New York: John Wiley & Sons, 1993.
- Study Group, *Recent Innovations in International Banking*, Basle: Bank for International Settlements, 1986.
- Walmsley, J., *The Foreign Exchange and Money Markets Guide*, New York: John Wiley & Sons, 1992.
- Weismeiller, Rudi, *Managing a Foreign Exchange Department*, Cambridge, UK: Woodhead-Faulkner, 1985.

Notes

1 For a discussion of gold points, see Leland Yeager, *International Monetary Relations: Theory and Policy*, 2nd edn (New York: Harper and Row, 1976), pp. 20–1 and 317–18.

2 An extensive discussion of the Bretton Woods intervention system can be found in Yeager, op. cit., chs 20 and 21. See also Robert Solomon, *The International Monetary System: 1945–1976: An Insider's View* (New York: Harper and Row, 1977), chs 5–7, for a discussion of the problems which the Bretton Woods system faced during the late 1960s. See also B. Diane Pauls, "US Exchange Rate Policy: Bretton Woods to Present," *Federal Reserve Bulletin*, November 1990, pp. 891–908.

3 The problems of such exchange control regimes are discussed in J.N. Bhagwati, *The Anatomy and Consequences of Exchange Control Regimes* (Cambridge, MA: Ballinger, 1978). See also Dunn, R.M. "The Misguided Attractions of Foreign Exchange Controls," *Challenge*, Sept./Oct. 2002, pp. 98–111. See IMF, *Annual Report on Exchange Arrangements and Exchange Controls* (Washington, DC: IMF), for information on practices being maintained by various countries.

4 For a discussion of official intervention in a regime of flexible exchange rates, see K. Dominguez and J. Frankel, *Does Foreign Exchange Market Intervention Work?* (Washington, DC: Institute for International Economics, 1993). See also R. Dunn, Jr., "The Many Disappointments of Flexible Exchange Rates," *Princeton Essays in International Finance*, no. 154, December 1983, pp. 13–15.

5 The institutional arrangements through which foreign exchange is traded are covered in M. Melvin, *International Money and Finance* (New York: Harper and Row, 1989), and in R. Kubarych, *Foreign Exchange Markets in the United States* (New York: Federal Reserve Bank of New York, 1983). See also, K.A. Chrystal, "A Guide to Foreign Exchange Markets," *Federal Reserve Bank of St. Louis Review*, March 1984, pp. 4–18. For a discussion of recent developments in foreign exchange trading, see *The Financial Times*, June 5, 1998, special survey on foreign exchange. See also "Do It Yourself Forex Deals," *The Financial Times*, July 9, 1998, p. 8.

6 Purchasing a local currency for dollars at an airport "bank" or other money exchange can be extremely expensive and the costs are often unclear to customers. The exchange office may offer an attractive exchange rate in large letters, but then place a notice in very small letters at the bottom of the sign which states the commission, which can be as high as 9.75 percent. You will generally get better rates at a commercial bank, but that is of little help on weekends or at night. If you are registered at a hotel, it may be possible to change money there without a commission, but often at a very unattractive exchange rate. It is a good idea to ask what the commission is before handing over your traveler's check or cash. Credit card transactions are usually processed within a percentage point or two of the interbank rate, which can save you considerable amounts of money. ATM machines also process transactions at, or close to, the interbank rate, usually with a fixed fee of about $2.50 per transaction. Using credit cards for most costs and ATM cards for cash needs (keeping each ATM transaction fairly large) can minimize costs, although you may want to check with your bank and credit card company before traveling to find out exactly how close to the interbank rate your transactions will be processed. See Robert M. Dunn, Jr., "Retail Foreign Exchange Trading in Prague: Are Tourists Rational?," *Journal of Socio-Economics* 26, no. 5, 1997, for a discussion of the apparently less-than-rational behavior of travelers in deciding where to exchange money.

7 If perfect competition prevails in markets for tradables, the law of one price holds and the domestic price of tradables equals the foreign price divided by the nominal exchange rate. This is simply an arbitrage condition. With domestic prices of tradables fixed by the nominal exchange rate and by foreign prices, the relevant price level for the measurement of domestic competitiveness is the price of nontradables, so the following conditions hold:

$$(1) \quad P_{dom} = P_{nt}$$

and

$$(2) \quad P_t = \frac{P_{row}}{XR_n}$$

and therefore,

$$(3) \quad P_{row} = P_t \cdot XR_n$$

Since the real effective exchange rate is:

$$(4) \quad XR_r = \frac{XR_n \cdot P_{dom}}{P_{row}}$$

Substituting (1) and (3) into (4) produces

$$(5) \quad XR_r = \frac{XR_n \cdot P_{nt}}{XR_n \cdot P_t}$$

which becomes:

$$(6) \quad XR_r = \frac{P_{nt}}{P_t}$$

8 The history of the purchasing power parity approach to exchange rate determination begins with G. Cassel, "Abnormal Deviations in International Exchanges," *Economic Journal*, September 1918. See also B. Belassa, "The Purchasing Power Parity Doctrine: A Reappraisal," *Journal of Political Economy*, December 1964, and K. Froot and K. Rogoff, "Perspectives on PPP and Long Run Real Exchange Rates," ch. 32 in G. Grossman and K. Rogoff, eds, *Handbook of International Economics*, Vol. III (Amsterdam: Elsevier, 1995).

9 The failure of nominal exchange rates to follow purchasing power parity in the short-to-medium term is analyzed in P. Kortweg, "Exchange Rate Policy, Monetary Policy, and Real Exchange Rate Variability," Princeton Essays in International Finance, no. 140, December 1980, and in J. Frenkel, "The Collapse of Purchasing Power Parities in the 1970s," *European Economic Review*, May 1981, pp. 145–65.

10 For a discussion of the asset market approach to exchange rate determination, see W. Branson, "Asset Markets and Relative Prices in Exchange Rate Determination," *Reprints in International Finance*, 20, 1980. See also Polly Allen and Peter Kenen, *Asset Markets, Exchange Rates, and Economic Integration* (New York: Cambridge University Press, 1980). For a discussion of empirical tests of alternative models of exchange rate determination, see R. Levich, "Empirical Studies of Exchange Rates: Price Behavior, Rate Determination, and Market Efficiency," in R. Jones and P. Kenen, eds, *Handbook of International Economics*, Vol. II (Amsterdam: North-Holland, 1985), ch. 19. See also J. Frankel and A. Rose, "Empirical Research on Nominal Exchange Rates," in Grossman and Rogoff, eds, *Handbook of International Economics*, Vol. III, ch. 33.

14 International derivatives

Foreign exchange forwards, futures, and options

Learning objectives

By the end of this chapter you should be able to understand:

- how forward foreign exchange contracts are used to hedge risks arising from foreign trade or investment transactions, and how these contracts can be used by speculators;
- the interest parity theory of forward rate determination, the forward rate as expected spot rate theory, and how the two can be reconciled;
- the difference between a forward contract and a foreign exchange futures contract;
- foreign exchange options: who buys puts or calls, who is willing to sell or write them, and the nature of the price or premium on such contracts; the large risks that can result from selling or writing uncovered options;
- how the premium or price of a foreign exchange option is determined;
- circumstances in which a company would use an international interest rate swap.

A derivative is a financial contract which gains or loses values with the movement of the price of a commodity or a financial asset. Commodities and financial futures contracts are examples of derivatives. Derivatives do not involve the direct ownership of an asset or the existence of a liability, and therefore do not typically appear on a balance sheet, but nevertheless do create the opportunity for speculative gains or losses. Many domestic financial derivatives have become quite controversial, due to large losses being suffered on such contracts by hedge funds (Long Term Capital Management), nonfinancial corporations (Procter & Gamble), and even local governments (Orange County, California) in recent years. Our concern, however, is only with international derivatives, such as foreign exchange forwards, futures, and options.

Forward exchange markets

Forward exchange markets allow the purchase or sale of foreign exchange today for delivery and payment at a fixed date in the future. Contracts typically have maturities of 30, 60, or 90 days to match payment dates for export sales and the maturities of short-term money market assets such as Treasury bills, commercial paper, and certificates of deposits (CDs). If, for example, a US importer is committed to pay euro 500,000 for German exports in 90 days, a forward purchase of euro is a convenient way to avoid the possibility that the currency may appreciate over that time, which would impose higher dollar costs on the importer.

Trading in forward contracts is carried on by the same banks and traders that do the spot trading described in the previous chapter. The arrangements are similar to those for spot trading, except that settlement takes place in 30, 60, or 90 days rather than in 2 days. For a few major currencies trading is common at 180- and 360-day maturities, and longer contracts are sometimes done on a negotiated basis. Forward contracts are binding in that someone buying forward sterling is required to complete that purchase at maturity, even if the spot exchange rate has moved to a level that makes doing so unprofitable. In contrast, a buyer of an option, may choose to complete or not to complete the transaction, depending on how the spot exchange rate has moved. Foreign exchange options will be discussed later in this chapter. Forward exchange rates for a number of currencies, along with the prevailing spot rates, can be found in Exhibit 14.1.

As can be seen, forward rates frequently differ from prevailing spot rates. If a currency is worth less in the forward than in the spot market, it is said to be at a "forward discount." A forward premium exists in the opposite situation. Although those involved in these markets on a day-to-day basis frequently quote such discounts or premiums in terms of cents, economists usually refer to annual percentages. This is done to make such discounts or premiums directly comparable to annual interest rates. If, for example, sterling were trading at $2.00 in the spot market and at $2.01 in the 90-day forward market, the premium would appear to be one-half percent (1/200), but that is for only 90 days or one-quarter of a year. The premium measured as an annual rate is four times one-half percent, which is 2 percent. The reasons for using annual rates rather than monetary units to measure this premium will become more apparent when we discuss the factors determining forward rates.

The forward market is similar to the futures market for commodities, where it is possible to buy or sell for future delivery at a price determined now. There are, however, small differences between the two types of arrangements. All futures contracts close on the same day of the month, whereas forward contracts close a fixed number of days after they are signed, which can be any day of the month. Futures contracts are relatively

EXHIBIT 14.1 EXCHANGE RATES: SPOT AND FORWARD

The foreign exchange mid-range rates below apply to trading among banks in amounts of $1 million and more, as quoted at 4 p.m. Eastern time by Reuters and other sources. Retail transactions provide fewer units of foreign currency per dollar.

Canada (Dollar)	.6381	.6360
1-month forward	.6373	.6352
3-months forward	.6358	.6337
6-months forward	.6334	.6313
Japan (Yen)	.008331	.008420
1-month forward	.008340	.008430
3-months forward	.008359	.008448
6-months forward	.008388	.008476
Switzerland (Franc)	.7131	.7239
1-month forward	.7136	.7243
3-months forward	.7146	.7253
6-months forward	.7160	.7267
U.K. (Pound)	1.5939	1.6097
1-month forward	1.5904	1.6061
3-months forward	1.5837	1.5996
6-months forward	1.5740	1.5898

Source: The Wall Street Journal. Republished by permission of Dow Jones, Inc. via Copyright Clearance Center, Inc. © 2003 Dow Jones and Company, Inc. All Rights Reserved Worldwide.

liquid, in that they can be resold in commodity exchanges before maturity, whereas forward contracts usually have to be held to maturity. Although forward contracts are traded by banks in large transactions, futures are traded in commodity exchanges such as the Chicago Board of Trade in smaller transactions and with sizable brokerage commissions.

A **futures market for foreign currencies** exists as the International Monetary Market (IMM) in Chicago (data for which can be found in Exhibit 14.2) where trading is carried on just as it would be for commodities such as copper or wheat. It is used both to hedge risks arising from relatively small trade transactions and to provide a vehicle for speculation.[1]

EXHIBIT 14.2 EXCHANGE RATE FUTURES

CURRENCY FUTURES

Jan 2		Open	Sett	Change	High	Low	Est. vol	Open int
€-Sterling*	Mar	0.6520	0.6519	-0.0018	0.6523	0.6505	18	4,635
€-Dollar*	Mar	1.0405	1.0330	-0.0140	-	0.0000	5	900
€-Yen*	Mar	123.86	123.54	-0.45	123.88	123.42	979	6,757
$-Can $ †	Mar	0.6342	0.6352	+0.0030	0.6362	0.6318	10,628	55,143
$-Euro € †	Mar	1.0444	1.0330	-0.0141	1.0444	1.0302	10,906	97,405
$-Euro € †	Jun	1.0393	1.0295	-0.0141	1.0400	1.0270	206	1,225
$-Sw Franc †	Mar	0.7226	0.7146	-0.0103	0.7226	0.7127	4,508	49,517
$-Sw Franc †	Jun	0.7224	0.7161	-0.0101	0.7225	0.7145	26	620
$-Yen †	Mar	0.8429	0.8358	-0.0089	0.8442	0.8341	14,706	99,231
$-Yen †	Jun	0.8408	0.8385	-0.0089	0.8464	0.8374	19	20,230
$-Sterling †	Mar	1.5992	1.5850	-0.0172	1.6006	1.5834	6,468	34,387
$-Sterling †	Jun	0.0000	1.5746	-0.0172	1.5810	1.5754	4	435

Sources: * FINEX; Sterling €100,000, Dollar: €200,000 and Yen: €100,000. † CME; Canadian $: C$100,000, Euro: €125,000; Swiss Franc: SFr125,000; Yen: Y12.5m ($ per Y100); Sterling: £62,500.
Contracts shown are based on the volumes traded in 2001.

Source: Fnancial Times, 3 January 2003.

Reasons for forward trading

The forward exchange market has three separate, but related, roles in international commercial and financial transactions. First, it is a way of hedging risks arising from typical credit terms on export/import business. In the first half of this book it was assumed that trade took the form of barter, or that if money was involved, payment was immediate. It is actually far more common for exports to be sold under credit terms which create a period of time before payment is due. This creates an exchange rate risk.

If, for example, Harrods agrees to pay 50 million yen for television sets to be sold from its UK stores, it will not make that payment when it becomes committed to the transaction or even when the sets are delivered. It will normally have 30-, 60-, or 90-day payment terms. Consequently, it faces the risk that the yen may appreciate during that period, resulting in higher sterling costs for the television sets. The yen might, of course, fall instead, which would save Harrods money, but if the company does not view itself as being in the business of speculating on the future exchange rate for the Japanese currency, a forward contract to purchase yen becomes a convenient way to avoid any uncertainty as to the cost of the sets in pounds sterling. As soon as the commitment to purchase the television sets is binding, the immediate purchase of 50 million yen in the forward market means that Harrods has hedged or covered the exchange risk arising from its delayed payment to the Japanese manufacturer.

When fixed parities existed under the Bretton Woods system and market exchange rates fluctuated only within a narrow band, many firms did not worry about such risks, and they frequently left accounts payable or receivable denominated in a foreign currency uncovered. The introduction of flexible exchange rates in the early 1970s greatly increased the perceived risk of such behavior and reportedly resulted in a sharp increase in the volume of forward contracts being traded as firms sought to eliminate such exposure.

It is worth noting that forward contracts are not the only way to cover risks arising from accounts payable or receivable that are denominated in foreign exchange. Changing the invoicing of another transaction is an alternative for large firms that undertake many export and import transactions every day. If, for example, Unilever in the United Kingdom purchases French goods worth 10 million euros with 90-day payment terms, it could cover this risk by invoicing its next sale to an EU country that was for about the same value in euros. If, within a short time after the agreement to purchase the French goods became binding, Unilever received an order for about 10 euro worth of goods from a German firm, it could offer to invoice that sale in euros rather than sterling. The German firm could be expected to agree, because it would be relieved of the need to cover a sterling account payable. If Unilever has both an account payable and an account receivable for 10 million euros with the same 90-day maturities, it is fully hedged. Some large multinational firms, which have many transactions in each currency every day, are reported to undertake such offsets frequently, and to use the forward market only for whatever exposure is left over, thereby saving bid-asked spreads and commissions on forward contracts.

The same result could be obtained by altering where one borrows or lends to offset a foreign exchange exposure. Returning to Unilever's 10 million euro account payable, if that firm also had about that sum in UK treasury bills, it could switch those funds to the euro equivalent of such bills for the 90-day period. If Unilever has both a 10 million euro account payable and 10 million euros in short-term paper, it is fully hedged. The cost to Unilever of this latter approach would be the difference between the interest income which it would earn on that sum in the United Kingdom and what it earns on euro paper. That cost would, of course, be negative if interest rates in euro exceed those in the United Kingdom.

Returning to forwards, the second major role of such contracts is to cover risks arising from international capital movements. When banks or other financial institutions seek to take advantage of higher interest rates available in foreign markets, they typically seek to avoid the risk that the currency in which they invest may depreciate. Undertaking a "**swap**" in which a currency is simultaneously bought spot and sold forward is a way of covering such risk. New York banks, for example, might hope to observe the following situation:

UK Treasury bill yield	14 percent
US Treasury bill yield	10 percent
Uncovered differential	4 percent favoring the UK
Forward discount on sterling	2 percent
Covered differential	2 percent favoring the UK

UK interest rates are 4 percentage points above those in New York, but switching into sterling for 90 days involves a sizable risk that the currency could depreciate by enough (or more than enough) to destroy the transaction's profitability. If, however, sterling is bought in the spot market (in order to purchase the 14 percent bills) and simultaneously sold forward, the cost is only 2 percent (measured as an annual rate), leaving a net profit of 2 percent. For reasons that will be discussed soon, this situation would be extremely unlikely, and banks would normally face a situation such as the following:

UK Treasury bill yield	14 percent
US Treasury bill yield	10 percent
Uncovered differential	4 percent favoring the UK
Forward discount on sterling	4 percent
Covered differential	0

Finally, forward contracts can be used to take on risk rather than to avoid it. If speculators believe that a currency will depreciate during the next 90 days to a level below the existing forward exchange rate, a forward sale of that currency is a convenient way to gamble on that outcome without investing large sums of money. If the exchange rate for sterling was $1.86 in the New York spot market and $1.85 in the 90-day forward market when a speculator believed that a depreciation of the spot rate of considerably more than 1 cent was likely during the next 3 months, he or she could sell forward sterling at $1.85 and wait. If the exchange rate was, for example, $1.83 at the end of the contract, the speculator would purchase the currency spot at that rate and deliver it on the forward contract, for a net profit of 2 cents times the number of pounds sterling in the contract. If, of course, sterling were $1.88 at the end of the contract, he or she would absorb a loss of 3 cents per pound.

Since this is not an option contract, the speculator is obligated to complete the losing transaction, and the bank with which he or she did business would normally have required that the speculator provide enough money as "margin" at the beginning of the contract to protect it against the possibility of an attempt to evade that obligation.

Factors determining forward rates: the interest parity theory and the role of speculators

The determination of forward exchange rates can be viewed in two separate ways, but the differences can be more apparent than real. The two approaches can be reconciled and finally regarded as a single approach under reasonable assumptions. First, forward rates are set through international capital flows. This approach is known as the interest parity theory of forward rate determination.

If New York banks faced the 2 percent covered interest rate spread that appears in the first set of numbers on page 315, they would purchase spot sterling in enormous volumes, driving the currency up, and they would simultaneously sell forward sterling in the same volumes, driving it down. The 2 percent forward discount on sterling should widen to 4 percent in the twinkling of an eye, eliminating the profitability of the swap transaction.[2] The arbitraging process will normally produce the following outcome, when forward rates are measured as annual percentage discounts or premiums:

$$\text{Sterling forward discount} = r_{UK} - r_{US}$$

Or, making the same statement for the opposite situation:

$$\text{Sterling forward premium} = r^{\cdot}_{US} - r_{UK}$$

Sterling should trade at a forward discount that equals the difference between British and US interest rates, and vice versa. Any time this is not true, the possibility for arbitrage profits exists and money can usually be expected to move in sufficient volume to force the forward rate to the level at which such profits are eliminated or at least reduced to a very low level. This adjustment of the forward rate should be instantaneous.

Sometimes financial markets produce data which do not match the interest parity condition. When sizable covered interest arbitrage profits have appeared to exist, it was often for one of the following reasons:

1   The two assets were not of the same perceived risk, so that a risk premium had to be paid on one of them. Commercial paper, for example, may be viewed as having a greater default risk in Canada than in the United Kingdom, resulting in a higher covered yield in Toronto than in London.
2   The possibility of double taxation existed because one country maintained a with-holding tax on interest payments to foreigners that could not be fully credited against taxes due in the investor's country.
3   Investors feared the imposition of exchange controls by the country with the higher covered interest rate, meaning that it might not be possible to enforce forward contracts as they matured in order to get money out of the country.

Sometimes the appearance of such profits has been created when interest and exchange rate data were not collected for the exact same times. Using average daily interest rates and daily closing exchange rates, for example, could produce the appearance of arbitrage profits when none actually existed.

The second approach to the forward rate is that it represents the exchange markets' consensus prediction of what will happen to the spot exchange rate over the period of the forward contract. If, for example, spot sterling is trading at $1.86 and the 90-day forward rate is $1.84, market participants on average expect spot sterling to depreciate by 2 cents during the next 3 months. If this were not the case, speculators would undertake transactions that would move the forward rate to a level that would represent their consensus expectation. If, for example, forward sterling were $1.84 when most market participants thought it would be no lower than $1.86 in 90 days, speculators would buy it heavily at $1.84 in expectation of a sizable profit. The volume of such purchases would be large enough to push the rate to the expected spot rate, when the buying pressure would end.

It is not necessary that everybody has the same expectation, for that is obviously impossible. It is only necessary that the average expectation matches the forward rate so that speculative purchases and sales roughly match. If, for example, 20 percent of the market participants expect the spot rate to be $1.86 in 90 days, whereas 40 percent think it will be lower and 40 percent think it will be higher, the forward market should clear at $1.86 because the number of people speculating that it will be higher will equal the number of people betting on the opposite outcome, and the market will clear. (For the sake of simplicity, this example assumes that each market participant is prepared to gamble the same amount of money.) To use an inelegant analogy, the forward rate is like the point spread on a basketball game; it represents the consensus prediction of how the game will end. Otherwise, bets on one team will greatly exceed those on the other, and the spread will be very quickly adjusted.

These two approaches to forward rate determination seem different, but they can be reconciled; both can be shown to result from differences in expected rates of inflation. If

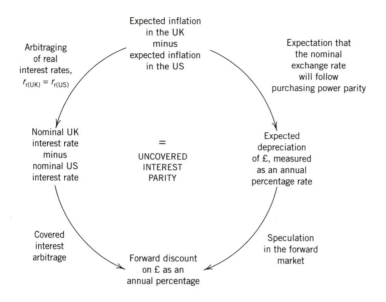

Figure 14.1 The determination of the forward discount on sterling. The fact that UK inflation is expected to exceed US inflation causes both an excess of UK nominal interest rates over US yields and an expectation that sterling will depreciate relative to the dollar. The difference between UK and US interest rates produces an offsetting forward discount on sterling through covered interest arbitrage. The expectation that sterling will depreciate causes the same forward discount on sterling through speculation in the forward market.

British interest rates exceed those in the United States by 4 percentage points, this suggests that investors expect 4 percentage points more inflation in the United Kingdom than in the United States. Real interest rates are thought to be arbitraged together because if people expect more inflation in one currency than another, a higher nominal interest rate will be required to attract them to hold assets in that currency. The following statement represents the arbitraging together of real interest rates:

$$r_{UK} - r_{US} = \text{expected UK inflation} - \text{expected US inflation}$$

The forward discount on sterling, which superficially reflects differing nominal interest rates, more fundamentally reflects the fact that more inflation is expected in the United Kingdom than in the United States.

Speculators can be viewed as forming exchange rate expectations on the basis of inflationary predictions. If national monies are ultimately claims on real goods and services, exchange rates should reflect the relative purchasing powers of those monies, which is to say that they should reflect purchasing power parity, as discussed earlier. If speculators expect nominal exchange rates to follow purchasing power parity, indicating that they expect a constant real exchange rate, they will form expectations of future spot rate behavior on the basis of forecasts of differences in rates of inflation. Trading forward sterling at a discount of 4 percent (annual rate) indicates the speculators' belief that the United Kingdom will experience 4 percentage points more inflation than will the United States, and therefore that spot sterling will have to depreciate at a 4 percent annual rate to maintain purchasing power parity.

Both the interest-arbitrage and the expected-spot-rate approaches to forward rate determination can be traced back to the same origins – expectations with regard to relative rates of inflation. The following statements summarize this conclusion:

Expected UK inflation – Expected US inflation = $r_{UK} - r_{US}$ = Forward discount on sterling

Expected UK inflation – Expected US inflation = Expected spot sterling depreciation = Forward discount sterling

Therefore:

Expected UK inflation – Expected US inflation = Forward discount sterling

This might be visualized more easily as in Figure 14.1. The forward rate reflects both differences in nominal interest rates and expected changes in the spot exchange rate, both of which result from differences in expected rates of inflation. The way inflationary expectations are formed is a more complex matter. It might begin with differences in the rates of growth of national money supplies, but that subject is beyond the scope of this chapter.

The relationship among expected rates of inflation, nominal interest rates, and forward exchange markets may be easier to understand with a somewhat more extreme example. If inflation during the next year is expected to be 40 percent in Brazil and 4 percent in the United States, nobody is going to be willing to hold fixed-interest assets denominated in Brazilian reals unless they are paid a great deal more than the US interest rate. Ignoring taxes, people will insist on being paid 36 percentage points more on Brazilian debt than they would be willing to accept on US dollar assets. The fact that Brazilian interest rates exceed US yields by 36 percentage points strongly suggests the expectation of 36 percentage points more inflation in Brazil than in the United States. In addition, the fact that inflation is expected to be so much higher in Brazil than in the United States indicates that the Brazilian currency will have to be devalued. The exact amount of that devaluation or **depreciation** cannot be known ahead of time, but a reasonable expectation is about 3 percent per month. That depreciation would just offset the differences in expected rates of inflation, thereby maintaining an unchanging real effective exchange rate for the Brazilian real. To summarize thus far, the fact that Brazilian inflation is expected to exceed US inflation by 36 percent per year will mean both that Brazilian interest rates will exceed US yields by 36 percentage points and that people will expect the Brazilian real to depreciate by an offsetting amount.

If a forward market for the real exists, that currency should trade at an annual rate forward discount of about 36 percent, both because the difference in interest rates is that wide and because of the expected depreciation of the real. The forward discount of about 36 percent on the real, however, ultimately reflects the fact that inflation is expected to be 36 percent higher in Brazil than in the United States. (The expected depreciation and the forward discount will be somewhat less than 36 percent because of the arithmetic problem of using the opening number as the base for any percentage change, meaning that the same change over the same range is a higher percentage if the number rises and a lower percentage if it falls; if a number rises from 80 to 100, that is 25 percent, but if it falls over the same range it is only 20 percent. If the price level in Brazil rises by 100 percent, that would not imply a 100 percent depreciation of the real, which would make it worthless, but instead a depreciation of 50 percent. The forward discount would also not be 100 percent, implying a worthless currency at maturity, but instead 50 percent. If a stockbroker tells you that a mutual fund made 100 percent one year, and then lost 50 percent the following year, that does not mean a net gain of 50 percent. It means a gain of zero.)

Two phrases have been used here which sound quite similar, but which are in fact different. Covered interest parity, which is almost always true, says that a currency will trade at a forward discount which equals the difference between the local and the foreign interest rate. If short-term interest rates are 6 percent in the United Kingdom and 4 percent in the United States, sterling will trade at a 2 percent forward discount. This is the interest parity theory of forward rate determination. Uncovered interest parity says that the difference between the local nominal interest rate and that prevailing abroad equals the rate at which the local currency is expected to depreciate. The difference between London and New York interest rates just referred to means that sterling is expected to depreciate at an annual rate of 2 percent. This may be the expectation, but as will be seen below it is seldom fulfilled.

Problems with the model

As the previous discussion suggests, countries that have high interest rates and therefore forward discounts, should have depreciating currencies. If that were not true, a trading rule could be devised which would earn profits most of the time. Surprising as it may seem, the model is not supported by the data, and such profits could have been earned in the past. In a total of seventy-five empirical studies, it was found that industrialized countries with high interest rates usually had appreciating, rather than depreciating, currencies, meaning that the expectations implied by uncovered interest parity were badly mistaken.[3]

Investors could therefore have made sizable profits by always buying fixed-interest securities in high-interest-rate, industrialized countries without covering in the forward market. On average, they would have received both a higher interest rate and the results of an appreciation of that currency. Buying US dollar assets in 1981, for example, and holding them for 4 years would have produced both extremely high nominal interest rates and a 60 percent appreciation in the nominal effective exchange rate. In addition, since the interest parity condition usually holds in the forward market, currencies with high interest rates typically had forward discounts but did not, in fact, depreciate and instead usually appreciated. This means that profits could have been earned most of the time by purchasing the currencies of industrialized countries in the forward market whenever they were at sizable discounts and simply waiting for maturity. If these currencies appreciated rather than depreciated in the spot market, the forward contracts would have been quite profitable. The same pattern was repeated in the euro/dollar market in 2002 and early 2003. Interest rates were higher in Europe than in the United States through a period in which the euro appreciated by 20 percent. A decision to replace dollar assets with euro assets, uncovered, would have made a huge profit in 2002 and early 2003.

It should be stressed that these are the results of studies of past data and that there is no guarantee, or even likelihood, that such profits will be available in the future. Nevertheless, these research results are surprising, and academic economists have not yet produced very convincing explanations of why this happened. They merely wish that they had known about it in the past, so that they could have taken advantage of this situation in the markets.

The earlier model, which produced a unified result for the forward rate via interest arbitrage and speculation, required that speculators determine their exchange rate expectations solely on the basis of differences in expected rates of inflation; that is, that they firmly believed in purchasing power parity. This, of course, may not be the case. Particularly for industrialized countries for which capital account transactions exceed current account transactions by a large multiple, exchange rate expectations may be set in a variety of ways. This creates the possibility that interest arbitragers and speculators will disagree as to what forward rate ought to prevail, and the actual outcome will depend on their relative numbers and the amounts of money they are prepared to commit. In some periods speculative activity may be modest, and interest arbitragers will dominate the market, producing the outcome predicted by the interest parity theory. In other periods, however, speculators may be so active as to move the forward rate away from that suggested by interest parity, despite the activities of arbitragers.[4]

Foreign exchange options

Futures or forward contracts obligate the holder to complete the transaction at maturity, unless it is sold in the meantime or offset by a contract in the opposite direction. A 90-day forward purchase of sterling, for example, could be canceled after 30 days through a sale of 60-day sterling. Otherwise the contract goes to maturity, whether or not the outcome is favorable. An option contract, in contrast, provides the opportunity to purchase or sell a fixed amount of a currency or a common stock during a fixed period of time at a guaranteed price (called the **strike price**), but the holder of the option has the alternative of not completing the purchase or sale.[5] A "**put**" gives the buyer of the contract the right to sell the asset, and a "**call**" provides the opportunity to buy. Because an option is a one-sided bet, an often sizable premium or price is required to purchase such a contract, as can be seen in Exhibit 14.3. Sterling, for which the spot exchange rate was US$1.5978, was available on 2 January 2003 as a call with a March 2003 expiration at a strike price of $1.60. The price or premium on that call is 1.50 cents. A March put was available at the same $1.60 strike price at a premium of 2.90 cents. The fact that the premium for the put was considerably higher than that on the call, despite the fact that the strike price was very close to the current spot exchange rate ($1.60 versus $1.5978) suggests that the put was viewed as being much more likely to be exercised than was the call, for reasons that will be discussed later.

Foreign exchange options are a useful means of covering possible exchange exposure from a transaction that may not occur. If, for example, a US firm were in the midst of negotiating a contract to purchase a British firm for £1 million sterling, it might want to lock in its US dollar price but not be bound to take delivery of the sterling if the negotiations were to fail. Purchasing sterling calls totaling £1 million will protect the firm against the possibility that sterling will appreciate before the deal is completed and paid for, but will still give the firm a means of avoiding purchasing the sterling if the transaction does not occur.

Foreign exchange options can also be used to insure a pre-existing financial position against loss without giving up the possibility of a profit. If, for example, a firm owned £1 million in sterling assets and had no sterling liabilities, it would be worried about a possible future depreciation of sterling, but would profit if the currency appreciated. Purchasing £1 million in sterling puts would protect the firm against the depreciation without depriving it of the possibility of making money if sterling rose. If the firm had sterling liabilities but no sterling assets, the same insurance would be provided by purchasing sterling calls. In both cases, however, the insurance comes at the cost of the premium on the option plus brokerage commissions.

Finally, purchasing puts or calls is a means of speculating on the future of the spot exchange rate with a limited risk of loss. If, for example, a speculator believed that spot sterling will

EXHIBIT 14.3 FOREIGN EXCHANGE OPTIONS

CURRENCY OPTIONS

■ **US $/€ OPTIONS** (CME)

Strike price Jan 2	·········· CALLS ··········			·········· PUTS ··········		
	Jan	Feb	Mar	Jan	Feb	Mar
10200	1.09	3.14	2.50	0.01	0.77	1.25
10300	0.45	1.38	1.90	0.19	1.18	1.56
10400	0.09	1.00	1.40	0.66	1.65	1.65
10500	0.05	0.68	1.12	0.00	0.00	2.02

Calls: 2,805 Puts: 1,062 . Volume: 3,867 . Previous day's Open Interest: 52,156 .

■ **US $/YEN OPTIONS** (CME)

Strike price Jan 2	·········· CALLS ··········			·········· PUTS ··········		
	Jan	Feb	Mar	Jan	Feb	Mar
8300	0.60	2.02	2.33	0.07	0.84	1.14
8400	0.07	0.90	1.20	0.40	1.04	1.68
8500	0.02	0.68	1.00	0.68	1.50	2.00
8600	0.04	0.40	0.68	-	-	2.80

Calls: 614 Puts: 488 . Volume: 1,102 . Previous day's Open Interest: 85,334 .

■ **US $/UK£ OPTIONS** (CME)

Strike price Jan 2	·········· CALLS ··········			·········· PUTS ··········		
	Jan	Feb	Mar	Jan	Feb	Mar
1590	0.34	1.34	-	0.58	1.82	-
1600	0.16	1.32	1.50	0.40	1.48	2.90
1610	0.05	1.36	1.16	-	-	-
1620	0.06	0.66	0.92	-	-	3.28

Calls: 50 Puts: 81 . Volume: 131 . Previous day's Open Interest: 12,195 .

Source: Financial Times, 3 January 2003.

fall well below $1.60 before the end of March, purchasing a sterling put with a strike price of $1.60 for 2.90 cents is a way of gambling on that outcome without taking a large risk. The problem is that sterling will have to fall below $1.5710 for the gamble to be profitable because, although the strike price is $1.60, the speculator already has spent 2.90 cents on the premium or price of the option. Since the contract size is £31,250, the total price of the option is $906.25 plus brokerage charges, which is the maximum loss that the speculator can experience. That will occur if spot sterling never goes below $1.60 before maturity, so it is never worth exercising. This put option is said to be "in the money" (or, sometimes, "above water") whenever the spot exchange rate is below $1.60, but it is only profitable at spot exchange rates below $1.5710.

If, for example, spot sterling is $1.58 as the expiration date of the put approaches, the option is certainly worth exercising at a strike price of $1.60. Two cents is earned per pound, but this does not offset the original cost of the option (2.90 cents per pound), leaving a loss of 0.9 cent per pound, or $281.25 plus brokerage commissions on the entire contract. If, however, sterling had fallen to $1.55 before the maturity of the option, a profit of 2.10 cents per pound, or $656.25 minus brokerage charges on a contract of £31,250, would have resulted. An option contract is said to be "out of the money" (or underwater) if it is not worth exercising, meaning that its holder will lose the full premium on the option plus commissions if circumstances do not improve before maturity.

It should be clear why one might be interested in purchasing puts or calls, but the question then arises as to why anyone would be willing to sell, or "write," such contracts. The seller of the option accepts the possibility of a large loss with no offsetting possibility of speculative gain. Those who sell options are willing to do so because they receive the premium or price of the option, which was $906.25 in the example in the previous paragraph. Those who sell puts on sterling with a strike price of $1.60 are gambling that sterling will not fall below $1.5710 before the option expires, so that even if the option is exercised, they will retain some profit. If sterling does not fall below $1.60, the option will be "out of the money" and will not be exercised. In that case, the seller retains the entire $906.25 minus brokerage charges.

The profit and loss outcomes from this put contract, measured as US cents per pound sterling, are illustrated in Figure 14.2. The buyer of the put makes a profit at any spot exchange rate below $1.5710 and loses above that rate, with the maximum loss being 2.90 cents if the put is "out of the money" and therefore not worth exercising. The writer or seller of this option faces the mirror-image situation; losses are absorbed if the spot price is below $1.5710, and a maximum profit of 2.90 cents is earned if the spot rate does not fall below $1.60.

Note that the buyer of the option has an almost unlimited possible profit and a limited loss, whereas the seller has a limited possible profit and an almost unlimited possible loss. The only reason why there is any limit to the possible profit to the buyer, and loss to the seller, of this put option is that spot sterling cannot go below zero in US funds.

The profit and loss outcomes for the previously discussed sterling call, which had a strike price of $1.60 and a premium of 1.50 cents, can be found in Figure 14.3. In this case, the buyer of the call absorbs a maximum loss of 1.50 cents if spot sterling never goes above $1.60,

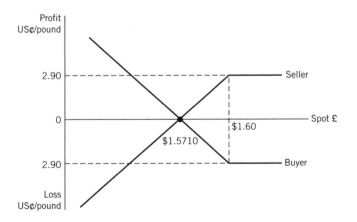

Figure 14.2 Profits and losses from a put option on sterling. A sterling put with a strike price of $1.60 and a premium of 2.90 cents will be profitable for a buyer if the spot price of sterling falls below $1.5710 before the option expires. The maximum loss for a buyer, which occurs if spot sterling does not fall below $1.60, is 2.90 cents per pound. The writer or seller of the option is in the mirror-image situation, facing a loss that rises as sterling falls below $1.5710 and a profit that is at a maximum of 2.90 cents per pound if spot sterling never falls below $1.60 before the option expires.

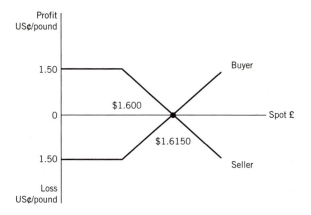

Figure 14.3 Profits and losses from a call option on sterling. A sterling call with a strike price of $1.60
and a premium of 1.50 cents will be profitable for a buyer if spot sterling rises above
$1.6150 before the option expires. The maximum loss for the buyer, which occurs if spot
sterling never exceeds $1.60, is 1.50 cents per pound. The seller of the option is in the
mirror-image situation, making a maximum profit of 1.50 cents per pound if sterling never
exceeds $1.60, and losing money as spot sterling rises above $1.6150 before the option
expires.

so the option is "out of the money" and not worth exercising. Profits begin at $1.6150 and
are unlimited as sterling rises beyond that level. The seller of the option again faces the
mirror-image outcomes. A maximum profit of 1.50 cents is made if spot sterling never rises
above $1.60. Losses begin at $1.6150 and rise without limit as sterling exceeds that level.
Transactions costs are ignored in these graphs, so profits will be slightly smaller and losses
bigger when brokerage commissions are included.

Those who write or sell options often have a cover or hedge; if, for example, someone
already owns £31,250 with no offsetting sterling liabilities, selling a sterling call contract
is not risky. If sterling rises sharply and the option is exercised, there is no out-of-pocket
loss, but instead merely a loss of what otherwise would have been a capital gain on sterling's
appreciation. If, however, someone owns no sterling and sells sterling calls, the risks can
be very large. If sterling rises sharply and the option is therefore exercised, the seller of the
option must purchase the necessary sterling at the higher spot exchange rate and absorb
whatever out-of-pocket loss results. Writing uncovered or "naked" options is extremely
dangerous, as many writers of puts on US common stocks discovered on 19 October 1987
when the Dow-Jones Industrial Average declined by over 500 points.

Determinants of options prices

The determination of the premiums on foreign exchange options depends on both intrinsic
and time value, that latter having a number of determinants. Intrinsic value is the extent
to which the option is currently "in the money." If a sterling call has a strike price of $1.60
and the current spot exchange rate is $1.63, the intrinsic value of the option is 3 cents, and
the premium must be at least that amount.

Time value results from the possibility of future exchange rate changes that could make
the option worth more than its current intrinsic value. Three factors determine an option's
time value: relative interest rates, expected volatility, and the length of time until the option
expires. Relative interest rates determine the forward premium or discount, which in turn

represents the expected change in the spot rate. If 90-day interest rates in the United Kingdom are above those prevailing in the United States, sterling will be at a forward discount in the 90-day market, meaning the market expects spot sterling to depreciate during that period. This set of circumstances existed at the beginning of 2003. This situation would reduce the time value and therefore the premium on a sterling call with a 3-month maturity, because the market views it as unlikely that this option will become more profitable to exercise by the time it matures. Higher interest rates in the UK and the resulting forward discount on sterling would, of course, increase the premium on a sterling put with the same maturity, because the market is saying that option is likely to be further in the money, and therefore more worth exercising, at maturity than it is now. This explains the 2.90 cents premium on the sterling put relative to the 1.50 cents premium on the call in the earlier examples which were drawn from 2 January 2003 data.

The second factor in determining time value is expected volatility, which is likely to be based on volatility in the recent past. Sterling puts and calls with strike prices of $1.60 will be worth more if the exchange rate for sterling is expected to be quite volatile, perhaps because it has been volatile during the last year or two. If, however, sterling has not moved above $1.62 or below $1.58 during that period, and there is no reason to expect that circumstance to change, both the put and the call will be worth considerably less. Purchasing options are sometimes referred to as buying price volatility, and the premium is the cost of that purchase.

The last factor is the amount of time left until an option expires; the longer that period, the greater the opportunity for an exchange rate change that will make the option more profitable, and the higher its current premium. An option which has a year until maturity will be considerably more valuable than one which expires in 3 months. As maturity approaches, time value declines rapidly, there being no time value at maturity, when the premium must be the intrinsic value of the option. If a sterling call has a strike price of $1.60 and the spot exchange rate is $1.62 when the option expires, its premium must be 2 cents. With the same spot rate, a sterling put with the $1.60 strike price would have a premium of zero at maturity because it is out of the money by 2 cents.

Informal trading in foreign exchange options has existed for some time, but formal trading on exchanges is fairly recent. It began in Amsterdam in 1978 and was extended to Montreal and Philadelphia in 1982. American options can be exercised at any time until maturity, while European options can only be exercised at the maturity date. European options can, however, be bought or sold in the secondary market, at the current premium or price, in the meantime.

Other international derivatives

The contracts described in the previous pages of this chapter are the most commonly used international derivatives, but there are many others. International interest rate swaps involve the exchange of interest payments in one currency and maturity for those of another currency and maturity. If, for example, a British corporation was borrowing in order to undertake a direct investment in Japan and wished to make its interest payments in yen, but was unknown to bankers outside the United Kingdom and therefore could not easily borrow in Tokyo, it could borrow sterling and then use an interest rate swap to solve its problem. Under the interest rate swap it would agree to pay in yen the Japanese short-term interest rate on a nominal amount equal to its UK borrowing, and to receive the UK short-term interest rate on the same amount in sterling. The latter funds would be used to pay interest on its UK borrowing. The firm would be paying interest as if its debt were denominated in yen, despite the fact that it actually borrowed dollars in London. If the firm exchanged both payments of interest and principle in this manner, the contract would be a currency swap rather than an interest rate swap.

A foreign exchange swap involves the spot purchase of a currency and its simultaneous sale in the forward market. If a US investor purchased spot sterling with dollars, and simultaneously sold the same amount of forward sterling for dollars, in order to undertake a short-term investment in London, that investor would have a foreign exchange swap into sterling.

A note issuance facility (NIF) provides its purchaser with the option to borrow a fixed sum of money in foreign or domestic currency under guaranteed terms, that is, at a fixed interest rate or at a rate tied to a market rate such as the US prime rate or **LIBOR** (**London Interbank Offer Rate** in the Eurodollar market). A single NIF might involve borrowing in more than one currency.

The variety and complexity of both domestic and international derivatives are limited only by the imagination of the officers of commercial and investment banks who are selling them in exchange for handsome fees.[6] Derivatives were originally seen as a way of offsetting risks from previous financial exposures, but have increasingly become ways of speculating. Many investors have become involved in such derivatives without fully understanding the risks, and have absorbed large financial losses when markets turned against them. This chapter might close by merely noting that if one is told by a banker or broker that a particular investment or derivative contract offers the certainty of a large profit at virtually no risk, that person should find a new bank or brokerage firm. Neither international nor domestic financial markets offer opportunities for large profits at no significant risk. International derivative markets have reinforced this unhappy lesson for numerous investors in recent years.

Summary of key concepts

1   Foreign exchange forwards, futures, and options are all international derivatives, that is, contracts which gain or lose value depending on the movement of another asset price.

2   Exchange risk arising from purchasing imports which are payable in the exporter's currency at a fixed later date can be hedged by purchasing that currency in the forward market. For small transactions, purchasing a futures contract in that currency can accomplish the same purpose.

3   The premium or discount on a currency in the forward market is normally determined by the interest parity condition; that is, a currency trades at a forward discount which equals the local interest rate minus the foreign interest rate.

4   This premium is also the expected change in the spot rate. These two seemingly separate theories can be reconciled as both representing the difference between rates of inflation in the two countries; that is, a forward discount ultimately reflects the difference between the expected local rate of inflation and that in the foreign country.

5   Foreign exchange options (puts and calls) provide a means of speculating on an exchange rate change with a limited down-side risk. They are also a means of insuring an existing asset or liability position against loss without losing the possibility of a speculative gain. The price of this one-way bet is the premium on the option.

6   The price or premium on an option has two components: intrinsic value, which is determined by the relationship between the current spot exchange rate and the strike price, and time value, which is based on the length of time until the option matures, the expected volatility of the exchange rate over that period, and the forward premium or discount on the currency as an indication of where the spot exchange rate is expected to be at the maturity of the option. Relative interest rates are, of course, important in determining that forward premium or discount on the currency and therefore the expected spot exchange rate.

Questions for study and review

1   Suppose you are a US bicycle dealer. You have signed a contract in which you agree to import 1,000 bicycles from a UK manufacturer and to pay £100,000 for them 6 months from today. How exactly can you use the forward exchange market to protect yourself against exchange rate risk?

2   What is the essential difference between a hedger and a speculator in the foreign exchange market?

3   Suppose 1-year US Treasury bills yield 10 percent, and 1-year German Treasury bills yield 6 percent. If the spot exchange rate is $0.50 = DM 1.00, what should be the forward exchange rate? Explain why.

4   "If the spot exchange rate is DM 4.00 = $1.00, and short-term interest rates are 10 percent in Germany, 6 percent in the United States, the forward exchange rate will probably be more than DM 4 for $1.00." Do you agree? Defend your answer.

5   If US short-term interest rates are 12 percent and Japanese rates are 9 percent and the Japanese yen is trading at a 3 percent (annual rate) discount in the forward market, what does that imply about the market's expectations with regard to US and Japanese inflation? Why?

6   In September of 1998 the following deposit interest rates were offered in Jakarta, Indonesia: US dollar deposits: 1 month 15 percent, 6 months 14 percent, 1 year 12 percent. Rupiah deposits: 1 month 50 percent, 6 months 30 percent, 1 year 20 percent. What discount or premium should exist on the rupiah in the forward markets at the three maturities? What other inferences can you make from these interest rates? If you later discovered that the US dollar deposits in the United States yielded 6 percent at all maturities, and that the central bank of Indonesia provided deposit insurance on rupiah deposits but not on dollar deposits, how would your conclusions change?

7   You work for an investment banking firm in Amsterdam. A new sterling call option is about to open for trading which will allow its purchasers to pay euros and receive sterling. You are asked to predict the price or premium at which this new option contract will trade at the end of its first day on the market. What information do you need to make this prediction, and how would you use that information?

8   What factors would cause the premium or price of a 6-month sterling put option with a given strike price to rise from 1 cent to 3 cents?

Suggested further reading

- Aliber, Robert, *The New International Money Game*, 6th edn, Chicago: University of Chicago Press, 2002.
- Fieleke, N., "The Rise of the Foreign Exchange Futures Market," *New England Economic Review*, March 1985.
- Froot, K., and R. Thaler, "Anomalies: Foreign Exchange," *Journal of Economic Perspectives*, Summer 1990, pp. 179–92.
- Giddy, I., *Global Financial Markets*, Lexington, MA: D.C. Heath, 1994.
- Lewis, K. "Puzzles in International Financial Markets," in G. Grossman and K. Rogoff, eds, *Handbook of International Economics*, Vol. III (Amsterdam: Elsevier), 1995, pp. 1913–72.
- Stokes, H. and H. Neuberger, "Interest Arbitrage, Speculation, and the Determination of the Forward Exchange Rate," *Columbia Journal of World Business*, Winter 1979.
- Study Group, *Recent Innovations in International Banking*, Basle: Bank for International Settlements, 1986.
- Thornton, D., "Tests of Covered Interest Rate Parity," *Federal Reserve Bank of St. Louis Review*, July 1989.

Notes

1   The Chicago market for foreign exchange futures is discussed in N. Fieleke, "The Rise of the Foreign Currency Futures Market," *New England Economic Review*, March 1985. See also I. Giddy, *Global Financial Markets* (Lexington, MA: D.C. Heath, 1994), pp. 191–8.

2   The first presentation of the interest parity theory of forward rate determination appears in J.M. Keynes, *A Tract on Monetary Reform* (London: Macmillan, 1923), pp. 113–39. See also P. Einzig, *The Dynamic Theory of Foreign Exchange* (London: Macmillan, 1967). For an empirical study of when interest rate parity does and does not hold, see D. Thornton, "Tests of Covered Interest Rate Parity," *Federal Reserve Bank of St. Louis Review*, July 1989, pp. 55–66.

3   K. Froot and R. Thaler, "Anomalies: Foreign Exchange," *Journal of Economic Perspectives*, Summer 1990, pp. 179–92. See also P. Jorion, "Does Real Interest Rate Parity Hold at Longer Maturities?," *Journal of International Economics*, February 1996, pp. 105–26.

4   A discussion of this approach to forward rate determination can be found in H. Stokes and H. Neuberger, "Interest Arbitrage, Forward Speculation and the Determination of the Forward Exchange Rate," *Columbia Journal of World Business*, Winter 1979, pp. 86–98.

5   A rather thorough discussion of markets for foreign exchange options can be found in I. Giddy, *Global Financial Markets* (Lexington, MA: D.C. Heath, 1994), ch. 8. See also Study Group, *Recent Innovations in International Banking* (Basle: Bank for International Settlements, 1986), chs 1–4.

6   Data on the volume of trading and the notional value of contracts outstanding in the international derivatives market can be found in the Bank for International Settlements, *Annual Report* (Basle: Bank for International Settlements, 1998), p. 156.

15 Alternative models of balance-of-payments or exchange-rate determination

Learning objectives

By the end of this chapter you should be able to understand:

- why large payments surpluses or deficits create major problems for a government or central bank, although the difficulties caused by deficits are more obvious;
- how a payments disequilibrium affects the domestic money supply and how this impact can be reversed, or "sterilized";
- the determination of a country's current account performance as a function of its terms of trade, its business cycle performance relative to that of its trading partners, and its real effective exchange rate;
- the behavior of the capital account as a response to expected yields and risks, or of recent changes in those variables in the portfolio balance model;
- monetarism as a quite different, general equilibrium-based approach, in which balance-of-payments deficits are the result of an excess supply of money which generates a parallel excess demand for goods and/or bonds; these excess demands spill over into the balance of payments as deficits on the current and/or capital accounts.

What causes changes in the sum of the autonomous items in the balance of payments, which in turn causes either payments disequilibria or alterations in exchange rates? Those factors that would cause a balance-of-payments deficit for a country maintaining a fixed parity would instead cause a depreciation of the currency if a floating exchange rate existed. Accordingly, we are seeking to explain exchange market pressures that can result in changes either in the balance of payments or in the market exchange rate.

Why are some countries frequently in deficit (or have depreciating currencies), whereas others experience constant surpluses (or long-term appreciations)? There is no single cause of such disequilibria; rather, several factors can produce such outcomes. There are also different theories, which sometimes overlap but sometimes conflict, in this area. First, we discuss these factors and theories in order to provide a broad understanding of what drives the balance of payments or the exchange rate. Next, we examine payments adjustment, that is, how payments disequilibria are resolved, and, finally, how flexible exchange rates operate.

The ordering of this discussion may seem odd in that the treatment of fixed exchange rates and payments disequilibria precedes that of flexible exchange rates, despite the fact that the

United States and many other countries maintain floating exchange rates. This ordering has been chosen both for pedagogical reasons and because many countries still maintain parities rather than having independent floating exchange rates. With regard to the pedagogical argument, the experience of teaching international economics has led to the conclusion that students find a system of fixed exchange rates to be easier to understand than a regime of floating exchange rates. The concepts of international finance will then be better understood if the more straightforward system is presented first and if the more difficult arrangements follow.

Since this chapter is long and rather complicated, we want to indicate at the outset the way in which it is organized. The presentation of alternative models of the balance of payments is preceded by a section on why the balance of payments or the exchange rate matters, that is, why governments and central banks are concerned about payments disequilibria and frequently adopt various policy measures to bring about payments adjustment. This section is followed by a discussion of balance-of-payments determination which views the current and capital accounts separately. The current account is modeled in a traditional or Keynesian framework. The capital account is then discussed as responding first to differences in levels of interest rates or risks in what is known as a "flow-adjustment model."

A more current view of the capital account, which is known as the "portfolio balance" or "stock-adjustment model," is the next topic. In this view of the capital account, international flows respond to recent changes in yields and risks rather than to differences in levels.

This item-by-item approach is followed by the monetarist model, which views the balance of payments as a whole as responding to differences between the domestic demand for money and the supply of money being created by the central bank. The monetarist model of the balance of payments and the portfolio balance model of the capital account are related in that both can be viewed as subcategories of the asset market approach to balance-of-payments or exchange-rate determination. The presentation of the monetarist model is followed by a discussion of some limitations or criticisms of that approach.

Readers may think of the factors affecting the balance of payments of a country on a fixed exchange rate as being quite different from the determination of the exchange rate for a country with a float, and may therefore be surprised to see the two concepts tied together. The relationship between the two is, however, based on a simple argument. If a country with a fixed exchange rate is in official reserve transactions balance-of-payments equilibrium, the exchange market clears without official intervention. If a country in that situation maintained a clean float, there would be no pressure for the exchange rate to appreciate or depreciate. Thus the circumstances that produce a balance-of-payments equilibrium for a country maintaining a fixed exchange rate would produce an unchanging exchange rate for a country on a float.

If one of the positive autonomous items in the balance of payments, such as exports, then increased significantly, a country with a parity would experience a payments surplus. If that country instead maintained a floating exchange rate, its currency would be in excess demand in the exchange market and would appreciate. The same circumstances that would produce a payments surplus for a country on a parity would produce an appreciation for a country with a float. The same argument holds in the opposite direction: an increase in the negative autonomous items in the balance of payments, such as domestic purchases of foreign securities, would produce either a payments deficit for a country on a parity or a depreciation for a country maintaining a floating exchange rate.

The conclusion of this argument is that, theoretically, a model that explains balance-of-payments deficits or surpluses in a world of fixed exchange rates should also explain depreciations or appreciations in a world of floating exchange rates. As will be seen later in this book, however, empirical research is at some variance with this theory in that the models that follow in this chapter do a considerably better job of explaining payments disequilibria than they do of explaining the behavior of floating exchange rates. Possible reasons for this research result also will be discussed later.

Why the balance of payments (or the exchange rate) matters

Before beginning a discussion of causes of balance-of-payments disequilibria, we might ask why anyone cares. That is, why are deficits or surpluses seen as a policy problem that requires attention, or, if a parity is not being maintained, why are large changes in exchange rates undesirable?

Balance-of-payments deficits, especially if they continue for long periods, present a variety of problems, some obvious and others more subtle. First, there is the question of the adequacy of foreign exchange reserves (FXR) and of what happens if reserves approach exhaustion. A payments deficit normally means that reserve assets decline, and such reserves are finite. If these reserves approach zero, the country becomes unable to make payment for imports, and deliveries may cease. It might be thought that no country would allow reserve depletion to continue to such an extreme, but it does happen and the results are not pleasant. If vital imports, such as petroleum, spare parts, or raw materials, become unavailable, the domestic economy slows dramatically. During the early 1980s Tanzania was in such a situation, and the operating rule for the delivery of imports was that ships did not come into Dar es Salaam to unload until the captain had received a radio message to the effect that payment had been received and had cleared the bank. There are no 30- or 60-day payment terms for such countries. As a result, imports are available only when export receipts arrive, and the modern economy barely operates. Sometimes this means a lack of imported medicines or insecticides, with obvious consequences for public health.

Countries that face the exhaustion of foreign exchange reserves often find themselves dependent on lenders such as the International Monetary Fund. The typical result is emergency loans extended under rather stringent terms, widely known as **conditionality**. The country's ability to manage its own economic and financial affairs can be compromised by such conditions, a situation that is politically embarrassing.[1]

In addition to the budgetary constraint implied by finite foreign exchange reserves and a limited ability to borrow, there is the problem of trade deficits as a recessionary factor in a Keynesian view of a macroeconomy. A loss of export sales that shifts the trade or current account toward deficit reduces aggregate demand in the economy and reduces total output and incomes through the multiplier process. If the economy was in an inflationary state at the time of the export decline, such a reduction in total demand might be desirable. If, however, the economy was already weak or tending toward recession, such a deficit would be harmful. Expansionary fiscal or monetary policies could be used to offset such an impact, but the trade deficit would still be a complicating factor in the domestic macroeconomy. The more open the economy of a country is, the more vulnerable it is to macroeconomic shocks from abroad through shifts in the trade balance.

Balance-of-payments deficits also affect the domestic money supply in ways which may not match the desires of the central bank, thus complicating the management of monetary policy. A payments deficit requires that the central bank sell foreign currency in the exchange market, with payment being made to the central bank in domestic money. The result is a reduction in the member bank reserves (MBR) of domestic commercial banks. It is exactly as if the central bank had sold domestic Treasury bills in a standard restrictive open-market policy, except that foreign money replaces the Treasury bills and the transaction was not voluntary. The central bank is required to sell foreign exchange reserves, thus reducing the stock of member bank reserves or **base money**, by its commitment to maintain a fixed exchange rate.

The reduction in the stock of base money works through the coefficient of monetary expansion or money multiplier (the reciprocal of the reserve ratio) to further reduce the domestic money supply and the availability of credit. Assuming a 20 percent reserve requirement and a payments deficit of $10 million, we can expect the banking system to be affected as shown in the balance sheets in Table 15.1.

Table 15.1 Impact on the domestic money supply of a balance-of-payments deficit shown through balance sheet changes

Central bank		One commercial bank		All commercial banks	
–$10m FXR	–$10m MBR	–$10m MBR	–$10m demand deposits	–$10m MBR –$40m loans	–$50m demand deposits

The money supply has fallen whether or not such a decline matches the wishes of the central bank. This effect could be canceled through a practice known as **sterilization**, namely, the open-market purchase of sufficient domestic Treasury bills (or other domestic assets) to return the stock of member bank reserves to its original level. In this case a purchase of $10 million in such domestic assets would be called for, as shown in the balance sheets in Table 15.2.

Table 15.2 The sterilization of effects of a payments deficit

Central bank		One commercial bank		All commercial banks	
+$10m Treasury bills	+$10m MBR	+$10m MBR	+$10m demand deposits	+$10m MBR +$40m loans	+$50m demand deposits

Sterilization is any open-market purchase or sale of domestic assets which has the effect of canceling or offsetting the monetary effects of a balance-of-payments disequilibrium. In the case of a payments deficit, an open-market purchase of domestic assets produces this effect; that is, it returns the money supply to the level prevailing before the payments disequilibrium. Although central banks widely practice sterilization, payments deficits still significantly complicate the management of a domestic monetary policy. Sterilization can be partial if a central bank uses open-market policy to offset less than all of the monetary impact of a payments disequilibrium.

Balance-of-payments surpluses present fewer and less pressing problems than deficits, but even surpluses are not without disadvantages. First, a trade surplus is a source of aggregate demand, and the sudden emergence of such a surplus can be inflationary. Countries with open economies often find sharp increases in export sales to be a mixed blessing at best. The resulting increases in domestic incomes can work through the multiplier process to cause serious inflation, particularly if the economy was close to full employment when the export increase began.

A balance-of-payments surplus also increases the domestic money supply through the same process described earlier for a deficit. The central bank's purchases of foreign exchange are paid for with domestic money which is deposited in commercial banks, thus adding to the stock of member bank reserves. The transactions are the same as those shown in the balance sheet summaries on page 332, except that all the signs are reversed. Sterilization is possible, but in this case domestic Treasury bills would be sold rather than purchased. If the central bank sells off all its domestic assets, control of the money supply might be threatened, but an increase in the reserve ratio would remain available as a way to control the money supply despite a payments surplus. The point remains that a payments surplus increases the money supply unless sterilization is pursued, and that large payments imbalances of either type complicate the management of monetary policy.

Sterilization may be quite difficult in the case of a payments surplus, particularly if the surplus is large. The central bank should sell domestic assets to offset the monetary effects of a surplus, and these assets are almost certain to be government debt such as Treasury bills in the United States. These sales are likely to be very unpopular with the finance ministry of the government, which is probably trying to sell debt in order to finance a budget deficit or to replace its outstanding securities which are maturing. The central bank is put in the position of selling debt securities in competition with its government, with predictable impacts on the interest rates that the government must pay to borrow.

In the case of a large and sustained surplus, the central bank could exhaust its holdings of government debt, having nothing to sell to offset the expansionary impact of a payments disequilibrium. As was noted above, the central bank could then raise reserve requirements to reduce the money supply, but this would anger commercial banks, which would be required to hold an increased percentage of their assets in nonearning forms.

This problem arose in a striking form in India during 1993–4. As a result of continuing economic reforms and speculative optimism about the Bombay stock market, a huge inflow of equity capital arrived, driving the payments accounts into a surplus of almost $9 billion during a 1-year period. The Reserve Bank of India faced a decidedly unpleasant set of choices: it could do nothing and allow inflation to accelerate, or it could revalue the rupee, harming India's export prospects, or it could sterilize. If it chose to sterilize, it would either create serious problems for the government of India by selling large volumes of government debt, or make life very difficult for commercial banks by raising reserve requirements. Reserve requirements were raised, but not by enough to fully offset the payments surplus; therefore money supply growth and inflation accelerated.[2]

A balance-of-trade surplus means that the country is producing more than it is using or absorbing domestically, which may not be in the interests of the local population. Let us return to the national income accounting identities of Chapter 12:

$$Y = C + I + G + (X - M) \tag{1}$$

$$(X - M) = Y - (C + I + G) \tag{2}$$

where C, I, and G are totals rather than only goods and services of domestic origin. A trade surplus of $10 billion means that the country is producing $10 billion more real output than its residents are utilizing, with the difference being sent to the rest of the world in exchange for financial assets. Those assets presumably earn a rate of return that will allow even more resources to be used later, but such assets are also subject to the effects of inflation.

The US price level more than tripled between 1967 and 1987, and during many of those years *ex post* real interest rates on US government securities were negative. Foreign governments that held foreign exchange reserves in the form of dollar assets during that period did not do well. Balance-of-payments surpluses run during the 1950s and early 1960s were used to purchase such securities, only to have inflation reduce their value. If a government's purpose is to maximize the utility or welfare of its citizens, it may not be desirable to use continuing current account or balance-of-payments surpluses to finance the accumulation of foreign assets, which are vulnerable to inflation.

Even when US inflation is low, foreign exchange reserves in the form of dollars are not necessarily the most productive use of a country's wealth. The People's Republic of China, for example, has run payments surpluses in recent years which have resulted in the accumulation of foreign exchange reserves of over $200 billion (more than $300 billion if Hong Kong is included). Those reserves are largely in the form of dollars earning less than 5 percent. Given China's poverty and need for infrastructure, physical investments would certainly return more than 5 percent per year. By running current and overall payments surpluses sufficient to accumulate these enormous reserves, China is giving up the difference between its internal marginal product of capital and the low interest rate that it is earning on its dollar reserve assets. This is not to argue that foreign exchange reserves are "bad," but merely that to the extent that they are in excess of a country's needs, as they certainly are in China, they can be expensive.

Finally, to the extent that some countries have chronic payments surpluses, they make it impossible for the rest of the world to eliminate deficits. The world's balance of payments totals zero; thus if some countries maintain and even defend surpluses, the rest of the world is necessarily in deficit. During the 1960s both the United States and the United Kingdom frequently found that their attempts to deal with payments deficits were frustrated by policies pursued by Japan, Germany, and other surplus countries which seemed designed to perpetuate their surpluses.

In a world of flexible exchange rates, the forces that would have caused large payments disequilibria instead produce exchange rate volatility, such as was experienced in the market for the US dollar in the early 1980s. The dollar rose by over 60 percent (nominal) from early 1981 to 1985 and then fell by a similar amount in the next few years. More will be said about flexible exchange rates in Chapters 19 and 20, but for now let us note that such exchange rate volatility has decidedly disruptive effects on a nation's economy. For a relatively open economy, the exchange rate is probably its most important single price, in that it affects almost everything, including the price level, production, and the distribution of incomes. Exchange rate volatility of the type experienced by the US during the early 1980s is certainly to be avoided. Either large payments disequilibria or large exchange rate changes are undesirable, and the next question is what causes them.

Alternative views of balance-of-payments (or exchange-rate) determination

This chapter presents two broad views of the forces that drive the autonomous transactions in the balance of payments; these forces produce either payments disequilibria or exchange rate movements. The first approach is more traditional and views the payments accounts in an item-by-item format. The trade account is examined in a Keynesian framework, and the capital account is then analyzed separately as being driven by expected relative rates of return and risk variables in the flow adjustment approach, and by recent changes in expected yields and risks in the stock adjustment or portfolio balance version. The second approach is considerably newer and looks at the accounts as a whole rather than at items within the accounts. It is the "monetarist model of the balance of payments," and it is an extension of the domestic neoclassical model for which the University of Chicago is so well known.

The non-monetarist view of the trade balance

The traditional view of the balance on goods and services, which will be referred to more briefly as the "trade balance" in what follows, begins with an accounting identity and then adopts a demand-driven or Keynesian approach to explain elements in that identity:

$$BOT = P_x \cdot Q_x - P_m \cdot Q_m \tag{3}$$

which says that the trade balance is defined as the world price of exports times the volume exported minus the world price of imports times the volume imported. For most countries world prices of traded commodities can be taken as given, in that the country in question cannot be expected to affect these prices. With given prices of exports and imports (and hence given terms of trade), the question then becomes: what determines the quantities of goods exported and imported? Taking imports first in this Keynesian approach,

$$Q_m = F(\overset{+}{Y_d}, \overset{+}{XR_r}) \tag{4}$$

which says that imports are a positive function of domestic incomes and of the real exchange rate, measured as the foreign price of domestic money. Imports rise with local incomes and when the domestic currency appreciates in real terms.

The **marginal propensity to import**, which is the percentage of extra income which is spent on additional imports ($\Delta M/\Delta Y$), provides the linkage from domestic incomes to imports, the idea being that when domestic incomes rise people will spend more on a variety of consumer goods and part of the marginal expenditures will be on imports. Imports tend to be cyclical, rising during domestic expansions and declining in recessions.

The real exchange rate reflects the attractiveness of foreign versus domestic goods in terms of relative costs. A real appreciation means that domestic goods have become more expensive relative to foreign alternatives, which encourages domestic residents to substitute toward imports. A real depreciation means that domestic goods become relatively cheaper, thus discouraging imports. To summarize, imports are determined by domestic incomes and relative prices, rising with incomes and falling as foreign goods become relatively more expensive. Other variables might be added, including some measure of tastes or fashion, as well as changing reputations for quality and prompt delivery, but those less important (and unmeasurable) factors will be ignored for the time being.

Turning to exports, we find that

$$Q_x = F(\overset{+}{Y_f}, \overset{-}{XR_r}) \tag{5}$$

which says that the volume of goods exported is positively related to foreign incomes and negatively related to the real exchange rate. An increase in foreign incomes causes rising purchases of a range of goods, some proportion of which will be exports from the home country. Export volumes are then tied to foreign business cycles, rising with expansions and declining in recessions. Foreigners also make purchases on the basis of relative prices, purchasing fewer of this country's goods when its currency is overvalued and more when it is undervalued. Rapid inflation in the home country, which is not offset by a nominal depreciation or devaluation, will make the home country's products less price-competitive and reduce export volumes.

Substituting equations (4) and (5) into equation (3):

$$BOT = P_x \cdot F(Y_f, XR_r) - P_m \cdot F(Y_d, XR_r) \tag{6}$$

or

$$BOT = F(\overset{+}{P_x}, \overset{-}{P_m}, \overset{-}{Y_d}, \overset{+}{Y_f}, \overset{-}{XR_r}) \tag{7}$$

which says that the trade balance is positively related to the home country's terms of trade (P_x/P_m), negatively related to domestic incomes (due to the impact of such incomes on import expenditures), positively related to foreign incomes (for the same reason), and negatively related to the real exchange rate. The last variable is an index of the home country's cost and price competitiveness in world markets. When it is high, the home country's currency is overvalued and its products are overpriced, resulting in depressed exports and a larger volume of imports, and vice versa.

A country's terms of trade are determined in world markets for its exports and imports. Such markets can be highly competitive and have volatile prices, or they can be oligopolistic and have more stable prices. Many developing countries export large volumes of a small number of primary products into highly competitive markets and find that their terms of trade are unstable. A country such as the Congo (former Zaire) or Zambia is dependent on the world price of copper, over which it has no control, whereas Sri Lanka is similarly dependent on tea prices. Diversifying exports makes a country's terms of trade more stable, but this is not easy for small developing countries. Highly industrialized countries, such as Japan, export a wide variety of products in largely oligopolistic markets with far more stable prices. The terms of trade of such countries can still be affected by particularly important import prices, such as the price of oil, but these countries have typically had far less unstable terms of trade than have developing countries. In the mid-1970s, however, many developed countries found their trade balances seriously worsened by terms-of-trade effects when the price of oil rose sharply. The year 1990 produced similar effects on a smaller scale.

The role of domestic incomes in this model suggests that a country's trade balance is negatively related to its own business cycle, but positively related to foreign cycles. When the domestic economy is in a strong expansion, rapidly rising imports worsen the trade account, but when foreign economies are booming, rising exports improve trade results. If the business cycles of all countries were in phase – that is, they all had expansions and recessions at the same time – these effects would largely cancel, but such cycles are seldom in phase. The impacts of business cycles on trade flows occur rather quickly in that a strong increase in domestic incomes can be expected to cause a parallel rise in imports within a few months.

Cost and price competitiveness, as measured by the real exchange rate, affects the trade balance with a longer lag. Consumers, being creatures of habit, do not immediately adjust to changing relative prices. Finding alternatives to previous purchases may take time, and trade in primary commodities is often managed through long-term contracts that set prices and quantities well into the future. The real exchange rate affects the trade account with a lag of as much as a year, or occasionally even longer. The US dollar, for example, started to depreciate in 1985, but the trade balance did not start to improve significantly until 1987.

Many of the services items in the current account are determined by the same factors that are relevant for merchandise trade. Tourism, which is a major source of foreign exchange for many developing countries, is determined largely by price competitiveness and the business cycle in developed countries. When a developing country's currency is overvalued, it becomes an expensive place to visit, and tourism declines, and vice versa. When, for example, the United Kingdom is in an economic expansion, its residents have more funds for vacations, and Caribbean and North African countries benefit from stronger tourism receipts. When the UK is in a recession, fewer of its citizens travel abroad, and tourist receipts in North Africa and the Caribbean are weaker.

Net dividend and interest transactions are determined first by whether a country is a net debtor or creditor, and second by prevailing interest rates. Brazil, for example, experienced a serious deterioration of its current account in the early 1980s because it was already a large net debtor when interest rates on that debt increased sharply.

Many developing countries, including India and Pakistan, have large current account receipts from remittances, which depend on the state of the economies that employ their workers. When countries along the Persian Gulf are prosperous and peaceful, India and Pakistan receive payments of more than $1 billion per year from their citizens employed abroad. The sharp decline in the world price of oil in the late 1990s reduced job opportunities in the Gulf region and seriously harmed the current account results for South Asian countries.

The capital account

Chapter 9, which dealt with factor mobility in general and multinational corporations in particular, suggested that international capital movements were the result of an arbitrage process. Funds are moved from countries in which expected rates of return (interest or profit rates) are low to countries in which they are high. Risks are an additional problem in that investors are assumed to be averse to risk and therefore to avoid countries where political or other risks are high. Capital then flows from low expected yields or high risks toward higher expected yields or lower risks. Unattractive expected yield/risk combinations drive money out of a country and vice versa. This would suggest that capital flows during any period, which constitute the capital account within the balance of payments, should be a simple function of relative expected yields and risks:

$$KA = F(\overset{+}{r_d}, \overset{-}{r_f}, \overset{-}{risk_d}, \overset{+}{risk_f}) \tag{8}$$

where KA is capital account, where risks may be measured as the variability of past yields in particular countries, including the effects of exchange rate movements, and as probabilities of political instability. This is known as a "flow-adjustment model" of the capital account and suggests that constant expected yield differentials should produce a steady flow of funds from one country to another. If US expected yields exceed those prevailing in Tokyo by 2 percentage points, a steady volume of funds should flow from Tokyo to New York; if the yield spread widens, the flow of funds should increase proportionally, and vice versa.

The availability of forward cover back into the investor's home currency, and the likelihood that covered yield differentials will be zero, as discussed in Chapter 14, is ignored in this model, so it is implicitly assumed that the investments in question are of such a long maturity that forward contracts are not available.

The flow-adjustment model was the dominant view of international capital flows for many years, and it remains implicit in some simple graphical analyses of the balance of payments (the IS/LM/BP curves that will be introduced in Chapter 16), but it turns out to be based on an unrealistic and oversimplified view of how investment managers behave.

The portfolio balance approach

More recent models of the capital account, which are known as stock-adjustment or **portfolio balance models**, have grown out of Tobin's and Markowitz's work on domestic financial behavior.[3] These models begin with the obvious point that an investment manager (banker or mutual fund director, for example) has a fixed stock of capital to invest at any time. That stock will hopefully grow as his or her institution attracts more funds, but investment behavior at any moment is based on the allocation of a fixed stock of funds with the goal of maximizing yield subject to a risk constraint.

The investment manager knows the current yields on the alternative assets and forms expectations with regard to future yields, but he or she cannot know actual future yields. An unexpected increase in interest rates, for example, will impose sizable capital losses on that part of the portfolio that is held in the form of bonds, but will produce higher returns on short-term assets. The manager also has opinions about the riskiness of each of the assets, with those opinions probably being formed on the basis of the degree of instability in past or historic yields. On the basis of expected yields and perceived risks, the manager constructs an ideal portfolio that is designed to maximize the expected yield on the portfolio subject to a risk constraint. The risk constraint is important, because without it the manager would simply put all the funds under his or her management into the asset with the highest expected yield.

Risk is reduced through portfolio diversification, that is, by not putting all portfolio funds into one asset or one type of asset. If, for example, the portfolio is divided between long-term bonds and short-term money-market funds, unforeseen increases in interest rates will produce a capital loss on the first half of the portfolio and an increased rate of return on the latter half. A decline in yields would produce the opposite result. As unexpected increases and decreases in interest rates occur, the portfolio as a whole will have a yield that is more stable than the return on either half of it. For this increase in yield stability to occur, the various parts of the portfolio must not have the same pattern of yield behavior. If, for example, the whole portfolio was invested in 30-year AT&T bonds and then half of it was shifted to 30-year IBM bonds, no significant reduction in yield instability would occur, because both assets would experience the same decline in value when interest rates rose, and the same increase in value when yields fell. Default risk would be reduced by holding claims on two separate firms, but the more serious risk arising from unforeseen changes in interest rates would not be reduced.

Reduction in yield instability requires that the portfolio contains assets that have performed quite differently over interest rate cycles and in response to other financial shocks. Dividing a portfolio between long- and short-term assets is one obvious way to reduce yield instability.

Another way to reduce risk is to diversify a portfolio internationally, that is, to hold claims denominated in more than one currency. Since changes in interest rates in various industrialized countries do not have the same timing, holding assets denominated in a number of national currencies can be expected to reduce risk in the portfolio as a whole. The fact that business cycles have had quite different timing patterns in various industrialized countries means that manufacturing corporations can reduce instability in profit rates by becoming multinational enterprises. When Europe is in a recession, the United States may be booming, so declining European profits are offset by higher profits here. In the early 1980s the Ford Motor Company was losing enormous amounts of money in the United States but had large profits in Europe, which may have been responsible for keeping the parent firm in business. As long as national business cycles do not follow the same timing pattern, foreign direct investments can be viewed as a form of portfolio diversification.

Returning to financial institutions such as mutual funds or banks, we can view the managers of such enterprises as facing different expected yields on classes of assets within their home country and abroad, as well as associating various degrees of risk with each of them.[4] Estimates of risk may be derived from the past behavior of each asset type. Based on the set of expected yields and perceived risks, the manager constructs a desired portfolio that reflects the institution's preference for yield versus risk, that is, its willingness to take higher risks to increase expected yields. A venture capital fund would presumably prefer a much riskier portfolio than would a commercial bank. The manager then compares the desired portfolio to that which the institution actually holds, and shifts funds among asset types to eliminate differences between the two. Once this portfolio adjustment process is complete – that is, the actual portfolio matches the desired portfolio – the manager has no further reason to shift funds between classes of assets despite the continuing existence of yield differentials. As long as the portfolio manager wants to limit risk and does not view foreign assets as perfect substitutes for domestic assets, the continued existence of international differences in interest rates will not cause a continuing or indefinite flow of funds from low- to high-yield markets. Once the actual portfolio matches the desired portfolio, where the desired portfolio reflects existing expected yields and risks, there is no reason to move funds from one country to another.

Investment managers determine the stock of assets which they wish to hold as claims on each country as a positive function of the level of expected yields in that country, a negative function of expected yields elsewhere, a negative function of perceived risks in that country and a positive function of perceived risks elsewhere. Since the capital account of the balance of payments records flows of transactions, it represents changes on the stocks of assets and therefore responds to changes in these variables. When expected yields in one country change, the desired portfolio is affected and the manager moves funds in response. That process should be completed fairly quickly, however, and then funds cease to flow. If, for example, expected rates of return rise in the United Kingdom and there are no changes in perceived risks, portfolio managers might conclude that an additional 5 percent of the funds under their control should be in sterling assets. Over the next few weeks or months, adjustments in the actual portfolio would be made until an extra 5 percent was in sterling claims. Then no further flows of funds to the United Kingdom would occur, despite the continuation of higher relative yields in that market.

If this is how managers of financial institutions behave, international capital flows, and therefore the capital account of the balance of payments, should respond to recent changes in expected yields and risks rather than to differences in the levels of such expected yields and risks. The capital account can then be viewed as follows:

$$KA = F(\overset{+}{\Delta r_d}, \overset{-}{\Delta r_f}, \overset{-}{\Delta risk_d}, \overset{+}{\Delta risk_f}) \tag{9}$$

where Δ is change.

The actual modeling of the capital account for purposes of econometric estimation would be far more complicated, but the basic idea is that capital flows are responses to recent changes in expected yields and risks rather than to continuing differences in the levels of such yields and risks.

Combining models of the capital and current accounts

If the earlier model of the trade and current accounts is combined with the above view of capital account determination, the balance of payments is determined as follows:

$$BOP = F(\overset{+}{P_x}, \overset{-}{P_m}, \overset{-}{Y_d}, \overset{+}{Y_f}, \overset{-}{XR_r}, \overset{+}{\Delta r_d}, \overset{-}{\Delta r_f}, \overset{-}{\Delta risk_d}, \overset{+}{\Delta risk_f}) \tag{10}$$

This rather lengthy expression says that a country's official reserve transactions balance of payments is:

1   Positively related to its terms of trade, that is, positively related to world prices of its exported commodities and negatively related to world prices of its imports.
2   Negatively related to domestic incomes and positively related to foreign incomes, because rising local incomes cause a parallel increase in imports through the marginal propensity to import. Rising foreign incomes cause increased export sales, for the same reason.
3   Negatively related to the real exchange rate, which is measured as the foreign price of the local currency adjusted for differing rates of inflation. An increase in a country's real exchange rate reduces the cost and price competitiveness of its products in world markets. If, for example, UK inflation is 7 percent when foreign inflation averages only 3 percent, a constant nominal exchange rate for sterling means a 4 percent real appreciation, which worsens the cost and price competitiveness of UK firms by 4 percent a year.
4   Positively related to recent changes in domestic expected interest rates, and negatively related to recent changes in foreign expected yields. When expected US interest rates rise relative to those prevailing abroad, capital will flow into the United States while financial portfolios are being adjusted to the new relative yield situation. Once that adjustment is complete, such flows should cease.
5   Negatively related to recent changes in domestic risk and positively related to recent changes in risks abroad. An increase in the likelihood of political instability in Latin America or elsewhere, for example, will typically cause large flows of capital into the United States as investors seek a safe haven.

This model, as well as the monetarist approach that follows, deals with the economic variables that affect a country's balance of payments, and ignores various external shocks to which items in the payments accounts may be subject. A drought, for example, would reduce a country's agricultural exports (or increase its imports), thereby moving both the trade account and the balance of payments toward deficit. A change in consumer tastes that resulted in the increased popularity of a country's exports would shift the trade account and the balance of payments toward surplus. A number of external shocks, including dock strikes as well as weather or taste shifts, can affect a country's payments results, in addition to the economic variables discussed in the models presented in this chapter.

Asset market approaches to the balance of payments and the exchange rate

As noted in Chapter 13, capital account transactions have become far larger than current account transactions as sources of supply and demand for foreign exchange in the United States and in many other industrialized countries. As a result, many economists have come to view the exchange market and the balance of payments solely as financial phenomena and largely (or totally) ignore real factors that determine trade and other current account transactions.

The exchange market is then viewed (and modeled) as reflecting the supply and demand for financial assets denominated in different currencies. Equilibrium in the balance of payments and the exchange market exists when these financial asset markets clear; payments deficits or depreciations occur when the relative demand for foreign financial assets rises, and vice versa.[5]

This broad class of **asset market models of the balance of payments** (or of the exchange rate) includes two subsectors. In one group of models, domestic and foreign assets are viewed as imperfect substitutes in financial portfolios because of uncertainty and risk constraints. This is the portfolio balance approach to the balance of payments, which was discussed earlier in this chapter as a model of only the capital account. In the second group of asset market models, problems of risk and uncertainty are ignored, thereby allowing domestic and foreign assets to be viewed as perfect substitutes in portfolios. This is known as the "monetarist approach" to the balance of payments, and a discussion of it follows.

The monetarist model of the balance of payments

The **monetarist model of the balance of payments** includes far fewer variables than do the models described earlier and is an outgrowth of the monetarist model of a domestic economy. It operates on the basis of that model's simplifying assumptions.

Markets are assumed to be perfectly competitive and therefore to move toward equilibrium rather quickly if they are shocked out of equilibrium. Money is neutral, meaning that purely monetary factors cannot have permanent effects on real variables. An increase in the money supply, for example, cannot permanently affect real output. The model has a long-run orientation in that short-run impacts of macroeconomic shocks receive less attention than in a Keynesian world. As was noted above, the monetarist model of the balance of payments adds the assumption that investors or portfolio managers view domestic and foreign financial assets as perfect substitutes. Therefore they are not constrained by portfolio balance considerations, and they can move far larger amounts of money in response to changes in expected yields. It is not suggested that these assumptions are realistic; they are necessary to construct the model in a rigorous fashion. The usefulness of the model is judged not by whether its assumptions are realistic (most economic theory would be abandoned if that were so), but by its ability to explain real-world payments flows. Although this model is not perfect in that regard, it does have a fairly good empirical track record in explaining payments disequilibria.[6]

A monetarist view of macroeconomics operates through a general equilibrium framework and therefore requires an understanding of **Walras's law**, which was developed by a French mathematical economist in the 1870s. This law states that if an economy is defined as an all-inclusive set of markets (a supply function, a demand function, and a market-clearing identity for each good, financial asset, etc., in the economy), where one market is for money, net excess demands must total zero. That rather complicated statement simply means that if something is in excess demand, something else must be in a parallel excess supply. Since nobody expects to be given anything for free (there is no charity in this model), an excess demand for one item necessarily implies an excess supply of whatever people are willing to give up to get what is in excess demand. If, for example, goods are in excess demand, that means people are willing to reduce their holdings of money (or of something else, such as other financial assets) in order to get more goods at current prices. An excess supply of bonds means that people want to reduce their holdings of bonds in order to increase their holdings of something else. That something else, which may be money, is in excess demand.

This point is sufficiently simple that we may wonder why it is so important. It is important because it implies that an economy cannot experience a single disequilibrium. Disequilibria always come in offsetting pairs. If there is an excess supply of goods, there must be a parallel excess demand for something, and it is frequently important to discern what that something is. To think in Walrasian terms is to have a mental reflex of always looking for the offsetting disequilibrium. If one market is observed to be out of equilibrium, the Walrasian response is immediately to seek the offsetting disequilibrium elsewhere in the system. For a monetarist, problems in the markets for goods or financial assets usually have their origin in the market for money. That is, an excess demand for goods is caused by an excess supply of money, which in turn results from unwise decisions by the central bank.

In the monetarist model of a closed economy, an excessive rate of monetary expansion causes price inflation which returns the real money supply (the nominal money supply divided by the price level) to its original equilibrium level. The demand for money is a stable function of GNP. If real growth is 3 percent, any attempt to increase the money supply beyond that rate will merely produce offsetting inflation. A rate of monetary expansion of 10 percent would produce 7 percent inflation and a rate of growth of the real money supply of 3 percent, which matches the growth of real GNP.

In a monetarist model of the balance of payments, or in open economy monetarism, monetary growth has somewhat different effects. Under the assumption of fixed exchange rates, no tariffs or transport costs, and perfect competition, the domestic prices of tradable goods are constrained by international arbitrage. If the exchange rate is 1.5 Swiss francs to the dollar and the Swiss price of wine is 40 francs, the US price must be $26.67. This is known as the **law of one price**:

$$P_d = \frac{P_{row}}{XR_n} \tag{11}$$

The domestic price of tradable goods must equal the foreign price divided by the nominal exchange rate. If that were not true, profits could be made arbitraging between the two markets, assuming no transport costs or tariffs. There is significant evidence that in less than perfectly competitive markets the law of one price is frequently violated, but it is a necessary assumption if the monetarist model is to be understood.[7] The existence of nontradables (goods and services not involved in international trade) is ignored for the moment.

Since domestic and foreign bonds are perfect substitutes, the law of one price holds in the bond market as well as in the market for goods. Because the exchange rate is rigidly fixed (and confidently expected to remain fixed), prices of bonds and therefore interest rates are arbitraged together.

$$r_d = r_f \tag{12}$$

Both goods and bonds move freely between countries to maintain the law of one price in both markets. Any increase of US prices above those prevailing in Canada would cause goods to flow south in sufficient volume to destroy that price difference. The same situation holds in the market for bonds. As a result, a disequilibrium in either the goods market or the bond market causes large balance-of-payments flows. An excess supply of goods quickly becomes a balance-of-trade surplus as the goods that are unsold at home are exported, and an excess demand for bonds causes a capital account deficit as bonds are imported from abroad to fill the domestic shortage.

In the monetarist model, the balance of payments can be viewed as a mechanism through which domestic market disequilibria are ended and through which excess supplies or demands for money are eliminated. Imagine an economy consisting of three markets: goods, bonds, and money. Both the goods and the bonds are traded internationally. If the three markets started in equilibrium and then the central bank increased the money supply by 10 percent, an excess supply of money would be created. Walras's law says that any such excess supply must create a mirror-image excess demand; hence the market for either goods or bonds (more likely, both) must be in excess demand. An excess demand for goods, with domestic prices that are fixed by the law of one price, must spill over into the trade sector as a balance-of-trade deficit. The shortage of goods is filled by imports without any significant increase in domestic prices. If the excess demand were in the bond market, it would be filled through an inflow of bonds from abroad, which would mean a capital account deficit. If the excess demand situation prevailed in both markets, both the trade and the capital account would go into deficit. In any of these cases, the official reserve transactions balance of payments moves into deficit.

If, starting from equilibrium in all markets, the central bank had reduced the money supply, the resulting domestic excess demand for money would have created an excess supply of goods and/or bonds, resulting in an outflow of the goods and/or bonds to foreign buyers and a balance-of-payments surplus. In the monetarist view, balance-of-payments dis-equilibria have a single dominant cause: disequilibria in the domestic market for money, usually caused by central bank errors, which cause mirror-image disequilibria in the domestic markets for goods and for financial assets such as bonds. These latter disequilibria spill over into the balance of payments, causing deficits or surpluses, depending on whether the money supply was too large or too small. If the law of one price does not quite hold in goods or bond markets, an excess supply of money may create some domestic inflation and/or declines in real interest rates, but these are not the ultimate causes of the resulting balance-of-payments deficit. Changes in the domestic price level or in interest rates are merely symptoms of the real cause of the payments deficit, which is an excess supply of money.

The balance-of-payments disequilibrium is not only a response to a nonequilibrium money supply; it is also the mechanism through which the market for money is brought back to equilibrium. Earlier in this chapter we noted that a balance-of-payments deficit auto-matically reduces the domestic money supply and that a surplus increases it. An excess supply of money causes a payments deficit, which reduces the money supply until equilibrium is restored. All that is required is that the central bank not sterilize the monetary impact of its loss of foreign exchange reserves. In the reverse case, an excess demand for money, caused by an excessively restrictive domestic monetary policy, causes a balance-of-payments surplus, which automatically increases the money supply as the central bank accumulates foreign exchange reserves. Again, all that is required is that the central bank not sterilize.

Balance-of-payments disequilibria are therefore both the result of monetary policy errors and the source of their reversal. An unwise increase in the money supply causes a payments deficit that drains the excess money out of the economy, and vice versa. All that is required for the system to be automatically restored to equilibrium is that the central bank avoid sterilization. If the central bank does sterilize, it merely recreates the original disequilibrium in the market for money and maintains the balance-of-payments disequilibrium. In the case of a balance-of-payments deficit, for example, sterilization means that the central banks purchase domestic assets, adding to the stock of the member banks' reserves and the money supply, thus avoiding the money supply reduction which is the normal result of a payments deficit. Since the money supply is not allowed to fall, the excess supply of money that caused the payments deficit cannot be eliminated. Therefore the market for money (and the markets for goods and bonds) cannot return to equilibrium.

The balance of payments will automatically return the markets for money, goods, and bonds to equilibrium if the central bank avoids interfering with the process. Sterilization is one form of such interference, and it merely maintains market disequilibria and the resulting balance-of-payments problems.

Criticisms or limitations of the monetarist model

Although the model described in the previous paragraphs has empirical support and is widely used in analyzing payments problems, it is not without disadvantages. First, it results in central banks being blamed for payments deficits without consideration of whether the central bank is actually an independent decision-making agency. Monetarists tend to assume that other countries have central banks that are similar to the Federal Reserve System or the European Central Bank in their independence from the executive branch of the government. The Open Market Committee of the Federal Reserve System can decide how rapidly to expand its holdings of domestic assets, and therefore the US stock of base money, without having to accept the "advice" of the White House or the Secretary of the Treasury. If the US money supply is badly managed, it is reasonable to blame the Federal Reserve System. The Governing Council of the European Central Bank has the same powers and therefore has the same responsibility for monetary policy errors.

Few other central banks enjoy such independence. It is far more common, particularly in developing countries, for the governor of the central bank to report to the minister of finance, and therefore to be unable to make independent decisions. The overriding concern of the finance ministry is the financing of budget deficits, and the central bank is often viewed as the obvious lender. If the finance ministry must borrow vast sums to cover a budget deficit, it is extremely tempting to order the central bank to purchase the required bonds and issue new money in exchange. When the government spends these funds, they enter the domestic banking system, and rapid monetary expansion results. It appears to be a typical expansionary open-market policy, except that the central bank purchases government debt directly from the finance ministry, and, more importantly, it does not do so voluntarily. The money supply expands, often at an inappropriate rate, not because the central bank decides on such a policy, but because it is forced to monetize large government budget deficits.

The resulting balance-of-payments deficits should be blamed not on the central bank, which has no policy independence, but on the fiscal authorities who allowed an excessive budget deficit that had to be financed by the central bank. In such a policy situation, the rate of growth of the central bank's domestic assets cannot be controlled unless the government budget deficit is constrained. Balance-of-payments deficits are therefore caused, not by unwise central bankers, but by excessively large government budget deficits that are monetized.

Box 15.1 Modeling the monetarist view of the balance of payments

A simple version of the monetarist model can be put in algebraic form, which makes it possible to understand how econometric tests can be run.

$$MD \quad = \quad \overset{+\ -}{F(Y, r)} \tag{13}$$

which says that the demand for money is positively related to domestic incomes (the transactions' demand for money) and negatively related to the cost of holding money, which is the interest rate.

$$MS \quad = \quad 1/RR(\text{base money stock}) \tag{14}$$
$$RR \quad = \quad \text{reserve ratio for commercial banks}$$

which says that the money supply equals the coefficient of monetary expansion (1 over the reserve ratio) times the stock of base money. Since the stock of base money is the total liability side of the central bank's balance sheet (ignoring currency in people's pockets), and since the balance sheet identity holds:

$$\text{base money} = DA + FXR \tag{15}$$

which says that the stock of base money equals the sum of the domestic assets of the central bank and its holdings of foreign exchange reserves. Substituting equation (15) into equation (14),

$$MS \quad = \quad (1/RR) \cdot (DA + FXR) \tag{16}$$

Equating money supply with money demand,

$$MS \quad = \quad MD \tag{17}$$

and therefore

$$F(Y, r) \quad = \quad (1/RR) \cdot (DA + FXR) \tag{18}$$

This equation is then put in the form of changes or first differences. Since domestic interest rates cannot change (the law of one price in the bond market) and since the reserve ratio is assumed to be fixed, the above equation becomes:

$$F(\Delta Y) \quad = \quad \Delta DA + \Delta FXR \tag{19}$$

where Δ = change. Because a balance-of-payments surplus causes an equal increase in foreign exchange reserves, and vice versa, the above can be reorganized as

$$\Delta FXR = BOP = F(\Delta Y, \Delta DA) \tag{20}$$

This equation, often in a more complicated form, can be estimated econometrically. The monetarist view of the balance of payments predicts a positive coefficient on the first independent variable and a negative coefficient on the second.

Box 15.2 Printing the budget deficit as a route to inflation

In many particularly backward developing countries, where the banking system is rudimentary and most money is currency, governments or central banks literally print paper money in the amount of the budget deficit. One of the authors of this volume was in Burma (Myanmar) in 1974 and was told that monetary policy in that country consisted of the following: estimate the government budget deficit for the next 12 months. Send an order to the engraving plant to have that amount of paper money, called kyats, printed up and brought to the finance ministry. Spend the paper money to cover the government budget deficit. If your forecasts are correct, you should be out of money in 52 weeks. In the early 1970s, however, Burma had a problem. It did not have sufficient foreign exchange reserves available to import the paper to print the money. Finally, a means of restraining inflationist governments has been found: do not give them any paper. The story ends badly. The government of West Germany gave them the paper to offset the political influence of East Germany, which had given Burma the engraving plant. A friend at the IMF later confirmed this story. The finance minister of Albania was recently quoted as saying, "We do not have the money to print money."

In Yugoslavia, the government of Slobodan Milosevic took the creating of money to finance deficits (and to provide free money for his friends) to a new level, producing an annual rate of inflation of 313 million percent during January of 1994. A friend made a gift of a handsome Yugoslavian bank note in the amount of 50 billion dinars; it was worth $2 when issued, but is now worthless.

Hyper-inflation, and the resulting collapse of the balance of payments and ultimately of the economy, always has the same cause: large government expenditures with grossly insufficient tax revenues, the resulting budget deficit being monetized.

Source: Adapted from *The Wall Street Journal*, April 28, 1999, editorial page, and *The Financial Times*, February 25, 1997, p. 7.

This situation is particularly common in the less developed economies. Such countries typically have very limited private financial markets; thus the government has few, if any, alternatives to borrowing from the central bank. If the Federal Reserve System does not purchase the new securities being issued by the Department of the Treasury, they can be sold to private banks, insurance companies, pension funds, and so on, in New York, but the finance ministry of the typical developing country does not have such alternatives. In addition, developing-country governments seem to have particular difficulties in controlling budget deficits. First, their economies make it difficult to collect a sizable percentage of total incomes as taxes. Much of the economy may be informal (subsistence hunting, fishing, and farming), which cannot be taxed easily. Even the market economy may be based in part on barter, which is hard to tax. When money is used, records may be incomplete, making it almost impossible to enforce an efficient income tax. Such countries often rely heavily on import and export tariffs, and have very limited tax revenues.

On the expenditure side, many developing countries have state-owned enterprises that lose vast sums of money with the necessary funds coming out of public resources.[8] Subsidies for consumer goods such as food and fuel often result in large expenditures. When the costs of a sizable military and a large civilian bureaucracy are added, the result is total government expenditures that cannot be financed with a very limited tax system. The resulting deficit is often monetized, causing an excessively rapid rate of growth of the money supply, which in turn leads to large balance-of-payments deficits.

This suggests why balance-of-payments adjustment programs for developing countries usually contain requirements for reducing government budget deficits as well as for limiting the growth of the money supply. Little is accomplished by requiring the central bank to promise that it will restrain excessive growth of the money supply unless the government budget deficit is also controlled.

The next problem with the monetarist view of payments disequilibria involves the stability of the demand for money, which means the velocity of money. A stable relationship between GNP (P.Q) and the demand for money, in the form of a fixed or at least a predictable velocity of money, is central to both domestic and international monetarism, but that stability is not as apparent as monetarists would like us to believe. The M1 velocity of money in the United States rose fairly steadily from 3.5 to about 7 between 1959 and 1980, but has moved erratically between 5 and 7 since then, and the US velocity for M2 has been only slightly less unstable. The British velocity for M1 has also been quite unstable, moving over a range from 4.5 to 7.5 in the 1960–86 period, before moving more narrowly during later years. The UK velocity for M2 has also moved over a fairly wide range. In Germany, both M1 and M2 velocities have moved over a range of about 50 percent and have trended downward in recent decades. Far fewer economists believe that there is a stable relationship between nominal GDP and the quantity of money which people wish to hold than was the case in the 1970s.

A major reason for the increased variability of money velocity is probably what has become known as **currency substitution**.[9] The monetarist view that the demand for a national currency is a stable function of that country's GNP is based on the implicit assumption that each currency has a monopoly as the circulating money within its national borders; that is, that only dollars are used in the US economy, only sterling is used in the United Kingdom, and so on. That may be true for paper currency but not for bank accounts. As barriers to international capital flows have declined and business has become more international, an increasingly large number of firms hold more than one currency in the form of bank deposits. They might hold each currency in proportion to the amount of business they do in that country, but if they observe that different interest rates are available on deposits in various countries and they form expectations as to likely exchange rate changes, they should make certain adjustments. Specifically, they should shift their portfolios of money balances toward currencies with high expected yields, after making allowance for likely exchange rate movements, and away from currencies where yields are low and/or a depreciation is expected. As a result, the demand for various currencies may be quite volatile as views change on likely exchange rate movements or other factors that affect expected yields.

Each company may have a demand for all monies that is a stable function of its total transactions volume, but it need not have a demand for any single currency that is a stable function of the amount of business it does in each country. Thus the total demand for a currency need not be a stable function of that country's GNP; instead, it can be far more volatile. This currency substitution argument may have been the cause of the exchange rate volatility that plagued many industrialized countries in the 1970s and early 1980s. The total demand for the monies of the major industrialized countries may be a relatively stable function of the total GNPs of those countries, whereas the demand for each currency is far less closely related to the GNP of that country.

It is argued, for example, that the rapid appreciation of the US dollar in the early 1980s was the result of currency substitution into the US dollar. High nominal interest rates, combined with widespread confidence among foreign investors in the ability of the new chairman of the Federal Reserve Board, Paul Volcker, to reduce the US rate of inflation, produced very high real interest rates on US dollar holdings. As a result, desired dollar balances by multinational firms increased sharply, as did the demand for the dollar and therefore the exchange rate for this currency. The observed velocity for both M1 and M2 fell in the United States as more dollars were held per dollar of US GNP, and monetary conditions may have been tighter than the Federal Reserve Board intended. If the Fed did not allow for increased foreign holdings of dollars, it would overestimate the volume of dollars held by Americans and underestimate the extent to which it had tightened domestic monetary conditions. The currency substitution argument remains controversial, but it is an interesting explanation for the increased volatility in the data for the velocity of money in the United States.

Despite these criticisms and problems, the monetarist model is widely used in analyzing balance-of-payments problems and in designing adjustment programs. It is particularly useful in developing countries that are suffering from serious inflation. Its emphasis on controlling the rate of growth of the money supply, which usually requires controlling the government budget deficit, is correct, and countries that are designing a payments adjustment program typically include a target for reduced growth in the money supply. That target may have been of their own choosing, or it may have originated with the International Monetary Fund. In either case, limiting the rate of growth of the domestic assets of the central bank is crucial to avoiding balance-of-payments deficits.

This discussion of monetarism has operated entirely under the assumption of a fixed exchange rate. The monetarist model includes views as to how devaluations affect the balance of payments and how a flexible exchange rate should behave. Those subjects are covered in later chapters.

Exchange rates and the balance of payments: theory versus reality

In theory, as was argued early in this chapter, models of the balance of payments in a world of fixed exchange rates should become models of exchange rate determination in a world of floating rates. The same forces that produce a payments deficit for a country on a fixed parity should produce a depreciation for a country on a float, and vice versa. The models, in theory, should have equal explanatory powers under either system; unhappily, this is not the case.

The models discussed in this chapter have a fairly strong track record in explaining payments deficits and surpluses for those countries that maintain fixed exchange rates. For the industrialized countries that have maintained floating exchange rates since 1973, however, these models perform poorly. It is not an exaggeration to say that academic economists do not, at present, have any models that do a consistently good job of explaining movements of flexible exchange rates over the short to medium term. It is not entirely clear why models that are successful in explaining balance-of-payments disequilibria cannot explain exchange rate movements, but the problem appears to lie in the differing roles of speculative capital flows in the two systems.

Except during infrequent periods of balance-of-payments crisis, when the possibility of parity changes exists, speculation is not a dominant factor in a world of fixed exchange rates. Parities are viewed as unlikely to change, and nonspeculative factors, such as those discussed previously in this chapter, dominate international transactions and balance-of-payments results. Underlying or fundamental economic forces largely determine transactions, and models that are based on such fundamentals perform well.

A world of flexible exchange rates, however, is very different. Enormous sums of money can be made or lost in brief periods of time as exchange rates move over a sizable range, and the exchange market becomes a huge casino. As was noted in Chapter 12, short-term capital flows now dominate international transactions and foreign exchange trading in the industrialized countries, and these short-term capital flows appear to be largely speculative in cause.

Economists have not been able to successfully model speculative behavior, so they remain unable to explain the behavior of floating exchange rates. The economic and financial fundamentals, as discussed in the models in this chapter, are still relevant, but their short-term impacts on exchange rates are largely obscured by massive speculative capital flows, the determinants of which are not known. More will be said about this matter in Chapter 20, which discusses the experience with flexible exchange rates since 1973. For now, it should merely be noted that, although a theory of the balance of payments ought to be a theory of exchange rates, existing models have a much better record of explaining payments disequilibria than they do in explaining the behavior of floating exchange rates. The next topic, however, is alternative views as to how balance-of-payments adjustment can occur within the confines of a fixed exchange rate.

Summary of key concepts

1   The same economic or financial forces which would create a balance-of-payments deficit for a country maintaining a fixed exchange rate would cause a depreciation of the local currency if a floating exchange rate existed. Factors causing a surplus with a parity would cause an appreciation with a float.

2   Although the problems created by large and chronic balance-of-payments deficits are more obvious, surpluses can also create serious difficulties, particularly if they are large enough to threaten the central bank's ability to control the money supply.

3   In the nonmonetarist approach, the current account of the balance of payments is positively related to the country's terms of trade, negatively related to its current level of income, positively related to foreign incomes, and negatively related to the level of its real effective exchange rate.

4   The capital account is driven by expected yields and risks, responding positively to recent increases in domestic expected yields and foreign risks, and negatively to recent increases in expected foreign yields and domestic risks.

5   The monetarist approach, which is associated with the University of Chicago, views payments disequilibria as entirely a monetary phenomenon. Deficits are caused by an excess supply of money which, by Walras's law, causes an excess demand for goods and/or bonds. These excess demands are satisfied from abroad, resulting in deficits in the current and/or capital accounts of the balance of payments.

Questions for study and review

1   What is the effect of a balance-of-payments surplus on a country's domestic money supply? How does this effect occur? How can it be offset or canceled by the central bank of the payments-surplus country?

2   If your employer, who studied economics at a British university where monetarism is disliked, asked you to explain why a particular country experienced a serious deterioration of its balance of payments, what aspects of that country's economy would you study in seeking to respond to that request? If your employer had studied economics at the University of Chicago, how would your approach change?

3   If interest rates in Japan rise relative to those prevailing in the United States, would you expect a steady flow of capital into Japan? Why, or why not?

4   Real output and incomes rise in Country A. How and why would a Keynesian analysis of the likely effect of that event on the balance of payments of Country A differ from that of a monetarist?

5   Why is the role of the terms of trade in current account determination of more concern to small developing countries than to larger developed countries?

6   In a monetarist model of the balance of payments, assuming a fixed exchange rate and starting from equilibrium in all markets, how would Country A's balance of payments react to each of the following events:

   (a) The central bank of Country A increases its domestic assets sufficiently to increase the stock of base money in the banking system by 10 percent.
   (b) Central banks in the rest of the world increase their domestic assets sufficiently to increase the stock of base money in the banking system of the rest of the world by 10 percent.
   (c) Because of a drought, GNP in the rest of the world declines by 10 percent.

7   Why is sterilization more difficult for a central bank when its country has a payments surplus than when it has a deficit?

Suggested further reading

- Branson, W. and D. Henderson, "The Specification and Influence of Asset Markets," in R. Jones and P. Kenen, eds, *Handbook of International Economics*, Vol. II, Amsterdam: North-Holland, 1985, ch. 15.
- Frenkel, J. and H.G. Johnson, eds, *The Monetary Approach to the Balance of Payments*, Toronto: University of Toronto Press, 1976.
- Frenkel, J. and M. Mussa, "Asset Markets, Exchange Rates, and the Balance of Payments," in R. Jones and P. Kenen, eds, *Handbook of International Economics*, Vol. II, Amsterdam: North-Holland, 1985, ch. 14.
- Hinkle, L. and P. Montiel, eds, *Exchange Rate Misalignment: Concepts and Measurement for Developing Countries*, Oxford: Oxford University Press, 1999.
- Kenen, P., "Macroeconomic Theory and Policy: How the Closed Economy Was Opened," in R. Jones and P. Kenen, eds, *Handbook of International Economics*, Vol. II, Amsterdam: North-Holland, 1985, pp. 625–78.
- Kreinen, M. and L. Officer, "The Monetary Approach to the Balance of Payments: A Survey," *Princeton Essays in International Finance*, no. 43, 1978.

- Levich, R., "Empirical Studies of Exchange Rates, Price Behavior, Rate Determination, and Market Efficiency," in R. Jones and P. Kenen, eds, *Handbook of International Economics*, Vol. II, Amsterdam: North-Holland, 1985, pp. 979–1040.
- McKinnon, R., "Currency Substitution and Instability in the World Dollar Standard," *American Economic Review*, June 1982, pp. 320–34.

Notes

1   The often demanding terms under which the IMF is willing to lend large sums of money to countries facing balance-of-payments crises are discussed in various works on the subject of conditionality, that is, on IMF loans being conditional upon certain policy changes. See Paul Mosely, "Conditionality as Bargaining Process: Structural Adjustment Lending 1980–1986," *Princeton Essays in International Finance*, no. 168, October 1987. See also J. Sproas, "IMF Conditionality: Ineffectual, Inefficient, and Mistargeted," *Princeton Essays in International Finance*, no. 166, December 1986. See also J. Polak, "The Changing Nature of IMF Conditionality," *Princeton Essays in International Finance*, no. 184, September 1991. For a more recent analysis, see H. James, "From Grandmotherliness to Governance: The Evolution of IMF Conditionality," *Finance and Development*, December 1998, pp. 44–7.

2   *Financial Times*, Editorial, 27 May 1994, p. 27.

3   H.P. Markowitz, "Portfolio Selection," *Journal of Finance*, May 1952, and J. Tobin, "Liquidity Preference as Behavior toward Risk," *Review of Economic Studies*, February 1958.

4   Early work on the effects of portfolio balance considerations on international payments includes W. Branson, *Financial Capital Flows in the US Balance of Payments* (Amsterdam: North-Holland, 1968). See also P. Kouri and M. Porter, "International Capital Flows and Portfolio Equilibrium," *Journal of Political Economy*, June 1974. For a survey of this literature, see W. Branson and D. Henderson, "The Specification and Influence of Asset Markets," in R. Jones and P. Kenen, eds, *Handbook of International Economics*, Vol. II (Amsterdam: North-Holland, 1985), ch. 15.

5   The asset market approach and alternative models are surveyed in R. Levich, "Empirical Studies of Exchange Rates: Price Behavior, Rate Determination, and Market Efficiency," in R. Jones and P. Kenen, eds, *Handbook of International Economics*, Vol. II (Amsterdam: North-Holland, 1985), pp. 979–1040. In the same volume, see J. Frenkel and M. Mussa, "Asset Markets, Exchange Rates, and the Balance of Payments," ch. 14.

6   A full listing of the important works in the monetarist approach to the balance of payments is impossible in the available space, but the J. Frenkel and H. Johnson (eds) volume is a good place to begin: *The Monetary Approach to the Balance of Payments* (Toronto: University of Toronto Press, 1976). For a useful and nontechnical survey, see M. Kreinin and L. Officer, "The Monetary Approach to the Balance of Payments: A Survey," *Princeton Essays in International Finance*, no. 43, 1978. See also S. Magee, "The Empirical Evidence on the Monetary Approach to the Balance of Payments and Exchange Rates," *American Economic Review*, May 1976, pp. 163–70.

7   For early evidence of the frequent failure of the law of one price to be maintained in real world markets, see R. Dunn, "Flexible Exchange Rates and Oligopoly Pricing: A Study of Canadian Markets," *Journal of Political Economy*, January 1970, pp. 140–51. For a more recent study that reaches the same conclusion, see M. Knetter, "Price Discrimination by US and German Exporters," *American Economic Review*, March 1989, pp. 198–210.

8   For data on the enormous financial losses of state-owned enterprises in developing countries, see M. Gillis, D. Perkins, M. Roemer, and D. Snodgrass, *Economic Development*, 3rd edn (New York: Norton, 1992), pp. 298–300.

9   Early elements in the discussion of currency substitution include C. Chen, "Diversified Currency Holdings and Flexible Exchange Rates," *Quarterly Journal of Economics*, 1973, pp. 96–111. See also L. Girton and D. Roper, "Theory and Implications of Currency Substitution," *Journal of Money, Banking, and Credit*, February 1981, pp. 12–30.

16 Payments adjustment with fixed exchange rates

Learning objectives

By the end of this chapter you should be able to understand:

- how David Hume's specie flow mechanism produces automatic, although potentially painful, adjustment of payments disequilibria;
- the relevance of the specie flow mechanism for countries operating currency boards rather than central banks, countries that lack their own currency, and regions within a country;
- the IS/LM/BP graph as a useful tool in understanding balance-of-payments adjustment and other macroeconomic events;
- the Bretton Woods adjustment process, and the greater relative efficiency of monetary policy over fiscal policy in that circumstance; why Bretton Woods failed;
- the policy assignment model as one possible way to balance the need for payments adjustment with the desire to manage the domestic economy to avoid undesirable business cycles;
- international policy coordination as a theoretically attractive, but realistically impractical, way of dealing with adjustment problems.

For much of the post-war era, the world has operated with fixed exchange rates, and even today many developing countries still maintain fixed parities. It therefore seems useful to discuss possible routes to balance-of-payments adjustment with a fixed parity before going on to devaluations and then to floating exchange rates. As will be seen, payments adjustment without use of the exchange rate is frequently painful and/or unsuccessful. This situation may explain why devaluations are so common in the developing world and why many of the industrialized countries have flexible exchange rates.

David Hume's specie flow mechanism

The **specie flow mechanism** for adjustment of payments that David Hume described as early as 1752 operated for many countries before World War I and is still relevant for a few countries and situations.[1] It has the advantage of being automatic, that is, of not depending on fallible central bankers or politicians for prudent decisions, but it leaves a country with very little ability to manage its own monetary affairs. Although they were not followed precisely,[2] the formal system is based on two rules:

1 National currencies are to be backed rigidly by gold; that is, the stock of base money is determined solely by the stock of gold held by the government or the central bank. The central bank therefore has no monetary policy discretion; it must create a money supply that is based on its holdings of gold.
2 Gold is to be the only foreign exchange reserve asset; that is, payments deficits cause a parallel loss of gold, and vice versa.

These two rules mean that the domestic money supply is determined by the balance of payments (and by the gold-mining industry). A payments surplus causes an inflow of gold and a parallel increase in the stock of base money. A deficit causes gold to flow out, and the money supply must fall proportionally. This is analogous to the monetarist world described in the previous chapter, except that sterilization cannot occur. The money supply must be allowed to fall when a country has a payments deficit and to rise in the case of a surplus.

These changes in the money supply produce payments adjustment through three linkages. In the case of a payments deficit, the resulting decline in the money supply:

1 raises domestic interest rates, which attracts capital inflows, thereby improving the capital account of the balance of payments;
2 puts downward pressure on the price level, thereby improving price competitiveness. Exports should rise and imports fall, improving the current account;
3 puts downward pressure on economic activity and on real incomes. Imports should fall by the marginal propensity to import times the decline in domestic incomes. A reduction in the money supply is recessionary and discourages imports, thereby improving the current account.

The first two of these linkages are not particularly difficult or painful; the third, however, is unpleasant or worse for deficit countries. To the extent that wages and prices are downward rigid or sticky in the short run, which appears to be the case in modern industrialized economies, the second linkage becomes largely inoperative, necessitating greater reliance on the third. This payments adjustment mechanism means that countries with payments deficits are likely to be forced into recessions and then be unable to use an expansionary monetary policy to escape such downturns.

For surplus countries, the same three linkages operate in the opposite direction. Interest rates fall, worsening the capital account, and prices rise, a condition that hurts the trade account. Output and incomes rise, thereby increasing imports. If the economy is fully employed, however, output and real incomes cannot rise. Thus inflation can become serious as the money supply rises without the central bank being able to control it.

This system means that the central bank has no policy discretion in the management of the money supply. The recessionary implications for deficit countries, and the prospects for inflation in the case of a surplus, suggest why this system was abandoned. In the late 1970s and early 1980s a few "gold bugs" argued for a return to this approach, but this discussion has now largely ended.

The pre-1914 gold standard has the additional disadvantage of being subject to shocks from the gold-mining industry. When major ore discoveries are made, the government or central bank is required to purchase gold and issue new money, resulting in inflation. Spain experienced disastrous inflation in the sixteenth century when its conquest of Latin America produced huge inflows of gold.

Dollarization or Euroization

The specie flow mechanism may seem to be an historic relic, but is remains quite relevant today, and may become more so in the near future. A number of small countries have always lacked their own currencies and have instead used the currency of another country, and there is a modest trend toward more countries adopting this approach. Panama and Liberia have always used the US dollar, and a number of small island countries in the South Pacific use Australian or New Zealand money. Kosovo and Montenegro are now largely or entirely "euroized," in that almost all circulating currency is euros, and most bank accounts, loans, and other transactions are denominated in euros. Ecuador recently abandoned its national currency and is now dollarized, and El Salvador is in transition to that circumstance.

A balance of payments deficit in such a country means that there is more money flowing out of the country than is flowing in, and there is no central bank to sterilize the outflows and restore the previous money supply level. A payments deficit reduces the money supply in the amount of the deficit, producing the specie flow adjustment process with the same three linkages discussed earlier. A payments deficit increases the money supply by the amount of the surplus, producing the same adjustment process in the opposite direction.[3]

Dollarization or euroization requires that the country start out with sufficient foreign exchange reserves to buy back from the public all outstanding base money. Foreign exchange reserves are turned into cash which is transported (with considerable security efforts) into the country and the local currency is simply bought back from the populace. Banks accounts and loans are denominated in dollars or euros, with reserves against deposits also being held in dollars. In adopting this approach, the country gives up the profit or seignoriage that comes from running a central bank and must live with the monetary policy adopted by the country whose currency it uses. Monetary policy in Kosovo is determined by the Governing Council of the European Central bank, and the policy prevailing in Ecuador is settled by the Federal Open Market Committee of the Federal Reserve System. Seignoriage for the two countries goes to the ECB and the Federal Reserve System.

One major disadvantage in the use of a foreign money, or with the operation of a currency board which is discussed below, is the lack of an apparent lender of last resort for commercial banks. One of the original and important functions of a central bank is to provide prompt loans to solvent commercial banks that are experiencing liquidity problems. The San Francisco Federal Reserve Bank cannot be expected to lend to banks in Quito, and banks in Kosovo are unlikely to find an accommodating loan officer at the European Central Bank in Frankfurt. Countries that dollarize or euroize must set up separate financial institutions to make such loans, and arranging adequate funding for such entities may be difficult.

One might wonder why a country would even consider giving up its own currency for the dollar or the euro. Often countries that do so have had a very poor history of economic and monetary policy management, and adopting a foreign money is a means of gaining credibility. Ecuador is a prime example of this circumstance; before it dollarized, its currency was held in very low regard by its citizens, and its economy was in crisis. Dollarization, although painful, calmed the economy and allowed a recovery to begin. When a country has a long and firmly established history of mismanaging monetary policy, maybe it should give up the effort and let someone else provide a policy for it. Argentina would then appear to be an obvious candidate for dollarization, but its recent debt crisis drained its foreign exchange reserves so thoroughly that it may lack sufficient dollars to undertake the effort.

Currency boards

Currency boards, which have recently drawn increased attention among policy makers and economists, create another situation in which balance-of-payments adjustment occurs through the specie flow mechanism. A currency board resembles a central bank with one very large difference: it is forbidden from purchasing assets other than foreign exchange reserves. It is prohibited by law from lending to the government or purchasing other domestic assets. This means that changes in foreign exchange reserves cannot be sterilized through purchases or sales of government debt. A loss of foreign exchange reserves, resulting from a balance-of-payments deficit, must create a parallel reduction in the stock of base money. If the reserve ratio is unchanged, which is supposed to be the case, a proportionate reduction in the money supply must occur. The money supply is regulated by changes in foreign exchange reserves that result from payments imbalances, and adjustment occurs through the specie flow mechanism.

In the past currency boards were maintained primarily by small countries with historic ties to the United Kingdom, such as the members of the United Arab Emirates, or by British dependencies. During the 1990s currency boards have been adopted in some high-inflation developing countries, such as Argentina, and in transition economies, such as Estonia and Bulgaria. In the latter two cases, such arrangements were very successful in bringing down what had been high rates of inflation.

Although a currency board would appear primarily to be a restraint on monetary policy, in practice it represents a more severe constraint on fiscal policy, because such a replacement for a central bank makes it impossible for the government to force the central bank to monetize its budget deficits. As was noted in the previous chapter, central banks in many developing and transition economies have little or no policy independence, but instead must create money to finance government deficits. In some underdeveloped countries, as was also noted earlier, the government actually orders the central bank to print paper money in the amount of its projected budget shortfall, which has typically meant large increases in the money supply and rapid inflation. A currency board is intended to absolutely end such behavior.

A currency board is a means of gaining credibility for a central bank and a currency which have had little in the past, because of high inflation driven by the monetization of government budget deficits. If the public understands that domestic money is backed by foreign exchange reserves rather than by domestic government debt, people will become willing to use and hold the local currency, reversing the common use of dollars or euros as a local currency.

Currency boards work best in small open economies where modest changes in the money supply will produce relatively prompt payments adjustment and where the foreign exchange requirements for financing such an enterprise are not prohibitive. In the case of Bulgaria, for example, the IMF strongly encouraged the creation of such a board and lent the foreign exchange which allowed it to begin operations. When such an arrangement was suggested for Indonesia, however, the IMF opposed such a decision because massive amounts of foreign exchange would have been required to finance its operations, and because the Indonesian economy is large and not very open, meaning that the specie flow mechanism would have been particularly painful. Suggestions that a currency board be adopted in Russia are likely to fail for the same reasons: the economy is too large and insufficiently open, and the financial requirements of such a board would be excessive. Currency boards may be set up, however, in more of the small countries which emerged from the USSR if it becomes clear that fiscal and monetary discipline cannot be realized through any other means.

The Estonian and Bulgarian currency boards have reportedly operated thus far in a traditional manner with fixed commercial bank reserve ratios, which result in domestic money supplies which rise and fall proportionately with changes in foreign exchange reserves, thereby producing the classic specie flow adjustment process. Perhaps because they followed the rules closely, these currency boards have been successful. Argentina's, however, collapsed in early 2002. The Argentinian board was reportedly somewhat more "creative" in finding ways to escape the intended constraints of the specie flow mechanism. Changes in reserve ratios for domestic commercial banks were sometimes used to offset changes in foreign exchange reserves, thereby allowing the money supply to remain unchanged despite balance of payments deficits or surpluses. As this and other means of evading the rules came to be understood by investors, confidence in Argentina's currency board deteriorated. More importantly, the expected constraints on government budget deficits never materialized, and various levels of government (particularly the provinces) borrowed enormous amounts of money, with many of the loans denominated in dollars.

As it became apparent that these loans could not be repaid, and that both fiscal and monetary policy were unsound, confidence collapsed and massive capital outflows quickly drained foreign exchange reserves. The fixed parity of the peso to the dollar had to be abandoned for a float which produced a massive depreciation. This created a broader financial and political crisis, which remains unresolved at the time of this writing. If a currency board is to be successful, its rules must be followed fully, and it must produce constraints on fiscal deficits as well as on money supply expansion. Neither occurred in Argentina.[4]

This same specie flow mechanism forces the balance of payments of a state or region within a country toward adjustment. We usually do not think of the balance of payments of Massachusetts, but there is one, and it must be adjusted when it is out of equilibrium. A deficit in the Massachusetts balance of payments means that residents of the state are making more payments to nonresidents than they are receiving from them. The stock of dollars held by Massachusetts residents must fall by the amount of that deficit. As checks are cleared against Massachusetts banks and in favor of out-of-state banks, the stock of member bank reserves in the local banking system declines, requiring a reduction of lending activity. A payments deficit reduces the money supply of a state, and imposes the same adjustment process as was described above for a country on the gold standard.

The implications of this mechanism are often quite severe. When a state or region suffers a major export loss, the resulting declines in output and incomes are not limited to the export industry. The resulting payments deficit drains money out of the local economy and banking system, deepening the resulting economic downturn. Eventually, local wages and other costs of doing business decline sufficiently to attract new businesses, and a recovery begins. The migration of unemployed people out of the state reduces both purchases of imports and the demand for local housing, which lowers real estate prices, making the state more attractive for incoming businesses. A sharp decline in the textile and shoe industries in Massachusetts during the 1950s caused such an adjustment process, and the state economy did not fully recover for many years. Declining expenditures on national defense and weak markets for the state's computer industry produced a similar process in Massachusetts during the early 1990s. The recent collapse of the dot com sector of the US economy means that the San Francisco area is now in the same unpleasant situation.

Box 16.1 The IS/LM/BP graph as a route to understanding balance-of-payments adjustment

A graphical technique that is widely used in domestic macroeconomics can be readily extended to an open economy framework. It allows a somewhat more rigorous, if still oversimplified, analysis of the effects of various policies designed to produce payments adjustment. For students who have had an intermediate macroeconomics course, the purely domestic portion of what follows will probably not be new, and even part of the international extension may be familiar. For those who have not been introduced to these graphs, an introduction follows.

The IS/LM graph

The domestic economy is modeled as a real sector and a market for money. The real sector is in equilibrium when $I_i = S$, that is, when intended investment equals savings, which is the standard definition of equilibrium in a simple Keynesian model. The market for money is in equilibrium when $MD = MS$, that is, when the demand for money equals the supply. If both the market for goods and the market for money are in equilibrium, then Walras's law implies that the market for bonds must also be in equilibrium. Thus to analyze equilibrium in the entire economy, we need consider only two markets, goods and money.

Returning to the real sector, which is to be represented by the **IS line**, we find that savings is a positive function of domestic income (Y) through the marginal propensity to save. Intended investment (I_i) is a negative function of the interest rate (r), so:

$$S \overset{+}{=} F(Y)$$

and

$$I_i \overset{-}{=} F(r)$$

The situation in which $S = I_i$ can then be represented as shown in Figure 16.1. Along IS, intended investment equals savings; therefore GNP is at its equilibrium level. To the left of IS intended investment is greater than savings, so GNP tends to rise. Interest rates are too low (which increases investment) or incomes are too low (which represses saving), resulting in the excess of intended investment over savings. The opposite situation holds to the right of IS. The economy automatically moves toward IS when it is out of equilibrium through changes in output up to the level of full employment, beyond which there is inflation which raises nominal GNP. A movement from point A to point B illustrates the offsetting impacts of an increase in Y and a decline in the interest rate. Starting from equilibrium at point A, an increase in output and incomes causes an increase in savings, making it exceed previously intended levels of investment. If interest rates fell by Δr, however, intended investment would rise to the new level of savings and the economy would be at point B.

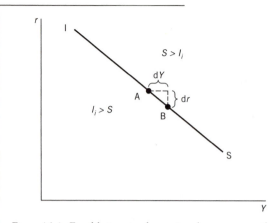

Figure 16.1 Equilibrium in the savings/investment relationship. Intended investment equals savings along the IS line because as interest rates decline, investment rises, and as output and incomes increase, savings rise. The slope of IS reflects the relative sensitivity of intended investment to interest rates and of savings to increases in output and incomes.

The slope of IS reflects the relationship between the size of the marginal propensity to save and the impact of changes of the interest rate on intended investment levels. If the marginal propensity to save was high or if intended investment was insensitive to changes in the interest rate, IS would be steep because a large change in interest rates would be required to offset the effect of a small change in incomes. A flatter IS would imply the opposite situation: that investment is highly sensitive to interest rates and/or that the marginal propensity to save is low, so that a large change in incomes would be required to offset the effect of a small change in the interest rate.

Since this graph has only two dimensions, the effects of only two variables (Y and r) on the savings/investment relationship can be shown. If any other relevant factor shifts, the IS line moves. A more expansionary fiscal policy, for example, would shift it to the right, as would an increase in export sales caused by an economic expansion abroad. Either event would increase the level of GNP that was consistent with a given level of the interest rate, because domestic savings would have to rise relative to private domestic investment to make room for the larger government budget deficit or the stronger current account. With a government sector and with international trade, the savings investment identity becomes:

$$I = S + (T - G) + (M - X)$$

It should be remembered that in this identity I is actual investment, including unintended changes in inventories. This identity must be true, but intended investment equals the sum of the items on the right-hand side of the equation only when the economy is at equilibrium, that is, when intended investment equals actual investment, because there are no unintended changes in inventories.

The market for money is in equilibrium when $MD = MS$, where the money supply is determined by the central bank. The demand for money is a positive function of income (the transactions demand for money, stressed by monetarists) and a negative function of the interest rate under the assumption that money does not pay interest and that therefore the interest rate is the opportunity cost of holding money rather than bonds. This can be shown as

$$MD = F\overset{+\ -}{(Y, r)}$$

$MS = \overline{MS}$, meaning that the money supply is determined outside the model, i.e. by the central bank.

$$MD = MS \text{ in equilibrium}$$

With a given money supply, which has been determined by the central bank, equilibrium exists in the market for money along the **LM line** shown in Figure 16.2.

Starting from point A, an increase in the interest rate reduces the amount of money people want to hold, creating an excess supply of money. An increase in incomes of ΔY would raise the transactions demand for money sufficiently to return the market to equilibrium with the pre-existing money supply. The slope of LM reflects the relative sensitivity of the demand for money to changes in incomes and in interest rates. A monetarist would believe that the role of income is far stronger and that the line is therefore very steep. A Keynesian would argue for a stronger role for the interest rate and would therefore believe that the line was flatter, particularly at low interest rates.

Since only the level of national income and the interest rate are shown on the two axes, any other factors that affect the market for money cause the LM line to shift. An increase in the money supply, for example, would cause it to shift to the right, whereas a decision of people to hold more money at every level of GNP (a reduction in the velocity of money) would cause LM to shift to the left.

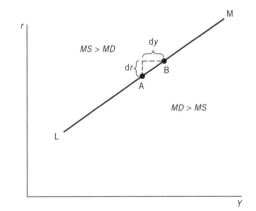

Figure 16.2 Equilibrium in the market for money. With a constant money supply, the market for money clears along LM. The demand for money is positively related to the level of output and negatively related to the interest rate, which is the opportunity cost of holding money. If the money supply were increased, LM would shift to the right. The slope of LM reflects the relative sensitivity of the demand for money to changes in output and in the interest rate.

If the two lines derived above are put on the same graph, it is possible to see where the economy is in equilibrium and how it reacts to policy changes (see Figure 16.3). At the equilibrium levels of Y and r, the real economy is at rest, because intended investment equals savings, and the market for money is in equilibrium, because the demand for money equals the supply. If a more expansionary fiscal policy were adopted, the situation shown in Figure 16.4 would hold. A more expansionary budget causes GNP to rise because a higher level of income is required to produce enough additional private saving to offset the decrease in government saving $(G - T)$. It also produces a higher interest rate owing to the effect of the higher level of incomes on the

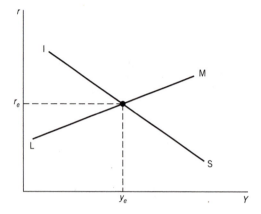

Figure 16.3 Equilibrium in the real and monetary sectors. In a closed economy equilibrium is reached where IS crosses LM because only at that level of output and of interest rates is intended investment equal to savings and the demand for money equal to the supply of money. There is no other situation in which both conditions hold.

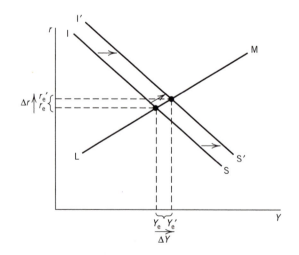

Figure 16.4 Impacts of fiscal expansion. An expansionary fiscal policy shifts IS to the right, producing a higher level of output and higher interest rates.

transactions demand for money. If the LM line were steeper, the expansionary effect on Y would be smaller. If the LM were vertical, as some monetarists would suggest, there would be no effect on Y; the expansionary fiscal policy is entirely crowded out through its effects on interest rates. The central bank's decision to increase the money supply would have the effects illustrated in Figure 16.5. The expansion of the money supply causes the interest rate to fall, which increases intended investment. At the resulting higher level of output, savings rise to the new level of investment and the economy is again at equilibrium.

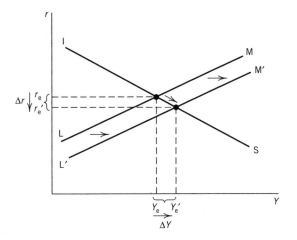

Figure 16.5 Impacts of an expansion of the money supply. An increase in the money supply shifts LM to the right, producing a higher level of output and lower interest rates.

Balance-of-payments equilibrium, as an additional line

If the balance of payments is added to this macroeconomy and if payments equilibrium is a goal or policy constraint, a new line is needed. If the balance of payments is viewed in the oversimplified form:

$$CA = F(\overset{-}{Y})$$

and

$$KA = F(\overset{+}{r})$$

with equilibrium where

$$CA + KA = 0$$

then the balance of payments is in equilibrium along the line shown in Figure 16.6. It would be in surplus to the left of BP and in deficit to the right of that line.

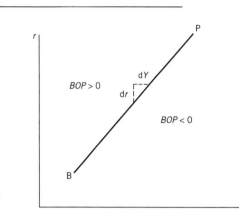

Figure 16.6 Equilibrium in the balance of payments. The balance of payments is in equilibrium along BP, in deficit to the right, and in surplus to the left. Higher interest rates attract capital, while higher levels of output and income increase imports, so increases in interest rates and output offset each other. The slope of BP reflects the relative sensitivity of the balance of payments to an increase in incomes and an increase in interest rates.

The slope of the **BP line** represents the relationship between the impact of the interest rate on the capital account and the impact of domestic incomes on imports. If the marginal propensity to import is very high or if international capital flows are unresponsive to changes in local interest rates, BP is steep.

If, instead, capital markets are closely integrated, so large amounts of capital flow in response to small interest-rate differentials, and/or if the marginal propensity to import is low, BP becomes much flatter. It is worth noting that the capital account is positively related to the level of domestic interest rates rather than to recent changes in yields. A flow-adjustment model of the capital account, rather than a stock-adjustment approach, is implicit in the BP line. It would not be possible to define the IS and LM lines, and therefore to combine the three functions, if changes in interest rates were on the vertical axis of this graph, as would be implied by a stock-adjustment or portfolio balance approach.

Since only the effect of interest rates and domestic income on the balance of payments can be shown directly on the graph, any other factor that shifts the payments situation causes BP to shift. An increase in foreign incomes, for example, that caused an increase in the demand for domestically produced exports would cause BP to shift to the right. A devaluation of the local currency, which strengthened the current account, would have the same effect.

If a devaluation was expected in the near-term future, BP would shift up because of speculative capital outflows. If, for example, a devaluation of 10 percent was expected in about 12 months, short-term interest rates would have to rise by enough to offset the expected devaluation, to compensate people for holding assets denominated in the currency that was going to be devalued. If such interest-rate increases do not occur, a large payments deficit will result from the withdrawal of speculative funds from the country.

In order to simplify the following discussion, exchange rate expectations will be put aside; that is, it will be assumed that investors expect existing exchange rates to continue. Readers should remember, however, that the expectation of exchange rate movements shifts BP; the expectation of a revaluation shifts BP down because investors would be willing to hold domestic currency assets at lower interest rates because of the expected gain from the future exchange rate change.

If the BP line is added to the previously discussed IS/LM graph, equilibrium in all three sectors exists at point A (see Figure 16.7). There is no reason, of course, for the economy to be in such an equilibrium state. In Figure 16.8 an economy with a fixed exchange rate operates at point A and has a balance-of-payments deficit.

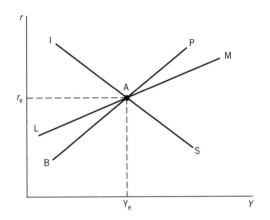

Figure 16.7 Domestic and international equilibrium. Where all three lines cross, the domestic economy and the balance of payments are both in equilibrium.

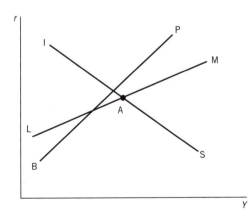

Figure 16.8 Domestic equilibrium with a balance-of-payments deficit. At point A the domestic economy is in equilibrium, but the balance of payments is in deficit because point A is to the right of the BP line.

Payments adjustment through specie flow

As was discussed in the main text, the specie flow mechanism requires that the domestic money supply be allowed to fall when a country has a balance-of-payments deficit until the deficit is fully adjusted. Such a decline in the money supply is shown as a leftward shift of LM (Figure 16.9). Balance-of-payments adjustment is automatic, but it produces higher interest rates and, more importantly, a lower level of GNP. If this exercise had begun with a payments surplus, LM would have shifted to the right until equilibrium was re-established. Nominal income would have been higher, which might have meant considerable inflation. LM moves to the right or left as required to produce equilibrium, whether or not the resulting effects on national income are desirable.

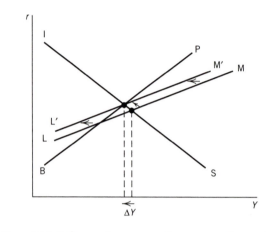

Figure 16.9 Balance-of-payments adjustment under specie flow. A balance-of-payments deficit will be automatically adjusted under specie flow because the money supply will decline as gold is lost, shifting LM to the left to cross IS and BP. This occurs, however, at a lower level of output, that is, at the cost of a recession.

The Bretton Woods adjustment mechanism: Fiscal and monetary policies

The post-World War II international financial system designed at the Bretton Woods conference in New Hampshire during the summer of 1944 was intended not only to avoid the rigidity and lack of policy autonomy of the specie flow system, but also to escape the relative chaos that resulted from the lack of a broadly accepted system during the interwar period. The result was a rather ingenious approach that functioned with varying degrees of success until the early 1970s.[5] The international financial history of that period is discussed in Chapter 20. For minor and presumably temporary payments imbalances, there was no expectation of active adjustment policies. Foreign exchange reserves would accumulate or be depleted, and their monetary impacts would be sterilized, until normal payments patterns returned. National macroeconomic policies were not to be diverted from their domestic goals by transitory and minor changes in balance-of-payments results.

If payments disequilibria were more serious, however, both monetary and fiscal policies were to be used to produce adjustment. Deficits called for a more restrictive set of policies, and payments surpluses were to be adjusted through more expansionary policies. The system was to be symmetrical in that both deficit and surplus countries were to bear the same responsibility for adjustment.

Because the timing and mix of policies were to be determined by individual governments, the rigidity of specie flow was avoided. If, however, countries were in sufficiently serious payments deficits to require large loans (drawings) from the International Monetary Fund, the design of an adjustment program would involve the Fund through what became known as "conditionality"; that is, large drawings from the IMF are conditional on the imposition of a policy program that can be expected to make repayment possible. Although national governments were not put under the binding constraints implied by the specie flow system, those countries (primarily LDCs) that rely heavily on IMF resources often complain that conditionality requirements leave them with considerably less than full control over national macroeconomic policies.

Box 16.2 IS/LM/BP analysis of adjustment under the Bretton Woods system

If a country tightens its monetary policy to adjust a payments deficit, the IS/LM/BP representation is the same as for the specie flow system presented earlier. The only difference is that the central bank decides to tighten monetary policy rather than having a reduction of the money supply result automatically from a loss of gold reserves (see Figure 16.10).

The effects of fiscal policy on the balance of payments are more complicated and depend on the relative slopes of the LM and BP lines. The case in which BP is steeper than LM, which implies much less than complete international capital mobility, is shown in Figure 16.11. Tightening of fiscal policy eliminates the payments deficit, but it does so at the cost of a larger loss of GNP than occurred in the case of the tightening

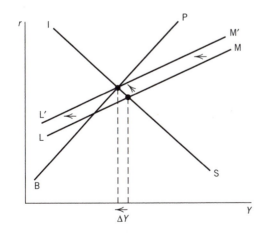

Figure 16.10 Payments adjustment through monetary policy. This is similar to the previous graph, except that the monetary tightening is not automatic but is undertaken by the central bank to eliminate the payments deficit. LM is shifted to the left, adjusting the balance of payments but reducing output.

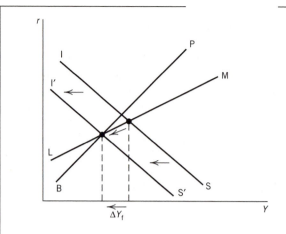

Figure 16.11 Payments adjustment through a tightening of fiscal policy. A balance-of-payments deficit can also be adjusted with a tighter fiscal policy, which shifts IS to the left. The cost of this approach, however, is a rather large decline in output.

of monetary policy in Figure 16.10. The two policies are compared in Figure 16.12. Monetary policy is more efficient as a route to payments adjustment in the sense that the resulting loss of GNP is smaller. This is because tightening the fiscal policy reduces domestic interest rates, which worsens the capital account. Hence a larger reduction in GNP is necessary to produce the required current account improvement. Tightening the monetary policy both reduces incomes and raises interest rates. The latter effect improves the capital account, which means that the required current account improvement, and therefore the reduction in GNP, is smaller.

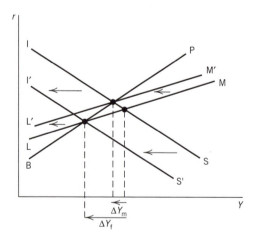

Figure 16.12 Comparing the effects of fiscal and monetary policies. The "efficiency" of the two approaches is compared in this graph, which shows that a given balance-of-payments deficit can be adjusted with a smaller loss of output through the use of monetary rather than fiscal policy. Monetary policy is the more efficient tool with which to adjust a payments disequilibrium under the assumptions of this graph. The critical assumption is that LM is flatter than BP.

If the BP line is flatter than the LM line, implying a great sensitivity of international capital flows to small interest-rate differentials, the effects of fiscal policy on the balance of payments become quite different (Figure 16.13).

A balance-of-payments deficit is adjusted, not by tightening the budget, but by a more expansionary fiscal policy. This odd conclusion results because BP is flatter than LM. Thus when the more expansionary budget increases the interest rate, the result is a huge inflow of capital that more than offsets any negative impact of higher GNP on the current account. The capital account dominates the balance of payments, and so changes in interest rates are far more important to balance-of-payments results than are changes in income.

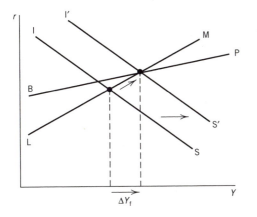

Figure 16.13 Adjustment of a payments deficit through expansionary fiscal policy. If the BP line is flatter than the LM line, an expansionary fiscal policy can be used to adjust a payments deficit because this approach raises interest rates and the flat BP line means that the balance of payments is very sensitive to interest rates.

The Bretton Woods participants did not foresee this case because strict controls on capital flows were expected to remain in effect. This would make the capital account relatively unresponsive to interest-rate differentials, causing the BP line to be much steeper than the LM line. In the 1960s and 1970s, however, controls on capital account transactions were eased or eliminated in most industrialized countries, creating the possibility that BP could be flatter than LM. Thus this seemingly perverse relationship between fiscal policy and the balance of payments could occur. This result would only be possible for a few highly industrialized countries such as the United States, Japan, and Germany, whose capital markets are highly integrated. During the early 1980s, for example, large US budget deficits were accompanied by a sharp appreciation of the dollar, which would have been a payments surplus in a fixed parity system. A larger budget deficit appeared to strengthen rather than weaken the US balance of payments. The conclusion is made uncertain by the fact that the US monetary policy was very tight at this time, which means that either the more expansionary budget or the tighter monetary policy could have pushed the dollar up. The BP line is probably flatter than the LM line for most highly industrialized countries, but the opposite situation prevails for most developing and transition economies, where financial linkages to the rest of the world are weak.

Although Bretton Woods was a fixed exchange rate system, it did have provisions for parity changes. Countries facing particularly large and chronic payments disequilibria were expected to change their parities, with deficits calling for devaluations and vice versa. Large exchange rate changes, however, were to occur only after consultations with the International Monetary Fund in order to avoid competitive devaluations (Country A undertakes a large devaluation, which Country B feels to be threatening to its payments situation, so Country B devalues, threatening Country C's payments position, and so on) or otherwise disruptive exchange rate changes. Exchange rate changes will be covered in more detail in the next chapter.

With regard to payments adjustment through fiscal and monetary policies, the tighter policies required for deficit countries were to have the same effects described for the specie flow system: prices and incomes were to be held down, thus improving the current account, and higher interest rates that resulted from a tighter monetary policy were to attract capital inflows. The more expansionary policies adopted by surplus countries were to produce the opposite effects, the thought being that if both sides of the disequilibrium followed the rules, neither side would have to shift policies very far from those desired for domestic purposes.

Critical flaws in the Bretton Woods adjustment process

The use of monetary and fiscal policies to adjust payments disequilibria was not particularly successful, especially in the latter part of the Bretton Woods era. This failure helped to bring about the collapse of the system in the early 1970s. Many surplus countries believed that they should not have to adopt more expansionary policies than they desired for domestic purposes in order to adjust payments disequilibria that were caused by excessively expansionary policies in the deficit countries.

Because the surplus countries were unwilling to adopt more expansionary macroeconomic policies, the entire adjustment burden fell on deficit countries. In such a situation payments adjustment required that they adopt very restrictive policies because they were getting no help from macroeconomic expansion in the surplus countries. The deficit countries found the required tightening of monetary and fiscal policies to be extremely painful and frequently resorted to protectionism or other distortions of international transactions as an alternative. Limits were put on the residents' ability to spend money abroad while traveling, exchange controls on capital transactions were reintroduced, and protectionism designed to reduce imports for payments purposes became more common.

In the 1950s a British economist, James Meade, described four situations in which a country could find itself.[6] Two of these cases, which are still widely known as the "Meade conflict cases," suggest why many countries found balance-of-payments adjustment through fiscal and monetary policy changes to be unacceptable:

1   A balance-of-payments surplus and a domestic recession.
2   A balance-of-payments deficit and domestic inflation.
3   A balance-of-payments surplus and domestic inflation.
4   A balance-of-payments deficit and a domestic recession.

Cases 1 and 2 do not present obvious problems for those managing domestic macro-economic policies. In case 1, both problems call for more expansionary policies. The more rapid growth of the money supply or larger government budget deficit that will adjust the payments surplus will also lead to recovery from the domestic recession. In case 2, the same situation holds, but the policies are to shift in the opposite direction. Tighter fiscal and monetary policies will both reduce domestic inflation and eliminate the payments deficit.

Cases 3 and 4, however, present problems for the management of macroeconomic policies. In case 3, the domestic economy calls for restrictive policies that would increase the payments surplus. Payments adjustment under Bretton Woods rules calls for expansionary policies that would exacerbate the domestic inflation. Whichever way the policies are shifted, one problem is eased while the other is aggravated. The choice between the two sides of this conflict is relatively easy, however. A balance-of-payments surplus may create annoying problems, but it is hardly a crisis. The domestic economy was typically viewed as far more important, and restrictive policies were used to stop the inflation at the cost of a larger payments surplus. The problems facing countries with payments deficits were, of course, made considerably worse, but that was of little concern to the surplus countries, for whom the dominant goal was the control of inflation.

Case 4 is the worst of the group. The balance-of-payments deficit calls for restrictive policies that would deepen the recession, whereas the domestic economy needs expansionary policies that would worsen the payments deficit. In this case, however, the balance of payments could not be ignored. If foreign exchange reserves were being depleted and confidence in the domestic currency was rapidly evaporating, the government could not risk the expansionary policies required for domestic recovery. In this situation the temptation to adopt protectionist policies, controls on capital account transactions, and a variety of other distorting interventions has often become irresistible.

The United States was in case 4 when the Kennedy administration took office in early 1961. The result was the 1962 adoption of the Interest Equalization Tax (a tariff on imported securities) and great caution in the adoption of expansionary macroeconomic policies, which produced a very slow recovery in 1961–3. Cases 3 and 4 occurred with sufficient frequency during the Bretton Woods era to make the use of domestic macroeconomic policies for payments adjustment largely unworkable. By the end of the 1960s the system was almost inoperative, which led to its collapse in the early 1970s and the adoption of floating exchange rates by many major industrialized countries in 1973.[7]

The policy assignment model: one last hope for fixed exchange rates

During the 1960s Robert Mundell and J. Marcus Fleming produced an interesting attempt to salvage payments adjustment with fixed exchange rates.[8] The **policy assignment model** was not successful, as indicated by the events of the early 1970s, but it remains intellectually useful. It is based on an older concept, associated with Jan Tinbergen, concerning the relationship between the number of policy goals being pursued by a government and the number of policy tools it has at its disposal. His idea was that if the government has at least as many policy tools as it has goals, it should be possible to design a set of policy positions that will reach all the goals simultaneously. The policy tools must have different relative strengths in affecting different goals, and it must be possible to run the policies separately or independently.

Each policy tool is directed at the goal on which it has the greatest relative impact, but allowance is made for the secondary effects of other policies on that goal. In theory it should then be possible to maneuver the policies toward a set that reaches all the goals.

Mundell and Fleming argued that because monetary policy had a great relative impact on the balance of payments while fiscal policy was more powerful in affecting domestic output (as was shown in Figure 16.12), it should be possible to solve the Meade conflict cases. Fiscal policy would be directed at maintaining the desired level of domestic output while the central bank pursued balance-of-payments equilibrium, with each policy being so managed that allowance was made for the secondary effects of the other policy on its goal. Figure 16.14, which is adapted from an article by Robert Mundell on this model, indicates how this may work.[9]

The DD line represents all the combinations of fiscal and monetary policies that will produce the desired level of domestic output. It therefore indicates how fiscal and monetary policy can be traded off against each other. The fact that DD is relatively flat indicates that a small adjustment of fiscal policy will have the same impact on the domestic economy as would a larger change in monetary policy. This point of view is decidedly Keynesian and would not be popular among monetarists. To the right of DD the policy set is too restrictive and the economy is in a recession, whereas to the left the policies are too expansionary and inflation results. DD can therefore be viewed as a frontier between two regions of the quadrant: inflation to the lower left and recession to the upper right, with the line representing sets of policies that will avoid both of these problems.

The FF line represents all the policy sets that will produce balance-of-payments equilibrium, and its slope again illustrates the manner in which the two policies trade off. The greater steepness of this line means that a small change in monetary policy will have the same impact on the balance of payments as a large change in fiscal policy. Hence monetary policy is powerful and fiscal policy less so in producing payments adjustment. To the left of FF the policies are too expansionary, creating a payments deficit, whereas to the right of the line the policies are too restrictive, producing a surplus. FF is also a frontier, in this instance between the lower left area of the quadrant where a payments deficit exists and the upper right where a surplus results. The four areas of disequilibrium correspond to the four Meade cases discussed above. The recession/surplus case is to the right of both lines, the deficit/inflation case is to the left of both lines, and the two conflict cases are the smaller areas between the equilibrium lines.

Both policy goals are met where the lines cross. Thus just one policy set will produce both payments equilibrium and the desired level of domestic output. If a government starts from a disequilibrium situation, its ability to find the point where the lines cross depends critically

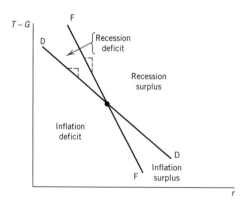

Figure 16.14 Internal and external balance. Along FF the balance of payments is in equilibrium; along DD the domestic economy is at the desired level of aggregate demand. Only where the two lines cross is the economy at both internal and external balance. The slopes of the lines reflect the relative impacts of monetary and fiscal policies on internal and external balance.

on the correct assignment of policies to goals (Figure 16.15). As this figure shows, the incorrect assignment of policies to goals can produce a disaster. If, starting from point A, fiscal policy is used to reach FF (payments equilibrium) and monetary policy is used to deal with the domestic economy (DD), things end badly. If, however, the correct assignment was made, the path reaches point B and the desired equilibrium for both goals fairly easily.

Problems with the policy assignment model

Although the policy assignment model is ingenious, it contains flaws and was not the salvation of the fixed exchange rate regime of Bretton Woods. Some of the problems lie with the theory behind the model, whereas others are more practical. First, the modeling of the balance of payments is extremely simple, and the capital account is viewed in a pure flow-adjustment perspective. In a stock-adjustment world, the model would not work because high but unchanging interest rates would attract capital inflows for only a brief period. Constant increases in interest rates would be necessary to produce continuing capital inflows, and such repeated yield increases would be inconsistent with domestic macro-economic equilibrium at a desired level of GNP. If a stock-adjustment model of the capital account is adopted, the definition of FF in the previous Mundell graph requires that the horizontal axis be labeled "change in the interest rate," which would make it impossible to define the DD line. The model is internally consistent only with a flow-adjustment model of the capital account.

The problem of the number of goals is more important. The model assumes that the government cares about only two things: balance-of-payments equilibrium and a desired level of current GNP. If additional goals are introduced, additional policy tools are required or the full set of goals cannot be reached. If, for example, the government is concerned about the long-term rate of economic growth, it will want to avoid excessively high interest rates that reduce the share of current GNP going into investment. A rate of growth of the capital stock that is sufficient to produce fairly rapid long-term economic growth may require a fiscal/monetary policy set that represses both private and public consumption sufficiently to

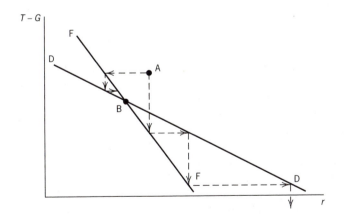

Figure 16.15 Balance-of-payments adjustment through policy assignment. If fiscal policy is assigned to reaching internal balance and monetary policy is assigned to reaching external balance, the joint equilibrium at point B is reached. If, however, the policies are misassigned, the economy does not move toward the equilibrium but instead away from it.

Box 16.3 The IS/LM/BP graph for the policy assignment model

The policy assignment approach to dealing with the two Meade conflict cases can also be seen with the IS/LM/BP graph that was introduced earlier. If, for example, a country faces a domestic recession and a balance-of-payments deficit (case 4), an expansionary fiscal policy is used to escape the recession, and tight money is used to adjust the payments deficit (Figure 16.16). The tightening of monetary policy shifts LM to the left, whereas the more expansionary budget moves IS to the right. The goal is to have them cross on the BP line above the desired level of GNP, represented in the figure as Y_{fe}.

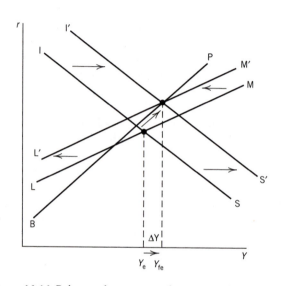

Figure 16.16 Balance-of-payments adjustments through policy assignment in the deficit recession case. A tightening of monetary policy, designed to solve the payments deficit, and an expansionary fiscal policy, to attack the recession, make it possible to solve both halves of this conflict case in the policy assignment model.

make room for more investment in plant and equipment. That implies a tighter fiscal policy, to reduce consumption, and a more expansionary monetary policy, to encourage investment. Monetary policy can no longer be assigned solely to the balance of payments because it is needed to pursue a desired level of domestic investment. When a third goal of long-term growth is introduced, two policy tools are no longer sufficient.

If the problem of the number of goals is pursued further, the distinction between goals and tools starts to break down. Goals are what the government cares about, and tools are what it is prepared to manipulate to reach those goals. Fiscal policy, however, contains government expenditure programs, about which the voters care a great deal. It also includes taxes, about which people have strong opinions which they feel free to express on election day. Voters do not want programs from which they benefit to be turned on and off over the business cycle, and they want their taxes to be stable and therefore predictable. Fiscal policy contains large elements of "goal," and is often unavailable to deal with short-term business-cycle problems, which seems to leave monetary policy as the only short-term macroeconomic tool available for cyclical stabilization. Even a central bank faces constraints. Monetary policy means interest rates, and voters very much dislike sharp increases in yields, because large losses are taken on bond and stock portfolios, and because mortgage loans become impossible to arrange at monthly costs that families can afford. There is certainly far more short-term flexibility in monetary policy than in the government budget, but even the central bank must operate within limits.

The policy assignment model is based on the assumption that both fiscal and monetary policy are readily available for rapid adjustment to pursue only two goals. That is not the case. There are more than two goals, and fiscal policy is seldom available for short-run adjustment.

Macroeconomic policy coordination

The discussion thus far has dealt with a single country trying to manage its own balance of payments and domestic macroeconomy without reference to policy changes in the rest of the world. This raises the question as to whether some of the problems discussed in the previous pages could be avoided if countries coordinated their macroeconomic policies in order to reach shared goals. If, for example, all of the major industrialized countries were in a recession, aggressive expansionary policies should be undertaken by those countries with payments surpluses. These expansionary policies would cause their economies to grow, and rising imports would follow. The expansion would then spread to payments-deficit countries through rapid export growth, and balance-of-payments disequilibria would decline. The countries that began with payments surpluses would play the role of "locomotive," pulling everybody out of the recession and adjusting their own payments surpluses back toward equilibrium.

If all of the industrialized countries were in an inflationary boom, the payments-deficit countries might be expected to lead in the adoption of restrictive policies, thereby slowing all of the economies and shifting payments balances toward equilibrium. Restrictive policies in the deficit countries would reduce their imports, spreading the contractionary impacts to surplus countries through declining exports, and reducing payments disequilibria. If, however, payments-surplus countries were experiencing inflation, while deficit countries were in a recession, the possibilities for a coordinated policy response within the confines of a fixed exchange rate would be less apparent. Some conflict cases, however, should be more easily managed through coordinated policies.

A sizable literature on the possibilities of policy coordination has developed in recent decades, but that literature and the historical experience of the industrialized countries are not encouraging to the hopes of solving policy conflicts through coordination.[10] There are a number of reasons for this pessimism, including the fact that, despite promises to the contrary, surplus countries are seldom eager to adjust toward equilibrium and want to avoid a movement to payments deficit at all costs. It has been extremely difficult to get such surplus countries to move sharply toward expansion, even when doing so appeared to serve their domestic interests.

There is also the institutional fact that the executive branch of the US government controls neither fiscal nor monetary policy. A president or a secretary of the Treasury can promise allied countries that the United States will undertake certain policy shifts, but the Congress controls the budget, and the Federal Reserve System controls monetary policy. Therefore these promises are not worth a great deal, a fact that is widely understood by the allies. In addition, broad goals may conflict; Germany and Japan, for example, have had a strong bias against any inflation whatever, whereas many other industrialized countries have been willing to accept some inflation in order to reduce unemployment, however doubtful that trade-off is beyond the short run. It is difficult or impossible to coordinate policies among the industrialized countries if Germany is determined to drive inflation to almost zero, while the United States and the United Kingdom are eager for expansion, even if it means moderate inflation for everyone. Conflicts of this type were common in the era of fixed exchange rates. This suggests why policy coordination may present interesting theoretical possibilities, but turned out to be of very limited practical use in maintaining a regime of fixed exchange rates for a large number of countries with diverse economies.

Monetary policy was very closely coordinated among the members of the Exchange Rate Mechanism of the European Monetary System during the 1980s and early 1990s, as it evolved toward full monetary union in 2000, but this subject will be deferred to Chapter 20. The industrialized countries which have maintained floating exchange rates since 1973 have sometimes maintained a loose coordination of monetary policies to either stabilize exchange rates or to move them in a desired direction, and that subject also comes up later.

In a world of parities, the adjustment of large balance-of-payments disequilibria without interference with domestic macroeconomic goals requires more than domestic fiscal and monetary policies, which leads us to the subject of changes in otherwise fixed exchange rates. Chapter 17 deals with devaluations and revaluations.

Summary of key concepts

1   Under the specie flow mechanism the money supply of a payments-deficit country automatically falls and this produces a return to payments equilibrium at the likely cost of a domestic recession.

2   Countries such as Estonia and Bulgaria which maintain currency boards rather than central banks operate with the specie flow adjustment mechanism, unless they find ways of cheating on the rules of a currency board, as Argentina reportedly did.

3   Under the Bretton Woods system countries were to have more discretion in adopting measures to adjust payments disequilibria, but deficit countries were still to tighten monetary and/or fiscal policies, with monetary policy having clear efficiency advantages.

4   The policy adjustment model of Mundell and Fleming appeared to offer a means of both adjusting payments disequilibria and maintaining a desired level of GDP, by using monetary policy to deal with the balance of payments and fiscal policy to manage the domestic economy. The model has serious problems, however, so the promise is more apparent than real.

5   International policy coordination offers only modest gains over a purely domestic approach, and is no longer seen as a means of salvaging a fixed exchange rate system.

6   As a result there are no approaches to balance-of-payments adjustment which do not rely on exchange rate changes that now appear to be promising for more than modest disequilibria. Another tool is needed, and this will lead us to a discussion of devaluations.

Questions for study and review

1   Under the pre-1914 gold standard, Country A has a large gold strike; that is, it becomes able to produce far more gold. What happens to the balance of payments of Country A? Why? How is it returned to equilibrium? What is the effect of this process on the rest of the world? What country can you think of which went through the experience of Country A a few hundred years ago? Did that country prosper from the experience?

2   Under the Bretton Woods system, a country with a balance-of-payments deficit is to make what changes in its domestic macroeconomic policies? Under what circumstances would these changes parallel the needs of the domestic economy? When would these policy changes conflict with those needs?

3   Why were payments-surplus countries under far less pressure to adopt the domestic macroeconomic policies called for by the adjustment process than were deficit countries under the Bretton Woods system? What effect did this situation have on the problems facing deficit countries as they tried to adjust?

4   Under the Mundell/Fleming policy assignment approach, what policies are called for if a country experiences a payments surplus and a domestic inflationary boom?

5   Use the IS/LM/BP graph to show what happens in the situations described in questions 1, 2, and 4, show the line-shifts, and explain why they occur.

6   Why are countries such as Bulgaria and Estonia giving up any monetary policy independence by adopting currency boards as replacements for their central banks? Explain how payments adjustment would occur if Bulgaria started in equilibrium and then experienced a large increase in exports due to a boom in Germany.

Suggested further reading

- Argy, V., *International Macroeconomics: Theory and Policy*, New York: Routledge, 1994.
- Eichengreen, B., *The Gold Standard in Theory and History*, 2nd edn, New York: Routledge, 1997.
- Frenkel, J. and M. Mussa, "The Mundell–Fleming Model a Quarter Century Later," *IMF Staff Papers*, December 1987, pp. 567–620.
- Hume, D., "On the Balance of Trade [1752]," in R. Cooper, ed., *International Finance: Readings*, Baltimore: Penguin Books, 1969.
- Meade, J., *The Balance of Payments*, New York: Oxford University Press, 1951.
- Mundell, R., *International Economics*, New York: Macmillan, 1968.
- Oudiz, G. and J. Sachs, "Macroeconomic Policy Coordination among Industrialized Countries," *Brookings Papers on Economic Activity*, no. 1, 1984, pp. 1–64.
- Person, T. and L. Svensson, "The Operation and Collapse of Fixed Exchange Rate Regimes," in G. Grossman and K. Rogoff, eds, *Handbook of International Economics*, Vol. III, Amsterdam: Elsevier, 1995, pp. 1865–911.
- Solomon, R., *The International Monetary System 1945–1976: An Insider's View*, New York: Harper and Row, 1977.

Notes

1 David Hume, "On the Balance of Trade," originally written in 1752, published in D. Hume, *Essays: Moral, Political, and Literary* (London: Longmans Green, 1898), reprinted in R. Cooper, ed., *International Finance: Selected Readings* (Baltimore: Penguin, 1969).

2 R. Triffin, "The Myths and Realities of the So-Called Gold Standard," in R. Triffin, *Our International Monetary System: Yesterday, Today, and Tomorrow* (New York: Random House, 1968), ch. 1. See also B. Eichengreen, ed., *The Gold Standard in Theory and History* (New York: Methuen, 1985). See also L. Yeager, *International Monetary Relations: Theory, History, and Policy*, 2nd edn (New York: Harper and Row, 1976), chs 15, 16, and 17.

3 For a discussion of balance-of-payments adjustment in a country or dependency that lacks its own currency, see J. Ingram, *Regional Payments Mechanisms: The Case of Puerto Rico* (Chapel Hill: University of North Carolina Press, 1962), pp. 113–33.

4 For a recent discussion of the newly popular currency boards, see C. Enoch and A. Gulde, "Are Currency Boards a Cure for All Monetary Problems?," *Finance and Development*, December 1998, pp. 40–3. This article contains citations to other research on this topic. See also "Currency Boards Circumscribe Discretionary Monetary Policy," *IMF Survey*, May 20, 1996. For a discussion of the possibility of introducing a currency board in Russia, see "Unpalatable Truths of a Currency Board," *The Financial Times*, August 31, 1998, p. 2.

5 The academic history of balance-of-payments adjustment under the Bretton Woods system can be found in P. Kenen, "Macroeconomic Theory and Policy: How the Closed Economy Was Opened," in R. Jones and P. Kenen, eds, *Handbook of International Economics*, Vol. II (Amsterdam: North-Holland, 1985), pp. 625–78. The history of international economic policy in this era is covered in R. Solomon, *The International Monetary System: 1945–1976: An Insider's View* (New York: Harper and Row, 1977), chs 2–13.

6 James Meade, *The Balance of Payments* (London: Oxford University Press, 1951).

7 Despite its problems, the system of fixed exchange rates retained some defenders. See S.I. Katz, "The Case for the Par Value System," *Princeton Essays in International Finance*, no. 92, 1972.

8 The literature on what became known as the Mundell–Fleming policy assignment model begins with R. Mundell, "The Appropriate Use of Monetary and Fiscal Policy for Internal and External Stability," *IMF Staff Papers*, March 1962, pp. 70–7, and J.M. Fleming, "Domestic Financial Policies under Fixed and under Flexible Exchange Rates," *IMF Staff Papers*, 1962, pp. 369–79. For an important early discussion of the problem of the number of policy goals versus the number of policy tools, see J. Tinbergen, *The Theory of Economic Policy* (Amsterdam: North-Holland, 1952), chs 4 and 5. For a review of the impact on international economics of the Mundell–Fleming approach, see J. Frenkel and M. Mussa, "The Mundell–Fleming Model a Quarter Century Later," *IMF Staff Papers*, December 1987, pp. 567–620.

9 R. Mundell, *International Economics* (New York: Macmillan, 1968), p. 235.

10 See J. Niehans, "Monetary and Fiscal Policies in Open Economies under Fixed Exchange Rates: An Optimizing Approach," *Journal of Political Economy*, 1968, pp. 893–920. See also K. Hamada, "A Strategic Analysis of Monetary Interdependence," *Journal of Political Economy*, 1976, pp. 677–700. Suggestions as to why policy coordination is likely to fail can be found in K. Rogoff, "International Economic Coordination May Be Counterproductive," *Journal of International Economics*, February 1985, pp. 199–217. For econometric work suggesting that any gains from policy coordination are likely to be very small, see G. Oudiz and J. Sachs, "Macroeconomic Policy Coordination among Industrialized Countries," *Brookings Papers on Economic Activity*, no. 1, 1984, pp. 1–64. For a more recent survey of this subject, see T. Persson and G. Tabellini, "Double-Edged Incentives: Institutions and Policy Coordination," in G. Grossman and K. Rogoff, eds, *Handbook of International Economics*, Vol. III (Amsterdam: Elsevier, 1995), ch. 38. See also M. Feldstein, "Thinking about International Economic Coordination," *Journal of Economic Perspectives*, Spring 1988, pp. 3–13.

17 Balance-of-payments adjustment through exchange rate changes

Learning objectives

By the end of this chapter you should be able to understand:

- the microeconomics of a devaluation; that is, how price elasticities of demand for exports and imports help determine the success or failure of a devaluation;
- the macroeconomics of a devaluation in the Keynesian absorption model; how the growth of domestic absorption of goods and services must be restrained after a devaluation if success is to be likely; why this constraint is particularly severe if the country is at or close to full employment at the time of the devaluation;
- the IS/LM/BP graph as a means of seeing the macroeconomics of a devaluation, particularly how appropriate fiscal and monetary policies can help;
- why monetarists view control of the growth of the nominal money supply as the only important requirement for the success of a devaluation;
- the often unpleasant side-effects of a devaluation, particularly when accompanied by tight fiscal and monetary policies as suggested by the theory and often required by the IMF; therefore why devaluations are often extremely unpopular.

The argument for using the exchange rate as the primary tool for balance-of-payments adjustment goes back to the first week of elementary economics. When a market is out of equilibrium, a price change is the preferred solution, and if a market remains in disequilibrium, it is typically because government intervention or some other rigidity has precluded the necessary price adjustment. If the market for foreign exchange is viewed as being analogous to the market for corn, the same argument holds, and exchange rate changes are the obvious answer for payments disequilibria. A supply and demand graph for foreign exchange may make this point clearer (see Figure 17.1).

A return to supply and demand

The autonomous demand for foreign exchange is derived from the domestic demand for foreign goods, services, and financial assets. The autonomous supply of foreign exchange represents the foreign demand for the local currency, and it is similarly derived from the rest of the world's demand for the home country's goods, services, and financial assets. If the local demand for foreign goods, services, and assets exceeds the foreign demand for the same items in the home country, the demand for foreign exchange exceeds the supply at the existing price, and a balance-of-payments deficit exists. The excess demand for foreign exchange is absorbed through central bank intervention as the deficit country loses foreign exchange reserves. If this loss of foreign exchange reserves is sizable relative to their level at the outset, something must be done.

All the adjustment mechanisms discussed in Chapter 16 represent attempts to force the demand function shown in Figure 17.1 to shift to the left and the supply function to shift to the right, producing equilibrium at the historic fixed parity. As was suggested in that chapter, the domestic effects of the policies required to produce such demand and supply shifts are painful and may not be politically acceptable. It might be wondered why a government would even consider imposing such difficulty on its economy, when the option of an exchange rate change is readily available. If there is excess demand for foreign exchange, then the best policy is to raise the price (lower the exchange rate) to a level at which the excess demand disappears, which is a devaluation if the new rate is to be fixed.

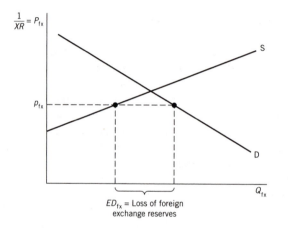

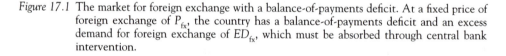

Figure 17.1 The market for foreign exchange with a balance-of-payments deficit. At a fixed price of foreign exchange of P_{fx}, the country has a balance-of-payments deficit and an excess demand for foreign exchange of ED_{fx}, which must be absorbed through central bank intervention.

Raising the price to clear the foreign exchange market, as indicated in Figure 17.2, and avoiding all the problems of payments adjustment discussed in the previous chapter, would seem to be an easy matter. Unfortunately, it is far from simple. **Devaluations** are difficult to impose and often fail, in the sense that improvements in the balance of payments are insufficient or so short-lived that the devaluation has to be repeated. The market for foreign exchange is not analogous to the market for corn. Merely adjusting a price to clear the market, which would succeed in the corn market, is not a guaranteed solution in the case of the market for foreign exchange, as will be discussed in this chapter.

For a country with a relatively open economy, the exchange rate can be its most important single price. The exchange rate directly or indirectly affects virtually everything in the economy, and many of the effects of exchange rate changes can be quite disruptive. Exchange rate changes have impacts on the level of aggregate demand, the price level, the interest rate, the distribution of income within the country, and many other aspects of the economy. Because changing an exchange rate in either direction will be unpopular with at least one

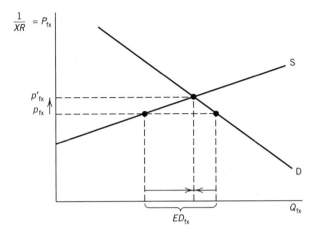

Figure 17.2 The market for foreign exchange when the local currency is devalued. Raising the price of foreign exchange from P_{fx} to P'_{fx}, which lowers the exchange rate, allows the exchange market to clear without the loss of foreign exchange reserves or painful attempts to force the supply and demand functions to shift.

major group in the economy, elected governments usually prefer to avoid such changes whenever possible.

For the sake of simplicity, the following discussion stresses devaluations, but it should be remembered that **revaluations** are also possible, if less frequent, and that the resulting impacts are in the opposite direction.

Requirements for a successful devaluation

For a devaluation to succeed in adjusting a chronic payments deficit, a number of conditions must be met. Devaluations have both microeconomic and macroeconomic effects that can complicate the payments adjustment process. The microeconomic requirements for a successful devaluation, which are typically less serious, will be discussed first. Macroeconomic problems, which are often much more demanding, follow.

The Marshall–Lerner condition: the desirability of high elasticities of demand

In the first half of this book, elasticities of demand for imports and exports played crucial roles in determining a country's terms of trade, the impacts of tariffs and quotas, and the impacts of economic growth on a nation's welfare. Once again, these elasticities are important – this time in determining how effective a devaluation will be in improving a country's balance of trade.

The primary objective of a devaluation is to change relative prices in ways that will encourage exports and discourage imports. To devalue a currency is to increase the local price of foreign money, thereby raising local prices of imports. If the US dollar were devalued by 10 percent, the price of the pound sterling would rise, for example, from $1.80 to $1.98, thereby causing US prices of British goods to increase proportionally. A British car with a price of £10,000 would have previously cost $18,000; now it will cost $19,800, which it is hoped will discourage US buyers of such vehicles, who will instead shift to domestic models.

The US price increase would be smaller only if the British manufacturer decided to absorb some of the effects of the devaluation in the form of a lower sterling price.

The effect of these increases in domestic prices on the volume of imports depends on the elasticity of demand. If that elasticity is high, a relatively large decline in import volumes occurs, and the devaluation has its intended effect. If the elasticity is less than one, however, the volume reduction will be insufficient to offset the price increase, and the local currency value of imports will rise. The higher the demand elasticity, the better the prospects for the success of the devaluation.

That elasticity depends on the strength of substitution and income effects. If domestic substitutes for imported goods are readily available, the substitution effect will be strong, suggesting a large decline in imports. If, however, imports consist largely of necessities for which domestic substitutes are not available, import reductions will be smaller, implying poor prospects for the success of the devaluation. This situation is more likely in developing countries, although even highly developed nations such as France, Germany, Japan, and the United States lack obvious substitutes for some imported products such as oil.

The income effect will be powerful if imports are a major part of the typical citizen's budget; it is easy to see, then, why devaluations are unpopular in this circumstance. If a devaluation raises the domestic prices of major items in consumer budgets, such as food and fuel, real incomes decline, which necessitates reduced purchases of imports and other goods. Devaluations reduce real incomes in relatively open economies, which makes both devaluations and the governments that impose them unpopular.

With regard to exports, a devaluation will produce some combination of a reduction in the foreign currency price and an increase in the local currency price, with relative elasticities of supply and demand determining the outcome. If the local currency price of exports is fixed, implying an infinitely elastic supply function, the foreign currency price falls by the full percentage of the devaluation, which should encourage foreigners to purchase more of the home country's goods. Returning to the earlier example, we see that when the pound sterling was at $1.80, a US product priced at $100 carried a price of £55.56 (100/1.80). The

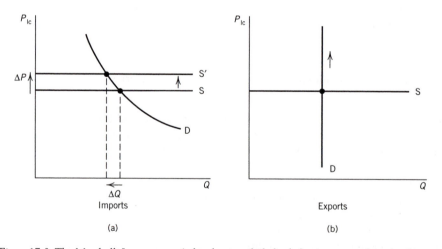

Figure 17.3 The Marshall–Lerner case. A devaluation shifts both foreign curves (supply of imports and demand for exports) up by the percentage of the devaluation. Since the demand curve is already vertical, it slides along itself. If the demand for imports is of unitary elasticity, there is no change in the trade balance.

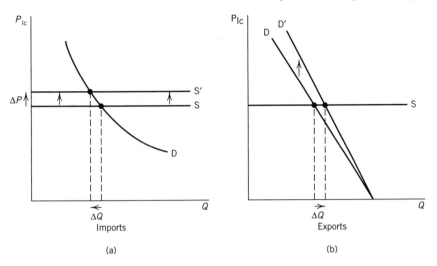

Figure 17.4 The Marshall–Lerner case where a devaluation succeeds. Continuing the case described
in the previous sets of graphs, the elasticity of demand for exports now exceeds zero and
the elasticity of demand for imports remains unitary, so the sum of the elasticities exceeds
one and the trade balance improves by the growth of export revenues.

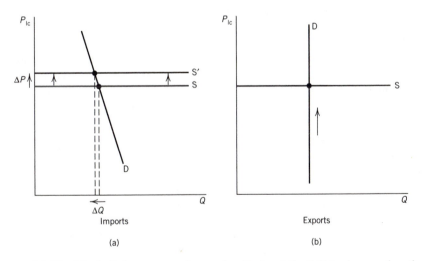

Figure 17.5 The Marshall–Lerner case where a devaluation fails. Still in the case described in the
previous two sets of graphs, now the elasticity of demand for exports is zero and the
elasticity of demand for imports is less than one, so the sum of the elasticities of demand
is less than one. The devaluation worsens the trade balance because export revenues do
not change and import expenditures rise.

devaluation of the US dollar by 10 percent produced a US cost of sterling of $1.98. Therefore
the US product carrying a price of $100 would now cost British residents only £50.51, which
should encourage UK purchases of American products.

If, instead, foreign currency prices of exports are fixed, implying an infinitely elastic foreign
demand for such goods, the local currency price of exports rises by the percentage of the
devaluation, which should encourage domestic firms to make greater efforts to sell abroad.

Returning to the above numerical example, we find that if a product carries an unchanging British price of £100, the $1.80 exchange rate means a US price of $180, and the 10 percent devaluation to $1.98 means a US price of $198, which both earns US firms more revenue for the same volumes of exports and encourages them to make greater efforts to increase those volumes.

If neither the demand nor the supply curve for exports is infinitely elastic, the foreign price of exports will fall by less than the full percentage of the devaluation, and the local price will rise by the rest of that percentage. The result will be an incentive for foreigners to purchase more of these goods and for exporters to make greater efforts to sell them. In all these cases, however, higher elasticities of demand for both imports and exports increase the desired impact of the devaluation on the balance of trade.

If the elasticities of demand for exports and imports are extremely low, a devaluation can worsen the trade balance rather than improve it. If prices are always fixed in exporters' currencies, which means that both elasticities of supply are infinite, the condition for the desired response of the trade account to the exchange rate is relatively simple: the two elasticities of demand (for imports and exports) must sum to more than one, that is, average more than 0.5. If they sum to exactly one, the trade account does not change when a devaluation occurs. The perverse trade account response to the exchange rate occurs only if they sum to less than one. This is known as the Marshall–Lerner condition.[1]

The effects of a devaluation on the trade balance can be seen in Figure 17.3. Prices are in the local currency; thus the devaluation causes a vertical shift in the foreign functions (demand for exports and supply of imports). A case in which the elasticities sum to exactly one is presented first. Since the foreign demand for exports is vertical, its shift upward means that it slides along itself, that is, that there is no change. Since the elasticity of demand for imports is one, the vertical shift of the supply function means that total expenditures on imports are the same before and after the devaluation, the decline in import volumes being just offset by the price increase. Neither export revenues nor import expenditures change, demonstrating that the trade balance is unaffected by the devaluation.

If the elasticity of demand for exports exceeds zero, which indicates that the elasticities sum to more than one, the results shown in Figure 17.4 will occur. Import expenditures remain unchanged, but export receipts have clearly increased. Thus the trade balance improves by the amount of the export revenue growth. The Marshall–Lerner condition is met, and a devaluation has its intended effect. If the elasticities sum to less than one, however, the outcome is quite different (see Figure 17.5). In this case, the trade account deteriorates. The vertical foreign demand for the home country's products means that export revenues do not change, and the fact that the domestic elasticity of demand for imports is less than one means that total expenditures rise. The decline in the volume of imports is insufficient to offset the price increase, so the local currency cost of imports increases. The trade account worsens by the amount of the import expenditure growth.

The assumption of infinitely elastic supply functions is unrealistic, but it makes possible the simple version of the Marshall–Lerner condition. (The demand elasticities must sum to more than one.) If the elasticities of supply are less than infinite, the Marshall–Lerner condition becomes far more complicated. It remains true, however, that the higher the demand elasticities, the better the prospects that a devaluation will improve the trade balance. If these elasticities sum to more than one, the prospects that the devaluation will produce the desired change in the trade account are quite good.

It may be useful to show two somewhat more realistic cases. First, a small country is one that is a perfect competitor in both export and import markets (Figure 17.6). It has neither

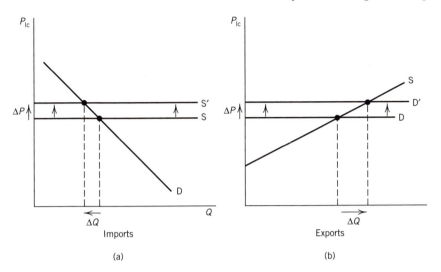

Figure 17.6 The small-country case. A small country is a perfect competitor in all markets, meaning that it faces a horizontal demand for exports and a horizontal supply for imports. It can buy or sell as much as it wishes in world markets without affecting any prices. In this case there is a strong presumption that a devaluation will improve the trade balance.

monopoly nor monopsony power, and it takes world prices of exports and imports as given. Imagine, for example, the role of Honduras in world trade. A dollar price of coffee exists in New York, over which Honduras has no control. Honduras can export as much or as little coffee as it chooses, without affecting that dollar price. The Honduras price of coffee is then the dollar price times the exchange rate, expressed as the number of Honduran lempiras per dollar. A 10 percent devaluation of the lempira leaves the dollar price of coffee unchanged and therefore raises the lempira price by 10 percent. Honduras faces an infinitely elastic demand for coffee at the world price translated into lempiras at the current exchange rate.

On the import side, Honduras faces a similar situation. Dollar prices are fixed, and the Honduras price is simply the dollar price times the number of lempiras per dollar. Honduras faces an infinitely elastic supply of imports at the world price translated into lempiras at the existing exchange rate. Since both export and import prices, measured in lempiras, rise by the percentage of the devaluation, there is no change in the terms of trade of Honduras.

Many, or perhaps even most, countries in the world are in this situation, particularly when we allow for the large number of small countries that has become independent during the 1980s and 1990s. In this case, a devaluation is almost certain to improve the trade account.

On the export side, both quantity and price rise, producing a large increase in revenues. With regard to imports, the volume falls, which helps, but prices rise, which does not. Import expenditures rise if the elasticity of demand is less than one, and they fall if it is more than one. Whatever happens to import expenditures, export revenues rise sharply. In this case the trade account fails to improve, and instead is unchanged, only if both the domestic demand for imports and the supply of exports are vertical. If either of the domestic elasticities exceeds zero, the trade account improves.

The second case is that of a country that is somewhat larger in the sense that it has some market or monopoly power in one or more export markets but has no monopsony power as an importer. Many of the larger developing countries export large volumes of a few goods and import smaller amounts of many things. In their major export markets, they have

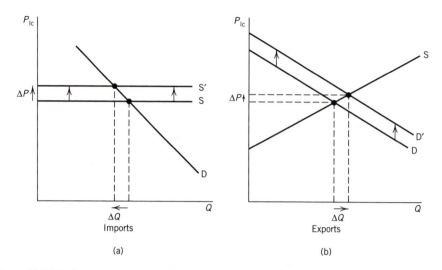

Figure 17.7 The larger-country case. This country has some monopoly power in its export markets but no monopsony power as an importer. The demand curve for its exports is no longer horizontal, but it still faces a perfectly elastic supply for imports. A devaluation is very likely to improve the trade balance in this case, unless both demand elasticities are very low.

significant market power and face downward-sloping demand curves, but as importers they have no market power and face infinitely elastic supply curves. Brazil is such a country because it is far from a perfectly competitive seller of coffee and a few other major commodities, but it has no ability to control or influence its import prices. Sri Lanka and India would be in a similar situation with regard to exports of tea, whereas Peru, Chile, and Zambia probably export enough copper to have some potential influence over prices. For such countries, the supply and demand curve shifts depicted in Figure 17.7 occur.

Again, there is a strong presumption that the balance of payments improves. On the export side, both price and quantity increase, implying significantly larger local currency revenues. It is worth noting, however, that the export price does not rise by the full percentage of the devaluation. World prices, denominated in foreign exchange, fall by the remainder of that percentage. Because import prices do rise by the percentage of the devaluation, there is a modest deterioration of the home country's terms of trade. With regard to import expenditures, the outcome depends solely on the elasticity of demand. If it is more than one, expenditures fall, and vice versa, which repeats the small-country case. Because export revenues clearly rise, whereas import expenditures rise or fall slightly depending on whether the elasticity of demand is greater or less than one, the balance of trade should improve. That would fail to be the case only if the elasticities of demand for both exports and imports were very low.

During the 1950s and 1960s "elasticity pessimism" was fairly common. Many economists feared that the relevant demand elasticities were sufficiently low for many countries to make devaluations an unlikely solution for payments deficits. Improved econometric estimates of these elasticities and ongoing studies of devaluations have made it clear that such pessimism is typically unjustified. Over reasonably long periods of time, demand elasticities are almost certain to be high enough to produce the desired effect of a devaluation on the trade account.

Over short periods, however, there can be problems. Buyers of imports are creatures of habit, in the sense that they are accustomed to dealing with the same suppliers and need time to find alternatives. In addition, trade in raw materials often involves contracts that set prices and quantities to be purchased per month for considerable periods. Buyers cannot respond to exchange rate changes until such contracts expire and new arrangements can be made. If, for example, a Japanese steel company is committed by contract to purchase its iron ore requirements from Australia when another country devalues and offers iron ore at a lower yen price, the Japanese firm can make no response until its contract with the Australian mines expires.[2]

The effect of the time required to find new sources, and of such contracts, is to produce what is widely known as the **J-curve effect**. After a devaluation, the trade balance follows a pattern that resembles a "J"; that is, it declines slightly for a brief period and then rises sharply. The period of worsening trade results may be 6 months or a year, but the trade account does respond in the intended manner if sufficient time is allowed to pass. Hence countries need enough foreign exchange reserves at the time of a devaluation to finance continuing trade deficits for that period, which suggests why IMF drawings often accompany such parity adjustments. Borrowing from the IMF is arranged to provide the foreign exchange needed to cover the period before the trade balance can be expected to improve.

Another complication is created if a country has maintained severe restrictions on imports during the period before the devaluation. Such import controls are quite common for countries with severe payments deficits which necessitate later devaluations. If these imports restraints are removed or eased at the time of the devaluation, imports will rise, or at least not fall as much as normally would be the case, partially offsetting the intended effect of the exchange rate change on the trade account. If a parity change is to be accompanied by the easing of previous import controls, the devaluation will have to be larger, and it is likely to take somewhat longer to have its intended effect on the trade balance than otherwise would be the case.

Returning to the earlier discussion of demand and supply elasticities, the Marshall–Lerner condition with non-infinite supply elasticities is as follows:

$$\frac{V_x}{V_m} \left(\frac{e_dx + 1}{\dfrac{e_dx}{e_sx} - 1} \right) - \frac{e_sm + 1}{\dfrac{e_sm}{e_dm} - 1} > 1$$

(V_x = previous value of exports, V_m = previous value of imports, e_sm = elasticity of supply for imports, e_dm = elasticity of demand for imports, e_sx = elasticity of supply for exports, and e_dx = elasticity of demand for exports.)

The trade balance improves if this condition holds, and vice versa. High demand elasticities increase the likelihood that a devaluation will succeed, but there is not a clear relationship between the size of the supply elasticities and the response of the trade balance to the exchange rate.[3]

Countries also worry about the impact of a devaluation on their terms of trade. Countries benefit if their terms of trade improve, and vice versa, as was discussed in Chapter 2 of this book. If readers return to the graphs on earlier pages in this chapter, it can easily be seen that in the first Marshall–Lerner case (the unrealistic situation in which both supply elasticities are assumed to be infinite), the devaluing country's terms of trade declined by the percentage of the devaluation, because the local price of imports rose by that percentage and export prices did not change. In the far more realistic small-country case, a devaluation had no effect on the country's terms of trade because local currency prices of both exports and imports rose by the percentage of the exchange rate change. In the larger-country case, which is also realistic, a devaluation produced a small worsening of the country's terms of trade, because local currency prices of imports rose by the full percentage of the devaluation while export prices rose by somewhat less.

The terms of trade of a country worsen after a devaluation, and vice versa, if the following condition holds:

$$e_s x \cdot e_s m > e_d x \cdot e_d m$$

Whatever the realities of a country's circumstances, the fear of worse terms of trade has been a frequent reason for governments of developing countries to resist pressures to devalue overvalued currencies.

Macroeconomic requirements for a successful devaluation

Devaluations typically fail, in the sense that any balance-of-payments improvement is small and/or temporary, not because of the microeconomic issues discussed above, but because of macroeconomic problems. As a result, the success of a devaluation generally depends on the adoption of appropriate fiscal and monetary policies.

Devaluations often seem to self-destruct, in the sense that the exchange rate change causes macroeconomic effects within the economy which cause the balance of payments to return to large deficit, requiring another devaluation. If these problems become sufficiently serious, a country may end up devaluing very frequently. Between 1991 and 1998, for example, Yugoslavia devalued the dinar 18 times.

There are two views of these issues, Keynesian and monetarist; the Keynesian analysis is widely known as the **absorption model**,[4] and deals with the current account. The response of the capital account to a devaluation will be discussed later.

The absorption approach to devaluation

The absorption approach begins with the fact that a devaluation is expected to have effects that sharply increase aggregate demand for domestic output. Production of exports and import substitutes rises, which leads to higher incomes and more consumption expenditures through the multiplier effect. Export- and import-competing industries become more profitable, which should encourage increased plant and equipment investment in those sectors. These expansionary forces may become excessive, particularly if the economy is close to full employment at the time of the devaluation, and result in inflation that destroys the effectiveness of the devaluation. As the export and import-competing sectors attempt to expand, they must bid for more labor and other inputs. If the economy is close to full employment, wage rates and other factor prices will increase, passing inflationary effects across the economy, thereby offsetting the intended effects of the devaluation. These effects can also be seen through simple national income accounting identities:

$$Y = C + I + G + (X - M)$$

Therefore:

$$(X - M) = Y - (C + I + G)$$

where C + I + G = absorption, which is the total domestic use of goods and services. Therefore:

$$\Delta(X - M) = \Delta Y - \Delta (C + I + G) \text{ or } \Delta Y - \Delta A$$

where Δ = change.

The trade account can improve (Δ (X – M) exceeds zero) only if domestic output grows by more than the growth in domestic absorption. This is a simple but important point. If an economy is producing $10,000 in output and is absorbing $11,000, the current account must be in deficit by $1,000. If, as a result of a devaluation, output increases to $12,000 but domestic absorption rises to $13,000, nothing has been accomplished. The trade account remains in deficit by $1,000. The $2,000 growth of output must be accompanied by sufficient restraint on domestic absorption to hold its growth to $1,000, thus producing output and absorption that are equal at $12,000 and a current account that is in balance. In this case the growth of absorption must be restricted to 50 percent of the growth of output, which implies a considerable tightening of fiscal and monetary policy.

In this case there is no suggestion that absorption must fall in absolute terms, but merely that its growth must be held well below the growth of output and incomes to allow the trade account to improve. If, however, the economy had been fully employed at the time of the devaluation, the implications of the absorption model would be more demanding. If output cannot rise, absorption must fall in absolute terms for the trade account to improve:

$$\Delta(X - M) = \Delta Y - \Delta(C + I + G)$$

If ΔY = 0, then

$$\Delta(X - M) = -\Delta (C + I + G) = -\Delta A$$

In this circumstance the trade account can improve only if absorption falls in absolute terms. Returning to the previous example, we see that if a country is producing its maximum potential output of $10,000 and absorbing $11,000 so that the current account is in deficit by $1,000, balance-of-payments adjustment requires that absorption fall to $10,000, which means extremely restrictive macroeconomic policies. It is much easier to devalue when the economy has excess capacity, because in that case the growth of absorption merely has to be held below the growth of output. If a devaluation is undertaken when an economy is fully employed, the implications for domestic absorption are unpleasant at best.

Many developing countries find the implications of this model to be particularly painful. They often face severe output bottlenecks in the form of limited transport and electricity-generating capacity, so that large numbers of unemployed workers do not represent additional potential output in the short run. Their absorption levels are already low enough to imply real suffering, and balance-of-payments adjustment means reducing absorption further. If full-capacity output, allowing for bottlenecks, is $350 per person and absorption has been $400 per person, returning the current account to balance requires squeezing $50 per person out of an already appallingly low level of absorption. Unless this country can find sources of foreign aid or loans, however, it faces the same budget constraint that applies to a poor family: it cannot absorb more than it can produce, no matter how miserable the standard of living implied by that level of income.

The requirements of the absorption condition can also be seen in the relationship between the trade balance and the savings/investment gap, which was discussed in Chapter 12. Returning to page 286, you will find:

$$I + (X - M) = S_p + (T - G)$$

which can be reorganized into:

$$(X - M) = S_p + (T - G) - I$$

Putting the previous statement in first differences:

$$\Delta(X - M) = \Delta S_p + \Delta(T - G) - \Delta I$$

or

$$\Delta(X - M) = \Delta S_t - \Delta I$$

where total savings equals private savings plus the government budget surplus (or minus the government deficit). This statement makes a simple but important point that a country's trade balance can improve only to the extent that total domestic savings rise relative to domestic investment. The policy implications of that statement are not pleasant: total domestic savings must grow rapidly, or severe restraint must be put on domestic investment, if a devaluation is to succeed.

Discouraging investment, particularly in the tradable goods sector, is an extremely unattractive idea, so savings must increase sharply. The sector of savings over which the government has clear control is $(T - G)$, which means that tight fiscal policies are likely to be necessary if a devaluation is to succeed. Government expenditures will probably have to be cut, taxes raised, or both, if a country's trade account is to improve. Such policy changes, following a devaluation, are standard elements in IMF stabilization programs for countries that are borrowing from the Fund. At a minimum, if the economy is able to grow rapidly, thereby generating more tax revenues, the growth of government expenditures must be repressed in order to allow $(T - G)$ to rise. If the economy is close to full employment and therefore cannot grow rapidly, government expenditures will have to be cut and/or tax rates increased if a devaluation is to succeed. It can easily be seen from this discussion why governments of poor countries find the requirements of orthodox balance-of-payments adjustment programs to be distasteful, and why they often fail to adopt policies that make a devaluation successful.

Box 17.1 IS/LM/BP analysis of a devaluation

Returning to the graphical analysis of the previous chapter, we observe that a devaluation shifts both the BP and IS lines to the right. The IS line shifts because the current account improves, thus increasing the level of GNP so that domestic savings rise relative to intended domestic investment. Domestic savings must rise relative to domestic investment by the amount of the current account improvement in order to maintain the identity that

$$S_t - I = X - M$$

where

$$S_t = S_p + (T - G)$$

Since $X - M$ has risen, S_T must rise relative to I, and it is the increase in GNP that produces that increase in savings. The BP line shifts to the right because the balance of payments improves, thereby increasing the level of GNP that is consistent with payments equilibrium (see Figure 17.8).

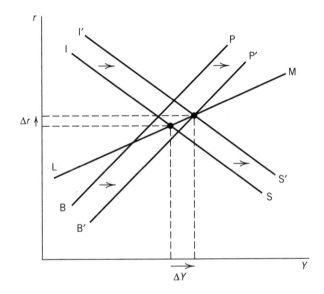

Figure 17.8 The effects of a successful devaluation. A devaluation shifts both BP and IS to the right, with the desired outcome being that all three lines cross at the same point, as shown above. If IS shifts too far to the right, the balance of payments will remain in deficit, necessitating a tighter fiscal policy to shift it back to the left.

The devaluation increases the equilibrium level of GNP, which may create capacity problems. If the new equilibrium level of GNP is above that which the economy can easily produce, the result will be worsening inflation, which will undermine the effectiveness of the devaluation. The rightward shift of IS must be limited to where BP and LM cross. If the IS line shifts too far to the right, the result is a return to payments deficit. Fiscal policy must be sufficiently restrictive to avoid that outcome. It is also worth noting that the devaluation increases the interest rate; this results from an increase in nominal GNP, which raises the demand for money.

The monetarist view of a devaluation

Monetarists, it was argued earlier, view balance-of-payments deficits as being caused by excessively expansionary monetary policies. An excess supply of money creates a parallel excess demand for goods or financial assets, which spills over into the balance of payments as a deficit. Since deficits have a single cause, they can be remedied only by a reversal of that problem.

The elasticity analysis is irrelevant because monetarists believe that all prices and costs in the devaluing country will ultimately rise by the percentage change in the exchange rate. Although they would not disagree with the desirability of budgetary restraint, the Keynesian analysis holds little attraction for monetarists. Balance-of-payments deficits can be adjusted only if the fundamental problem of an excess supply of money is remedied.

In the monetarist view, a devaluation has only one important effect on the balance of payments: it raises the price level and thereby reduces the **real money supply**. Put in nominal terms, a devaluation raises nominal GNP because of an increase in the price level, and it thereby increases the demand for nominal money balances. In either form, the conclusion is the same: the problem of the excess supply of money is solved. Short-term elasticities of demand and Keynesian absorption conditions are unimportant. The only important role of a devaluation is to raise the price level, thereby reducing the real money supply (or increasing the demand for nominal money balances) and eliminating the excess supply of money that caused the deficit.[5]

According to this model, devaluations fail when they are followed by further increases in the nominal money supply that recreate the original disequilibrium. Repetitive cycles of balance-of-payments deficit, devaluation, price increases, money supply growth, payments deficit, and devaluation are the common result. Some Latin American countries, for example, frequently face huge payments deficits and have to devalue. The prices of imports, and then of other goods and services, rise, thereby reducing the real money supply and moving the balance of payments toward equilibrium. The central bank, however, then allows the money supply to grow too rapidly, probably because it is compelled to monetize a government budget deficit, thereby recreating the excess supply of money and the excess demand for goods and financial assets. The balance of payments returns to deficit, and soon another devaluation is needed, starting the cycle all over again.

Only when the central bank sustains a restrictive monetary policy, which typically means when the government no longer forces the central bank to monetize large budget deficits, can any balance-of-payments adjustment program be successful. With or without exchange rate adjustments, fiscal and monetary austerity is necessary if payments deficits are to be resolved, which again suggests why stabilization programs are so unpopular in developing countries. The medicine may be necessary, but that fact does not make it pleasant.

If inflationary momentum exists, encouraged by labor unions and oligopolistic firms, it becomes even more difficult to make a devaluation successful. If monetary policy really is tightened, but wage and price increases continue (perhaps because people do not trust the central bank to actually pursue a tight policy), the real money supply falls sharply, which is likely to produce a nasty recession. Many countries in this situation have found that temporary wage and price controls can be useful while the central bank builds credibility for its tighter policies. These so-called heterodox adjustment programs, which combine temporary wage and price controls with restrictive fiscal and monetary policies, have had some success in Latin America and Israel. It is critical to the success of this approach, however, that the wage and price controls be temporary and that the macroeconomic policy tightening be convincing. Any suspicion that fiscal and monetary discipline is lacking will renew inflationary expectations and speculative capital outflows, thereby guaranteeing the failure of the adjustment program.[6]

Managing a central bank during such an adjustment program becomes particularly difficult if the demand for the local currency becomes volatile. Local money demand may have been previously depressed by the expectation of a devaluation, producing a very high velocity of money for the local currency. If the devaluation occurs, and people believe that the central bank will avoid future inflation and a repetition of the devaluation, the demand for the local currency will rise sharply as people try to rebuild local cash balances. Since the money supply is not being allowed to grow, this sharp increase in the demand for local money (i.e. a reduced velocity of money) can produce a severe tightening of monetary conditions and a recession. The central bank must somehow allow the money supply to grow fast enough to allow for increases in money demand, thereby avoiding severe contractionary pressures, but not fast enough to renew inflationary expectations. This is sometimes made easier by the maintenance of temporary capital controls to limit the impact of international capital flows on domestic financial markets.

Effects of the exchange rate on the capital account

The discussion thus far has stressed the response of the current account to the exchange rate, and it may have created the incorrect impression that there are no additional effects of the exchange rate on the capital account. Since a devaluation increases nominal GNP, it should increase the demand for money and raise interest rates. The result should be an inflow of capital and an improvement in the balance of payments.

In addition, the devaluation was probably preceded by a period of speculative capital outflows, creating the possibility of large reverse flows after the parity change. If investors had suspected that a devaluation would occur, they would have shifted large sums of money into foreign financial assets before that event. When the devaluation is complete, they might be expected to return these funds to the home market. This reflow of speculative capital will occur, however, only if the devaluation is large enough, and if macroeconomic policies are sufficiently restrictive, to convince investors that the devaluation will not be repeated soon. If, for example, the market consensus is that a 20 percent devaluation is needed, an announcement of a 10 percent parity adjustment will not cause a return of speculative funds. Investors will suspect that another 10 percent devaluation will occur relatively soon, and so they will merely wait. A devaluation that is followed by a continuation of inflationary monetary and fiscal policies will also fail to attract speculative capital reflows, because investors will see such a parity change as the first of a potentially endless series.

Direct investment will also be affected by a devaluation, but again this reaction depends critically on strict control over later inflation. Direct investment is based to a considerable degree on relative production costs in different countries, and a devaluation improves a country's cost competitiveness as a location for factories or other production facilities.

A 10 percent devaluation of the Czech koruna, for example, lowers the cost of hiring Czech labor by 10 percent compared to the cost of hiring labor elsewhere. This should encourage both foreign and domestic firms to locate more factories in the Czech Republic, but this effect will occur only if Czech wages and other costs do not rise sufficiently to offset the devaluation. A 10 percent increase in koruna wages and other costs, relative to such costs elsewhere, would fully offset the devaluation, and leave the competitive situation of the Czech Republic unchanged. The devaluation must be real, rather than merely nominal, to have the effect of attracting direct investment funds.

Capital losses and other undesirable effects of a devaluation

As noted earlier, devaluations are unpopular; the restrictive fiscal and monetary policies that must accompany such parity changes are only part of the reason for this public response. Devaluations produce across the economy a range of disruptive side-effects that add to this reaction. First, the prices of a wide range of imports and exportables rise, lowering the real incomes of domestic residents who purchase them. In an open economy, this decline in real incomes can be sizable.

Second, the local currency required to service foreign debts increases, imposing large losses on anyone with outstanding liabilities that are denominated in foreign exchange. Any resident who has borrowed abroad, and whose debt is denominated in a foreign currency, will find that the local-currency cost of paying the interest and the principal on such a loan will have increased by the percentage of the devaluation. People suffering such losses will be unhappy about the decision to devalue.

The largest foreign debtor in developing countries is frequently the government, and the budgetary cost of servicing public debts to foreigners increases by the percentage of the devaluation. The government of Brazil, for example, owes over $100 billion to foreign banks and governments, and virtually all of that debt is denominated in dollars or other foreign currencies. Whenever the real, which replaced the cruzeiro, is devalued, the cost to the Brazilian government budget of servicing that debt increases proportionately.[7] That cost increase makes it more difficult to maintain the restrictive fiscal policy that is necessary to make the devaluation succeed.

If unhedged foreign currency denominated debts, which are often referred to as currency mismatches, are large enough, and if many sectors of the economy have undertaken such borrowing, a devaluation can become extremely contractionary in its effects because of widespread insolvencies and bankruptcies.

Thailand in 1997–9 and Argentina more recently are particularly unpleasant examples of this problem. Thai commercial banks, unwisely believing the government's promise to defend the parity for the baht, and attracted by wide spreads between the high interest rates to be earned on local baht loans and the low yields at which yen could be borrowed, brought in massive deposits and other loans denominated in yen. These funds were converted into baht, without forward cover back into yen, which were loaned out locally at spreads of 6 to 8 percentage points. It looked like a gold mine, and would have been if the exchange rate for the baht could have been maintained. When the debt crisis of 1997 forced a large devaluation of the baht, however, many of these commercial banks became insolvent, producing a sharp reduction in the availability of credit across the economy and worsening the recession which followed.

Argentina was even worse. Believing that the currency board guaranteed that the local currency could never be devalued, many sectors of the economy, including commercial banks, borrowed dollars to finance peso assets without forward cover. Large public sector deficits, and serious doubts about whether the currency board rules were actually being followed, produced a financial panic in the winter–spring of 2002. When the currency board then collapsed, and the peso depreciated by over 60 percent, large sectors of the economy became insolvent. Massive numbers of bankruptcies followed, the banking system was closed, and Argentina went into a depression rather than a recession.

The debt crises of South East Asia and Argentina will be discussed further in Chapter 20, but for now the conclusion is that a government or central bank must never promise to protect a parity if there is the slightest possibility that the promise cannot be kept. What has become known as a "soft peg" is a likely disaster because it encourages gullible local banks

---

Box 17.2 The "success" of Mexico's 1994–6 adjustment program

It would be hard to find a more successful IMF stabilization program than that for Mexico in the mid-1990s. After the debt crisis of late 1994, the peso was devalued sharply (from 3.1 pesos to the dollar in 1993 to 7.6 by the end of 1995) and decidedly restrictive monetary and fiscal policies were adopted, as the IMF and other lenders provided about $40 billion. It worked. Mexico's current account moved from a deficit of about $30 billion in 1994 to only $1.6 billion in 1995, and remained strong in later years. Capital flows came back into the country and foreign exchange reserves, which had fallen from $25 billion to about $6 billion during 1994, recovered to $17 billion in 1995 and $25 billion by the end of 1997. Real output has grown strongly, particularly in the form of exports to the United States, which have boomed.

But there were enormous costs. Consumer price inflation, fed by higher local currency costs for imports and exportables, accelerated to an annual rate of about 35 percent in 1995–6, before declining to 21 percent in 1997. Wage rates did not keep up, so the real wage fell by 25 percent in 1995, and did not recover in 1996–7. Four million workers moved from being merely poor to being in extreme poverty, this being defined as living on $2 or less per day per person. Previously, only 14 percent of all workers were in such poverty; that number rose to 20 percent in 1995–7.

These numbers are now beginning to improve, but it was a brutal 4 years for many Mexicans. The problem is the lack of an apparent alternative program. Mexico's 1994 current account deficit of almost $30 billion meant that its citizens were literally living beyond their means in the amount of about 8 percent of GDP. Absorption had to be brought back down to what the economy produced; that happened, but it was not pleasant.

Source: Adapted from *The Wall Street Journal*, March 8, 1999, p. 1, and *The Financial Times*, February 12, 1997, p. 11.

---

and other firms to borrow abroad unhedged. When the weak promise is broken and the currency is devalued, financial chaos is likely to follow.

If a peg is to be maintained, it must a "hard peg," meaning one that is certain to be maintained. A currency board where the rules are followed or full dollarazation (or euroization) are means of imposing such a "hard peg." Another part of this lesson is that private businesses and government agencies must become less gullible, and pay little attention to promises to maintain a parity unless the evidence is overwhelming that it is a very hard peg; borrowing dollars, euros, or yen to finance local currency assets, without forward cover, is a quick route to bankruptcy unless the peg is as strong as the Rock of Gibralter. If the peg is that hard, however, local interest rates should be no higher than those prevailing abroad, making such foreign borrowing marginally profitable at best.

Where pegs are not sufficiently hard, governments and central banks may need to regulate uncovered borrowing in foreign currencies. Since the solvency of the commercial banking system is central to the operations of any economy, strict limits on uncovered foreign borrowing by commercial banks is advisable. Since the banks lend to domestic firms, whose bankruptcy would threaten their solvency, limits may also be necessary on unhedged foreign currency borrowing by nonbanking firms. Merely making it very clear that the government cannot guarantee that the currency will not depreciate or have to be devalued, however, may be sufficient because it puts all domestic firms on clear notice that they had better not become involved in large currency mismatches. The worst situation is when the government promises to maintain the exchange rate, which encourages firms to borrow abroad without forward cover, when that promise cannot be kept. Large currency mismatches, which result from foreign borrowing which is denominated in foreign exchange to finance local assets, can be very dangerous to a country's economic health and need to be avoided if there is any chance that the currency will have to be devalued.

Although those who have debts denominated in foreign currencies lose, those who hold assets abroad gain; this situation creates another political problem. Private speculators who suspect that a devaluation is coming frequently move large sums of money into a foreign currency in anticipation of the parity change. When the devaluation occurs, they receive large capital gains in terms of local currency. Such speculators, who make large profits while the rest of the economy is suffering, are likely to be unpopular. As a result, the decision to devalue, which allows such profits, may not be popular. A government can minimize such problems by devaluing as soon as it believes the payments deficit is serious, rather than waiting to be forced to devalue. If such a decision can be made and implemented before investors suspect what is under way and move large sums of money, large speculative profits can be avoided.

In addition to capital gains and losses, devaluations also produce more long-lasting income redistribution effects. Those industries that produce exports and import substitutes gain, and the rest of the economy loses. As was noted at the beginning of this chapter, the first effect of a devaluation is to raise the local price of imports, which allows price increases for competing domestic goods. Export prices denominated in the local currency are also likely to increase, as was discussed in the small- and larger-country cases described earlier in this chapter.

If the economy is viewed as containing two sectors, one of which produces tradables (exports and import-competing goods), with the other producing nontradables (mostly services, including government ones, along with highly protected goods-producing industries), a devaluation increases the real incomes of those in the first sector and imposes losses on those in the second. These losses occur through an increase in the prices that must be paid for tradable goods and the lack of an offsetting increase in nominal incomes. Eventually, prices and incomes in the nontradables sector may rise to match the increase in the prices of tradables, which is the monetarist prediction, but that final equilibrium may be long in coming.

In the meantime, these effects can sometimes have regional implications. In Canada, for example, the western part of the country specializes in the production of exports, while Ontario has a heavier concentration of service and other nontradables industries. Whenever the Canadian dollar has depreciated (depreciation is the same as a devaluation but in a flexible exchange rate regime), western Canada has prospered at the expense of Ontario, creating considerable unhappiness in a province with a large population and significant political power.

In many developing countries the tradables/nontradables distinction exists between the rural and urban sectors. Rural areas in such countries typically produce agricultural products that are exported (coffee, tea, cocoa, jute, etc.) and food products that compete with imports. In addition, export-oriented mineral extractive industries are generally located in rural areas. In contrast, urban areas typically have a far heavier concentration of nontradables. Government, banking, insurance, and a range of other urban service industries are usually nontradables. Because manufacturing industries are often highly protected by tariffs and other import barriers, they are not greatly affected by the exchange rate. A devaluation in such a country raises the prices of tradables (including food) relative to the prices of non-tradables and shifts real incomes from the cities to the rural areas. Such income shifts, particularly in the form of sharp increases in the local prices of food, sometimes result in civil disturbances in the cities of developing countries.

Finally, devaluations are unpopular because they are a public admission that the policies of the government or central bank have not been successful in defending the value of the currency. The creation and maintenance of a currency is one of the basic roles of a national government, and the announcement that that currency is being reduced in value relative to foreign currencies suggests that the government and the central bank have not managed that role prudently. Governments, preferring to avoid such admissions, often delay devaluations as long as possible.

Some countries devalue the way some movie stars get married: over and over again. Other countries, however, make devaluations and the accompanying adjustment programs succeed, and have become models for IMF stabilization programs. There is no easy way to predict who will succeed and who will fail, but the ability and willingness to stay with a program for a considerable period of time is critical. Balance-of-payments adjustment programs produce considerable pain and very few, if any, benefits in the short run. If such programs can be sustained for a period of time, however, the pain eases and the benefits become more apparent. The problem is surviving the short run.

This has led some observers to suggest that "firm" (nondemocratic) governance can be helpful, because it means that short-run political popularity can be ignored. Many countries with a history of nondemocratic governments, however, such as Yugoslavia and Nigeria, have had poor records of making adjustment programs succeed, while Mexico, India, and other countries with regular elections have been more successful. Whatever the political institutions, a willingness to manage short-run economic policies on the basis of long-run goals is vital to the success of payments adjustment programs. Short-run maximizing is an almost certain road to failure and to repetitive devaluations, followed by a "currency reform," in which a new currency is created that is worth 1,000 units of the old currency.

Before this section closes, a bit more should be said about the pain which is imposed on much of the population by devaluations and the policies which accompany them in developing countries. Tighter fiscal and monetary policies impose obvious costs across the economy, but the most striking impact may be higher prices for food (a tradable) in urban areas, which sharply reduces the real incomes of poor people in cities. There is abundant evidence that nutritional standards and other measures of health deteriorated in many Latin American cities after balance-of-payments adjustment packages were imposed during the early 1980s.

This pattern has recently been repeated in Asia. In Indonesia, for example, farmers did reasonably well in 1998 because the devaluation of the rupiah raised local-currency prices of food and other primary products, but life for poor and middle-class Indonesians in Jakarta and other urban centers became much worse. School enrollments declined sharply because higher food costs meant that parents could not afford to pay school fees, and instead had to put their children into the labor force.

The maintenance of exchange rates which overvalues the currency of a developing country is often and correctly seen as a way of subsidizing an urban elite at the expense of a much larger population of poor people in rural areas. There are, however, poor people in the cities who are injured by a devaluation, and the tight fiscal and monetary policies which must follow a devaluation harm both urban and rural populations.

It is easy to blame the International Monetary Fund, which designs and imposes the adjustment packages, but critics typically lack any realistic alternative policy proposals. It does seem clear, however, that somewhat closer coordination between the IMF and the World Bank, which are across the street from each other in Washington, would be very helpful. If the Bank were to fund programs to help the poorest and most vulnerable parts of the population when IMF programs are being implemented, the pain resulting from payments adjustment programs might be greatly reduced.

A brief consideration of revaluations

Thus far this discussion has stressed devaluations, in part because they are far more frequent than revaluations. Even so, revaluations do occur, and they have the same effects that have been presented above but in the opposite direction.[8] Assuming that the relevant elasticities of demand are high enough, the trade balance declines as imports rise and exports fall. The decline in the trade account works through the Keynesian multiplier to produce potentially large recessionary effects, which may have to be offset with expansionary fiscal and monetary policies. If the economy is fully employed and threatened by rising prices, a revaluation helps reduce aggregate demand and contain inflation. If the economy is in a recession, however, a revaluation worsens the situation. Revaluations are easier to impose on a fully employed economy, and are very painful if the economy is already operating at less than full capacity. In this case, macroeconomic policies would have to be strongly expansionary to avoid a serious recession.

Revaluations also reverse the pattern of capital gains and losses discussed above. Those who own assets denominated in foreign exchange lose, whereas those with foreign debts discover that the local currency costs of repaying such obligations decline. Such gains or losses for an individual have to be measured, of course, on the basis of a net foreign exchange position. If a firm has $10 million in foreign assets and $7 million in foreign liabilities, its net foreign exchange position is $3 million and it will lose if the local currency is revalued. Companies frequently try to maintain roughly equal volumes of assets and liabilities in each foreign currency so that their net position in each is close to zero. Hence they do not face such exchange rate risks.

A revaluation results in a decline in the internal prices of tradable goods. Imports are less expensive, and the local currency prices received for exports typically decline. This results in a decline in incomes received from the production of tradables, but an increase in real incomes in the nontradables sector. This real income increase takes the form of lower prices for tradables paid by those working in the nontradables sector. Revaluations are extremely unpopular with export- and import-competing industries.[9] Such industries often argue that the decline in local-currency prices that they receive for their output will force them into bankruptcy. Owners and managers of firms producing tradables, together with their labor unions, can be expected to argue forcefully against any consideration of a revaluation. As a result, changes in exchange rate are often delayed until long after it is apparent that a country's balance of payments is in fundamental and chronic surplus.[10]

The Meade cases again

In Chapter 16 we argued that fiscal and monetary policies can deal with combinations of inflation/deficit or recession/surplus quite successfully, but that they encounter serious conflicts in the recession/deficit or inflation/surplus situations. In this chapter we have suggested that devaluations are much more likely to succeed in adjusting a payments deficit if the economy is in a recession at the time the exchange rate change is undertaken and that revaluations are more likely to succeed at reasonable domestic cost if the economy is fully employed. Returning to the four Meade cases listed on page 368, a possible solution to each situation now exists:

Set of problems	Policy response
1 Balance-of-payments surplus and a domestic recession	Expansionary fiscal and monetary policies
2 Balance-of-payments deficit and domestic inflation	Restrictive fiscal and monetary policies
3 Balance-of-payments surplus and domestic inflation	Revaluation of the local currency
4 Balance-of-payments deficit and a domestic recession	Devaluation of the local currency

Real-world policy choices may not be as simple as this list would suggest. For example, the degree of domestic policy tightening which the balance of payments calls for in case 2 may differ from that required by the domestic business cycle, and fiscal policy may simply be unavailable as a short-run macroeconomic policy because of political constraints, but the direction of suggested policies is clear. Countries facing deficits and recessions should devalue, but they may have to adjust domestic macroeconomic policies to produce the desired level of aggregate demand. In the deficit/inflation case, the primary emphasis must be on restrictive domestic policies. If a devaluation is necessary, the fiscal and monetary tightening will have to be quite severe. The surplus cases are somewhat easier because there is no threat of foreign exchange reserves being exhausted. If the surplus is combined with a recession, there should be no thought of a revaluation; instead, the adoption of more expansionary domestic policies should be pursued. If inflation is a problem, however, a revaluation will both adjust the surplus and put downward pressure on prices, thus easing both difficulties, but again adjustments to fiscal or monetary policy may be necessary to produce the desired level of aggregate demand.

This problem of managing a combination of exchange rate changes and domestic aggregate demand management to find both balance of payments equilibrium and the desired level of GDP is best seen through a graph which was developed by Trevor Swann in 1963.[11]

In the original graph the vertical axis was the exchange rate, but that was with the past practice of defining that phrase as the local price of foreign money. With the current usage in which the exchange rate is the foreign price of local money, the vertical axis must be the inverse of the exchange rate. Moving up that axis is a devaluation, and vice versa. Absorption is domestic aggregate demand, which is to be managed with fiscal and monetary policies; a tightening moves the country to the left, and vice versa. The external and internal balance lines are both equilibrium functions, in that each represents a trade-off between two relationships. EB stands for external balance, which is defined as trade account being in equilibrium; as one moves to the north-east along that line, a devaluation improves the trade account, but rising domestic absorption, by raising imports, worsens it. To the left of that line, a trade surplus exists, and vice versa. IB, or internal balance, is defined as the desired level of aggregate demand, including both domestic absorption and the current account. As a country moves south-east along that line, the revaluation of the currency worsens the trade account, thereby reducing aggregate demand, but rising domestic absorption increases

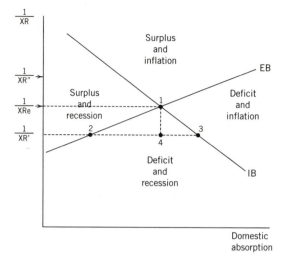

Figure 17.9 The Swann diagram. EB represents external balance, meaning that the balance of trade is in equilibrium anywhere on it. IB similarly represents internal balance, meaning the desired level of aggregate demand. Both goals are met only at Point 1. At 1/XR', the currency is clearly overvalued, but reaching Point 1 will require both a devaluation and an adjustment of fiscal or monetary policy, unless the country starts from Point 4. At 1/XR" the currency is undervalued, but reaching Point 1 will require changes in macro-economic policies as well as a revaluation, unless the country starts from directly above Point 1.

aggregate demand. A recession exists to the left of the line, and in an inflationary boom to the right. There is only one set of an exchange rate and a level of domestic absorption, point 1, at which the economy is at the desired level of output and the trade account is in balance. The four area of disequilibria correspond to the four Meade cases.

At 1/XR', the currency is clearly overvalued; the country cannot have both the desired level of output and balance in its trade account. At point 2 it has a trade balance at the cost of a severe recession. Alternatively, at point 3, it would have the desired level of domestic output at the cost of a huge trade deficit. Between points 2 and 3, it has both problems at more modest levels. The country would have a trade surplus only if it had an awful recession, being to the left of point 2. Only if this country is at point 4, directly below point 1, will a devaluation alone solve its problems. Anywhere to the right of point 4, a tightening of fiscal or monetary policy must be combined with a devaluation to get to point 1. Between points 2 and 4, when the country is far to the left of IB and therefore in a serious recession, a modest easing of macroeconomic policies would be combined with a devaluation to get to point 1. The reader can also see that the currency would be undervalued at 1/XR", and that similar requirements to adjust fiscal or monetary policy, as well as the exchange rate, would exist unless the country starts directly above point 1.

In the deficit/inflation region, to the right of both lines, a tightening of domestic macro-economic policies will clearly be called for, but exchange rate changes are also likely to be necessary. Only if the country were directly to the right of point 1 would fiscal or monetary tightening alone suffice to solve both problems and get to where the two equilibrium lines cross. Readers can visualize other sets of disequilibria with this graph, and see how both the exchange rate and domestic macroeconomic policies are likely to be needed to solve the problems.

This analysis brings us back to the earlier Tinbergen conclusion; if you have two goals, internal and external balance, you are almost certainly going to need two policies, the exchange rate and domestic aggregate demand management, to solve both of them. The broader conclusion is that, while exchange rate changes may appear to be simple, they are actually very complex in their effects, and quite difficult to make work in real-world policy settings.

Summary of key concepts

1   The argument for using a devaluation to adjust a payments deficit is analogous to the argument for using a price change to clear any market disequilibrium.
2   Devaluations are much more likely to succeed if the price elasticities of demand for a country's exports and imports are high than if the opposite circumstance holds.
3   The larger problems in making a devaluation work are macroeconomic in nature, the first requirement being that the growth of domestic absorption be held well below the growth of domestic output. This is a particularly difficult requirement to meet if the economy is close to full employment at the time of the devaluation.
4   Monetarists argue that since the cause of the payments deficit was an excess supply of money, the only important impact of a devaluation is to raise the price level and thereby reduce the real money supply. A devaluation will succeed only if it is followed by severe restraint on the growth of the nominal money supply.
5   If inflation can be strictly controlled, a devaluation results in a reduction in local costs of labor and other inputs when measured in terms of foreign exchange. This should make the country a more attractive location for direct investments, thereby helping payments adjustment in the capital account.
6   Devaluations raise real incomes in the tradables sector of the economy, but reduce them in the nontradables sector, which may cause regional and political problems.
7   The reductions in absorption levels which are required by a devaluation and a variety of other unpleasant side-effects make this adjustment approach very unpopular. Devaluations and the required macroeconomic policies often impose particular costs on the poor, adding to the unpopularity of IMF-sponsored adjustment programs.
8   When exchange rate changes are used to adjust a payments imbalance, shifts is fiscal and/or monetary policies will typically become necessary if an acceptable level of domestic aggregate demand is to be maintained.

Questions for study and review

1   Draw the supply and demand graphs for exports and imports for a small country that revalues. Do the same for a larger country. Explain the shifts that occur in the lines.
2   Why might a typical poor developing country be more worried about whether the price elasticities of demand for its exports and imports will be high enough to meet the Marshall–Lerner condition than would an industrialized country?

3 Explain why it is easier for a country to revalue its currency if it has a fully employed economy and faces inflationary pressures than if it is in a recession. Why is it similarly easier for a country to devalue if it has a recession than if it is fully employed?

4 Why do developing countries often find the macroeconomic policy requirements for the success of a devaluation to be particularly painful and politically unpopular?

5 From the perspective of a monetarist, what is the only really important effect that a revaluation has on a surplus country? How does this affect the surplus? What must the central bank do in order to avoid interfering with the intended effects of the revaluation?

6 "One problem with achieving balance-of-payments equilibrium through devaluation is that the therapy may be addictive. That is, additional devaluations become necessary." Why might this be true? How can a country avoid such an outcome?

7 What are so-called heterodox adjustment programs? Are they a sound long-term approach?

8 Use the IS/LM/BP graph to illustrate the effects of a revaluation. Show the fiscal and monetary policy changes that would make it more likely that a revaluation will succeed in eliminating a payments surplus.

Suggested further reading

- Agenor, P. and P. Monteil, *Development Macroeconomics*, Princeton, NJ: Princeton University Press, 1996.
- Alexander, S., "The Effects of a Devaluation on the Trade Balance," *IMF Staff Papers*, 1952, pp. 263–78.
- Alexander, S., "Effects of a Devaluation: A Simplified Synthesis of Elasticities and Absorption Approaches," *American Economic Review*, March 1959, pp. 22–42.
- Frankel, J., *On Exchange Rates*, Cambridge, MA: MIT Press, 1993.
- Goldstein, M., and M. Khan, "Income and Price Effects in International Trade," in R. Jones and P. Kenen, eds, *Handbook of International Economics*, Vol. II, New York: North-Holland, 1985, pp. 1041–106.
- Kamin, S., "Devaluation, External Balance, and Macroeconomic Performance. A Look at the Numbers," *Princeton Studies in International Finance*, no. 62, August 1988.
- Khan, M., "The Macroeconomic Effects of Fund-Supported Adjustment Programs," *IMF Staff Papers*, September 1990, pp. 195–231.
- Kiguel, M. and N. Liviatan, "Progress Reports on Heterodox Adjustment Programs," *Finance and Development*, March 1992, pp. 22–37.
- Solomon, R., *The International Monetary System 1945–1976: An Insider's View*, New York: Harper and Row, 1977, chs 6, 9, 11, 12, and 13.
- Yeager, L., *International Monetary Relations, Theory, History and Policy*, 2nd edn, New York: Harper and Row, 1976, chs 6–11.

Notes

1 The discussion of the problem of low demand elasticities begins with Alfred Marshall, *Money, Credit, and Commerce* (London: Macmillan, 1923), and Abba Lerner, *The Economics of Control* (London: Macmillan, 1944). The mathematical derivation of the more complicated case in which elasticities of supply are not infinite can be found in J. Vanek, *International Trade: Theory and Economic Policy* (Homewood, IL: R.D. Irwin, 1962). For a survey of more recent research on this topic, see M. Goldstein and M. Kahn, "Income and Price Effects in International Trade," in R. Jones and P. Kenen, eds, *Handbook of International Economics*, Vol. II (Amsterdam: North-Holland, 1985), pp. 1041–106. For more recent econometric estimates of the elasticities see Hooper, P., Johnson, K. and Marquez, J., "Trade Elasticities for the G-7 Countries," *Princeton Studies in International Economics*, No. 87, August 2000.

2 The J-curve problem is discussed in S. Magee, "Currency Pass Through and Devaluation," *Brookings Papers in Economic Activity*, no. 1, 1983. See also S. Magee, "Contracting and Spurious Deviations from Purchasing Power Parity," in H. Johnson and J. Frenkel, eds, *The Economics of Exchange Rates* (Boston: Addison-Wesley, 1993). See also K. Backus, P. Kehoe, and F. Kydland, "Dynamics of the Trade Balance and the Terms of Trade: The J Curve?," *American Economic Review*, March 1994, pp. 84–104.

3 The derivation of this version of the Marshall–Lerner condition originally appeared in J. Vanek, *International Trade: Theory and Policy* (Homewood, IL: R.D. Irwin, 1962). It can also be found in P. Lindert and T. Pugel, *International Economics*, 10th edn (Chicago: Irwin, 1996), pp. 619–21.

4 The discussion of the absorption condition for the success of a devaluation begins with S. Alexander, "The Effects of a Devaluation on the Trade Balance," *IMF Staff Papers*, 1952, pp. 263–78. A combination of the elasticities and the absorption approaches can be found in S. Alexander, "Effects of a Devaluation: A Simplified Synthesis of Elasticities and Absorption Approaches," *American Economic Review*, March 1959, pp. 22–42. The savings/investment relationship is discussed in S. Black, "A Savings and Investment Approach to Devaluation," *Economic Journal*, June 1959, pp. 267–74.

5 The monetarist analysis of the impacts of a devaluation on the balance of payments can be found in M. Kreinen and L. Officer, "The Monetary Approach to the Balance of Payments: A Survey," *Princeton Essays in International Finance*, no. 43, 1978, pp. 20–6. The effects of price level changes on the real money supply, which became known as the "real balances effect," was brought back to the attention of economists by D. Patinkin in his volume *Money, Interest, and Prices* (New York: Harper and Row, 1956 and 1965). An early application of the concept of the real balance effect to balance-of-payments adjustment can be found in Per Meinich, *A Monetary General Equilibrium Theory for an International Economy* (Oslo: Univeritetsforlaget, 1968). See also M. Michaelly, "Relative Prices and Income Absorption Approaches to Devaluation: A Partial Reconciliation," *American Economic Review*, March 1960, pp. 144–7.

6 For an analysis of the successes and failures of heterodox adjustment programs, see M. Kiguel and M. Liviatan, "Progress Reports on Heterodox Stabilization Programs," Finance and Development, March 1992, pp. 22–37. See, by the same authors, "When Do Heterodox Stabilization Programs Work?," *World Bank Research Observer*, January 1992.

7 For countries with severe inflation, occasional currency reforms are necessary to reduce the number of zeros in most prices to a level which cash registers can handle. Replacing an old currency with a new one, at a ratio of 1,000:1 has been a frequent occurrence in some Latin American and transition countries. Mexico, for example, replaced its old peso with a new peso at a 1,000:1 ratio in the early 1990s.

8 An unintended revaluation can occur if a major trading partner devalues. If, for example, 40 percent of Ireland's trade is with the United Kingdom and sterling were devalued by 20 percent, the Irish punt, measured in terms of its nominal effective exchange rate, would have been revalued by 8 percent. Large devaluations by major trading countries are often seen as threatening by their trading partners, sometimes encouraging such countries to devalue for defensive reasons. When sterling was devalued in 1967, for example, a number of its major trading partners, including Spain and Australia, felt threatened and devalued in response. This had the effect, of course, of reducing the nominal effective devaluation of sterling below the intended 15 percent.

9 For a discussion of the income distribution effects of revaluations, and of the resulting political obstacles facing governments considering such exchange rate adjustments, see R. Dunn,

"Exchange Rate Rigidity, Investment Distortions, and the Failure of Bretton Woods," *Princeton Essays in International Finance*, no. 97, 1973.

10 For a study of the effectiveness of a large number of devaluations, see S. Kamin, "Devaluation, External Balance, and Macroeconomic Performance: A Look at the Numbers," *Princeton Studies in International Finance*, no. 62, 1988. For a review of the effects of IMF stabilization programs, see M. Kahn, "The Macroeconomic Effects of Fund-Supported Adjustment Programs," *IMF Staff Papers*, June 1990, pp. 195–231. For a broad range of issues concerning exchange rates, see J. Frankel, *On Exchange Rates* (Cambridge, MA: MIT Press, 1993).

11 Swann, T. "Longer Run Problems In The Balance of Payments," in *The Australian Economy: A Volume Of Readings*, Arndt, H. and M. Corden eds, Melbourne: Chesire Press, 1963. pp. 384–395. Reprinted in Caves, R. and H. Johnson, eds, *Readings In International Economics*, Homewood, IL: Irwin, 1968, pp. 455–64.

18 Open economy macroeconomics with fixed exchange rates

Learning objectives

By the end of this chapter you should be able to understand:

- the impacts of foreign trade on a standard Keynesian income determination model: exports as a new source of exogenous shocks to demand, and the marginal propensity to import as a new leakage from the multiplier process, thereby making the multiplier smaller; the larger the role of trade in the economy, the larger the reduction in the size of the domestic multiplier;
- the transmission of business cycles through trade flows among countries maintaining fixed exchange rates;
- the $S - I/X - M$ graph as a means of illustrating responses to foreign or domestic shocks in this simple Keynesian world;
- why a fixed exchange rate and an open economy severely limit the ability of a country to use a domestic monetary policy to manage the domestic macroeconomy when that monetary policy differs significantly from that prevailing elsewhere;
- how domestic fiscal policy can be made more effective by a fixed exchange rate if international capital market integration is extensive, but less effective if capital market integration is very limited;
- how the IS/LM/BP graph can be used to clarify the arguments in the two previous items;
- why a monetary policy shift abroad imposes a parallel shift in monetary policy at home when a fixed exchange rate exists.

The second half of this book has thus far dealt almost entirely with the balance of payments and with exchange markets. It is now necessary to turn to the effects of international trade and capital flows on the behavior of a domestic macroeconomy, with particular emphasis on business cycles and on the usefulness of monetary and fiscal policies in dealing with them. This chapter will first add international trade to a typical Keynesian national income determination model to see how such trade affects the cyclical behavior of the economy. It turns out that the effects are sizable, particularly for an economy that is relatively open to trade, that is, for a country in which exports and imports play a large role. Macroeconomic shocks that originate within the economy are somewhat milder, because the Keynesian multiplier is smaller, but business cycles are transmitted from one economy to another through trade flows. Although this Keynesian approach might reasonably be viewed as oversimplified, it is surprisingly useful in understanding real-world macroeconomic events.

The Keynesian approach to foreign trade will be followed by the introduction of international capital flows and the overall balance of payments, which will allow a more thorough analysis of the prospects for successful management of business cycles with monetary and fiscal policies. The IS/LM/BP graph, which was introduced in Chapter 16, will be an important part of that discussion. In the section of this chapter that deals with the Keynesian model, the phrase "**open economy**" will refer only to the role of trade in the economy; later it will refer to the roles of both trade and capital movements.

The Keynesian model in a closed economy

Before introducing international trade, it may be useful to review briefly the closed-economy Keynesian model, in part because it is no longer included in some introductory or intermediate macroeconomics courses.

Our economy is assumed to have two sectors: a business sector and households. We assume for the time being that it has no government, meaning no taxes or public expenditures, and no transactions with the rest of the world, and that prices remain unchanged. The model will, of course, soon be extended to include international trade. If the government were included, its expenditures would be an additional source of demand for goods and services, and taxes would be a drain on demand because they reduce consumption spending power well below earned incomes.

Determination of the level of income

The gross national product of our economy is defined as the money value of all final products (goods and services) produced in a period of time, usually a year. This product can be divided into two categories, consumption (C) and investment (I). Thus we have the following definitional equation:

$$Y = C + I \tag{1}$$

where Y stands for GNP.

In the production of goods and services making up the GDP, an equal amount of income is generated in the form of wages, rent, interest, and profit. All income earned is either spent for consumption or saved. Thus we have another definitional relation to state the disposition of income:

$$Y = C + S \tag{2}$$

Setting equations (1) and (2) equal to each other, we obtain:

$$C + S = Y = C + I$$

and thus

$$C + S = C + I$$

Subtracting C from both sides yields the important identity which states that savings equals investment:

$$S = I \tag{3}$$

Equations (1), (2), and (3) express *ex post*, or realized, relationships. They hold true, by definition, for any past period. I is actual investment, which may contain an unintended component in the form of the accumulation of unsold inventories. Intended investment equals savings only when the economy is in equilibrium.

The amount of investment expenditure is assumed to be exogenously determined (i.e. it is independent of the level of income).

Consumption, on the other hand, is a function of income: when income increases, consumption also increases, but not by as much as the increase in income. This gives us a relationship (a "consumption function") such as the following:

$$C = C_a + cY \tag{4}$$

where C_a is the amount of consumption expenditure that is not a function of income, and c is the fraction of extra income $(0 < c < 1)$ that is spent on additional consumption. This fraction (c) is the marginal propensity to consume, defined as

$$c = \frac{\Delta C}{\Delta Y} \tag{5}$$

the change in C divided by the change in Y. For convenience we will assume that the marginal propensity to consume is a constant fraction.

We can obtain an expression for the equilibrium level of income by substituting equation (4) into (1), as follows:

$$Y = C + I \tag{1}$$

$$C = C_a + cY \tag{4}$$
$$Y = (C_a + cY) + I$$
$$Y - cY = C_a + I$$
$$Y(1 - c) = C_a + I$$

$$Y = \left(\frac{1}{1-c}\right)(C_a + I) \tag{6}$$

Equation (6) states that the equilibrium level of income is equal to a multiplier $[1/(1-c)]$ times autonomous consumption plus investment.

A numerical example can be used to illustrate the determination of the equilibrium level of income. We assume the following consumption function:

$$C = 50 + 0.60Y \tag{7}$$

where $C_a = 50$, and $c = 0.60$. Thus we assume that 60 percent of any increase in income will be spent for consumption.

This relationship is depicted in Figure 18.1a, which also shows the determination of Y for a given amount of investment. The consumption function, $C = 50 + 0.60Y$, shows how much is spent for consumption (vertical axis) at various levels of income (horizontal axis). The slope of the consumption function represents the marginal propensity to consume, $c = \Delta C / \Delta Y = 0.60$. The 45° line in Figure 18.1a is a geometric device, which represents all points which are equidistant from the vertical and horizontal axes; thus the level of income can be measured either horizontally or vertically. Since all income is either spent for consumption or saved, the vertical difference between the consumption function (labeled C) and the 45° line represents the amount of saving at any level of income. At point B, where the two lines intersect, all income is spent for consumption; hence saving equals zero. At lower levels of income, saving is negative – that is, people are dis-saving, or dipping into past savings in order to spend more than their current incomes.

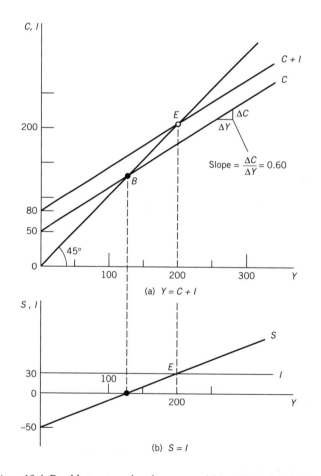

Figure 18.1 Equilibrium in a closed economy: (a) $Y = C + I$, (b) $S = I$. The top half of this graph, which presents the standard "Keynesian cross" diagram, indicates that equilibrium output is 200 because only at that level does total demand for goods and services, measured vertically, equal total output, which is measured horizontally. The bottom half of the figure illustrates that, at this equilibrium level of income, savings equals intended investment.

Given the amount of planned investment expenditures, which is assumed to be the same for all levels of income, we can now draw a line representing total expenditures $(C + I)$ for every level of income. In Figure 18.1a, we assume $I = 30$, and that amount is added vertically to the consumption function to give us the $C + I$ line, also called the "aggregate expenditure function." The equilibrium level of income is that level at which aggregate expenditure just equals the level of income as indicated by the 45° line. In Figure 18.1a, the $C + I$ line intersects the 45° line at E, indicating an equilibrium level of income of 200. It is clear that only one such point exists: at lower levels of Y, aggregate expenditure $(C + I)$ is above the 45° guideline; at higher levels of Y, aggregate expenditure is below the 45° guideline.

The solution can also be obtained by substituting equation (7) into equation (1), setting $I = 30$, and solving, as follows:

$$Y = C + I \tag{1}$$

$$C = 50 + 0.60Y \tag{7}$$
$$Y = (50 + 0.60Y) + I = (50 + 0.60Y) + 30$$
$$Y = 0.60Y + 80$$
$$Y - 0.60Y = 80$$
$$Y(1 - 0.60) = 80$$

$$Y = \left(\frac{1}{1 - 0.60} \right) 80 = 200$$

The equilibrium level of income may also be defined as the level at which intended investment just equals the amount of saving people are willing to take out of income. In Figure 18.1b, we show the saving function (S), obtained from the upper part of the diagram by taking the vertical difference between consumption at the 45° line at each level of income. The saving function can also be obtained by substituting equation (7) into equation (2), as follows:

$$Y = C + S \tag{2}$$

$$C = 50 + 0.60Y \tag{7}$$
$$Y = (50 + 0.60Y) + S$$

$$S = -50 + 0.40Y \tag{8}$$

The saving function shows that saving increases as income increases. Equation (8) indicates that 40 percent of any increase in income will be saved. The fraction, 0.40, is the marginal propensity to save, defined as

$$s = \frac{\Delta S}{\Delta Y} \tag{9}$$

As noted earlier, we assume that there are no taxes so that all income is either spent for consumption or saved. Thus it is clear that the marginal propensities to consume and save add up to 1.00, that is:

$$c + s = 1 \tag{10}$$

In our example, of each $1.00 of additional income, $0.60 will be spent for consumption and $0.40 will be saved.

The level of planned investment is shown in Figure 18.1b by a horizontal line at $I = 30$. The equilibrium level of income, at which $S = I$, is indicated by point E, where $Y = 200$.

Algebraically, this solution entails substituting equation (8) into equation (3) and setting $I = 30$, as follows:

$$S = I \tag{3}$$

$$S = -50 + 0.40Y \tag{8}$$
$$-50 + 0.40Y = 30$$
$$0.40Y = 80$$
$$Y = \left(\frac{1}{0.40}\right) 80 = 200$$

The two parts of Figure 18.1 contain the same information and thus yield the same outcome, although the lower part is especially useful for the case of an open economy, as we will see.

The multiplier in a closed economy

We are now in a position to explain how a change in investment expenditure (actually, any autonomous change in expenditure) will affect the level of income, consumption, and saving. To continue the given example, suppose planned investment increases by 10. This change appears as an upward shift in the aggregate demand function) to $(C + I')$ in Figure 18.2a, and as an upward shift in the horizontal investment line (to I') in Figure 18.2b. In both diagrams we see that the equilibrium level of income rises by 25, from 200 to 225. Thus income rises by a multiple of $2\frac{1}{2}$ times the initial increase in investment ($25 \div 10 = 2\frac{1}{2}$).

The size of this multiplier is determined by the division of an increment to income between consumption and saving – that is, the value of the marginal propensities to consume and save. In this case, with $c = 0.60$, when investment rises by 10, thus generating an initial increase in income of 10, 60 percent of that increase in income is spent for consumption. Therefore the first-round increase in consumption is 6. That increase in consumer expenditure is income to those who produce and sell consumer goods, and they in turn spend 60 percent of their increased income, so in the second round $\Delta C = 6 \times (60\%) = 3.6$. This process generates a sequence:

$$\Delta Y = 10 + 10(0.60) + 10(0.60)^2 + \dots$$
$$\Delta Y = 10(1 + 0.60 + 0.60^2 + \dots)$$

$$\Delta Y = 10\left(\frac{1}{1 - 0.60}\right) = 10(2.5) = 25$$

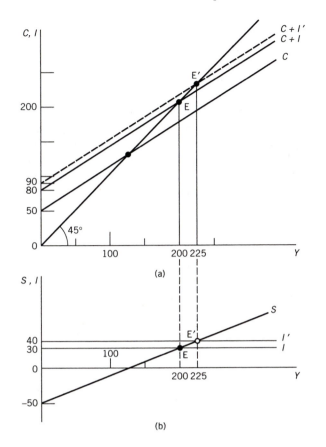

Figure 18.2 The multiplier in a closed economy. Continuing from the previous figure, if intended investment increases, C + I shifts up to C + I' in the top half of the figure and I shifts up to I' in the bottom half, both producing an increase in output which is based on the multiplier process. This is based on the marginal propensity to consume, which is the slope of the C line and therefore the C + I line.

More generally:

$$\Delta Y = \Delta I \left(\frac{1}{1 - c} \right)$$

where c is the marginal propensity to consume. The multiplier is the expression in parentheses:

$$k = \frac{1}{1 - c} \tag{11}$$

Since c + s = 1, we can replace (1 – c) in the denominator and write the multiplier as

$$k = \frac{1}{s} \tag{12}$$

This last formulation focuses on the so-called leakage from the circular flow of income. When people use their income to buy goods and services, their expenditure represents income to the seller and is thus returned to the income stream. That part of income which is not spent, namely the part saved, causes subsequent increments to income to be smaller, and thus reduces the size of the multiplier. In equation (12), the larger the value of s, the smaller is the multiplier, k.

If a government sector were included in the model, the marginal propensity to consume becomes lower because taxes make less of earned income available for consumption spending. This, of course, lowers the size of the multiplier. Government expenditures become an additional source of exogenous demand, playing a role in the model which is very similar to that of investments. Government budget deficits, whether from expenditure increases or tax cuts, are expansionary and potentially inflationary. Budget surpluses produce the opposite impacts.

An open economy

To extend this analysis to an economy that is engaged in trade with the outside world, we must allow for an additional sector, the foreign sector. Thus we will now include a third category of final product – exports of goods and services – and a third use of income – imports of goods and services.

Determination of the level of income

The gross domestic product is still defined as the money value of all final products produced in a given period of time. Since we are still omitting the government sector, the gross domestic product can be divided into three categories, and we have the following definitional equations for the product:

$$Y = C_d + I + X \tag{13}$$

and for the disposition of income:

$$Y = C_d + S + M$$

where X and M represent exports and imports of goods and services, respectively, and C_d is consumption of domestically produced goods and services.

In equation (13), we define Y as the value of final product produced domestically – that is, net of imports. In the case of consumption this is denoted by C_d, with the subscript d serving as a reminder that we mean consumption of domestically produced goods and services. However, we are also assuming that I and X are net of imports.

Now we can set equations (13) and (14) equal to each other and subtract C_d from both sides, as before:

$$C_d + S + M = C_d + I + X$$

$$S + M = I + X \tag{15}$$

Equation (15) states that, *ex post*, saving plus imports (leakages) must equal investment plus exports (the exogenous injections of expenditure). Although this relationship is a definitional one, it has interesting and useful interpretations. For example, when written in the form

$$S - I = X - M$$

it indicates a necessary relation between the trade balance and domestic saving and investment. If domestic investment exceeds saving in any period, imports must exceed exports. Similarly, if a country has an export surplus, its domestic saving must exceed investment; it is making savings available to the rest of the world, or acquiring claims on the rest of the world in exchange for the excess exports.

Note that this relationship can also be written as

$$S = I + (X - M) \tag{16}$$

In Chapter 12 we observed that the balance of trade in goods and services $(X - M)$ is equal to the change in the home country's net creditor/debtor position relative to the rest of the world, which can also be regarded as net foreign investment.[1] Consequently, the familiar identity between saving and investment still holds, with investment including both domestic and foreign investment. That is:

$$S = I_d + I_f \text{ where } I_f = X - M$$

Now we are ready to explain how income is determined in an open economy. We assume that exports, like investment, are exogenous – that is, the level of exports does not depend on domestic income. Imports, on the other hand, are a function of income: an increase in income leads to an increase in imports. This gives us a relationship (an import function) such as the following:

$$M = mY \tag{17}$$

where m represents the "marginal propensity to import," the fraction of additional income that is spent for imports. That is:

$$m = \frac{\Delta M}{\Delta Y} \tag{18}$$

For the purposes of this example, we will assume that m is 0.20. The import function is then simply:

$$M = 0.20Y \tag{19}$$

It is depicted in Figure 18.3, which shows how much is spent for imports (vertical axis) at various levels of income (horizontal axis). If it is assumed that exports are determined externally (on the basis of foreign levels of foreign GDP) and that the exchange rate is fixed, the graph shown in Figure 18.3 leads to Figure 18.4. The latter shows how the trade balance behaves as domestic GNP increases. With given exports and with imports rising by the marginal propensity to import times any increase in income, there is an inverse relationship between GNP and the trade balance. As can be seen, a trade surplus exists at low levels of income, but the surplus declines and becomes a deficit as the economy expands.

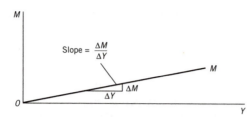

Figure 18.3 The propensity to import, and the marginal propensity to import. Imports rise with
income, the marginal propensity to import being the share of additional income which is
spent on imports and the slope of the M line.

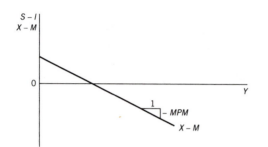

Figure 18.4 The trade balance as income rises. With a given level of exports, the trade balance declines
as imports rise due to an increase in domestic incomes.

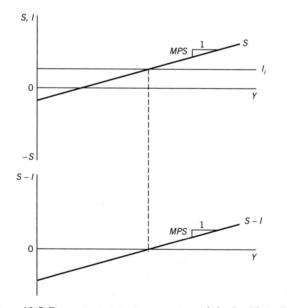

Figure 18.5 Domestic savings, investment, and the S – I line. Saving increases with income through
the marginal propensity to save, which is the share of additional income that is saved and
the slope of the S line. Intended investment is determined outside the model and is
assumed to be fixed at the level indicated by the I_i line. S – I is generated in the bottom
half of the diagram by subtracting the fixed level of investment from the savings line in
the top half.

Returning to Figure 18.2, we observe that we can derive Figure 18.5 by deducting the fixed level of investment from the savings line. An equation on page 411 expressed the following identity:

$$S - I = X - M$$

That expression can be presented graphically by combining two graphs derived previously. Figure 18.6 shows an equilibrium level of national income at which $S = I$ and $X = M$; that is, the trade account is in balance so that domestic savings equals domestic investment. Figure 18.7 illustrates what would occur if the economy were to experience an internal shock in the form of an increase in domestic investment.

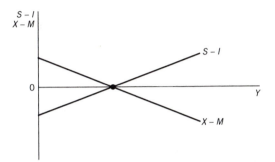

Figure 18.6 Savings minus investment and the trade balance with both at equilibrium. Putting the $S - I$ and the $X - M$ lines on the same graph produces an equilibrium point where they are equal. For the purpose of the illustration, they are both zero, but that does not have to be the case.

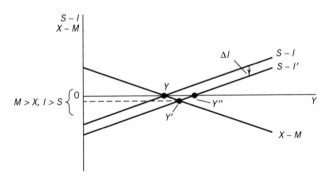

Figure 18.7 The impact of an increase in domestic investment. If intended investment increases, $S - I$ shifts down, producing a new equilibrium level of income at Y' and a trade deficit. If the economy had been closed, output would have increased to Y'' because there would have been no increase in imports to reduce the strength of the multiplier process.

The multiplier in an open economy

If the economy had been closed, national income would have increased to Y''', but because trade exists and imports increase with income, the resulting increase in national income is considerably smaller, as shown at Y'. An expansionary domestic shock produces both a trade

---

Box 18.1 Japan's chronic current account surplus: savings minus investment

During every year since 1980 Japan has run a current account surplus, and during the 1990s, these surpluses averaged about $100 billion per year. The reason for the surplus is straightforward: the Japanese save 30 percent of GDP, compared to 16 percent in the United States, and only 20 percent on average for the G-7 countries other than Japan. As a mature and highly industrialized country, it would be difficult for Japan to invest 30 percent of GDP in the domestic economy, so a huge and chronic current account surplus results. During the Japanese recession of 1998–9, investment in Japan was far from buoyant, but the savings rate has remained very high, so the current account surplus exceeds $100 billion per year. Complaints by the United States and other industrialized countries about Japanese protectionism as the reason for the surplus are simply wrong: as long as Japan saves such an enormous percentage of GDP, and cannot find profitable investment projects in the domestic economy to absorb that savings flow, a large current account surplus must result.

Despite being a developing country with enormous needs for domestic investment, China is following the Japanese pattern. The citizens of China outdo the Japanese, saving 40 percent of GDP. Even with an investment rate of 35 percent of GDP, a current account surplus must result. China's current account surplus averaged just about $10 per year in the 1990s, and if domestic investment ever slows, it will become larger, which will mean larger bilateral trade deficits for the United States with China and more complaints about Chinese protectionism, which are again irrelevant. Singapore is the apparent champion of excess savers: the savings rate has recently been as high as 51 percent of GDP when domestic investment was 37 percent, resulting in a current account surplus of 14 percent of GDP. What causes these enormous savings rates in East Asia is not clear, but as long as they continue, it will be very difficult for the United States, which has a current account deficit of over $400 billion per year, to return to current account equilibrium.

Source: Adapted from *The Financial Times*, June 4, 1996, p. 16, and Table 13 of the World Bank's *Annual Development Report* (Washington, DC) for 1998–9, p. 214.

---

deficit and a smaller increase in GDP than would have occurred in a closed economy, or in an economy with barter trade where exports always equal imports. The smaller increase in GDP implies a smaller multiplier, inasmuch as imports are an additional leakage from the income stream. In a closed economy without a government sector, savings are the only leakage, so a marginal propensity to save of 0.20 implies a multiplier of 5. With an open economy and a marginal propensity to import of 0.20, total leakages become 0.40 and only 60 percent of marginal income is spent on domestically produced goods, so the multiplier falls to 2.5. The multiplier is now defined as follows:

$$K = \frac{1}{MPS + MPM} = \frac{1}{1 - MPC_{dom}}$$

where *MPS* is marginal propensity to save, which would include the marginal tax rate on income if government were included; *MPM* is marginal propensity to import; MPC_{dom} is marginal propensity to consume domestic goods and services.

The marginal propensity to import in the United States is less than 0.20. Thus its impact on the multiplier is not large, but in a smaller and therefore more open economy such as that of Belgium, where the marginal propensity to import could be 0.40 or more, the so-called foreign trade multiplier would become quite small. The more open the economy, that is, the larger the marginal propensity to import, the smaller the multiplier.

The fact that domestic investment can have an import component provides another reason for more stability in the domestic economy in response to domestic shocks. If, for example, 20 percent of US capital goods are imported, a decrease in machinery investment of $1 billion would reduce domestic demand by only $800 million in the first round of the multiplier process, with the other $200 million in lost output occurring abroad. The greater the percentage of domestic investment that consists of imported goods, the larger is this dampening effect.

Another effect of trade in this model is that the domestic economy becomes vulnerable to external macroeconomic shocks that affect export sales. A recession abroad, for example, will reduce foreign demand for imports, which means declining exports for the home economy. A decline in export sales has the same effect on national income as does a decline in domestic investment (see Figure 18.8).

The decline in exports, which resulted from a foreign recession, caused domestic GDP to decline. Therefore the home economy imported the recession. The trade balance did not deteriorate by as much as the decline in exports because the domestic recession caused imports to fall. A shift in export sales will be partially offset by a parallel change in imports, resulting from changes in domestic national income. Hence the trade balance will not fluctuate as sharply as export sales.

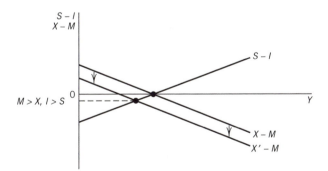

Figure 18.8 The impact of a decline in exports. If exports decline, due to a recession abroad, X – M shifts down to X′ – M, producing a lower level of output and a trade deficit. The trade deficit is less than the decline in exports, however, because at a lower level of output and income, imports decline.

The international transmission of business cycles

An important conclusion of this chapter is that business cycles of major trading partners tend to be linked through trade under the assumption of fixed exchange rates. A recession that begins in one large importer will tend to spread to its trading partners through declines in their exports. Small countries do not export cycles, because their imports are not sufficiently important in the other countries' economies to produce such an impact, but big importers such as the United States, Germany, and Japan certainly do export cycles.[2]

The short-term business-cycle prospects of the large trading countries are therefore of intense interest around the world. A cyclical turn in any of the largest importers brings the likelihood of a parallel cycle in many other countries; accordingly, the large countries are expected to manage their economies in such a way as to avoid destabilizing other economies. When such a country does a poor job of managing its cycles, as when, for example, the United States had an excessively expansionary set of policies during the Vietnam War, other affected countries become displeased. In such cases considerable diplomatic pressure may be brought to bear on the country that is causing the problems to improve its performance. The United States has frequently been the target of such pressure, which is often exerted through international organizations such as the Organization for Economic Cooperation and Development (OECD) or the **Bank for International Settlements (BIS)**.

Governments often try to predict the cyclical behavior of their major trading partners in order to adopt timely domestic macroeconomic policies to offset their impacts. If, for example, the Canadian government believes that the United States will enter a recession within a year, it may prepare to adopt more expansionary fiscal or monetary policies to maintain GDP despite the loss of export sales. If Canada were to use a more expansionary monetary policy to increase domestic investment expenditures, the situation depicted in Figure 18.9 would occur.

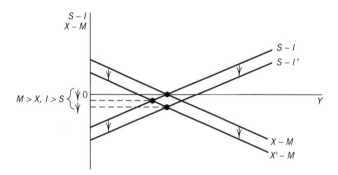

Figure 18.9 Impacts of a decline in exports and an increase in domestic investment. A decline in export sales shifts $X - M$ down to $X' - M$, as in the previous graph. If an expansionary domestic macroeconomic policy is used to recapture the lost output, $S - I$ shifts down to $S - I'$. The recession is avoided, but the resulting trade deficit is larger.

Although Ottawa was successful in avoiding the US recession, it did so at the cost of a larger trade deficit. A recession that originates in the United States can produce a difficult choice for Canada in a world of fixed exchange rates: it can avoid the recession at the cost of a serious deterioration of the trade account, or it can limit the trade balance deterioration by accepting the recession.

Foreign repercussions

This discussion has avoided one complication in its discussion of multipliers and of the transmission of business cycles from one country to another. That complication is bounce-back effects or repercussions. A recession in the United States, for example, will reduce Canadian exports and therefore Canadian GDP. The recession in Canada will reduce that country's demand for imports, which means a decline in US exports, which is a repercussion back to the US from its original recession working through Canada. This secondary loss of US export sales would deepen the US recession, which would further reduce imports from Canada, adding to the Canadian recession, cutting Canadian imports from the United States, and so on. These repercussions tend to be fairly small, and the rounds decline in size because each country has a positive marginal propensity to save. Thus only part of each repercussion is passed back to the trading partner.

The size and nature of the foreign repercussions, and of the multipliers that include them, depend on the values of the marginal propensities to save and import in both countries, where the marginal propensity to save includes the marginal tax rate on national income.[3] If there is a change in domestic investment, the domestic multiplier, allowing for repercussions, becomes:

$$\frac{1 + \dfrac{MPM_{row}}{MPS_{row}}}{MPS_{dom} + MPM_{dom} + MPM_{row}\left(\dfrac{MPS_{dom}}{MPS_{row}}\right)}$$

If, instead, there were an increase in autonomous demand for domestic goods and an equal reduction in autonomous demand for foreign goods (an expenditure switch rather than an expenditure change), the domestic multiplier, with repercussions included, would become:

$$\frac{1}{MPS_{dom} + MPM_{dom} + MPM_{row}\left(\dfrac{MPS_{dom}}{MPS_{row}}\right)}$$

Any multiplier formula rests on a number of assumptions, including assumptions about the influence of economic policy. Thus when US imports rise, inducing a rise in Canada's exports and income, authorities in Canada may take action to stabilize its national income. Then the repercussive chain is broken, because, with no change in income, there is no change in Canada's imports and thus no subsequent effects flowing back to the United States.

These alternative policy stances cannot be easily encompassed in multiplier formulas, except arbitrarily, but they are extremely important in practice. In an interdependent world, economic changes in one country can be and are transmitted to others. Economic policy in any one country must take account of these external influences.

Some qualifications

In the preceding discussion we have concentrated on the relationship between national income and the balance of trade. In the attempt to isolate that one relationship, we have made the simplifying assumption, common in economic analysis, that a number of other things remain unchanged. But in the real world, some of these other things do not remain unchanged when income changes, and we need to take note of the implications of that fact for our analysis. We will mention only two qualifications of this kind.

First, we have made no allowance for the effect of a change in income on money market conditions, especially the effect on the rate of interest. We have implicitly assumed that the interest rate remains unchanged. Actually, an increase in income is likely to lead to an increase in the demand for money and a rise in the interest rate. A rising interest rate would tend to check or restrain expenditure (for business investment, consumer durables, and housing) and thus constrain the rise in income. In omitting this influence, we have implicitly assumed that the money supply is being increased just enough to leave interest rates unchanged.

If the money supply were held constant, an increase in autonomous expenditure would lead to a rise in interest rates and thus tend to hold down the resulting increase in income. With a smaller increase in income, the induced rise in imports would also be smaller than we have shown.

Second, we have assumed that prices remain unchanged. In our analysis an increase in aggregate demand simply brings about an increase in output. This implies that idle resources exist and that supply is perfectly elastic at the existing price. In the real world, an expansion of aggregate demand is likely to lead to some upward pressure on prices and wages. For a given stimulus, such price increases will mean a smaller rise in real output, but they may make foreign prices more attractive and thus lead to a larger increase in imports than we have allowed for in our analysis. Here, too, conditions in the money market become important, as does the nature of expectations at home and abroad. The interaction among all these factors becomes extremely complex. Our only recourse is to simplify and deal with two or three variables at a time.

Despite these simplifying assumptions, the central conclusions of this discussion do operate in the real world. If fixed exchange rates are maintained, foreign trade does have the effect of reducing the size of domestic Keynesian multipliers, and the more open an economy is, the larger the reduction. Trade also links the business cycles of countries, with large countries that import a great deal tending to pass their domestic cycles on to their smaller trading partners.

Capital flows, monetary policy, and fiscal policy

Introducing international capital flows allows a more realistic analysis of how, and whether, macroeconomic policies can be used to minimize or avoid business cycles in a world of fixed exchange rates. Monetary and fiscal policies work quite differently in open economies where there are both trade and capital flows. This section deals with such policies under the assumption of fixed exchange rates, and its conclusions will be significantly altered with the introduction of flexible exchange rates in Chapter 19.

International capital flows will be assumed to respond to differences in the level of expected interest rates, as in the flow adjustment model of Chapter 15. This assumption allows the use of the IS/LM/BP graph which was introduced in Chapter 16. The portfolio balance model of Chapter 15 is intellectually more attractive, but would make the use of this graph impossible. In addition, the portfolio balance model has fit empirical data rather poorly, and the flow adjustment model, however oversimplified, often seems to be a more realistic representation of what actually occurs in international capital markets.

Monetary policy

The adoption of an expansionary monetary policy, which lowers interest rates, will encourage capital outflows. If international capital market integration is close, as is certainly the case for the major industrialized countries, these flows can be quite large. In addition, an expansionary monetary policy can be expected to increase domestic incomes and/or the price level, both of which would worsen the current account. For industrialized countries, the capital account response is very likely to be far larger and more prompt than the current account shift, and capital flows will be stressed in the following discussion. It ought to be remembered, however, that an expansionary monetary policy can be expected to worsen both the current and capital accounts, with the former impact being of greater importance in developing countries.

The resulting balance-of-payments deficit will cause a parallel loss of foreign exchange reserves, which the country may not be able to afford. Central banks are often constrained from pursuing an expansionary domestic monetary policy by a fear that foreign exchange reserves might be exhausted by such payments deficits, particularly if reserves were low at the outset. More importantly, a balance-of-payments deficit, as was discussed in Chapter 15, automatically reduces the money supply, which reverses the original expansion, thereby returning the economy to the circumstances prevailing before the central bank attempted an expansionary policy. An attempt to sterilize the monetary effects of the payments deficit will merely recreate the payments deficit, the loss of foreign exchange reserves, and the decline of the money supply toward its original level.[4]

A central bank has very little ability to manage an autonomous domestic monetary policy in a world of fixed exchange rates, unless the other countries to which it is tied happen to want the same policies that it adopts. If, for example, Canada adopts an expansionary monetary policy at the same time that the US Federal Reserve System is doing so, Ottawa can expect few if any problems, but an expansionary Canadian policy at a time of restrictive US monetary policy is doomed to failure. The following diagram, which emphasizes the capital account, indicates how an attempt by the Bank of Canada to adopt an expansionary monetary policy would be frustrated by balance-of-payments flows in a world of fixed exchange rates:

$$\uparrow \Delta MS_{cn} \rightarrow \downarrow \Delta r_{cn} \rightarrow \uparrow \Delta I_{cn} \rightarrow \uparrow \Delta Y_{cn}$$
$$\downarrow$$
$$\rightarrow \downarrow \Delta KA_{cn} \rightarrow \downarrow \Delta BOP_{cn} \rightarrow \downarrow \Delta FXR_{cn} \rightarrow \downarrow \Delta MBR_{cn} \rightarrow \downarrow \Delta MS_{cn} \rightarrow \uparrow \Delta r_{cn} \rightarrow \downarrow \Delta I_{cn} \rightarrow \downarrow \Delta Y_{cn}$$

(In this and later flow diagrams in this and the following chapter, the horizontal arrows are lines of causation and the vertical arrows indicate the direction of the change. Downward vertical arrows between lines indicate that what occurred above caused what appears below, and upward arrows between the lines indicate that what occurred below caused what happened above. Some of the later diagrams are too long to fit on one line, so where a lower line begins at the far left, it is a continuation of the far right of the previous line. Delta means change, Y is GDP, MS is the money supply, r is the interest rate, I is intended investment, MBR is member bank reserves of the domestic banking system, BOP is the balance of payments, and FXR is foreign exchange reserves. The subscripts refer to the country, the United States or Canada.)

The practical effect of this analysis is that a regime of fixed exchange rates ties the monetary policies of countries together, and these ties are particularly constraining if the countries have close financial and trade ties. The largest and strongest countries may be able to do as they wish, and their smaller counterparts are largely compelled to follow along. A Dutch central banker was reported to have said, before the European Monetary Union began operations but during a period in which the guilder was pegged to the DM, that monetary independence meant being able to wait an hour before changing interest rates to match changes introduced by the Bundesbank.

When the monetary policy needs of Germany paralleled those of the Netherlands and when the Bundesbank was well managed, this was not necessarily a bad arrangement for the Dutch, but if either of these conditions had not prevailed, a combination of fixed exchange rates and extensive economic integration with Germany would not have been pleasant for the Netherlands. Now that the European Monetary Union (a subject which is discussed in Chapter 20) is in operation, there is a single central bank determining monetary policy for Germany, the Netherlands, and the other ten members.

Box 18.2 IS/LM/BP analysis of monetary policy with fixed exchange rates

To return to the graphical analysis of the previous two chapters, a monetary policy expansion shifts LM to the right (Figure 18.10). With a fixed exchange rate, the result is a balance-of-payments deficit that results in a loss of foreign exchange reserves and a reduction of the money supply, which shifts LM to the left. Equilibrium is re-established at the original level of GDP, which means that the expansionary monetary policy was unsuccessful in increasing output and incomes. A tightening of monetary policy would have shifted LM to the left, creating a payments surplus, an increase in foreign exchange reserves and the money supply, shifting LM back to the right. Domestic monetary policy, when it differs from the policy being maintained abroad, accomplishes little or nothing in a world of fixed exchange rates.

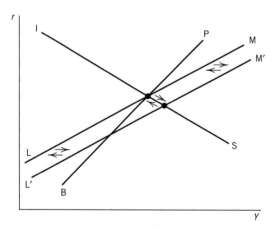

Figure 18.10 Effects of an expansionary monetary policy with fixed exchange rates. A monetary expansion cannot succeed because it causes a payments deficit and a loss of foreign exchange reserves, which automatically reduces the money supply, shifting LM back to the left.

The same circumstance that operated for the Netherlands and Germany in the past would now exist for Canada and the United States if the Canadian dollar were on a parity. Fixed exchange rates will work well for Canada if the monetary policy needs of that country typically match those of the United States, and if the Federal Reserve Open Market Committee can be expected to make sound and prudent decisions. If either or both of these conditions does not hold, however, Canada will face serious problems in maintaining a monetary policy which meets the needs of its economy while on a fixed exchange rate.

The decision by the United Kingdom to leave the Exchange Rate Mechanism (ERM) of the European Monetary System in the summer of 1992 was a direct result of this problem. The UK was in a recession and needed an expansionary monetary policy when the Bundesbank was pursuing tight money. As long as sterling remained within the ERM and therefore had an exchange rate which was fixed to the DM and other ERM currencies, the Bank of England could not adopt the expansionary policy which its economy required. The decision to float sterling created the necessary independence for the Bank of England, as will be discussed in Chapter 19. The later decision by the United Kingdom not to join the European Monetary Union was almost certainly the result of a continued desire to maintain the independence of the Bank of England in setting the country's monetary policy. The problems created by the creation of a monetary union are discussed in Chapter 20.

Fiscal policy with fixed exchange rates

While the conclusion of the previous section was quite clear, namely that domestic monetary policy is made much weaker by a combination of fixed exchange rates and an open economy, the conclusions in this section are more complicated and ambiguous. Introducing international trade and capital flows in a world of fixed exchange rates may make fiscal policy stronger or weaker as a tool of domestic business cycle management, depending on the relative strengths of two relationships. If capital account transactions dominate the balance of payments and if capital flows are sensitive to interest-rate changes, fiscal policy is made considerably stronger if fixed exchange rates are maintained. This situation might be expected to prevail for highly industrialized countries. If, however, capital market integration is quite limited and the balance of payments is largely dominated by trade flows, with imports being sensitive to changes in domestic incomes, fiscal policy becomes quite weak if a fixed exchange rate is maintained. Most developing and transition economies could be expected to fit this circumstance.

For the industrialized countries, where capital flows are likely to dominate the balance of payments, the conclusion that fiscal policy is powerful in a world of fixed exchange rates depends on the following line of reasoning: an expansionary fiscal policy will raise domestic incomes, which produces a parallel increase in the demand for money. With an unchanged domestic monetary policy, interest rates rise, which would tend to reduce or cancel the expansion of a closed economy, a process which is known as "crowding out." Since, however, the economy is open and the balance of payments is dominated by the capital account, large capital inflows will result from higher interest rates, causing a balance-of-payments surplus. A payments surplus, as was discussed in Chapter 15 and earlier in this chapter, will cause foreign exchange reserves and the stock of domestic base money to rise. The money supply increases, bringing interest rates back down, thereby avoiding crowding out, and allowing the expansionary impact of the fiscal policy to be quite powerful.

If, however, international capital market integration is quite limited and the balance of payments is dominated by trade flows, as might be expected to be the case for less developed countries, the line of reasoning is quite different. An expansionary fiscal policy increases incomes, which operates through the marginal propensity to import to increase imports and push the balance of payments into deficit. Foreign exchange reserves are lost and the stock of domestic base money declines. The money supply falls, further increasing interest rates, making the crowding-out process even more powerful than it would be in a closed economy. In this situation, fiscal policy is quite weak as a domestic macroeconomic tool. If foreign exchange reserves were low at the beginning of this process, the government may reasonably fear that it cannot afford the loss of reserves which an expansionary fiscal policy would cause, further limiting its policy flexibility. Developing countries are frequently precluded from adopting expansionary budgets during recessions by a quite reasonable fear that the resulting payments deficit would cause an unacceptable loss of already limited foreign exchange reserves.

The outcomes of an expansionary fiscal policy in these two quite different situations are summarized in the following diagrams.

Fiscal expansion with fixed exchange rates and extensive capital market integration

$$\uparrow\Delta(G-T)\rightarrow\uparrow\Delta Y\rightarrow\uparrow\Delta r\rightarrow\downarrow\Delta I\rightarrow\downarrow\Delta Y$$
$$\downarrow$$
$$\rightarrow\uparrow\Delta KA\rightarrow\uparrow\Delta BOP\rightarrow\uparrow\Delta FXR\rightarrow\uparrow\Delta MBR\rightarrow\uparrow\Delta MS\rightarrow\downarrow\Delta r\rightarrow\uparrow\Delta I\rightarrow\uparrow\Delta Y$$

Fiscal expansion with fixed exchange rates and little capital market integration

$$\uparrow\Delta(G-T)\rightarrow\uparrow\Delta Y\rightarrow\uparrow\Delta M\rightarrow\downarrow\Delta BOP\rightarrow\downarrow FXR\rightarrow\downarrow\Delta MS\rightarrow\uparrow\Delta r\rightarrow\downarrow I\rightarrow\downarrow\Delta Y$$

(In these diagrams, which are similar to that presented in the previous section on monetary policy, M is imports and KA is the capital account.)

As was noted earlier, an autonomous shift in domestic investment has the same impact on the domestic economy as does a fiscal policy shift, so the previous conclusions hold for such investment changes. If international capital market integration is extensive, an increase in domestic investment, which might be caused by a major technical breakthrough, would lead to higher interest rates and a payments surplus, which would increase the money supply and augment the expansionary impact of the investment surge. If, however, capital market integration is very limited and trade flow responses dominate the balance of payments, the same autonomous increase in investment would lead to a balance-of-payments deficit which would reduce the money supply, thereby limiting the expansionary impact of the original increase in investment.

The practical implication of this argument is that highly industrialized countries, for which international capital market integration is extensive, do have one domestic macroeconomic tool that can be used to manage GDP in a world of fixed exchange rates. A domestic monetary policy that differs from that prevailing abroad will accomplish little or nothing, as was suggested earlier in this chapter, but fiscal policy is quite powerful and is not likely to be seriously constrained by balance-of-payments considerations (a tight budget would cause a payments deficit, reducing foreign exchange reserves, which might be a problem). Although industrialized countries are not powerless in dealing with domestic business cycles, the circumstances facing developing countries, for which capital market integration is very limited, are difficult at best. Neither fiscal nor monetary policy can be expected to work well, and if either of them is used in an expansionary direction, one can

Box 18.3 IS/LM/BP graphs for fiscal policy under fixed exchange rates

Changes in fiscal policy are represented by shifts in the IS line because an expansionary budget increases the level of GDP at which total savings (private plus government) would equal intended investment. An autonomous positive shock to domestic investment would produce the same rightward shift of IS. In either case GDP must increase sufficiently to increase private savings to offset either lower government savings or increased private investment. The slope of the BP line relative to the slope of the LM line indicates whether international capital market integration is sufficiently close to strengthen fiscal policy with fixed exchange rates. Perfect capital market integration (where BP is horizontal) means that fiscal policy is highly effective with fixed exchange rates, as shown in Figure 18.11.

The fiscal expansion raises interest rates, which causes large capital inflows, producing a payments surplus that increases the money supply, shifting LM to the right and reversing the increase in interest rates. The result is a large increase in GDP. Increases in imports, resulting from the higher level of GDP, which might seem to imply a payments deficit, are overwhelmed by the large capital inflows.

If capital market integration is less than complete but still sufficient to make BP flatter than LM, international repercussions still make fiscal policy quite powerful in a world of fixed exchange rates. The fiscal expansion still produces higher interest rates and capital inflows that lead to a payments surplus, causing a money supply increase that supports the purpose of the larger budget deficit as shown in Figure 18.12.

The case in which capital market integration is weak, so that the current account response to fiscal policy changes dominate the capital account response, is represented by the BP line being steeper than the LM line. A fiscal expansion leads to a payments deficit, causing the money supply to fall, thereby shifting the LM line to the left. This

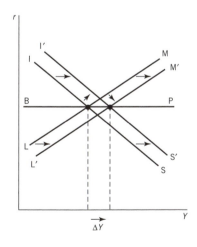

Figure 18.11 Effects of fiscal policy expansion with perfect capital mobility. If a fixed exchange rate is maintained and capital is perfectly mobile internationally, fiscal policy is very powerful. An expansionary policy increases interest rates, which causes large capital inflows and a payments surplus. The money supply then increases, shifting LM to the right, producing a large increase in GDP at the world interest rate.

significantly reduces the impact of a fiscal expansion on GDP as can be seen in Figure 18.13.

If there were no capital market integration, so that the balance of payments consisted only of the trade account and flows of foreign exchange reserves, BP would be vertical. Readers can adapt Figure 18.13 to that circumstance to see why fiscal policy would be totally ineffective in changing GDP.

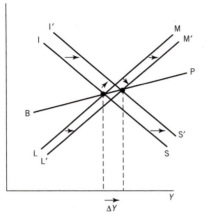

Figure 18.12 Effects of fiscal policy expansion when BP is flatter than LM. With a high degree of capital mobility, but not perfect mobility, fiscal policy remains quite powerful. With a fixed exchange rate, an expansionary fiscal policy shift causes interest rates to rise, attracting capital inflows that produce a payments surplus and an increase in the money supply, which shifts LM to the right, thereby increasing the expansionary impact on GDP.

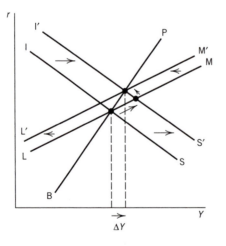

Figure 18.13 Effects of fiscal policy expansion when BP is steeper than LM. With very limited capital mobility, meaning that BP is steeper than LM, fiscal policy is quite weak with a fixed exchange rate. An expansionary policy causes a payments deficit, which causes the money supply to contract, shifting LM to the left and reducing the expansionary impact on GDP.

expect a loss of foreign exchange reserves that could threaten a payments crisis. A regime of fixed exchange rates leaves developing countries with very little domestic macroeconomic policy autonomy.

Domestic macroeconomic impacts of foreign shocks

In the first part of this chapter it was argued that a cyclical expansion abroad, which could be caused either by an autonomous increase in investment or by an expansionary fiscal policy, would cause an improvement in the home country's trade account and an expansion of its economy. This Keynesian approach allowed only for trade account effects; if capital flows and the effects of balance-of-payments disequilibria on the domestic money supply are introduced, the analysis becomes more complicated and the conclusions potentially ambiguous.

If international capital market integration is extensive, so the expanding foreign economy goes into payments surplus because of interest rate increases and large capital inflows, the home country obviously goes into payments deficit, which will reduce the money supply. The home country's trade account, however, went into surplus, as explained by the Keynesian approach, because higher foreign incomes result in higher imports which are the home country's exports. The overall impacts on the home country's GDP are uncertain. The trade account has improved, which is expansionary, but large capital outflows have resulted in a balance-of-payments deficit, which reduces the money supply, with restrictive results. The net impact on domestic GDP depends on the relative strengths of these two forces, as illustrated in the diagram below, in which the impacts on Canada of a shock originating in the United States are presented.

$$\uparrow \Delta Y_{us} \rightarrow \uparrow \Delta M_{us} \rightarrow \uparrow \Delta X_{cn} \rightarrow \uparrow \Delta Y_{cn}$$
$$\downarrow$$
$$\rightarrow \uparrow MD_{us} \rightarrow \uparrow \Delta r_{us} \rightarrow \uparrow \Delta KA_{us} \rightarrow \downarrow \Delta KA_{cn} \rightarrow \downarrow \Delta BOP_{cn} \rightarrow \downarrow \Delta FXR_{cn} \rightarrow$$
$$\downarrow \Delta MBR_{cn} \rightarrow \downarrow \Delta MS_{cn} \rightarrow \uparrow \Delta r_{cn} \rightarrow \downarrow \Delta I_{cn} \rightarrow \downarrow \Delta Y_{cn}$$

Box 18.4 Impacts of an expansion abroad with extensive capital market integration

Students wishing to analyze this case with the IS/LM/BP graph should start with BP being flatter than LM. The IS line shifts to the right (the trade account improves) and the BP line shifts to the left (higher interest rates abroad result in large capital outflows). LM and the new IS cross to the right of BP, indicating a payments deficit, which causes LM to shift left. The overall impact on GDP is unclear, the only certain conclusion being that domestic interest rates increase.

If international capital market integration is not extensive, meaning that trade flows dominate capital account transactions, the domestic impacts of foreign real-sector shocks become clearer. An expansion abroad, caused by an expansionary budget or an autonomous increase in investment, will cause the home country's trade account and balance-of-payments account to go into surplus. The trade account surplus increases domestic output directly, and the payments surplus increases the money supply, with further expansionary impacts. In this case a macroeconomic expansion abroad has unambiguously expansionary impacts on the domestic economy. The following diagram illustrates this situation, again in terms of the effects on Canada of a shock originating in the United States.

$$\uparrow\Delta Y_{us}\rightarrow\uparrow\Delta M_{us}\rightarrow\uparrow\Delta X_{cn}\rightarrow\uparrow\Delta Y_{cn}$$
$$\downarrow$$
$$\rightarrow\uparrow\Delta BOP_{cn}\rightarrow\uparrow\Delta FXR_{cn}\rightarrow\uparrow\Delta MBR_{cn}\rightarrow\uparrow\Delta MS_{cn}\rightarrow$$
$$\downarrow\Delta r_{cn}\rightarrow\uparrow\Delta I_{cn}\rightarrow\uparrow\Delta Y_{cn}$$

Box 18.5 Macroeconomic expansion abroad with little capital market integration

The IS/LM/BP analysis of this case is more straightforward. Start with BP being steeper than LM. Both IS and BP shift to the right with the expansion abroad, because both the trade account and the overall balance of payments of the home country improve. The crossing point of LM and the new IS must be to the left of BP, indicating the payments surplus which causes the money supply to increase, shifting LM to the right. The final equilibrium point must be to the right of the initial situation, meaning a higher level of nominal GDP.

Domestic impacts of monetary policy shifts abroad

It was argued earlier in this chapter that a single country facing a large world with a system of fixed exchange rates cannot pursue an independent monetary policy, unless the country in question is very large and can compel others to match its policy changes. For a more typical nation, this leads to the conclusion that monetary policy shifts in the much larger "rest of the world" will be imposed on it. A monetary policy shift abroad cannot be avoided at home. Returning to the earlier US/Canada example, if the Federal Reserve System switches to a tighter monetary policy stance, higher interest rates in the United States will attract capital inflows from Canada and lower US incomes will reduce imports, causing the Canadian trade account to go into deficit. For both reasons, Canada's balance of payments goes into deficit, causing a loss of foreign exchange reserves and a decline in the Canadian money supply. Tight money in the United States becomes tight money in Canada, as indicated by the following diagram:

$$\downarrow\Delta MS_{us}\rightarrow\uparrow\Delta r_{us}\rightarrow\downarrow\Delta I_{us}\rightarrow\downarrow\Delta Y_{us}\rightarrow\downarrow\Delta M_{us}\rightarrow\downarrow\Delta X_{cn}\rightarrow\downarrow\Delta BOP_{cn}$$
$$\downarrow$$
$$\longrightarrow\uparrow\Delta KA_{us}\rightarrow\downarrow\Delta KA_{cn}\rightarrow\downarrow\Delta BOP_{cn}\rightarrow\downarrow\Delta FXR_{cn}\rightarrow\downarrow\Delta MBR_{cn}\rightarrow$$
$$\downarrow\Delta MS_{cn}\rightarrow\uparrow\Delta r_{cn}\rightarrow\downarrow\Delta I_{cn}\rightarrow\downarrow\Delta Y_{cn}$$

The situation described for the United States and in the previous flow diagram parallels the problems facing the Bank of England in 1992, as discussed earlier. With a fixed exchange rate for sterling, the Bundesbank's decision to tighten monetary policy imposed tight money on the UK until sterling was floated in the late summer.

<hr>

Box 18.6 Impacts on Canada of a tighter US monetary policy

Readers wishing to apply the IS/LM/BP approach to this case should begin with BP shifting considerably to the left and IS slightly to the left, creating a crossing point for LM and the new IS which is to the right of the new BP. The implied balance-of-payments deficit causes the money supply to fall, shifting LM to the left. The new equilibrium is at a considerably lower level of nominal GDP.

<hr>

Conclusion

Fixed exchange rates imply a great deal of macroeconomic interdependence, and the previous pages indicate just how constraining such interdependence can be. The domestic economy is vulnerable to shocks from foreign business cycles, and has little or no monetary policy independence in dealing with them. Fiscal policy is available for countries with capital markets which are highly integrated with those of foreign countries, but for those developing countries that lack such integration, even fiscal policy is unavailable to manage the domestic macroeconomy.

Relatively open economies have very little macroeconomic independence in a world of fixed exchange rates, and the constraints on developing or transition economies are particularly severe. This lack of macroeconomic independence, which grew as economies became increasingly open in the decades after World War II, was a major cause of the collapse of the Bretton Woods system of fixed parities in the early 1970s and of the growing popularity of flexible exchange rates, particularly among developing countries.

The following chapter deals with the theory of floating exchange rates, with particular emphasis on the open economy macroeconomics of such an exchange rate regime. The theory (the views of monetarists excepted) suggests a large increase in national autonomy in macroeconomics as a result of the adoption of floating exchange rates; the reality since the early 1970s has been less conclusive. Although some of the policy constraints described in this chapter and in Chapter 16 are eased by exchange rate flexibility, new problems have arisen that have meant that business cycles and macroeconomic policies are still linked when flexible exchange rates exist, although not as closely as under fixed exchange rates.

<hr>

Summary of key concepts

1   The closed economy Keynesian model is considerably altered by the introduction of international trade: export volatility becomes a new source of exogenous shocks that cause business cycles and the marginal propensity to import is a new leakage from the multiplier process, which reduces the size of the multiplier, particularly in a small open economy where the multiplier may not be much larger than unity.

2   Business cycles are transmitted among countries through trade flows, particularly from large relatively closed economies to smaller, more open economies. The Netherlands imports German business cycles, but Germany does not import cycles which originate in the Netherlands.

3   In a world of fixed exchange rates, a domestic monetary policy that differs from that prevailing abroad is not likely to have much success, particularly in a small open economy.

4   A domestic fiscal policy is likely to be more successful if the capital markets of a country are closely integrated with those of foreign countries, but rather unsuccessful if such capital market integration is lacking.

5   The IS/LM/BP graph is a convenient means of illustrating these cases.

6   A foreign monetary policy shift is likely to produce the same change in monetary conditions in the home economy, particularly if this economy is small and relatively open.

Questions for study and review

1   In Country X, the marginal propensity to save is 0.10 and the marginal propensity to import is 0.15. If only the income effect is operating, what would the effect be on X's balance of trade of an increase in domestic investment of $200 million? Explain.

2   In a two-country world of the United States and Canada, if a recession begins in the United States, will the existence of repercussions increase or decrease the depth of the US decline? Why?

3   Use the $S - I/X - M$ graph to show how a country in current account equilibrium responds to a recession abroad. What happens in this graph if the government then adopts a change in fiscal policy to restore the previous level of GDP? Why may this situation be unsustainable?

4   Use the IS/LM/BP graph to show why a domestic monetary contraction will not be effective if a fixed exchange rate is maintained.

5   Under what circumstances will a domestic fiscal policy expansion be successful in increasing GDP if a fixed exchange rate is maintained? When will it be unsuccessful? Illustrate with the IS/LM/BP graph.

6   What is the effect on Country A's macroeconomy of the adoption of an expansionary monetary policy by the rest of the world in a world of fixed exchange rates?

Suggested further reading

- Argy, V., *International Macroeconomics: Theory and Policy*, New York: Routledge, 1994.
- Baxter, M., "International Trade and Business Cycles," in G. Grossman and K. Rogoff, *Handbook of International Economics*, Vol. III, Amsterdam: Elsevier, 1995.
- Bryant, R., David A. Currie, Jacob A. Frenkel, Paul R. Masson, and Richard Portes, eds, *Macroeconomic Policies in an Interdependent World*, Washington, DC: Brookings Institution, 1989.
- Dornbusch, R., *Open Economy Macroeconomics*, New York: Basic Books, 1980.
- Filatov, V., B. Hickman, and L. Klein, "Long-term Simulations of the Project Macroeconomic Interdependence," in R. Jones and P. Kenen, *Handbook of International Economics*, Vol. II, Amsterdam: North-Holland, 1985.
- Mundell, R., *International Economics*, New York: Macmillan, 1968.

Notes

1 Strictly speaking, it is the current account balance that is equal to net foreign investment. Here we assume no unilateral transfers.

2 A great deal of econometric research has been done on foreign trade multipliers, linkages among business cycles of countries, and other macroeconomic ties among national economies. Much of this work was done through Project LINK and Eurolink. For a review of this literature and its main conclusions, see J. Helliwell and T. Padmore, "Empirical Studies of Macroeconomic Interdependence," in R. Jones and P. Kenen, eds, *Handbook of International Economics*, Vol. II (Amsterdam: North-Holland, 1985), pp. 1107–51. See also M. Baxter, "International Trade and Business Cycles," in G. Grossman and K. Rogoff, eds, *Handbook of International Economics*, Vol. III (Amsterdam: Elsevier, 1995), pp. 1801–64. See also S. Norton and D. Schlagenhauf, "The Role of International Factors in the Business Cycle: A Multi-Country Study," *Journal of International Economics*, February 1996, pp. 85–104.

3 Econometric estimates of foreign trade multipliers are far from fully dependable, but it may be useful to note the available numbers. According to estimates based on Project LINK, an increase in US investment equal to 1 percent of GDP can be expected to cause an increase of 1.60 percent in GDP in the first year and a cumulative increase of 2.73 percent, including allowance for repercussions from abroad. Canadian GDP should rise by a cumulative total of 0.63 percent due to the stronger export sales resulting from the US growth. Japanese GDP should rise by 0.22 percent and German GDP by 0.33 percent over 3 years for the same reason. See V. Filatov, B. Hickman, and L. Klein, "Long-term Simulations of the Project Macroeconomic Interdependence," in Jones and Kenen, eds, *Handbook of International Economics*, Vol. II, pp. 1117–19.

4 Much of the original work on this subject was done by Robert Mundell in terms of comparisons between regimes of fixed and flexible exchange rates. The latter regime will be discussed in the following chapter. See R. Mundell, "The Monetary Dynamics of International Adjustment under Fixed and Floating Exchange Rates," *Quarterly Journal of Economics*, May 1960, and "Capital Mobility and Stabilization Policy under Fixed and Flexible Exchange Rates," *Canadian Journal of Economics*, November 1963. These articles can also be found in R. Mundell, *International Economics* (New York: Macmillan, 1968). See also A. Takayama, "The Effects of Fiscal and Monetary Policies under Flexible and Fixed Exchange Rates," *Canadian Journal of Economics*, May 1969.

19 The theory of flexible exchange rates

Learning objectives

By the end of this chapter you should be able to understand:

- the difference between a "clean" and a "dirty" or managed floating exchange rate regime, the latter being much more common;
- factors determining whether the exchange rate is extremely volatile or instead more stable;
- why the business-cycle transmission mechanism, which was so powerful with fixed exchange rates, is greatly weakened by the adoption of a float;
- the far greater independence and effectiveness of national monetary policy with flexible exchange rates; why that independence, which is so apparent in the theory, is less apparent in the real-world management of central banks in countries with floating rates; the monetarist view as to why monetary policy shifts are likely to have real impacts that are short-lived at best;
- the impact of fiscal policy in a world of floating exchange rates; why fiscal policy loses effectiveness if capital markets are highly integrated, but becomes more powerful if such integration is very limited.
- how the IS/LM/BP graph illustrates the arguments in the previous two points;
- why monetary policy shifts abroad produce reverse impacts at home; that is, why an expansionary policy abroad produces restrictive impacts at home through an appreciation of the currency;
- why mercantilist trade policies, which make little sense in any exchange rate regime, are particularly unwise and self-defeating if a floating exchange rate exists.

In the decades since World War II, one of the most important debates in international finance has been between those favoring flexible exchange rates and those advocating fixed parities. Bankers and others directly involved in international transactions often had a strong preference for fixed exchange rates, whereas academic economists typically supported floating exchange rates.[1] In 1973 many of the major industrialized countries decided to adopt floating rates. This was not a victory of the professors over the men of affairs, but rather it followed the collapse of the previous system and the lack of a feasible alternative. At the time it was thought that floating exchange rates would be replaced by a return to parities within a few months, but the OPEC price shock and other sources of financial turmoil made that return impossible.

Flexible exchange rates have been retained not because they performed as well as academic supporters predicted they would, but in spite of unforeseen problems which they have created. They are still in operation primarily because there are no attractive alternatives. Fixed parities still pose the major problems that became apparent in the late 1960s and early 1970s, and none of the proposals for new or reformed systems, which will be discussed in Chapter 20, has thus far seemed feasible. There is now relatively little serious discussion of abandoning flexible rates.

This chapter emphasizes the theory of a floating exchange rate system; the experience of the last two decades is discussed in Chapter 20.

Since this chapter is one of the more demanding of the book, it may be useful to indicate at the outset how it is organized and what it is intended to accomplish. It begins with three brief sections that deal with the contrast between a clean and a dirty or managed float, factors determining the volatility of exchange rates, and the impacts of introducing floating rates on how international business is done. These sections lead to the dominant topic of the chapter: the effect of a regime of floating exchange rates on a domestic macroeconomy, or the open economy macroeconomics of a regime of flexible exchange rates.

The first topic within the open economy macroeconomics discussion is the mechanism through which business cycles are transmitted from one economy to another, which was introduced in Chapter 18. That linkage is significantly weakened by the existence of floating exchange rates; therefore this exchange rate regime may make a national economy less closely tied to its trading partners and more independent. This material is followed by a discussion of the impacts of floating exchange rates on the management of monetary policy. Domestic monetary policy shifts have more powerful effects on aggregate demand under floating than under fixed exchange rates, but this strengthening of the ability of central bankers to manage the domestic macroeconomy depends upon their willingness to accept a large increase in exchange rate volatility.

Floating exchange rates also affect the management of fiscal policy, although the nature of the effects will vary from economy to economy. IS/LM/BP graphs are used throughout the discussion of monetary and fiscal policies under alternative exchange rate regimes to illustrate the main conclusions. The effect of floating rates on a protectionist policy designed for mercantilist purposes is also discussed. Using protection to increase aggregate demand is unwise under any exchange rate regime, but it is particularly foolish with a floating exchange rate. The exchange rate can be expected to respond to policies designed to restrict imports in ways that will cancel the intended effects on aggregate demand and output. The chapter concludes with a brief discussion of the expectation (which ultimately proved mistaken) among many economists that floating exchange rates would follow purchasing power parity, thus producing relatively constant real effective exchange rates.

Clean versus managed floating exchange rates

A floating exchange rate supposedly eliminates any central bank intervention in the exchange market. Since, as was discussed in Chapter 12, all items in the balance of payments must sum to zero, the lack of any transactions that result in the movement of foreign exchange reserves means that the Official Reserve Transactions balance of payments must be in equilibrium. Balance-of-payments surpluses or deficits simply become impossible. The exchange market, and therefore the balance of payments, clears in the same way the market for copper clears – through constant price changes. The academic literature and the existing theory of flexible exchange rates typically discuss such a clean or pure float.

The real world of floating exchange rates, however, is quite different. Because managed or dirty floats do exist, central banks retain the option of intervening in the exchange market when the exchange rate moves too rapidly or in a direction the government does not like. There is considerable debate over whether such intervention accomplishes much, but it does mean that the balance of payments is not kept in exact equilibrium by the exchange rate.[2] The major industrialized countries which have floating rates exist in a sort of halfway house, in that exchange rates are allowed to move roughly to adjust the balance of payments, but intervention occurs whenever rates become volatile or move beyond what is considered a reasonable range. The goal of such intervention has been to produce not fixed exchange rates but less volatile rates. Some developing countries have carried the management of floating exchange rates to the point of operating something very close to a fixed parity. Such countries announce that they are on a float, but their central banks intervene so actively in the exchange market that rates move very little, but foreign exchange reserves are quite volatile.

For the sake of simplicity, the theoretical discussion of this chapter assumes a clean float; accordingly, it is assumed that the exchange rate moves sufficiently to maintain equilibrium in the payments accounts. These assumptions permit rather clear distinctions between the workings of a flexible and a fixed exchange rate system. The broad conclusions of this theory hold for the real world, though in a less precise way.

The stability of the exchange market

The volatility of the exchange rate depends on how items in the payments accounts react to shocks in the form of major transactions shifts. If, for example, a $500 million capital inflow occurs, how far will the exchange rate have to rise to produce offsetting transactions totaling $500 million? If trade flows and other transactions respond weakly to the exchange rate, a large appreciation might be necessary to absorb the $500 million, while a strong responsiveness implies a small or even infinitesimal rise.

The trade account's response to the exchange rate depends on the same elasticity conditions that were discussed in Chapter 17. Low demand elasticities imply a weak or perhaps even perverse response of the trade account to the exchange rate, which would make the rate more volatile. As was implied in the J-curve discussion earlier, the short-term response of the trade account to the exchange rate is unlikely to be very stabilizing. Thus other items in the payments accounts will have to be the primary source of stabilizing reactions to transactions shifts.

Stabilizing flows of capital, based largely on speculative motives, are the most likely source of such payments response. If market participants believe that the currency is basically sound (because the central bank is prudently managed), they will typically view any sizable exchange rate movements as temporary and as likely to be reversed. If, for example, the market viewed the British pound as being worth approximately $1.80 and had confidence that the policies of both the Federal Reserve System and the Bank of England were stable, any significant movement of the market away from $1.80 would be resisted by speculative capital flows. A rate of $1.83, for example, would be viewed as too high, encouraging sales of sterling that would drive it back toward $1.80. If a large flow of capital out of the United Kingdom pushed the rate down to $1.77, speculators would view sterling as likely to rise, generating flows of short-term funds into the currency, thereby stabilizing the rate. As long as market participants have confidence in the future of the exchange rate, speculation will be stabilizing. Accordingly, shocks to the market, such as large capital flows, will be absorbed with only modest exchange rate movements.

If, however, speculators lack such confidence and instead fear that exchange rates may face large unpredictable changes, speculation can be destabilizing. A decline in sterling from $1.80 to $1.77, for example, might create fears that this was the beginning of a trend, setting off a speculative bandwagon effect in the form of sales of sterling, thereby driving the currency lower. If such uncertain expectations exist, the exchange rate can be quite volatile.

How such expectations are formed by market participants is uncertain, but the degree of confidence in the relevant central banks is a critical factor. If speculators view monetary policy in one or both countries as unpredictable and subject to large changes, their behavior is likely to be destabilizing. They may view small exchange rate changes as the result of monetary policy shifts, and move out of the currency that is depreciating, thereby encouraging further changes in the same direction. Confidence in the soundness of monetary policy is important in any exchange rate regime, but particularly in a floating rate system. If the market fears the adoption of an unsound expansionary monetary policy, any sign of weakness in the currency will be seen as a reason to move to alternatives. Confidence in the stability of monetary policy produces the opposite result: a depreciation is seen as an opportunity to make profits by moving funds into that currency before it recovers to its normal exchange rate.

In a managed float, central bank intervention can be a source of stabilizing capital flows. A depreciation may encourage the central bank to support the weakening currency, and vice versa. If private participants in the exchange market believe that the central bank will behave in such a stabilizing way, they may be encouraged to follow the same pattern, that is, to support a declining currency in expectation that the central bank will push it back up, thus making their transactions profitable. Central bank intervention is sometimes intended to encourage such stabilizing behavior by other investors.

Impacts of flexible exchange rates on international transactions

Opponents of flexible exchange rates have frequently expressed the fear that the abandonment of fixed parities would discourage trade and other international transactions. Additional transactions costs (wider bid/asked spreads in exchange markets) and risks would encourage businesses to emphasize domestic activities and avoid international business. Studies of international trade during the period since 1973 provide little support for these fears. Some studies show no reduction in trade volumes, whereas others show small impacts.[3] Capital flows have become so enormous that they appear to dominate exchange markets; consequently, additional risks do not appear to have discouraged international investors.

Despite the increased risks implied by flexible exchange rates, trade and other transactions have continued to grow, in part because it is possible to hedge or cover such risks through the forward market and other routes. Conversations with exchange traders and other market participants indicate that the volume of forward contracts increased sharply after the adoption of flexible exchange rates in the early 1970s. Firms that were previously willing to accept the risks implicit in the narrow band within which spot exchange rates were allowed to move decided that these risks became too large when rates could move over an indefinite range. Rather than reduce or abandon their international business, however, they made heavy use of the forward market and other hedging techniques to avoid unacceptable increases in exchange risks.[4]

The adoption of flexible exchange rates had far less impact on the management of international business than many people had feared. Such business continued normally and has grown. Opportunities for speculation certainly increased as exchange rates moved over ranges that provided large opportunities for profits or losses on uncovered positions. For those wishing to avoid such risk, forward markets and other hedging techniques made such avoidance possible for many transactions.

Open economy macroeconomics with a floating exchange rate

Some of the most interesting aspects of the economics of floating exchange rates involve the domestic economy rather than international transactions. Many important relationships in macroeconomics are altered by the adoption of flexible exchange rates, including the effectiveness of monetary and fiscal policy shifts. The mechanisms through which fiscal and monetary policies affect aggregate domestic demand, for example, are quite different under a flexible exchange rate regime, as will be discussed later in this chapter.

The critical difference between systems of fixed and flexible exchange rates that generates these impacts is the absence of balance-of-payments disequilibria in the flexible system. Any economic relationship or process that is dependent on shifts of the balance of payments to surplus or deficit is eliminated because there are no such shifts. Since a clean float is assumed for this discussion, the balance of payments on official reserve transactions is always zero. That is, it is always in equilibrium, which means that movements in that balance cannot affect anything.

Since the exchange rate, rather than the balance of payments, moves constantly, domestic prices of traded goods are affected. As argued in Chapter 17, a devaluation increased local currency prices of tradable goods, whereas a revaluation reduced them. A depreciation has the same effect on prices as a devaluation, whereas an appreciation replicates the price effects of a revaluation. The domestic prices of tradables should rise when the local currency depreciates, and vice versa. If the markets for these goods are oligopolistic, however, these price changes may be smaller than the exchange rate movements and may occur with a considerable lag, because, as noted in Chapter 15, the law of one price often does not hold in less than perfectly competitive markets.

Business cycle transmission with flexible exchange rates

As shown in Chapter 18, international trade provides a mechanism through which business cycles are transmitted from one country to another. For example, a recession in the United States reduces US demand for Canadian exports, which reduces output in Canada, thus transmitting the recession to the north. This argument assumes a fixed exchange rate. With a flexible exchange rate this process becomes more complicated, and the transmission process is weakened, because the exchange rate absorbs at least some of the macroeconomic shock that would otherwise be passed through to Canada.

The decline in US demand for Canadian exports, which results from a US recession, causes a parallel decline in the exchange market demand for Canadian dollars to pay for those exports. With a fixed exchange rate, Canada would have a payments deficit and incur a loss of foreign exchange reserves. With a floating exchange rate, however, the Canadian dollar would depreciate sufficiently to return the balance of payments to equilibrium. Canada does not have a balance-of-payments deficit, but instead a lower exchange rate. The depreciation of the Canadian dollar should encourage exports and discourage imports, producing a recovery of the trade account. Low short-term demand elasticities may delay this response, but after the J-curve lag has passed, Canada's trade account should recover to approximately its previous position. In the meantime, if speculators view the US recession and its impact on the exchange rate as temporary, they can be expected to support the Canadian dollar. The contrast between macroeconomic linkages under the two systems can be seen in the following diagrams:

Fixed exchange rates

$$\downarrow\Delta Y_{us}\rightarrow\downarrow\Delta M_{us}\rightarrow\downarrow\Delta X_{cn}\rightarrow\downarrow\Delta Y_{cn}$$

Flexible exchange rates

$$\downarrow\Delta Y_{us}\rightarrow\downarrow\Delta M_{us}\rightarrow\downarrow\Delta X_{cn}\rightarrow\downarrow\Delta XR_{cn}\rightarrow\uparrow\Delta X_{cn}\rightarrow\uparrow\Delta(X-M)_{cn}$$
$$\downarrow\qquad\qquad\uparrow$$
$$\rightarrow\downarrow\Delta M_{cn}\rightarrow$$

If the trade account were the sole source of adjustment to the exchange rate, the improvement in the Canadian current account that completes the diagram should exactly match the original loss of Canadian exports, leaving the current account and Canadian aggregate demand unaffected by the US recession. If stabilizing speculative capital flows, or central bank intervention under a managed float, supports the Canadian dollar, the current account reaction to the exchange rate will be less than the original loss of export sales, leaving a current account deterioration and some recessionary impacts in Canada. The exchange rate and the resulting response of the current account, however, will still absorb part of the macroeconomic shock from the United States, leaving Canada somewhat less vulnerable to recessions that originate in the United States. If international trade were the only source of supply and demand in the market for foreign exchange, a clean float would mean that the trade account was always in balance. Such a situation would completely isolate total demand in a domestic economy from foreign business cycles transmitted through the trade account. In a more realistic world which includes speculative capital flows and central bank intervention, floating exchange rates reduce the extent to which business cycles are passed from one country to another but do not eliminate the mechanism.

It should be noted that price effects of foreign business cycles are passed through the exchange rate. In the previous example, the depreciation of the Canadian dollar, which resulted from the US recession, could be expected to increase the Canadian prices of tradable goods. Since Canada has a decidedly open economy, this means considerably more inflation, which the Bank of Canada may find unacceptable. Some combination of intervention in the exchange market and a tightening of monetary policy, with the purpose of avoiding a depreciation of the Canadian dollar, may follow.

The greater the extent to which stabilizing speculation and/or central bank activities stop the exchange rate from moving in response to shifting trade flows, the closer we are to the fixed exchange rate situation in which such cycles are fully transmitted. If countries such as Canada wish to avoid the aggregate demand impacts of US cycles, they must be willing to allow their currencies to depreciate in response to a US recession and appreciate when the US has an expansionary boom. Any attempt to stabilize the exchange rate over the business cycle will increase Canadian vulnerability to US recessions.

Monetary policy with flexible exchange rates

One of the most striking macroeconomic effects of the introduction of flexible exchange rates is an increase in the independence and effectiveness of monetary policy. As was argued in the previous chapter, a regime of fixed exchange rates means that a central bank is constrained by balance-of-payments considerations (it cannot adopt an expansionary policy that would result in the exhaustion of foreign exchange reserves) and often finds that payments disequilibria tend to offset its intended changes in the money supply. In contrast, under flexible exchange rates the balance of payments is no longer a constraint, and movements of the exchange rate tend to enhance, rather than reverse, the impacts of monetary policy on aggregate demand.[5]

The reasoning behind the conclusion that floating exchange rates make monetary policy more powerful is as follows: an expansionary monetary policy still lowers interest rates and encourages capital outflows, but a balance-of-payments deficit and a loss of foreign exchange reserves no longer occur. Instead, the domestic currency depreciates, which improves the trade balance, thus increasing domestic output of exports and import substitutes. This depreciation also increases domestic prices of tradable goods. Since there is no loss of foreign exchange reserves, there is no decline in member bank reserves or of the money supply. The original increase in the domestic money supply remains intact, and the depreciation of the local currency adds to the intended expansionary effect on domestic output and incomes.

The following diagram, which can be usefully compared to that on page 419 in the previous chapter, illustrates these impacts with a clean floating exchange rate, again for an expansionary policy by the Bank of Canada:

$$\uparrow\Delta MS_{cn}\rightarrow\downarrow\Delta r_{cn}\rightarrow\uparrow\Delta I_{cn}\rightarrow\uparrow\Delta Y_{cn}$$
$$\downarrow$$
$$\rightarrow\downarrow\Delta KA_{cn}\rightarrow\downarrow\Delta XR_{cn}\rightarrow\uparrow\Delta X_{cn}\rightarrow\uparrow\Delta(X-M)_{cn}\rightarrow\uparrow\Delta Y_{cn}$$
$$\downarrow\qquad\qquad\uparrow$$
$$\rightarrow\downarrow\Delta M_{cn}\rightarrow$$

The international effects of monetary policy shifts enhance rather than undermine the intended effects of such policy changes. Flexible exchange rates have frequently been seen as a way of increasing the power and influence of the central bank in managing domestic aggregate demand, as is argued in Exhibit 19.1. Consequently, flexible rates are more popular among those who have strong confidence in the management of that institution. In contrast, fixed exchange rates are seen as a mechanism for restricting the power of the central bank and are therefore supported by those who distrust the central bankers. If the governor of a country's central bank is thought to be sensible and prudent, flexible exchange rates are acceptable; if that governor is thought to be incompetent and given to unwise policy shifts, fixed exchange rates are a better option.

EXHIBIT 19.1 WHY IS THE FED SUDDENLY SO IMPORTANT?

The question of Paul Volcker's reappointment generated controversy beyond anything in the history of the Federal Reserve Board. William McMartin was reappointed chairman a number of times with a minimum of fuss. Arthur Burns and William Miller arrived and departed without great debate. But suddenly the chairmanship had become President Reagan's most important appointment since he put Sandra Day O'Connor on the Supreme Court – and that term is for life, not a mere 4 years.

One reason for this extraordinary rise in interest in the Fed is that the constant acrimony between the two ends of Pennsylvania Avenue on the subject of the budget has produced chaos in the form of unmanageable deficits, and the widespread view here and abroad that the United States merely has a fiscal result rather than any policy. This makes the Federal Reserve Board the only source of thoughtful macroeconomic planning in Washington. With the federal budget out of control, monetary policy is the only game in town, and the chairmanship of the Fed becomes correspondingly more critical to the future of the economy.

A more interesting but less widely understood reason for the increased importance of the Federal Reserve chairmanship is that the existence of a regime of flexible exchange rates during recent years has made monetary policy a far more powerful tool for the management of the economy than it was in the previous era of fixed exchange rates.

With flexible exchange rates, the adoption of a restrictive monetary policy, which raises interest rates and attracts foreign capital inflows, will cause an appreciation of the dollar. This increase in the exchange rate for the dollar makes imports cheaper in the United States and American products more expensive abroad. As domestic and foreign consumers respond to these shifts in relative prices, US imports rise and exports fall, reducing aggregate demand and production in this economy.

The decline in the price of imports also forces US firms that compete with imports to restrain their prices, and US exporters are under strong pressure to reduce US dollar prices to remain competitive abroad. Flexible exchange rates make monetary policy an awesome macroeconomic tool. Tight money produces an appreciation of the dollar that literally forces a reduction in a wide range of prices of traded goods, and sharply reduces aggregate demand through a decline in the trade balance.

If a fixed exchange rate for the dollar had been maintained, the effects of tight money would have been less impressive. Higher interest rates would have had restrictive impacts within the economy through their effects on investment expenditures, but the foreign capital inflows that resulted from higher yields would not have caused an appreciation of the dollar, which forced down prices and reduced production and employment in the export and import-competing sectors.

Instead, the US balance of payments would have been pushed into surplus by the inflow of foreign funds, and this surplus would have increased the US money supply, partially canceling the Fed's original tightening. Although this undesired increase in the money supply could be reversed through domestic monetary policy shifts, it remains true that a tightening of monetary policy would not directly affect the exchange rate, the domestic prices of traded goods or the trade balance. A fixed exchange rate makes monetary policy a far more limited tool for the management of the economy.

Flexible exchange rates have the additional effect of reducing the expansionary impacts of federal budget deficits and of thus weakening fiscal policy. An increase in government expenditures that raises federal borrowing and interest rates, for example, will attract foreign capital inflows and lead to an appreciation of the dollar. As the trade balance responds to the exchange rate, the expansionary effect of the government expenditure is largely offset by the loss of output in the export and import-competing sectors. The intended effects of the expansionary fiscal policy are "crowded out" through the exchange rate and the trade balance. In any conflict between an expansionary budget and a restrictive monetary policy, the central bank will win easily. The success of the Federal Reserve System in dramatically reducing the US rate of inflation during the last 3 years is largely the result of a 35 percent appreciation of the dollar during 1981 and 1982. This exchange rate change was also a major cause of the huge costs of this disinflation in terms of output and employment. The appreciation had particularly harsh impacts on export sectors such as agriculture and heavy machinery.

The recovery of these sectors depends on a depreciation of the dollar that has been expected for some time by many economists but that has not yet occurred.

Whether one supports or opposes the "cold shower" approach to fighting inflation of the last 3 years, it is clear that the great importance of Federal Reserve policy to the economy results in large part from the nature of the exchange rate regime. If the United States maintained a fixed exchange rate, the impacts of shifts in Fed policy would be far less dramatic, and there would probably have been far less interest in whether Paul Volcker was reappointed.

Source: *The Washington Post*, Robert M. Dunn, Jr., © 1983, Op. Ed. page, June 22, 1983. Reprinted with permission.

Box 19.1 Canadian monetary policy in mid-1999

The Canadian dollar depreciated sharply in mid-1998, leading the Bank of Canada to raise interest rates by a full percentage point to defend the currency. By early 1999, the recovery of the Canadian dollar to almost 70 cents US was seen as threatening to export growth and to the continued growth of the economy. The Bank of Canada reduced interest rates by 25 basis points on 4 May 1999, and announced that it was doing so because of the recent appreciation of the Canadian dollar. The Canadian dollar depreciated by 30 basis points in one day, so the Bank of Canada appears to have produced exactly the impact which it wished. The flexible exchange rate allowed the Bank of Canada to pursue this course of action, which would have been impossible with a fixed parity, as was argued in Chapter 18.

Source: Adapted from *The Wall Street Journal*, May 5, 1999, p. A–8.

The conclusion that a flexible exchange rate greatly enhances the independence and power of the central bank in its management of domestic aggregate demand is not without problems. First, it requires that the government be willing to accept the implications of potentially large exchange rate changes. It was argued in Chapter 17 that such exchange rate movements can be very disruptive, and that remains true in a regime of flexible exchange rates. If the government concludes that these disruptions are unacceptable, the central bank will have to design its policies to stabilize the exchange rate rather than produce an ideal level of GNP. If the avoidance of exchange rate volatility becomes a dominant goal, monetary policy may not be significantly more independent in a regime of flexible exchange rates than it would be with fixed parities.

Monetarists argue that the adoption of flexible exchange rates will have no more than short-run impacts on the effectiveness of monetary policy in managing GNP because price-level changes will return the real money supply to its equilibrium level.[6] An expansionary monetary policy, for example, will create an excess supply of money which causes a parallel excess demand for goods and bonds. These excess demands spill over into international transactions, creating an excess demand for foreign exchange. The local currency depreciates, which increases domestic prices of tradable goods. Eventually, all prices rise by the percentage of the depreciation, reducing the real money supply to its previous level. Real output and incomes are unaffected. The following diagram illustrates this argument for an expansionary monetary policy pursued by the Bank of Canada:

$$\uparrow \Delta MS_{cn} \rightarrow \uparrow ESM_{cn} \rightarrow \uparrow EDG\&B_{cn} \rightarrow \downarrow \Delta XR_{cn} \rightarrow \uparrow \Delta Pt_{cn} \rightarrow \uparrow \Delta P_{cn} \rightarrow \downarrow \frac{\Delta MS_{cn}}{P_{cn}}$$

(*ESM* is an excess supply of money, *EDG&B* an excess demand for goods and bonds, and *Pt* the price of tradables.)

Box 19.2 IS/LM/BP analysis of monetary policy under floating exchange rates

In the previous chapter this graph, which is reproduced here for convenience as Figure 19.1, was used to illustrate why a monetary expansion must fail with a fixed exchange rate, because the balance-of-payments deficit which results from a money supply increase causes LM to shift back to the left, reimposing the original level of GDP.

If a flexible exchange rate is being maintained, in contrast, the rightward shift of LM does not create a payments deficit; instead it produces a depreciation of the local currency that shifts BP and IS to the right (Figure 19.2). IS shifts to the right because the depreciation improves the trade account, thereby increasing the level of GNP at which domestic savings equals intended investment.

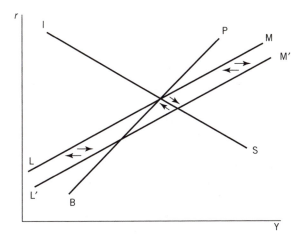

Figure 19.1 Effects of an expansionary monetary policy with fixed exchange rates. A monetary expansion cannot succeed because it causes a payments deficit and a loss of foreign exchange reserves, which automatically reduces the money supply, shifting LM back to the left.

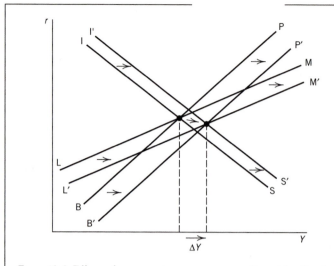

Figure 19.2 Effects of an expansionary monetary policy with a floating exchange rate. Monetary policy is far more powerful in this situation. The local currency depreciates, which shifts IS and BP to the right, producing equilibrium at a considerably higher level of output. Y is, however, nominal GNP, so some part of this "growth" may be mere inflation.

Any effects of monetary policy on output are temporary. When prices have fully adjusted to the exchange rate, the real money supply returns to its original level, leaving all real variables unaffected by the central bank's policy change. The late Rudiger Dornbusch maintained that, to the extent that prices adjust to the exchange rate with a significant time lag, the exchange rate will **overshoot** its long-term equilibrium. When prices do adjust fully, the rate will return to that equilibrium, but in the meantime the exchange rate will be quite volatile.[7]

An example may clarify the process of overshooting. Assume that 50 percent of the weights in the Consumer Price Index are assigned to tradable goods and services and that 50 percent are assigned to nontradable goods and services. Starting from equilibrium in all markets, assume that the central bank increases its domestic assets by a sufficient amount to increase the money supply by 10 percent, creating an excess supply of money of that amount. According to Walras's law, there is an excess demand for goods and bonds, which creates an excess demand for foreign money in the exchange market. The domestic currency starts to depreciate.

If the law of one price holds, prices of tradables should rise quickly when the currency falls, but nontradables prices will not respond quickly. If the currency has depreciated by 10 percent, prices of tradables will have risen by 10 percent, but nontradables prices will not have changed, producing a 5 percent increase in the overall price level and a 5 percent decline in the real money supply. This leaves the real money supply 5 percent above its equilibrium level, creating further downward pressure on the domestic currency in the exchange market. When the currency has depreciated by 20 percent, as shown in Figure 19.3, domestic prices of tradables will have risen by 20 percent, prices of nontradables will still not have changed, and the overall price level will have risen by 10 percent, returning the real money supply to its equilibrium level. There is no longer an excess supply of money,

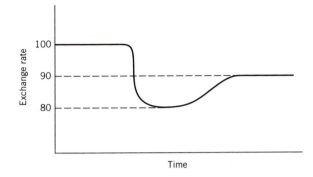

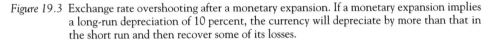

Figure 19.3 Exchange rate overshooting after a monetary expansion. If a monetary expansion implies a long-run depreciation of 10 percent, the currency will depreciate by more than that in the short run and then recover some of its losses.

so there is no longer an excess demand for goods and bonds, and a temporary equilibrium is established.

Eventually, this equilibrium is disturbed by an increase in the price of nontradables. This increase occurs for two reasons. First, tradables and nontradables are gross substitutes, which means that the 20 percent increase in the price of tradables causes consumers to substitute toward nontradables, driving their prices up. Second, the production of tradables and nontradables uses the same factors of production. Firms that produce tradables respond to increased prices by attempting to expand production; thus they must bid for more land, labor, and capital. Because full employment is assumed, the prices of these inputs increase, putting upward pressure on costs in all sectors of the economy. The prices of nontradables rise as the costs of inputs increase.

The increase in the price of nontradables moves the overall price level more than 10 percent above its original equilibrium. If nontradables prices rise by 10 percent while tradables prices are still 20 percent above their original level, the overall price level has risen by 15 percent, reducing the real money supply 5 percent below its equilibrium level. The earlier excess supply of money is replaced by an excess demand for money and by a parallel excess supply of goods and bonds. There is now an excess demand for the local currency in the exchange market, and an appreciation begins. Prices of tradables start to fall. Eventually, the currency rises by 10 percent from its lowest level, leaving a net depreciation of 10 percent from the original level, as shown in Figure 19.3. The prices of both tradables and non-tradables have risen by 10 percent from their original level, the real money supply returns to its equilibrium level, and the system is at rest.

After the initial depreciation of 20 percent, it is expected that the currency will appreciate, so domestic interest rates will have to be lower than those abroad to produce the same net yields in both countries. If, for example, the 10 percent appreciation, which follows the initial depreciation, is expected to occur at an annual rate of 5 percent over 2 years, local short-term interest rates should be 5 percentage points below foreign yields to meet the uncovered interest parity condition, which was discussed in Chapter 14; nominal interest rate differentials equal expected exchange rate changes, with lower nominal yields in the country whose currency is expected to appreciate.

Dornbusch overshooting is based on the fact that, although tradables prices may respond to the exchange rate quickly (and even that assumption is doubtful because the law of one price may not hold, as was noted in Chapter 15), nontradables prices will respond with a considerable lag. Thus the overall price level moves by less than the exchange rate in the short run. This requires a larger movement of the exchange rate to produce an adjustment of the average price level which will return the real money supply to a temporary equilibrium. Eventually, prices of nontradables adjust, producing a partial reversal of the earlier exchange rate movement and a permanent equilibrium.

This is the best-known explanation of exchange rate volatility, but there are other explanations, including the responses of capital flows to interest-rate changes in the portfolio balance model of Chapter 15. During the time in which pre-existing portfolios are being adjusted to recent changes in expected yields or risks, large capital movements will occur which will cause large exchange rate changes. When the adjustment of portfolios is largely completed, capital flows will become far smaller, and the exchange rate will move back toward its original level. Exchange rate volatility is also attributed to the activities of speculators. Enormous sums of money can be made or lost by moving short-term capital between currencies in a timely fashion, and the huge growth of such capital flows since 1973 suggests that speculation has become far more important in exchange market activity. It is not known how speculators form expectations, but they clearly move large sums of money and thereby encourage exchange rate volatility.

The impossible trinity or 'trilemma'

Countries often desire sets of economic outcomes which are impossible, that is, having one or two makes another unattainable. Monetary policy under alternative exchange rate regimes represents such a conflict. Many governments want fixed exchange rates because they strongly encourage price stability, particularly in open economies where tradables dominate the price structure. But they also want an independent monetary policy which can be used to minimize the problems arising from domestic business cycles. Finally, these countries may also value free capital mobility, that is, the avoidance of capital controls, because such mobility increases efficiency, as was argued in the chapter on international factor mobility in the first half of the book, and may result in large capital inflows which will accelerate economic growth.

These three goals cannot all be reached; any two may be available, but the third must then be abandoned. As was noted in the previous chapter, a rigidly fixed exchange rate and free capital mobility are possible if monetary policy independence is foregone. In previous pages in this chapter it was argued that free capital mobility and an independent monetary policy are possible if a country maintains a floating exchange rate and is willing to accept the likelihood that its price level may be volatile. Finally, a country might have both a fixed exchange rate and an independent monetary policy if capital controls were maintained and could be fully enforced. If, however, as was suggested in Chapter 12, capital controls are virtually impossible to enforce and generally become less effective the longer they are in place, the real choices facing a country are two: a fixed exchange rate with no monetary policy independence, or an independent national monetary policy and a floating exchange rate with what may be considerable price level volatility.

Fiscal policy with a flexible exchange rate

It was argued in the previous chapter that the effectiveness of fiscal policy in managing domestic business cycles under a fixed exchange rate depends on whether a country's capital markets are closely integrated with those of the rest of the world. Fiscal policy is relatively powerful if capital markets are closely tied to those of foreign countries, but weak if trade flows dominate the balance of payments.

If a regime of flexible exchange rates is introduced, these conclusions are exactly reversed. Fiscal policy becomes weak if capital market integration is extensive, but is more powerful if trade flows are dominant.[8]

In understanding this argument, it is vital to remember one distinction between the two regimes: with a fixed exchange rate a balance-of-payments deficit causes a decline in the money supply, with restrictive impacts to follow, and vice versa. Under a flexible exchange rate, however, forces which would otherwise cause a payments deficit instead cause a depreciation and no change in the money supply, and the depreciation is expansionary. Forces which would otherwise cause a surplus instead cause an appreciation, with restrictive impacts on GDP.

If capital market integration is extensive, the conclusion that fiscal policy is weakened by the adoption of a flexible exchange rate rests on the following reasoning: a fiscal expansion still increases GDP, the demand for money, and the interest rate. Large capital inflows, attracted by the increase in yields, cause the local currency to appreciate, which weakens the trade account, thereby weakening the intended expansionary effects of the fiscal policy shift.

The following diagram, which is similar to those used earlier, illustrates the situation in which fiscal policy is ineffective with floating exchange rates because capital market integration is extensive:

$$\uparrow\Delta(G-T)\rightarrow\uparrow\Delta Y\rightarrow\uparrow\Delta r\rightarrow\downarrow\Delta I\rightarrow\downarrow\Delta Y$$
$$\downarrow$$
$$\rightarrow\uparrow\Delta KA\rightarrow\uparrow\Delta XR\rightarrow\downarrow\Delta X\rightarrow\downarrow\Delta(X-M)\rightarrow\downarrow\Delta Y$$
$$\downarrow\qquad\qquad\uparrow$$
$$\rightarrow\uparrow\Delta M\rightarrow$$

The top line represents the traditional crowding out argument. The second line shows an appreciation of the currency, and a worsening of the trade account which, rather than canceling crowding out as was the case in the previous chapter, enhances it. Flexible exchange rates greatly weaken fiscal policy, unless a cooperative monetary policy accompanies the budgetary shift. If the central bank had increased the money supply sufficiently to avoid an increase in interest rates in the previous example, both forms of crowding out would have been avoided and the fiscal expansion would have succeeded. If the central bank refuses to cooperate, however, the adoption of a flexible exchange rate greatly weakens fiscal policy if international capital markets are closely integrated, as is the case for the major industrialized countries.

If instead capital markets are not closely integrated and trade flows, which are sensitive to changes in incomes, dominate the balance of payments, this conclusion is reversed. In this case, which is particularly relevant for developing and transition economies, the adoption of a flexible exchange rate makes fiscal policy more effective in managing domestic business cycles. An expansionary budget, for example, increases domestic incomes and imports, which causes the local currency to depreciate. The decline in the exchange rate, with a J-curve time lag, will strengthen the trade account, adding to domestic output and enhancing the effectiveness of the fiscal expansion. There is also no loss of foreign exchange reserves to threaten a balance-of-payments crisis, thereby precluding the adoption of fiscal stimulus. The introduction of a flexible exchange rate makes fiscal policy both more independent and more powerful if income growth has a more powerful effect on imports than it does on the interest rate and international capital flows. The following diagram illustrates this case:

$$\uparrow\Delta(G - T)\rightarrow\uparrow\Delta Y\rightarrow\uparrow\Delta M\rightarrow\downarrow\Delta XR\rightarrow\uparrow\Delta X\rightarrow\uparrow\Delta(X - M)\rightarrow\uparrow\Delta Y$$
$$\downarrow\qquad\qquad\uparrow$$
$$\rightarrow\downarrow\Delta M\rightarrow$$

There is no clear theoretical conclusion as to whether flexible exchange rates strengthen or weaken fiscal policy. It depends on the relative strengths of the two linkages discussed above, which will differ between countries. The circumstances in which fiscal policy is weakened by the adoption of a floating exchange rate are much more likely to prevail among industrialized countries which maintain full convertibility of their currencies for capital as well as current account. Developing and transition countries are far more likely to face the circumstances in which flexible exchange rates strengthen fiscal policy, because many of them maintain convertibility for current account, but not for capital account, transactions.

Box 19.3 IS/LM/BP analysis of fiscal policy with floating exchange rates

As was discussed in the similar box in Chapter 18, a change in fiscal policy is represented as a shift of the IS line because an expansionary budget increases the level of GDP at which total savings (private plus government) would equal intended investment. The slope of the BP line relative to the slope of LM indicates whether international capital market integration is sufficient to make fiscal policy stronger with fixed exchange rates and weaker with a float. The extreme case of perfect capital market integration, where BP is horizontal and fiscal policy is totally ineffective, is illustrated in Figure 19.4. The expansionary fiscal policy shift produces a temporary equilibrium above the BP line where LM and I'S' cross. The currency then appreciates because of large capital inflows attracted by higher domestic interest rates. That appreciation worsens the trade account, shifting I'S' back to the left. BP also shifts to the left, but since it is horizontal, it moves along itself. Equilibrium is restored at the original crossing point of LM and BP. The fiscal expansion has no impact on GDP.

If capital market integration is less than complete but still sufficient to make BP flatter than LM, fiscal policy is weakened by international repercussions in a world of flexible exchange rates, but it is not made totally ineffective. This case can be seen in Figure 19.5. The fiscal expansion shifts IS to I'S', where a higher interest rate again attracts large capital inflows. The currency again appreciates, causing I'S' and BP to shift to the left, producing a new equilibrium where LM, I"S" and B'P' cross. Fiscal policy is weakened by the appreciation and the worsening trade account, but it still has some impact on GDP.

The case in which capital market integration is weaker than the trade account linkage can be seen in Figure 19.6, where BP is steeper than LM. In this case fiscal policy is strengthened by international impacts under floating exchange rates. The fiscal expansion shifts IS to I'S', producing a temporary equilibrium to the right of BP. The currency depreciates because a large increase in imports generated by an increase in incomes overwhelms any capital inflows caused by higher interest rates. The depreciation of the local currency causes I′S′ to become I″S″ and BP to become B′P′, producing an equilibrium even farther to the right. GDP increases by even more, and fiscal policy becomes stronger because of the existence of a flexible exchange rate.

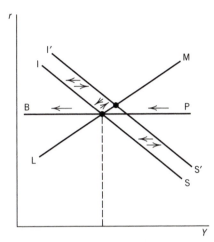

Figure 19.4 Effects of fiscal policy expansion with perfect capital mobility. If a floating exchange rate is maintained, perfect capital mobility means that fiscal policy has no impact. The inflow of capital resulting from the higher interest rates causes the domestic currency to appreciate, shifting IS and BP back to the left, returning the equilibrium to its original position.

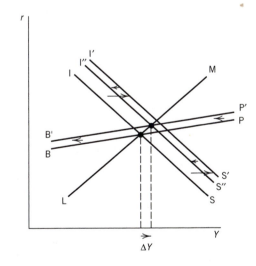

Figure 19.5 Effects of fiscal policy expansion when BP is flatter than LM. With flexible exchange rates, large capital inflows cause the local currency to appreciate, shifting IS and BP to the left, reducing the final expansionary impact.

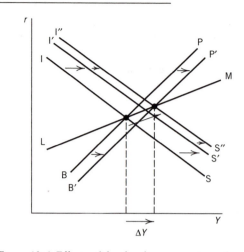

Figure 19.6 Effects of fiscal policy expansion when BP is steeper than LM. With a flexible exchange rate, the fiscal expansion causes the local currency to depreciate, shifting BP to the right and IS farther to the right, resulting in a greater expansionary impact.

The figures and accompanying discussion in this section and in the previous chapter may seem confusing; therefore it may be useful to summarize the conclusions with regard to the effectiveness of fiscal policy under fixed flexible exchange rates (see Table 19.1).

Table 19.1 Strength of fiscal policy in affecting GNP under alternative exchange rate regimes

	BB flatter than LM (extensive capital market integration)		BB steeper than LM (only limited capital market integration)
With:		Fiscal policy is:	
Fixed rates	Powerful		Weak
Flexible rates	Weak		Powerful

The practical implications of this theory begin with the conclusion that fiscal policy is not likely to be very effective for industrialized countries that maintain floating exchange rates, unless the fiscal policy is accompanied by a cooperative monetary policy. With a high degree of capital market integration, floating exchange rates mean that the central bank will dominate macroeconomic policy-making. For developing countries, in contrast, the adoption of a flexible exchange rate means that fiscal, as well as monetary, policy can be quite effective. The threat of lost foreign exchange reserves no longer precludes expansionary policies, and both monetary and fiscal policies have strengthened impacts on the domestic economy. It is hardly surprising that more developing countries have moved toward some degree of exchange rate flexibility in recent years.

The domestic impacts of foreign monetary and fiscal policy shifts with flexible exchange rates

Monetary policy

It was noted earlier that a domestic monetary policy shift is particularly effective with a flexible exchange rate because it encourages a depreciation of the local currency, and this strengthens the trade account. This means that the rest of the world experiences an appreciation which weakens its trade account, with restrictive effects on output and incomes. Viewing this issue in a two-country world consisting of Canada and the United States, a decision by the Federal Reserve System to adopt an expansionary monetary policy will lead to a depreciation of the US dollar which is an appreciation of the Canadian currency. The Canadian trade account will weaken, which causes a decline in total output and incomes in Canada. Monetary policy shifts in the United States produce the opposite or mirror-image impacts in Canada if a flexible exchange rate is being maintained. This is, of course, the exact opposite of the outcome with fixed exchange rates, as discussed in the previous chapter, where an increase in the money supply in the United States imposed a similar monetary expansion on Canada through a balance of payments disequilibrium. This line of reasoning is summarized in the following:

$$\uparrow \Delta MS_{us} \rightarrow \downarrow \Delta r_{us} \rightarrow \downarrow \Delta KA_{us} \rightarrow \downarrow \Delta XR_{us} \rightarrow \uparrow \Delta XR_{cn} \rightarrow \downarrow \Delta(X-M)_{cn} \rightarrow \downarrow \Delta Y_{cn}$$

The rather paradoxical conclusion of this discussion is that although floating exchange rates make domestic monetary policy both independent of balance-of-payments constraints and more powerful, such an exchange rate regime does not insulate a country from foreign monetary shocks. Canada can pursue any monetary policy it wishes, but is still affected by the actions of the Federal Reserve System. A tightening by the US central bank produces expansionary impacts in Canada, which could, of course, be offset with a modest tightening by the Bank of Canada. Canada is free to pursue its own domestic monetary policy goals, but it still must respond to policy shifts by the Federal Reserve System.

The same problem faces the Bank of England. If the new European Central Bank of EMU, which will be discussed at some length in Chapter 20, decides to adopt an expansionary monetary policy, the resulting capital flows from the continent to the UK will cause an appreciation of sterling which will worsen Britain's trade balance and reduce GDP. Easy money in EMU has recessionary effects in the UK.

Another example of this problem involves the attempts of Japan to escape from a recession during 1998: the United States wanted an expansionary fiscal rather than monetary policy from Tokyo because the latter would cause the yen to depreciate, which means an appreciation of the US dollar, followed by a worsening of the US trade account, with recessionary implications.

Foreign fiscal policy shifts with a floating exchange rate

The effect of a fiscal policy shift abroad on the home country depends on whether capital markets are highly integrated, so that capital account responses dominate the balance of payments, or whether instead the current account dominates the payments accounts.

If capital market integration is extensive, a fiscal expansion in the rest of the world will have expansionary effects on the home country in a world of flexible exchange rates. The reasoning behind that conclusion is as follows, again using the United States and Canada as the example. If the United States adopts an expansionary budget, the increase in GDP will raise the demand for money and the interest rate. Large capital inflows from Canada will be attracted, causing the US dollar to appreciate and the Canadian dollar to depreciate. The Canadian trade account will improve in response to the more competitive exchange rate, producing an expansionary impact north of the border. In this case, of course, the fiscal expansion was not very powerful in the United States, precisely because of the appreciation of the US dollar and the worsening of the trade balance. The point of this discussion is that the expansionary impact of the US fiscal policy was not lost; it was merely shifted in part from the United States to Canada through the depreciation of the Canadian dollar and the improvement of Canada's trade balance. The following diagram summarizes this argument:

$$\uparrow\Delta(G-T)_{us}\rightarrow\uparrow\Delta Y_{us}\rightarrow\uparrow\Delta r_{us}\rightarrow\downarrow\Delta I_{us}\rightarrow\downarrow\Delta Y_{us}$$
$$\downarrow$$
$$\rightarrow\uparrow\Delta KA_{us}\rightarrow\uparrow\Delta XR_{us}\rightarrow\downarrow\Delta XR_{cn}\rightarrow\uparrow\Delta(X-M)_{cn}\rightarrow\uparrow\Delta Y_{cn}$$

This argument makes it easy to see why the United States wanted Japan to adopt an expansionary fiscal policy during its recession of 1998; such a policy in Tokyo would have caused the yen to appreciate, meaning a depreciation of the dollar, a stronger US trade account, and continued growth of the US economy.

If capital markets are not closely integrated and instead the trade account dominates the balance of payments, this conclusion is reversed: now an expansionary fiscal shift abroad has little or no effect on the home economy because the exchange rate moves in the opposite direction from the previous case. Continuing with the US/Canada example, an expansionary budget in Washington would raise GDP and imports from Canada. The US dollar would depreciate, however, meaning an appreciation of the Canadian dollar which would return the Canadian trade account toward its original level. Canada would be largely isolated from the impacts of US fiscal policy changes if trade dominates payments flows in a world of flexible exchange rates. The following diagram summarizes this line of reasoning:

$$\uparrow\Delta(G-T)_{us}\rightarrow\uparrow\Delta Y_{us}\rightarrow\uparrow\Delta M_{us}\rightarrow\uparrow\Delta X_{cn}\rightarrow\uparrow\Delta Y_{cn}$$
$$\downarrow$$
$$\rightarrow\uparrow\Delta XR_{cn}\rightarrow\downarrow\Delta(X-M)_{cn}\rightarrow\downarrow\Delta Y_{c}$$

The first line represents the standard argument for business cycle transmission through the trade account, as discussed in the previous chapter. The second line, which occurs because of the flexible exchange rate, largely cancels the impact of the first line, leaving Canada protected at least to some degree from the impacts of US fiscal policy shifts. This result, of course, only holds if the balance of payments is dominated by trade flows; if large capital flows occur in response to interest rate changes, we return to the earlier argument that an expansionary fiscal policy in the United States will have expansionary effects in Canada. That is the more likely outcome for industrialized countries such as the United States, Canada, Japan, and the members of the European Union.

Returning to the earlier example of the United Kingdom and the continent of Europe, a decision by the EMU countries to adopt an expansionary fiscal, rather than monetary, policy would have expansionary, rather than restrictive, effects in the UK. Expansionary budgets on the continent would increase interest rates, attracting capital flows from London, which would cause sterling to depreciate. The resulting improvement in the UK's trade balance would increase output, employment, and incomes. Under floating rates, expansionary monetary policy on the continent has restrictive effects in the United Kingdom, but expansionary budgets in the rest of Europe have expansionary effects in the UK.

Mercantilism and flexible exchange rates

One of the arguments for protectionism that was discussed in the first half of this book is that domestic output and incomes may be increased by replacing imports with domestic products. It was suggested that this is a weak argument under any circumstances, but flexible rates make it even weaker. The introduction of a tariff that reduces imports, for example, produces a parallel reduction in the domestic demand for foreign exchange needed to pay for those imports. The local currency appreciates and foreign currencies depreciate until balance-of payments equilibrium is re-established. The appreciation of the local currency reduces exports and increases other imports, leaving the trade balance and the level of domestic aggregate demand largely unaffected. Any benefits received by domestic producers of the protected goods occur at the cost of losses in production and employment in other domestic industries that produce tradable goods.[9] The following diagram outlines this process, where T represents the tariff rate:

$$\uparrow\Delta T\rightarrow\downarrow\Delta M\rightarrow\uparrow\Delta(X-M)\rightarrow\uparrow\Delta Y$$
$$\downarrow$$
$$\rightarrow\uparrow\Delta XR\rightarrow\uparrow\Delta M\rightarrow\downarrow\Delta(X-M)\rightarrow\downarrow\Delta Y$$
$$\downarrow\qquad\qquad\uparrow$$
$$\rightarrow\downarrow\Delta X\rightarrow$$

The decline in domestic output with which the diagram ends should largely cancel the increase in output on the top line, leaving domestic production and output unaffected.

Some supporters of flexible exchange rates believed that the widespread understanding of this argument might eliminate much of the political pressure for protectionist policies, because those who would be injured by the adoption of restrictions would argue forcefully against them. If, for example, the US textile and garment industries asked the Congress for sharp increases in tariffs on textile and garment imports, other US industries that produce tradables would understand that the dollar would appreciate and they would be injured if this policy were adopted. These industries could then be expected to offer strong opposition to the demands of the textile and garment interests, making it much less likely that the tariff proposal would become law. This argument is discussed in Exhibit 19.2.

EXHIBIT 19.2 SAVE AN AUTO WORKER'S JOB, PUT ANOTHER AMERICAN OUT OF WORK

People who support domestic-content (or "local content") laws for imported automobiles argue that they would reduce unemployment in the United States. They are wrong.

As long as the United States maintains a floating exchange rate, the adoption of protectionist measures to help one industry will merely shift jobs from elsewhere in the economy to the favored sector, with no significant effect on total employment.

Changes in the exchange rate for the dollar are the mechanism through which output and jobs are lost in the unprotected industries. Protectionism is never a sensible way to increase domestic employment, but it is wholly self-defeating for a country with a floating exchange rate.

Under fixed exchange rates, it might be possible to view the short-term effects of a tariff solely in terms of impact on the protected industry, because there would be no exchange rate movement to cause undesirable effects elsewhere in the economy. If foreign countries did not retaliate against US restrictions on car imports, for example, employment would increase in Detroit without loss of jobs elsewhere in the United States.

But since the exchange rates began to float in 1973, this is no longer true. A decision to apply domestic-content rules to cars sold in the United States, for example, would greatly reduce imports from Japan, causing a parallel decline in the US demand for yen to pay for those cars. The yen would then depreciate and the dollar would appreciate until the balance in international transactions was restored. As consumers in the United States and abroad responded to this change in relative prices by purchasing fewer US goods and more foreign products, sales and employment would be lost in a range of US industries. The US car industry might gain from the imposition of domestic-content rules, but other domestic industries that must compete in world markets would lose. Total employment in the US economy would not increase.

With fixed exchange rates among currencies, the worldwide employment effects of US protectionism would be a "zero-sum game," in that job gains in the United States would be offset by job losses abroad. Under the existing system of floating exchange rates, the effects of protectionism on employment are a "zero-sum game" within the United States. Job gains in Detroit are matched by job losses in Boston and Seattle, with exchange rate changes imposing the losses on unprotected parts of the US economy.

A statistical study has recently been completed in the Labor Department supporting this argument. It concludes that the original form of the domestic-content bill would create about 300,000 jobs in automobile manufacturing and related industries, but that about the same number of jobs would be lost elsewhere in the US economy as the exchange rate for the dollar rose.

The study indicates that the apparel and electronic components industries would be particularly injured by the exchange rate change, and that computers and commercial aircraft would be seriously affected. The study suggests that because the US auto industry uses fewer workers per million dollars in sales than do many other affected industries, the adoption of the domestic-content bill for cars might actually cause a slight net loss of employment in the United States.

It is surprising that industries such as apparel and computers have not realized that protectionism for automobiles would hurt them, and entered the lobbying battle against the domestic-content bill. The late Harry Johnson of the University of Chicago argued many years ago that floating exchange rates were a good idea precisely because they would destroy the traditional argument for tariffs and encourage an era of free trade. He optimistically assumed that politicians and lobbyists would understand that protection for one industry was merely a tax on other domestic industries under floating exchange rates. But it doesn't seem to be working out that way. Walter Mondale's conversion to protectionism is a particularly unfortunate example.

If Washington wants to help US industries compete against foreign firms, the first goal must be to reverse the sharp increase in the exchange rate for the dollar that has occurred during the last 18 months. A decline of the dollar to more realistic levels would be expensive for American tourists abroad, but it would greatly help US industries that compete against imports, such as cars and apparel, and those that export, such as computers and aircraft.

Bringing down the exchange rate for the dollar requires a continuing decline in US interest rates. Although interest rates are determined by a number of factors, predictions of huge federal deficits have been a dominant element in maintaining high US yields since early 1981. Gaining permanent control over federal deficits requires decisions that are painful and politically risky. It is far easier for politicians to promise help for US workers and industries through domestic-content rules and other protectionist policies. Such an approach will actually produce no increase in employment or any other help for the economy, but that result would be apparent only in the long run. Election results are always in the short run.

Source: The Washington Post, Robert M. Dunn, Jr., © The Washington Post, Op. Ed. page, October 28, 1982. Reprinted with permission.

Readers may have understandably been a bit overwhelmed by all of the open economy macroeconomics conclusions in the two exchange rate regimes of this and the previous chapter. It may therefore be useful to briefly summarize these conclusions in one table.

Table 19.2 Summary of open economy macroeconomics conclusions fixed versus flexible exchange rates

	Fixed	*Flexible*
Business cycle transmission via trade	Strong	Weak
Domestic monetary policy	Weak	Strong
Domestic fiscal policy with:		
A high degree of capital mobility	Strong	Weak
A low degree of capital mobility	Weak	Strong
Expansionary domestic impacts of Protectionism	Strong	Weak
Domestic impacts of foreign macro policy changes Monetary policy	Strong in same direction	Strong in opposite direction
Fiscal policy with:		
A high degree of capital mobility	Uncertain	Strong in same direction
A low degree of capital mobility	Strong in same direction	Uncertain

Purchasing power parity and flexible exchange rates

Finally, many supporters of flexible exchange rates predicted that nominal exchange rates would move roughly to offset differing rates of inflation, leaving real exchange rates relatively constant. If US inflation continued at 4 percent while the rest of the world's price level rose at an average annual rate of 7 percent, the dollar would appreciate by about 3 percent per year, leaving the cost- and price-competitive position of US producers of tradables largely unchanged. The adoption of flexible nominal exchange rates would then be a route to relatively constant real exchange rates.

As will be seen in Chapter 20, the experience with flexible exchange rates since 1973 has differed in a number of ways from the theory presented here. Nominal exchange rates have not moved to offset differences in rates of inflation, and large changes in real exchange rates have been frequent and persistent. Such changes in real exchange rates have been quite disruptive, and since 1987 the governments of the major industrialized countries have tried to limit such changes. As a result, national monetary policies are not as independent or powerful as the theory discussed in this chapter would imply. In addition, pressures for protectionism in the United States have not disappeared but seem to have become stronger. As was stated earlier, academic and other supporters of flexible exchange rates have to be described as "sadder but wiser."

Summary of key concepts

1   In a clean or pure float the official reserve transactions balance of payments is in equilibrium at all times. In a "dirty" or managed float, that is not true.

2   A float greatly weakens the business cycle transmission mechanism described in Chapter 18, because the exchange rate moves to limit any changes in a country's trade account. A recession in the United States, for example, will cause the Canadian dollar to depreciate, thereby limiting or eliminating any decline in the Canadian trade account.

3   Flexible exchange rates make domestic monetary policy independent of balance-of-payments constraints and more powerful. A decision by the Bank of England, for example, to adopt an expansionary monetary policy will cause sterling to depreciate, strengthening the British trade balance, which further increases output and incomes in the United Kingdom.

4   In the real world this independence and power of the central bank may be quite limited. In the previous example, the Bank of England might feel constrained from an expansionary policy by a fear that the depreciation of sterling would cause an unacceptable acceleration of British inflation.

5   Fiscal policy can be made more or less effective by a float, depending on the extent of international capital market integration. If that integration is extensive, fiscal policy is weakened by a float, and vice versa.

6   A flexible exchange rate means that an expansionary monetary policy abroad has restrictive effects at home. If, for example, the European Central Bank were to adopt an expansionary policy, the euro would depreciate, meaning that sterling appreciates, which would worsen the British trade balance, weakening the UK economy.

7   Any attempt to increase aggregate demand through protectionist policies is doomed to failure with a float because the reduced demand for foreign exchange to pay for imports will cause the local currency to appreciate, worsening the trade account and reversing the intended expansionary impacts of the protectionism.

Questions for study and review

1   When a country has a floating exchange rate, the domestic money supply is not affected by shifts in its international payments. Is this statement true or false? Why?

2   Starting from an initial position of payments equilibrium, suppose that foreign demand for Country A's exports suddenly rises. If a flexible exchange rate exists, explain what would happen and how equilibrium would be restored.

3   How does the existence of a flexible exchange rate affect the impact of monetary policy shifts on a domestic economy? Explain, and illustrate for a tightening of monetary policy using the IS/LM/BP graph.

4   What effect does the adoption of a flexible exchange rate have on the impacts of fiscal policy shifts in a country whose capital markets are closely integrated with those of the rest of the world? Use the IS/LM/BP graph to illustrate for a fiscal tightening.

5   Why is the mercantilist argument for protection weakened by the adoption of a flexible exchange rate?

6   In what sense does a flexible exchange rate encourage national macroeconomic independence as opposed to the macroeconomic interdependence implied by a fixed parity?

7   A Keynesian views an appreciation as deflationary, whereas a monetarist views the same appreciation as expansionary. Why?

8   If a contractionary monetary policy is expected to be temporary, what happens to the effectiveness of that policy under flexible exchange rates? Why?

9   How does a restrictive monetary policy abroad affect the domestic economy under a float? How does this mechanism operate?

Suggested further reading

- Argy, V., *International Macroeconomics: Theory and Policy*, New York: Routledge, 1994.
- Cooper, R., "Dealing with the Trade Deficit in a Floating Rate System," *Brookings Papers on Economic Activity*, no. 1, 1986, pp. 195–208.
- Dornbusch, R., *Open Economy Macroeconomics*, New York: Basic Books, 1980.
- Dornbusch, R., "External Balance Correction: Depreciation or Protection?," *Brookings Papers on Economic Activity*, no. 1, 1987, pp. 249–70.
- Dunn, R., "The Many Disappointments of Flexible Exchange Rates," *Princeton Essays in International Finance*, no. 154, December 1983.
- Frankel, J., *On Exchange Rates*, Cambridge, MA: MIT Press, 1993.
- Friedman, M., "The Case for Flexible Exchange Rates," in *Essays in Positive Economics*, Chicago: University of Chicago Press, 1953.
- MacDonald, R., *Floating Exchange Rates: Theory and Evidence*, London: Unwin Hyman, 1988.
- Mundell, R., *International Economics*, New York: Macmillan, 1968, chs 17, 18, and 19.
- Sohmen, E., *Flexible Exchange Rates*, Chicago: University of Chicago Press, 1969.

Notes

1   Milton Friedman produced one of the most influential early defenses of flexible exchange rates in "The Case of Flexible Exchange Rates" in *Essays in Positive Economics* (Chicago: University of Chicago Press, 1953). An early discussion of the payments adjustment process under floating exchange rates can be found in Joan Robinson's "The Foreign Exchanges," in her volume, *Essays in the Theory of Employment* (Oxford: Blackwell, 1947). See also E. Sohmen, *Flexible Exchange Rates* (Chicago: University of Chicago Press, 1969). A more recent study of flexible exchange rates, which references much of the published work on this topic, can be found in R. MacDonald, *Floating Exchange Rates: Theory and Evidence* (London: Unwin Hyman, 1988).

2   An influential study of official intervention under flexible exchange rates grew out of the 1982 Versailles G-7 economic summit: Working Group on Exchange Market Intervention, Report, 1983. For a review of the evidence that sterilized intervention does not affect market exchange rates beyond the short run, see W. Weber, "Do Sterilized Interventions Affect the Exchange Rate?," *Federal Reserve Bank of Minneapolis Quarterly Review*, Summer 1986, pp. 14–23.

3   Rachel McCulloch, "Unexpected Real Consequences of Floating Exchange Rates," *Princeton Essays in International Finance*, no. 154, 1983, p. 6. See also D. Cushman, "The Effects of Real Exchange Rate Risk on International Trade," *Journal of International Economics*, August 1983, pp. 44–63. For a more recent study, see J. Gagnon, "Exchange Rate Flexibility and the Level of International Trade," *Journal of International Economics*, May 1993, pp. 269–87.

4   Michael Duerr, *Protecting Corporate Assets under Floating Exchange Rates* (New York: The Conference Board, 1975). See also R. Dunn, *The Canada–US Capital Market* (Washington, DC: National Planning Association, 1978), pp. 95–102.

5   Much of the theoretical work on this subject was done by Robert Mundell during the 1960s. See his "The Monetary Dynamics of International Adjustment under Fixed and Floating Exchange Rates," *Quarterly Journal of Economics*, May 1960. Also "Flexible Exchange Rates and Employment Policy," *Canadian Journal of Economics*, November 1961, and "Capital Mobility and Stabilization Policy under Fixed and Flexible Exchange Rates," *Canadian Journal of Economics*, November 1963. These and other related articles by Mundell are gathered in his *International Economics* (New York: Macmillan, 1968). See also A. Takayama, "The Effects of Fiscal and Monetary Policies under Flexible and Fixed Exchange Rates," *Canadian Journal of Economics*, May 1969.

6   R. Dornbusch, *Open Economy Macroeconomics* (New York: Basic Books, 1980), chs 11 and 12. See also L. Girton and D. Roper, "A Monetary Model of Exchange Market Pressure Applied to Post-War Canadian Experience," *American Economic Review*, September 1977, pp. 537–48.

7   R. Dornbusch, "Expectations and Exchange Rate Dynamics," *Journal of Political Economy*, December 1976, pp. 1161–76. Also R. Dornbusch, *Open Economy Macroeconomics* (New York: Basic Books, 1980), ch. 12. For alternative arguments for overshooting, see R. Dunn, "The Many Disappointments of Flexible Exchange Rates," *Princeton Essays in International Finance*, no. 154, 1983, pp. 19–23. See also J. Levin, "Trade Flow Lags, Monetary and Fiscal Policy, and Exchange Rate Overshooting," *Journal of International Money and Finance*, December 1986.

8   R. Mundell, "Capital Mobility and Stabilization Policies under Fixed and under Flexible Exchange Rate," *Canadian Journal of Economics*, November 1963.

9   H. Johnson, "The Case for Flexible Exchange Rates," in G. Halm, ed., *Approaches to Greater Exchange Rate Flexibility: The Burgenstock Papers* (Princeton, NJ: Princeton University Press, 1970), pp. 100–1. See also R. Cooper, "Dealing with a Trade Deficit in a Floating Rate System," *Brookings Papers on Economic Activity*, no. 1, 1986, pp. 195–208, and R. Dornbusch, "External Balance Correction: Depreciation or Protection?," *Brookings Papers on Economic Activity*, 1987, pp. 249–70.

20 The international monetary system

History and current controversies

Learning objectives

By the end of this chapter you should be able to understand:

- The history of the international financial system before 1973, with particular emphasis on why the Bretton Woods system of 1947–71 failed;
- the ways in which the experience with flexible exchange rates has not met expectations (far more volatility in both nominal and real exchange rates than thought likely);
- the failure of various models which are based on economic and financial fundamentals to explain movements of floating rates (econometric results very disappointing);
- why the proposed alternatives to floating exchange rates have failed to gather support, leaving us with floating rates, not as an ideal system, but as the best available;
- the European Monetary Union: why it has such wide support, how it is organized and operates, and its potential problems if business-cycle timing differs sharply among member countries;
- the problems of developing country debt crises, with particular emphasis on what happened in East Asia in 1997–9 and in Argentina in 2002. What attempts are being made to reduce the likelihood of future crises, and the prospects for the success of these attempts;
- why balance of payments crises are contagious, that is, why they often spread from one country experiencing a negative payments shock to others in the region which were not affected by the original shock;
- the issues relating to the phrase "new international financial architecture," including the problem of debt relief for heavily indebted poor countries;
- prospective issues in international trade and finance during the next decade.

Events before 1973

The gold standard

Although the United Kingdom adopted the gold standard in the early eighteenth century, the period in which the system operated for the large majority of the industrialized countries was from 1880 to 1914. The United States returned to the gold standard in 1879, having abandoned it during the Civil War. Few countries rigidly followed the rules of the specie flow system as described in Chapter 16, but the system did operate in an approximate sense. The operative rule was that whenever a balance of payments deficit occurred and gold was lost, interest rates were raised sufficiently to stop the gold outflow. There was not a rigid linkage between the loss of gold and a proportionate reduction in the stock of base money, as presumed by the specie flow system, but there was a clear linkage from payments dis-equilibria to monetary policy changes which produced adjustment. The system worked with considerable success because this was a period of relatively free trade, capital account convertibility, peace, and highly competitive markets for both goods and labor. As a result even modest changes in monetary policy produced responses in both the current and capital accounts which shifted the balance of payments back toward equilibrium.

Capital controls prevailed during World War I, effectively suspending the system, and when attempts were made to restore the gold standard after that war, it was considerably less successful. Goods and labor markets had become less competitive, due to the growth of labor unions and oligopolistic industries, free trade was in decline due to growing protectionist sentiment, and surplus countries increasingly failed to follow the "rules of the game" by refusing to ease monetary policy as gold inflows occurred. The United Kingdom, which had experienced serious inflation during the war, tried to return to the gold standard at sterling's pre-1914 parity. This required extremely tight monetary policy in the early and mid-1920s, which seriously harmed the British recovery from the war. By the time the gold parity was restored in 1925, the United Kingdom had suffered from unemployment rates of over 10 percent for years. Tight money had to be retained in the UK for the rest of the decade to protect the country's gold stocks, keeping the country's output well below full capacity and deepening the depression which followed.

The gold standard collapsed in the early and mid-1930s, in part because surplus countries (particularly the United States) sterilized gold inflows, making the adjustment process far more severe for deficit countries. Defections from the gold standard were followed by competitive devaluations and the general collapse of anything that might be called an international monetary system. Economic nationalism prevailed as tariff rates were raised to try unsuccessfully to generate domestic demand and output increases. The outbreak of World War II led to the reimposition of exchange controls. As the war progressed allied leaders started to consider how a new international monetary system might be constructed after the end of hostilities.

The Bretton Woods system

The leaders of the allied countries very much wanted to avoid the international economic anarchy of the 1930s but realized that a return to the rigidities of the gold standard was unlikely and probably undesirable. A conference was held at Bretton Woods, New Hampshire in the summer of 1944 which produced, in the form of the founding documents for the International Monetary Fund, the outlines of the international financial system which functioned from the late 1940s until the early 1970s. The World Bank was also founded at that conference.

Under the Bretton Woods system the US dollar was tied to gold at $35 per ounce, and other countries were pegged to the dollar. The United States promised to buy or sell gold in unlimited amounts at the $35 price, but only dealing with foreign governments or central banks. Americans were prohibited by US law from owning gold under a law from the 1930s that was not repealed until the early 1970s.

Foreign exchange reserves were held as gold, dollars and a few other reserve currencies, and as positions at the IMF. SDRs, as discussed in Chapter 12, were introduced at the end of the 1960s, but have never become a significant part of the world's reserves. The primary purpose of the IMF was to lend hard currencies to countries experiencing excessive foreign exchange reserve losses. Its activities were financed by the quotas which member countries paid in, the size of national quotas being based on the size of their economies. Part of the quota was paid in the form of gold or convertible foreign currencies, with the remainder paid in the form of each country's domestic currency. The first part of the quota, known as the gold tranche, counted as part of a country's reserves and could be borrowed without question. Each country could also borrow beyond its gold tranche under terms of conditionality, which meant adjustments in macroeconomic policies which would make the loan repayable within a reasonable period of time. The core elements of standard conditionality packages were discussed in Chapters 16 and 17.

The adjustment process which was foreseen under the Bretton Woods system had three stages, depending on the seriousness of payments problems:

1   For what were believed to be temporary or transitory imbalances, unpleasant policies were to be avoided, and financing was to be pursued. Deficit countries ran reserves down, surplus countries accumulated them, and both were presumed to sterilize.
2   For more serious problems, deficit countries were expected to adopt more restrictive monetary and/or fiscal polices, and surplus countries had an equal and parallel responsibility to adopt more expansionary policies. The system was explicitly designed to avoid the contractionary bias of the gold standard when surplus countries refused to expand and instead sterilized gold inflows, thereby requiring severely restrictive policies by the deficit countries.
3   For what were referred to as fundamental payments disequilibria, deficit countries were expected to devalue, but only to do so after consultations with the IMF to see to it that the devaluation was not excessive or designed primarily for mercantilist purposes. The competitive devaluations of the 1930s were not to be repeated. A country with a large and persistent surplus would be expected to revalue.

The system, if it can be called that, that evolved in the 1950s and 1960s was quite different from that described above, and turned out to be deeply flawed. It can also be viewed as having three stages:

1   Merely financing disequilibria, and avoiding painful adjustment policies, went on for far longer than could be justified by the original plan. Central banks found ways to borrow from each other and thereby avoid conditionality, and the quotas of the IMF were expanded, making larger loans by that institution possible.
2   Surplus countries simply refused to adopt more expansionary policies than they preferred for domestic reasons, thereby eliminating the intended outcome that deficit and

surplus countries would both adjust macroeconomic policies, thereby making the necessary changes more modest on each side. Deficit counties received little or no help from surplus counties, making the tightening of policies which they would have to pursue quite severe. The Meade conflict cases, as described in Chapter 16, occurred frequently; since the surplus/inflation countries pursued the domestic goal of reducing aggregate demand, the situation facing the deficit/recession counties was almost impossible. The latter group of countries often responded with a retreat from capital account convertibility and from liberal trade policies. Deficit/recession countries, including the United States in the early 1960s, introduced capital controls and frequently sought ways to restrict imports of goods and services. By the end of the 1960s, the post-war regime of open trade and capital flows was in serious danger of collapse.

3   Despite what were obviously large and chronic payments disequilibria, surplus countries refused to revalue. They viewed an undervalued currency as useful in spurring exports and restricting imports, meaning that exchange rates were used for mercantilist purposes. Chronic deficit countries, like the United Kingdom, put off devaluations until a balance of payments crisis, which included massive speculative capital outflows, compelled a parity change. It was obvious by the early 1960s that sterling was overvalued at $2.80, but London fought off a devaluation until the fall of 1967, when its reserves were largely exhausted.

The United States, because other currencies were pegged to the dollar, faced a unique problem, sometime known as N-1. If there are N currencies in the world, there are N-1 dollar exchange rates, meaning that if N-1 governments peg their currencies to the dollar and actively defend those parities, the United States has no control over its exchange rate. The US dollar could not be devalued; the dollar price of gold could be increased, which would be of interest to nations with gold mines, but that action would not affect any bilateral exchange rate. As other countries in crisis devalued, but surplus countries refused to revalue, the dollar appreciated without Washington having any control over that outcome. The N-1 problem became particularly serious in the late 1960s when it became quite apparent that the dollar was badly overvalued, but the US government was unable to move toward a more realistic exchange rate.

Returning to the beginning of the Bretton Woods system, the United States had massive reserves and an unrivaled financial and economic position in the late 1940s, in part because its capital stock had not been injured by the war. The rest of the world lacked sufficient reserves, a situation which was referred to as a "dollar shortage." During the 1950s the United States started to run consistent payments deficits, both because many countries had devalued sharply against the dollar at the end of the 1940s, thereby gaining cost competitive advantages, and because Americans were making large investments and loans in Europe and elsewhere abroad. In the early 1950s, the US deficits were seen as desirable because they allowed other countries to accumulate foreign exchange reserves that had previously been badly depleted. By the end of the 1950s, however, the US deficits were sufficiently large as to create the impression of a "dollar glut." By the early 1960s, the United States had a serious payments deficit.

In 1964 the United States adopted capital controls in the form of the Interest Equalization Tax, which was nothing but a tariff on foreign bonds and other debt instruments. This tax, combined with quite restrained US macroeconomic policies, produced a sufficient improvement in the US payments results that many observers thought the US problem was largely solved. The Johnson administration, however, decided to pursue a war in Vietnam and enhanced social welfare expenditures, under the Great Society program, without a tax increase to pay for either of them. US monetary policy remained relatively expansionary in the late 1960s, despite large budget deficits. The results were predictable. The US current account deteriorated, and capital outflows accelerated. The Johnson administration responded with a far more thorough set of capital controls, which created a brief respite. Late in the decade and at the beginning of the 1970s, however, major questions developed concerning the quality of the leadership of the Federal Reserve Board and the management of US fiscal policy, and it became clear that the exchange rate for the dollar could not be sustained.

A massive speculative run against the dollar began, rapidly draining US gold holdings, but the N-1 problem meant that the Nixon administration could not devalue the dollar. The result was the shock of 15 August 1971 when the Nixon administration suspended gold sales, imposed a surtax on US import tariffs, and urgently requested an international conference to negotiate a new set of exchange rates. The result was the Smithsonian Conference of December 1971 in Washington, which produced a devaluation of the dollar relative to gold and a revaluation of the currencies of the surplus countries, the latter being accepted because the apparent alternative was a severe worsening of US protectionism.

The new exchange rate schedule survived for just over a year. At the end of 1972 US trade numbers were not much better, monetary policy was obviously too expansionary, and there was a growing perception that the Nixon administration was largely preoccupied with the growing Watergate scandal. The result was another speculative run on the dollar, and the adoption of floating exchange rates by the major industrialized countries in early 1973.

The Eurocurrency market

An important innovation in international banking occurred during the Bretton Woods era when commercial banks in several countries began to accept deposits and to extend loans in currencies other than their own national currency. We will briefly describe this activity, which was known as the "Eurodollar market." As currencies other than the dollar became more central to its operation this became known as the "Eurocurrency market," or merely as "offshore banking."As noted in earlier chapters, creation and control of a nation's money are among the most sensitive and jealously guarded attributes of national sovereignty. Traditionally, it has been accepted that every nation has an exclusive right to coin and print its own money. When money actually took the form of coins and currency, this exclusive national privilege was generally respected, except by counterfeiters, and even when bank deposits became the principal form of money, the primacy of national control was respected – at least until recently.

In 1960, however, European commercial banks discovered that they could earn handsome profits by accepting deposits in US dollars and by engaging in banking operations in terms of dollars. Since they were dealing almost entirely in bank deposits, or bookkeeping money, it was easy enough to keep accounts in dollars, whether the bank was located in London, Paris, or Zurich.

From a modest beginning in 1960, commercial banks proceeded to increase their foreign currency deposits at a rapid rate. Although this market is sometimes referred to as the **Eurodollar market**, banks in world financial centers now accept deposits and make loans in several other national currencies as well (euros, pounds, and yen are important examples), and commercial banks throughout the world are participating in this market. There is an Asian US dollar market centered in Singapore, and many banks collect deposits in branches located in the Bahamas. Thus even the term "Eurocurrency" is not really adequate, although it is much used. Our discussion will primarily concern the Eurodollar portion of the market. US commercial banks are heavily involved through their branches and subsidiaries in foreign financial centers, especially in Europe.

The rise of the Eurodollar market may be interpreted as an evolutionary response of the private banking sector to the need for an international money market. Since no international money exists, commercial banks have proceeded to internationalize some of the national monies, particularly the US dollar. These have been made to serve as international monies, and a huge, highly competitive money market has been created. Every important nation is linked into this vast money market, and every nation is influenced by it with respect to credit conditions, interest rates, and so on. Thus it has become a major force pulling toward a more closely integrated world economy. One of the most striking facts about the development of this important institutional form is that it was entirely unplanned. Central bankers watched it grow with some apprehension, but they did not try to suppress it.

How the Eurodollar market works

Transactions in the Eurodollar market are extremely simple, in essence. Suppose Firm A, which has a $10 million deposit in a US bank, decides to place that sum in a bank in London (a "Eurobank," as we will call any commercial bank in the rest of the world that accepts deposits denominated in dollars and other currencies besides its own national currency). Firm A simply writes a check on its US bank and deposits the check in the Eurobank. The effects of this transaction may be shown in balance sheets, as in Table 20.1. In the US bank, the deposit is simply switched from Firm A to Eurobank 1, leaving its total deposit liabilities unchanged. Firm A now has a time deposit in Eurobank 1, on which it may earn a higher rate of interest (say, 4 percent) than it could earn in a domestic time deposit, and Eurobank 1 now has a $10 million demand deposit in the US bank.

Table 20.1 The creation of a Eurodollar deposit

US bank			
Assets		*Liabilities*	
		Demand deposit, Firm A	–$10 million
		Demand deposit, Eurobank 1	+$10 million

Eurobank 1			
Assets		*Liabilities*	
Demand deposit in US bank	+$10 million	Time deposit, Firm A	+$10 million

Eurodollar deposits are time deposits, with maturities ranging from 1 day to many months, and they earn interest. (Until the early 1980s, banks in the US were not allowed to pay interest on deposits of less than 30 days' duration, which is one reason Eurodollar deposits have been attractive to firms holding large cash balances.)

Now Eurobank 1 has a $10 million time deposit liability on which it pays 4 percent, and a $10 million asset (demand deposit in a US bank) on which it earns little or nothing. To hold such a nonearning asset is like holding a hot potato – one wants to get rid of it as quickly as possible. Thus Eurobank 1 will be anxious to convert that deposit into an interest-bearing asset, say by making a loan or buying an asset. For example, it may place $10 million in a time deposit at 4½ percent interest with an Italian commercial bank (Eurobank 2) that is temporarily in need of funds. (Eurobank 1 may keep a small portion of the demand deposit as a reserve, but in practice reserve ratios are quite small in the Eurodollar market, and we will omit them.) The spreads between interest rates received and paid are very small in the Eurodollar market, as low as ¼ or ⅛ of 1 percent. It is a wholesale market, with large transactions and low margins.

Table 20.2 A Eurodollar redeposit

	US bank		
Assets		*Liabilities*	
		Demand deposit, Firm A Eurobank 1	–$10 million
		Demand deposit, Eurobank 2	+$10 million

	Eurobank 1		
Assets		*Liabilities*	
Demand deposit in US bank	–$10 million		+$10 million
Time deposit in Eurobank 2	+$10 million		

	Eurobank 2		
Assets		*Liabilities*	
Demand deposit in US bank	+$10 million	Time deposit from Eurobank 1	+10 million

This second transaction can also be shown in balance sheets, as in Table 20.2. In the US bank, the deposit is again simply switched from one holder to another. Eurobank 1 acquires an earning asset, while Eurobank 2 incurs a time deposit liability in return for which it acquires the dollar demand deposit. Note that Eurodollar deposits of $20 million now exist: $10 million payable to Firm A by Eurobank 1 (Table 20.1), and $10 million payable to Eurobank 1 by Eurobank 2 (Table 20.2). This process could be repeated several times, with the amount of Eurodollars increasing each time. The cycle will stop, however, if the dollar demand deposit is used to make a direct payment to a firm in the United States. We can illustrate by taking our example one step further.

The Italian Bank, Eurobank 2, now has the demand deposit in the US bank. It too will want to convert this deposit into an earning asset. Let us suppose it lends $10 million to an Italian leather producer (Firm B) at 5 percent interest, and Firm B uses the money to pay for hides it has bought from a US exporter (Firm C). Now the $10 million demand deposit in the US bank is switched from Eurobank 2 to Firm C, an American firm. Firm C may draw checks on this deposit to pay for wages and other expenses, but if these are paid to domestic persons and firms, they will involve monetary circulation within the United States. There is no basis for further rounds of credit creation in the Eurodollar market. However, Eurobank 1 still has a $10 million time-deposit liability to Firm A, matched by a time-deposit claim on Eurobank 2; and Eurobank 2 still has a $10 million time-deposit liability to Eurobank 1, matched by a loan receivable from Firm B. The expansion process in the Eurodollar market stopped because the funds lent to the Italian leather producer were not redeposited in a Eurobank, but were paid to a firm that deposited them in a US bank.

Much discussion has occurred about the extent to which multiple creation of deposits can and does take place in the Eurodollar market. In the absence of any formal reserve requirements, there is no definite limiting value for the multiplier. However, it seems clear that an important factor determining how much multiple expansion of deposits can occur is the extent to which funds lent by Eurobanks are redeposited in the Eurobank system. The larger the ratio of redepositing, the greater the potential for multiple expansion of deposits in the Eurocurrency system.

Although simple in essence, Eurodollar transactions can become intricate in details, with a complex variety of links to trace out. We need not pursue these complications. The main point is that a large external money market now exists, based on dollars. Many governments, persons, and business firms (American, foreign, and multinational) find it to their advantage to place funds (i.e. hold deposits) in Eurobanks, and many governments, persons, and firms borrow in that market.

Why the Eurodollar market exists

An obvious question is probably floating through the reader's mind at this point: why did this money market develop outside the United States? Why aren't banks within the United States doing all this business in dollar loans and deposits?

The first and principal answer is that the Eurodollar market provides a way to circumvent the many regulations and controls that national governments have placed on domestic money markets and bank operations. In the exercise of their sovereign power to operate monetary, fiscal, and other economic policies at the national level, governments have imposed numerous restrictions, regulations, and controls on the use of money and on the operations of commercial banks. The opportunity to escape from this maze of legal restrictions provided much of the stimulus and incentive for the Eurodollar market. We will mention a few examples:

1   Until the mid-1980s US banks were subject to Regulation Q of the Federal Reserve System, which specified the maximum interest rates American banks could pay on time deposits. In the early 1960s the maximum rate was 4 percent. Eurobanks, not subject to Regulation Q, were willing to pay 6 to 8 percent at that time. Consequently, persons and firms with large sums to place in time deposits were induced to hold dollar deposits in the Eurodollar market.

2   During the 1960s and early 1970s the United States imposed a tax on foreign bond issues in New York and placed restrictions on loans to foreigners by US banks. The natural result was that foreigners borrowed money from Eurobanks instead. Furthermore, US firms, facing restrictions on the transfer of funds to finance their subsidiaries in Europe and elsewhere, also turned to Eurobanks for loans. (Note that the US regulations generated both a supply of funds to the Eurodollar market and a demand for loans from it.)

3   Other nations had even more exchange controls and legal restrictions on their citizens than did the United States. Consequently, the opportunity to hold funds in Eurobanks was extremely attractive to firms and individuals in those countries. Eurodollar deposits were subject to no controls, they could be exchanged into any currency, they could be

used for payments anywhere in the world, and they were largely beyond the reach of the tax collector.

4   US banks are required to maintain reserves against their deposit liabilities, but Eurobanks are not required to maintain such reserves. Since reserves earn no interest, the requirement to hold them has adversely affected the ability of US banks to compete with their Eurobank rivals. (This factor may be less important now. In 1981, the Federal Reserve System authorized US banks to establish international banking facilities through which they may conduct banking business with foreigners, exempt from domestic regulations such as reserve requirements.)

A second reason for the rapid growth of the Eurodollar market is that it is a highly competitive and efficient market. Eurobanks pay attractive interest rates on time deposits placed with them, and they charge competitive rates of interest on loans they make. As we noted, spreads are small in this market – considerably smaller than in US banks. Eurobanks can operate in this way because they are dealing in large sums, their clerical costs are low because they do not operate a retail banking business, they have no legal reserve requirements to meet, and they are dealing mostly with blue-chip clients whose credit ratings are excellent. If a Eurobank accepts a 1-year time deposit of $100 million at 4 percent and simultaneously makes a 1-year loan of $100 million to IBM at 4⅛ percent, its gross profit is $125,000. Operating costs would be low and risk practically nil.

The effect of the Eurocurrency market on national monetary autonomy

The existence of this huge, highly competitive money market has tended to reduce the ability of any individual nation to operate an independent monetary policy while maintaining a fixed exchange rate. Such a policy usually entails an attempt to raise or lower the domestic interest rate. But, as Geoffrey Bell observed, "short-term funds, like water, find their own level, and there is little that even Canute-minded central bankers can do to arrest the forces of the market."[1] In the 1960s, for example, Germany tried to maintain a tight money policy to restrain inflationary pressures. But when interest rates rose in Germany and credit became scarce, German banks had an incentive to seek funds in the Eurodollar market where lower interest rates prevailed. To block that channel, the German central bank placed restrictions on commercial bank access to outside funds, but then German business firms themselves borrowed the funds they needed in the Eurodollar market. The German central bank tried to insulate the German economy by imposing various additional rules and regulations, but these proved to be difficult to enforce. The financial markets have shown great ingenuity in discovering new ways to get around the regulations.

Similarly, if a single country tried to stimulate its economy by pursuing an easy-money policy and reducing interest rates, funds would tend to flow out of that country. If its time-deposit rates dropped, firms would shift deposits to the Eurobanks. Borrowers would increase their borrowing in the low-interest-rate country and use the proceeds to repay higher-cost loans in other places. These actions tend to equalize interest rates in the various financial markets. The United States was in this position in the 1960s. The authorities wanted to keep interest rates low in order to stimulate economic activity and reduce unemployment. Regulation Q was used to limit the rate of interest paid on time deposits. But that led to an outflow of funds to the Eurodollar market, and forced the authorities to introduce a variety of regulations and restrictions designed to curb that outflow. Then, in 1969, the Federal Reserve instituted an extremely tight monetary policy in an effort to stop inflation. Interest rates rose sharply and US banks were put in a double bind – they could not raise their own time-deposit rates to attract and hold funds, but short-term interest rates were rising sharply and inducing depositors to switch to other types of assets. In their desperate search for funds, the banks turned to the Eurodollar market. They borrowed $15 billion in 1969, a huge sum at that time. This heavy demand for funds drove up interest rates in the Eurodollar market and, through it, put upward pressure on interest rates in countries in Europe and elsewhere. Their access to Eurodollar funds enabled US banks to escape or at least to moderate the tight-money pressure from the Federal Reserve, but it also transmitted that pressure to the rest of the world.

The advent of floating exchange rates has not greatly changed the role of the Eurocurrency market and the functions it performs. It has continued to grow at a rapid rate since floating began. To a considerable extent, the Eurocurrency market has become a world money market. National money markets are linked into it in many ways. Some scope for an independent monetary policy still exists for countries that maintain a flexible exchange rate, but the monetary authority in one country cannot change its policy without taking account of conditions in this world money market. Through arbitrage, domestic interest rates are kept in line with Eurocurrency interest rates in the same currency.

Interest rates in the US money market are closely linked to interest rates on comparable maturities in the Eurodollar market. For example, at any given time the interest rate on 3-month Eurodollar market deposits is about equal to the interest rate on 3-month certificates of deposit or Treasury bills in New York. Similarly, interest rates on Euro-Swiss franc deposits are closely linked to interest rates in the Swiss money market. But interest rates on financial assets denominated in euros can and do diverge from rates on assets denominated in dollars. As noted in Chapter 14, these differences are related to spot/forward exchange rate differentials and to the possibility of exchange rate changes. We will return to this matter later in this chapter.

Recycling oil payments

The Eurocurrency market played a major role in financing the huge current account imbalances that followed the oil shocks of the 1970s. The resulting build-up of international debt produced another difficult problem, however. After the sharp increases in oil prices in 1973 and in 1979, much concern was expressed about the ability of the international monetary system to handle the enormous flows of funds that would be involved. Many experts feared that a crisis or collapse of the system would occur, so massive was the disturbance to which it had to adjust. As it turned out, the system accommodated itself very smoothly to this major shift in direction and amount of international payments. Basically, the mechanism is quite simple, and it could possibly be compared to a game of musical chairs. The Eurocurrency markets played a major role in the mechanism through which payments were made from the oil-importing countries to the oil exporters, especially to members of OPEC. We will explain briefly what the problem was and how it was handled.

The oil price increase meant that oil-importing countries had to pay about $50 billion per year to the OPEC countries. This is an estimate of their current account deficit relative to OPEC; that is, the $50 billion represents OPEC exports minus their imports of goods and services. It was clear that OPEC nations could not quickly increase their imports to match the sudden huge rise in their exports.

Oil-importing countries had to pay for the oil largely in dollars. Thus in making payments they drew checks on their dollar deposits in US banks. OPEC countries then had to decide what to do with these large receipts of dollars. They chose to place a large part of them in the Eurodollar market – that is, they placed time deposits in Eurobanks. This gave the Euro-banks an immediate increase in their lending capacity, and they were eager to make new loans to match their new deposit liabilities. (Remember, they were paying perhaps 8 percent on those time deposits, and they could not afford to hold non-earning assets.)

Many oil-importing countries, having just drawn down their dollar balances and facing the need to pay for next month's oil as well, were eager to borrow dollars from the Eurobanks. When they did borrow, they paid the dollars to OPEC nations, who redeposited them in Eurobanks, thus making possible further loans to oil importers who could then pay for more oil, and so on. This process is what came to be called "recycling the petrodollars." The Eurocurrency market served as a financial intermediary between the oil importers and OPEC. OPEC nations could have made loans directly to oil importers (i.e. sold the oil on credit), but they much preferred to be paid in dollars and then to place deposits in large, prestigious commercial banks such as Barclays, Chase Manhattan, Bank of America, Lloyds, and other major participants in the Eurocurrency market. Furthermore, these banks then had to assume the risks of lending to the oil-importing countries. The borrowers were not only industrial countries, but also oil-importing underdeveloped countries throughout the world.

Very large sums were recycled in this way during the 1970s. The process involved a rapid build-up of debt, especially in certain Latin American countries such as Brazil and Argentina. When interest rates rose sharply in the 1980s and exports fell as a result of the world-wide recession, many debtor countries became unable to service their debt – that is, to pay the interest and repay the principal when it became due. The problem was aggravated by the fact that much of the debt was in short-term forms. Even if these loans were renewed (rolled over), the required interest payments rose sharply. This was a factor in the creation of the Latin American debt crisis of the early 1980s, which is discussed later in this chapter.

Floating exchange rates

As was noted earlier, the industrialized countries that adopted flexible exchange rates in 1973 did not do so because the academic arguments prevailed, but instead because the fixed exchange rate regime had failed twice in a period of less than 2 years, and because it was not clear what set of parities would succeed. Many countries, however, did not float, but instead pegged to other currencies or to the SDR. A number of European countries pegged to each other, and then floated as a group relative to the rest of the world. These countries later formed the European Monetary Union, a subject which will be discussed later in this chapter. The number of countries maintaining fixed or flexible rates, or various other arrangements as of early 2002 can be found in Table 20.3.

A very brief history of the US float

The March 1973 adoption of flexible exchange rates by the major industrialized countries was widely expected to be temporary. Fixed exchange rates were still viewed as the normal and preferred system, and it was thought that when the floating rates settled in a narrow range they could be re-fixed. The IMF had already begun discussions about how to reform the system through the Committee of Twenty (C-20). It was expected that those discussions would simply proceed under the new temporary arrangements.

Table 20.3 Exchange rate regimes of IMF member countries, as of 31 December 2001

Exchange regime	Number of countries
No separate legal tender (includes members of EMU)	40
Fixed rate with a currency board	8
Other conventional fixed pegs	41
Pegged within horizontal bands	5
Crawling pegs	4
Crawling or non-horizontal bands	6
Managed floating with no announced path for the exchange rate	42
Independently floating	40
Total	186

Source: 2002 IMF *Annual Report*, pp. 118–9.

For evidence that many developing countries that claim to maintain floating exchange rates actually manage them so closely as to almost produce a fixed parity, see Calvo, G. and Reinhart, C., "Fear of Floating," *Quarterly Journal of Economics*, May 2002.

The oil embargo of late 1973 and the 1974 increase in the price of oil from \$3 to \$8 per barrel changed everything. The OPEC countries suddenly had a huge current account surplus (over \$70 billion in 1975, declining to the \$40 billion range in following years), and there was no way to predict how or where this money would be invested. In light of the payments instability that could result from shifts in OPEC investment patterns, as well as other uncertainties resulting from higher oil prices, it did not appear feasible to return to a set of fixed parities. As a result, flexible exchange rates were accepted as the normal system for industrialized countries, despite widespread opposition among central bankers and finance ministry officials. This change was formalized in amendments to the IMF Articles of Agreement that were adopted in Kingston, Jamaica, in 1976.

The US dollar, which had depreciated in 1973, recovered in the following 3 years, and the system had settled into a relatively stable pattern by 1975–6. In 1977, however, a new US secretary of the treasury publicly stated that he thought the dollar was too strong and that it should depreciate. This unfortunate statement, combined with considerable un-certainty about the new leadership of the Federal Reserve Board, led to a decline in the dollar, which came under speculative attack by the summer and fall of 1978. A number of US allies organized a rescue package for the dollar in late 1978, but worsening US inflation continued to create doubts about its future. In late 1979, however, the newly appointed chairman of the Federal Reserve Board, Paul Volcker, presided over a sharp tightening of US monetary policy.

In early 1981, in part because of increasing market confidence that Chairman Volcker's policies would succeed in breaking the US inflation, a large volume of capital began flowing into the United States and the dollar began a long appreciation. By the time it peaked in early 1985, the dollar had appreciated by over 60 percent in nominal effective terms and by approximately 40 percent in real terms. A 40 percent real appreciation of the dollar meant a disastrous decline in the cost and price competitiveness of US firms operating in inter-national markets. Exports stagnated and imports grew enormously, resulting in huge trade and current account deficits.

This appreciation can be seen as resulting primarily from an extremely unusual set of macroeconomic policies in the United States. The Kemp–Roth tax cut of 1981 combined with a large increase in military expenditures to produce large federal budget deficits. The resulting increase in the US Treasury borrowing coincided with a tight monetary policy, resulting in very high interest rates. These high rates, combined with the widespread conviction that US inflation was being controlled, caused capital inflows that bid the dollar up to levels at which US products were uncompetitive in world markets. Fiscal and monetary policies were being taken in opposite directions, and the result was an exchange rate that severely damaged large parts of the US tradable goods sector. The industrial and agricultural Midwest, which is particularly dependent on export markets, was injured severely by this situation and suffered through a slow recovery from the early 1980s recession. One benefit of the overvalued dollar, however, was that it did force US tradable goods prices down and helped to end the inflation that had plagued the US economy in the late 1970s and early 1980s. For US producers of tradable goods and for their employees, however, this benefit of an overvalued dollar was difficult to appreciate.

In early 1985 the dollar, then widely viewed as overvalued, finally peaked and started to depreciate. This was in part the result of an earlier easing of US monetary policy, which had helped generate a recovery from the 1982 recession. This decline was encouraged by US official intervention in the exchange market, which had been lacking during the period of appreciation. In late 1985, the secretary of the treasury met with the finance ministers of the major industrialized countries at the Plaza Hotel in New York, where it was agreed that the dollar was still too high and that coordinated intervention should be used to produce a further depreciation.

The other industrialized countries accepted this view in part because enormous US trade deficits had led to a rapid increase in protectionist sentiment in the United States. It was feared that if the dollar did not fall to levels at which the US trade account could recover, the Congress would pass protectionist legislation with a sufficient majority to override a presidential veto, thus threatening a breakdown of the carefully constructed post-war trading system.

The dollar continued to decline in 1986 and early 1987, leading to another meeting of the finance ministers at the Louvre in Paris, at which it was decided that existing exchange rates were approximately correct and that no further depreciation of the dollar was needed. The goal of intervention, and perhaps of loose coordination of monetary policies, was then to be to stabilize exchange rates at close to existing levels.

Despite this intention, the dollar appreciated by over 10 percent in 1988–9, which was seen as a threat to the further recovery of the US trade balance. In 1989–90, however, this appreciation was reversed, and by the end of 1990 the dollar had fallen slightly below its 1988 lows. Despite declining US interest rates, the dollar rose slightly during the first part of 1991, perhaps owing to the effect of the rapid conclusion of the Gulf War on market confidence. The dollar weakened modestly in 1992, rose in 1993, and then declined in 1994. It then appreciated from late 1999 to the end of 2001, having risen by about 35 percent from its 1995–7 lows, before depreciating by about 10 percent in 2002 and early 2003.

US current account deficits, which had been in the $100–$200 billion range in the 1980s and early 1990s, worsened late in the decade, reaching levels of over $400 billion by 2001–2. As was argued in Chapter 12, these deficits are ultimately the gap between US investment and domestic savings rates. Investment has not been a particularly high percentage of US GDP, but national savings rates have been very low. During the 1980s and early 1990s large public sector dis-saving (budget deficits) offset much of an otherwise normal private savings rate. When the reduction of US military expenditures, which followed the end of the Cold War, and large tax increases in 1990 and 1993 brought budget deficits down and actually produced brief surpluses late in the decade, private saving rates declined to offset the public sector gain. The gap between modest investment rates of 16–18 percent of GDP and national savings rates of only 12–14 percent persisted, thereby requiring a current account deficit of about 4 percent of GDP.

Continuing questions about flexible exchange rates

As suggested in Chapter 19, flexible exchange rates have not performed as their supporters predicted. The period of almost two decades of floating has produced a number of problems, the most important being unexpectedly large volatility in both nominal and real exchange rates. Supporters of this system had widely predicted that nominal rates would move only to approximately offset differing rates of inflation, leaving real exchange rates largely unchanged. This expectation was not realized, and changes in real rates were both large and disruptive. Even during the 1970s, real exchange rates were far from constant, but the dollar became far more volatile in the 1980s, before becoming less so in the 1990s. Between 1973 and 1979, the average real exchange rate change for 16 currencies of industrialized countries was 6.8 percent, but the larger shock was the real appreciation of the dollar by over 40 percent in 1981–5, followed by an equally large real depreciation in 1985–8.[2]

Real exchange rate movements of these magnitudes are quite disruptive, and there has been a growing desire among central bankers and finance ministry officials to avoid them. A real depreciation raises the prices of tradable goods relative to those of nontradables, thus redistributing income within the economy. The tradables sector gains, at the cost of losses of real income to the nontradables sector. A real appreciation has the opposite effect, as the tradables sector loses real income. The 1981–5 appreciation of the dollar devastated the tradables sector of the US economy, and some of the affected industries took years to recover.

This redistribution of incomes can sometimes have sizable regional impacts across an economy. The US Midwest, for example, has a particularly heavy concentration of export industries in both agriculture and manufacturing, so the appreciation of the dollar in the early 1980s was very damaging to that region. As noted in Chapter 17, most of western Canada is oriented toward the production of exports (oil, metals, grain, forest products), whereas Ontario produces more nontradables such as services. Therefore a real depreciation of the Canadian dollar shifts real incomes from Ontario toward the west.

If these movements of real exchange rates were long run or permanent responses to terms-of-trade movements or changes in competitiveness, they might be accepted as necessary, but this has not been the case. Large changes in real exchange rates have often been caused by temporary factors and have later been reversed, the rise and fall of the dollar during the 1980s being the most striking example of that pattern.

The widespread desire to avoid or at least limit such real appreciations and depreciations has increasingly constrained national monetary policies, which cancels one of the strongest original arguments for floating exchange rates. The Meade conflict cases, which were discussed in Chapter 16 for a regime of fixed exchange rates, are reappearing in a new form. The desire to limit the depreciation of a currency strongly implies the need for a tighter domestic monetary policy, which may conflict with a domestic goal of macroeconomic expansion. Similarly, a real appreciation could be stopped with an expansionary monetary policy, which could conflict with a desire to control inflation.

If a currency is depreciating when a recession appears to be starting, the central bank faces a clear conflict: the desire to stabilize the exchange rate implies tighter money, whereas the desire to expand the domestic economy implies the opposite. An appreciation during a period in which inflation is a threat creates the same type of conflict.

Under fixed exchange rates, monetary policy had to be managed to avoid unacceptable payments disequilibria, which often meant conflicts with domestic macroeconomic goals. Under flexible exchange rates, monetary policy may have to be managed to avoid unacceptable exchange rate volatility, which can also create frequent conflicts with domestic macroeconomic goals. It is not clear that domestic monetary policies are much more independent in a regime of flexible exchange rates than they were under the parities of Bretton Woods.

The difficulties attributed to this experience with flexible exchange rates should not be taken as suggesting that the system has somehow failed. The volume of international trade has continued to grow faster than world output since the early 1970s, as was noted in Chapter 1, so flexible exchange rates have not significantly discouraged trade. Capital flows have exploded in volume, and tourism and other international transactions have expanded rapidly. Flexible exchange rates have not, as some observers feared, repressed the continued growth of the international economy, but they have produced a few surprising and disruptive effects, particularly large movements of real exchange rates.

Trying to explain exchange rate movements

A number of models of exchange rate determination have been presented at various points in the second half of this book. Since econometric studies have been done on these models, it may be useful now to see how they have performed empirically. Although it may be necessary to summarize this research, it is not enjoyable for economists who expect academic models to explain what happens in the real world. The models, to put it mildly, have a poor track record. Floating exchange rates have moved in ways that are not easily explained by any of the models. To summarize:

1   *Cassel's purchasing power parity model.* Any expectation that floating exchange rates would move to just offset differing rates of inflation has been sadly disappointed. As was noted earlier, movement of real exchange rates has been large and persistent. Cassel was not the only economist to argue for the likelihood of relatively constant real exchange rates; Milton Friedman's classic defense of floating exchange rates predicted that purchasing power parity would hold, so he, too, was wrong.[3]

2   *Uncovered interest parity.* In the section of Chapter 14 that dealt with forward exchange markets, it was argued that spot exchange rates should move to just offset differences in nominal interest rates; countries with high nominal interest rates should experience depreciations, and vice versa. As noted earlier, this model has performed very badly. According to a survey of research by Kenneth Froot and Richard Thaler, industrialized countries with high nominal interest rates usually have appreciating currencies. Seventy-five studies were surveyed, and the average coefficient on the interest rate differential was –0.88, when it should have been +1.0.[4]

3   *The monetarist model.* According to this approach, as was argued in Chapter 15, currencies should depreciate in response to an increase in the domestic assets of a country's central bank (or a country's money supply) and appreciate in response to an increase in a country's total output, which is a proxy for money demand. Rudiger Dornbusch tested this model for five major industrialized countries, and it performed badly. Some coefficients were of the wrong sign, and others were insignificant. Dornbusch concluded that the monetarist model was "an unsatisfactory theory of exchange rate determination."[5]

4 *The portfolio balance model.* Jeffrey Frankel tested this model for five major industrialized countries. Out of 20 coefficients, 11 were of the wrong sign, and very few were significant.[6]

5 *Filter rules.* If academic models of exchange rate determination, which emphasize economic and financial fundamentals, are put aside, and the market is instead viewed as responding to random shocks, the question arises as to how the market incorporates such shocks or new information into exchange rates. If it does so instantly, that is, if the current exchange rate fully reflects all available information, the exchange rate should follow a random walk as such information arrives. It has often been suggested, however, that the market may not be very efficient and that exchange rate patterns can therefore be found. If, for example, the market absorbs new information slowly, then the exchange rate will follow short-to-medium-term trends. If that were true, money could be made by taking a long position in any currency that has recently risen by some amount and by shorting currencies that have recently declined. An alternative view is that the exchange market overreacts to new information, and therefore recent changes are likely to be partially reversed. If that were true, it would be profitable to sell currencies that have recently risen, and purchase those that have declined. Statistical tests are frequently undertaken to discover trading or **filter rules** that would have made money in the past, with the hope that they will do so in the future. The first approach (buy a currency that has recently risen, and sell a falling currency) would have made money for speculators trading the dollar in the 1980–7 period, because it would have suggested buying dollars in 1981 and selling them in mid-1985. Both decisions would have been highly profitable.

This rule, however, would probably have lost money in the 1988–94 period, when the dollar moved within a narrow range. Econometric studies have been done on such filter rules with mixed results. Some studies find that the first of the two trading rules described above would have made money during some specific periods, but other models show that these models more often lose money if transactions costs are fully allowed for. Nobody should think it safe to gamble on future exchange rates using such a filter rule just because it appears to fit past data.

None of the academic models explains exchange rates well, and speculative filter rules have only sporadic success, leading one student of this subject to conclude that "Economists do not yet understand the determinants of short to medium-run movements in exchange rates."[7] It should be noted, however, that if any economist did understand, and therefore could accurately predict, how exchange rates behave, that fortunate person would be unlikely to tell anybody but would instead "buy low and sell high."

Protectionism and flexible exchange rates

To return briefly to the subject of protectionism and mercantilism, the adoption of flexible exchange rates has not had the effect of reducing political pressures for restrictions on imports. These pressures have instead continued and sometimes seem to have worsened. The fact that protection for one industry produces exchange rate impacts that harm other tradable-goods industries is not widely understood, and this argument is seldom raised in political debates over import restrictions. The hope that the existence of flexible exchange rates would discourage or eliminate protectionist campaigns has not yet been realized. None the less, the 1994 passage of the Uruguay Round agreement by the US Congress, and the recent renewal of fast-track negotiating authority for the Bush administration as it enters the Doha WTO round, are encouraging to those still hoping for open trade.

Alternatives to flexible exchange rates

It is easier to conclude that the existing system of managed floats has performed imperfectly than it is to design an attractive replacement. Widespread unhappiness with the experience of the last two and a half decades has led to a variety of proposals for reform, but none of them has gained sufficient support to threaten current arrangements. It may be worthwhile, however, to review briefly some of the proposals.

Since the exchange rate volatility of recent years has been widely blamed on enormous speculative capital flows, it is occasionally suggested that such transactions be prohibited, taxed, or otherwise discouraged. Exchange market controls could be used to make such capital flows illegal, or an exchange market tax could be used to discourage them.[8] A closely related alternative would be the maintenance of a dual exchange rate, with all capital transactions segregated into a market that operated on the basis of a clean float.[9] Capital flows would then have to balance, meaning that net capital flows would equal zero. A fixed, or at least a more stable, exchange rate would be maintained for current account transactions. The goal of all such proposals is to protect current account transactions, and therefore real economic activity, from shocks resulting from large shifts in the capital account.

All these proposals have at least two major disadvantages. First, international capital flows move a scarce productive resource from less to more productive locations. Prohibiting or discouraging such flows must result in a less efficient allocation of the world's capital stock, thereby making the world economy less productive. Second, exchange controls or taxes on capital account transactions are easily evaded, and the imposition of such systems therefore invites widespread cheating.

False invoicing or transfer pricing, as discussed in Chapter 13, is one of the more obvious ways of moving capital despite such rules. This involves the use of false or misleading prices on international trade transactions in order to move capital. If, for example, an investor in India wants to purchase assets in the United States despite legal prohibitions on such transactions, he could simply understate export prices on invoices. If this investor is exporting to the United States garments that have a value of $250,000 and the investor has a cooperative importer in New York, the invoice may show exports of only $150,000, which is the amount actually remitted back to India. The cooperative importer then invests the other $100,000 in the United States on behalf of the exporter.

There is no way of knowing how common such under-invoicing is, but many believe it is a widespread means of evading both exchange controls and *ad valorem* tariffs. With regard to the latter, if, for example, Australia maintains a 10 percent import tariff on foreign cars, invoicing a car at $9,000 which is actually worth $10,000 saves the importer $100, unless this ruse is discovered by the Australian customs agents. This is why customs valuation procedures are often so controversial. In addition, multinational firms can use transfer pricing to shift profits from high-tax to low-tax jurisdictions. If, for example, a British firm owns a subsidiary in Germany, where the corporate tax rates are considerably higher than in the UK, a great temptation will exist to overprice any parts, components, or services that are sold to the subsidiary, and to underprice anything the parent firm purchases from that subsidiary. Doing so shifts profits away from Germany and into the UK, saving the parent firm the difference in the tax rates.

This has been a large source of conflict between the Internal Revenue Service of the United States and various Japanese multinational firms which have US subsidiaries. Washington accountants, lawyers, and tax economists have a sizable business working for each side in settling these disputes.

Exchange controls have generally been found to become less effective the longer they are in operation because people find more ways to evade them.[10] Dual exchange rates have the same problems because false invoicing can be used to shift capital account transactions into the current account market. When Belgium maintained such a dual rate system, with a higher value for the Belgian franc for current account than for capital transactions, it was widely rumored that Belgium's trade statistics for one year showed imports of eggs from the Netherlands that exceeded the number of eggs laid by all Dutch hens that year. The story may be apocryphal, but its underlying point is valid: both exchange controls and dual exchange rates encourage graft and cheating, and therefore ought to be avoided.

A **crawling peg** that follows purchasing power parity is sometimes proposed as an alternative to either fully fixed or flexible rates. Under this approach a fixed exchange rate is maintained, but frequent parity changes are made to offset the difference between local and foreign rates of inflation. If, for example, Brazilian prices are rising by 40 percent per year, while inflation in the rest of the world averages 4 percent, the Brazilian government can devalue the currency by 3 percent per month, for an annual total of 36 percent, which equals the difference between local and foreign rates of inflation.

This approach has been used with some success in developing countries with high rates of inflation, but it has the disadvantage of not allowing for other sources of balance-of-payments disequilibria. If differing rates of inflation were the only source of payments problems, this reform proposal would be attractive, but that is obviously not the case. Changing terms of trade, shifts in rates of return to capital, and a variety of other factors affect the balance of payments, and a purchasing-power-parity crawl does not provide a route to payments adjustment when they occur. A purchasing-power-parity crawl also eliminates any discipline on the central bank, which no longer has to limit inflation in order to avoid balance-of-payments deficits. Theoretical arguments have also been developed that suggest that a purchasing-power-parity crawl may respond to random real shocks in a destabilizing manner, that is, that domestic prices may increase and the exchange rate may decrease without limit. This depends importantly on how the central bank responds to the shock, the point being that such a crawling rate lacks a nominal anchor unless the central bank provides one.[11]

Finally, there is the option of returning to rigidly fixed exchange rates. In the early 1980s there was considerable public discussion of reviving the gold standard, but that proposal is no longer under active consideration, in part because of fears that unstable gold production in South Africa or Russia could result in unstable monetary policies in the countries that were tied to gold. Ronald McKinnon's proposal for close coordination of monetary policies between the major industrialized countries has received more serious consideration. He would have these countries set target exchange rates based on current purchasing power parities, and then use coordinated shifts in monetary policy to keep market rates close to those parities.[12]

This proposal has disadvantages that are similar to those of the Bretton Woods system. It would leave national central banks with little or no independence in managing domestic aggregate demand, particularly in the Meade conflict cases discussed in Chapter 16. What would the Federal Reserve System do, for example, if the dollar fell significantly below its target parity just as the US economy entered a recession? The coordination rules would call for a tightening of US monetary policy when the domestic economy called for the opposite.

It is not clear that such a system of monetary policy coordination could survive a series of such policy conflicts, particularly if they occurred shortly before national elections. It is sometimes suggested facetiously that the major industrialized countries should first co-ordinate the timing of their elections, perhaps setting them at the same time every 4 years. Close monetary policy coordination and stable exchange rates could be maintained for 3 years, with each country being allowed to do whatever it wanted during the year before elections.

The current system of managed floating exchange rates will likely be maintained for the foreseeable future, but if exchange rates return to the volatile behavior of the early and mid-1980s, fixed exchange rates could be considered more seriously. Loose and informal coordination of monetary policies and of exchange market intervention will probably continue as a way to reduce exchange rate volatility, with countries being allowed to act more independently if faced with clear conflict situations.

The broad lesson of recent experience is that open economies cannot escape some degree of vulnerability to macroeconomic shocks that originate abroad, and that policy independence will always be partially constrained by balance-of-payments or exchange rate considerations. The only way to avoid these costs of interdependence is to maintain an isolated economy. The economic performance of countries that have tried to remain in autarky suggests the enormous costs of such economic isolation. Trade and other international transactions produce huge efficiency gains and other advantages. Vulnerability to foreign economic shocks and constraints on macroeconomic policies are unavoidable costs of these benefits. Some degree of exchange rate flexibility and modest reforms of the international monetary system can be used to limit these problems, but it does not appear that they can be eliminated.

The European Monetary Union

Early history

Shortly after the breakdown of the IMF par value system, several European countries began to operate a joint float, a scheme in which they linked their currencies together by limiting the range of exchange rate fluctuation between any two currencies in the group. The result was that the currencies of participating countries moved together relative to the dollar, rising or falling as a group. The moving band, its width fixed by the permitted range of fluctuation between member currencies, traced a snake-like path as it floated against the dollar; financial journalists promptly dubbed it the "European snake."

The active participants in this scheme varied as countries joined or withdrew. The joint float led to the creation, in 1979, of a European Monetary System, which was a major step toward the **European Monetary Union**. Members agreed to maintain the exchange value of their currencies within 2.25 percent of each other (except for Italy, which was allowed a 6 percent range). At the end of 1991, the members of the European Union agreed to the **Maastricht Treaty**, which was to accelerate movement toward full monetary union, as well as advance European unity in a number of other areas such as social policies and immigration. As of the end of 1992 there were nine full EMS members (Belgium, Denmark, France, Ireland, Italy, Germany, the United Kingdom, the Netherlands, and Luxembourg).[13]

In 1992–3 the System encountered serious problems. The Bundesbank adopted very tight money to offset the inflationary effects of the unification of East and West Germany. This tightening required that other members follow the Bundesbank in order to maintain narrow exchange rate bands. The United Kingdom entered a recession in 1991–2, and found the Bundesbank-determined policies to be almost impossible to accept. The British withdrew from the exchange rate band, known as the "Exchange Rate Mechanism," in the summer of 1992. Then other countries, including France and Italy, encountered recessions, making the tight German monetary policy very painful. As a result the narrow bands of the System were temporarily widened to 15 percent, the guilder being an exception because it remained within a narrow band relative to the DM.[14] Nonetheless, the Maastricht Treaty became legally binding late in 1993, and movement toward monetary unification continued. The European Monetary Union and its central bank began operations in January of 1999.

Recent developments

European Union members were allowed to join EMU if they met five convergence criteria:

1   The rate of inflation in the country must not exceed the average of the three lowest-inflation members by more than 1.5 percentage points.
2   Long-term interest rates in the country must not exceed the average of such yields in the three lowest-inflation-rate countries by more than 2.0 percentage points.
3   The government budget deficit must not be greater than 3 percent of GDP.
4   Outstanding government debt must not exceed 60 percent of GDP.
5   The exchange rate for the country within the Exchange Rate Mechanism must not have been changed within the previous 2 years.

Eleven countries were formally designated in May 1998 to be the founding members of EMU, despite the fact that not all of them quite met all the criteria, number 4 being a particular problem. The 11 countries which started EMU in January 1999 were Germany, France, Italy, the Netherlands, Belgium, Luxembourg, Ireland, Spain, Austria, Finland, and Portugal. Greece failed to meet the convergence criteria when EMU began, but soon did reach the criteria and joined. Denmark, Sweden, and the United Kingdom decided not to join, at least for the time being. Denmark, however, has an agreement with EMU under which the krone has a parity relative to the euro and is kept within a band of plus or minus 2.25 percent.

The European Central Bank, which emerged from the European Monetary Institute, began operations in January 1999. Exchange rates among the member currencies were rigidly fixed to the euro, which is the legal currency, during 1999–2001. Local currencies were withdrawn from circulation and were replaced by euro notes and coins in January 2002, fully completing the monetary union. The twelve national central banks have not been closed, but instead play roles which are similar to those of the twelve Federal Reserve Banks in the United States. Each of the twelve central bank governors is a member of the Governing Council of the ECB, which determines monetary policy in a manner similar to that of the Federal Open Market Committee within the Federal Reserve System. Short-term management of the ECB is provided by the Executive Board which has six members, who are also members of the Governing Council, which therefore has 18 members. Six countries (Germany, the Netherlands, Finland, Greece, Spain, and Italy) now have two votes on the Governing Council, while the other six EMU members each have one vote. The Executive Board resembles the seven-member Board of Governors of the US Federal Reserve System.

EXHIBIT 20.1 One Currency, but Not One Economy

By Robert M. Dunn Jr.

WASHINGTON

With euro bills and coins now circulating across much of Europe, the European Monetary Union is fully in place. The post-World War II European leaders' dream of an economically and politically unified continent is one large step closer to realization, and membership in the monetary union could easily grow to 20 or more countries from the current 12 as the larger European Union, of which it is an offshoot, expands to the east.

The Euro nations have their own business rhythms.

A fully operational European Monetary Union does not come, however, with a guarantee of success. There is one enormous problem: This union creates a single monetary policy for a group of quite different national economies that often experience divergent business-cycle patterns.

During most of the last three years, while the European Central Bank managed monetary policy for the 12 member countries even without common coins and paper money, Germany's economy was decidedly soft – a situation that lower interest rates could be expected to ease. The Netherlands, Ireland and a few other small countries, however, were booming; for them, lower interest rates would have encouraged inflation. The Governing Council of the European Central Bank, which plays the role that the Federal Reserve's Open Market Committee, under Alan Greenspan, plays in the United States, kept interest rates low in 1999 but raised them in 2000 and early 2001. (A modest and overdue easing has recently begun.)

The central bank's policy reportedly pleased the Germans and displeased the Dutch and Irish in 1999; vice versa in 2000 and 2001.

As long as business-cycle conditions differ significantly among European Monetary Union countries, there is no way for the central bank's policies to avoid creating serious problems for some members. There have been widespread rumors of controversy within the bank's Governing Council, which includes the governors of all the member nations' individual central banks. But since that board, unlike the Open Market Committee of the Fed, does not publish minutes of its meetings or records of its votes, there is no way to know just how displeased various members may have been.

In the United States, the Federal Reserve System sometimes has similar problems in designing a monetary policy for the country's 12 districts. In 1986 and 1987, for example, most of the American economy was booming but the Dallas district was in a severe recession due to collapsing oil and gas prices. The Fed kept interest rates fairly high, and the local recession in the oil-producing states got worse instead of better. More typically, however, this country behaves as a single national economy and shares cyclical shocks across its regions.

The patterns of economic ups and downs remain far more diverse in the European Monetary Union countries, and it is not clear that this will change soon. The designers of the monetary union thought that the imposition of a single monetary policy, combined with free trade among the members, would cause cyclical conditions to converge quickly, producing a unified group of economies that would closely resemble the United States econ-

Thomas Fuchs

omy. While this may eventually occur, so far evidence of such convergence remains rather scarce.

A 1997 agreement also limits the power of the individual nations in the European Monetary Union to use government spending or tax cuts to ease national downturns. They can be fined if they run budget deficits of more than 3 percent of their gross domestic products. No fines have been levied yet, but the threat is there.

Even if the economies of the original European Monetary Union members become more similar in their cyclical behavior, it will take far longer for the convergence to include the new member nations expected to come in within the next 10 or 15 years. The chances for consensus on the Governing Council, however thin now, will become far more distant with more members representing divergent national economies. And the larger nations, like Germany, France and Italy, might well resent the power of representatives from much smaller nations to outvote them on monetary policy.

All of this does not mean that the European Monetary Union is likely to fail. But clearly the arrival of the euro as the standard currency – momentous as it is for the average European consumer – does not guarantee the union's success.

Source: New York Times, Op-Ed Page, January 3, 2002. © *New York Times*. Reprinted with permission.

The euro was expected to be a strong currency, but doubts about the firmness of the European Central Bank's monetary policy in the face of high unemployment rates in Europe led to speculative pressures which caused it to depreciate from $1.17 to about 85 US cents in 1999–2001, before it recovered to about $1.15 between the spring of 2002 and mid-2003. Eight new countries (Hungary, the Czech Republic, Poland, Estonia, Latvia, Lithuania, Slovenia, and Malta) are scheduled to join the European Union in 2004, and to join EMU in 2006.

Although the monetary union began operations in January 1999, its success is far from assured. The problems facing any large monetary union are best seen through what has become known as the theory of **optimum currency areas**. The question to be addressed by this literature is what is the ideal area over which either a single currency or rigidly fixed exchange rates should prevail. This question was first raised in this form by Robert Mundell and Ronald McKinnon in the early 1960s.[15] Mundell argued that an optimum currency area should be no larger than the region over which labor was mobile, so that localized recessions could be eased by having workers move to where jobs were more plentiful. If France was a currency area, for example, a localized recession in Paris could be handled in part by having workers move to other regions of the country. A currency area consisting of almost all of the continent of Europe, however, potentially faces serious difficulties because it is not easy for people to move between countries seeking work. If there is a recession in southern Europe, for example, it is far from easy for Italian workers to move to the Netherlands to find jobs. Differences in language, culture, and national retirements systems make such mobility quite difficult in Europe. The addition of eight new members, which will extend EMU far to the east and somewhat to the south, will make this problem more serious.

This problem exists in any geographically large monetary union, including the United States. During the mid-1990s, for example, New England was in a recession due to defense expenditure cutbacks while the rest of the country was quite prosperous. The fact that the Federal Reserve Bank of Boston is part of a monetary union of twelve districts meant that it was impossible to design a monetary policy that would produce prompt recovery in New England without encouraging inflation elsewhere in the country. Since it is difficult or impossible for large numbers of workers to move quickly from New England to other parts of the country, the United States may be larger than an optimum currency area in terms of Mundell's argument. Countries which are members of the European Monetary Union can be expected to face problems which are similar to those faced by the Boston Federal Reserve District in the mid-1990s, as is suggested in Exhibit 20.1.

McKinnon's view of an optimum currency area is that it must be large enough to stabilize the internal price level despite changes in the external exchange rate. A small currency area has the major disadvantage of an internal price level that is dominated by tradables. These prices change whenever the exchange rate moves, destabilizing the overall price structure. Imagine a currency area consisting of New York City. Almost all products produced or consumed by residents of the city would be either exported or imported, meaning that when the New York City dollar depreciated, virtually all prices would rise, and vice versa. A flexible exchange rate for New York City would produce such price-level instability that the local currency would lose its ability to function as a stable store of value. New York residents might refuse to use such a currency and instead move toward a foreign currency (New Jersey dollars) which they viewed as having a more stable purchasing power. The McKinnon approach would suggest that Europe would be a far better currency area than France or any other single European country, and that the movement to a full monetary union of twelve members was a good idea.

The problem is that the Mundell and McKinnon views conflict, and therefore no currency area can meet both goals. Both Europe and the United States are too large for the Mundell approach. This means that regional recessions remain a major problem, but they are both big enough to largely stabilize internal prices, as McKinnon suggests. Smaller currency areas, such as the United Kingdom outside of the EMS, might ease the problem of localized recessions at the cost of creating a less stable price level than would be ideal. There is no perfect solution to this conflict, as the Europeans have discovered.

If it is so difficult to form a currency union, one might wonder why the Europeans have tried so hard. In addition to stabilizing the internal price level, a single currency in Europe provides a number of other advantages, including the following:

1   It is far easier to manage European Union institutions, such as the Common Agricultural Policy, with a single currency. In the past, if the franc depreciated against the DM, either French agricultural support prices had to rise or German prices had to fall. The CAP was in constant flux when such exchange rate changes occurred, which made its costs difficult to predict.

2   EMU is intended to impose anti-inflationary discipline on countries, such as Italy, Spain, and France, which have had histories of serious inflation. A single currency, of course, encourages a single rate of inflation across Europe, which has been quite low.

3   A single currency is a powerful symbol of European unification, and a major step toward a federation of Europe, although citizens of European countries who are of more nationalistic views see this as a disadvantage rather than an advantage of EMU. For many senior European politicians who have favored such unification since shortly after World War II, this is the dominant reason for EMU. Some have recognized the economic difficulties of EMU, as implied by the Mundell argument, and have simply said that the political goals of European unity are far more important than any economic problems resulting from EMU.

4   The euro may become a strong rival to the dollar for the role as the dominant world currency, thereby strengthening the competitive position of financial centers such as Frankfurt and Amsterdam against New York. This is viewed as a major argument for eventual British entry, because it would make London a far more powerful financial center.

5   Having a single currency across much of Europe produces large savings in transactions costs in exchanging one currency for others. A Dutchman is said to have traveled to each of the other EMU members a few years ago, exchanging money into the currency of each country as he traveled. He started with 1,000 guilders. By the time he got back to the Netherlands, he had 275 guilders. Commissions had used up almost 75 percent of his money in eleven transactions. Thousands of people were employed trading one European currency against another, and are now hopefully employed doing something more productive.

6   Since there is only one currency for the EMU members, it will be impossible for any single country to use its exchange rate for mercantilist purposes. France cannot devalue to gain a competitive advantage against Germany and Italy. The British decision to leave the exchange rate mechanism of the European Monetary System during the summer of 1992 was widely resented on the Continent, because sterling depreciated sharply, helping the UK to recover from a recession at the expense of its competitors elsewhere in Europe. Members of EMU cannot use their exchange rate in this manner.

Despite these advantages of EMU, a major question remains whether a single monetary policy can be successfully implemented across such a divergent group of countries. A "one size fits all" monetary policy will have serious problems when the business cycle in one region of EMU differs sharply from that prevailing in the majority of the member countries. If, for example, all of northern Europe is quite prosperous and favors a restrictive monetary policy, while Italy, Spain, and Portugal are in a serious recession, life will be quite difficult for EMU. One can foresee strong disagreements within the EMU management boards when such cyclical differences exist, as various members argue for policies fitting their country's needs against opposition from members whose countries are in different cyclical circumstances.

Monetary unions are very difficult to create, but, as the experience of the Soviet Union and Czechoslovakia made clear in the early 1990s, they are quite easy to take apart.[16] The fact that EMU is operating successfully at present does not mean that it will necessarily retain all of its members permanently. Countries whose business cycle patterns very frequently differ from those of the majority of the members may face a strong temptation to attempt to leave.

Changes in the role of the SDR

The 1976 amendments to the Articles of Agreement of the IMF included changes in the definition of the SDR and in the interest rate charged for its use. Originally, the SDR was defined as the gold content of 1 US dollar, but that definition became unacceptable to other countries when the link to gold was cut. The SDR is now equal to a basket of currencies that are most important in world trade. As of 30 April 2002 the value of the SDR equaled the total of the following amounts of each of five currencies:

euro	0.4260
US dollar	0.5770
Yen	21.0000
Sterling	0.984

An SDR was worth U.S. $1.2677 at that time.

Source: IMF *Annual Report*, 2002, p. 64.

The interest rate that is applied to countries using their SDR allocations is a weighted average of short-term yields in the five countries whose currencies make up the SDR. New allocations of SDRs occurred in 1979, 1980, and 1981, but there have been none since then. When US inflation was very serious in the late 1970s and early 1980s, there was some thought that the SDR would replace the dollar as the dominant reserve asset, but the return to relative price stability in the United States has restored the dollar to its previous position as a widely acceptable reserve asset, and the SDR has not become as important in the international financial system as was expected a decade or two ago.

Two decades of developing country debt crises

Although there is a long history of developing and other countries encountering balance of payments crises which made it impossible for them to meet make scheduled interest or principle payments on foreign debts, the period since 1982 has produced an unusual concentration of these unhappy events. Mexico, Brazil, and many other Latin American countries experienced a payments collapse in 1982–3 which lasted much of the decade; it resulted in large losses being imposed on US and other banks which had lent to them, and a period of serious hardship in these countries as the policies described in Chapter 17 were applied to turn the situation around. Mexico experienced a repeat crisis at the end of 1994, but a financing package provided by the United States and the IMF avoided serious losses to the banks, and adjustment policies worked quickly, allowing Mexico to return to relative economic health in less than 2 years.

A massive payments crisis broke out in South East Asia in 1997; it started in Thailand in the summer of 1997, but quickly spread to Malaysia and Indonesia, before moving north to Korea. At the time of this writing South Korea and Malaysia have largely recovered, Thailand is a bit behind them, and Indonesia is still in some trouble. Russia experienced serious trouble in 1998 and suspended payments on foreign debts. In early 2002 Argentina defaulted on almost $100 billion in foreign debts, and is now mired in a depression which almost rivals that experienced by the United States in the 1930s. That crisis may be spreading to Uruguay and Brazil, and could become a broader regional conflagration. It has been a very difficult two decades, both for the troubled developing countries and for the commercial banks which, perhaps unwisely, lent them money.

Although details obviously vary among crises, most countries encountering such trouble share a number of characteristics:

1   They have run current accounts into the distant past which have resulted in their being large net debtors, with much of the money being owed to commercial banks in New York, London, Tokyo, and a few other industrialized country financial centers. The debts are denominated in dollars, sterling, yen, or another hard currency, meaning that the devaluation of an LDC currency imposes large capital losses on the debtor government and on others in the country who have borrowed abroad.

2   This debt typically has short average maturities, meaning that the countries must "roll over" or refinance the debts rather frequently. This gives the foreign banks opportunities to at least try to withdraw their funds if they feel that the country's risk profile has deteriorated badly. Interest rates on this debt are well above prime yields, and are adjusted up whenever monetary policy is tightened in the creditor country or if the perceived riskiness of the debtor country increases.

3   At the time of the crisis the debtor country is running a large current account deficit, which is likely to have been caused by the combination of a fixed nominal exchange rate and serious domestic inflation. The inflation results from excessively expansionary fiscal and monetary policies, with the government and central bank showing insufficient self-discipline. Large budget deficits are often monetized, producing predictable results. Sometimes the current account has also been worsened by recent negative shocks to the country's terms of trade. A sharp decline in the world price of a country's dominant export commodity may be a sign of trouble to come, but the dominant problem is typically an inflation-driven upward crawl (or trot) of the real effective exchange rate which has continued for sufficient time to make the local currency badly overvalued.

4   The domestic banking system of the country is often deeply troubled. It probably has a high percentage of nonperforming loans, badly inadequate equity capitalization, and weak supervision from the central bank or other regulatory authorities. The circumstances of domestic commercial banks may have been worsened by weak or nonexistent bankruptcy laws which make it impossible for the banks to seize assets from debtors who refuse to repay loans. In far too many countries borrowers can simply ignore the demands

from banks for prompt payment because they know that the banks cannot force them into bankruptcy or use any other means to compel repayment. These commercial banking problems were probably at their worst in the Asian crisis of 1997–9, and included the following:

a   Insufficient net worth as a share of total liabilities, meaning that even modest losses from bad loans threatened insolvency. These banks had grown rapidly without selling more common stock, or retaining sufficient earnings, to build net worth as fast as deposit liabilities grew.

b   Nonperforming loans were not written down and loans in default were not written off, meaning that asset values and net worth were badly overstated. Combined with the previous item on this list, this meant that many banks were insolvent if accurate accounts were used. The problem of nonperforming loans was made worse by the lack of sound bankruptcy laws which would make it possible for banks to seize assets from debtors who refuse to pay. In many crisis countries weak or unenforced bankruptcy laws made it impossible for banks to compel payment from debtors who were fully able to pay.

c   Many of the banks had excessively concentrated their lending to a few industries or customers. This was a particular problem in Korea where a few chaebols (huge conglomerates) dominate the economy. Such loan concentration by banks means that if a few firms or industries encounter financial difficulties, a bank can face insolvency. Prudent banking requires loan diversification.

d   Many banks, particularly in Thailand, noted a wide spread between the high interest rates prevailing in their domestic markets and very low yields in Japan. They "arbitraged" between these yields by borrowing yen in Tokyo, switching the funds into baht, and making local currency loans without forward cover back into yen, thereby creating a serious currency mismatch on their balance sheets. This was very profitable as long as the baht did not depreciate relative to the yen. When the baht had to be allowed to depreciate sharply against both the dollar and the yen in 1997, disastrous losses followed, which made many of these banks insolvent. A currency mismatch, such as that which occurs when a bank borrows yen to fund loans in baht, without forward cover back into yen, is extremely risky.

e   In some cases, particularly in Indonesia, bank loans were simply fraudulent and represented a looting of the institutions by their officers and owners. Because of the high ratio of deposits to net worth on the right side of the balance sheet of any commercial bank, unregulated banking creates an enormous moral hazard. A controlling equity interest in a bank can be purchased for a small percentage of the value of its total assets. Owners and officers can then "lend" large sums of money to themselves and their associates, allow the bank to fail, and leave the depositors (or the deposit insurance authorities) with huge losses. Prudential regulation of banks, as practiced in the industrialized countries, is designed to prohibit such behavior, although instances of such fraud certainly occurred in the US savings and loan crisis of the late 1980s. Banks in the United States are prohibited from lending more than modest sums to anyone with a management role in the institution, although sometimes means have been found of evading this rule. In many of the Asian crisis countries, there was no serious attempt at prudential regulation of the banks, many of which were owned by industrial firms which were their largest borrowers. Speculative and under-collateralized loans were made by the banks to their owners, and when the loans were not repaid, the banks failed or had to be rescued by governments. In some cases, particularly in Indonesia, banks made large loans to politically important people where no repayment was ever expected. The "loans" were really bribes.

This rather daunting list of troubles leads to the obvious question of why commercial banks in New York, London, and elsewhere would even consider lending to such countries. One possibility is that the bank officers who made the lending decision were dim-witted, or at least that they have very short memories, having forgotten all of the losses that their and other banks have absorbed in these and similar counties over past decades. A more realistic answer is that the high fees and interest rates on these loans are very attractive, particularly when loan demand in the industrialized country is weak. The bankers hope that the loans can be rolled forward forever, or that if a crisis does occur, the IMF, the United States, or somebody will lend the government of the crisis country enough money to allow the banks to escape with few, if any, losses, which is exactly what happened in Mexico in 1994–5. Many commentators have argued that the fact that the foreign banks were fully bailed out in the Mexican crisis encouraged them to lend irresponsibly in Asia, leading to the crisis of 1997–9, when they were not so well protected and lost large sums.

Although the characteristics of likely crisis countries are widely understood, the timing of the collapse is not. In early 1997 nobody was predicting trouble in Thailand and its neighbors, but during the summer foreign lenders suddenly refused to roll over loans and instead withdrew large sums of money. Speculators such as George Soros concluded that a wider crisis was coming, and took massive short positions in Malaysian ringit. Other lenders started taking money out of Indonesia and South Korea, and the route was on. For some reason lenders who were satisfied with circumstances in a country in one month decide the next month that they are more than dissatisfied, and that they want their money *now*. As the foreign exchange reserves of the debtor country decline rapidly and approach being exhausted, the local currency is devalued or allowed to float. Local citizens and foreign lenders now fear even larger financial losses, and a flight of capital out of the country which approaches a panic follows. The currency depreciates sharply or is devalued again. With foreign exchange reserves having declined sharply and with large debts due to be paid, interest and principle payments on foreign debt are at least temporarily suspended. Now that the conflagration is complete, the fire department, in the form of the IMF, arrives on the scene.

EXHIBIT 20.2 $40 BILLION FOR WALL STREET

Carla Hills argued on this page Monday that Congress should approve a $40 billion Mexican loan guarantee program because our neighbor to the south faces a "three alarm economic blaze" that will cause untold catastrophe if the United States does not put it out. The facts of the matter are that Mexico faces a debt problem which is similar to that faced by Latin American countries many times in the past, and that the people who are most threatened by the difficulty, and who would therefore benefit from the proposed arrangement, are primarily in New York (and to a lesser extent Tokyo and elsewhere) rather than Mexico.

The proposed $40 billion bail-out is really a rescue package for investment bankers and mutual fund managers in New York and other financial centers, who took huge risks in exchange for very high interest rates in Mexico during the early 1990s, and who now want the rest of us to pay for their mistakes. If US taxpayers are to subsidize unfortunate investors in Mexico, why not losers in the stock market, or Orange County or people who bought houses that went down in value?

To understand why it makes no sense for US taxpayers to guarantee $40 billion in Mexican debt, it may be useful to understand how this mess developed. Back in 1992–1993, when short-term yields in the United States fell to 3 percent, which was about zero in real terms, US investors became extremely eager to find assets that paid more.

Throughout history such searches for high yields have resulted in investors taking excessive risk, and history repeated itself. Many managers of hedge funds used borrowed money to buy 30-year bonds with higher yields, meaning that if interest rates went up, they would take large losses on the bonds. Other investment managers were attracted by Mexican short-term debt that paid 12 percent or more.

Since these Wall Street operators were not amateurs, they had to understand that Mexican debt paid such high yields because of sizable exchange rate and default risk. The investment managers accepted these risks, on behalf of their clients, in exchange for the high yields.

As nervousness about the exchange rate increased, Mexico switched these loans to a dollar guaranteed form at somewhat lower yields. About $30 billion was borrowed at short maturities with principal and interest payable in pesos, but with such payment to be adjusted for any exchange rate change. This meant that the debt was really denominated in dollars.

Mexico needed these funds to finance an annual current account deficit that exceeded $25 billion, or about 8 percent of GNP. Such huge deficits would have appeared unsustainable to most observers, but as long as US interest rates remained low, relatively high Mexican yields, combined with euphoria over NAFTA, attracted the necessary money.

The party ended when the Federal Reserve System tightened US monetary policy last year. As US short-term yields rose by three percentage points and long-term Treasury yields approached 8 percent, a lot of risky assets, including Mexican debt, became less attractive. Just as money goes into high-risk assets in periods of low interest rates, a tightening of monetary policy always produces a "flight to quality." While the Dow-Jones industrial average, which represents large firms, remained almost unchanged over 1994, stocks of smaller companies declined sharply. Junk bonds became garbage bonds, and risky borrowers, like Mexico, started to have great difficulty in rolling over their debts.

As Mexico's foreign exchange reserves fell to a small fraction of the country's outstanding short-term debt, investors started to flee, and a depreciation of the peso became necessary. Now the New York investment managers want to be paid. Mexico does not have the money, so they will have to wait. But no, the US taxpayer will come to the rescue with $40 billion in loan guarantees. We now have a wonderful recipe for prosperity on Wall Street: When risky assets pay, keep the money and complain about high taxes. When such high-risk assets approach default, get the US Treasury to cover the losses.

There is no reason for US taxpayers to provide $40 billion for Wall Street. Mexico needs to wait for the depreciation of the peso to improve its trade balance and prevail upon its creditors to be patient. The three-month debt should have a zero added to become a 30-month debt, while Mexico tightens domestic fiscal and monetary policies to augment the effects of the lower exchange rate for the peso on its current account. If more help is needed, it should come from the International Monetary Fund with standard conditionality terms.

The Wall Street investment bankers and mutual fund managers will not be happy, but they accepted the risks in exchange for high Mexican yields, so they deserve little sympathy. Mexico borrowed too much money to finance an excessive current account deficit and should not be protected from the costs of that decision.

Republicans in Congress tell us that everybody needs to be responsible for his actions and that welfare is going to be reformed to make that clear to the poor. If we are going to have a Personal Responsibility Act for welfare mothers, maybe it should be applied to Wall Street and to Mexico City.

Source: The Washington Post, Robert M. Dunn, Jr. © The Washington Post, January 24, 1995, Op-Ed Page, Reprinted with permission.

The role of the IMF in such a crisis is to lend the afflicted country enough money to pay for normal imports and to at least cover interest payments on outstanding debts. The loan from the IMF is, however, conditional upon the adoption of policies which will make the loan repayable within a reasonable time period. As was argued in Chapter 17, these policies typically include a devaluation or downward float, and a severe tightening of fiscal and monetary policies. In recent years the Fund has also "encouraged," or required, reforms of bank regulation and of bankruptcy laws, movement toward a central bank which is independent of short-term politics, repression of corruption, and increased transparency in fiscal decision. The requirements of conditionality are painful and highly controversial. The Fund has been accused of having been far too harsh in the Asian crisis, but few of the critics have believable alternative approaches. A particularly unpleasant event in this controversy was the publication of a book by Joseph Stiglitz, who had been the chief economist of the World Bank, which denounces Fund policies in Asia and elsewhere. The chief economist of the IMF, Kenneth Roggoff, presented a stinging rebuttal of Stiglitz's writings at an open meeting at the Fund. This rebuttal was widely reported in the press and can be found in the IMF Survey.[17]

While Stiglitz and his friends are attacking the IMF as being too harsh on debtor countries, another group of critics has suggested that the Fund simply allow the crisis countries to fail and let the banks absorb the resulting losses as a lesson against imprudent lending in the future. This group of critics includes Allan Meltzer and a number of economists who joined the new Bush administration in early 2001. They firmly believe that IMF bail outs create a serious moral hazard by allowing commercial banks to avoid the costs of their unwise lending practices, thereby encouraging them to make more imprudent developing country loans in the future. Since the crises are typically the result of a long history of bad economic policies in the debtor countries, and since the banks lent there knowing how the country was run, one might reasonably ask why the countries and the banks ought not to be allowed to absorb the full costs of their poor decisions. One answer is that the level of suffering among citizens of such a country can become truly appalling, as can readily be seen in the recent experience of Argentina; the other is the problem of contagion.

Crisis contagion

As was noted earlier, balance of payments problems often appear to spread from one country to others in the same regions. Most of Latin America faced crises in the early 1980s, and the Asian crisis began in Thailand in 1997 before spreading to Indonesia, Malaysia, and South Korea. Argentina's problems worsened after Brazil was forced to devalue in 1999, and the 2002 collapse of Argentina has harmed both Uruguay and Brazil.

Crisis contagion is the phrase that economists use to describe a debt crisis which begins in one country and spreads to neighbors who did not encounter the negative shock which harmed the first country. Contagion would not apply to a situation in which a number of neighbors, who all export oil, encounter serious payments problems because the price of oil declines sharply. It would be relevant if one country has a domestic banking collapse, causing massive capital outflows and a payments crisis, which spreads to nearby countries that did not have the original problems with their domestic banks.[18]

Analysis of how such contagion might occur began after the Asian crisis of 1997–9. A number of linkages has been noted, some of which operate through the current account. The more important ones, however, instead involve international capital flows. Turning to the trade and current accounts first, the policies required to deal with a crisis are almost certain to cause a recession and will very probably include a devaluation or depreciation of the local currency, both of which will harm the trade balances of neighboring countries that both export to, and compete with, the original crisis country. When Mexico had to devalue and adopt severe macroeconomic austerity in 1994–5, nearby countries faced serious problems. First their exports to Mexico declined sharply, and then Mexico's new exchange rate put them at a great disadvantage in exporting to the United States. Mexico's current account improved rapidly, but a sizable part of that improvement was at the expense of other countries in the region. As was noted earlier, the Brazilian devaluation of 1999 put Argentina at a serious cost competitive disadvantage and helped to move that country toward its crisis in 2001–2.

The causes of contagion through the capital account begin with fear caused by the likely deterioration of the current account described in the previous paragraph. When Thailand enters a payments crisis, the likelihood that Indonesia and Malaysia will suffer current account losses will cause lenders in Tokyo to fear a crisis in the latter countries and to try to withdraw funds before it becomes impossible to do so. In addition, the bankers in Tokyo may have little detailed knowledge of individual countries in the region but suspect that they are all fairly similar. Seeing Thailand in trouble, they fear that Indonesia and Malaysia might have the same underlying problems, and have a second reason to reduce loan exposure in these countries. Finally, there is just a herd instinct among bankers and speculators; when they see a crisis begin to spread from one country to its neighbors, they join the bandwagon and seek to get every dollar possible out of the region. Everybody understands that those who wait to reduce loan exposure may not get paid, so they try to be at the head of the line.

This process is similar to what happened in the US banking system in the early 1930s. A few unsound banks failed and were closed; depositors at other banks, which were actually sound, feared the worst and wanted their funds immediately. Even sound banks cannot liquidate assets overnight, so perfectly healthy banks encountered deposit runs which they could not sustain, and were forced to close. Banks in Tokyo and New York are analogous to the depositors in the 1930s, Thailand and Indonesia were the unsound banks, and Malaysia and South Korea were the otherwise sound banks that were thrown into crisis.

Box 20.1 Argentina: snatching defeat from the jaws of victory

At the end of World War II Argentina had approximately the same GDP per capita as Canada. At present its GDP per capita is about one tenth of Canada's, and Canada has not done that well during the last 57 years. Argentina went from first world to third world in half a century, despite having a highly educated population of Spanish, Italian, and German origins, a temperate climate, and an extremely rich endowment of natural resources. It should be prosperous, but it is desperately poor. How can such an awesome defeat be snatched from the jaws of victory?

Economic policies really do matter, and if they are bad enough for long enough, even the most promising economy can be wrecked. In the case of Argentina the bad policies had major balance of payments effects, the responses to which made the domestic situation worse.

Argentina's government sector, including provincial and local levels, has run consistent and large deficits. The country has a long history of an utter lack of fiscal discipline. The deficits were typically financed by the central bank, i.e. they were monetized. During a visit to Buenos Aires in 1980, one of the authors of this book was told by an official at the Bank of Argentina that the Ministry of Finance would print up bonds in the morning, and send them to the central bank by noon. The offsetting funds were in the government's account by 2 p.m. and were spent by 5 p.m. When spent by the government, these funds entered the commercial banking system. Given the volume of money thus created, the result was serious inflation, which sometimes became hyperinflation, requiring that the local currency be devalued sharply.

Since 1968 the Argentinian currency, which has had many names as 3 or 4 zeros were removed every few years, has been devalued relative to the US dollar by a factor of 114 billion to one. That is not a typo. 114 billion to one. Every time the currency fell relative to the dollar, Argentinian residents that had borrowed dollars without forward cover took capital losses. Between 1984 and 1990, a mere 6 years, the price level rose by a factor of 100,000 to one. Overnight interest rates reached 9 million percent annual rate for a brief period in 1990.

This was all to end in the 1990s when Argentina adopted a currency board. Now the exchange rate would be permanently fixed at $1 = 1 peso, with Argentinian base money backed 1 to 1 by US dollar foreign exchange reserves. As was discussed in Chapter 16 balance of payments deficits would produce a decline in the money supply, with automatic adjustment via specie flow. More importantly, the fact that the currency board could not purchase domestic assets would impose fiscal discipline on all levels of government. It was a lovely dream, but it failed because the Argentinians cheated on the currency board rules. Government debt which was denominated in dollars somehow got on the asset side of the currency board's balance sheet, and various other gimmicks were used to frustrate the automatic payments adjustment process. Fiscal policy discipline was a bit better at the federal level, but the provinces continued to run large deficits. Despite these failings, many Argentinians unwisely trusted the 1:1 exchange rate and borrowed dollars without forward cover or other hedges. Currency mismatches, as discussed earlier in Chapter 17, pervaded the economy. When this house of cards collapsed in early 2002, and the currency had to be allowed to depreciate to 3.6 pesos to the dollar, large sectors of the economy instantly became insolvent.

Then the government displayed a breathtaking lack of respect for contracts or for private property by forcing the commercial banks to switch all dollar deposits into pesos at 1.4:1 but all dollar loans into pesos at 1:1. The banks, most of which were foreign owned, became insolvent and had to be closed. The economy collapsed. The unemployment rate rose above 20 percent, as did the decline in real GDP. The IMF, which had loaned large sums in the past based on "promises to reform," refused to provide more money. Finance ministers and presidents came and went. Argentina was in a depression by mid-2002, with press reports of food riots, widespread poverty, and threats of civil disturbances.

If a nation's economic policies are really bad for a long period of time, even the most promising of economies can be turned into a rusting hulk. One can only hope that other countries will learn from Argentina's tragedy.

In this circumstance, the role of the IMF is to try to limit a payments crisis to the country in which it began by being prepared to lend large sums to soundly managed countries in the region who may be hit by contagion. In mid-2002, for example, the IMF would not advance more money to Argentina, whose policies it still believed to be unsound, but did lend large sums to Uruguay and Brazil, whose policies it believed to be sound, in order to limit the threat of crisis contagion. Crisis contagion was a massive problem in the 1930s, and the IMF was founded after World War II precisely in order to avoid a repetition of the disasters of that decade. While the Fund undoubtedly has made occasional errors in lending money to countries with doubtful policies, or by imposing conditionality policies which were less than fully appropriate, it has had a very strong record of limiting the spread of crises, and of helping countries, if they were willing to pursue sound macroeconomic and exchange rate policies over a number of years, return to economic health.

Despite the noisy complaints of its critics, the only reasonable conclusion from recent international monetary experience is that if the IMF did not exist, it would have to be invented. Quickly.

The new financial architecture

The Basel accords: I and II

As a result of the threatened insolvency of many US and other industrialized-country banks that occurred during the Latin American debt crisis of early 1980s, questions were raised about the adequacy of the prudential regulation of international banks. In particular there was fear that banks were "jurisdiction shopping" to find countries from which they could operate with little or no oversight. The collapse of banks in the 1930s made it all too clear that an unregulated banking system was very dangerous, leading to the idea of international standards in bank regulation, at least for the industrialized countries.

Basel I

The threat to the solvency of many large banks, which resulted from the Latin American debt crisis of the early 1980s, intensified already growing doubts as to whether major international banks were being regulated properly by governments and central banks. A rapid increase in international banking, as banks branched or set up subsidiaries outside the borders of their home countries, made it almost impossible for a single government or central bank to regulate its banks. They could merely set up subsidiaries in a jurisdiction with looser regulations. "Jurisdiction shopping" became a common practice as banks set up operations wherever they would escape regulations they did not like.

The bank regulatory authorities of the industrialized countries began discussions in 1986 at the Bank for International Settlements in Basle, Switzerland, which were intended to coordinate their efforts in improving the safety of the banking system.[19] The resulting negotiations were directed at four problems facing international banks, each of which potentially threatened their solvency and the stability of the world's banking system:

1   *Capital adequacy.* Many of the largest banks had grown very rapidly throughout the 1970s and 1980s without selling more common stock or retaining large earnings. As a result, their net worth declined as a percentage of their total assets, meaning that even rather modest losses, owing to bad loans, could threaten their solvency. This created enormous risks for government insurance agencies such as the Federal Deposit Insurance Company in the United States.
2   *Excessively risky loans.* Latin America was not the only area in which very risky loans, which produced huge losses, had been made. US banks lost large sums of money in Zaire and the Sudan, while the decline in the US commercial real-estate market late in the 1980s imposed large losses on banks from a number of countries, including Japan. Many banks simply did not appear to be sufficiently prudent in making large loans.
3   *Excessively concentrated loans.* Partially in order to reduce administrative costs, banks prefer making a few very large loans to making a large number of small ones. In addition, they too often concentrate lending in a few industries or countries. Such concentration greatly increases the risk that the bank will fail if a single country or industry experiences serious financial problems. At one time Citibank had 75 percent of its net worth loaned in Brazil and over 100 percent of its net worth loaned in Latin America.
4   *Exposure from off-balance-sheet items.* International banks were becoming increasingly involved in foreign exchange forwards, futures, and options contracts, and many of these activities created potentially large risks for these banks which did not appear on their balance sheets. The question arose as to how these risks could be evaluated and limited.

The Basle Accord on Capital Adequacy of July 1988 began to address some of these problems. Most importantly, it set a minimum level of 8 percent for capital as a share of risk-adjusted assets. That 8 percent included both net worth and subordinated (nondeposit) debt. At least half of the 8 percent had to be stockholders' equity, including accumulated reserves. Loan types were ranked according to riskiness, with loans to OECD governments least risky and loans to developing-country governments in the riskiest class. These risk weights were used to determine minimum capital requirements; if a bank makes more risky loans, it must maintain more net worth. The 1991 failure of the Bank for Credit and Capital International (BCCI) and the more recent problems of many large Japanese banks make it clear that the Basel Accord has not solved all of the problems of excessive risk (and sometimes of fraud) in international banking, but the agreement was an important step in the right direction.

Basel II

Perceived inadequacies in the original Basel Accord have led to negotiations over revising some of its terms. What is now called "Basel II" is scheduled for completion in 2003 and for full implementation by 2006. The risk-weighted capital requirements on banks are to become more complex in order to more accurately reflect the risks in various asset types. Basel I, for example, treats loans to all OECD members as equally low in risk, despite the fact that both Turkey and the United Kingdom are members. It also views all loans to developing countries as being riskier than loans to any OECD member, despite the fact that Hong Kong is listed as a developing country. In addition, Basel II will require far more public disclosure by banks of their risk profiles, making it easier for the market (stockholders and depositors) to impose risk-reducing discipline. It will also increase the role of prudential regulation by central banks and other financial authorities in overseeing the risks that banks are allowed to undertake. The problem in Basel II will be to produce an enhanced international regulatory system that really does reduce the risk of major bank failures without creating a massively complicated system that unreasonably stifles bank lending and burdens taxpayers and bank stockholders.

Sovereign bankruptcy for heavily indebted crisis countries

Another aspect of what may become a new financial architecture for international finance is a proposal by Anne Kreuger, the Deputy Managing Director of the IMF, that something rather like corporate bankruptcy be possible in developing countries with overwhelming debts that face a payments crisis. The goal of this effort is to avoid chaotic attempts by banks to get their dollars before a country's foreign exchange reserves are exhausted, and to have some binding system for creditors to negotiate partial payments and/or longer-term structures for old debts. US, UK and other industrialized country bankruptcy laws are being studied to find whose approach might work best for sovereign nations that cannot service their debts promptly.

This effort is now in its early stages, and it is far from clear that it will succeed. What is obvious, however, is that the crises of the last two decades, beginning with Latin America in 1982 and continuing through Mexico in 1994–5, Asia in 1997–9, Russia in 1998, and Argentina in 2002 have created a strong desire to somehow improve the international financial system to reduce the likelihood of more destructive collapses.

The idea of broad debt forgiveness for so-called "Highly Indebted Poor Countries" has also been proposed as part of the new financial architecture. There obviously are very poor countries that simply will never be able to pay their debts, and forgiveness has few if any alternatives. To extend this idea to a broad range of poor countries, however, has major problems. Most of the debts of the poorest countries would have to be written off by the World Bank and the IMF, which would severely constrain the ability of these institutions to lend to other countries who need help in the future.

If the World Bank has to write off a large number of loans, its credit rating, which has been excellent, will decline and it will only be able to borrow at higher interest rates, which will have to be passed on to the borrowing countries. If private lenders, to the limited extent that they have made loans to very poor countries, are compelled to write off loans that in fact could eventually be repaid, they will never lend in these or similar countries again. For countries that simply cannot repay debts, forgiveness will have to occur, but to extend this idea to a far larger number of countries that can repay their debts in time, would be very dangerous. It would mean that these and similar countries would be unable to borrow in the future, which is hardly a prescription for success in their future development.

Prospective issues in international economic policy in the next decade

Economic forecasting is an extremely risky enterprise. (An elderly colleague once advised: "If you are going to forecast, do so very frequently. That way, you will occasionally be correct.") However, if one were to ask what the major policy issues in international economics will be during the next decade, the following questions come to mind:

1   Does the success of President Bush in getting fast-track authority, after President Clinton's failure to do so, mean that what appeared to be growing economic isolationism in the US Congress has faded, and that the Doha Round has strong prospects for success? In the Doha WTO Round, will the United States be willing to seriously negotiate an easing of its extremely unpopular dumping and subsidy codes, and if the United States does so, will the Congress, which likes the dumping and subsidy codes, be willing to pass the agreement into law? Will the EU and the United States be willing to scale back their production-distorting agriculture support programs which injure farmers in developing countries so severely? Can further progress be made in liberalizing trade in services? Can a compromise be found on issue of the protection of intellectual property which will allow poor countries access to patented medicines at reasonable prices without severely damaging market incentives for research and development, which is both risky and expensive, on new medicines? This is only the beginning of the list of issues for the Doha Round.

2   Can the European Union successfully absorb a series of Eastern European countries as new members? Eight new members are scheduled to enter in 2004. Given the large farm sectors of these countries, particularly Poland, how can the Common Agricultural Policy be maintained in its existing form without huge increases in costs, which taxpayers in Europe will oppose? Many in the United States have disliked the CAP from its beginning, because of its negative impact on US agricultural exports, and would be pleased to see it become unsustainable due to the entry of Poland and other large agricultural producers. France, Ireland, and other major beneficiaries, however, can be expected to firmly oppose any phase-out of, or even serious cutbacks in, the CAP.

3   Will MERCOSUR survive the crisis in Argentina and become a free-trade bloc which includes more of Latin America? Or, instead, will President Bush's desire for free trade in the Americas be the route to western hemisphere trade liberalization? Or will attempts at further regional trade liberalization fail, leaving the Doha Round as the primary route to expanded trade? Or will the United States negotiate a series of bilateral free-trade arrangements, such as those recently signed with Singapore and Chile? Or some combination of the above?

4   Will the phase-in of the Uruguay Round agreement, which is to be completed in January 2005, occur as scheduled? The "back-end-loaded" nature of the tariff cuts and the quota removals virtually guarantees a great deal of pain among import-competing industries in the United States and elsewhere in the years 2003–4, and serious attempts to delay or stop these eliminations of import barriers can be expected. If the United States or other industrialized countries were not to meet their obligations under the Uruguay Round agreement, developing countries could be expected to back away from their promises with regard to trade in services and enforcement of rules on protection of intellectual property. The agricultural sector of the Chinese economy can expect serious pain as imports of food are liberalized under China's agreement to enter the WTO, and Beijing may be tempted to delay those provisions.

5 Will the WTO trade dispute settlement system, which is far stronger than its GATT predecessor, function successfully? The United States has been angry over some of its losses in Geneva, and the European Union is now similarly annoyed over the banana and beef cases. There is always the danger that if the United States or the European Union loses enough cases about which either cares deeply, they may try to limit the powers of the WTO or avoid its jurisdiction. That would leave the world without an institutional arrangement for settling trade disputes, which would be quite dangerous.

6 Will the terms of trade of primary-product-producing developing countries, particularly in Africa, finally recover? The deterioration of these prices in the previous 25 years has been devastating for many of the poorest countries in the world, and they badly need a recovery of demand for these products, or they need to diversify away from reliance on such commodities for export revenues.

7 When will Russia and the other countries emerging from the former Soviet Union continue a recovery from their economic decline of the 1990s? With the exception of the Baltic republics (Estonia, Lithuania, and Latvia), the fifteen former Soviet republics experienced a very difficult period. The contrast between the failures of most of the former Soviet republics and the successes of China and countries in Eastern Europe such as the Czech Republic, Hungary, and Slovenia in implementing a transition program is striking, and is not entirely understood. The problems of the transition process are largely outside the scope of this book, but the difficulties encountered by the former Soviet republics are having major harmful effects on the world financial system, with the Russian bond default of the summer of 1998 coming as a particularly destructive shock.

8 Will the European Monetary Union succeed, or will the macroeconomic diversity of the members, particularly if it adds eight countries in 2006, mean that a "one size fits all" monetary policy becomes unacceptable for some members, which then attempt to withdraw? If a few countries were to leave, would EMU continue with a smaller membership, or would it collapse and its members return to their national currencies?

9 Will the recent pattern of frequent LDC debt crises continue, with its destructive impacts on both the economies of those countries and the balance sheets of banks which have loaned to them? In trying to reduce the likelihood of such crises, will the attempts to design a "new financial architecture," which includes both Basel II and plans for something approaching a sovereign bankruptcy system for heavily indebted poor countries, succeed?

10 Can a mechanism be devised to provide debt relief for poor countries that are unable to repay without weakening the finances of the World Bank, the IMF, and other international lenders? In particular, can this be done without destroying the willingness of financial institutions to lend to these countries in the future?

11 Will the war on terrorism and other difficulties between the middle east and the west cause a disruption of international financial markets? Can the techniques which terrorists use to secretly move money internationally, as discussed in Chapter 13, be unraveled and ultimately be stopped? Will the 2003 invasion of Iraq ultimately result in stability in Persian Gulf oil production, upon which so many countries critically depend, or will it be a prelude to more troubles and supply interruptions in the region?

12 Will there be a new Bretton Woods conference to reform the World Bank and the IMF, and to create a new financial architecture? Considerable unhappiness has been expressed with the performance of these institutions in recent years, particularly with regard to the Asian crisis and the transition economies. A few politicians, and fewer

economists, have even suggested that these institutions be abolished, but that idea has faded from attention fairly quickly. The danger of an international conference to redesign these institutions is that various groups of countries may arrive with such divergent goals that no agreement is possible and the world will end up, not with a reformed international financial system, but with no system.

Perhaps this volume can be closed by merely noting that the last time the world was in such a "no system" situation, with regard to both trade and financial matters, was 1931–9, which was not an era which many would care to repeat. The arrangements which grew up after World War II for handling the liberalization of international trade, lending for reconstruction and development, and international monetary relations, may be imperfect, but a return to unbridled economic nationalism, as we saw in 1931–9, would be tragic.

Summary of key concepts

1   Both nominal and real exchange rates have been far more volatile than had been expected when floating rates were adopted, and this volatility has been very disruptive, the 1981–5 appreciation of the dollar being particularly harmful to the tradables sector of the United States.

2   The models of exchange rate determination which were presented earlier in this book have a very poor econometric track record in explaining exchange rate movements during the period since 1973. Economists at present do not have any successful means of predicting movements of flexible exchange rates.

3   Various alternatives to floating exchange rates have been proposed, including a return to the fixed rates of the Bretton Woods era, but none of the proposals appears to be likely to perform better than floating rates so the current system of managed floats is likely to remain in operation for the foreseeable future.

4   The European Monetary Union, which began operations in January 1999, has a number of major advantages for its members, but one large disadvantage. It is no longer possible for a member country to use monetary policy to deal with a domestic business cycle which is not shared by a majority of the membership. Whenever the business-cycle patterns of the member countries differ significantly, some countries will have to accept a monetary policy that is the opposite of what their domestic economies need.

5   Almost all of the major Latin American countries in the early 1980s went through a debt crisis which was quite threatening to the US banks which had lent them large sums of money. Eventually, the crisis was eased, but the banks absorbed large financial losses and the Latin American countries had a decade of very slow growth and other painful results of the payments adjustment process.

6   Mexico went though a debt crisis in 1994–5, but it did not spread to other countries and was contained fairly quickly. The adjustment process, under IMF guidance, was very painful and real incomes fell for many Mexicans due to restrictive macroeconomic policies and the price increases caused by the devaluation of peso.

7   The Asian crisis of the late 1990s has some similarities to the episodes in Latin America, but one large difference. The financial institutions in Asia (particularly the banks) were discovered to be in very bad condition. When assets were entered on the balance sheet at what they were worth, many of the banks were insolvent. Prudential regulation of the banks had obviously been careless or nonexistent, leading to lending and accounting

practices which should never have been allowed. In some cases the banks had simply been looted by their owners, a situation which also arose in the US savings and loan crisis of the late 1980s. The IMF found the Asian crisis to be more difficult to deal with than those in Latin America because of the financial institution problems, which it had not previously encountered in such an extreme form.

Questions for study and review

1 The United States has allowed the dollar to float since 1973, yet the United States has reported large balance-of-payments deficits on a reserve settlements basis. What is the explanation for this apparent paradox?

2 "If nations have different rates of inflation, then exchange rates between their currencies cannot remain fixed." Do you agree? Explain.

3 What are the principal arguments against a system of floating exchange rates? How do these stand up in the light of experience with floating rates since 1973?

4 Exchange rate fluctuations since 1973 appear to be larger than warranted by the underlying economic circumstances in the nations involved. What reasons have been offered to explain this experience?

5 Academic supporters of flexible exchange rates began the 1970s with some strong expectations as to how that system would operate. Which of those expectations have and which have not been realized?

6 "Flexible exchange rates, like democracy, is not the best system; it is merely the least bad." Explain.

7 How can central banks be caught in a new version of the Meade conflict cases under floating exchange rates?

8 On what grounds might one conclude that the current membership of the European Monetary System is too large to be an optimum currency area?

9 "Latin America lived very well in the 1970s, but the region paid for its sins in the 1980s." Explain. Who else paid for those sins?

10 What is the Basel Accord? What problems was it intended to solve or at least ease?

11 If you were going to forecast the dollar/sterling exchange rate, how would you do it? Might you expect to have better results in predicting the dollar/Brazilian real exchange rate? Why?

12 In what ways is the Asian debt crisis similar to, and different from, the difficulties which Latin America experienced in the early 1980s?

13 If you were asked to predict which developing or transition countries might be expected to experience balance of payments or debt crises, what statistical variables would you look for in seeking evidence of trouble to come?

14 One developing country has a payments and debt crisis. Through what linkages might this crisis spread to other countries in the region that did not experience the original shock to the first country to experience trouble?

Suggested further reading

- Branson, W., "Exchange Rate Policy after a Decade of Floating," in J. Bilson and R. Marston, eds, *Exchange Rate Theory and Practice*, Chicago: University of Chicago Press, 1984.
- Collins, S., "Multiple Exchange Rates, Capital Controls, and Commercial Policy," in R. Dornbusch, *The Open Economy: Tools for Policy Makers in Developing Countries*, New York: Oxford University Press, 1988.
- Crockett, A., "The Theory and Practice of Financial Stability," *Princeton Essays in International Finance*, no. 203, April 1997.
- Cuddington, J., "Capital Flight: Estimates, Issues, and Explanations," *Princeton Essays in International Finance*, no. 58, December 1986.
- de la Dehasa, G. and P. Krugman, *EMU and the Regions*, Washington, DC: Group of Thirty, 1992.
- Dornbusch, R., "Exchange Rates Economics: Where Do We Stand?," *Brookings Papers on Economic Activity*, no. 1, 1980, pp. 143–85.
- Dunn, R., "Likely Conflicts Within the European Central Bank's Management during 1999," *Challenge*, July/August 1999.
- Eaton, J. and R. Fernandez, "Sovereign Debt," in G. Grossman and K. Rogoff, eds, *Handbook in Economics*, Vol. III, Amsterdam: Elsevier, 1995, pp. 2031–74.
- Eichengreen, B., "European Monetary Integration," *Journal of Economic Literature*, September 1993, pp. 1321–57.
- Elliott, A. ed., *Corruption and the World Economy*, Washington: Institute for International Economics, 1997.
- Frankel, J. and A. Rose, "Empirical Research on Nominal Exchange Rates," in G. Grossman and K. Rogoff, eds, *Handbook of International Economics*, Vol. III, Amsterdam: Elsevier, 1995, pp. 1689–730.
- Froot, T. and K. Rogoff, "Perspectives on PPP and Long-Run Real Exchange Rates," in G. Grossman and K. Rogoff, eds, *Handbook of International Economics*, Vol. III, Amsterdam: Elsevier, 1995, pp. 1647–88.
- Froot, T. and R. Thaler, "Anomalies: Foreign Exchange," *Journal of Economic Perspectives*, Summer 1990, pp. 179–92.
- Goldstein, M., Reinhardt, C., and Kaminsky, G., *Assessing Financial Vulnerability: An Early Warning System*, Washington: Institute for International Economics, 2000.
- McKinnon, R., "Monetary and Exchange Rate Policy for International Financial Stability: A Proposal," *Journal of Economic Perspectives*, Winter 1988.
- McLeod, R. and R. Garnaut, eds, *East Asia in Crisis: From Being a Miracle to Needing One?*, London: Routledge, 1998.
- Meese, R., "Currency Fluctuations in the Post-Bretton Woods Era," *Journal of Economic Perspectives*, Winter 1990, pp. 3–24.
- Mussa, M., *Argentina and the Fund: From Triumph to Tragedy*, Washington: Institute for International Economics, 2002.
- Pauls, B. Diane, "US Exchange Rate Policy: Bretton Woods to Present," *Federal Reserve Bulletin*, November 1990, pp. 891–908.
- Sachs, J., ed., *Developing Country Debt and Economic Performance: The International Financial System*, Chicago: University of Chicago Press, 1989.
- Sachs, J., "Making the Brady Plan Work," *Foreign Affairs*, Summer 1989, pp. 87–104.

Notes

1 G. Bell, *The Euro-dollar Market and the International Financial System* (London: McMillan, 1973) p. 70.

2 P. Korteweg, "Exchange Rate Policy, Monetary Policy, and Real Exchange Rate Variability," *Princeton Essays in International Finance*, no. 140, 1980.

3 M. Friedman, "The Case for Flexible Exchange Rates," in *Essays in Positive Economics* (Chicago: University of Chicago Press, 1953), pp. 157–203. For more recent surveys of exchange rate economics that fail to support purchasing power parity in the short to medium term, see K. Froot and K. Rogoff, "Perspectives on PPP and Long-Run Real Exchange Rates," and J. Frankel and A. Rose, "Empirical Research on Nominal Exchange Rate," both in G. Grossman and K. Rogoff, *Handbook of International Economics*, Vol. III (Amsterdam: Elsevier, 1995), chs 32 and 33. For a more recent discussion of purchasing power parity, which suggests that deviations from its predicted exchange rates are partially reversed in the very long run but that such deviations are large in the short-to-medium term, see K. Rogoff, "The Purchasing Power Parity Puzzle," *Journal of Economic Literature*, June 1996, pp. 647–68. See also C. Crownover and D. Steiger, "Testing for Absolute Purchasing Power Parity: A Survey," *Journal of International Money and Finance*, October 1996, pp. 783–96.

4 See K. Froot and R. Thaler, "Anomalies: Foreign Exchange," *Journal of Economic Perspectives*, Summer 1990, pp. 179–92.

5 R. Dornbusch, "Exchange Rate Economics: Where Do We Stand?," *Brookings Papers on Economic Activity*, no.1, 1980, pp. 143–85.

6 J. Frankel, "Tests of Monetary and Portfolio Balance Models of Exchange Rate Determination," in J. Bilson and R. Marston, eds, *Exchange Rates in Theory and Practice* (Chicago: University of Chicago Press, 1984), p. 250. For equally poor econometric results for this model, see R. Meese, "Currency Fluctuations in the Post-Bretton Woods Era," *Journal of Economic Perspectives*, Winter 1990, p. 125.

7 R. Meese, "Currency Fluctuations in the Post-Bretton Woods Era," *Journal of Economic Perspectives*, Winter 1990, pp. 3–24. For a more recent survey, which is only slightly less pessimistic on this subject, see M. Taylor, "The Economics of Exchange Rates," *Journal of Economic Literature*, March 1995, pp. 13–45. See also S. Blomberg, "Politics and Exchange Rate Forecasts," *Journal of International Economics*, August 1997, pp. 189–205.

8 Such proposals can be found in J. Karekin and N. Wallace, "International Monetary Reform: The Feasible Alternatives," *Federal Reserve Bank of Minneapolis Quarterly Review*, Summer 1978, pp. 2–7, and in J. Tobin, "A Proposal for International Monetary Reform," in his *Essays in Economics: Theory and Policy* (Cambridge, MA: MIT Press, 1982), pp. 488–94. See J. Stotsky, "Why the Two Tier Tobin Tax Won't Work," *Finance and Development*, June 1996, pp. 28–9.

9 For a discussion of dual and multiple exchange rate systems, see S. Collins, "Multiple Exchange Rates, Capital Controls, and Commercial Policy," in R. Dornbusch and L. Holmes, eds, *The Open Economy: Tools for Policy Makers in Developing Countries* (New York: Oxford University Press, 1988), pp. 128–64.

10 R. Dunn, "The Misguided Attractions of Foreign Exchange Controls," *Challenge*, Sept./Oct. 2002, pp. 98–111.

11 R. Dornbusch, "PPP Exchange Rate Rules and Macroeconomic Stability," *Journal of Political Economy*, February 1982, pp. 158–65. See also V. Argy, *International Macroeconomics: Theory and Policy* (London: Routledge, 1994), pp. 406–7.

12 R. McKinnon, "Monetary and Exchange Rate Policies for International Economic Stability: A Proposal," *Journal of Economic Perspectives*, Winter 1988, pp. 83–103. See the comments following the McKinnon article by R. Dornbusch and J. Williamson for doubts about this proposal.

13 For a discussion of the prospects for the EMS before the events of 1992, see A. Giovannini, "The Transition of European Monetary Union," *Princeton Essays in International Finance*, no. 178, 1990, and P. Kenen, *EMU after Maastricht* (Washington, DC: Group of Thirty, 1992). For a more doubtful view, see G. de la Dehesa and P. Krugman, *EMU and the Regions* (Washington, DC: Group of Thirty, 1992).

14 For a discussion of the problems which EMU faced during and after 1992, see B. Eichengreen, "European Monetary Unification," *Journal of Economic Literature*, September 1993. See also W. Buiter, G. Corsetti, and P. Pesenti, "Interpreting the ERM Crisis: Country Specific and Systemic Issues," *Princeton Studies in International Finance*, no. 84, 1998.

15 R. Mundell, "The Theory of Optimum Currency Areas," *American Economic Review*, September 1961, pp. 657–65, and R. McKinnon, "Optimum Currency Areas," *American Economic Review*, September 1993, pp. 717–25.

16 For an econometric analysis of which members of EMU would be likely to agree or disagree on a joint monetary policy, which is based on the Mundell approach to optimum currency areas, see R. Dunn, "EMU without Britain: Reasons for Scepticism," *Economic Affairs*, September 1998, pp. 45–52.

17 K. Rogoff, "An Open Letter From Kenneth Rogoff to Joseph Stiglitz, Author of Globalization and Its Discontents," *IMF Survey*, July 8, 2002, p. 209–11, and by the same author, "The IMF Strikes Back," *Foreign Policy*, Jan./Feb. 2003, pp. 39–46. See also, J. Stiglitz, *Globalization and Its Discontents* (New York: Norton, 2002) and by the same author, "What I Learned at the World Economic Crisis," *New Republic*, April 17, 2000.

18 For discussions of balance of payments crisis contagion, see, G. Kaminskyj, and C. Reinhart, "The Twin Crises: The Causes of Banking and Balance of Payments Problems, *American Economic Review*, June 1999. Also, G. Calvo and E. Mendoza, *Rational Herd Behavior and the Globalization of Securities Markets* (College Park: University of Maryland Press, 1998.

   Also, R. Dunn, "The Routes to Crisis Contagion," *Challenge*, Nov./Dec. 2001, pp. 45–58. With regard to the recent collapse of Argentina, see M. Mussa, *Argentina and the Fund: From Triumph to Tragedy*, Washington: Institute for International Economics, 2002.

19 On the problem of banks tendency to make excessively risky loans despite having absorbed losses on similar loans in the past, see J. Guttentag and R. Herring, "Disaster Myopia in International Lending," *Princeton Essays in International Finance*, no. 164, 1986. For a discussion of the Basel Accord and of the problems of capital adequacy in commercial banking, see I. Giddy, *Global Financial Markets* (Lexington, MA: DC Heath, 1994), pp. 266–8. The views of the current General Manager of the Bank for International Settlements on this subject can be found in A. Crockett, "The Theory and Practice of Financial Stability," *Princeton Essays in International Finance*, no. 203, 1997. See also M. Goldstein, *The Case for an International Banking Standard* (Washington, DC: Institute for International Economics, 1997). For a discussion of how to predict debt crises, see M. Goldstein, C. Reinhardt, and G. Kaminsky, *Assessing Financial Vulnerability: An Early Warning System for Emerging Markets*, Washington: Institute for International Economics, 2000.

20 For a recent discussion of the issues in the new financial architecture debate, see P. Kenen, *The New Financial Architecture: What's New? What's Missing?* (Washington: Institute for International Economics, 2001). See also, B. Eichengreen, *Toward a New International Financial Architecture: A Practical Post-Asia Agenda* (Washington: Institute for International Economics, 1999).

Glossary

Absolute advantage The argument, associated with Adam Smith, that trade is based on absolute differences in costs. Each country will export those products for which its costs, in terms of labor and other inputs, are lower than costs in other countries.

Absorption model A Keynesian analysis of the conditions necessary for the success of a devaluation, namely, that output must grow relative to the domestic use of goods and services, and that domestic savings must grow faster than investment. Associated with Sidney Alexander.

Accommodating transactions Those items in the balance-of-payments accounts which occur in order to offset imbalances in the total of the remaining items. Flows of foreign exchange reserves are the dominant accommodating transaction.

Ad valorem tariff A tariff that is measured as a percentage of the value of the traded product.

Appreciation An increase in the value of a currency, measured in terms of other currencies, in a regime of floating exchange rates. If the dollar/sterling exchange rate moved from 1 pound = $1.50 to 1 pound = $1.75, that would be an appreciation of sterling.

Arbitrage Purchase of a good or an asset in a low-price market and its riskless sale in a higher-price market. If arbitrage is possible, prices should be forced together, differing by no more than transport or transactions costs.

Articles of Agreement of the IMF The founding document of the International Monetary Fund that defines the Fund's functions. Agreed to at the Bretton Woods conference in 1944 and amended since then.

Asset market model of the balance of payments A group of models of the balance of payments or the exchange rate which views foreign exchange as a financial asset rather than as a claim on real goods. Capital transactions, rather than current account transactions, dominate these models. Foreign exchange is bought or sold in order to facilitate financial transactions rather than merchandise trade, and the models are based on supply and demand functions for financial assets.

Autonomous transactions Those items in the balance-of-payments accounts which occur for commercial or financial reasons, and not to balance other items. The sum of the autonomous items is offset by accommodating items. International trade and long-term capital flows are autonomous transactions.

Balance of payments A set of accounts that represents all transactions between residents of one country and residents of the rest of the world during a period of time, normally a year.

Bank for International Settlements (BIS) A financial institution located in Basle, Switzerland, which provides a range of services for the central banks of the industrialized countries. The BIS was founded in 1930 to manage problems in German reparations payments from World War I. Some central banks hold part of their foreign exchange reserves as deposits at the BIS. Representatives of the central banks of the industrialized countries frequently meet at the BIS for consultations on monetary and exchange-market policies.

Base money The total volume of member bank reserve accounts and currency created by a central bank. The stock of base money, sometimes known as "high-powered money," is central in determining the money supply of a country.

Basic balance A balance-of-payments surplus or deficit measured as the sum of the current account and the long-term capital account. Excludes short-term capital and flows of foreign exchange reserves.

Bilateral exchange rate The price of the local currency in terms of a single foreign currency.

BP line Combinations of interest rates and levels of domestic output which will produce equilibrium in the balance of payments.

Brady Plan A plan, named after the secretary of the Treasury during the Bush administration, to ease the Latin American debt crisis by encouraging banks to write off some of these debts and lengthen those maturities that remained.

Brain drain The movement of scientists, engineers, and other highly educated people from developing to industrialized countries, which imposes a loss on public investments in education on the developing country.

Bretton Woods Agreement The conclusion of the Bretton Woods conference, held at a resort of that name in New Hampshire during the summer of 1944. The World Bank and the International Monetary Fund were founded as a result of the Bretton Woods Agreement. The phrase "Bretton Woods system" is often used to describe the international monetary system of fixed exchange rates which prevailed until the crises of 1971 and 1973.

Cable transfer A means of transferring foreign exchange from one economic agent to another. An electronic message instructs a bank to transfer funds from the account of one party to that of another.

Call An option contract that allows the owner to purchase a specified quantity of a financial asset, such as foreign exchange, at a fixed price during a specified period. The owner is not required to exercise the option. The price at which the option can be exercised is known as the "strike price."

Capital account A country's total receipts from the sale of financial assets to foreign residents minus its total expenditures on purchases of financial assets from foreign residents. These assets include both debt and equity instruments.

Cartel A collusive arrangement among sellers of a product in different countries, which is intended to raise the price of that product in order to extract monopoly rents.

c.i.f. Cost, insurance, and freight. This measurement of the value of imports includes the cost of the goods itself, insurance, and freight.

Clean floating exchange rate A rate that exists when an exchange rate is determined solely by market forces. The central banks not only fail to maintain a parity, but also refrain from buying or selling foreign exchange to influence the rate.

Clearing House International Payments System (CHIPS) The electronic system among banks in New York and other major foreign financial centers, which is used to transfer foreign exchange, that is, to complete foreign exchange market transactions.

Commercial policy Government policies that are intended to change international trade flows, particularly to restrict imports.

Common market A group of countries that maintain free trade in goods among the membership, share a common external tariff schedule, and allow mobility of labor and capital among the members.

Common property resource A resource for which use by one individual reduces the amount available for other individuals, but one from which no individual can be excluded.

Community indifference curve A line that shows all the combinations of two goods which provide the community with the same level of welfare, that is, to which the community would be indifferent. A set of these curves can be used to show increases in community welfare as more goods are made available.

Comparative advantage The argument, developed by David Ricardo in the early nineteenth century, that mutually beneficial balanced trade is possible even if one country has an absolute advantage in both goods. All that is required is that there be a difference in the relative costs of the two goods in the two countries and that each country export the product for which it has relatively or comparatively lower costs.

Conditionality The policy under which the International Monetary Fund makes large loans (drawings) to member countries only if they pursue exchange rate and other policies that can be expected to improve the borrowing country's balance-of-payments performance and make the repayment of the loan possible.

Consumers' surplus The difference between what a consumer would be willing to pay for a product and its market price.

Contagion When a balance of payments or debt crisis begins in one country and then spreads to similar countries, often in the same region, that did not experience the original negative payments shock to the first country. Thailand had such a crisis in the summer of 1997, which soon spread to Malaysia, Indonesia, and South Korea.

Countervailing duty A tariff imposed by an importing country which is intended to increase the price of the goods to a legally defined fair level. Often used in export subsidy and dumping cases.

Covered return The rate of return on an investment in a country after allowance for the cost of a forward contract to move the funds back to the country of the investor.

Crawling peg An exchange rate system in which a fixed parity is maintained, which is changed quite frequently (sometimes weekly) to maintain balance-of-payments equilibrium and/or offset differing rates of inflation among countries.

Credit A transaction that results in a payment into a country. Exports, receipts of dividend and interest payments, and purchases of local assets by foreigners are all credits in a country's balance-of-payments accounts.

Crowding out The argument that government budget deficits do not increase GNP because the deficits crowd out or discourage other private transactions, perhaps through higher interest rates resulting from government borrowing.

Currency basket A weighted average of a group of currencies to which the currency of a country is pegged. India, for example, has maintained a fixed exchange rate for the rupee relative to a basket of currencies of India's major trading partners.

Currency board An institution that fulfills the role of a bank but is not allowed to own domestic financial assets. Its only financial assets are foreign exchange reserves, meaning that its ability to create base money, and thereby increase the domestic money supply, is strictly regulated by the balance of payments.

Currency mismatch When an enterprise or government borrows heavily in one foreign currency but does not maintain offsetting assets in that currency or undertake other hedging techniques. If the home currency is later devalued relative to the currency in which the borrowing occurred, large capital losses are imposed on the debtor. If such currency mismatches are widespread, the local economy may experience a large number of bankruptcies that can create a serious recession or depression. Argentina experienced this circumstance in 2002, as did Thailand in 1997.

Currency substitution The argument that national currencies are often viewed as substitutes and that firms switch from holding one currency to another in response to changes in expected yields and risks.

Current account A country's total receipts from exports of goods and services minus its local expenditures on imports of goods and services. Also includes unilateral transfers such as gifts and foreign aid.

Customs union A group of countries that maintain free trade in goods among the membership and a common external tariff schedule.

Deadweight loss The loss from a tariff or other restrictive policy that is a gain to nobody. A pure efficiency loss.

Debit A transaction that results in a payment out of a country. Imports and purchases of foreign securities are debits in a country's balance-of-payments accounts.

Debt/equity swap An exchange that occurs when a bank sells financial claims on a foreign government to another firm at a discount, and that firm allows the debtor country to pay the debt in local currency, which it uses to finance a direct investment in the debtor country. Frequently used in Latin America to ease the burdens of excessive debt.

Depreciation A currency's decline in exchange market value in a flexible exchange rate system.

Destination principle A tax is levied on a good in the country where it is consumed. Under GATT rules the destination principle is applied to indirect taxes, and rebated on exports but imposed on imports.

Devaluation A condition that arises when a government or central bank changes a fixed exchange rate or parity for its currency in a direction that reduces the value of the local currency compared to foreign currencies.

Direct tax A tax levied on individuals or income.

Dumping Selling a product in an export market for less than it sold for in the home market or for less than the importing country views as a fair value, which is usually based on estimates of average cost.

Economic union An agreement among a group of countries to maintain free trade among themselves, a common external tariff, mobility of capital and labor among the members, and some degree of unification in their budgetary and monetary systems.

Economies of scale Conditions characterized by the decline of long-run average costs as an enterprise becomes larger. Economies of scale frequently exist when fixed costs are particularly important in an industry.

Effective rate of protection A measurement of the amount of protection provided to an industry by a tariff schedule which allows for tariffs on inputs that the industry buys from others, as well as for the tariff on the output of the industry. The effective tariff can be negative, which means that the government policy is discriminating against local firms and in favor of imports, if tariff levels on inputs are sufficiently higher than the tariff on the final good.

Embargo A complete prohibition of trade with a country. US trade with Libya and Cuba, for example, has been under an embargo.

Escape clause A provision of US law which allows temporary protection for US industries that are under particular pressure from imports.

Euro   The new currency of the European Monetary Union (EMU), the membership of which includes 12 members of the European Union. It became an accounting currency in January 1999, and replaced the 12 national currencies for all uses in 2002. A euro was worth about $1.15 in mid-2003.

Eurobonds   Bonds sold in one or a group of countries which are denominated in the currency of another country, such as dollar-denominated bonds sold in Europe.

Eurodollar market   Banking markets in Europe, and elsewhere outside the United States, in which time deposits are accepted and loans are made in US dollars. Similar arrangements exist for such offshore banking in other currencies.

European Economic Community   An association of European countries, established in 1957, that agreed to free trade among its members and imposed a common external tariff on trade with nonmembers. As of 1995 there were 15 member countries. In 1967 the EEC joined with the European Coal and Steel Community and Euratom to become the European Community. In 1993 an agreement to achieve even closer economic cooperation was ratified, which established the European Union.

European Monetary System (EMS)   The phased unification of the monetary systems of the members of the European Union. Fixed exchange rates and coordinated monetary policies existed until 1992–3 when the system encountered major problems. The EMS became a full monetary union in January of 1999.

European Monetary Union (EMU)   The monetary union which grew out of the European Monetary System. In January of 1999 the exchange rates of the original 11 members were irrevocably fixed relative to each other and the euro was introduced as an accounting currency. EMU is run by the European Central Bank, which is headquartered in Frankfurt. Its management structure is very similar to that of the US Federal Reserve System, with the governors of the national central banks sitting on the Governing Council, along with six members of the Executive Board, and acting as the Federal Open Market Committee does in the United States. The euro fully replaced the 12 national currencies in 2002.

Exchange market intervention   Purchases or sales of foreign exchange by a central bank which are intended to maintain a fixed exchange rate or to affect the behavior of a floating rate.

Exchange Rate Mechanism (ERM)   The arrangement through which the members of the European Monetary System maintained fixed exchange rates before 1992–3 when a much wider band was at least temporarily adopted.

Export-led growth   Policies in developing countries that are designed to encourage economic growth which is based on rapid growth of exports sales. Widely used in East Asian countries.

Export tariffs   Taxes or tariffs that are applied to export receipts. Such tariffs are frequently used by developing countries as a revenue source, but have the effect of discouraging exports of the tariffed products.

External economies of scale   Greater production by one firm in an industry allows costs of production for other firms in the industry to decline. This benefit from greater production represents a positive externality that an individual firm will ignore in deciding how much to produce. In such circumstances some advocate a subsidy to give the firm an incentive to expand output.

Externality   Benefits or costs from a transaction that affect those who are not parties to the transaction. A positive externality from more flu vaccinations given is better health for those exposed to inoculated individuals.

Factor intensity reversal A situation in which it is impossible to rank clearly or identify the relative factor intensities of two products, because one is more labor-intensive at one set of relative factor prices, but the other becomes more labor-intensive at another set of relative factor prices. Factor intensity reversal can occur when it is far easier to substitute one factor for the other in one industry than it is in the other industry.

Factor-price equalization The argument that international trade that is based on differences in relative factor endowments, as predicted by the Heckscher–Ohlin theorem, will tend to reduce or eliminate international differences in factor prices. Free trade between Australia and Japan, for example, would reduce land prices in Japan and increase them in Australia until land prices in the two countries became equal or at least similar. Associated with Paul Samuelson and Wolfgang Stolper.

f.a.s. Free alongside ship. This measurement of the value of exports includes the price of the goods shipped to the side of the ship, but without loading costs.

Filter rule An approach to speculation in which an asset is bought or sold on the basis of the recent behavior of its price. One such "rule" would be to buy a currency that had recently appreciated by some percentage or sell it if it had depreciated. Another would be to sell currencies that had recently appreciated and vice versa. If exchange markets are fully efficient, such filter rules should not be consistently profitable.

Floating exchange rate An exchange rate for which a government or central bank does not maintain a parity or fixed rate, but instead allows to be determined by market forces.

f.o.b. Free on board. This measurement of the value of exports includes the price of the goods loaded on the ship, but without the cost of international shipping and insurance.

foreign exchange reserves Foreign financial assets held by a government or central bank which are available to support the country's balance of payments or exchange rate. Includes holdings of gold, the country's reserve position in the International Monetary Fund, and claims on foreign governments and central banks.

Foreign trade multiplier The Keynesian multiplier adjusted to allow for the existence of foreign trade. The marginal propensity to import makes this multiplier lower than that which would prevail for the economy without trade.

Forward exchange market A market in which it is possible to purchase foreign exchange for delivery and payment at a future date. The quantity and exchange rate are determined at the outset, but payment is made at a fixed future date, frequently in 30, 60, or 90 days.

Free-trade area A group of countries that maintain free trade among the membership, but where each country maintains its own tariff schedule for trade with nonmembers.

Free-trade zone An area within a nation where manufacturing can be carried out with imported parts and components on which no tariffs have been paid. The output of such manufacturing efforts must then be exported if it is to remain duty-free. Many developing countries have free-trade zones, which are also known as "duty-free zones," as a way of encouraging export activities, which require imported inputs, without eliminating protection for domestic industries that produce such inputs for the rest of the economy.

Futures market for foreign currencies A market that is similar to the forward market except that all contracts mature on the same day of the month, a secondary market for the contracts exists, and the amounts of money in the contracts are smaller. Futures contracts are traded in commodity markets rather than through commercial banks.

General Agreement on Tariffs and Trade (GATT) An agreement reached in 1947 that established principles to govern international trade in goods. Also, until 1995 the GATT was an organization based in Geneva to administer this trade agreement, to settle trade disputes between member countries, and to foster negotiations to liberalize trade. It was replaced by the WTO in 1995.

Generalized System of Preferences A preferential trading arrangement in which industrialized countries allow tariff-free imports from developing countries while maintaining tariffs on the same products from other industrialized countries.

Gold standard A monetary system in which governments or central banks maintain a fixed price of gold in terms of their currencies by offering to purchase or sell gold at fixed local currency prices. Exchange rates are then determined by relative national prices of gold.

Heckscher–Ohlin theorem The argument, developed by two Swedish economists in the 1920s, that international trade patterns are determined by the fact that countries have different relative factor inputs. Each country will export those products that require a great deal of its relatively abundant factor of production.

Hedging Undertaking a financial transaction that cancels or offsets the risk existing from a previous financial position.

Immiserizing growth Economic growth that is so strongly biased toward the production of exports, and where the world demand for these exports is so price-inelastic, that the world price falls sufficiently to leave the country worse off than it was before the growth occurred.

Import substitution A development policy in which economic growth is to be encouraged by repressing imports and by encouraging the domestic production of substitutes for those imports.

Indirect tax A tax levied on production or consumption of goods and services.

Industrial strategy The argument that the growth of industries within an economy should not be left to market forces but should instead be guided by government policies. The government should choose industries that have strong prospects and encourage their growth, perhaps by maintaining barriers to imports.

Infant-industry protection The argument that an industry's costs will be high when it is beginning, and it will therefore need protection from imports to survive. If provided with a period of protection, the industry's costs will decline and it will be able to prosper without protection.

Intellectual property Property developed through research and other creative efforts. Forms of protection include patents, copyrights, and trademarks.

Interest parity theory The forward discount on a currency, measured as an annual rate, should equal the local interest rate minus the foreign interest rate.

International Bank for Reconstruction and Development (IBRD) An institution founded in 1944 that lends money to developing countries. Located in Washington DC, it was originally to finance both reconstruction from World War II and development projects in poor countries. This institution also carries on research and provides advice in the area of development economics. Also known as the "World Bank."

International Finance Corporation A division of the IBRD which carries on equity financing of private projects in developing countries.

International Monetary Fund (IMF) An institution that was founded at the Bretton Woods conference in 1944 and lends money to countries facing large balance-of-payments deficits. Located in Washington DC, across the street from the IBRD, it also oversees the exchange rate system and provides research and advisory services for member countries in the areas of monetary economics and international finance.

Intra-industry trade Trade that occurs when a country both exports and imports the output of the same industry. Italy exporting Fiat automobiles to Germany and importing VWs from Germany would be an example of intra-industry trade.

IS line Combinations of interest rates and levels of domestic output which will equate savings and intended investment, thus producing equilibrium in the market for goods.

Isoquant A curve representing all the combinations of two factors of production which will produce a fixed quantity of a product. A set of isoquants can be used to represent a production function for two inputs.

J-curve effect The possibility that after a devaluation or depreciation, a country's balance of trade will deteriorate modestly for a brief period of time before improving by far more than enough to offset that loss.

Law of one price The argument that international differences in prices for the same commodity should be arbitraged away by trade. If the exchange rate is 5 pesos per dollar, a product that costs $1 in the United States should cost 5 pesos in the other country. This law is frequently violated in oligopolistic markets.

Learning curve A relationship showing the tendency for a firm's marginal cost of production to fall as its cumulative output rises. This relationship has been especially important in aircraft and semiconductor production.

Leontief paradox The 1953 research finding by Wassily Leontief that US exports were more labor-intensive than US imports, which contradicts the predictions of the Heckscher–Ohlin theorem.

Letter of credit A document issued by a commercial bank which promises to pay a fixed amount of money if certain conditions are met, such as the delivery of exported goods to a customer. If firm A wishes to purchase goods from firm B in a foreign country, firm B may require that firm A provide a letter of credit for the amount of the purchase. If such a letter is provided, firm B is guaranteed by a known commercial bank that it will be fully paid a certain number of days after firm A takes delivery of the goods.

LM line Combinations of interest rates and domestic output which, given a money supply, will clear the domestic market for money.

London Interbank Offer Rate (LIBOR) The market-determined interest rate on short-term interbank deposits in the Eurodollar market in London, frequently used as the basis for floating interest rates on international loans. A country might borrow at LIBOR plus 1 percent, for example.

Long position Owning an asset or a contract to take delivery of an asset at a fixed price with no hedge or offsetting position. A long position is profitable if the price of the asset rises, and vice versa.

Maastricht Treaty An agreement among the members of the European Community which was completed in Maastricht, the Netherlands, in December 1991. This treaty led to the European Monetary System becoming a full monetary union in early 1999, the euro to fully replace the national currencies of the 12 members in 2002. The treaty also included provisions to make it easier for nationals of one EU member to migrate to another seeking work, and moved Europe toward a full union in other ways.

Managed [or dirty] floating exchange rate A policy in which a government or central bank does not maintain a parity, and instead allows the exchange rate to change to some degree with market forces. The government or central bank buys or sells foreign exchange, however, when it is displeased with the behavior of the market. Such intervention is intended to produce exchange market behavior that the government prefers.

Marginal propensity to import The percentage of extra or marginal income which residents of a country can be expected to spend on imports.

Marginal rate of substitution The rate at which an individual or a group of people would be willing to exchange one good for another and be no better or worse off. Equals the ratio of the marginal utilities of the two goods, which equals the slope of an indifference curve.

Marginal rate of transformation The rate at which an economy can transform one good into another by moving productive resources from one industry to another. Equals the ratio of the marginal costs of the two goods, which equals the slope of the production-possibility curve.

Marshall–Lerner condition The elasticity of demand and supply conditions that are necessary for a devaluation to improve a country's balance of trade.

Mercantilism The view that a government should actively discourage imports and encourage exports, as well as regulate other aspects of the economy.

Monetarist model of the balance of payments A view of the balance of payments, or the exchange rate, which emphasizes excess demands for, or supplies of, money as causes of exchange market disequilibria. An asset market approach to the balance of payments in which domestic and foreign assets are viewed as perfect substitutes.

Moral hazard An institutional or legal situation which, perhaps unintentionally, encourages people to behave badly. If, for example, the IMF always provides financial packages for developing countries that face debt crises and this results in the lenders being fully compensated, i.e. "bailed out," banks in industrialized countries may be encouraged to lend less than prudently. The expectation of an IMF "bail-out" encourages irresponsible lending in developing countries, which makes a later debt crisis more likely.

Most-favored-nation status (MFN) When a country promises to offer the country having most-favored-nation status the lowest tariff which it offers to any third country.

Multi-Fibre Arrangement (MFA) A system of bilateral quotas in the markets for textiles and garments in which each exporting country is allowed to send a specified quantity of various textile or garment products to an importing country per year.

New International Economic Order A list of requests by the underdeveloped countries for improvements in their trading and development prospects, to be largely financed by the industrialized countries. The agenda was actively discussed during the 1970s, but interest in it declined in the 1980s. The most important element in the agenda was a system of price support programs for primary products which are exported by developing countries. Fears of enormous costs and resource allocation inefficiencies led the industrialized countries to resist this and other parts of the NIEO program.

Newly industrialized countries (NICs) A group of previously poor countries that experienced very rapid economic growth during the 1970s and 1980s, based primarily upon greater production of manufactured goods that were exported to developed countries. South Korea, Taiwan, Hong Kong, and Singapore were the original NICs but in the 1990s China, Thailand, Malaysia, and Indonesia were added to that group.

Nominal effective exchange rate A weighted exchange rate for a currency relative to the currencies of a number of foreign countries. Trade shares are frequently used as the weights.

Nontariff barrier Any government policy other than a tariff which is designed to discourage imports in favor of domestic products. Quotas and government procurement rules are among the most important nontariff trade barriers.

North American Free Trade Agreement (NAFTA) An agreement to establish a free-trade area consisting of the United States, Canada, and Mexico. A US–Canada free-trade area began operations in 1989, and was extended to Mexico at the beginning of 1994.

Offer curve A curve that illustrates the volume of exports and imports that a country will choose to undertake at various terms of trade. Also known as a "reciprocal demand curve."

Official reserve transactions balance A measurement of a country's balance-of-payments surplus or deficit which includes all items in the current and capital accounts. It excludes only movements of foreign exchange reserves. Also known as the "official settlements balance of payments" and occasionally as the "overall balance."

Open economy macroeconomics Macroeconomic models that explicitly include foreign trade and international capital-flow sectors.

Opportunity cost The cost of one good in terms of other goods which could have been produced with the same factors of production.

Optimum currency area The area within which a single currency or rigidly fixed exchange rates should exist.

Optimum tariff A tariff that is designed to maximize a large country's benefits from trade by improving its terms of trade. Optimum only for the country imposing the tariff, not for the world.

Organization for Economic Cooperation and Development (OECD) An organization consisting of the governments of the industrialized market economies, headquartered in Paris. It provides a forum for a wide range of discussions and negotiations among these countries, and publishes both statistics and economic research studies on these countries and on international trade and financial flows.

Origin principle A tax is levied on the good in the country where it is produced. No tax adjustment is made at the border when a good is exported or imported.

Overshooting A condition that occurs when the price of an asset, such as foreign exchange, is moving in one direction but temporarily moves beyond its permanent equilibrium, before coming back to its long-run value. Associated with Rudiger Dornbusch's analysis of the response of a floating exchange rate to a shift in monetary policy.

Par value A fixed exchange rate, denominated in terms of a foreign currency or gold.

Policy assignment model A model of balance-of-payments adjustment under fixed exchange rates in which it is possible to reach both the desired level of domestic output and payments equilibrium through the use of fiscal and monetary policies. Associated with J. Marcus Fleming and Robert Mundell.

Portfolio balance model A view of the capital account or of the overall balance of payments which emphasizes the demand for and supply of financial assets. Concludes that capital flows in response to recent changes in expected yields rather than in response to differing levels of expected yields. That part of the asset market approach to the balance of payments in which domestic and foreign assets are viewed as imperfect substitutes.

Predatory dumping Temporary dumping designed to drive competing firms out of business in order to create a monopoly and raise prices.

Preference similarity hypothesis The argument that trade in consumer goods is often based on the fact that a product that is popular in the country in which it is produced can most easily be exported to countries with similar consumer tastes. Associated with Stefan Burenstam Linder.

Principle of second best The argument, associated with Richard Lipsey and Kelvin Lancaster, that when it is not possible to remove one economic distortion, such as an imperfectly competitive product or factor market, eliminating another distortion, such as a trade barrier, may not increase economic efficiency. Many arguments for protection are based on this principle.

Producers' surplus The difference between the price at which a product can be sold and the minimum price which a seller would be willing to accept for it.

Production function A graphical or mathematical representation of all the combinations of inputs which will produce various quantities of a product. Can be represented with an isoquant map if only two inputs exist.

Purchasing power parity The argument that the exchange for two currencies should reflect relative price levels in the two countries. If yen prices in Japan are on average 200 times as high as dollar prices in the United States, the exchange rate should be 200 yen = $1. Associated with Gustav Cassel.

Put An option contract that allows its owner to sell a specified amount of a financial asset, such as foreign exchange, at a fixed price during a specified period of time. The owner of the option is not required to exercise the option. The price at which the asset can be sold is known as the "strike price."

Quota A government policy that limits the physical volume of a product which may be imported per period of time.

Quota rents The extra profits that accrue to those who get the right to bring products into a country under a quota. Equal to the difference between the domestic price of the product in the importing country and the world price, multiplied by the quantity imported.

Real effective exchange rate The nominal effective exchange rate adjusted for differing rates of inflation to create an index of cost and price competitiveness in world markets. If a country's nominal effective exchange rate depreciated by 5 percent in a year in which its rate of inflation exceeded the average rate of inflation in the rest of the world by 5 percentage points, its real effective exchange rate would be unchanged.

Real interest rate The nominal interest rate minus the expected rate of inflation. Current saving and investment decisions should be based on the real interest rate over the maturity of the asset.

Real money supply A nation's money supply divided by the price level in that country. The real money supply, which represents the purchasing power of the nation's money supply, is critical in determining the demand for goods and services, as well as for financial assets, in a monetarist model.

Relative factor endowments The relative amounts of different factors of production which two countries have. India has a relative abundance of labor, while the United States has a greater relative abundance of capital.

Relative factor intensities The relative amounts of different factors of production that are used in the production of two goods. Textiles and garments are relatively labor-intensive, whereas oil refining is relatively capital-intensive.

Residence principle A tax is imposed on the income of a country's residents, regardless of where the income is earned.

Revaluation An increase in the value of a currency in terms of foreign exchange by changing an otherwise fixed exchange rate.

Rybczynski theorem The argument, associated with Thomas Rybcyznski, that if the supply of one factor of production increases, when both relative factor and goods prices are unchanged, the output of the product using that factor intensively will increase and the output of the product using the other factor of production intensively must decline.

Section 301 A provision of US trade law which allows retaliation against the exports of countries maintaining what the United States views as unfair trade practices such as allowing the theft of US intellectual property by local firms.

Settlement date The date at which payment is made and an asset received. Normally two business days after the trade is agreed to for spot foreign exchange transactions. If General Motors purchases DMs from Citibank on Wednesday, payment will be made in both directions on that Friday, which is the settlement date.

Short position Having a liability or a contract to deliver an asset in the future at a fixed price with no hedge or offsetting position. A short position is profitable if the asset declines in price, and vice versa. A short position in sterling would exist if someone owed a sterling debt without offsetting sterling assets, or if that person had sold sterling in the forward or futures market while not holding offsetting sterling assets.

Singer–Prebisch hypothesis The argument developed by Hans Singer and Raul Prebisch that developing countries face a secular decline in their terms of trade owing to a trend toward lower prices for primary commodities relative to prices of manufactured goods.

Smoot–Hawley tariff A very high level of tariffs adopted by the United States in 1930 which caused a dramatic decline in the volume of world trade. It is widely believed to have worsened the great depression.

Society for Worldwide Interbank Financial Telecommunication (SWIFT) An electronic system maintained by large international banks for transmitting instructions for foreign exchange transfers and other international transactions.

Source principle A tax is imposed on the income earned in a country, regardless of whether a resident or nonresident earns it.

Special Drawing Rights (SDRs) A foreign exchange reserve asset created by the International Monetary Fund. The value of the SDR is based on a weighted average of the US dollar, the DM, the yen, sterling, and the French franc.

Specie flow mechanism A balance-of-payments adjustment mechanism in which the domestic money supply is rigidly tied to the balance of payments, falling in the case of deficits and rising when surpluses occur. Associated with David Hume.

Specific factors model A factor of production is specific to an industry, or immobile, when its productivity in one industry exceeds its productivity in other industries at any price. A specific factors model predicts that immobile factors that produce import-competing goods will be harmed by free trade. The text refers to the case where capital is immobile between industries, but labor is mobile, as a specific factors model.

Specific tariff A tariff that is measured as a fixed amount of money per physical unit imported – $500 per car or $10 per ton, for example.

Spot market The market for an asset, such as foreign exchange, in which delivery is in only one or two days.

Statistical discrepancy Also known as "net errors and omissions," this is the number that must be entered in the balance-of-payments accounts of a country to make them sum to zero. Logically, the accounts must sum to zero, but many of the entries are estimates of actual transactions that contain many errors, so these estimates seldom do sum to zero. The statistical discrepancy number is frequently placed at the end of the table and is simply the sum of all the other entries in the account with the sign reversed.

Sterilization A domestic monetary policy action that is designed to cancel or offset the monetary effect of a balance-of-payments disequilibrium. When a payments surplus increases the domestic money supply, an open-market sale of domestic assets by the central bank will cancel this effect and will constitute sterilization.

Stolper–Samuelson theorem   The argument that in a world of Heckscher–Ohlin trade, free trade will reduce the income of the scarce factor of production and increase the income of the abundant factor of production in each country.

Strategic trade policy   The argument that trade policy, including protection, should be used to encourage the growth of domestic industries which the government feels to have strong prospects in world markets. This usually involves trying to choose industries in which rapid technical advances are likely and where growing world markets exist.

Strike price   The price at which an option can be exercised before the expiration date. Such an option is said to be "at the money" if the strike price equals the current market price, and "in the money" if the market price exceeds the strike price, so a call option is worth exercising. A call option is "out of the money" if the current market price is below the strike price, so the option is not worth exercising.

Swap   A transaction in which one security or stream of income is exchanged for another, frequently with a contract to reverse the transaction at a date in the future. In foreign exchange, a swap means the purchase of a currency in the spot market and its simultaneous sale in the forward market.

Tariff   A tax on imports or exports imposed by a government. Tariffs are frequently a major source of revenue for developing countries, but are primarily used for protectionist reasons in industrialized countries.

Tariff rate quota   A trade restriction which places a low tariff rate on a fixed volume which is imported per period of time and a higher tariff rate on imports above that level. Alternatively, there may be no tariff on the fixed volume, and a tariff above that level.

Terms of trade   The ratio of a country's export prices to its import prices. High terms of trade imply large welfare benefits from trade, and vice versa.

Trade Adjustment Assistance (TAA)   The practice of providing financial aid for industries injured by growing imports or for their employees. When tariffs are reduced, trade adjustment assistance is sometimes promised for import-competing industries.

Trade balance   A country's total export receipts minus its total import expenditures during a period of time, usually a year.

Trade creation   An efficiency gain that results from the operation of a free-trade area because more efficient firms from a member country displace less efficient local producers in the domestic market.

Trade diversion   An efficiency loss that results from the operations of a free-trade area because less efficient firms from a member country displace more efficient producers from a nonmember country. It occurs because of the discriminatory nature of the tariff regime. The member country faces no tariff in the import market, whereas the nonmember still faces a tariff.

Trade-related investment measures (TRIMs)   Government policies in which foreign direct investments in a country are allowed only if the investing firm promises to meet certain trade performance goals. The Uruguay Round agreement prohibits TRIMs that require firms to use a certain amount of domestically produced inputs or maintain a certain balance between imports and exports.

Transfer pricing   The practice of using false or misleading prices on trade documents in order to evade *ad valorem* tariffs or exchange controls, or to shift profits within a multinational firm from a high-tax-rate jurisdiction to a low-tax-rate jurisdiction. Also known as "false invoicing."

United Nations Conference on Trade and Development (UNCTAD)   A series of conferences carried on through the United Nations since 1964 at which the developing countries discuss trade and development issues. The New International Economic Order agenda for reform of the world economy grew out of these conferences.

Uruguay Round A round of negotiations on trade liberalization held under GATT auspices which was completed in 1993. The agreement reached reduces tariffs and addresses trade practices not previously covered by GATT rules. It also replaces GATT with the World Trade Organization.

US Trade Representative An official of the executive branch of the US government who is responsible for carrying on negotiations with foreign governments on foreign trade issues. Previously known as the "Special Trade Representative."

Vernon product cycle The observation that a country such as the United States will frequently export a product that it has invented only for as long as it can maintain a technical monopoly. When the technology becomes available abroad, perhaps because a patent has expired, production grows rapidly in foreign countries where costs are lower, and the inventing country experiences a decline in its production of the product because of a rapid growth of imports. Associated with Raymond Vernon.

Voluntary export restraint (VER) An agreement by a country to limit its export sales to another country, frequently in order to avoid a more damaging protectionist policy by the importing country. Sometimes known as an "Orderly Marketing Agreement" (OMA). VERs are severely restricted by the Uruguay Round agreement.

Walras's law The idea that excess demands must net out to zero across an economy in a general equilibrium framework, because if there is an excess demand in one market, there must be an offsetting excess supply in another market. Associated with Leon Walras.

World Trade Organization (WTO) A successor organization to the GATT established in 1995, as agreed upon in the Uruguay Round. The WTO provides a stronger administrative framework, more streamlined dispute resolution provisions, and a trade-policy review procedure, all of which suggest more effective implementation of the agreements reached.

Index